PAUL E. FERTIG, *PhD, CPA*
The Ohio State University

DONALD F. ISTVAN, *DBA, CPA*
Northern Illinois University

HOMER J. MOTTICE, *PhD, CPA*
The Florida State University

Second Edition

USING
ACCOUNTING
INFORMATION

AN INTRODUCTION

Harcourt Brace Jovanovich, Inc.
New York   Chicago   San Francisco   Atlanta

THE HARBRACE SERIES IN BUSINESS AND ECONOMICS

Editorial Advisory Board

William J. Baumol PRINCETON UNIVERSITY
William F. Massy STANFORD UNIVERSITY
Robert K. Mautz UNIVERSITY OF ILLINOIS
Leonard R. Sayles COLUMBIA UNIVERSITY
Martin K. Starr COLUMBIA UNIVERSITY

ISBN: 0-15-594454-1

Library of Congress Catalog Card Number: 79-141605

Printed in the United States of America

PREFACE

This book reflects our belief that the strength of an accounting system lies in the usefulness of its applications, rather than in the information-gathering and processing aspects. Although the procedures for preparing accounting information are important, we feel that an introductory accounting course should concentrate on the uses of accounting information inside and outside the business firm. We believe that the study of accounting should begin with its relationship to the nature and objectives of business decisions—what information is necessary to make them, what data are relevant, and what the uses and limitations of these data are.

This "user" approach to the introductory accounting course has been classroom-tested for over a decade. The first edition of this book resulted from extensive classroom research at The Ohio State University, and experience gained with that edition convinced us that students appreciate and are challenged by learning "why" before "how." This revision reflects further field testing at colleges and universities across the country.

While maintaining the user orientation and analytical approach of the first edition, we have reorganized the new edition to enhance its applicability to a variety of courses. The book has four parts: Introduction (Chapters 1–3); Managerial Uses of Accounting Reports (Chapters 4–11); All-Purpose Financial Statements (Chapters 12–16); and Nonmanagerial Uses of Accounting Reports (Chapters 17–19). The first two chapters of the original edition have been supplemented by a new Chapter 3 ("Recording and Reporting Events") to form Part I, which serves as a basis for a full understanding of the remainder of the book. The new chapter describes the bookkeeping cycle and process and, for those who wish still more emphasis on the mechanics of accounting, includes two appendixes ("The Accounting Process Illustrated" and "Asset Control"). Although these appendixes are not essential for an understanding of the subsequent chapters, they are a valuable enrichment of the book. They provide examples of bookkeeping in manufacturing firms and in merchandising firms, and they illustrate the uses of bookkeeping as a tool of asset control.

In Part II we now treat performance measurement in two chapters and have expanded the discussion. Chapter 6 ("Cost Control: Special Considerations") has a new appendix, which illustrates accounting records using standard costs and flexible budgets, and it is useful for a fuller understanding of this difficult topic.

In Part III an appendix added to Chapter 12 presents actual financial reports from industry. The old chapter on "Investments, Long-lived Assets, and

Long-term Liabilities" has also been split into two chapters and the discussion has been extended.

Part IV is substantially the same as in the first edition, with the exception of an appendix to Chapter 17 on accounting for income taxes.

It is fair to say that the book has been almost entirely rewritten. In every instance we have worked toward greater clarity, more discussion of difficult topics, and more concrete examples. The problems at the end of each chapter have been reviewed, and numerous problems have been added. Solutions to most of the problems are given in the Instructor's Manual in complete form.

Since the book does not have a traditional design, chapters need not be studied consecutively, nor need all chapters be studied in all courses. The following table outlines the manner in which the book might be used in various courses:

Course	Course length	Suggested application
Introductory accounting (first course for majors and nonmajors)	Two terms	Parts I–IV consecutively, or Parts I, III, IV, II
Financial accounting for nonmajors (undergraduate or graduate)	One term	Part I (excluding Appendixes 3A and 3B); Part III; Part IV (Chapter 17 optional); Part II (selected sections at instructor's option)
Managerial accounting for majors and nonmajors (prerequisite: one term of financial accounting)	One term	Part II, all chapters consecutively (including appendixes)
Managerial accounting for nonmajors (undergraduate or graduate)	One term	Part I; Part II, all chapters consecutively (Appendix 6A optional)

The outline above indicates that we expect students will come to this book, as they did to the first edition, without knowledge of accounting or an extensive background in mathematics or statistics. For most students we expect this book to provide a first glimpse of course work in business. It is written accordingly and assumes that study of data-collection procedures can profitably be put off until the second course (for accounting majors) or by-passed (for those not majoring in accounting). Widespread experience with the first edition has demonstrated that accounting majors can study intermediate accounting and accounting systems in fewer course hours once they understand how accounting data are used. We are grateful to our colleagues whose comments have led to the changes incorporated in this edition.

Paul E. Fertig, Donald F. Istvan, Homer J. Mottice

CONTENTS

Chapter Five PERFORMANCE MEASUREMENT: COST CONTROL 172

Chapter Six COST CONTROL: SPECIAL CONSIDERATIONS 197

Chapter Ten PLANNING ALTERNATE COURSES OF OPERATIONS   *349*

Chapter Eleven PLANNING THE ACQUISITION OF FACILITIES   *375*

Part Four   NONMANAGERIAL USES OF ACCOUNTING REPORTS   631

Chapter Seventeen   ACCOUNTING REPORTS FOR GOVERNMENT USERS   633

Chapter Eighteen   ACCOUNTING REPORTS FOR CREDITORS   672

Part One INTRODUCTION

This is a book about the uses of accounting information and therefore about the users of that information as well. There are several groups of people that use accounting information. Some are skilled in the profession of accounting; others are not. The successful user of an accounting report need not be an accountant or even a bookkeeper (just as the user of an electric light need not be an electrical engineer or even an electrician). He should be a person, however, who knows how to conduct business activity, understands how accounting information can help him apply his abilities, and is willing to use the information for all it is worth.

Chapter 1 discusses the various kinds of users of accounting information and the informational needs each has. Chapter 2 presents the role of profits and earnings in business enterprise, shows how accounting is focused on calculation of profits and earnings, and outlines the concepts that accountants have developed for this purpose. Chapter 3 builds upon the concepts developed in Chapter 2 and formulates the model of the accountant's recording and reporting system. Appendixes 3A and 3B expand this model for the student who wants to delve more deeply into the mechanics of accounting.

Chapter One USERS OF ACCOUNTING INFORMATION

INTRODUCTION

This chapter describes what managers and nonmanagers do with accounting reports. The manager, as the next few pages will show, uses accounting information in two ways: he measures performance (assesses past history) and he plans for the future (gauges how he can best perform his job in the months ahead). The nonmanager may use accounting information to decide whether to invest in a company or lend it money, whether it will be a good customer or supplier, or how to regulate its activities.

MANAGERIAL USERS

Every business enterprise has a manager. In the local pizza parlor the manager is probably also owner, cook, and chief waiter; but above all he is the manager, because he makes every decision that affects his enterprise. He sets menu prices, places orders for more tomato sauce and cheese, hires and fires waiters and dishwashers, and decides whether to borrow money to install an additional baking oven.

Decision making is the prime job of the manager. Not all businesses are owner-managed or as relatively simple to operate as a pizza parlor. Large groups of people working toward a common goal often make up a business enterprise. Such group activity can take several different legal forms, the most common of which are the partnership and the corporation.

Many professional people, such as accountants, doctors, and lawyers, operate their business activity in partnership. Each partner is an owner and perhaps even

3

a manager. When the group of partners becomes too large for effective inter-communication among the group, a manager or management group is appointed to run the firm and make the business decisions for the group.

A corporation is legally different from either the owner-manager enterprise or the partnership. The owners of a small corporation may also be its managers, but they need not be. The advantage of the corporate form is that it is a versatile form of organization that makes possible extensive operations under varying conditions. It typically embodies a separation of owners and managers. The shareholder-owners elect company directors who become the highest-level managers of the corporation. The board of directors delegates its authority to the officers of the corporation, whom it appoints or elects. These officers are responsible to the board for conducting the affairs of the corporation, just as the board of directors is responsible to the shareholder-owners.

As the business activities of an enterprise expand, the top-level managers must delegate responsibility and then authority to subordinates. It would be impossible, for instance, for the president of the General Motors Corporation to make decisions about buying more nuts and bolts for use at the Cleveland assembly plant. The delegation of authority may extend through several managerial levels until it reaches the individual who has the authority to make the decision and will bear the responsibility for it.

Even the local pizza parlor will have to undergo a delegation of responsibility and authority when the manager hires additional personnel. For example, when delivery operations are begun, the man in charge of deliveries might be permitted to make decisions about delivery routes, gasoline purchases, and auto repairs. Similarly, the new dishwasher might be in charge of all aspects of buying and using supplies as well as of scheduling the working hours of his helpers. In firms the size of the General Motors Corporation or the United States Steel Corporation, the network of managerial delegation becomes more complex. Delegating managerial responsibility and authority gives rise to the need for managerial accounting reports.

Business activity consists of a continuing series of transactions, which in turn provide a flow of raw data that will be converted into accounting reports. The information contained in the accounting reports assists managers at all levels to form conclusions and reach decisions.

Business managers need accounting information for two purposes:

1. to measure performance
2. to facilitate planning

Performance Measurement

Performance measurement is a broad concept. It includes measurement of the performance of individuals, such as that of a particular machinist operating a grinding machine in the production line of an automobile parts manufacturing plant. It includes measuring group activity, such as that of the entire grinding machine department of the plant. The accounting system can also provide information about the performance of a machine or groups of machines, measuring, for example, their efficiency of operation, their product quality, and their need for repair.

Performance measurement can be as simple or as complex as the situation demands. The simplest form of performance measurement entails a determination of what actually happened. A more sophisticated method requires a comparison of what did happen with what the manager thinks should have happened. In either case, the manager's ability to reach conclusions and make decisions according to them is enhanced by accounting reports that provide information about past performance. This is true regardless of the level at which the decision is made. Of course, at the higher levels of management more raw data is available, requiring greater summarization—that is, less detail in reporting the information.

The foreman in charge of the grinding machine department can measure the performance of a particular machinist by studying the minute details of that man's work record. The plant supervisor, to whom the foreman is responsible, does not have time to study each individual machinist but instead measures the performance of the grinding department and the foreman according to the summarized results of the department as a whole. The company's president measures the performance of the vice president in charge of production by analyzing the accounting reports for the entire plant. In these reports, the information pertaining to the individual machinist, or even to the grinding department, is included only as part of a summary item.

It is vital to remember that an individual's performance should be measured only in terms of those activities over which he exercises control. For example, the supervisor of the grinding department is concerned with the quantity and quality of his product and with the labor and material costs of production, but not with the selling of the product to customers.

At some level in the firm one or more managers have responsibility for selling the products or services as well as for producing them. Such managerial responsibility provides a second aspect to performance measurement, because the revenues derived from sales to customers, as well as the costs of these sales, must be considered. In this case performance measurement becomes more difficult and the role of the accounting report more important in helping the manager make decisions about the actions he must take.

Most accounting reports provide information about the past performance of individuals, machines, or departments. A manager cannot erase mistakes made in the past, but his conclusions about past performance provide a basis for anticipating and avoiding similar mistakes in the future. Accounting reports of past performance are therefore a vital part of the management process.

Planning

The job of the manager goes far beyond mere correction of past mistakes. He must continually forecast outside influences that he cannot control on the business activities of his enterprise. He must also establish realistic goals for those activities for which he is responsible. Most of a manager's time, particularly in larger enterprises, is devoted to this planning activity. Planning reports, usually different from those that report past performance, are indispensable for this purpose.

There are two kinds of planning for which the business manager is responsible. The first, *budgeting*, deals with planning for all activities within his control for a specified future period. For budgeting purposes, the manager makes predictions about the operating conditions he can reasonably expect in a future period. He then establishes the goals he can hopefully expect to accomplish under these conditions. Accounting reports assist the manager in making his predictions and establishing his goals. Reports also reveal the expected results of the plans he has made. These reports then permit him to determine whether the goals are satisfactory or whether other decisions might improve his chances of achieving the goals he has established. A manager, for example, must predict his cash needs during a coming period. He knows that his present bank balance is $300. After predicting the reactions of customers during the future period, he estimates that his cash revenues from the sale of his products will be $2,000 more than his cash expenditures for running the company. He also estimates that he will need a cash balance of $700 to allow for unexpected expenditures or emergencies. His budgeting shows that he will have excess cash of $1,600 ($300 plus $2,000 minus $700) as a result of business operations in the future period. He can then plan to invest the excess cash profitably, pay his debts, or plow the excess back into his enterprise.

The second kind of planning is closely related to period budgeting but calls for a different kind of accounting report. This kind of planning is in terms of particular *projects*, rather than in terms of periods of time. These projects are usually concerned with possible changes in the conditions that are assumed for period budgeting purposes. The manager in the above example may envision a project relating to the purchase of new equipment for a particular phase of his production process. The equipment will cost $10,000 but will lower production costs by $500 per year. It will also require a cash down payment of at least $2,000. By relating his project planning to his period budgeting the manager can revise his estimates to choose the best course of future action. In this case the manager might plan to borrow the money for the down payment in order to buy the new machinery immediately. With the new machinery his operating expenditures would be reduced by $500 and his excess cash would be $2,100, or more than enough to pay back the amount borrowed to make the down payment. In addition he would have made an investment that would save him $500 per year throughout the life of the new equipment.

Accounting reports dealing with managerial project planning are particularly useful for the continued long-range success of a business enterprise. Such reports are receiving more and more consideration by managers.

NONMANAGERIAL USERS

Many people in addition to managers are interested in the activities of a business enterprise. These "outsiders" include government officials, actual and potential lenders of money, customers, suppliers, and owners. These nonmanagerial users employ accounting reports about an enterprise to draw conclusions and make decisions about their future relationships with the company. They are not concerned with the details of day-to-day operations. Instead they want information about overall enterprise performance.

Financial Investors

People invest money in business enterprises to earn a return on their money. Investment always involves some risk that the expected return will not materialize or that all or part of the amount invested will be lost. Investors differ widely in the risks they are willing to accept. For example, a millionaire might invest $10,000 in an oil venture that would be far too risky for a bank handling depositors' funds or for a widow who has only $10,000 to invest. While these investors each have different investment objectives, all require accounting reports about the oil venture, both to evaluate the risk and the potential earnings and to compare investment alternatives.

There are two common ways in which people invest in a business. The first is to become a part owner of the business. If the business is a corporation, the investor must buy one or more shares of stock to become a part owner. Stock ownership usually permits the purchaser to share fully in any return that the enterprise may earn. For this opportunity the investor is willing to risk losing his entire investment should the venture fail.

The second common way of investing in a business enterprise is to lend it money. The lenders, considered creditors by the enterprise, may include financial institutions, such as banks or insurance companies, as well as individuals. Loans may take the form of bonds or short- or long-term promissory notes. Creditors, though interested in risk and earnings, are primarily interested in whether the enterprise will be financially able to repay the principal and interest when due. Accounting reports provide information vital to these conclusions.

One of the basic problems in interpreting financial statements is that they represent a financial history of the enterprise, while the owners and creditors of the enterprise are primarily concerned with the future. For example, the investor is interested in future earnings and the creditor is interested in debt-paying ability at some future time. In a very real sense financial statements covering past periods are useful only to the extent that they permit predictions of the future.

Financial statements are also very important because they permit the investor or the creditor to appraise the performance of the firm's management. The managers of business enterprises, and in particular the managers of large corporations, are responsible to financial investors for efficient administration of the assets placed in their care. Therefore, corporate managements owe investors, and society as well, reports on how successfully they have discharged this responsibility. Past performance of management is the best indication of how management will perform in the future.

The separation of corporate managements from corporate owners in our society adds emphasis to the importance of this reporting function. Most stockholders (ordinarily not creditors) have a voice in the management of the enterprise through their right to vote for the directors of the corporation. Relatively few stockholder groups of American corporations, however, are sufficiently well organized to participate actively in the management of the firm. Corporate managements, therefore, are relatively independent of their owners; in general the owners are permitted to measure the performance of management merely in their decision to buy or sell shares. Accounting reports permit these owners to appraise management performance but rarely to improve it.

Accounting reports to financial investors also inform potential owners and potential lenders, as well as people who make a living advising owners and lenders. In some respects potential enterprise investors make more use of accounting reports on that enterprise than do investors who have already committed themselves. Once people have invested in an enterprise they will usually keep informed of its activity only periodically, but they tend to investigate an investment possibility very thoroughly before they choose among several alternatives. An entire industry of financial analysts and investment counselors examines published accounting reports of companies and makes investment recommendations to potential investors.

Other Nonmanagerial Users

Two kinds of users of accounting reports are neither managers nor financial investors. The first group has an interest in a business enterprise because it benefits from a beneficial relationship with the business. The second group has in some way been designated by a government to oversee some aspect of the enterprise's operations.

The Beneficial Relationship

A beneficial relationship with a business enterprise consists of buying from it, selling to it, or working for it. Customers, suppliers, and employees use accounting reports to judge the degree of benefit they can expect from their relationship with a business activity.

Customers will use accounting reports to judge the ability of the enterprise to produce desired products or services in sufficient quantity, of adequate quality, and with the required continuity. A sound source of supply is a vital requirement for many business concerns. Customers who are dependent on an enterprise for their own financial well-being use the accounting reports of that enterprise continually to draw conclusions and make decisions about its status as a source of supply.

Similarly, every supplier of products or services wants to deal with a customer who will continue a fairly stable relationship and pay his bills on time. It is common for suppliers to check thoroughly into the financial status and reputation of potential customers before entering into a credit relationship with them. If you have ever applied for a gasoline-company credit card you realize that the application form required detailed personal financial information. In this respect a supplier has an interest in his customers that is similar to that of a lender of money.

Employees make similar use of accounting reports about their employers. These reports are especially important in those cases in which the employees have obtained a degree of bargaining power through labor unions. Here the emphasis is placed on determining the terms under which the union will continue its relationship with the employer enterprise. News reports of wage and bargaining talks give ample indication that unions keep a close watch on employers. The information provided by accounting reports is the focal point of many of these employee-employer bargaining sessions and promises to play an increasingly important role in the years ahead.

The Overseer Relationship

Government plays as large a part in the affairs of business enterprises as in the lives of individuals. Some people are concerned that the role of government is becoming too great, but the fact remains that today government does oversee certain aspects of business activity and depends very largely upon accounting reports to help accomplish its objectives.

The way in which government affects business activity most visibly is through its powers to impose and collect taxes. Every business enterprise is subject to some form of taxation. The list of taxes is formidable: for example, there are income, real estate, property, and excise taxes. The taxation problem is complicated by the fact that most businesses are taxed by states and municipalities as well as by the federal government. A typical business enterprise may file several dozen tax returns in the course of a year. Each of these is an accounting report.

The tax return type of accounting report is used by the government to draw conclusions about the business enterprise and to decide what action, if any, need be taken. The government decides whether the tax paid by the reporting enterprise conforms to the requirements of the law. If it concludes that the enterprise has not complied with the law, it then decides what kind of action must be taken. This action usually takes some legal form to ensure collection of a proper tax.

Governments set forth rules and regulations pertaining to the financial affairs of business. These rules are designed to protect the financial rights of investors, customers, employees, and the public, in situations where they may not be able to protect themselves. The rules are usually administered by special government agencies charged with regulating certain areas of business activity. These regulatory agencies require business enterprises under their jurisdiction to file accounting reports at regular intervals on their financial activities and status.

Typical of such government agencies are the federal Securities and Exchange Commission (SEC) and the public utility commissions (PUC) of the various states. The SEC is generally responsible, among other things, for regulating the sale and purchase of the bonds and stocks of most of our large corporations. The commission has set forth a series of regulations that require periodic accounting reports from those businesses under its jurisdiction. These regulations specify the accounting information that corporations must provide and are designed to require full disclosure and to prevent fraud. The SEC uses these accounting reports to draw conclusions about the activities of the reporting enterprises and to decide what regulatory actions it must take to protect investors from illegal practices. The commission has the authority to suspend transactions in a particular security for a short period; it may take action against any of the security exchanges, against the corporation whose securities are being traded, or against the accounting firm whose opinion accompanies the financial statements of the firm.

The state PUCs regulate the electric, gas, transportation, and communications enterprises within their respective states. In addition to overseeing the services performed by businesses and the financial well-being of these enterprises, regulatory agencies often participate in the establishment of rates for services performed. The accounting reports required by these agencies are numerous, and the reports eventually affect the daily lives of us all.

In addition to taxing and regulating business activity, government bodies serve as information collectors. The United States Department of Commerce, for example, collects financial information from many business firms in order to prepare and publish such economic statistics as the Consumer's Price Index. This is a very important government service and is the basis for much of the economic policy of our nation. Statistical information is gathered primarily from accounting reports submitted by many different business enterprises.

The number and nature of accounting reports required by governmental agencies has expanded markedly in recent years and will undoubtedly play an increasing role in the future.

SUMMARY

All users of accounting reports seek information about the business activities of the enterprise being reported upon. They use the accounting information to draw conclusions. These conclusions, in turn, help them to make decisions. The raw material from which accounting reports are made is the data flowing from business transactions. The manner in which the information is presented in the accounting report will depend on the user and the nature of the decision he has to make.

A summary of the users of accounting reports would look somewhat like this:

A. Managerial users at various levels of responsibility and authority who use accounting reports for:
1. Measuring performance
2. Planning

B. Nonmanagerial users, who include:
1. Financial investors (and their advisers)
   a. Owners
   b. Lenders
2. Those who are not financial investors
   a. Those with a beneficial relationship:
      1. Customers
      2. Suppliers
      3. Employees
   b. Those with an overseer relationship:
      1. Taxation agencies
      2. Regulatory agencies
      3. Statistics collectors

The purpose of this book is to develop in detail the exact nature of the accounting reports that are required by each of these users as well as the meaning of the information that the reports provide.

Questions for Review

1-1. In what kind of management decisions do accounting reports assist the manager? Be as specific as you can in describing the nature of the assistance provided.

1-2. What kind of measurements would be of particular importance if you wished to evaluate the performance of
    a. the foreman of the cutting department in a shirt factory?
    b. the sales manager of a paint company?
    c. the vice president in charge of production in a soft-drink factory?
    d. the president of an airline?

1-3. Performance measurement tries to answer questions of how well a particular job was accomplished or how well a department or company fared over a period of time. These judgments are necessarily comparative (that is, how well the department performed measured against a yardstick). Think of some yardsticks that are often used for performance measurement, and comment on their validity and usefulness.

1-4. A plant superintendent asks for accounting statements that measure the performance of each department in the plant. Which decisions of the plant superintendent will presumably be affected by these performance statements?

1-5. What uses would you make of accounting reports
    a. as the owner-manager of a service garage for the repair of automobiles?
    b. as a financial analyst for a large mutual investment fund?
    c. as a prospective investor in stock of a leading automobile manufacturer?

1-6. You have just secured a government contract for the manufacture and delivery of degassers to be attached to the carburetors of its fleet of vehicles. You decide to subcontract a portion of the work to a firm that you have never before done business with. What uses would you make of the accounting reports of the potential subcontractor?

1-7. Jim Smith, a mechanical engineer, works for a leading electrical equipment company. He has received an offer of employment as supervisor of an engineering department from a young, aggressive firm in the electrical manufacturing industry. What uses might Mr. Smith make of the accounting reports of his prospective employer?

1-8. Briefly describe the major uses of accounting reports for each of the following:
    a. A nonmanagerial shareowner who owns 75 per cent of the outstanding shares of the reporting firm.
    b. An insurance company that has lent the reporting firm $25 million for ten years at 8 per cent.
    c. A shareholder who owns just a few shares out of several million shares outstanding.

1-9. Briefly describe the financial information that will help a manager decide:
    a. Whether the firm will have to borrow on a short-term basis from the bank next year.

b. Whether to buy or to rent a computer (after it has been decided to acquire one).

c. Whether the firm should invest $10 million in a program of research and development of new uses for its product.

1-10. Name at least three federal agencies that require periodic financial reports from business firms, and indicate the uses these agencies make of the reports.

Chapter Two THE PURPOSE OF BUSINESS ACTIVITY

INTRODUCTION

Business enterprises, like individuals, wish to increase their ability to acquire and hold goods and services, and in general they seek to maintain as high a level of economic power as possible. Business firms are able to do this as long as they are able to use their financial resources profitably. Thus the primary motivating factor behind our economy is called the *profit motive*. We feel that the profit motive has been, and will continue to be, the major factor contributing to our high standard of living in this country. The desire for making sustained profits has brought this nation technological and economic progress beyond that of any other country.

The majority of business firms exist primarily to earn a profit in a manner consistent with ethical social mores. This is true for retailers, wholesalers, and product manufacturers, as well as for an almost unlimited variety of firms offering services. The sole purpose of the activity is to bring the owner-investors of the enterprise optimal profits over the longest possible time span while providing for society a needed product or service. Other purposes of these enterprises, even those that seem to conflict temporarily with the profit motive, are really intermediate steps in accomplishing the long-run goal of *optimizing profit*.

The term profit optimization is used, rather than the more common term profit maximization, because it better describes the way most businessmen react to their environment. The profit optimizer allows his decisions to reflect social and cultural attributes of society. His thought processes weigh qualitative as well as quantitative criteria. His goals are formulated with the realization that in the long run they are reachable only if they mesh with those of his fellows.

14

A substantial minority of enterprises, of course, do not have profits as a primary goal. These are hospitals, churches, public schools, government units, and many others. These *nonprofit* enterprises will be discussed later in this chapter. For now, attention will be directed to the more typical kind of business activity, the profit-making activity.

ACCOUNTING AND THE PROFIT MOTIVE

Accountants assume that business managers try to optimize long-run profits for the enterprise. Accountants, by means of the reports they prepare, measure the extent to which the managers succeed in achieving this goal.

Readers of accounting reports sometimes doubt the validity of the accounting assumption. Much of this doubt is caused by confusion over words. The key term is *long run*. When one reviews the actions of business managers over a single year, it is difficult to remember that they are trying to optimize their profits. When the owners of the General Electric Company, for example, created the General Electric Foundation, which donates money for furthering college education, they were still acting to increase profit in the long run. The company reasoned that in the long run people will be better educated and thus better able to create, use, and enjoy General Electric products. At the same time, people will feel kindly toward a firm that acts charitably in the short run.

A business enterprise will do many things in the short run that may seem contrary to profit optimization. Better working conditions, paid vacations, contributions to charity, product improvements, and lower-than-possible prices are just a few examples of apparently nonprofitable short-run actions that are really designed to optimize long-run profits.

The assumption of the long-run profit-optimization objective is valid, but is of limited usefulness in the control and management of the business enterprise. Neither managers nor accountants are equipped with a crystal ball that tells them whether a particular decision is consistent with the long-run profit objective. Only an examination of accomplished fact can provide the final answer, and at that point it is too late to change past earnings.

Accountants do not justify their existence by pointing out to management what should have been done after the enterprise has failed to optimize past profits. Accounting is useful insofar as it assists in improving future performance. This means that accounting deals with the short run: Any mistakes uncovered are short-run errors that can be corrected before major impairments to long-run profit have occured. In this sense, accounting reports are like the white line on a highway. Once the firm is on the road to long-run profit optimization, the accounting report can show the managers how well they are staying on that road. Accounting reports can indicate the need for corrective action and help managers reach decisions about when and how much to turn the wheel, step on the gas, or apply the brakes. Accounting reports do not, however, ensure that the firm is on the right road to profit optimization. That is the function of management, not accounting.

BASIC ACCOUNTING CONCEPTS

This section of the chapter deals with accounting definitions. It will require very close attention because definitions are learned only by understanding, rather than remembering, what is said. It is as important to understand the definitions in a book on accounting as it is to have the proper tubes in a radio set. Without them there can be no communication. (The glossary at the end of the book contains definitions of key terms and phrases found throughout the text.)

Assets. A firm's assets include all items of value to the firm that are available for current or future use and that are measurable in money terms. There are two kinds of assets:

1. *Monetary assets,* which are usually not income producing, including cash and claims to future cash.

2. *Nonmonetary assets,* including merchandise, real estate, equipment, and the like, which are used by a business in the process of earning a profit.

Equities. Equities are claims against the assets of the enterprise. If the claimant is not an owner, his equity is a liability to the firm. An owner's equity is his share of the net assets of the firm.

1. *Liabilities.* A firm's liabilities are its commitments, arising out of past transactions, to make future payments. These may include more than just legal liabilities (i.e., those currently enforceable in a court of law), if there is reasonable evidence that a future payment will be made, and if the amount is measurable in money.

2. *Owners' equity or net assets.* Owners' equity is the excess of a firm's assets over its liabilities and is sometimes called *net assets.* As we shall see below, earning profits is an important way of increasing the net assets of the firm. The term "net assets" is very important because it is used in most of the definitions given below.

Revenue. Revenue is one of the sources of a firm's net assets, and it is measured by assets received (or liabilities discharged), resulting from the process of providing goods and services to customers.

Expense. Expense is measured by the amount of assets consumed (or liabilities assumed) for the purpose of generating revenue for the business.

Profit. Profit is the excess of revenue over expense. Therefore, the effect of a profitable transaction is to increase the net assets of the firm. If the net assets given up (expense) exceed the net assets received (revenue), a *loss* has occurred.

Earnings. Earnings are the excess of revenue over expense (i. e., the increase in net assets) during a specified period of time, such as a month or a year. The word "earnings" differs from "profit" in that the latter refers to a single transaction. Net-asset changes are usually measured by time periods, rather than single transactions, and therefore the concept of earnings is extremely important. An excess of expenses over revenues (i.e., a decrease in net assets) for a period is called a *net loss.* The word "income" is often used as a synonym for earnings, but income has so many meanings that "earnings" will be used here instead.

Cost. The word "cost" is sometimes used to mean "expense"; it is a mistake to use the word this way, and considerable confusion results from doing so. Cost means outlay, measured in assets given up (and/or liabilities assumed) to acquire another asset. Thus the *cost* of an asset is the amount that has been or will be paid to gain useful possession of the asset. If and when this asset is later consumed, or given up, to obtain revenue, the asset becomes an *expense.*

Cost is, of course, related to expense: The amount of assets given up to earn revenue is usually measured by the former's cost, that is, the amount paid for the assets when they were acquired. For instance, when a retailer buys merchandise for $1.00, he becomes the owner of an asset having a *cost* of $1.00 (whether he pays for it at the time or not). When he later sells it for $1.25, the *expense* (merchandise given up in the sale) is measured by its original *cost* of $1.00. The revenue is $1.25, and the profit is $.25.

The ideas conveyed by these definitions are relatively simple. The definitions themselves, however, are difficult because the words are often used inconsistently in our everyday language. And accountants themselves are not as precise or consistent as they should be. This makes it even more important for the student to gain a firm understanding of accounting terms.

THE RELATIONSHIP
BETWEEN ASSETS AND PROFIT

The relationship between the profit arising from a transaction (or the earnings of a given period) and the net assets of the firm is a basic concept in accounting. If a farmer sells a truckload of eggs, he gives up an asset (the eggs) and he receives an asset (either a claim against the customer for the selling price of the eggs or, in a cash-and-carry transaction, cash). Whether the transaction results in a profit or a loss depends on the value placed on the asset received (revenue) compared with the asset given up (expense). The value of the asset received is a relatively simple matter if the cash is received immediately or if the claim against the customer is to be collected soon.

The value of the eggs to the farmer just prior to the sale may not be so simple. Accounting practice dictates that the value placed on the eggs be based on the *cost* of the eggs to the farmer. The ease of computing this cost varies with the case. If the farmer is really a wholesaler who buys the eggs from other farmers and who has few selling, delivery, or other expenses, it is fair to say that the cost of the eggs is his purchase price. On the other hand, if the farmer built the hen houses and feeders, raised or purchased the chickens, raised or purchased the feed, and performed a variety of other functions required in producing the eggs, then the cost to him of a particular truckload of eggs is a difficult calculation indeed. Nevertheless, the cost of the truckload of eggs can theoretically be computed: If the accountant determines that the claim against the purchaser is $175 and that the cost to the farmer of the truckload of eggs is $150, the sale transaction increases the farmer's net assets by $25—the profit on the sale.

THE RELATIONSHIP BETWEEN ASSETS AND EARNINGS

Very rarely is it possible for the accountant to compute with any assurance the profit attributable to a given transaction. Normally the cost allocations are necessarily so arbitrary that the resulting profit is unreliable; a manager who did not understand accounting might be misled by such profit figures to make poor decisions. It is customary, therefore, to compute earnings for given time periods rather than profits for specific transactions. It is true that the earnings of time periods are merely the sum total of the profits of all transactions occurring during that period, but when these transactions are added together, the need for arbitrary cost allocations begins to disappear. It may not be a difficult task, for example, for the farmer to compute the cost of the feed consumed by his chickens for a month or a week, if he finds this information useful. In any case this task is far simpler than determining the feed cost included in one egg or a dozen eggs or even a truckload. By shifting the basis of accounting from the transaction to the time period, many difficult problems are solved. Similarly, the longer the time period the more reliable the measurement of earnings becomes. The accountant can compute the earnings attributable to the egg business of the farmer over the farmer's lifetime with a high degree of assurance. This is because all of the costs attributable to the egg business can be allocated to this single time period and are therefore expenses. The earnings computation is a simple matter of deducting total expenses from total revenues.

The obvious limitation of this computation is that it is in no way useful to the farmer. The farmer is interested in accounting reports that he can use to conduct his egg business in the most profitable manner. Thus he must have timely reports at regular intervals covering relatively short periods. The optimum reporting period is therefore long enough so that the arbitrary cost allocations become relatively small and unimportant, and yet short enough to keep the farmer informed in time to operate his business properly.

As might be expected, habit and the calendar also have a great deal to do with the selection of the length of the accounting period. Managers receive the most frequent reports, but even for them, reports of earnings are rarely prepared for periods shorter than a month. Large corporations ordinarily report to stockholders annually, with very brief tentative reports prepared quarterly.

Assets and Earnings Illustrated

Assume that several individuals form the Good Neighbor Corporation and contribute $150,000 cash to it in exchange for its shares of stock. The corporation purchases an apartment house for $200,000, using $125,000 of the corporation's cash and borrowing $75,000 from a local bank, giving the bank a mortgage as collateral for the loan. An accounting report (called a *statement of financial position,* or *balance sheet*) of the corporation after these transactions is shown in Exhibit 2–1.

E X H I B I T 2 – 1

GOOD NEIGHBOR CORPORATION
STATEMENT OF FINANCIAL POSITION
As of June 1, 19xx

Assets		Equities	
Cash	$ 25,000	Mortgage note payable (liability)	$ 75,000
Apartment house	200,000	Owners' equity	150,000
Total assets	$225,000	Total equities	$225,000

Determining the source of the items in this statement is not a difficult matter. The corporation began business with $150,000 in cash and used $125,000 of that amount to acquire the apartment house, leaving a balance of $25,000. The bank contributed the remainder of the purchase price, and as a result, the corporation has a liability of $75,000 that must be paid, with interest, at a specified future time. Note also that the apartment house is valued at cost, regardless of what anyone might think it to be worth. Finally, the net assets are represented by the owners' equity. It is this amount that the corporation will try to optimize by operating the apartment house profitably.

Assume that in the first month of operations the apartment house tenants pay the corporation one month's rent of $5,000 in cash, and that at the beginning of the month the corporation buys a three-year fire insurance policy, paying $7,200 in cash. At the end of the month, $1,000 principal and $375 June interest on the mortgage note are paid. Assume also that we estimate the useful life of the apartment house to be fifty years. In addition, we can reasonably anticipate that semiannual property taxes of $1,200 will have to be paid six months from now. The financial position statement as of the end of the first month's operations is shown in Exhibit 2–2.

EXHIBIT 2-2

GOOD NEIGHBOR CORPORATION
STATEMENT OF FINANCIAL POSITION
As of June 30, 19xx

Assets		Equities	
Cash (1)	$ 21,425	Liabilities:	
Prepaid insurance (2)	7,000	Taxes payable (4)	$ 200
Apartment house (3)	199,667	Mortgage note payable (5)	74,000
		Total liabilities	$ 74,200
		Owners' equity	$153,892
Total assets	$228,092	Total equities	$228,092

Deciding where these items came from is not as simple as it was in the statement made at the beginning of the month. Before you read the explanations given below, examine the statement carefully and see if you can decide what each item represents. The numbers in parentheses are keyed to the explanations.

1.   The corporation began the month with $25,000 cash, collected $5,000 from tenants, paid the insurance company $7,200 and the bank $1,375, leaving a balance of $21,425.

2.   When the corporation paid the insurance premium, it acquired a three-year asset, consisting of the protection against loss due to fire, and so on, which had a *cost* of $7,200. With the expiration of the first month of the policy, $\frac{1}{36}$ or $200 of this cost became *expense*, that is, this portion was "used up" in the process of earning the first month's revenues. At the end of the month, $7,000 remains to be assigned to revenues over the next thirty-five months.

3.   The same reasoning is applied to the apartment house, except that the fifty-year life is obviously an estimate. Because of this and because of the large number of dollars often involved, *depreciation* (the using up over a period of time of an asset such as the apartment house) causes accountants much difficulty. Nevertheless, here the accountant reasons that $\frac{1}{12}$ of $\frac{1}{50}$ of the $200,000 cost has been consumed in the process of earning the first month's revenues.

4.   The "taxes payable" item represents $\frac{1}{6}$ of the semiannual property tax bill. Even though the tax bill will not be paid until some later date, it is important

to recognize that each month's operations must bear its share of property tax expense.

5. A $1,000 payment was made on the principal of the mortgage note during the month. Note that when payments on any liability are made, both the assets and liabilities are reduced, and the owners' equity (the net assets) is unaffected. Like the property taxes, interest expense would have to be recognized even if no cash payment had been made in June.

6. The owners' equity (net assets) is the difference between assets and liabilities at the end of the month. Comparing this figure with the net assets at the beginning of the month, we have:

Net assets, end of month	$153,892
− Net assets, beginning of month	150,000
Increase in net assets	$ 3,892

Since we know all the transactions that occurred and all the conditions that prevailed during the month, we should be able to determine the factors that caused the change in net assets. We know, for example, that the corporation received assets, cash in this case, from tenants for the month's rent. This is the revenue for the month. We know that in the process of earning one month's rent, $200 of the cost of the insurance premium and $333 of the cost of the apartment house were used up, according to the rules for recording consumption of assets of this type. We know that liabilities of $200 for taxes and $375 for interest were assumed, the former remaining unpaid at June 30. These four items make up the total expenses of the first month's operations. An accounting report° showing the monthly earnings appears in Exhibit 2–3.

EXHIBIT 2-3

GOOD NEIGHBOR CORPORATION
STATEMENT OF EARNINGS
For June 19xx

Revenues:		
Apartment rentals		$5,000
Expenses:		
Insurance	$200	
Depreciation	333	
Taxes	200	
Interest	375	
Total expenses		1,108
Net earnings		$3,892

°For the sake of simplicity we have made no attempt to present a realistic illustration. Obviously, operating an apartment house involves many other expenses not considered here, such as maintenance, utilities, and income taxes.

From the illustrations concerning the egg farmer and the apartment house operation, you have already learned a very important fact: The profit resulting from a single transaction, or the earnings of an accounting period ($3,892 for June, in the case of the Good Neighbor Corporation), have the effect of increasing the business enterprise's net assets, the excess of its assets over its liabilities ($153,892 in the case of the Good Neighbor Corporation). The accountant's definition of an asset depends to a great extent upon his ability to measure it; his measurement in turn affects his definition of earnings. These measurements often depend on rough estimates and are therefore subject to sizable error (e.g., the depreciation of $333 is extremely arbitrary). Difficult and vague as they are, the accountant's definitions are rather widely accepted by the business community, and *earnings* has achieved a position of considerable importance as a measure of the performance of an enterprise.

The illustrations also showed that increasing net earnings is not the only way to increase the net assets of a business. The other principal way is to issue shares of stock to the original owners ($150,000) or to new owners. Obviously, assets received by the enterprise in this manner do not constitute revenue. An enterprise may also borrow assets (e.g., the $75,000 mortgage loan). Borrowing increases enterprise assets, but since it also increases enterprise liabilities, net assets are unchanged.

In addition, you have learned something about the flow of net assets out of the enterprise. For example, if expenses were to exceed revenues (i.e., a net loss for the period), the net assets would be reduced. When assets and liabilities are reduced in like amounts (e.g., the $1,000 payment on the mortgage), the firm's net assets are unaffected. Although they are not illustrated, there are several other types of transactions that do reduce net assets. Among these are the repurchase of shares from the owners and the distribution of dividends to the owners. (Neither of these types of transactions has an effect on earnings. Dividends are a distribution of earnings, not a reduction in earnings, and thus payment of dividends is not an expense.)

Finally, you have learned that costs incurred as assets are acquired for future consumption, and that these assets are measured in dollars by the amount of cash given up (as in the case of the insurance premium of $7,200) or liability incurred (if payment is not made immediately). The consumption of the asset is measured by the cost of the consumed portion and is called *expense* (as in the case of the $200 June insurance expense, or the $333 June depreciation). Sometimes the asset is consumed before it is recognized in the financial statements; i.e., the existence of the asset is acknowledged only by the cost of the consumed portion. In the above illustration, both the right to use the premises (evidenced by the $200 property tax liability) and the right to the use of borrowed money (evidenced by the $375 interest payment) are assets that are recognized only in the process of consumption. Accountants must be careful to recognize this consumption as expense in the statement of earnings of the period of consumption, even though the asset is not recognized in the statement of financial position.

OPTIMIZING PROFIT

Single-transaction profit and period earnings both deal with the excess of revenues over expenses. Obviously, then, the long-run profitability of the firm depends on how well the managers are able to increase revenues and decrease expenses. However, since an increase in revenues almost always involves an increase in expenses, management must try to increase revenues proportionally more than expenses are increased. Profitability may be increased even when revenues decrease, so long as expenses decrease proportionally more. This is an important idea to remember. Business managers may forget that profitability is a relationship between the two factors, and mistakenly stress increasing revenues while ignoring the corresponding expenses. Or they may think they are able to decrease expenses without any corresponding decrease in revenues; this tactic may result in a short-run false economy. If the farmer, for example, were to use a less costly and less potent chicken feed, he might reduce expenses for a few months without impairing revenues. Eventually, however, the chickens would start laying fewer and poorer-quality eggs, and his long-run earnings picture would grow dimmer. Failure of the apartment house firm to incur maintenance expense might mean that long-run profitability is being unwisely sacrificed for short-run profitability. The relationship between revenues and expenses is the tightrope upon which all managers must perform. Properly timed accounting reports help maintain the necessary balance.

THE ACCOUNTANT: MEASURER OR RECORDER?

The discussion to this point has represented measurement of periodic earnings, assets, and liabilities of the firm as one of the important roles of the accountant. The importance of this function is apparent, for we have already seen many of the uses to which these measurements are put, both by users outside the firm and by internal managers. Many accountants assert that this is the most important thing accountants do.

In view of this, it may be surprising to learn that for the accountant to measure assets and earnings is a relatively recent development. Other professional groups, such as economists, engineers, statisticians, and appraisers, all perform functions that must be considered highly relevant to the measurement of the assets and earnings of a business firm, and most accountants deny competence in or responsibility for the functions these groups perform, which include measurements of the current value of business assets. Most accountants deny that it is part of their responsibility to measure what assets are "worth." Instead, as we have already seen in the Good Neighbor Corporation illustration, accountants measure assets, and periodic consumption of assets, in terms of the *cost* (defined above) of the assets to the firm, rather than by what the assets are currently "worth." (The word "worth" is in common usage, but is obviously ambiguous, making the quotation marks necessary.)

Usually the difference between the current value of assets and their recorded cost is not large in the case of assets recently acquired, or assets that are consumed rapidly. But in other cases, the difference can be large, and this difference is a serious matter. In the Good Neighbor illustration, the accountant will continue to report the apartment house year after year at the cost of $200,000 (reduced by the cost consumed to date, or *accumulated depreciation*) during the entire useful life of the building. Only in extraordinary circumstances, such as uninsured loss by flood or riot, would the accountant recognize an unexpected drop in value of the building, and under *no* circumstances (except in the event of actual sale) would he recognize an increase in current value due solely to increase in prices of real estate in the neighborhood. It is not difficult to see that after many years the original cost of the apartment house, less depreciation, may have no relation to the current value of the building. Nevertheless, the accountant does not ordinarily attempt to determine this "worth," or to disclose it even if he knows what it is.

The basic reasons for this are not difficult to understand. Determining the current value of many types of assets is an extremely difficult, costly procedure. Most business assets are not bought and sold regularly, and established market prices do not exist. The current value of these assets is usually a matter of opinion, based on many assumptions that might or might not be acceptable to a reader of financial statements. Accountants as a group are not yet willing either to determine these values by their own procedures or to accept without question the opinions of experts such as engineers and appraisers. As a result, the user of statements of financial position and statements of earnings of business firms is forced to make decisions without the benefit of current-value information.

The controversy over the responsibility of accountants for current-value information has gone on for many years and will apparently continue for many more. Periods of more rapid inflation, which tend to hasten the obsolescence of originally recorded costs, strengthen the case of these who favor some kind of change in reporting procedures, but we have not yet experienced the degree of inflation that would force accountants to adjust asset values to reflect a lower value of the dollar. Although tax and other governmental reporting requirements do not control general-purpose financial reporting, they do exert a strong influence on accountants. Almost without exception, these requirements call for financial statements based on historical cost. In any case, accountants are not yet willing to accept responsibility for financial statements containing assets and liabilities that have been revalued to reflect current conditions.

Traditionally, the bookkeeper has viewed himself as the recorder of the transactions to which the firm is a party, defining *transactions* as events in which money, goods, or services are exchanged with other persons or firms. This recording function is considered a part of accounting, since bookkeeping includes interpretation and classification of the events' effects on the firm's assets and liabilities, but the accountant's responsibilities in measuring assets, liabilities, and earnings are broader than this. For example, the accountant recognizes the need to record (1) changes in financial position that could be assumed to be a function of the passage of time (even though there is no specific event), such as depreciation; (2) anticipated future events that affect current financial position, such as anticipated sale of an item of merchandise at a loss, or anticipated default on an account receivable by a customer, or anticipated payment of property taxes at a specified future time, such taxes being applicable to the current period; and (3) internal exchanges among subunits within the firm, reflecting movements of goods and services resulting particularly from internal (usually manufacturing) activities.

On the other hand, accountants ignore other events and conditions that many believe should have an effect on financial position and earnings. Long-term investments in intangible assets, as evidenced by personnel training costs, research and development costs, and advertising costs, are accounted for as if the costs were being consumed in the period of expenditure. For example, although the apartment building (a tangible asset) is recognized as an asset that will last fifty years, an equally large expenditure for research would usually be treated as current expense, even though it may be obvious that *none* of the expenditure is beneficial to the earnings of the current year. Although the cost of the research is obviously incurred for the purpose of bringing in revenues in the future, there is no certain way of measuring how successful this effort will be. Similar difficulties of measurement occur with many long-term investments.

One of the problems arising from valuing assets at the original cost to the firm, rather than at current value, can be demonstrated with an illustration. Assume that a prospective investor wishes to compare firms A and B by examining their statements of earnings for the year 19x1 and statements of financial position at December 31, 19x1. Assume further that during the year 19x0 both firms purchased adjoining parcels of land at a cost of $10,000 to each firm and that the market price of each parcel rose to $12,000 by the end of 19x1. On December 30, 19x1, firm A sold its parcel, recording the profit, or increase in net assets, of $2,000. Firm B did not sell, and at December 31, 19x1, it valued its land at $10,000. In comparing the financial statements, it would very likely appear to the investor that firm A had the advantage, when in fact the only difference between them was that firm A sold its land and firm B decided to hold its land for sale at some later date. With the meager information at hand, there is no way to determine which decision was the wiser. This judgment depends on expectations on the market price in 19x2 and later years: if these are expected to be high, we could easily conclude that firm B deserves to be judged the better firm, but the financial statements do not provide this information. This invalid comparison could be avoided only by valuing B's land at the market price of $12,000 at December 31, 19x1, thus allowing it to record the gain of $2,000, even though it did not sell.

Another aspect of the problem is the fact that, in its decision to sell, firm A might have been strongly influenced by the knowledge that the profit on the sale would be reported in the financial statements, and under certain circumstances this desire to appear profitable might have been the primary motivating factor in the decision, rather than long-run profit optimization.

Obviously, the reverse situation is also possible. If land prices had dropped between 19x0 and 19x1, firms wishing to conceal the fact of the loss from the users of the statements might hold on to the land unwisely. In either case, periodic net earnings, as defined and measured by the accountant, is not a good criterion for comparing the performance of the managements of the two firms, since the management might be influenced to make decisions which would not be consistent with the long-run profit-optimizing objectives of the firm.

BUSINESS VERSUS PERSONAL OBJECTIVES

While the objective of business enterprises seems to be long-run money making, we must remember that these enterprises are made up of individuals who have all sorts of personal objectives. As managers and employees of an enterprise they may be thought of as profit optimizers, but as people they are family men and women, church members, voters and politicians, patriots, individual money accumulators, and money spenders. These objectives conflict with one another as well as with the enterprise objectives.

It is almost impossible to sort out objectives in the owner-manager situation or, to a lesser degree, in partnerships. Accounting reports designed to help an enterprise strive for optimum profits mean little if their users do not take advantage of their recommendations. The somewhat painful and obviously unprofitable persistence of many owner-managed corner grocery stores is a case in point. Changing times have dictated the market shift to supermarket buying. The accounting reports of the corner grocery men have indicated this change in enterprise environment and long-run profit potential, yet some of these businessmen refuse to change their ways. Tradition, lack of investment incentive, family ties, and similar personal reasons outweigh the enterprise objectives of long-run profit optimization, which would dictate drastic changes in operating methods and increased investment. The result is eventual failure, even bankruptcy, for many owner-managed corner grocery stores.

The conflict of personal objectives with the enterprise's long-run profit objective exists in corporations as well as in owner-manager situations. Because the corporation is a distinct legal entity, the enterprise can be more easily separated from the individuals in it; and because more people are involved, a greater effort is made to achieve this separation. Such separation makes the enterprise objective easier to recognize and achieve. Nevertheless, even in a corporation, employees and managers are still people with objectives that are different from those of the business enterprise itself. For instance, the assistant cost accountant of an automotive parts manufacturing enterprise may be more interested in playing the stock market than he is in optimizing company profit. He may tend, therefore, to spend time on the job reading the stock quotations in the *Wall Street Journal*. If he were genuinely concerned with optimizing the profits of the enterprise, he would not think of loafing on the job. These differing objectives of a business enterprise itself and of the people that make it up provide an additional reason for management's use of accounting reports.

THE NONPROFIT ENTERPRISE

A substantial amount of organization theory is based on the rather obvious proposition that organizations are mindless and therefore do not have objectives. Only individual owners, managers, and employers of the firm have objectives, it is contended, and these may be diverse, inconsistent, and shifting in importance from one time to another. Nevertheless it is still necessary and useful, if not completely accurate, to distinguish between *profit* and *nonprofit* organizations, based on the assumption that the profit motive is dominant among management in some firms, and social, political, or religious motives are dominant in others. No single set of accounting reports covering the operations of an entire firm can take into account all of the motives of the individuals within the firm. Accountants assume, instead, that users of financial statements are interested in the profit-making ability of firms organized primarily for that purpose, and that secondary objectives may be ignored, or dealt with outside the financial statements. Furthermore, most nonprofit goals are highly subjective and qualitative, and accountants take the position that dollar measurements of these goals are not possible.

This means that the contribution of accounting reports to the operations of so-called nonprofit organizations, and to performance measurement, is not as important as it is in profit-seeking firms. Since objective measurements are not possible, the accountant usually returns to his more traditional role of recording and classifying financial transactions so that summaries of these transactions will provide an adequate description of the operations (if not the basic objectives) of the organization, and also of collecting and reporting other quantitative information that management may need. In addition, however, we find that accountants do provide a variety of accounting services for nonprofit firms. Examination of some of these services gives important insights into the broad scope of accounting activity.

Nonprofit Objectives

About the only generalization one can make about the objectives of nonprofit organizations is that they exist to provide some service, or to fulfill some social need, that cannot be provided adequately or efficiently by unorganized individuals. This generalization is not very helpful, because such organizations range all the way from the Red Cross, which is a worldwide organization with thousands of full-time employees, organized to alleviate suffering and privation in case of war or other disaster, to a local fraternity of college students, organized to provide certain social and economic benefits (e.g., from operating a fraternity house) for the members themselves.

Even these extremes in organizational patterns exhibit some common attributes, however. It seems clear, for instance, that the concepts of revenue and expense, as applied to profit-seeking firms, are not particularly useful in nonprofit firms. The Red Cross, for instance, is organized for the purpose of spending money; practically all of the services it provides call for expenditures of large sums, sometimes over extended periods. Obviously, this cannot be accomplished unless the money is first collected from contributors; but the amount of the collections, and the fund-raising drive that resulted in the collections, are based on the projected expenditures. If the objectives of the Red Cross are to be expressed in financial terms, description of these expenditures provides the best method of doing so.

A Charitable Fund

To illustrate the contrast in objectives, Exhibit 2–4 presents the condensed operating statement of a hypothetical charitable fund compared with the corresponding statement of a profit-seeking firm.

In the first place, the statements are of different kinds: one (White Feather) is a statement of cash and securities contributions and distributions, and the other (XYZ Manufacturing) is a statement of earnings. The difference in concept between these two statements should be apparent from the definition of earnings and the Good Neighbor illustration given earlier in this chapter.* Our interest here is to demonstrate how the difference in basic objectives between profit and nonprofit organizations is reflected in the financial statements of the two firms. These points should be noted:

1. Sales of the XYZ Company include both cash sales and sales on credit, but contributions to the White Feather Fund do not include promises or pledges for future contributions. Noncash contributions, such as securities, are included.

---

*The full significance of retained earnings in the XYZ Company statement, and its relationship to double-entry bookkeeping and the statement of financial position for profit-seeking firms, are discussed in detail in Chapter 3.

EXHIBIT 2 - 4

THE WHITE FEATHER FUND
STATEMENT OF FUND CONTRIBUTIONS AND EXPENDITURES
For the Year 19x0

Contributions:		
From donors		$100,000
From special projects:		
Revenues	$250,000	
Expenses	100,000	150,000
Total contributions		$250,000
Administrative expenses		17,500
Net contributions		$232,500
Cash & securities,		
January 1, 19x0		10,000
Available for distribution		$242,500
Distributions:		
Boy scouts	$100,000	
Heart fund	75,000	
Home for the aged	60,000	
Total distributions		$235,000
Cash and securities,		
December 31, 19x0		$ 7,500

THE XYZ MANUFACTURING COMPANY
STATEMENT OF EARNINGS
For the Year 19x0

Sales revenues		$500,000
Expenses:		
Materials used	$250,000	
Wages & salaries	100,000	
Depreciation	100,000	
Total expenses		450,000
Net earnings before		
income tax		$ 50,000
Income tax		20,000
Net earnings after		
income tax		$ 30,000
Retained earnings,		
January 1, 19x0		205,000
Available for dividends		235,000
Dividends		25,000
Retained earnings,		
December 31, 19x1		$210,000

2. Expenses of special projects (for example, the cost of serving a $100-a-plate dinner) and administrative expenses (salaries of fund employees, office rent, and so forth) are properly called "expenses" to the extent that they are incurred for the purpose of increasing fund contributions. But expenses are viewed very differently by contributors to the fund and by XYZ customers. Contributors insist that the smallest possible part of their contribution be absorbed in promotion and administration, and that a maximum proportion be available for distribution to worthy casuses. As a result, charitable funds tend to give wide publicity to their low administrative expenses. The XYZ Company, on the other hand, is not likely to boast to customers about its low expense and high profits.

3. Depreciation is clearly a determinant of net earnings of the XYZ Company but such is not the case in the White Feather statement. Although charitable funds are not likely to have large investments in depreciable assets, other non-profit firms, such as churches and educational institutions, do. These firms must exert careful control over their long-lived assets, just as profit-seeking firms must do, and they may prepare a financial statement in which these assets are listed. Generally, some measure of current value of these assets is of greater interest

to nonprofit firms than is cost, because the insurance coverage, loan values, and cost of replacement are the major concerns of the management. Earnings measurement in the accounting sense, which calls for depreciation based on cost, is of no importance to the nonprofit firms.

4. Some rough analogy may be drawn between the $242,500 available for distribution in the White Feather statement, and the $235,000 available for dividends of the XYZ Company, but there is great danger in carrying the analogy too far. All or most of the $242,500 is likely to be in a distributable form, but much of the $235,000 of the XYZ Company is likely to be in the form of income-producing assets, and it might be unwise or impossible for management ever to distribute such an amount to stockholders as a dividend. Many theorists would seriously question whether optimizing dividend payments to stockholders is a primary objective of profit-seeking firms. White Feather Fund, on the other hand, is not concerned with accumulating income-producing assets, and distribution of its reserves is its only basic reason for existence. Obviously, the fact that in 19x0 White Feather distributed more than its net contributions is in no way to be interpreted as a sign of unsuccessful operation.

5. The basic distinction between the two types of firms is recognized by the Internal Revenue Service, in that nonprofit firms are not subject to income tax.

From the accounting point of view, the differences in objectives between these two firms seem much more important than the similarities. This is particularly true in the case of the charitable fund, which clearly has no important profit motives. We have already seen, however, that there are many kinds of so-called nonprofit firms, some with diverse objectives in which the profit motive may be partially involved or in which the managers often behave much as they would in a profit-seeking firm. A few examples will be covered briefly to illustrate the wide diversity among nonprofit firms.

A State-assisted University

Very few educational institutions are supported entirely by tuition receipts. Those that are should be considered profit-seeking firms for accounting purposes. It is generally conceded that it is socially inadvisable and/or economically impossible to support educational programs in this manner. In a state-assisted university, for instance, it is appropriate to consider tuition as revenue, but these fees are usually only a fraction of the total cost of education. The institution is organized not to make a profit, but to fulfill a broad social purpose: to provide college education to people who can afford to pay only a portion of the cost. State-assisted universities are obviously nonprofit institutions.

From an accounting standpoint, however, these institutions have some important differences when compared with charitable organizations. One of these is heavy expenditure for long-lived assets such as land, buildings, and equipment that must be financed and cared for. These assets require commitment of funds for many years into the future and also create circumstances that make long-term borrowing possible. There is a tendency for institutions to behave as profit-oriented firms in this regard, that is, to maximize the services to be gained from the plant and equipment at minimum cost. However, this policy must always be consistent with the much more basic educational purpose that cannot be measured in dollars.

Educational institutions also have substantial payrolls of professional, administrative, and staff personnel. Some of the accountants' cost control procedures, highly useful in profit-seeking firms, are applicable here, particularly in nonprofessional categories, but whether they should be used in control of professional salaries is controversial. Low salaries for teachers have usually been interpreted as a sign of a poor educational institution, rather than as a sign of efficient, low-cost operation. Educational administrators are more likely to boast about high cost as a sign of excellence (as well as a sign of inflation), and the mark of a "good" academic administrator or institution is often how much, rather than how little, money is spent. For administrators to complain of insufficient funds, pointing out how much better the academic program would be if only the money were available, is standard practice. These nonprofit criteria for measuring performance raise serious questions not only about the applicability of standard accounting practices in these institutions but also about the broader questions of how society can ever decide whether or not it is getting its money's worth in education. This is a particularly serious question in state-assisted educational institutions, because the tax levied in support of these units is not a voluntary contribution. Since taxpayers are forced to contribute to state-supported institutions, they should have the right to ask if the tax dollars devoted to education are wisely spent.

Although accounting can make only limited contributions to educational institutions in quantifying objectives and performance measurement, substantial assistance is provided in these areas:

1. Asset control—controlling cash, securities, receivables, supplies, and long-lived assets, much as in profit-seeking firms. The purposes are to promote efficiency and reduce loss through error or fraud.

2. Expenditure control—limiting expenditures by means of a decentralized system of expenditure budgets.

3. Performance measurement—establishing norms or standards of performance for certain routine, nonacademic kinds of services.

In addition, all major universities carry on certain activities that must make a recognizable profit to justify their continuation. Activities such as research under industrial or government contracts, certain adult educational programs, some cultural programs open to the public, and a host of other activities rely on accounting measurements to decide whether they "stand on their own feet" (are profitable) and whether these should be continued or abandoned.

Governmental Units

Since a state-assisted university is partly a governmental unit, any discussion of the accounting contribution to a county, state, or federal government simply involves changing the degree to which the governmental administrators are responsible to the taxpayers. This responsibility becomes greater as the proportion of tax receipts becomes greater, and the accounting function becomes more important to the control and measurement of the administration. Fiscal solvency and efficiency in the conduct of governmental activities rank high among the objectives of all governmental units. The budget is the primary instrument by which governmental policy is communicated and controlled and by which financial responsibility is implemented. As channels of communication between voters and governmental units improve (i.e., as accounting reports on the financial responsibility of governmental administrators become more widely read and understood), we should expect a more direct participation of taxpayers in governmental financial affairs through the voting process.

Pseudo-nonprofit Institutions

A significant number of institutions have profit objectives in the accounting sense, but are called nonprofit primarily because the ultimate beneficiaries of the profit-seeking operation are related to the organization in an unusual way. In farm cooperatives, for example, the farmer-members are both owners (or participants) in the cooperative and customers of it. Profits of the organization are returned to them periodically as rebates or dividends.

Mutual insurance companies and mutual savings and loan associations arrange to have customers or depositors also receive profits from the operation. From a managerial point of view, these firms are managed just as profit-seeking firms are managed, with the same criteria for measurement of performance. Distribution of the profits, and the fact that these go to customers, present no special problems.

SUMMARY

The business objective of long-run optimum profitability is a legitimate and necessary part of the American way of life. Without it, innovation and a high standard of living would not exist.

Special terms are used by the accountant to describe different concepts of profit:

> Profit = Revenues − Expenses, for a single transaction
> Earnings = Revenues − Expenses, over a period of time

Profit may also be described as the increase in the net assets arising from a single revenue-producing transaction. Earnings result in an increase in net assets from all the revenue-producing transactions over a period of time. Revenues and expenses are narrower terms than most laymen believe. Certain types of asset inflows and outflows can occur without resulting in revenues or expenses.

Periodic measurement of earnings requires allocations of revenues and expenses based on estimates and predictions. This process grows more difficult as the time period involved becomes shorter. Accounting reports are most useful, however, when they are timely, and accountants continually make short-period allocations.

Accounting reports also facilitate the management of a business enterprise by relating the efforts of individuals to the objectives of the enterprise. This relationship is necessary in any form of business, whether it is owner-managed, a partnership, or a corporation.

Accounting reports in the profit-seeking business firm are directed primarily at helping to optimize long-run profits. The nonprofit enterprise, on the other hand, uses accounting reports primarily for asset and expenditure control, because the primary objective of such an enterprise is the satisfaction of social need.

Questions for Review

2-1. Use a personal experience or a situation that you know about at first hand to demonstrate the concept of profit from a transaction and/or earnings from a series of occurrences over a period of time. What methods would you recommend for the measurement of profit or earnings?

2-2. In each of the instances cited below, give an argument showing that each company's objective is long-run profit optimization:

    a. A company contributes $5,000 to the local United Appeals drive.

    b. A company spends $10,000 for landscaping the grounds surrounding the factory building.

    c. A pharmaceutical firm contributes $100,000 in drugs to be shipped to Cuba in exchange for prisoners.

    d. A company voluntarily institutes a retirement plan for retired employees at an estimated cost of $50,000 per year.

2-3. In each of the cases in 2–2, suggest a possible objective other than profit optimization. Which type of objective seems most plausible? Why?

2-4. What effect do the following items have on revenue?
   a. investment by the owner
   b. commission from the sale of real estate
   c. sale of merchandise on account by a department store

2-5. What effect do the following items have on expenses?
   a. payment of a dividend to stockholders
   b. office supplies used by a real-estate broker
   c. cost of merchandise sold by a department store

2-6. Discuss the possible effect of the following decisions on short-run profits and on long-run profits:

   a. A local manufacturer of paints and varnishes has been approached by the United Appeals, which is soliciting new contributors to its general drive. A severe recession has cut into the manufacturer's yearly profits; the company nevertheless decides to make a sizable contribution to the drive.

   b. A medium-sized appliance manufacturer has experienced extreme difficulty in keeping its prices in line with other appliance manufacturers. The company has just decided to lower its quality-control standards throughout the manufacturing process.

   c. A soap company has just perfected a new detergent for automatic washing machines. While the product was being developed, the company decided to conduct a high-pressure advertising campaign including unsubstantiated claims for the product that have not materialized.

2-7. Sam and Mike, first-year accounting students, are debating business objectives. Sam states that profit optimization is the only logical objective for most businesses. Mike contends that business survival, rather than profit optimization, would be the logical objective for most businesses. State and defend your position regarding Sam and Mike's discussion.

2-8. Dan Smith and his three sons sell Christmas trees each year. They rent a plot of ground on a busy street in their community. They operate from December 1 to December 25 each year.
   a. What need would they have for accounting reports?
   b. At what times during their operating season would accounting reports be most helpful?
   c. What measurements would be necessary if they wished to know how well they were doing (1) on December 15 and (2) on December 26?

2-9. Assets are often defined as a pool of wealth. In your opinion, what kinds of assets would be included in this "pool of wealth" for the following types of business operations?
   a. the leading department store in a community of 1 million people
   b. a textile manufacturer that has had unprofitable operations during the past three years

c. a professional football team enfranchised with the National Football League

2-10. Indicate the basic similarities and differences in the nature of the assets included in the three businesses above. Do you think that each of these three businesses could exercise the same degree of control over its assets?

2-11. The text has stated that accounting deals primarily with the short run. How, then, does accounting contribute to long-run profit optimization? Be specific in describing its contribution.

2-12. The text has indicated that both revenues *and* expenses have to be considered when trying to optimize profits. As the manager of a retail store, which of the following two courses of action would you prefer? An increase in sales revenue of $1.00, or a $1.00 decrease in real estate taxes. (The merchandise cost associated with the additional sales revenue is $.60.)

2-13. The president of a local chain of six restaurants has recently been selected as a campaign manager for the annual Red Cross drive for funds.

a. What type of accounting reports will the campaign manager need to conduct the fund drive?

b. How would these accounting reports and their purposes differ from those he might use in conducting his restaurant operations?

Problems for Analysis

2-14. Assume that the Arrow Corporation neither issued nor redeemed any ownership shares during a certain period and declared $10,000 in dividends. How much were their earnings during the period if their assets and liabilities were as follows?

	Beginning	Ending
Total assets	$150,000	$165,000
— Total liabilities	45,000	40,000
Net assets	$105,000	$125,000

2-15. "Our earnings won't be very good next year. We've got a large bond liability to pay off." Comment.

2-16. The Chatham Company received revenues of $100,000, incurred expenses of $70,000, declared dividends of $25,000, issued new shares for a total of $15,000, and gave up $5,000 to redeem shares during the year. If its assets were $100,000 and liabilities were $40,000 on January 1, how much were net assets on December 31?

2-17. The Blenheim Corporation's net assets were $25,000 on March 1 and $28,000 on March 31, and you know that March earnings were $8,000 and dividends $10,000. What are the possible explanations for the difference?

2-18. The Northridge Company had net assets of $125,000 by the end of 19x5. If 19x5 earnings were $40,000, 19x5 dividends declared were $15,000, and no shares were issued or redeemed in 19x5, what had its net assets been at the beginning of 19x5?

2-19. Fill in the missing figures in the table below.

	Case 1	*Case 2*	*Case 3*	*Case 4*
Total assets, beginning	$100,000	$140,000	$210,000	$165,000
Total assets, ending	125,000	135,000	190,000	180,000
Total liabilities, beginning	30,000	65,000	15,000	70,000
Total liabilities, ending	60,000	40,000	25,000	60,000
Revenues	150,000	?	240,000	125,000
Expenses	120,000	62,000	?	85,000
Dividends	?	10,000	0	10,000
Assets received from shares issued	10,000	12,000	0	0
Assets given up for shares redeemed	25,000	5,000	0	?

2-20. Write a correct equation using all the symbols below.

A_{t-1} = Total assets at the beginning of the period

A_t = Total assets at the end of the period

L_{t-1} = Total liabilities at the beginning of the period

L_t = Total liabilities at the end of the period

R = Net assets received from sales of goods and services rendered to customers (revenue) during the period

E = Net assets consumed in bringing in revenue (expense) during the period

D = Net assets given to shareowners as dividends during the period

SI = Net assets received from issue of shares to owners during the period

SR = Net assets given up to redeem outstanding shares during the period

Guide for Problem Solutions

In many of the following problems, you will be asked to compute the earnings of an enterprise for a period of time, which means that you will have to determine the revenues and the expenses associated with them for that period. For this purpose, we suggest that your answers appear in the following form:

(NAME OF ENTERPRISE)

STATEMENT OF EARNINGS

(Period Covered)

Revenues:	
(description of revenue item)	$(amount)
(description of revenue item)	(amount)
(etc.)	(etc.)
Total revenues	$Total
— Expenses associated with revenues:	
(description of expense item) $(amount)	
(description of expense item) (amount)	
(description of expense item) (amount)	
(etc.) (etc.)	
Total expenses	$Total
Earnings for period covered	$(difference)

This is similar in form to many earnings reports found in the regular financial reports of business enterprises. You need not show the arithmetic computations you use to arrive at the dollar amounts appearing in the report.

2-21. Joe Diamond, a plumber, has made an agreement with the owner of an apartment building to conduct routine weekly inspections of the plumbing in the building at a flat rate of $600 per year, payable at the beginning of the year. Additional repair work is billed to the owner separately as the work is done, and Joe usually collects the cash for repair work in the month following the one in which the work is done.

    a. From the data given below, show how much revenue you would report in Joe's monthly earnings statements for each of the first three months of 19x5:

	Billings for repair work	Cash collected
January	$ 75	$640[a]
February	0	75
March	125[b]	0

[a] $40 of this is for repair work done in December.
[b] Joe expects to collect this in April.

b. What information would Joe need in order to decide whether it is worthwhile to continue the routine inspection contract for another year?

2-22. Jake Corbin repairs radios and television sets. He collects cash for his services as the repair work is done, but he finds it necessary to maintain a supply of repair parts. He buys these parts from a wholesale house that grants large discounts for purchases of large quantities. In addition, Jake gets 2 per cent off if he pays the wholesaler by the tenth day of the month following the date of purchase. Jake's records show the following for the first three months of 19x5:

	Cash collections for repair work	*Cost of repair parts purchased*	*Cash payments to wholesaler*	*Cost of parts used in repairs*
January	$1,400	$490	$588	$340
February	900	0	490	190
March	1,050	686	0	270

a. Ignoring expenses other than repair parts, compute Jake's earnings for January, February, and March.

b. Suppose Jake said he had $800 invested in repair parts on hand on January 1 ($588 of which he did not pay for until January 10). How much would he have invested on January 31? On February 28? On March 31?

c. What information would Jake need in order to decide whether (1) he should purchase in large quantities and (2) he should pay his bills in time to get the 2 per cent discount?

2-23. James Fisher is a real-estate agent who collects, from the seller of the property, 5 per cent of the sales price of the property sold. His normal operating expenses are for advertising, running an automobile (he uses his own car—50 percent for personal use, 50 percent for business), and his office. During July, four houses were sold for which he was the agent. His July records show the following:

Houses sold	*Sales price*	*Advertising expenses*
1	$20,000	$ 50
2	15,000	400
3	30,000	5
4	25,000	20

Total car expenses:[a]	
Gas, oil, & routine maintenance	$ 50
Total July office expenses:	
Office rent	100
Secretary's salary	300
Office supplies used	10
Telephone & utilities	75

[a] The car was purchased two years ago at a cost of $4,600. Normally Mr. Fisher uses a car for four years. He will probably get $1,000 for it when he trades it in two years from now.

a. Compute Mr. Fisher's earnings for July. Indicate what additional information you would need to do this more accurately.

b. Compute Mr. Fisher's profit on the sale of house 1. Indicate the additional information you would need to do this more accurately.

c. Would you recommend to Mr. Fisher that he try to compute his profit on the sale of each house? Why?

d. Suppose you were thinking of going into the real-estate business and Mr. Fisher offered to give you any information his records would provide. What information would you ask for?

2-24. The Aubry Supply Company is a wholesaler of merchandise sold to hardware stores. Merchandise is purchased from manufacturers, usually on thirty-day credit terms. Sales are made to retail hardware stores, usually on thirty-day credit terms, although the company insists on cash payment at the time of delivery from a few stores having a poor credit standing in the community. A review of the company's checkbook for July reveals the following summary of the cash transactions:

AUBRY SUPPLY COMPANY

STATEMENT OF CASH RECEIPTS AND DISBURSEMENTS

For July 19xx

Cash provided from:		
Collections from credit customers on June sales		$25,000
Collections from cash customers		6,100
Proceeds from bank loan		2,000
Total cash provided		$33,100
— Cash used for:		
Payments to manufacturers for June purchases	$18,500	
Payments of July salaries to employees	9,200	
Loan to John Aubry, president	1,000	
Dividend to stockholders	500	
July payment on mortgage loan on warehouse	2,500	
Payment of 1-year fire insurance policy on warehouse (policy coverage begins 8/1)	750	
Total cash used		32,450
Increase in cash for July		$ 650

a. Which of the above cash receipts represent July revenue?

b. Explain why you have excluded the other items from July revenue.

c. Have you reason to believe that the company has earned additional revenue in July not shown above? Explain.

d. Which of the above cash disbursements represent July operating expenses?

e. Explain why you have excluded the other items from July operating expenses.

f. Have you reason to believe that the company has incurred other expenses not shown above? Explain.

2-25. Jerry Ebert owns a race track that he rents to a corporation to operate. The rental charge is $200 per month or 10 per cent of the monthly gate receipts, whichever is larger each month. Mr. Ebert's only operating expenses are property taxes, fire insurance on the grandstand, and repairs. Mr. Ebert has nothing invested in the land or the grandstand, except for the new roof, because he inherited the place from his father in 19x0. During 19x5, the following occurred:

	Gate receipts	Property taxes[a]	Fire insurance[b]	Repairs[c]
January	0	0	0	$ 100
February	0	$1,200	0	0
March	0	0	0	2,100
April	$10,000	0	$2,400	50
May	40,000	0	0	0
June	0	0	0	0
July	0	0	0	0
August	0	1,200	0	0
September	25,000	0	0	40
October	20,000	0	0	0
November	0	0	0	1,600
December	0	0	0	0

[a] The semiannual property tax payment has been $1,200 for many years.
[b] The fire insurance premium is due every April. The 19x4 premium was $3,000, but it was reduced in 19x5 because in November 19x4 Mr. Ebert put a fireproof roof on the grandstand at a cost of $1,500.
[c] The major repair outlays come before the opening of the spring season and after the close of the fall season, largely because workers are more available during these times and the weather is suitable.

a. Compute Mr. Ebert's earnings for 19x5. What reservations do you have about the accuracy of the statement?

b. Suppose Mr. Ebert wanted to engage you to prepare monthly earnings statements for him. Why might you hesitate to do so?

c. What is the shortest period for which a useful statement could be prepared? What length accounting period do you consider optimal for measuring the profitability of Mr. Ebert's property? Why?

2-26. Jacques Haefner has been elected chairman of his community's Amalgamated Fund drive for 19x6. The drive represents a number of different charitable organizations that request funds according to needs expressed in the form of one-year budgets.

Contributions are solicited in the name of the Amalgamated Fund, but its literature lists the names of the charities to which the money is allocated. Furthermore, contributors are invited to "earmark" their contributions for particular charities, if they wish to do so. In addition, some of these charities raise funds independently of the Amalgamated Fund by selling household products (the Home for the Handicapped, for example, sells brooms, rag rugs, and small wooden furniture made in the Home), candy and baked goods, secondhand goods, etc.

Mr. Haefner is responsible for (1) recommending to the board of directors of the fund an annual goal for the drive, (2) supervising the fund-raising activities, (3) allocating money to the various charities, (4) controlling costs of administration, and (5) reporting to the board of directors all of the activities of the fund.

a. What information would Mr. Haefner need from financial reports in order to carry out his administrative responsibilities, including his report to the board?

b. What major difficulties does Mr. Haefner face in (1) establishing a goal for the fund and (2) deciding how much money each charity should get?

2-27. In the earnings statement of a profit-oriented firm, such as a retail store, all sales for the period are included as revenue, whether or not the customer pays in cash at the time. In the statement of fund contributions and expenditures of a charitable organization, pledges are not included as contributions until they are received in cash (or perhaps in securities). In your opinion, what are the reasons for this? Are they sound?

Similarly, commitments of the charitable organization for future support of worthy causes are not recorded as distributions until the period in which the distribution is actually made in cash. However, does the same principle apply to future payment of employee wages that have already been earned or to liabilities incurred by the fund to trade creditors in the ordinary course of business (e.g., for purchase of equipment or supplies)? Explain.

2-28. Assume that a charitable fund received securities having a market value of $1,000 from a contributor. The transaction was recorded as a $1,000 contribution at that time. At the end of the reporting period, the securities had a market value of $1,200.

a. What recognition, if any, would you give to the increase in value of the securities in the financial reports of the fund? Why?

b. Would your answer have been different if the market value had been $800 at the time of the report? Explain.

2-29. Shown below, in comparative form for the year 19x0, are the statements of fund contributions and expenditures of the March of Quarters Funds of two counties.

MARCH OF QUARTERS
STATEMENT OF CASH CONTRIBUTIONS AND EXPENDITURES
For the Year 19x0
(in thousands of dollars)

	Brown County		Green County	
Contributions:				
From donors		$100		$125
From special projects:				
Revenues	$64		$79	
Expenses	27	37	40	39
Total Contributions		$137		$164
Administrative expenses		10		26
Net contributions		$127		$138
Cash balance, 1/1		25		2
Available for distribution		$152		$140
Distributions		125		139
Cash balance, 12/31		$ 27		$ 1

Assume that the two counties have the same potential for support of this fund, and that the differences between the statements are attributable to differences between the management practices of the two organizations.

a. Point out the particular items or ratios you consider most important in measuring performance of the two organizations, and give the reasons why you think they are important.

b. Which of these two organizations is better managed? Why?

2-30. The director of a particular bureau in the state government has $600 allotted to him annually in the budget for office supplies. You, an auditor, discover that in 19x1 only about $300 was spent in the first eleven months, and about $300 was spent in December, 19x1, for office supplies. The same thing happened in 19x2. You also discover that office supplies are used at a uniform rate throughout the year, and at physical inventory on November 15, 19x3, the date of your audit, office supplies having a cost of $750 are on hand. You ask the director to explain, and he answers "I have to handle it this way. If I don't spend my allotment each year, the budget director will cut it the next year."

Point out the basic defects in the budgetary control system, and make suggestions on how you think they can be corrected.

2-31. "The only fundamental difference in objectives between so-called profit and nonprofit organizations is that the former attempts to optimize profit and the latter attempts to achieve a zero profit." Do you agree with this statement? Why or why not?

Chapter Three RECORDING AND REPORTING EVENTS

INTRODUCTION

Accounting systems vary widely from one business to another, depending on the nature of the business and the transactions in which it engages, the size of the firm and the volume of data to be handled, and the particular informational demands that management and others place on the system. We will not cover all possible variations in this chapter. Instead, we will limit our discussion to those characteristics of accounting systems that are generally common to all business firms.

The broadest definition of an accounting system includes all of the activities required to provide management with the quantified (numerical) information it requires for the planning and control purposes described in Chapter 1. In this chapter we will describe only that part of the system required for the preparation of the statement of financial position for the firm as a whole, and other statements, principally the earnings statement, that are based directly on the statement of financial position. The system described here is known as a *double-entry bookkeeping system*.

The main body of this chapter presents the accounting model, concepts, and rules that comprise a basic double-entry system. The accounting cycle is demonstrated in a step-by-step example. The student who seeks only to become acquainted with the subject need not study either Appendix 3A or 3B.

Appendix 3A presents two more detailed illustrations of the accounting system and should be studied by the reader desiring greater understanding of event analysis, record keeping, and financial statement preparation. Additional problems accompanying Appendix 3A provide an opportunity for practice in bookkeeping beyond that made possible by the problems at the end of the basic chapter.

Appendix 3B is also available for the student who wishes to learn more about accounting systems. It illustrates the ways in which the accounting system can help the manager to control the assets placed at his disposal.

In Part II of this book, you will encounter many illustrations of planning and control reports for management that require more information than is provided by the examples used in this chapter and its appendixes. Nevertheless, the information stored in the bookkeeping system is essential to the successful operation of any business firm. Many questions that managers must answer depend on the bookkeeping system's record of the past:

What volume of sales can I expect next month, next quarter, or next year?

Which lines of merchandise are the most profitable? Which are the most popular with customers?

How long does it take the average credit customer to pay his account after he has been billed?

How much cash can I expect to collect next month from this month's sales?

How much cash will I have to pay out each month next year?

How can I tell which customers fail to pay their bills?

How can I minimize losses from errors in cash transactions or from theft of cash?

How can I be sure I receive all the merchandise I pay for?

These and many similar questions can be answered when there is an efficient bookkeeping system to provide the data.

Research reveals convincing evidence that inadequate accounting information has been a major cause of business failures in the United States in recent years. In light of this finding, it is unfortunate that managers of business firms often do not completely recognize the usefulness of adequate systems for collecting event data.

THE ACCOUNTING MODEL

Accounting rests on a system of rules for interpreting, recording, classifying, and reporting event data relating to the business firm. These rules derive from the concepts (particularly assets, liabilities, owners' equity, revenue, and expense) discussed in Chapter 2. With them, accountants are able to set up a classification scheme consisting of a language of *account titles*. Classification schemes and titles vary widely from one firm to another, depending on the characteristics of the transactions, the needs of the statement users, and trade practice within an industry. Definitions of some titles in general use appear later in the chapter.

The accountant also establishes procedures for periodic reporting of recorded event data in the form of financial statements, in an organized, repetitive way. These procedures are usually referred to as the steps in a bookkeeping *cycle*.

We shall discuss all these elements of the accounting model in this chapter. Let us begin by extending the basic accounting equation given in Chapter 2 to derive rules of accounting.

Financial Position

The most general accounting equation is

(1)   Assets (A_t) = Equities (E_t)

where t indicates a moment in time.

Although it appears too general to be very useful, equation (1) provides accountants with a basic rule:

Interpret and record all events in such a way that the total assets and total equities of the firm are equal.

Strictly speaking, expression (1) merely says that the assets of a firm at time t are equal to the equities of the various contributors of those assets. *Equities* have been interpreted by theorists as *claims against* assets, as suggested in Chapter 2, and as *contributions* or *sources of* assets, as indicated above. Both concepts serve useful purposes, but as we shall see in Part II of this book, the concepts are not the same, and the difference creates controversies.

Expanding the equities side of equation (1) gives us

Assets (A_t) = Liabilities (L_t) + Owners' Equity (OE_t)

which produces another basic rule:

Interpret and record all events in such a way that the total assets equal the sum of the totals of liabilities and owners' equity.

Some theorists would prefer to write this equation as

(2) $A_t - L_t = OE_t$

because this arrangement emphasizes the *owners* of the firm and interprets the concept of liabilities as claims against assets or perhaps negative assets, rather than as sources of assets. Indeed, Chapter 2 was intended to impress you with the facts that earnings measurement is a focal point of much accounting activity, and that periodic earnings is a major source of change in the *owners' equity*, or *net assets*, as it is usually called. Acceptance of this approach makes it crucial to separate *creditors'* equities (liabilities) from *owners'* equities.

It is useful to refine the idea of owners' equity, or net assets, by writing the equation as

(3) $A_t = L_t + CS_t + RE_t$

where CS stands for Contributed Capital and RE for Retained Earnings.

The accounting rule is apparent:

Interpret and record all events in such a way that the total assets equal the sum of the totals of liabilities, of owners' contributed capital, and of owners' capital earned and retained in the business.

Equation (3), by subdividing owners' equity into contributed capital (CS_t) and retained earnings (RE_t), emphasizes the fact that owners can acquire an equity in the firm (1) by contributing capital to the firm and receiving shares of stock as evidence of that contribution (hence the notation CS) and (2) by not withdrawing all of the past earnings of the firm in the form of dividends as the earnings are recorded. This form of the equation applies only to a corporation (rather than to a proprietorship or partnership). Actually, the distinction between "contributed capital" and "earned but not distributed" capital is difficult to preserve even in a corporation. It is presented here only because it will be useful to us later in the chapter.

Financial Position and Changes in Retained Earnings

The next step in expanding the accounting model is to analyze the effect of time on retained earnings (RE):

(4) $\quad A_t = L_t + CS_t + RE_{t-1} + Y - D$

The accounting rule is now more difficult to state:

Interpret and record all events in such a way that the total of assets equals the sum of the totals of liabilities, of owners' contributed capital, of retained earnings at the end of the previous period, and of increases and decreases in retained earnings since that time.

This equation shows that retained earnings at time t, the end of the accounting period, is the algebraic sum of retained earnings at the end of the *previous* period (RE_{t-1}), the earnings for the period (Y), and the dividends declared during the period (D).

Since the financial position statement is solely a statement of the firm's assets and equities at any time t, changes in retained earnings for a period from $t-1$ to t must be expressed in a separate statement, usually called the statement of retained earnings. This statement is symbolically expressed by equation (5):

(5) $\quad RE_t = RE_{t-1} + Y - D$

where $t-1$ is the moment in time at which the period began, Y is the earnings for the period, and D is the dividends declared during the period.

Not all accountants agree that equation (5) is correct. Some argue that retained earnings may be affected by events which are neither a part of earnings (Y) nor a dividend (D). This argument will be discussed in Chapter 12. In the meantime, we will assume that equation (5) is correct.

In passing, we might point out that RE_t may be negative (in which case it is called a deficit) either because the periodic earnings have been negative or because dividend distributions have exceeded accumulated periodic earnings over time.

Financial Position, Retained Earnings, and Earnings

Finally, we will substitute revenues (R) — expenses (E) for earnings (Y) in equation (4) to get equation (6). This is consistent with the definition of periodic earnings given in Chapter 2. In terms of the accounting model, revenues and expenses are simply subdivisions of the retained earnings, as expressed in this equation of financial position at time t.

(6) $\quad A_t = L_t + CS_t + RE_{t-1} + (R - E) - D$

The corresponding accounting rule is

Interpret and record all events in such a way that the total of assets equals the sum of the totals of liabilities, owners' contributed capital, and retained earnings—the last consisting of the sum of retained earnings at the end of the previous period, plus revenues, expenses, and dividends since that time.

Summary of the Accounting Model

Equation (6) is as far as we shall go in expanding the basic financial position equation, $A_t = E_t$. Only through equation (3) were we concerned with financial position at time t. When the time dimension is introduced, two additional statements are needed: the statement of retained earnings and the statement of earnings.

The equations that do include the time dimension (equations 4, 5, and 6) focus on retained earnings because changes in these earnings are especially important to financial statement users. The statements of retained earnings and of earnings greatly enhance the value of the financial position statement to users, because they provide some evidence of how the financial position at time t was achieved. It is for this reason that the accountant expands his basic equation to include the time dimension in his analysis of retained earnings. Alternatively, he could expand any other item from the financial position statement if the statement users considered it of sufficient importance.

The accounting model requires us to interpret business events in terms of the firm's assets, liabilities, capital stock, retained earnings, and the changes in retained earnings, consisting of revenues (R), expenses (E), and dividends (D). It is this model that enables accountants to prepare a financial position statement at any time t and to prepare statements of retained earnings and statements of earnings covering the period from $t - 1$ to t.

TRANSACTION ANALYSIS

Transaction analysis is the accounting process of interpreting the effect of events on the accounting equations in such a way that the equalities will always be maintained. Let us return to equation (6):

$$A_t = L_t + CS_t + RE_{t-1} + R - E - D$$

and consider the Model Firm as an example, beginning at time $t - 1$.

MODEL FIRM

STATEMENT OF FINANCIAL POSITION

At Time t — 1

Assets		Equities	
		Liabilities	$20,000
		Capital stock	25,000
		Retained earnings	5,000
Total assets	$50,000	Total equities	$50,000

The firm's financial position would be stated as follows: "The Model Firm has $50,000 in assets, $20,000 contributed by and owed to creditors, and $30,000 contributed by owners. Of the $30,000 contributed by owners, $25,000 came from contributions in exchange for stock, and $5,000 from earnings of the firm which have not been distributed to the owners." We are not concerned here with the events that resulted in this financial position, or with the breakdowns of total assets and total liabilities. Our concern is to see how the accounting equations apply. At time $t - 1$,

$$A_{t-1} = L_{t-1} + CS_{t-1} + RE_{t-1} + R - E - D$$
$$\$50,000 = \$20,000 + \$25,000 + \$5,000 + \$0 - \$0 - \$0$$

Since this equation is at time $t - 1$, R, E, and D are all zero, for their function is to measure changes in retained earnings from time $t - 1$ to time t. Now consider what happens as events occur in the Model Firm.

Event a: The firm purchases $5,000 of assets on credit.

Since we have moved away from time $t - 1$, we drop the $t - 1$ subscripts (from all terms except RE_{t-1}). The effect of event a is to increase both assets and liabilities by $5,000:

$$A = L + CS + RE_{t-1} + R - E - D$$
$$\$55,000 = \$25,000 + \$25,000 + \$5,000 + \$0 - \$0 - \$0$$

Event b: The firm issues new shares to stockholders for $10,000 in assets:

$$A \quad = \quad L \quad + \quad CS \quad + RE_{t-1} + R - E - D$$
$$\$65,000 = \$25,000 + \$35,000 + \$5,000 + \$0 - \$0 - \$0$$

Event *b* increases both assets and capital stock by \$10,000.

Event c: The firm pays liabilities amounting to \$8,000:

$$A \quad = \quad L \quad + \quad CS \quad + RE_{t-1} + R - E - D$$
$$\$57,000 = \$17,000 + \$35,000 + \$5,000 + \$0 - \$0 - \$0$$

Assets and liabilities are both decreased \$8,000 by this event.

Event d: The firm issues new shares to creditors in satisfaction of debts amounting to \$5,000. Thus, these creditors now become owners:

$$A \quad = \quad L \quad + \quad CS \quad + RE_{t-1} + R - E - D$$
$$\$57,000 = \$12,000 + \$40,000 + \$5,000 + \$0 - \$0 - \$0$$

Liabilities are reduced and capital stock is increased by \$5,000. Assets are unchanged.

Event e: The firm sells assets (listed on the books at \$7,000) to customers who promise to pay \$12,000 for these assets:

$$A \quad = \quad L \quad + \quad CS \quad + RE_{t-1} + \quad R \quad - \quad E \quad - D$$
$$\$62,000 = \$12,000 + \$40,000 + \$5,000 + \$12,000 - \$7,000 - \$0$$

Assets are increased by \$12,000, reflecting the value of the customers' promise to pay, and also decreased by \$7,000, the "value" (probably the purchase price) of the assets given up in the sale. Hence event *e* could be thought of as two events, rather than one. The increase in revenue of \$12,000 reflects the source of the asset received, and the increase of \$7,000 in expense reflects the disposition of the asset given up.

Event f: Employees earn \$2,000 in wages this period, which will be paid early next period:

$$A \quad = \quad L \quad + \quad CS \quad + RE_{t-1} + \quad R \quad - \quad E \quad - D$$
$$\$62,000 = \$14,000 + \$40,000 + \$5,000 + \$12,000 - \$9,000 - \$0$$

Interpreting these wages as expense involves the assumption that the services of the employees were used up in the earning of the \$12,000 revenue.

Event g: The firm declares a \$1,000 dividend to stockholders, to be paid early next period:

$$A_t \quad = \quad L_t \quad + \quad CS_t \quad + RE_{t-1} + \quad R \quad - \quad E \quad - \quad D$$
$$\$62,000 = \$15,000 + \$40,000 + \$5,000 + \$12,000 - \$9,000 - \$1,000$$

The dividend affects retained earnings in the same way as expenses, but the dividend is not expense, since it was not incurred for the purpose of earning revenue.

These relatively simple events should be sufficient to demonstrate how the accounting model is used for interpreting the effect of events on the financial position of the firm. Notice that the purchase of an asset on credit (event *a*), the sale to a customer on credit (event *e*), the earning of wages by the employees even though not paid (event *f*), and the promise to pay a dividend (event *g*) all are sufficiently definite to qualify as "events" for recording purposes, and in the cases of events *e* and *f*, for recognition as revenue and expense.

The inherent self-balancing, or "equilibrium" that is characteristic of the accounting equations stems from the fact that we are accounting for the firm's assets (*A*) and its sources of assets (*E*), which by definition are equal (equation *1*). It is from this characteristic that the term "double-entry bookkeeping" originates. It means, of course, that any change in any asset or equity item is balanced by one or more changes in other asset or equity items so that the equilibrium is maintained.

Financial Statements

Now that the firm has arrived at time *t* (note the subscripts after event *g*), financial statements are desired. These statements are as follows:

THE MODEL FIRM

EARNINGS STATEMENT

For Period from t − 1 to t

Revenues	$12,000
Expenses	9,000
Net earnings	$ 3,000

THE MODEL FIRM

STATEMENT OF RETAINED EARNINGS

For Period from t − 1 to t

Retained earnings, at time $t-1$		$5,000
Net earnings for the period	$3,000	
Dividends	1,000	
Increase in retained earnings		2,000
Retained earnings, at time t		$7,000

The starting point for the financial statements for the next period, which will end at $t + 1$, is as follows:

$$A_t = L_t + CS_t + RE_t + R - E - D$$
$$\$62,000 = \$15,000 + \$40,000 + \$7,000 + 0 - 0 - 0$$

THE MODEL FIRM

STATEMENT OF FINANCIAL POSITION

At time t

Assets		Equities		
		Total liabilities		$15,000
		Owners' equity:		
		Capital stock	$40,000	
		Retained earnings	7,000	
		Total owners' equity		47,000
Total assets	$62,000	Total equity		$62,000

The revenue, expense, and dividend amounts, having measured changes in retained earnings during the period ended at time t, are no longer needed now that t has passed and financial statements covering the period $t - 1$ to t have been prepared. These three items are therefore added (algebraically) to RE_{t-1} ($5,000) to give RE_t ($7,000).

This illustration is useful only as a demonstration of accounting concepts; it has little relevance to the "real-world" problems of transaction analysis and collection of data on business events. The reason, of course, is that it is not sufficient simply to interpret business events in terms of *total* assets, *total* liabilities, *total* revenues, or *total* expenses. A good accounting system must provide finer breakdowns of these general categories. The amount of detail required varies with the statement user. Because of their need for detailed planning and control information, internal managers of the firm require finer breakdowns than, say, external users whose interests are often limited to more general classifications.

A system that will fulfill managerial requirements must incorporate three devices: the *account*, the *general ledger*, and the *journal*. The account stores event data in the form of debit and credit entries, and reports account balances. The general ledger and the chart of its accounts form a system of classifying the assets and equities required for financial statements. Subsidiary ledgers are also required for management planning and control. Finally, the journal contains a chronological listing of business events, interpreted within the framework of the accounting equations. We shall now consider each of these devices in detail.

The Account—Debit and Credit

The function of the account is to receive and preserve event data that have changed (i.e., increased or decreased) the amount of any asset or equity item, and to preserve them in such a way that the new balance of that item is readily available whenever financial statements are needed. Accounts take a variety of forms in mechanized and manual systems, but the essential features are contained in the form called a *T-account:*

Account Title	
Debit, or left side	*Credit,* or right side

Whatever form the account may take, it should provide an organized way of recording dollar increases and decreases in the item being measured, cross-references that indicate any relationships to other records, and the balance (the excess of the sum of the amounts on the larger side over the smaller side) of the account at any time. Another form of account is also quite common in manual systems:

(Account Title)				Page No. _____
Date		L. F.	Debit	Credit	Balance

This form calls for the calculation of a new balance after each entry. (The L. F. column stands for ledger folio. It provides for cross-referencing to the ledger.) The title of an account should be descriptive of the item being measured in that account. In this discussion, we assume that the titles of the bookkeeping accounts are also used to describe those account balances appearing in the financial statements.

The words "debit" and "credit" (abbreviated DR and CR) cause a good deal of needless confusion. Trouble is avoided if you remember that *they refer to the left and right sides, respectively, of any T-account.* The relationship between debits and credits and increases and decreases in financial position items is very simple, but it is important in bookkeeping, and must be remembered:

1. Debits (left-hand entries) *increase* asset items; debits *decrease* equity items.

2. Credits (right-hand entries) *decrease* asset items; credits *increase* equity items.

A common error is to think of debits as increases and credits as decreases; but this is true only for asset accounts and accounts that reduce equities. The opposite rule holds for equity accounts and accounts that reduce assets.

A good way to remember this is to visualize the financial position statement of the Model Firm at time *t*. Assets appear on the left and equities on the right, as if the statement were a single account. This kind of financial position statement is in fact known as the *account form.* Applying the rules indicates that assets are increased by additions to the left side, or debits, and equities increased by additions to the right side, or credits. The rules for recording decreases then follow logically.

There are several corollaries to these rules that deserve special attention.

3. *Revenue* accounts, since they measure *increases* in retained earnings resulting from the *creation* of assets in the process of earning revenue, are equity accounts and therefore are increased by *credit* entries and have *credit* balances.

4. *Expense* accounts, since they measure *decreases* in retained earnings resulting from the *consumption* (rather than creation) of assets in the process of earning revenue, are also equity accounts but are increased by *debit* entries and have *debit* balances.

5. Special accounts are set up to measure deductions from principal accounts when it is desirable to retain these accounts at their originally recorded amount. Called *contra* accounts, they follow rules opposite to those applicable to the principal accounts. Examples of contra accounts are as follows:

Contra Account Title	*Principal Account Title*
Allowance for depreciation—buildings	Buildings
Allowance for credit losses	Accounts receivable
Sales allowances	Sales
Discount on capital stock	Capital stock

The T-account, the rules for debit and credit, and the equality of assets and equities in the statement of financial position constitute a sort of "shorthand" language of accounting. You should be able to communicate with these devices and understand the relationship of the analysis to the financial statements, even though it is often unstated.

The General Ledger Versus Subsidiary Ledgers

The general ledger is the entire group of accounts necessary for reporting the statement of financial position, statement of changes in retained earnings, and statement of earnings. It is supplemented by *subsidiary ledgers,* which are groups of accounts that describe the details of general ledger accounts. Ordinarily, the information provided by subsidiary ledgers is useful only for managerial purposes, and only the general ledger accounts are reported in the basic financial statements. The use of subsidiary ledgers is illustrated in Appendix 3B. Here our principal interest is in how general ledger accounts are used in event analysis, and in storing and reporting event information.

The "Chart" of Accounts

The essence of the system for reporting in the basic financial statements is the list, or chart, of general ledger account titles. Some examples of account titles that commonly appear in the chart of accounts of a typical industrial firm are given in the list that follows. You need not memorize this list; it should serve as a reference instead. The titles should be useful to you in problem solutions. Many of these accounts will be discussed in later chapters.

Typical Titles Used in a General Ledger Chart of Accounts

Asset Accounts

Cash (possibly separate accounts for "cash on hand" and "cash in bank")

Temporary investments (also called "marketable securities")

Notes receivable—trade (i.e., notes arising from operating revenue transactions)

Notes receivable—nontrade (e.g., notes arising from loans to employees)

Accrued interest receivable (interest earned but not collected in cash)

Accounts receivable—trade

Accounts receivable—nontrade

Allowance for credit losses (a contra account, reported as a deduction from trade receivables)

Merchandise (used by wholesalers or retailers to describe goods held for resale to customers; also called "inventory")

Direct materials (used by manufacturers to describe inventory of goods purchased for use in the manufacturing process; also called "raw materials")

Work in process (inventory of partially manufactured products; also called "goods in process")

Finished goods (inventory of manufactured products held for sale to customers)

Office supplies or store supplies (inventory of supplies used in nonmanufacturing activities)

Prepaid insurance (i.e., the portion of premiums paid that applies to future periods)

Prepaid rent, or prepaid advertising, etc.

Investment in subsidiary company (stock held in another firm for control purposes)

Investments in bonds (or stocks, or real estate, etc., held for income, rather than resale)

Land (i.e., the site of the store or factory—not subject to depreciation)

Buildings (factory, store, or office buildings owned and used in operations)

Allowance for depreciation—buildings (a contra account, reported as a deduction from "buildings"; also called "accumulated depreciation")

Equipment

Allowance for depreciation—equipment

(Many other assets subject to depreciation could be listed here.)

Patents (an intangible asset, subject to amortization [reduction in value, over time], that is usually treated as a direct deduction from the asset account, and therefore a contra account is not used)

Liability Accounts

Accounts payable (amounts owed for purchases of materials, or service received)

Notes payable (arising either from purchase transactions or cash borrowing)

Accrued interest payable (on bonds or notes)

Accrued wages, accrued taxes, or accrued rent (i.e., amounts owed for services received
—these may be recorded as "accounts payable")

Advances from customers (e.g., for products to be delivered, service to be rendered in
the future, or overpayments to be refunded)

Bonds payable (amounts payable from bonds issued in the past)

Mortgage note payable (amount payable on loans, for which some asset has been
pledged as collateral)

Owners' Equity Accounts

Capital stock (shares held by owners, issued in exchange for contributions of assets)

Retained earnings (an account balance brought forward from the previous accounting
period, not used to record event data, except in summary form at the end of a
period)

Dividends (the reduction in retained earnings for dividends declared this period)

Income summary (An account that is used only in the period-end closing procedure
described later in this chapter. It measures the effect of all revenues and expenses
on retained earnings during the period.)

Sales revenue (or simply "sales"; i.e., revenue from delivery of products to customers)

Sales returns and allowances, or sales discounts (i.e., contra accounts to "sales")

Commissions earned, fees earned, rent earned, or interest earned, etc. (revenue from
services)

Gain or loss on sale of land, or any noninventory asset (this account measures profit
or loss, i.e., the difference between cost and sales price, rather than revenue)

Cost of goods sold (an expense account measuring the manufacturing or purchase cost
to the seller of inventory items sold to customers)

Store supplies expense (i.e., store supplies used)

Salesmens' salary expense (services rendered by salesmen this period)

Advertising expense (advertising resources used this period)

Depreciation of store equipment

Officers' salary expense

Office supplies used

Depreciation of office equipment
(Many other examples of specific selling and administrative expense items could be
given. The above are illustrative only.)

Interest expense

It is good accounting practice to use special account titles to reflect special
events or conditions. It is also good practice to use words such as "receivable,"
"payable," "revenue," or "expense," even at the risk of some redundancy, if
ambiguity is reduced by doing so.

The Journal

The simplest form of journal is merely a chronological listing of transactions,
expressed in terms of debits and credits to the particular accounts in the ledger.
This type of journal is called a *general journal*.

THE XYZ CORPORATION

GENERAL JOURNAL   *Page No.* _____

Date	Accounts	L. F.	DR	CR
October 14	Cash	1	1,000	
	Capital stock	13		1,000
	Issued capital stock for a			
	cash contribution			
October 15	Merchandise	3	500	
	Accounts payable	11		500
	Purchased merchandise from the X Co.,			
	terms 10 days			

The journal permits the firm to establish control over events by providing a convenient method for original recording of the event, and to make easier the tasks of tracing the entries through the ledger to the financial statements. The event is first recorded in the journal (also called the *book of original entry*) at the time it occurs. The recorded debits and credits are then *posted* to the appropriate accounts in the general ledger.

Journals can take many different forms. Even small firms may have several special journals, designed to expedite the original recording of various classes of events. The general journal, as shown here, is usually limited to nonroutine, complicated transactions, period-end adjustments, and *closing* entries, to be described below. In addition to serving as books of original entry, special journals are designed to perform much of the preliminary data classification and summarization.

THE ANNUAL ACCOUNTING CYCLE

It is now useful to summarize and illustrate the accounting operations over a one-year period with respect to the business events occurring during the year. These operations are repeated in a regular annual cycle:

1. Interpretation and journalizing. When an event occurs, the event's effect on financial position is determined, expressed in terms of debits and credits to particular general ledger accounts, and recorded in the appropriate journal.

2. Posting. Individual debits and credits (in the general journal) or aggregated debits and credits (in the specialized journals) are posted to the appropriate general ledger accounts.

3. Balances (excess of debits over credits, or vice versa) of general ledger accounts are computed.

4. A trial balance of all general ledger accounts is prepared.

5. A statement of earnings for the year, a statement of retained earnings for the year, and a statement of financial position at year end are prepared from the trial balance.

6. Closing entries (to eliminate balances from revenue, expense, and dividend accounts and to bring the retained earnings account up to date) are recorded in the general journal and posted to the general ledger.

7. A trial balance of the remaining accounts (i.e., financial position accounts) is prepared to prove the technical accuracy of the entries and the arithmetic.

We shall illustrate the annual cycle using The Model Firm and events *a* through *g* shown earlier in the chapter. The starting point is the *trial balance* of the general ledger at time $t - 1$, the beginning of the current accounting period.

THE MODEL FIRM

GENERAL LEDGER TRIAL BALANCE

At time t — 1

Acct. No.	Title	DR	CR
1	Assets	$50,000	
2	Liabilities		$20,000
3	Capital stock		25,000
4	Retained earnings		5,000
5	Dividends	0	
6	Income summary		0
7	Revenues		0
8	Expenses	0	
	Totals	$50,000	$50,000

These dollar amounts are the *balances* of the accounts in the general ledger immediately after the books were *closed* at time $t - 1$. Now we are ready to follow the bookkeeping cycle for the period from $t - 1$ to t.

Step 1. The events are interpreted in terms of their effect on the accounts and this effect is recorded in the general journal.

Steps 2, 3, and 6. These steps are illustrated in Exhibit 3–1, which shows the eight ledger accounts affected during the period $t - 1$ to t.

Step 2. Event data (keyed with the letters *a* through *g*) are posted to the ledger.

Step 3. Account balances are calculated at time t before closing. (This calculation is automatic with the particular form of ledger account used in Exhibit 3–1.)

Step 6. The closing entries (keyed with the letter *t*) are posted in the ledger. (They are also transferred to the journal; this is shown below.)

THE MODEL FIRM
GENERAL JOURNAL

Date	Account Titles	L. F.	DR	CR
a	Assets	1	5,000	
	Liabilities	2		5,000
	Purchased assets on credit, $5,000			
b	Assets	1	10,000	
	Capital stock	3		10,000
	Issued stock certificates in exchange for $10,000 assets			
c	Liabilities	2	8,000	
	Assets	1		8,000
	Paid debts of $8,000			
d	Liabilities	2	5,000	
	Capital stock	3		5,000
	Issued stock certificates in payment of debt, $5,000			
e	Assets	1	12,000	
	Revenue	7		12,000
	Expense	8	7,000	
	Assets	1		7,000
	Sold $7,000 of assets for $12,000			
f	Expense	8	2,000	
	Liabilities	2		2,000
	Use of employee services earned but not paid			
g	Dividends	5	1,000	
	Liabilities	2		1,000
	Dividend declared but not paid			

Usually, ledger and journal entries are keyed by journal page number and date, rather than by letter as in this example. In either case, the purpose is the same: to be able to trace posted entries whenever necessary. Customarily, the

EXHIBIT 3-1

Assets					No. 1		Liabilities					No. 2
Date		L. F.	DR	CR	Bal.		Date		L. F.	DR	CR	Bal.
t-1	Brought forward				50,000 DR		t-1	Brought forward				20,000 CR
		a	5,000		55,000				a		5,000	25,000
		b	10,000		65,000				c	8,000		17,000
		c		8,000	57,000				d	5,000		12,000
		e	12,000		69,000				f		2,000	14,000
		e		7,000	62,000 DR				g		1,000	15,000 CR

	Capital stock				No. 3	
Date		L. F.	DR	CR	Bal.	
t-1	Brought forward				25,000	CR
		b		10,000	35,000	
		d		5,000	40,000	CR

	Retained earnings				No. 4	
Date		L. F.	DR	CR	Bal.	
t-1	Brought forward				5,000	CR
	Closing	t		3,000	8,000	CR
	Closing	t	1,000		7,000	CR

	Dividends				No. 5
Date		L. F.	DR	CR	Bal.
		g	1,000		1,000
	Closing	t		1,000	0

	Income summary				No. 6
Date		L. F.	DR	CR	Bal.
	Closing	t		12,000	12,000
	Closing	t	9,000		3,000
	Closing	t	3,000		0

	Revenues				No. 7
Date		L. F.	DR	CR	Bal.
		e		12,000	12,000
	Closing	t	12,000		0

	Expenses				No. 8
Date		L. F.	DR	CR	Bal.
		e	7,000		7,000
		f	2,000		9,000
	Closing	t		9,000	0

transaction date is placed in the appropriate ledger account, and the ledger account number is entered in the L. F. column of the journal.

Step 4. After the balance in each account is computed, a trial balance of the general ledger as of time *t* is prepared.

THE MODEL FIRM
GENERAL LEDGER TRIAL BALANCE
At time t

Acct. No.	Title	DR	CR
1	Assets	$62,000	
2	Liabilities		$15,000
3	Capital stock		40,000
4	Retained earnings		5,000
5	Dividends	1,000	
6	Income summary		0
7	Revenues		12,000
8	Expenses	9,000	
	Totals	$72,000	$72,000

Step 5. From the account balances in the trial balance, statements of earnings, retained earnings, and financial position are prepared. These statements were included earlier in this chapter and are not repeated here.

Step 6. The closing entries are made and are transferred from the ledger to the journal.

THE MODEL FIRM

GENERAL JOURNAL

(Continued)

Date	Account Titles	L. F.	DR	CR
t	Revenues	7	12,000	
	Income summary	6		$12,000
t	Income summary	6	9,000	
	Expenses	8		9,000
t	Income summary	6	3,000	
	Retained earnings	4		3,000
t	Retained earnings	4	1,000	
	Dividends	5		1,000

Step 7. The final (sometimes called *postclosing*) trial balance is made. This provides the starting point for period $t + 1$.

THE MODEL FIRM

FINAL GENERAL LEDGER TRIAL BALANCE

At time t

Acct. No.	Title	DR	CR
1	Assets	$62,000	
2	Liabilities		$15,000
3	Capital stock		40,000
4	Retained earnings		7,000
5	Dividends	0	
6	Income summary		0
7	Revenues		0
8	Expenses	0	
		$62,000	$62,000

ACCRUAL ACCOUNTING

If you desire to become more familiar with the accounting cycle, you may turn to Appendix 3A for a consideration of double-entry bookkeeping as it applies to two fictitious business enterprises: a merchandising firm and a manufacturing firm. Before you do, however, we must discuss the principles of *accrual* accounting, a term which cannot be precisely defined.

Accrual accounting implies, among other things, a system of accounting in which revenue is recorded and reported by the firm in the period it is *earned*, which means the period in which an asset is created, or a liability reduced, through a productive activity in which the firm engages. Similarly, accrual accounting attempts to record and report expense in the period in which an asset is consumed, or a liability created, in the conduct of that activity.

As you have already learned, fixing the exact time when an asset or liability is created or consumed can be a matter of opinion, and the accounting problems of measuring the *amounts* of the assets or liabilities created or consumed (and hence, revenue and expense) can be difficult.

Nevertheless, accrual accounting is useful in spite of its ambiguities. We know, for example, that an asset is created (and revenue is earned) when a retailer sells a product to the customer, whether the customer pays for it at the time or not, and that the delivered product is consumed (from the standpoint of the retailer) and expense is incurred at that time, whether the retailer has paid his suppliers for it or not. In other words, accrual accounting is distinguished from cash accounting simply by recognizing inventories and accounts receivable as assets, and accounts payable as liabilities. Accounting on a cash basis records revenue only when cash is received, and expense only when cash is paid out.

There are different interpretations of what accrual accounting means and different opinions of how accrual accounting should be applied in a given case. The two examples in Appendix 3A demonstrate conventional applications of accrual accounting.

SUMMARY

A double-entry bookkeeping system is a framework of rules for interpreting, recording, classifying, and reporting event data related to the business enterprise. The basic rule is as follows: Interpret and record all events in such a way that the total of assets equals the sum of the totals of liabilities, owner's contributed capital, and retained earnings—the last consisting of the sum of retained earnings at the end of the previous accounting period, plus revenues, expenses, and dividends since that time. Transaction analysis is the accounting process of interpreting the effect of events in such a way that the equality will always be maintained.

Procedures for the periodic reporting of recorded event data in the form of financial statements are referred to as the steps in the bookkeeping cycle. The cycle commences by recording events in books of original entry called journals. The information is then periodically transferred to accounts that are maintained in the ledger. Accounts are maintained using debit (left-hand) and credit (right-hand) entries. The closing process assists the accountant in periodically preparing financial statements from the accounts.

The accounting system usually employs the concept of accrual accounting. Accrual accounting records events in a manner that recognizes revenues when earned, and expenses when incurred, regardless of when associated cash payments are made.

Questions for Review

3-1. The bookkeeping system can be described in terms of inputs and outputs. What are the inputs and what are the outputs?

3-2. Define and give an example of each of the following terms as they relate to transactions and events: identifying, interpreting, recording, and reporting.

3-3. What is meant by double-entry bookkeeping as distinguished from single-entry bookkeeping?

3-4. Define accrual accounting.

3-5. What purpose do T-accounts serve in the accounting system?

3-6. Why are the transactions and events entered in revenue and expense accounts rather than directly in the retained earnings account?

3-7. Explain the purpose of each of the following items or activities in the accounting cycle:

a. Journal
b. General ledger accounts
c. Posting
d. Balancing general ledger accounts
e. Specialized journals
f. Trial balance (preclosing)
g. Accruals of revenue and expense
h. Preparation of financial statements
i. Closing entries
j. Trial balance (postclosing)

Problems for Analysis

3-8. The financial position statement of the XYZ Corporation at June 30 is as follows:

THE XYZ CORPORATION

STATEMENT OF FINANCIAL POSITION

As of June 30, 19x0

Assets	
Total assets	$7,500

Equities		
Liabilities		$2,500
Owners' equity:		
Capital stock	$3,000	
Retained earnings	2,000	
Total owners' equity		5,000
Total equities		$7,500

a. Demonstrate the application of equation (6) in this chapter by recording the effect on the accounting model of the July transactions:

	A	=	L	+	CS	+	RE	+	R	−	E	−	D
June 30	$7,500	=	$2,500	+	$3,000	+	$2,000	+	0	−	0	−	0

July 1 Issued shares of capital stock in exchange for assets received, $1,500

July 5 Purchased assets on credit, $2,300

July 7 Paid out assets to shareowners as a dividend, $500

July 10 Paid out assets to certain shareowners who surrendered their shares, $700

July 12 Received assets from clients for services rendered in July, $900

July 15 Consumed assets in rendering July services to clients, $400

July 18 Incurred liabilities in rendering July services to clients, $250

July 24   Paid liabilities to certain creditors by rendering July service to them, $550

| | | | | | | | | | | | | | |

July 27   Paid out assets to creditors in satisfaction of liabilities, $700

| | | | | | | | | | | | | |

July 28   Paid liabilities by issuing shares of capital stock, $350

| | | | | | | | | | | | |

  b. Prepare financial statements for July.

3-9. The financial statements of the MNO Company at June 30 are as follows:

MNO COMPANY

STATEMENT OF FINANCIAL POSITION

As of June 30, 19x1

Assets		
Total assets		$10,000
Equities		
Total liabilities		$ 4,200
Owners' equity:		
Capital stock	$5,000	
Retained earnings	800	
Total owners' equity		5,800
Total equities		$10,000

MNO COMPANY

**COMBINED STATEMENT OF EARNINGS
AND RETAINED EARNINGS**

Eleven Months Ended June 30, 19x1

Revenues	$7,900
Expenses	5,200
Net earnings	$2,700
Retained earnings, August 1, 19x0	1,000
Total	$3,700
Dividends	2,900
Retained earnings, June 30, 19x1	$ 800

  a. Demonstrate the application of equation (6) in this chapter by recording the effect on the accounting model of the July transactions:

	A	=	L	+	CS	+	RE	+	R	−	E	−	D
June 30	$10,000	=	$4,200	+	$5,000	+	$1,000	+	$7,900	−	$5,200	−	$2,900

July 3   Purchased assets on credit, $1,200

July 7   Received assets in exchange for capital stock issued, $500

July 8   Received $2,600 of assets from customers in exchange for assets sold to them that were valued at $1,800

July 12   Consumed $400 of assets (in addition to the $1,800 on July 8) in earning July sales revenue

July 19   Received advance payments from customers of assets amounting to $700 for sales to be made to them at a later date

July 24   Incurred liabilities of $250 in earning July sales revenue

July 27   Paid off liabilities of $500 by disbursing assets to creditors

July 29   Sold assets valued at $450 in satisfaction of the advance payments of $700 received on July 19

July 30   Declared a dividend of $100, to be paid to creditors early in August

    b. Prepare
        1. the financial position statement at July 31.
        2. the combined statement of earnings and retained earnings for the year ended July 31.
    c. If you wished to prepare a statement of earnings for the month of July only, where would you find the information on July revenue and expense?
    d. Assuming that July 31 is the end of the MNO Company's fiscal year, write the accounting equation that will serve as a starting point for analyzing and recording August transactions.

3-10. Analyze the following transactions of the Nu-Model Corporation, and for each transaction, prepare a statement of financial position showing its effect.

March 1: The company was organized, and the shareholders contributed $40,000 for capital stock.

March 2: The company acquired land and a building for $27,500 cash. The portion allocable to the land was $2,500.

March 3: The company purchased merchandise inventory for $11,500 on account.

March 4: It acquired a three-year fire insurance policy for $1,800 cash.

3-11. Analyze the following transactions of the Zero Corporation, and for each transaction, prepare a statement of financial position showing its effect.

April 1:   The shareholders contributed $35,000 for capital stock.

April 2:   The company acquired land and a building for $22,000. Of this amount, $7,000 was paid in cash and $15,000 was borrowed from the local bank. The loan was covered by a ten-year promissory note with interest of 5 per cent per year.

April 3:   The company purchased merchandise inventory for $14,500 on account.

April 3;   The company acquired a one-year fire insurance policy for $600 cash. The premium is due in thirty days.

April 12: The company paid $8,500 on account for the merchandise inventory purchased on April 3.

3-12. The following events relate to the Olympia Corporation, a newly organized corporation. Analyze these transactions, and prepare a statement of financial position as of May 15.

May 1:   The company issued 1,000 shares of $30 par-value capital stock for $30,000 cash.

May 4:   It purchased land for $8,000 cash.

May 6:   It purchased supplies for $750 on account.

May 9:   It sold one-half of the land purchased on May 4 for $4,000 cash.

May 15: It paid $400 on account for the supplies purchased on May 6.

3-13. The following transactions pertain to the operations of Pioneer International, Inc., for the month of August:

1. Purchased supplies on account for $900.

2. Sold merchandise on account for $3,000. Cost of the merchandise sold was $2,200.

3. Received $10,000 cash on account from customers for goods sold in a previous period.

4. Paid suppliers $6,000 on account.

5. Received a $2,000 promissory note from a customer in full settlement of his account.

6. Issued a $1,200 promissory note and a check for $700 to a supplier on account.

7. Issued common stock for $10,000 cash.

8. Purchased merchandise for $7,000 cash.

9. Received $1,000 from a customer as a deposit on a contract for future sale.

10. Shipped merchandise to a customer for which the sales price of $2,000 had been paid in advance in a previous accounting period. Cost of the merchandise sold was $1,400.

11. Purchased land for $10,000 cash.

On a sheet of notebook paper, draw up the following form:

Trans. No.	Increase (I) or Decrease (D)	Asset (A) or Equity (E)	Specific Title	Affect Earnings? (I) (D)	Amount

Analyze each of the transactions by filling in this form. For this problem, use only those specific titles that regularly appear in the statement of financial position, and indicate in the appropriate space whether the item has an effect on August earnings.

3–14. The following transactions and events relate to the operations of Twin Flames Company for the month of February:

1. Issued common stock for $20,000 cash.

2. Paid employees $1,100 for salaries earned and recorded in a previous accounting period.

3. Purchased merchandise for $6,000 on account.

4. Collected $4,000 on account from customers.

5. Sold merchandise as follows:

For cash, $2,200

On account, $7,000

Total cost of merchandise relating to these sales was $5,920.

6. Paid $1,400 to suppliers on account.

7. Received a $12,000 down payment for a special order of items that have not been produced yet.

8. Paid cash dividend of $650.

9. Completed and shipped items related to a special order. Total sale price was $22,000, of which $5,000 had been advanced by the customer in a previous period.

10. Purchased land for $15,000. This included a down payment of $4,000 and the assumption of an $11,000, 7 per cent note payable.

11. Recorded depreciation of $800 on buildings.

12. Recorded accrued salaries of $1,140.

On a sheet of notebook paper, draw up the following form:

Trans. No.	Increase (I) or Decrease (D)	Asset (A) or Equity (E)	Specific Title	Affect Earnings? (I) (D)	Amount

Analyze each of the transactions by filling in this form. For this problem, use only those specific titles that regularly appear in the statement of financial position, and indicate in the appropriate space whether the item has an effect on February earnings.

3–15. Shown below are seven successive statements of financial position of Orange Enterprises, Inc., numbered 0 through 6. Statement 0 is the starting point. Statements 1 through 6 each give effect to one or more transactions or events that occurred after the previous statement was prepared.

	0	1	2	3	4	5	6
Assets							
Cash	$ 1,300	$ 850	$ 1,750	$ 1,750	$ 4,450	$ 4,450	$ 1,600
Accounts receivable (net)	1,400	1,400	3,400	3,400	700	700	700
Supplies	1,250	1,700	1,000	1,000	1,000	1,000	1,000
Prepaid insurance	325	325	325	300	300	300	300
Land	1,650	1,650	1,650	1,650	1,650	1,650	1,650
Buildings (net)	9,400	9,400	9,400	9,325	9,325	9,325	9,325
Machinery (net)	4,850	4,850	4,850	4,750	4,750	5,750	5,750
Total assets	$20,175	$20,175	$22,375	$22,175	$22,175	$23,175	$20,325
Equities							
Accounts payable	$ 2,450	$ 2,450	$ 2,450	$ 2,450	$ 2,450	$ 3,450	$ 1,650
Note payable—6%	5,000	5,000	5,000	5,000	5,000	5,000	4,800
Wages payable	250	250	250	250	250	750	200
Accrued interest Payable	100	100	100	100	300	300	0
Capital stock	10,000	10,000	10,000	10,000	10,000	10,000	10,000
Retained earnings	2,375	2,375	4,575	4,375	4,175	3,675	3,675
Total equities	$20,175	$20,175	$22,375	$22,175	$22,175	$23,175	$20,325

a. Compare each statement of financial position shown above with the one at its left (i.e., 1 with 0, 2 with 1, etc.) and determine the transaction or transactions that apparently occurred in each case and caused the change in the items shown. Describe each transaction in a sentence.

b. Prepare a statement of earnings for the periods 0 through 6.

3-16. a. Show the effect of the following transactions on the statement of financial position of the Ninety-Nine Corporation by preparing a statement of financial position as of September 30.

September 1: Issued 500 shares of $20 par-value capital stock for $10,000 cash.

September 30: Billed customers for services rendered during September for $1,350.

September 30: Paid the following items applicable to September operations:

Salaries, $550

Rent, $200

Advertising, $150

b. Prepare a combined statement of earnings and retained earnings for September.

3-17. The following events relate to the Sigma Seventeen Corporation, a newly organized corporation.

October 1: Issued 700 shares of no-par value stock for $12,000 cash.

October 10: Issued 200 shares of no-par stock in exchange for a tract of land. The fair market value of the stock is determined to be $18 per share.

October 12: Purchased supplies on account at a cost of $200.

October 31: Paid the invoice for the supplies purchased on October 12.

October 31: Revenue from the performance of service for October was as follows:

Bills to customers on account, $650

Additional services rendered to customers on account, but not billed, $900

October 31: Expenses for the month were as follows:

Salaries paid in cash, $625

Rent paid in cash, $250

Supplies used, $120

a. Prepare statements of financial position on October 12 and on October 31.

b. Prepare a combined statement of earnings and retained earnings for October.

3-18. The following events relate to the Green Fir Corporation for December:

December 1: Issued 100 shares of no-par stock for $900 in cash.

December 4: Purchased Christmas trees for $675 in cash.

December 10: Paid $35 cash for operating supplies.

December 26: Total cash sales amounted to $1,150 for the entire inventory purchased December 4.

December 31: Paid the rent for December, amounting to $100.

December 31: Used supplies during December, amounting to $35.

December 31: Paid salaries for December, amounting to $400.

a. Prepare statements of financial position at December 15 and at December 31.

b. Prepare a combined statement of earnings and retained earnings for December.

3-19. The following events relate to Dapper Dan Clothing Stores, Inc.:

January 25: The Dapper Dan Clothing Stores, Inc. received its charter from the Secretary of State, and the organization contributed $50,000 cash in exchange for 1,000 shares of $50 par-value stock.

January 31: The company negotiated a one-year lease on a building suitable for its operations. The lessor has granted the company (the lessee) the option of renewing the lease for an additional three years. Cash of $1,200 was paid to cover the rental charge for the first three months.

January 31: A one-year fire-and-liability insurance policy was purchased for $1,200 cash.

January 31: Dapper Dan purchased store and office equipment on account for $2,300.

February 1: It purchased merchandise inventory for $12,000 cash.

February 1: It hired two salesmen effective February 1.

February 15: It paid the invoice for the store and office equipment purchased on January 31.

February 19: It sold, on account, merchandise amounting to $9,000; cash sales amounted to $7,500.

February 19: It incurred a cost of $9,700 for merchandise sold for cash and credit during February.

February 28: It paid salaries for February, which amounted to $1,200.

February 28: It recorded the rent expense for February.

February 28: It recorded the insurance expense for February.

February 28: The store and office equipment depreciated during February. (The estimated life of the equipment is seven years, with a salvage value of $200.)

a. Analyze each event, showing its effect on the statement of financial position by preparing statements of financial position at January 31, and at February 28.

b. Prepare the following financial statements for the January–February period:

   1. Statement of earnings and retained earnings.
   2. Statement of cash receipts and disbursements.

c. What amount did you show for retained earnings after reflecting the January events?

3-20. The following events affected the statement of financial position of Doan's, Inc.:

November 1: Doan's issued 150 shares of no-par value stock for $6,000.
November 1: It purchased supplies for $700 on account.

November 5: It purchased office equipment for $450 in cash.

November 10: It paid for the supplies purchased on November 1.

November 30: It billed customers for $2,750 in services rendered during November.

November 30: It paid the following expense items for November:

Salaries, $925

Rent, $275

Utilities, $70

Other, $320

November 30: The following items relate to November business:

Supplies used, $275

Depreciation expense,

office equipment, $30

a. Prepare a statement of financial position at November 30.

b. Prepare a statement of earnings and a statement of retained earnings for November.

3-21. The statement of financial position for the Ryder Company as of July 31 of the current year is as follows:

RYDER COMPANY

STATEMENT OF FINANCIAL POSITION

As of July 31, 19xx

Assets		*Liabilities and Owners' Equity*		
Current assets:		Current liabilities:		
Cash	$1,250	Accounts payable		$ 670
Accounts receivable	970	Owners' equity:		
Inventory	2,150	Capital stock	$4,000	
Prepaid rent	900	Retained earnings	600	
		Total owners' equity		4,600
		Total liabilities		
Total assets	$5,270	and owners' equity		$5,270

The following transactions pertain to August. Analyze each, showing its effect on the statement of financial position of the Ryder Company:

August 1: Ryder Company purchased land with the issuance of a six-month noninterest-bearing note payable of $4,000.

August 5: It collected $790 on accounts receivable.

August 10: It purchased $3,500 in inventory on account.

August 31: It made sales on account for the month totaling $6,100.

August 31: It paid the following items related to August business:
Salaries, $1,400
Property taxes, $300
Utilities, $150
Other, $95

August 31: The following items relate to August business:
Cost of goods sold, $4,500
Rent, $300

a. Prepare statements of earnings and retained earnings for August.
b. Prepare a statement of cash receipts and disbursements for August.
c. Prepare a statement of financial position at August 31.

3-22. The statement of financial position for Green Light, Inc., as of September 30 of the current year follows:

GREEN LIGHT, INC.

STATEMENT OF FINANCIAL POSITION

As of September 30, 19xx

Assets		Liabilities and Owners' Equity	
Current assets:		Current liabilities:	
Cash	$ 425	Accounts payable	$ 400
Accounts receivable	750	Owners' equity:	
Inventories	1,200	Capital stock	$2,200
		Retained earnings	(225)
		Total owners' equity	$1,975
		Total liabilities and	
Total current assets	$2,375	owners' equity	$2,375

The following transactions pertain to October. Analyze each transaction, showing its effect on the statement of financial position of Green Light.

October 1: Green Light purchased merchandise on account for $2,200.
October 5: It collected accounts receivable amounting to $695.
October 31: Its sales for the month were as follows:
Cash, $3,400
On account, $950
Cost of goods sold, $2,600

October 31: It made a payment on accounts payable of $1,700.
October 31: It paid the following items related to October business:
Salaries, $700
Rent, $125
Utilities, $80
Other, $175

a. Prepare statements of earnings and of retained earnings for October.
b. Prepare a statement of cash receipts and disbursements for October.
c. Prepare a statement of financial position as of October 31.

3-23. The statement of financial position for the Red Oak Company as of April 30 is as follows:

RED OAK COMPANY

STATEMENT OF FINANCIAL POSITION

As of April 30, 19xx

Assets		Liabilities and Owners' Equity	
Current assets:		Current liabilities:	
Cash	$ 900	Accounts payable	$ 2,420
Accounts receivable	550	Other liabilities	790
Inventories	1,150	Total current liabilities	$ 3,210
Prepaid insurance	110	Owners' equity:	
Total current assets	$ 2,710	Capital stock	$20,000
Long-lived assets:		Retained earnings	3,200
Land	$ 2,400	Total owners' equity	$23,200
Buildings (net)	17,500		
Equipment (net)	3,800		
Total long-lived assets	$23,700	Total liabilities and	
Total assets	$26,410	owners' equity	$26,410

The following events pertain to May. Write a sentence about each transaction, explaining its effect on the statement of financial position of the Red Oak Company.

May 1: Red Oak purchased inventory on account, $3,900.
May 2: It made payments on accounts payable, $420.
May 5: It made payments on other liabilities, $560.
May 10: It collected accounts receivable, $500.
May 31: Its sales of merchandise for the month were as follows:
    Cash sales, $2,400
    Sales on account, $3,150
May 31: The following items relate to May business:
    Cost of goods sold, $3,270
    Depreciation expense:
      Buildings, $150
      Equipment, $100
    Insurance expense, $10

May 31: Red Oak paid the following items related to May business:
Salaries, $1,100
Rent, $100
Utilities, $140
Other, $75

a. Prepare a statement of earnings and of retained earnings for May.
b. Prepare a statement of cash receipts and disbursements for May.
c. Prepare a statement of financial position as of May 31.

3-24.   PART I

The five problems that follow represent all of the transactions of Auto Service Shop, a small retail store. Provide the missing data in each case.

a. Accounts receivable, January 1	$2,190
January services rendered on credit	3,720
Cash collections on accounts receivable in January	3,510
Accounts receivable, January 31	?
b. Prepaid insurance, January 1	$ 470
Insurance premiums paid in January	2,005
January insurance expense	190
Prepaid insurance, January 31	?
c. Repair parts inventory, January 1	$ 220
Repair parts purchased in January for cash	175
Repair parts used, January	110
Repair parts inventory, January 31	?
d. Accrued salaries and wages, January 1	$ 170
Salaries and wages expense for January	865
Salaries and wages paid in January	890
Accrued salaries and wages in January 31	?
e. Accrued rent payable, January 1	$ 100
Rent expense for January	200
Rent paid in cash in January	400
Prepaid rent, January 31	?

PART II

From each of the problems in Part I, fill in the following financial statement forms:

AUTO SERVICE SHOP

STATEMENT OF CASH RECEIPTS AND DISBURSEMENTS

For January 19xx

Cash Receipts:		
Collections on accounts receivable		$
Cash disbursements:		
Insurance premiums paid	$	
Repair parts purchased for cash		
Salaries and wages paid		
Rent paid		
Total cash disbursements	─────	
Excess of receipts over disbursements		$ ────
(Disbursements over receipts)		
Cash balance, January 1		$2,360
Cash balance, January 31		$ ═══

AUTO SERVICE SHOP

STATEMENT OF EARNINGS

For January 19xx

Revenue from services		$
Operating expenses:		
Insurance	$	
Supplies used		
Salaries and wages		
Rent		
Total operating expense	─────	
Earnings		$ ═══

AUTO SERVICE SHOP

STATEMENT OF OWNERS' EQUITY

For January 19xx

Owners' equity, January 1	$
Earnings in January	─────
Owners' equity, January 31	$ ═══

AUTO SERVICE SHOP

COMPARATIVE STATEMENT OF FINANCIAL POSITION
As of January 1 and January 31, 19xx

Assets	January 1	January 31
Cash	$2,360.00	$
Accounts receivable		
Repair parts inventory		
Prepaid insurance		
Prepaid rent		
Total Assets	$	$
Liabilities and Owners' Equities		
Accrued salaries and wages	$	$
Accrued rent		
Total liabilities	$	$
Owners' equity		
Total liabilities and owners' equity	$	$

3-25.   PART I

The following data summarize all the transactions of Blue's Novelty Store, Inc., for July. Supply the missing data for these independent transactions.

a.	Accounts receivable, 7/1	$ 3,695
	Credit sales	?
	Cash collections on accounts receivable	10,015
	Accounts receivable, 7/31	3,905
b.	Prepaid insurance, 7/1	$ 1,965
	Insurance premiums paid	?
	Insurance expense	685
	Prepaid insurance, 7/31	3,780
c.	Accounts payable, 7/1 (for merchandise)	$ 2,820
	Merchandise credit purchases	6,320
	Cash payments on accounts payable	?
	Accounts payable, 7/31	3,420
d.	Supplies inventory, 7/1	$ 620
	Supplies purchased for cash	575
	Supplies used	?
	Supplies inventory, 7/31	670
e.	Accrued salaries & wages, 7/1	$?
	Salaries & wages expense	1,335
	Salaries & wages paid	1,260
	Accrued salaries & wages, 7/31	515
f.	Merchandise inventory, 7/1	$ 4,490
	Merchandise purchases	6,320

Cost of goods sold	6,530
Merchandise inventory, 7/31	?
g. Accrued rent payable, 7/1	$ 350
Rent expense	?
Rent paid in cash	975
Prepaid rent, 7/31	375
Cash balance, 7/1	3,520

PART II

Select the appropriate data from the transactions in Part I and prepare the following financial statements:
   a. Statement of cash receipts and disbursements for July.
   b. Statement of earnings and owners' equity for July.
   c. Comparative statement of financial position as of July 1 and July 31.

3-26. Supply the missing data for the following independent transactions for April:

	A	B	C	D
a. Accounts receivable, 4/1	$1,000	$ 1,400	$ 1,700	$
+ Sales on account	4,000	4,700		8,700
Total accounts receivable	$	$	$	$
— Cash collections				
from charge customers	3,800		5,600	7,500
Accounts receivable, 4/30	$	$ 1,300	$ 2,200	$ 3,700
b. Accounts payable, 4/1	$1,540	$ 1,900	$ 1,260	$
+ Purchases on account	7,270	9,250		10,460
Total accounts payable	$	$	$	$
— Cash payments on				
accounts payable[a]	6,820		7,120	9,890
Accounts payable, 4/30	$	$ 1,870	$ 1,490	$ 3,760
c. Inventory, 4/1	$2,000	$ 4,100	$ 9,150	$
+ Purchases	9,000	9,700		46,230
Total cost of goods				
available for sale	$	$	$	$
— Inventory, 4/30	3,000		7,690	12,150
Cost of goods sold	$	$10,550	$26,230	$49,370
d. Prepaid rent, 4/1	$ 100	$ 950	$ 4,685	$
+ Rent paid	200	770		2,165
Total rent paid	$	$	$	$
— Rent expense	240		2,705	2,480
Prepaid rent, 4/30	$	$ 825	$ 1,980	$ 1,760

[a] Assume that all accounts payable are for inventory purchases.

	A	B	C	D
e. Accrued rent payable, 4/1	$ 450	$ 795	$ 995	$
+ Rent expense	700	875		260
Total rent payable	$	$	$	$
− Rent paid	1,400		450	345
Accrued rent payable, 4/30	$	$ 650	$ 1,275	$ 170
f. Accounts payable, 4/1	$1,500	$ 7,165	$ 3,765	$
Accounts payable, 4/30	1,700	7,470		6,250
Inventory, 4/1	3,100	6,575	9,200	9,255
Inventory, 4/30	3,400		7,650	8,675
Cost of goods sold	9,600	11,800	12,670	12,500
Purchases		12,560		
Cash payments on accounts payable[a]			13,600	14,625
g. Accrued rent payable, 4/1	$ 100	$ 245	$ 155	$
Accrued rent payable, 4/30	150	220	170	275
Prepaid rent, 4/1	275	350	400	375
Prepaid rent, 4/30	260	410	450	400
Rent expense	750	1,200		1,400
Cash payments for rent:				
Rent payments in advance[b]		650	1,200	425
Rent payments on account[b]	300		750	1,300

[a] Assume that all accounts payable are for inventory purchases.
[b] There are two rental properties; one rental is paid in advance and the other rental is paid on account.

3-27. Supply the missing data for the following independent situations in January:

a. Accrued payroll, 1/1	$ 1,650
Accrued payroll, 1/31	1,710
Wages expense	10,460
Cash paid for wages	?
b. Accrued payroll, 1/1	$ 1,500
Wages paid	21,950
Accrued payroll, 1/31	1,310
Wages expense	?
c. Supplies inventory, 1/1	$ 460
Supplies purchased	290
Supplies inventory, 1/31	485
Supplies used	?
d. Accounts receivable, 1/1	$ 1,210
January collections on account	1,060

	January cash sales	410
	Accounts receivable, 1/31	1,425
	Sales revenues	?
e.	Prepaid insurance, 1/1	$ 710
	Prepaid insurance, 1/31	490
	Insurance expense	220
	January insurance cash payments	?
f.	Prepaid rent, 1/1	$ 190
	Accrued rent payable, 1/31	360
	Rent expense	1,000
	Rent paid	?
g.	Cash advances from customers, 1/1	$ 1,100
	Cash advances from customers, 1/31	1,460
	Sales revenues	9,120
	Collections in advance from customers[a]	?
h.	Accrued interest receivable, 1/1	$ 400
	Accrued interest receivable, 1/31	290
	Interest income	520
	Interest collected	?
i.	Accounts receivable (net), 1/1	$ 1,940
	Cash collections on accounts receivable	3,890
	Cash sales revenues	890
	Credit losses (1% of credit sales)	?
	Accounts receivable (net), 1/31	2,010
	Gross sales revenues	?
j.	Plant & equipment (net), 1/1	$11,000
	Plant & equipment additions	1,600
	Original cost of plant abandoned ($1,500 loss)	7,000
	Plant & equipment (net), 1/31	10,200
	Depreciation	?
k.	Retained earnings, 1/1	$ 1,590
	Dividend payments	940
	Retained earnings, 1/31	860
	Net earnings[b]	?
l.	Long-lived assets (net), 1/1	$12,400
	Long-lived assets (net), 1/31	11,900

[a] Assume that sales are made only to customers who have paid in advance.

[b] Assume that all items of profit or loss flow through the statement of earnings, even if they arise from other than normal operations.

Long-lived assets purchased	1,400
Depreciation	?

m.

Accounts payable, 1/1ᶜ	$ 2,800
Accounts payable, 1/31	2,600
Inventories, 1/1	11,150
Inventories, 1/31	13,170
Cash payments on accounts payable	9,260
Cost of goods sold	?

n.

Accounts payable, 1/1ᶜ	$ 870
Payments on accounts payable	1,680
Accounts payable, 1/31ᶜ	690
Cash merchandise purchases	360
Total merchandise purchases	?

o.

Accounts payable, 1/1ᶜ	$ 1,420
Accounts payable, 1/31	1,610
Inventory, 1/1	11,270
Inventory, 1/31	9,900
Cost of goods sold	4,660
Purchases	?
Cash payments on accounts payable	?

ᶜ Assume that all accounts payable are for inventory purchases.

3-28. John Q. Entrepreneur formed a company called Com-Consult for the purpose of rendering managerial advisory services. The transactions for the first month of operation, September, 19x1, are as follows:

September 1: Investment of cash by owner, $3,000.
September 1: Rent payment for three months, $900.
September 1: Payment of insurance premium for one year, $360.
September 15: Payment for purchased office supplies for $50.
September 20: Paid an employee $600 for September.
September 30: Rendered services during September amounting to $5,000, all of which were on account.
September 30: Utilities expense of $100—payable October 15.
September 30: Office supplies costing $35 were on hand at this date.

a. Record the transactions in T-accounts.
b. Prepare a trial balance at September 30.
c. Prepare a statement of earnings for September and a statement of financial position at September 30.

3-29.   PART I

Joe Cameron owned and operated a corner drugstore for many years. The only bookkeeping system he maintained was his cash book, or checking account, in which he carefully recorded all cash receipts (at the time of bank deposit) and all cash payments (at the time the checks were written). Some of the more significant operating policies, to which Joe strictly adhered, were the following:

1. He was always careful to get his credit customers to pay their bills before the end of the month, even though this meant occasionally dropping credit customers who could not pay by this time.

2. He deposited all cash receipts at or before the end of the month (except for a $20 change fund that he left in the cash register).

3. He always paid all of his bills for a given month before or at the end of that month. These were primarily for merchandise purchases but also included store and equipment rent, utilities, and store supplies each month, as well as other items that had to be paid less frequently (insurance, taxes, minor repairs, etc.).

4. Taxes and premiums on insurance policies were paid once a year.

5. Merchandise inventory on hand at the end of every month was maintained at a fairly constant level of $5,000. Because of many years of experience in the business, Joe knew approximately how much of various items to purchase every month to maintain a fairly constant inventory level. (This was verified by periodic physical counts.)

6. Because the building and all major equipment were rented, there was no depreciation.

After all cash payments and receipts were recorded for the month, Joe would cash a check for whatever balance remained in his account, considering this his monthly profit. This check might be as small as $400, following a month in which one or more of the less frequent bills were paid, or as high as $1,500. Over the years these withdrawals averaged $1,000 monthly.

a. What do you consider to be the primary objectives of Joe's bookkeeping system? Do you think his system fulfills these objectives?

b. Would a statement of monthly cash transactions provide an approximation to a monthly income statement? Explain your answer. Would a yearly statement of cash transactions approximate a yearly income statement? Explain.

c. Assume that Joe is interested in increasing his profit. Which of his operating practices might be objectionable? Why? How might a better bookkeeping system contribute to better operating practices?

PART II

When Joe decided to retire, he turned the management of the drugstore over to his nephew Henry although Joe retained sole ownership. It was agreed that Henry should be paid a salary of $400 per month, and then he would write Joe a check for the balance, considered the monthly profit. However, since his profit had averaged $1,000 monthly when he managed the business (without paying himself a salary), Joe felt that Henry should be paid a bonus if he increased the profits of the drugstore. Therefore, the maximum amount that Henry would send Joe in any month would be $600 ($1,000 − $400), keeping any amount over $1,000 ($400 salary + $600 check to Joe) as a bonus.

Henry, who had worked in the drugstore on a part-time basis for a year, felt that managing the drugstore was a great opportunity to make some money for himself, considering the generous bonus Joe was offering. Realizing that he would someday be managing the drugstore, Henry noticed how other drugstores operated, and developed some ideas that he intended to employ when he began running the business. The more important of these were the following:

1. Credit customers were no longer required to pay their bills by the end of the month. Henry felt that an easier credit policy would help increase sales, especially because credit customers who purchased goods near the end of the month would no longer be annoyed by having to pay their bills within a few days.

2. Henry did not feel that it was necessary to pay all bills at the end of each month. In fact, it seemed to him that it would be better always to delay payment until the due date, which was usually 30 days after purchase.

3. To compete with local supermarkets, Henry reduced prices on items that both types of concerns sold, such as soap, toothpaste, and cigarettes. He also added certain product lines that the supermarkets didn't carry, such as cameras, hi-fi records, baby clothes, and women's hosiery.

The practices adopted by Henry had some drawbacks, though. Not knowing any bookkeeping, Henry kept track of the money owed by credit customers by placing IOU's on a spindle. After he had been managing the business for three months, these IOU's added up to about $1,500. The expansion of product lines had forced Henry to increase inventories to about $7,500. Since his creditors insisted on prompt payment even though some of his customers were slow, a cash shortage occurred during the third month. In order to pay himself a salary and send Joe a check, Henry was forced to delay paying some of his suppliers. He kept his unpaid bills on another spindle, and at the end of the third month they totaled $2,200. Moreover, he had taken out a bank loan of $500 to meet the demands of some of his more persistent suppliers. The statement below covers the cash transactions for the three months that Henry had managed the drugstore.

a. From the information available, prepare an estimated statement of financial position at the beginning and at the end of the first quarter of the year, a statement of earnings for the quarter, and a statement of changes in owners' equity for the quarter. (You may want to refer to Part I in answering this question.) Consider checks sent to Joe and bonuses paid to Henry as distributions of earnings and not expenses. Assume that the insurance premium and property taxes paid are for the calendar year.

b. Would you consider Henry's operating practices to be more or less objectionable than Joe's? Why?

c. Consider your answer to question *b* of Part I. Would your answer

	January	February	March
Cash receipts:			
Collection from customers	$8,000	$8,500	$8,800
Bank loan			500
Total receipts	$8,000	$8,500	$9,300
Cash Disbursements:			
Merchandise invoices paid	$6,300	$7,100	$7,900
Store and equipment rent	200	200	200
Utilities	50	75	40
Salary—Henry Cameron	400	400	400
Withdrawal—Joe Cameron	600	500	400
Repairs to neon sign		225	
Fire insurance premium	200		
Property taxes paid			360
Bonus—Henry Cameron	250		
Total cash disbursements	$8,000	$8,500	$9,300

Notes: 1. The rent, utilities, withdrawal, salary, and bonus each apply to the month in which they are paid.
2. The fire insurance policy is for one year, beginning January 1.
3. Property tax payment applies to the July 1–December 31 period in the previous year. You may assume that the current year's taxes will be the same as last year.

regarding yearly statements be applicable in light of Henry's expansion practices? Why or why not?

d. What procedures would you recommend to Henry for keeping track of the receivables, payables, and inventory?

e. Define "financial control" and state what contribution accrual accounting makes to it.

APPENDIX 3A

The Accounting Process Illustrated

INTRODUCTION

This appendix provides two additional examples of the accounting cycle for the student interested in reinforcing his understanding of the concepts and rules involved. Luther's, Inc., represents a typical merchandising firm, whereas Samuels Manufacturing Company illustrates some basic aspects of the accounting cycle for manufacturing firms. Both examples are greatly simplified as compared to real accounting systems.

You may find it advantageous to study the Luther's, Inc., example in detail at this time since no new concepts are introduced, and to delay detailed analysis of the Samuels Manufacturing Company until you have studied Chapters 5–8. To understand the Samuels Manufacturing Company example requires a few new concepts that are explained briefly here but are more thoroughly examined in later chapters.

A MERCHANDISING FIRM: LUTHER'S, INC.

Luther's, Inc., holds an exclusive retailer franchise in a small city for Ajax automatic washers and driers. The firm sells for cash or on thirty-day credit terms. All merchandise and supplies are purchased on sixty-day credit terms from the Ajax distributor in the area. Luther's fiscal year ends December 31. The trial balance of the general ledger accounts on January 1, 19x1 follows:

LUTHER'S, INC.

POSTCLOSING TRIAL BALANCE

As of January 1, 19x1

Acct. No.		DR	CR
1	Cash in bank	$1,050	
2	Accounts receivable	2,700	
3	Merchandise—washers	1,500	
4	Merchandise—driers	1,200	
5	Store supplies	250	

LUTHER'S, INC. (CONT.)

Acct. No.		DR	CR
6	Accrued salaries		$ 600
7	Accounts payable—Ajax		4,500
8	Capital stock		1,000
9	Retained earnings		600
10	Sales—washers		0
11	Sales returns—washers.................................	0	
12	Sales—driers		0
13	Sales returns—driers....................................	0	
14	Cost of goods sold—washers	0	
15	Cost of goods sold—driers	0	
16	Salaries expense...	0	
17	Rent expense...	0	
18	Supplies expense..	0	
19	Loss on damaged merchandise	0	
	Totals	$6,700	$6,700

The January 1 merchandise inventory consists of ten washers valued at the purchase cost of $150 each and twelve driers valued at the purchase cost of $100 each. The accounts receivable are from a number of different customers for December purchases of varying amounts. The bookkeeper keeps a subsidiary ledger consisting of the individual accounts. Store supplies include store and advertising materials, office and bookkeeping materials, etc. The store building and fixtures are rented. The *accrued salaries* liability is the debt to employees for salaries earned in December.

The General Journal

The following general journal entries record the January transactions of Luther's, Inc., in the form of monthly totals. In an actual case there would be many transactions of each kind, journalized as they occur.

	L. F.	DR	CR
(a) Merchandise—washers	3	2,240	
Merchandise—driers	4	2,400	
Accounts payable	7		4,640

Event a: Luther's purchased fourteen washers at $160 each and twenty driers at $120 each from the distributor. These prices include transportation and handling cost, for which the distributor must be reimbursed.

Event b: Luther's sold all the washers and driers on hand at January 1, and some that were bought in January as well:

Sales	For cash	30-day terms	Total
Washers	4 @ $200 = $ 800	8 @ $200 = $1,600	$2,400
Driers	3 @ 150 = 450	11 @ 150 = 1,650	$2,100
Total	$1,250	$3,250	$4,500

The cost of the washers and driers sold was as follows:

	Washers	Driers
From beginning inventory	10 @ 150 = $1,500	12 @ 100 = $1,200
From January purchases	2 @ 160 = 320	2 @ 120 = 240
Total	$1,820	$1,440

Event *b* and the cost of the goods sold are entered in the accounts as follows:

	L. F.	DR	CR
(b) Cash in bank	1	1,250	
Accounts receivable	2	3,250	
Sales—washers	10		2,400
Sales—driers	12		2,100
Cost of goods sold—washers	14	1,820	
Cost of goods sold—driers	15	1,440	
Merchandise—washers	3		1,820
Merchandise—driers	4		1,440

Event c: Store supplies on credit:

	L. F.	DR	CR
(c) Store supplies	5	120	
Accounts payable	7		120

Event d: Luther's collected $3,400 cash from customers, of which $2,700 applied to credit sales made in December:

	L. F.	DR	CR
(d) Cash in bank	1	3,400	
Accounts receivable	2		3,400

Event e: The Ajax distributor was paid for credit purchases of merchandise and supplies, made in November:

	L. F.	DR	CR
(e) Accounts payable—Ajax	7	2,900	
Cash in bank	1		2,900

Event f: December salaries were paid in January. (In this illustration we ignore payroll taxes and deductions):

	L. F.	DR	CR
(f) Accrued salaries	6	600	
Cash in bank	1		600

Event g: The January payroll (again ignoring taxes and deductions), payable in February, is as follows:

Store manager		$ 400
Salesman		200
Bookkeeper		100
		$ 700
(g) Salary expense	16	700
Accrued salaries	6	700

Event h: Luther's paid the January rent.

(h) Rent expense	17	150	
Cash in bank	1		150

Event i: One of the washers, purchased in December and sold for $200 on credit in January, was damaged during installation. The washer was returned to Luther's; it was estimated that repair costs of $20 would be necessary if the washer was to be sold again as new. The customer refused to take delivery on another washer, and the sale was cancelled:

(i) Sales returns—washers	11	200	
Accounts receivable	2		200
Merchandise—washers	3	130	
Loss on damaged merchandise	19	20	
Cost of goods sold—washers	14		150

Event j: Paid repair cost on damaged washer.

(j) Merchandise—washers	3	20	
Cash in bank	1		20

Event k: The physical inventory count at January 31 reveals the following:

Repaired washer—1 (see *i* and *j*)—cost	$ 150
New washers—12—cost $160 each	1,920
Driers—18—cost $120 each	2,160
Supplies	210

Note that the appliance inventory count agrees with the number of appliances that should be on hand according to the general ledger, and therefore no entry is required. In this case, the inventory count demonstrates that no error has been made in the merchandise accounts. The inventory of store supplies is necessary as a means of measuring the amount of supplies used in January. The entry is based on the assumption that all supplies not on hand at January 31 were used in January, and the entry reduces the asset account "Store supplies" to $210.

	L. F.	DR	CR
(k) Supplies expense	18	160	
Store supplies	5		160

In an actual firm, an entry would be made to record the estimated federal income tax expense applicable to January earnings. This entry has been omitted here.

The General Ledger

Luther's general ledger accounts (in T-account form) are shown in Exhibit 3A–1. The January 1 account balances are entered in accounts 1 through 9. Since December 31 is the end of the fiscal year, closing entries as of December 31, 19x0, were made at that time in all revenue and expense accounts, reducing them to zero and updating the balance in the retained earnings account to the correct balance of $600.

EXHIBIT 3A-1

LUTHER'S, INC.
GENERAL LEDGER

Cash in Bank (1)				Accounts Receivable (2)			
1/1 bal.	$1,050	(e)	$2,900	1/1 bal.	$2,700	(d)	$3,400
(b)	1,250	(f)	600	(b)	3,250	(i)	200
(d)	3,400	(h)	150	(2,350)	5,950		3,600
		(j)	20				
(2,030)	5,700		3,670				

Merchandise—Washers (3)				Merchandise—Driers (4)			
1/1 bal.	$1,500	(b)	$1,820	1/1 bal.	$1,200	(b)	$1,440
(a)	2,240			(a)	2,400		
(i)	130			(2,160)	3,600		1,440
(j)	20						
(2,070)	3,890		1,820				

Store Supplies (5)

1/1 bal.	$250	(k)	$160
(c)	120		
(210)	370		160

Accrued Salaries (6)

(f)	$600	1/1 bal.	$600
		(g)	700
	600	(700)	1,300

Accounts Payable—Ajax (7)

(e)	$2,900	1/1 bal.	$4,500
		(a)	4,640
		(c)	120
	2,900	(6,360)	9,260

Capital Stock (8)

1/1 bal.	$1,000

Retained Earnings (9)

1/1 bal.	$600

Sales—Washers (10)

(b)	$2,400

Sales Returns—Washers (11)

(i)	$200

Sales—Driers (12)

(b)	$2,100

Sales Returns—Driers (13)

Cost of Goods Sold—Washers (14)

(b)	$1,820	(i)	$150
(1,670)	1,820		150

Cost of Goods Sold—Driers (15)

(b)	$1,440

Salaries Expense (16)

(g)	$700

Rent Expense (17)

(b)	$150

Supplies Expense (18)

(k)	$160

Loss on Damaged Merchandise (19)

(i)	$20

Exhibit 3A–1 shows all the January general journal entries posted to the ledger accounts. The appropriate ledger account numbers have been entered in the L. F. column in the journal to indicate the fact. For the reader's convenience, we show lower case letters keying the transactions posted in the ledger, but this is not common procedure. Real ledger accounts show only the journal page number from which the transaction was posted; journal entries are not usually given individual designations.

Once the data are posted to the ledger, an account balance of each account is computed by adding up each side, deducting the smaller side from the larger, and circling the difference (the account balance). This step is, of course, unnecessary in accounts having only one entry.

The General Ledger Trial Balance

Now the trial balance can be drawn:

LUTHER'S, INC.

GENERAL LEDGER TRIAL BALANCE

As of January 31, 19x1

Acct. No.		DR	CR
1	Cash in bank	$ 2,030	
2	Accounts receivable	2,350	
3	Merchandise—washers	2,070	
4	Merchandise—driers	2,160	
5	Store supplies	210	
6	Accrued salaries		$ 700
7	Accounts payable—Ajax		6,360
8	Capital stock		1,000
9	Retained earnings		600
10	Sales—washers		2,400
11	Sales returns—washers	200	
12	Sales—driers		2,100
13	Sales returns—driers	0	
14	Cost of goods sold—washers	1,670	
15	Cost of goods sold—driers	1,440	
16	Salaries expense	700	
17	Rent expense	150	
18	Supplies expense	160	
19	Loss on damaged merchandise	20	
	Totals	$13,160	$13,160

The trial balance serves two purposes: It demonstrates that certain kinds of mechanical and arithmetic errors have been avoided (it does not assure accuracy, however), and it is a convenient device for the preparation of financial statements.

Financial Statements

LUTHER'S, INC.

COMBINED STATEMENT OF EARNINGS AND RETAINED EARNINGS

For January 19x1

	Washers	Driers	Total
Sales	$2,400	$2,100	$4,500
Less: Sales returns	200	0	200
Net sales	$2,200	$2,100	$4,300
Cost of goods sold	1,670	1,440	3,110
Margin	$ 530	$ 660	$1,190
Operating expenses			
Salaries		$ 700	
Rent		150	
Supplies expense		160	
Loss on damaged merchandise		20	
Total			1,030
Net earnings			$ 160
Retained earnings, January 1			600
Total			$ 760
Dividends			0
Retained earnings, January 31			$ 760

LUTHER'S, INC.

STATEMENT OF FINANCIAL POSITION

As of January 31, 19x1

Assets		Equities		
Cash in bank	$2,030	Liabilities		
Accounts receivable	2,350	Accrued salaries		$ 700
Merchandise—washers	2,070	Accounts payable—Ajax		6,360
Merchandise—driers	2,160	Total liabilities		$7,060
Store supplies	210	Owners' equity		
		Capital stock	$1,000	
		Retained earnings	760	
		Total owners' equity		1,760
Total assets	$8,820	Total equities		$8,820

Notice that the January 31 balance of retained earnings, which appears in both financial statements, is the net result of the January 1 balance of $600, as shown in the ledger, plus all revenues and minus all expenses (and dividends, had there been any) for January. This amount of $760 does not appear in the ledger as a single figure because closing entries are not made at this time, but it demonstrates the fact that all temporary accounts (numbers 10 through 19 in this case) are subdivisions of the retained earnings account and are used to measure periodic changes in retained earnings (i.e., revenues, expenses, losses, and dividends).

LUTHER'S, INC.

STATEMENT OF CASH RECEIPTS AND DISBURSEMENTS

For January 19x1

Cash receipts		
From cash sales		$1,250
Collections on account		3,400
Total receipts		$4,650
Cash disbursements		
On accounts payable	$2,900	
For payroll	600	
For rent	150	
For merchandise repairs	20	
Total disbursements		3,670
Excess of receipts over disbursements		$ 980
Cash balance, January 1		1,050
Cash balance, January 31		$2,030

Although the dollar amounts for the cash receipts and disbursements statement for one month can be obtained from the ledger, it is necessary to refer to the journal for adequate descriptions. Note also that it would be most difficult to prepare this statement for a period longer than one month, since the system does not provide a convenient way of accumulating the information for a longer period.

MANUFACTURING PROCESSES AND COST ACCOUNTING

Manufacturing operations differ from mercantile operations primarily in that the former result in a product created from materials, labor, and the services provided by the factory and related facilities, whereas merchandising operations do not alter the product sold, but instead provide locational utility to the customer. Manufacturing operations vary widely in complexity, depending on the product, the extent to which the process is automated, and other factors; but even the simpler products incorporate some combination of these three classes of inputs.

Tracing the costs of these inputs through the manufacturing process is the task of the cost accountant. Cost accounting, a very important segment of accounting, is useful in all firms, including nonmanufacturing and "not-for-profit" firms, but its basic application is accounting for the cost of manufactured products. Its purpose is not only to permit comparison of actual manufacturing costs with some standard (i.e., with what the cost "should have been"), in order to reduce waste and increase efficiency, but also to measure the manufacturing cost of finished products and partly finished products, so that periodic gain or loss, and cost of inventories to be assigned to future periods, can be determined.

Some aspects of cost comparison are discussed in Chapters 5 and 6; cost measurement is examined in Chapters 7 and 8. In the Samuels Manufacturing Company example, we demonstrate how accrual accounting, with the double-entry bookkeeping system, is adapted to a typical manufacturing firm. The primary task is to measure and trace the basic cost elements through the inventory asset accounts in the firm's general ledger.

Every manufacturing firm has three basic cost elements: materials, both direct and indirect; labor, both direct and indirect; and overhead. Direct materials and labor are identified directly with the finished product. For example, the glass in a mirror obviously is identified with the product, as would be the labor of the man who cut the glass to proper size. On the other hand, the powder used in polishing the mirror is a material that was used in finishing the product, but it is not easily identified with the individual mirror; thus it is called an indirect material. Similarly, the labor of the operator of the grinding machine is treated as an indirect labor cost. Indirect costs are usually considered a type of overhead and are assigned to the product by using an allocation formula.

The three primary elements (materials, labor, and overhead) are all handled through three types of inventory asset account: materials and supplies, work in process, and finished product. Two temporary ("suspense") accounts are used to accumulate direct labor and manufacturing overhead costs temporarily. Let us see how and when entries are posted to the three inventory accounts.

1. Materials and supplies.   Purchases and use of materials and supplies are recorded in this account as they occur. Purchases are recorded as debits (increases) and uses are recorded as credits (decreases).

2. Work in process.   The costs of direct materials used, direct labor used, and manufacturing overhead (which includes indirect materials and indirect labor) are entered as debits (increases) when these inputs enter the manufacturing process. The total product costs are entered as credits (decreases) as the product is finished and leaves the factory.

3. Finished product.   The cost of finished product is entered in this account as a debit (increase) as the product is finished. These debits correspond to the

CHART OF COST FLOWS IN MANUFACTURING INVENTORIES

Materials and Supplies Inventory (an asset)

Cost of materials and supplies on hand, beginning of periods	Cost of direct materials used
Cost of materials and supplies purchased	Cost of indirect materials used
	Cost of materials and supplies on hand, end of period

Manufacturing Overhead (a suspense account)

No balance, beginning of period	Manufacturing overhead applied to product
Cost of indirect materials used	No balance, end of period
Cost of indirect labor	
Cost of facilities	

Direct Labor (a suspense account)

No balance, beginning of period	Direct labor cost, applied to product
Direct labor cost incurred	No balance, end of period

Work in Process (an asset)

Cost of unfinished product on hand, beginning of period	Cost of product finished this period
Cost of direct materials used	Cost of unfinished product on hand, end of period
Manufacturing overhead applied to product	
Direct labor cost applied to product	

Finished Product (an asset)

Cost of finished product on hand, beginning of period	Cost of product sold this period
Cost of product finished this period	Cost of finished product on hand, end of period

Cost of Goods Sold (an expense)

Cost of product sold this period

credits in the work in process account. When the products are sold to customers, the cost of finished product is entered as a credit (decrease).

These three inventory accounts, together with the two temporary accounts for direct labor and manufacturing overhead, are shown in Exhibit 3A–2. We shall examine the accounts in more detail when we turn to the Samuels Manufacturing Company.

Since cost of goods sold is usually such an important item in the earnings statement of a manufacturing firm, it is often the subject of a financial statement of its own. This statement is more appropriately described as a *supporting schedule* explaining the cost of goods sold item in the earnings statement. It is essentially a summary of the entries and the beginning and ending balances in the work in process and finished product inventory accounts, in the same way that the statement of cash receipts and disbursements is a summary of entries and beginning and ending balances in the cash in bank account. The schedule is called *cost of goods manufactured and sold,* and in skeleton form, looks like this:

THE XYZ COMPANY

SCHEDULE OF COST OF GOODS MANUFACTURED AND SOLD
(Period)

Direct materials used	xxx
Direct labor used	xxx
Manufacturing overhead	xxx
Total manufacturing cost	xxxx
Add: Work in process inventory, beginning of period	xx
Total	xxxx
Deduct: Work in process inventory, end of period	xx
Cost of goods manufactured	xxxx
Add: Finished product inventory, beginning of period	xx
Total	xxxx
Deduct: Finished product inventory, end of period	xx
Cost of goods sold	xxxx

A MANUFACTURING FIRM ILLUSTRATED

The Samuels Manufacturing Company produces a single product in a small factory building that also houses the sales and administrative offices. There are fifteen employees, including ten direct laborers, two maintenance men, one supervisor, one salesman, and two officers. The manufacturing process requires an average of about one month. Finished product is stored until it is sold (on credit), at which time the revenue from sales and the expense of cost of finished product sold is recognized. Selling and administrative expenses, and income taxes, are recognized as they are incurred. The fiscal year ends June 30.

The general ledger trial balance as of May 31, 19x1 follows:

SAMUELS MANUFACTURING COMPANY
GENERAL LEDGER TRIAL BALANCE
As of May 31, 19x1

Acct. No.		DR	CR
1	Cash in bank	$ 14,000	
2	Accounts receivable	11,000	
3	Materials and supplies	8,000	
4	Goods in process	17,000	
5	Finished product	10,000	
6	Prepaid insurance	5,000	
7	Plant and equipment	80,000	
8	Plant and equipment—allowance for depreciation		$ 25,000
9	Accounts payable		20,000
10	Accrued property taxes		1,000
11	Accrued utilities payable		0
12	Accrued payroll		8,000
13	Accrued income tax payable		16,000
14	Capital stock		50,000
15	Retained earnings		11,000
16	Dividends	9,000	
17	Sales		185,000
18	Cost of goods sold	105,000	
19	Manufacturing overhead	0	
20	Selling and administrative expenses	35,000	
21	Federal income tax expense	22,000	
	Totals	$316,000	$316,000

The Journal

Here are the June transactions and other events in general journal form:

		L. F.	DR	CR
a.	Materials and supplies	3	5,000	
	Accounts payable	9		5,000

Purchased materials and supplies on account.

		L. F.	DR	CR
b.	Goods in process	2	7,000	
	Manufacturing overhead	19	3,000	
	Selling and administrative expenses	20	4,000	
	Accrued payroll	12		14,000

Payroll for June (ignoring payroll taxes and deductions) consists of direct labor $7,000, indirect labor $3,000, selling and administration $4,000.

		L. F.	DR	CR
c.	Goods in process	4	4,000	
	Manufacturing overhead	19	2,000	
	Materials and supplies	3		6,000

Used direct materials $4,000 and indirect materials $2,000 in the manufacturing operation in June.

		L. F.	DR	CR
d.	Manufacturing overhead	19	400	
	Selling and administrative expense	20	100	
	Plant and equipment—allowance for depreciation	8		500

Depreciation cost of plant and equipment for June allocated 80 per cent to manufacturing, 20 per cent to selling and administration.

		L. F.	DR	CR
e.	Manufacturing overhead	19	800	
	Selling and administrative expense	20	200	
	Accrued utilities payable	11		200
	Prepaid insurance	6		500
	Accrued property taxes payable	10		300

June utilities, insurance, and property tax cost for June allocated 80 per cent to manufacturing, 20 per cent to selling and administration, as follows.

	Utilities	Insurance	Property Taxes	Total
Manufacturing	$160	$400	$240	$ 800
Selling and administration	40	100	60	200
	$200	$500	$300	$1,000

		L. F.	DR	CR
f.	Goods in process	4	6,200	
	Manufacturing overhead	19		6,200

To record entire manufacturing overhead for June as an addition to goods in process inventory.

		L. F.	DR	CR
g.	Finished product	5	19,100	
	Goods in process	4		19,100

The cost accounting system (not illustrated here) reveals that $19,100 is the cost of product finished during June and that $15,100 remains in process on June 30.

		L. F.	DR	CR
h.	Accounts receivable	2	25,000	
	Sales	17		25,000
	Cost of goods sold	18	16,500	
	Finished product	5		16,500

To record sales revenue and cost of goods sold for June.

	L. F.	DR	CR
i. Federal income tax expense	21	2,000	
Accrued income tax	13		2,000

To record estimated income taxes based on June income.

	L. F.	DR	CR
j. Cash in bank	1	22,000	
Accounts receivable	2		22,000

To record June cash collections from customers.

	L. F.	DR	CR
k. Dividends	16	3,000	
Accounts payable	9	11,000	
Accrued payroll	12	15,000	
Accrued utilities payable	11	200	
Cash in bank	1		29,200

To record June cash payments.

The Ledger

The general ledger accounts of Samuels Manufacturing Company are shown in Exhibit 3A–3. Note that Samuels does not use a direct labor account but adds these costs directly to the goods in process account.

In these accounts, running totals of the debit and credit sides are maintained, with the balance at any time shown in a circle on the appropriate side of the account. The running totals that comprise the May 31 balances are assumed for illustration purposes. (This is just one of several ways that ledger accounts are actually maintained.)

EXHIBIT 3A-3

SAMUELS MANUFACTURING COMPANY
GENERAL LEDGER

Cash in Bank (1)

(14,000)	$248,000		$234,000
(j)	22,000	(k)	29,200
(6,800)	$270,000		$263,200

Accounts Receivable (2)

(11,000)	$321,000		$310,000
(h)	25,000	(j)	22,000
(14,000)	$346,000		$332,000

Materials and Supplies (3)

(8,000)	$96,000		$88,000
(a)	5,000	(c)	6,000
	$101,000		$94,000
(7,000)			

Goods in Process (4)

(17,000)	$198,000		$181,000
(b)	7,000	(g)	19,100
(c)	4,000		
(f)	6,200		
(15,100)	$215,200		$200,100

Finished Product (5)

(10,000)	$176,000		$166,000
(g)	19,100	(h)	16,500
(12,600)	$195,100		$182,500

Prepaid Insurance (6)

(5,000)	$6,600		$1,600
		(e)	500
(4,500)	$6,600		$2,100

Plant and Equipment (7)

(80,000)	$82,000		$2,000

Plant and Equipment—Allow. for Depr. (8)

	$1,000	(25,000)	$26,000
		(d)	500
	1,000	(25,500)	$26,500

Accounts Payable (9)

	$245,000	(20,000)	$265,000
(k)	11,000	(a)	5,000
	$256,000	(14,000)	$270,000

Accrued Property Tax Payable (10)

	$900	(1,000)	$1,900
		(e)	300
	$900	(1,300)	$2,200

Accrued Utilities Payable (11)

	$4,200		$4,200
(k)	200	(e)	200
	$4,400		$4,400

Accrued Payroll (12)

	$94,000	(8,000)	$102,000
(k)	15,000	(b)	14,000
	$109,000	(7,000)	$116,000

Accrued Income Tax Payable (13)

	$33,000	(16,000)	$49,000
		(i)	2,000
	$33,000	(18,000)	$51,000

Capital Stock (14)

	$5,000	(50,000)	$55,000

Retained Earnings (15)

	July 1, 19x0 bal.	
		$11,000

Dividends (16)

	$ 9,000	
(k)	3,000	
	$12,000	

Sales (17)

		$185,000
(h)		25,000
		$210,000

Cost of Goods Sold (18)

	$105,000	
(h)	16,500	
	$121,500	

	Manufacturing Overhead (19)				Selling and Administrative Expense (20)	

	$340,000	(f)	$340,000		$35,000
(b)	3,000		6,200	(b)	4,000
(c)	2,000			(d)	100
(d)	400			(e)	200
(e)	800				
	$346,200		$346,200		$39,300

Federal Income Tax Expense (21)

	$22,000
(i)	2,000

The closing entires required for the preparation of the postclosing trial balance are left as an exercise. To help you figure them out, both the preclosing and postclosing trial balances are shown below. (The closing entries would affect only those accounts whose balance changes between preclosing and postclosing.) In actual practice, closing entries are journalized and posted to the ledger.

The Trial Balance

SAMUELS MANUFACTURING COMPANY
PRECLOSING AND POSTCLOSING TRIAL BALANCES
As of June 30, 19x1

Acct. No.		Preclosing DR	Preclosing CR	Postclosing DR	Postclosing CR
1	Cash in bank	$ 6,800		$ 6,800	
2	Accounts receivable	14,000		14,000	
3	Materials and supplies	7,000		7,000	
4	Goods in process	15,100		15,100	
5	Finished product	12,600		12,600	
6	Prepaid insurance	4,500		4,500	
7	Plant and equipment	80,000		80,000	
8	Plant and equipment—allow. for depr.		$ 25,500		$ 25,500
9	Accounts payable		14,000		14,000
10	Accrued property tax payable		1,300		1,300
11	Accrued utilities payable		0		0

SAMUELS MANUFACTURING COMPANY (CONT.)

Acct. No.		*Preclosing* DR	*Preclosing* CR	*Postclosing* DR	*Postclosing* CR
12	Accrued payroll............................		7,000		7,000
13	Accrued income tax payable...............		18,000		18,000
14	Capital stock		50,000		50,000
15	Retained earnings		11,000		24,200
16	Dividends..............................	12,000		0	
17	Sales...................................		210,000		0
18	Cost of goods sold	121,500		0	
19	Manufacturing overhead..................	0		0	
20	Selling and administrative expense...........	39,300		0	
21	Federal income tax expense	24,000		0	
	Totals.............................	$336,800	$336,800	$140,000	$140,000

The Financial Statements

The financial statements of Samuels Manufacturing Company follow:

SAMUELS MANUFACTURING COMPANY
STATEMENT OF EARNINGS AND RETAINED EARNINGS

	For the Month June 19x1	*For the Year Ended June 30, 19x1*
Sales...................................	$25,000	$210,000
Cost of goods sold.......................	16,500	121,500
Margin.............................	$ 8,500	$ 88,500
Selling and administrative expenses	4,300	39,300
Net operating earnings..................	$ 4,200	$ 49,200
Federal income tax expense...............	2,000	24,000
Net earnings	$ 2,200	$ 25,200
Retained earnings, beginning of period	25,000	11,000
Total.............................	$27,200	$ 36,200
Dividends	3,000	12,000
Retained earnings, June 30, 19x1	$24,200	$ 24,200

SAMUELS MANUFACTURING COMPANY
STATEMENT OF FINANCIAL POSITION
As of June 30, 19x1

Assets			Equities			
Cash in bank		$ 6,800	Liabilities			
Accounts receivable		14,000	Accounts payable			$ 14,000
Materials and supplies		7,000	Accrued property tax payable			1,300
Goods in process		15,100	Accrued payroll			7,000
Finished product		12,600	Accrued income tax payable			18,000
Prepaid insurance		4,500	Total liabilities			$ 40,300
Plant and equipment	$80,000		Stockholder's equity:			
Allow. for depr.	25,500	54,500	Capital stock		$50,000	
Total assets		$114,500	Retained earnings		24,200	
			Total stockholder's equity			74,200
			Total equities			$114,500

SAMUELS MANUFACTURING COMPANY
STATEMENT OF CASH RECEIPTS AND DISBURSEMENTS
For June 19x1

Cash receipts:		
Collections from customers		$22,000
Cash disbursements:		
On accounts payable	$11,000	
For payroll	15,000	
For utilities	200	
For dividends	3,000	
Total cash disbursements		29,200
Excess (deficiency) of receipts over disbursements		$(7,200)
Cash balance, June 1		14,000
Cash balance, June 30		$ 6,800

The difficulty in obtaining the data for the statement of cash receipts and disbursements is the same as in the case of the statement of cost of goods manufactured and sold described above. Cash in bank provides only monthly receipts and disbursement figures *in total,* and it is necessary to refer to the journal to get the breakdown of cash disbursements. Furthermore, it would obviously be difficult to get sufficient information to prepare the cash receipts and disbursements statement for the entire year. If management felt that such a statement were important, the accounting system should be changed to provide it. Apparently Samuels does not report cash receipts and disbursements regularly, or for periods longer than one month.

Problems for Analysis

3A-1. The Twin Oaks Company was organized April 1, 19x1, for the purpose of purchasing and operating an eighty-unit apartment complex. The following events occurred during the first month of operations:

April 1: Received $120,000 cash in exchange for shares of stock issued.

April 1: Purchased the apartment complex for $600,000. $100,000 of this cost was for the land and $500,000 was for the buildings. This included a cash payment of $100,000 and the assumption of a $500,000, 6 per cent, twenty-five-year mortgage. Payments of $4,500 (including principal and interest) are due the first of each month, beginning May 1.

April 1: Paid $900 cash for a one-year fire- and extended-coverage-insurance policy.

April 1: Collected $8,000 cash from tenants for April rent.

April 15: Paid $50 cash for grounds maintenance services for April.

April 25: Paid $600 cash for supplies.

April 30: Paid $400 management fee for the month of April.

Note: The above data reflect exchanges of cash, goods, and services between The Twin Oaks Company and others for the month of April. The passing of the month of April causes the following changes in its statement of financial position:

April 30: 1. The $8,000 cash collected from tenants on April 1 has been earned and the liability to tenants has been satisfied.

2. One month of the insurance policy cost has expired.

3. One month of the apartment buildings' usefulness has expired. The buildings have an estimated life of forty years. (Compute to the nearest dollar.)

4. Semiannual property taxes of $1,200 on the land and buildings are payable on October 1 and April 1 of each year.

5. $150 of the supplies is used up during the month of April.

6. The $4,500 mortgage payment due May 1 includes $2,500 for interest and $2,000 for principal repayment.

7. Estimated cost of electricity, gas, and water for April is $300.

a. Analyze and record the events of the Twin Oaks Company in a general journal.

b. Set up a general ledger (use T-accounts).

c. Post the transactions from the general journal to the appropriate general ledger accounts. Use transaction dates as cross-references.

d. Determine the general ledger account balances.

e. Prepare a trial balance of the general ledger accounts.

f. Prepare the following financial statements:
   1. Statement of earnings and statement of retained earnings for April.
   2. Statement of financial position at April 30.
   3. Statement of cash receipts and disbursements for April.

3A-2. The preclosing trial balance for the Twin Oaks Company after the first month of operations follows:

THE TWIN OAKS COMPANY

PRECLOSING TRIAL BALANCE

As of April 30, 19x1

	DR	CR
Cash	$ 26,050	
Prepaid insurance	825	
Supplies inventory	450	
Land	100,000	
Building	500,000	
Accumulated depreciation		$ 1,042
Accrued property taxes payable		200
Accrued interest payable		2,500
Accrued utilities payable		300
Rent received in advance		0
Mortgage payable		500,000
Capital stock		120,000
Retained earnings		0
Rent earned		8,000
Grounds maintenance expense	50	
Management expense	400	
Insurance expense	75	
Depreciation expense	1,042	
Property tax expense	200	
Supplies expense	150	
Interest expense	2,500	
Utilities expense	300	
	$632,042	$632,042

The following transactions and events occurred during the second month of operations:

May 1: Paid utilities for April, $300.
May 1: Collected $8,700 from tenants for rent.
May 1: Paid $4,500 on the mortgage payable (including April interest).
May 15: Paid $75 cash for grounds maintenance services.
May 20: Paid $525 cash for supplies.
May 31: Paid $435 management fee for the month of May.
Note: The above data reflect exchanges of cash, goods, and services between

The Twin Oaks Company and others for the month of May. The passing of the month of May causes the following changes in its statement of financial position.

May 31: 1. $8,000 of the cash collected from tenants on May 1 has been earned and the liability to tenants has been satisfied. Rentals earned but not collected in May amount to $400.

2. One month of the insurance policy cost has expired.

3. One month of the apartment buildings' usefulness has expired. The buildings have an estimated life of forty years.

4. Semiannual property taxes of $1,200 on the land and buildings are payable on October 1 and April 1 of each year.

5. Supplies used during the month amount to $320.

6. The $4,500 mortgage payment due June 1 includes $2,490 for May interest.

7. Estimated cost of electricity, gas, and water for May is $275.

a. Analyze and record the events of the Twin Oaks Company in a general journal.

b. Set up a general ledger (use T-accounts).

c. Post the entries to the general ledger accounts. Use transaction dates and account numbers for cross-references.

d. Determine the general ledger account balances.

e. Prepare a preclosing trial balance of the general ledger accounts.

f. Prepare the following financial statements:

1. A combined statement of earnings and retained earnings for the two-month period of April 1–May 31.

2. Statement of financial position at May 31.

3. Statement of cash receipts and disbursements for May. Assume that management has decided that this statement is important and should be reported monthly. What procedures do you recommend for simplifying its preparation?

3A–3. Par Driving Range, Inc., was organized July 1, 19x1, for the purpose of purchasing and operating an existing golf driving range. The following events occurred during the first month of operations:

July 1:   Received $100,000 cash in exchange for shares of stock issued.

July 1:   Purchased the golf driving range for $175,000. $125,000 of this cost was for the land and $50,000 was for the buildings and other improvements. This included a cash payment of $75,000 and the assumption of a $100,000, 7 per cent, twenty-year mortgage. Payments of $1,000 (including principal and interest) are due the last day of each month.

July 1:   Purchased a one-year insurance policy for $1,200. Payment is due in fifteen days.

July 10: Purchased supplies on account amounting to $700.

July 16: Paid the premium on the insurance policy purchased July 1.

July 20: Paid $250 cash for maintenance of grounds.

July 31: Revenue collected from customers for the month of July amounted to $5,800.

July 31: Amounts owed to employees for July salaries is $950.

July 31: Paid the first monthly mortgage installment. $583 was for interest and $417 for principal.

Note: The above data reflect exchanges of cash, goods, and services between Par Driving Range, Inc., and others for the month of July. The passing of the month of July causes the following changes in its statement of financial position.:

July 31: 1. One month of the insurance policy cost has expired.

        2. One month of the buildings and of other improvement costs has expired. These items have an estimated useful life of ten years. (Compute to the nearest dollar).

        3. Semiannual property taxes of $600 are payable on January 1 and July 1 of each year.

        4. $350 of the supplies is used up during the month of July.

        5. Estimated cost of utilities, $175.

  a. Analyze and record the events of Par Driving Range, Inc., in a general journal.

  b. Set up a general ledger (use T-accounts).

  c. Post the entries to the general ledger accounts.

  d. Prepare a trial balance of the general ledger accounts.

  e. Prepare the following financial statements:

    1. Statement of earnings and retained earnings for July.

    2. Statement of financial position as of July 31, 19x1.

    3. Statement of cash receipts and disbursements for July.

3A-4. The trial balance for Par Driving Range, Inc., after the first month of operations follows:

PAR DRIVING RANGE, INC.

PRECLOSING TRIAL BALANCE

As of July 31, 19x1

	DR	CR
Cash	$ 28,350	
Prepaid insurance	1,100	
Supplies inventory	350	
Land	125,000	
Buildings and improvements	50,000	
Accumulated depreciation		$ 417
Accounts payable		700
Accrued utilities payable		175
Accrued salaries payable		950
Accrued property taxes payable		100
Mortgage payable		99,583
Capital stock		100,000
Service revenue		5,800

PAR DRIVING RANGE, INC. (CONT.)

	DR	CR
Grounds maintenance expense	250	
Salary expense	950	
Interest expense	583	
Insurance expense	100	
Depreciation expense	417	
Property tax expense	100	
Supplies expense	350	
Utilities expense	175	
	$207,725	$207,725

The following events occurred during the second month of operations:

August 1: Paid cash for July utility bills, $175.

August 2: Paid July salaries of $950.

August 5: Purchased supplies for cash, $240.

August 10: Paid $175 cash for the maintenance of grounds.

August 31: Revenue collected from customers for the month of August amounted to $6,100.

August 31: Amounts owed to employees for August salaries is $975.

August 31: Paid the second monthly mortgage installment. $581 was for interest.

Note: The above data reflect exchanges of cash, goods, and services between Par Driving Range, Inc., and others for the month of August. The passing of the month of August causes the following changes in its statement of financial position.

August 31: 1. One month of the insurance policy cost has expired.

2. One month of the buildings and of other improvement costs has expired. These items have an estimated useful life of ten years. (Compute to the nearest dollar.)

3. Semiannual property taxes of $600 are payable on January 1 and July 1 of each year.

4. $300 of the supplies is used up during the month of August.

5. Estimated cost of utilities for August, $200.

a. Analyze and record the events of Par Driving Range, Inc., in a general journal.

b. Set up a general ledger (using T-accounts).

c. Post the transactions from the general journal to the appropriate general ledger accounts.

d. Prepare a trial balance of the general ledger accounts.

e. Prepare the following financial statements:

1. Statement of earnings and retained earnings in comparative form for July and August.

2. Statement of financial position as of August 31, 19x1.

3. Statement of cash receipts and disbursements for July and August. (See problem 3A–3.)

3A–5. Park Lanes, Inc., was organized September 1, 19x2, for the purpose of purchasing and operating a thirty-lane bowling alley. The general ledger accounts, containing the results of the first month's transactions, are shown on the following pages.

PARK LANES, INC.

GENERAL LEDGER

Cash

19x2		19x2	
Sept. 1	$300,000	Sept. 1	$250,000
30	16,300	1	2,400
		25	250
	$316,300		$252,650
Balance	$63,650		

Equipment

19x2		
Sept. 1	$450,000	

Accumulated Depreciation—Equipment

	19x2	
	(2)	$3,750

Supplies Inventory

19x2		19x2	
Sept. 16	$1,250	(4)	$625
Balance	$625		

Accounts Payable

	19x2	
	Sept. 16	$1,250

Prepaid Insurance

19x2		19x2	
Sept. 1	$2,400	(1)	$200
Balance	$2,200		

Accrued Property Taxes Payable

	19x2	
	(3)	$300

Land

19x2		
Sept. 1	$150,000	

Accrued Salaries Payable

	19x2	
	(6)	$1,300

Buildings

19x2		
Sept. 1	$900,000	

Accrued Interest Payable

	19x2	
	(5)	$8,333

Accumulated Depreciation—Buildings

	19x2	
	(2)	$2,500

Accrued Utilities Payable

	19x2	
	(7)	$700

Mortgage Payable

		19x2	
		Sept. 1	$1,250,000

Depreciation Expense—Equipment

19x2		19x2	
(2)	$3,750		

Capital Stock

		19x2	
		Sept. 1	$300,000

Property Tax Expense

19x2		19x2	
(3)	$300		

Retained Earnings

19x2	

Supplies Expense

19x2		19x2	
(4)	$625		

Service Revenue

19x2		19x2	
		Sept. 30	$16,300

Interest Expense

19x2		19x2	
(5)	$8,333		

Maintenance Expense

19x2		19x2	
Sept. 25	$250		

Salaries Expense

19x2		19x2	
(6)	$1,300		

Insurance Expense

19x2		19x2	
(1)	$200		

Utilities Expense

19x2		19x2	
(7)	$700		

Depreciation Expense—Building

19x2		19x2
(2)	$2,500	

PART I

a. Copy the ledger accounts, including the September transactions, on ledger or analysis paper, leaving ten blank lines in the cash account and four lines in each of the other accounts, for the October transactions.

b. Prepare a trial balance of the general ledger as of September 30, 19x2.

PART II

The following events occurred during the second month of operations:

October 1: Paid $10,000 (includes $8,333 September interest) on mortgage.

October 1:   Paid $1,300 for September salaries.
October 5:   Paid $700 for September utility costs.
October 10: Paid $1,250 for supplies previously purchased on account.
October 15: Paid $1,350 for salaries for the first half of October.
October 20: Paid $310 for the maintenance of alleys.
October 31: Cash revenues for the month of October totalled $18,900.

Note: The above data reflect exchanges of cash, goods, and services between Park Lanes, Inc., and others for the month of October. The passing of the month of October causes the following changes in its statement of financial position.

October 31: 1. One month of the insurance policy cost has expired ($200).
   2. One month of the building and equipment usefulness has expired:

   a. The building has an estimated life of thirty years.
   b. The equipment has an estimated life of ten years.
   3. $1,800 of property taxes on the real estate is due on February 28 and August 31 of each year.
   4. $400 of the supplies is used up during the month of October.
   5. The mortgage is payable on the first of each month. The $10,000 payment due November 1 includes $8,322 for interest.
   6. Salaries for the last half of October are $1,400.
   7. Estimated utility costs for October are $750.

a. Record the October events of Park Lanes, Inc., in a general journal.
b. Post the transactions from the general journal to the appropriate general ledger accounts, as supplied in Part I.
c. Prepare a trial balance of the general ledger accounts as of October 31.
d. Prepare the following financial statements:

1. Comparative combined statement of earnings and retained earnings for September and October.
2. Comparative statement of financial position.
3. Comparative statement of cash receipts and disbursements for September and October.

e. Prepare closing entries to bring the retained earnings account up to date and post these entries to the general ledger. (Closing entries are usually made only at the end of the fiscal year, i.e., when the need for preserving historical revenue and expense information in the ledger no longer exists. These entries are required here for illustrative purposes only.)
f. Prepare a trial balance after closing.

3A-6. Using the appropriate data below, prepare a statement of cost of goods manufactured and sold for Gayhawk Fabricators, Inc.:

Raw materials, February 1	$ 12,000
Work in process, February 1	9,000
Finished goods, February 1	35,000
Purchases	80,000

Sales		450,000
Direct labor		120,000
Indirect labor		45,000
Heat, light, and power—factory		6,000
Heat, light, and power—administrative		1,700
Insurance (70 per cent apportioned to factory)		1,500
Repairs to machinery and equipment		1,100
Salesman's salaries		30,000
Depreciation—factory building		3,000
Depreciation—machinery and equipment		4,200
Real estate and personal property taxes		3,100
(75 per cent apportioned to factory)		

The raw materials used cost $77,000, the cost of goods manufactured was $248,000, and the cost of goods sold was $235,000.

3A–7. Supply the missing information for Syron Manufacturing:

Raw Materials

Jan. 1	Balance	$10,000		Jan. 31	Requisitions	22,000
31	Purchases	?				

Work in Process

Jan. 1	Balance	$ 8,000		Jan. 31	Cost of goods manufactured	?
31	Raw materials used	?				
31	Direct labor	12,000				
31	Manufacturing overhead	?				

Finished Goods

Jan. 1	Balance	$16,000		Jan. 31	Cost of goods sold	?
31	Cost of goods manufactured	?				

Cost of Goods Sold

Jan. 31	?	

Manufacturing Overhead

Jan. 1	Balance	0		Jan. 31	Costs applied to work in process	?
31	Costs incurred	16,000				

January 31 balances:

Raw materials	$ 9,000
Work in process	10,500
Finished goods	18,000
Cost of goods sold	?
Manufacturing overhead	0

3A–8. Capitol Manufacturing Company had the following inventories on November 1:

Finished goods (300 units), $15,000

Work in process, $6,200

Materials and supplies, $7,500

November events are as follows:

1. Materials and supplies purchased on account, $12,000
2. Materials requisitioned for use:

    Direct, $10,000

    Indirect, $1,200
3. Factory payroll used: $12,000, of which $10,200 was used in the direct manufacture of product
4. Manufacturing overhead costs incurred on account:

    Utilities, $300 (will be paid next month)

    Insurance, $400 (one-year premium of $4,800 was paid last August)

    Property taxes, $450 (will be paid in February of next year)
5. Depreciation on machinery and equipment, $600
6. Entire manufacturing overhead recorded as an addition to goods in process inventory
7. Goods finished during the month, $22,500 (450 units)
8. Sales on account (600 units), $60,000
9. Cost of sales?

Record journal entries for the above transactions and events.

3A–9. The trial balance for Two-Way Manufacturing Company as of November 30, 19x1, follows:

TWO-WAY MANUFACTURING COMPANY
GENERAL LEDGER TRIAL BALANCE
As of November 30, 19x1

	DR	CR
Cash in bank	$ 17,000	
Accounts receivable	12,000	
Materials and supplies	7,000	
Work in process	14,000	
Finished goods	12,000	
Prepaid insurance	5,000	
Plant and equipment	78,000	

TWO-WAY MANUFACTURING COMPANY (CONT.)

	DR	CR
Plant and equipment—allowance for depreciation		$ 27,000
Accounts payable		22,000
Accrued property taxes		2,000
Accrued utilities payable		0
Accrued payroll		7,000
Accrued income tax payable		14,000
Capital stock		50,000
Retained earnings		10,000
Dividends	8,000	
Sales		187,000
Cost of goods sold	106,000	
Manufacturing overhead	0	
Selling and administrative expenses	37,000	
Federal income tax expense	23,000	
Totals	$319,000	$319,000

December transactions and other events are as follows:

1. Purchased materials and supplies on account, $8,000
2. Payroll for the month (ignoring payroll taxes and deductions):
    Direct labor, $6,000
    Indirect labor, $3,500
    Selling and administration, $4,000
3. Materials used for the month:
    Direct, $4,500
    Indirect, $1,500
4. Depreciation cost of plant and equipment for the month, $1,000—70 per cent to manufacturing and 30 per cent to selling and administration
5. Utilities, $300; insurance, $600; and property tax expense, $400 for the month—70 per cent manufacturing and 30 per cent selling and administration.
6. Record entire manufacturing overhead for December as an addition to goods in process inventory
7. Cost of goods finished during the month, $14,000
8. Sales on account for the month, $30,000; cost of sales, $22,000
9. Estimated income taxes for December income, $1,700
10. Cash collections on account from customers, $26,000
11. Cash payments for December:
    Dividends, $4,000
    Accounts payable, $10,000
    Accrued payroll, $12,000
    Accrued utilities payable, $300

a. Prepare general ledger T-accounts for each account in the trial balance and enter the November 30 balances.

b. Record the December transactions in journal form and post to the general ledger.

c. Prepare a statement of earnings and retained earnings for December and for the year.

d. Prepare a statement of financial position at year end.

e. Prepare a statement of cash receipts and disbursements for December.

f. Journalize and post closing entries.

g. Prepare a postclosing trial balance.

APPENDIX 3B

Asset Control

In this appendix we consider asset control, which is an organized way of making sure that a manager receives all of the assets he is entitled to receive, and that he does not lose assets unintentionally, through theft or error. We discuss three typical instruments of asset control: bank accounts, imprest funds, and subsidiary ledgers.

Bank Accounts

Bank accounts offer many advantages as a means of cash control. First, the bank keeps its own set of records of deposits and withdrawals, independently of the firm. Additional control is provided by having one person in the firm responsible for approval of cash receipts and disbursements (usually this person is the company's cashier) and another person in the firm responsible for keeping the cash receipts and disbursements records. The cashier should also be forbidden access to the documents that give the bookkeeper the information he needs to record transactions in the accounting records. In these circumstances the records provide another independent check on the cashier. Finally, for good control, a person other than the cashier or bookkeeper should be made responsible for reconciling the bank account at the end of each month.

In order to review the working of a bank account, we shall take as an example Bacy's, Inc., which opened a checking account at the First National Bank on August 1, 19x0. Bacy's reduces the danger of theft or loss of cash by depositing in the bank on a regular basis all cash and checks received. (The only exception is a small petty cash fund kept in the office for minor disbursements.)

The bank keeps a running set of cash records on the account, and at the end of each month sends a bank statement to Bacy's. The controller's secretary reviews the monthly statement. In addition, all mail from the bank is addressed directly to her. Since she has no responsibility for handling or recording cash receipts or disbursements, she is unbiased in reconciling the statement and in reporting unusual items to the proper authority.

The bank statement that Bacy's receives on September 1 is shown in Exhibit 3B–1, and Bacy's own records of cash receipts and disbursements are shown in Exhibit 3B–2. According to Bacy's records, there is $47,000 − $30,345 = $16,655 in the account, whereas the bank's records show a balance of $23,570. To reconcile these two sets of records is to determine why they do not agree.

EXHIBIT 3B-1

THE FIRST NATIONAL BANK
STATEMENT OF ACCOUNT WITH BACY'S, INC.

Charges	Deposits		Balance
			19x0
	$ 2,000	8/1	$ 2,000
$ 3,200	5,000	8/10	3,800
475	350a	8/13	3,675
12,400	12,000	8/16	3,275
1,490		8/19	1,785
	7,200	8/21	8,985
110		8/28	8,875
	14,700	8/31	23,575
5b		8/31	23,570

a Promissory note of a customer collected by the bank and deposited in the account.
b Bank service charge for maintaining the bank account for the month of August.

The first step in the reconciliation is to compare cash receipts on Bacy's books with deposits on the bank statement. Each book entry should be checked off against the corresponding bank-statement entry. Any unchecked items on either bank statement or books is an *item of difference* and must be investigated. Some items of difference are caused by the bank's delay in recording deposits (usually one or two days). Occasionally some deposit items on the bank statement will be unchecked, such as the proceeds of items collected for the depositor by the bank.

The next step in reconciliation is to compare the cash payments shown in the books with the payments reflected on the bank statement. The cancelled checks should be put in numerical order and compared with the checks recorded on the books for check number, amount, date, payee, and signature. This comparison will reveal any errors that occurred in writing the checks as well as any differences between the cash disbursement records and the bank statement. There are usually unchecked items on the cash records that represent checks outstanding (that is, not yet presented for payment). There may also be items of difference that result from errors made by the depositor or the bank.

On the bank statement, there are usually some unchecked payment items for bank service charges or nonsufficient fund (NSF) checks, which were originally recorded in Bacy's account but which have "bounced."

The results of the reconciliation for Bacy's, Inc., are shown in Exhibit 3B-3.

To sum up, there are four types of items of difference. The first two appear on the book portion of the reconciliation:

1. Items deposited by the bank but not recorded as cash receipts on the books.

CASH RECEIPTS SUMMARY[a]

		Amount Deposited
August 1	Bank loan	$ 2,000
10	Cash sales	5,000
15	Collection on account	12,000
20	Cash sales	7,200
30	Collections on account	14,700
31	Cash sales	6,100
	Total	$47,000

[a] Normally, receipts would be deposited daily; they are summarized here for reasons of space.

CASH DISBURSEMENTS SUMMARY

Date	*Check No.*	
August 10	1	$ 3,200
12	2	475
15	3	12,400
16	4	355
17	5	1,490
20	6	965
26	7	110
30	8	11,350
		$30,345

2. Items charged by the bank but not recorded as disbursements on the books.

If financial statements are to be prepared as of the date of the reconciliation, these items must be included. Since they have not been recorded on the books, the following journal entry is required to adjust the cash account:

Cash	345	
Expenses	5	
Notes receivable		350

The next two types of items of difference appear on the bank portion of the reconciliation:

3. Items recorded as cash received on the books but not yet received by the bank.

EXHIBIT 3B-3

BACY'S, INC.

CASH PER BOOK

Balance, August 31 ($47,000 − $30,345)	$16,655
Deposit by bank not recorded in the books: Promissory note collected	350
	$17,005
Charges by bank not recorded on books: Service charge	5
Balance, August 31, as adjusted	$17,000

CASH PER BANK

Balance, August 31			$23,570
Add: Deposits in transit			6,100
			$29,670
Less: Outstanding checks (recorded on books, not yet received by bank)			
	#4	$ 355	
	#6	965	
	#8	$11,350	12,670
Balance, August 31, as adjusted			$17,000

4. Items recorded as disbursements on the books but not yet charged by the bank.

Since these items, and any errors on the bank's part, will be processed by the bank, no adjustment is required on the books.

The use of a bank account has several advantages from an asset control standpoint. The danger of theft or loss of cash is reduced by depositing in the bank on a regular basis all cash and checks received. The formal procedure of preparing a check and having an authorized person sign it reduces the possibility of unauthorized disbursements. Finally, when the person reconciling the bank account is not responsible for processing cash or maintaining records, differences between the depositor's records and the bank's records will be handled in an unbiased manner.

Imprest Funds

An imprest fund is a fixed amount of assets for which one individual is held responsible.

Such a fund is often used in the control of petty cash. At Bacy's, Inc., the receptionist is custodian of a petty cash fund of $100, which is used in making small disbursements for a specified list of approved expenditures, such as postage, office supplies, and emergency funds for business entertainment.

The general manager of Bacy's, Inc., has decided to limit the fund to $100 in order to minimize the financial responsibility of the receptionist. He realizes that the fund will require reimbursement every two or three weeks but considers this an acceptable frequency.

To establish the fund, a $100 check is drawn and cashed. The journal entry to establish the fund is as follows:

Petty cash	100	
Cash in bank		100

As the receptionist disburses money to various individuals, she requires signed receipts from them. Three weeks after the fund is established, the receptionist has the following receipts for petty cash disbursements:

Postage	$22.00
Supplies	24.50
Entertainment	34.75
Total	$81.25

A count of the petty cash on hand indicates cash and currency of $18.40, and a cash shortage of $.35. The receptionist submits a request to the office manager for $81.60 to restore the fund to the original amount and sends along the receipts for expenditures of $81.25. The office manager examines invoices and other receipts for fund disbursements to determine whether they are reasonable and proper.° A check is drawn on the operating cash account to the receptionist. The journal entry to record the replenishment of the petty cash fund is as follows:

Postage expense	22.00	
Supplies expense	24.50	
Entertainment expense	34.75	
Cash over and short	.35	
Cash in bank (Operating Account)		81.60

The "cash over and short" account appears on the statement of earnings as an expense if it has a debit balance at the end of the period or as revenue if it has a credit balance (meaning that cash overages exceeded cash shortages). The office manager normally is not concerned with cash overages and shortages unless they become material and unless shortages appear regularly.

Accounting for an imprest fund has some special characteristics. The expenditures from the petty cash fund are not recorded in the accounts until the fund is replenished, and the entry to replenish the fund does not affect the petty cash account. Therefore, the balance in the petty cash account on Bacy's books

° Note that the office manager is approving these expenditures *after* they were made. For disbursements by check, approval is given *before* the disbursement is made.

does not change, except when the amount of the fund is increased or decreased by managerial decision. The fund custodian is responsible at all times for the physical custody of $100.00—in the form of currency, or receipts for expenditures, or a combination of the two.

Imprest funds can be used in many ways to facilitate the control of assets. Several examples follow.

Payroll disbursements. An organization with a large number of employees may establish a payroll bank account for processing employee checks. Assume that the amount of cash required for the August 22 pay of four hundred employees is $6,486. The company officer responsible for signing checks on the operating account examines the payroll register (a listing of each employee, gross wages, deductions, and net pay) and indicates his approval on the payroll register. He then signs a check on the operating account for transfer to the payroll cash account. The journal entry to record the transfer is:

Salaries and wages expense (gross wages)	7,960	
Accrued liabilities (deductions)	1,474	
Cash in bank (operating account)		6,486

Checks for each employee, totaling $6,486, are drawn on the payroll bank account. The amounts deducted from employees' pay are remitted from the operating account as they fall due. These deductions are for income and social security taxes withheld, union dues, hospitalization insurance premiums, etc.

What does the imprest payroll bank account accomplish? Generally, the person approving invoices and signing checks for an operating cash account is someone of high organizational rank. Since the signing of payroll checks is routine and there is frequently a large number of checks, it is desirable to delegate this responsibility to a person of lesser organizational rank, so that the officer responsible for the operating cash account can concentrate on less routine disbursements. Furthermore, the task of monthly bank reconciliations can be similarly subdivided because the payroll account can be reconciled independently of the operating account.

Imprest funds can be useful in any disbursements situation where a large number of checks of a fairly uniform amount are required, as in the case of dividend checks to stockholders.

Disbursements from a branch. Many organizations have branch operations, often in other cities. The home office can control disbursements by establishing an imprest cash account for the branch manager, i.e., a bank account of a predetermined amount in a local bank. The branch manager makes disbursements by check as required. Periodically, he submits receipts for disbursements to the home office together with a request for a reimbursement check. The responsible officer in the home office approves the expenditures made by the branch manager before signing the check to replenish the imprest fund for the branch.

Inventory control. Organizations in which the salesmen must be trusted with considerable inventory (dairies are one example) can use the imprest fund concept to control inventory and sales for each salesman. In the case of a dairy, each morning the driver-salesman is given a preestablished amount of inventory (an imprest fund). At the end of the day, he is accountable for inventory and/or sales of inventory.

Subsidiary Records

It is easy enough for a firm to find out how much inventory it has on hand. It is much more difficult, however, to tell how much *should be* on hand. A *perpetual inventory system* is used by many businesses to provide an answer to this question. In the perpetual system, an individual record showing purchases and issues in physical quantity, and frequently in dollar amounts as well, is kept for each item in the inventory. Periodically, a physical count is made of each item in the inventory and the amount on hand is compared with the quantity indicated on the perpetual record. If there are no more than, say, three or four items in the inventory, each item can be controlled by an individual inventory account in the general ledger. With a larger number of items, however, it becomes desirable to have only one inventory account in the general ledger (called a *control* account), with the individual inventory items controlled by separate accounts in a subsidiary ledger. Most perpetual inventory systems are maintained as subsidiary records to the inventory account in the general ledger.

Assume that Nimbel's, Inc., a retailer of sporting goods, begins operations on August 1. The firm decides to maintain perpetual inventory records. Since the firm estimates that it will handle twenty different items, the use of a subsidiary ledger for merchandise is indicated. In this illustration we shall make the simplifying assumptions that all units of the same item of merchandise are purchased at the same purchase price, all sales of that unit are made at the same selling price, and all purchases of merchandise and sales of merchandise for the month are made in single transactions. Nimbel's purchases and sales for August are as shown in Exhibit 3B–4.

EXHIBIT 3B-4

NIMBEL'S, INC.
MERCHANDISE PURCHASES AND SALES
For August 19x0

	Purchases			Sales			Cost of goods sold		
	Units	Per Unit	Amt.	Units	Per Unit	Amt.		Per Unit	Amt.
Golf clubs (irons), ea.	600	$ 6.00	$ 3,600	510	$10.00	$ 5,100		$ 6.00	$ 3,060
Tennis racquets, ea.	250	8.00	2,000	210	15.00	3,150		8.00	1,680
Baseball gloves, ea.	100	4.50	450	70	8.00	560		4.50	315
Golf balls, doz.	300	5.00	1,500	250	8.00	2,000		5.00	1,250
Golf bags, ea.	25	10.00	250	20	15.00	300		10.00	200

NIMBEL'S, INC., (CONT.)

	Purchases			Sales			Cost of goods sold	
	Units	Per Unit	Amt.	Units	Per Unit	Amt.	Per Unit	Amt.
Golf carts, ea.	10	20.00	200	7	25.00	175	20.00	140
Golf umbrellas, ea.	12	7.00	84	10	8.00	80	7.00	70
Tennis balls, doz.	150	7.00	1,050	120	9.00	1,080	7.00	840
Baseballs, doz.	25	12.00	300	18	20.00	360	12.00	216
Baseball bats, ea.	40	2.50	100	32	5.00	160	2.50	80
Baseball caps, doz.	20	9.00	180	15	10.00	150	9.00	135
Golf caps, doz.	15	10.00	150	12	12.00	144	10.00	120
Golf shoes, pr.	20	10.00	200	16	18.00	288	10.00	160
Baseball shoes, pr.	10	12.00	120	8	20.00	160	12.00	96
Golf shirts, ea.	60	2.00	120	—	—	—	—	0
Golf tees, doz.	100	.10	10	100	.10	10	.10	10
Baseball socks, pr.	50	1.00	50	40	1.50	60	1.00	40
Golf gloves, ea.	24	2.00	48	20	2.50	50	2.00	40
Golf clubs (woods), ea.	200	10.00	2,000	160	12.00	1,920	10.00	1,600
Golf club covers, ea.	100	1.00	100	85	1.20	102	1.00	85
Total			$12,512			$15,849		$10,137

Information on purchases is obtained from the purchase invoices of suppliers. This information is posted to the subsidiary ledger, shown in Exhibit 3B–5, as the debit postings designated ①. Information on sales comes from copies of sales slips, which are prepared in duplicate, with the original given to the customer at the time of the sale. This sales slip will specify the item sold, price per unit, and total selling price. The information on cost of goods sold is obtained later by multiplying the number of units sold by the cost price of the units. These amounts are posted to the subsidiary ledger as credit entries, designated ②.

The entries in the general journal to record purchases and sales for August are as follows:

		L. F.		
① Merchandise		5	12,512	
Accounts payable (or cash)				12,512
To record purchases of merchandise for August				
② Accounts receivable (or cash)			15,849	
Sales revenue				15,849
Cost of goods sold			10,137	
Merchandise		5		10,137
To record August sales				

The posting of these entries to the merchandise control account gives the following result:

Merchandise (control account)   *No. 5*

August purchases ①	$12,512	August cost of goods sold ②	$10,137
Balance, August 31	$ 2,375		

EXHIBIT 3 B - 5

NIMBEL'S, INC.

SUBSIDIARY LEDGER—MERCHANDISE

Golf Clubs (Irons)		*Tennis Balls*	
Aug. 600 ea. ① $3,600	Aug. 510 ea. ② $3,060	Aug. 150 doz. ① $1,050	Aug. 120 doz. ② $840
Bal. 8/31 $ 540		Bal. 8/31 $ 210	

Tennis Racquets		*Baseballs*	
Aug. 250 ea. ① $2,000	Aug. 210 ea. ② $1,680	Aug. 25 doz. ① $300	Aug. 18 doz. ② $216
$ 320		Bal. 8/31 $ 84	

Baseball Gloves		*Baseball Bats*	
Aug. 100 ea. ① $450	Aug. 70 ea. ② $315	Aug. 40 ea. ① $100	Aug. 32 ea. ② $80
Bal. 8/31 $135		Bal. 8/31 $ 20	

Golf Balls		*Baseball Caps*	
Aug. 300 doz. ① $1,500	Aug. 250 doz. ② $1,250	Aug. 20 doz. ① $180	Aug. 15 doz. ② $135
Bal. 8/31 $ 250		Bal. 8/31 $ 45	

Golf Bags		*Golf Caps*	
Aug. 25 ea. ① $250	Aug. 20 ea. ② $200	Aug. 15 doz. ① $150	Aug. 12 doz. ② $120
Bal. 8/31 $ 50		Bal. 8/31 $ 30	

Golf Carts		*Golf Shoes*	
Aug. 10 ea. ① $200	Aug. 7 ea. ② $140	Aug. 20 pr. ① $200	Aug. 16 pr. ② $160
Bal. 8/31 $ 60		Bal. 8/31 $ 40	

Golf Umbrellas		*Baseball Shoes*	
Aug. 12 ea. ① $84	Aug. 10 ea. ② $70	Aug. 10 pr. ① $120	Aug. 8 pr. ② $96
Bal. 8/31 $14		Bal. 8/31 $ 24	

	Golf Shirts	
Aug.	60 ea. ① $120	
Bal. 8/31	$120	

Golf Gloves			
Aug.	24 ea. ① $48	Aug.	20 ea. ② $40
Bal. 8/31	$ 8		

Golf Tees			
Aug.	100 doz. ① $10	Aug.	100 doz. ② $10
Bal. 8/31	0		

Golf Clubs (Woods)			
Aug.	200 ea. ① $2,000	Aug.	160 ea. ② $1,600
Bal. 8/31	$ 400		

Baseball Socks			
Aug.	50 prs. ① $50	Aug.	40 pr. ② $40
Bal. 8/31	$10		

Golf Club Covers			
Aug.	100 ea. ① $100	Aug.	85 ea. ② $85
Bal. 8/31	$ 15		

① Purchases
② Cost of goods sold

The general ledger account for inventory functions as a control account for the subsidiary ledger. While the subsidiary ledger accounts are kept in detail, only a summary of the inventory transactions is posted to the merchandise control account. The subsidiary ledger balances are compared with the control account balance periodically to determine whether they agree.

A schedule of subsidiary ledger balances for August 31 is given in Exhibit 3B–6. A comparison of the balance shown there with the inventory control account balance in the general ledger reveals that the control account and subsidiary ledger are in balance. If they were not in balance, an attempt would be made to find the error. An adjustment would then be required to bring the ledgers in balance.

In addition to the perpetual inventory records we have discussed, a business manager would take a periodic inventory (count) of all goods on hand and compare the count with the perpetual records. The inventory for Nimbel's, Inc., was counted on August 31. The schedule in Exhibit 3B–7 summarizes the results of the inventory count and compares the physical inventory with the perpetual inventory records. As the schedule shows, there is an inventory shortage of $115. The journal entry to record this shortage is as follows:

Inventory loss (or cost of goods sold)	115	
Merchandise		115

This entry is posted to the merchandise account in the general ledger, and the detail differences indicated by the inventory summary are posted to the subsidiary ledger account for each item in the inventory for which a difference is indicated.

Management now knows how much inventory they should have (from the

EXHIBIT 3 B - 6

NIMBEL'S, INC.

SCHEDULE OF SUBSIDIARY LEDGER
INVENTORY BALANCES
As of August 31, 19x0

Golf clubs (irons)	$ 540
Tennis racquets	320
Baseball gloves	135
Golf balls	250
Golf bags	50
Golf carts	60
Golf umbrellas	14
Tennis balls	210
Baseballs	84
Baseball bats	20
Baseball caps	45
Golf caps	30
Golf shoes	40
Baseball shoes	24
Golf shirts	120
Baseball socks	10
Golf gloves	8
Golf clubs (woods)	400
Golf club covers	15
Total	$2,375

perpetual records) as well as how much is actually on hand. An inventory count usually differs from the perpetual records. The manager then needs to decide whether the differences are great enough to warrant a follow-up. At Nimbel's, there was a shortage of eight golf woods, at a total cost of $80. Investigation of this difference might reveal a discrepancy in the inventory records or a loss of merchandise. If a loss of merchandise is indicated, perhaps the manager would decide to strengthen the inventory control procedures over the golf clubs.

In addition to facilitating the control of assets, a subsidiary ledger permits a further segregation of duties among employees within an organization. For example, the subsidiary ledger for inventory could be maintained by an employee who might have no other record-keeping responsibility.

The general ledger control account–subsidiary ledger concept can facilitate asset control for any asset. The concept is frequently used for accounts receivable and equipment. For example, unit records for accounts receivable are useful for billing and credit-management purposes, and unit equipment records are helpful in the control of maintenance expense.

EXHIBIT 3B - 7

NIMBEL'S, INC.
INVENTORY SUMMARY
As of August 31, 19x0

	Physical Count		Perpetual Records		Difference (over) (under)	
	Units	Dollars	Units	Dollars	Units	Dollars
Golf clubs (irons)	90 ea.	$ 540	90 ea.	$ 540	0	$ 0
Tennis racquets	37 ea.	296	40 ea.	320	3	24
Baseball gloves	28 ea.	126	30 ea.	135	2	9
Golf balls	52 doz.	260	50 doz.	250	(2)	(10)
Golf bags	5 ea.	50	5 ea.	50	0	0
Golf carts	3 ea.	60	3 ea.	60	0	0
Golf umbrellas	0	0	2 ea.	14	2	14
Tennis balls	35 doz.	245	30 doz.	210	(5)	(35)
Baseballs	6 doz.	72	7 doz.	84	1	12
Baseball bats	8 ea.	20	8 ea.	20	0	0
Baseball caps	5 doz.	45	5 doz.	45	0	0
Golf caps	2 doz.	20	3 doz.	30	1	10
Golf shoes	4 pr.	40	4 pr.	40	0	0
Baseball shoes	2 pr.	24	2 pr.	24	0	0
Golf shirts	52 ea.	104	60 ea.	120	8	16
Golf tees	5 doz.	5	0	0	(5)	(5)
Baseball socks	10 pr.	10	10 pr.	10	0	0
Golf gloves	4 ea.	8	4 ea.	8	0	0
Golf clubs (woods)	32 ea.	320	40 ea.	400	8	80
Golf club covers	15 ea.	15	15 ea.	15	0	0
Totals		$2,260		$2,375		$115

Problems for Analysis

3B-1. The following data pertain to the cash account and bank account for Newman's, Inc., for September:

1. Balance on bank statement at September 30, $2,490.65
2. Balance on books at June 30, $2,260.42
3. Deposit in transit, $450.00
4. Bank service charges, $4.90
5. Total of outstanding checks, $400.13
6. Proceeds from customer's promissory note collected by the bank and not recorded on the books, $300.00
7. A check for $185.00 in payment of rent was erroneously recorded as a cash payment of $170.00

a. Prepare a bank reconciliation.

b. List and discuss the control provided by

1. a bank account.

2. having the bank account reconciled by a person who does not handle cash or maintain cash records.

3B-2. The controller of Odum's, Inc., has decided to establish an imprest petty cash fund for $150.00. The controller's secretary will be the custodian of the fund. The following fund transactions and events occurred during the first three months:

March 1: Issued a check for $150.00 to establish the fund.

March 20: Issued a check for $121.19 to replenish the petty cash fund for the following disbursements: postage, $26.50; office supplies, $36.95; miscellaneous expenses, $19.48; and employee travel expenses, $36.50.

April 15: Issued a check for $87.41 to replenish the petty cash fund for the following disbursements: postage, $29.00; office supplies, $32.50; and miscellaneous expenses, $27.10.

April 30: Issued a check for $56.90 to replenish the petty cash fund for the following disbursements: postage, $21.00; office supplies, $17.50; miscellaneous expenses, $18.40.

May 1: Reduced the petty cash fund to $125.00.

a. Record journal entries for the transactions and events listed above.

b. List and discuss the control decisions that were apparently made by the controller in establishing the fund.

c. Assume that on March 31 there were receipts of $37.50 for postage and cash and currency of $112.50 in the fund. What journal entry, if any, would be required if financial statements were to be prepared on this date?

3B-3. On October 1, Hilltop Company of Florida establishes an organization in Atlanta to act as a sales agency. A working fund of $2,000, to be operated under the imprest system, is established on this date. On October 31, the agency working fund is replenished. Receipts submitted by the agency are as follows:

Travel expenses	$ 520
Advertising expenses	745
Miscellaneous expenses	97
	$1,362

a. Prepare the journal entries to record the imprest fund transactions on the home office books.

b. List and discuss the control features of establishing the agency fund on an imprest basis.

3B-4. Certain sales-on-account transactions and cash-collection-on-account transactions are summarized below:

Sales Journal	
Able	$ 400
Baker	350
Charlie	700
Davis	1,350
Egbert	610
	$3,410

Cash Receipts Journal (partial)	
Baker	$ 350
Charlie	510
Davis	900
Egbert	610
	$2,370

a. Set up an accounts receivable subsidiary ledger in T-account form and a general ledger control account for accounts receivable.

b. Post the appropriate transactions from the sales journal and the cash receipts journal to the control account and the subsidiary ledger accounts for accounts receivable.

c. List and discuss the advantages and several uses of a subsidiary ledger in a business.

3B–5. Joel Garber has been appointed chairman of the 19x6 March of Dollars campaign to raise money for the aged. Included in the projects to be supported are homes for the aged, maintenance of centers for instruction in hobbies and crafts, and financing of medical care for people over seventy years old.

The annual March of Dollars drive begins in February with the mailing of circulars to the entire community. This is followed in March with a second mailing, accompanied by spot radio and television announcements (donated by the broadcasting stations). The deadline for reaching the goal is March 31.

The only full-time employee of the March of Dollars is a secretary who handles year-round correspondence, writes checks, and keeps books on expenditures, which are made throughout the year. This secretary supervises two part-time assistants who are hired to work only during February, March, and April. Since Mr. Garber is not salaried, the only administrative costs are the salaries of the one full-time and two part-time employees, printing and mailing costs, office rent, office supplies, and bank service charges.

About 95 per cent of the contributions comes through the mail, most of it in the form of dollar bills. The remainder comes from individuals who bring contributions in person. The checking account is maintained throughout the year.

a. Write up a procedure for Mr. Garber to use for handling the cash receipts. If you were Mr. Garber, what would be your primary concern?

b. The local organization of Certified Public Accountants (CPA) has volunteered to audit the cash receipts at no charge. Would you accept this offer? What would you expect them to do?

c. What procedure do you recommend to Mr. Garber for controlling cash disbursements for projects for the aged and administrative costs?

d. What financial information should be included in a report by Mr. Garber to his board of directors at the end of the year?

Part Two **MANAGERIAL USES OF ACCOUNTING REPORTS**

*Accounting reports are important to the operations of a business
firm in two respects: control and planning. Part II describes the
ways in which accounting assists management in achieving these
objectives. Management affects control by measuring the performance of departments and individuals who have accepted responsibility in accordance with the organizational structure of the firm.
A typical organization is presented in Chapter 4. Responsibility
may be expressed in terms of output, standard costs, expense
budgets, or earnings. Accounting reports measure performance in
these situations by comparing the accomplishment (output or revenues) with the effort (input or costs). Performance measurement is
covered in Chapters 5 through 8.*

*Accounting reports assist management in business planning by
(a) reporting data of past periods so that they are useful in making
predictions, (b) reporting the projected results of predictions and*

goals of the firm in financial statements called budgets, *and (c) reporting the possible outcomes of alternative decisions affecting the immediate and long-range future plans of the firm. The accounting aspects of planning are dealt with in Chapters 9, 10, and 11.*

Appendixes 6A and 11A are included for the student who wishes to learn more about their respective subjects.

Chapter Four

THE FLOW OF RESPONSIBILITY IN A BUSINESS ENTERPRISE

INTRODUCTION

The accounting system discussed in Chapter 3 enables the accountant to record business events, summarize them meaningfully, and periodically prepare financial reports helpful in the decision-making process. Later chapters will discuss in detail the different types of accounting reports that can flow from the system, and the uses to which they can be put by managers and others interested in the enterprise. However, before we can fully comprehend the meaningfulness of accounting information, we must understand the organizational relationships in business firms. Proper organization is vital to the success of any business enterprise. It is the nerve network through which people in positions of responsibility order all actions and obtain the information they need to meet their responsibilities. This chapter is devoted to the organizational problems this network assists in solving.

Establishing the proper organizational structure for any enterprise is difficult. It is usually the result of trial and error, rather than initial creation, and it should be continually evolving to meet the changing needs of the enterprise. The organizational structure of the General Motors Corporation is certainly different today from what it was when Louis Chevrolet was building "those new-fangled horseless carriages" in his neighbor's carriage house, and it still changes often. It is impossible to outline specifically the kind of structure needed for any enterprise, because it is an organization of people, and people are, above all else, individuals with varying capabilities and weaknesses. Their efforts must be linked together in an ever changing manner by the organizational structure.

The simplest organizational structure is that of the owner-managed enterprise. The owner-manager of the corner pizza parlor is the entire organization and the entire management. He draws all conclusions and makes all decisions. The moment he hires others to work in his enterprise, however, he is complicating his organizational structure, because he then has at least two levels of organization—boss level and dishwasher level, for example.

Most partnerships, except very large ones, also have relatively simple organizational structures.

Corporations, on the other hand, are more complex, because they usually consist of at least several people, and often tens of thousands of individuals, ranged throughout an organization. Since most business enterprise is conducted within the corporate form and since this form best demonstrates the value of accounting reports as an aid to management and nonmanagement alike, we will be discussing the incorporated enterprise throughout the remainder of this book.°

MATCHING RESPONSIBILITY
WITH AUTHORITY

No two corporate enterprises are exactly alike, but there are similarities in all organizational structures, just as there are similarities in the nervous systems of all human beings. The common elements of all organizational structures are *responsibility* and *authority.*

Every individual in an enterprise has responsibility. It may be nothing more than the responsibility for keeping the floors swept clean of metal chips and other litter, or it may be the responsibility for every facet of the enterprise activity vested in the board of directors. Whether the responsibility is for accomplishing simple tasks, for making recommendations, or for drawing conclusions and making decisions, individuals are judged by how well they meet the responsibility.

To meet their responsibilities, individuals must have an appropriate amount of authority. Even the floor sweeper must have the right to enter the plant after working hours and to recommend the purchase of supplies needed to keep the floors clean. His authority is extremely limited, but then so usually is the responsibility for floor sweeping. The board of directors, on the other hand, has the authority to take any necessary action, so long as it is legal and does not violate the bylaws of the enterprise.

An ideal organizational structure allows each person just enough authority to match his responsibilities. Mismatching can hinder the efforts of the enterprise, because too much authority, for instance, will interfere with the authority of others to perform more important tasks. If the responsibility for floor sweeping

---

° A more detailed discussion of these three organizational structures appears in Chapter 12.

is minor, it would be a mistake to give the floor sweeper authority to interfere in any way with the production process. If, on the other hand, clean floors were somehow essential to the production of an acceptable product, then the responsibility for clean floors would be a major one and it might be appropriate to give the floor sweeper authority to interrupt production in order to carry out his responsibility.

The sum of the responsibility and authority that makes up the organizational structure must be allocated among people at several levels of management. This gives rise to the need for the same superior-subordinate relationships that are found in a family, an army, or a government. Division of responsibility and authority among several levels of management enables the enterprise to strive effectively for the long-run profit objective even when the individuals involved have different personal objectives. Such an organizational structure, however, requires performance measurement of the various individuals as well as of the enterprise itself.

The accounting system facilitates the job of measuring performance and helps maintain a proper balance between responsibility and authority. It is not, however, the function of the accounting system, or of the accountants themselves, to establish the organizational structure of the enterprise. Management establishes the organization, allocates responsibility and authority, and suggests appropriate relationships between superior and subordinates. The accountant accepts the structure as given and designs an accounting system to gather data and provide accounting reports that will best help management achieve long-run profits. Accounting reports may indicate changes needed in an organizational structure, but it is management's job to make the changes.

CONCEPTS IN PERFORMANCE MEASUREMENT

The accountant's approach to performance measurement is based on concepts that are really quite simple. Unfortunately, the words used to describe these concepts differ from accountant to accountant. The terms we use here are found in the accounting literature, but they are by no means universally employed. Thus, care should be taken to understand the concepts themselves as well as the language in which they are stated.

1. *Performance.* The performance of a subunit of a firm is defined as the relationship between *accomplishment* (output) and *effort* (input) of the subunit.

2. *Accomplishment.* Accomplishment is defined as the *output* of the subunit during the period. This output is measured in terms of the particular responsibility assigned the subunit in the organizational structure of the firm. Accomplishment may be measured in terms of revenue in dollars, i.e., dollar value of product

transferred or service rendered to customers or other subunits, or in terms of units produced, hours of operation, or number of customers called on; or any other suitable unit of measure.

3. *Effort.*   Effort is defined as the *input* to the subunit in order to achieve output. As in the case of accomplishment, the units of measurement of effort depend on the units in which the responsibility of the subunit is expressed. If the subunit has been assigned responsibility for earnings optimization as measured by accountants, effort is measured in terms of dollars of expenses incurred during the period.

Briefly, then, periodic performance measurement of a unit is a matter of comparing periodic unit inputs with outputs in a manner that corresponds to the responsibility assigned the unit by the firm.

At least three major problems are encountered in performance measurement. First, simply measuring the performance of a unit implies nothing about whether performance is good or bad. In order to form a judgment of that kind, some sort of standard or goal must be used to provide a basis for comparison. Setting such goals is no easy matter.

Second, a unit may have more than one criterion for performance at a time, and these criteria may not be consistent. A production department in a factory may have the responsibility of maintaining a given level of production, expressed, say, in units of output per day, in order that production in other departments not be delayed. However, it may also have the responsibility of keeping costs near or below a given standard, expressed in terms of cost per unit of output. For example, if it becomes necessary to work overtime to maintain the required level of output, thus increasing labor cost per unit, the department foreman may have to decide which criterion is more important, because the overtime may increase the unit cost above the desired standard.

Finally, a particular measurement may at times be a measure of output and at other times a measure of input. For example, if the organizational structure delegates to salesmen the responsibility for optimizing dollar sales per customer call, customer calls are a measure of input. But if it is the salesman's responsibility to minimize selling expense per customer call, then customer calls become a measure of output. Of course, it would be entirely possible to measure the performance of a salesman by both of these criteria (as well as others) at the same time.

PERFORMANCE MEASUREMENT AND THE ORGANIZATION

In Chapter 2 we pointed out that accounting assumes long-run earnings optimization to be the primary goal of the firm as a whole, and that the accountant's measurement of periodic earnings, with all its imperfections, is used by managers and others as a measure of performance of the firm. If we now assume further that management wishes to organize the firm into subunits in such a way as to make as much earnings as possible, it would seem logical to delegate this responsibility for earnings optimization to the subunits in the organization; that is, top management could visualize the entire firm as simply a collection of small firms and assign to each the responsibility (and the authority) to buy, make, and sell products or perform services in order to add as much as possible to the total earnings of the firm.

In many of our very large corporations in this country, this is generally what happens. Major divisions of the firm are considered to be autonomous, self-sufficient units that are operated most efficiently if the division management is permitted to make (almost) all decisions without interference from the "home office." Many present-day corporations (called conglomerates) are comprised of divisions that were once independent firms and that may have little or no relationship to the other divisions except that all have earnings as a basic objective. In cases when top management of the firm has delegated responsibility for earnings to divisional management, the measure of each division's performance is expressed by the accountant's earnings calculation:

Revenues (accomplishment) − Expenses (effort) = Earnings (performance)°

This measurement is completely valid only if the subunit has complete earnings responsibility delegated to it, which means authority to do whatever is necessary to optimize earnings, subject only to constraints imposed by the market mechanism external to the firm, and the social legal requirements that all independent firms must observe.

Such complete decentralization of earnings responsibility is seldom possible or desirable in actual practice. Complete decentralization of earnings responsibility would tend to deny or nullify the efficiencies and economies that can be achieved by interrelated subunits of firms working together for a common purpose. One of the principal reasons that large firms are economically justified is the fact that a single set of top-management decisions can provide coordination among subunits that could never be achieved if each subunit manager were permitted to decide for himself how he should optimize his earnings. Thus, top management almost always wishes to retain for itself authority to make certain types of decisions affecting the earnings. In these cases, managers of subunits take on only the responsibility delegated to them, and performance must be measured in terms of the responsibility delegated.

° As we shall see in Chapter 7, a more complete measure is

$$\frac{\text{Earnings}}{\text{Total assets}} \quad \text{or} \quad \frac{\text{Revenue} - \text{Expenses}}{\text{Total assets}}$$

so that performance is measured in terms of a rate of return, rather than in dollar earnings. One way of incorporating the concept of total assets into the Revenue − Expense framework is to include *implicit* interest on total assets as an expense. Then the formula becomes Revenues (accomplishment) − [Explicit expenses + Implicit interest on total assets (effort)] = Excess earnings (performance).

This means that for most of the subunits of the firm, performance must be measured in terms other than periodic earnings and must conform to the nature of the function performed by the subunit. Sometimes these measures of accomplishment and effort (output and input) are expressed in dollars, sometimes in physical units. In the more difficult cases, quantitative measurements, whether in dollars or units, can provide only a limited, and possibly biased, picture of performance of the subunit, which must be carefully qualified and explained by supplementary information.

SELECTING MEASURES OF ACCOMPLISHMENT AND EFFORT

The problems in selecting the proper measures of effort and accomplishment for performance measurement of a subunit of a firm can best be demonstrated by an illustration. Assume that the firm in question is an aspirin manufacturer and that the problem is to measure the performance of the advertising department. That the advertising function is immensely important to the earnings of aspirin manufacturers may be inferred from the large sums they spend on it.

The first major step in measuring the performance of the advertising department is to determine the responsibilities assigned this department in the organizational structure of the firm. It is a common error to assume that the title "Advertising Department" means that the department assumes complete responsibility for all of the firm's advertising. Many possibilities exist, from which we select three:

1. The advertising department could be completely independent, i.e., treated as if it were an outside agency developing complete advertising campaigns which it would "sell" to the top management for a fee. In the extreme case, the department could be considered to be in competition with outside agencies and could offer its services for a fee to outside firms. The top management could also hire an outside agency, thus refusing the bids of its own department. (Of course, this extreme is rarely encountered in practice.) In this case, the advertising department is in fact an earnings optimizing subunit, and its accomplishment should be measured by the fees it earns each period, and its effort by the expenses it incurs. Performance would be measured by periodic earnings, as if the department were in fact an independent advertising firm.

2. The advertising department could be responsible only for negotiations and transactions with advertising media, e.g., purchase of radio and television time, space in newspapers, and billboards. The responsibility for developing advertising campaigns could be retained by top management. In this case the accomplishment of the advertising department would be measured by the prices at which advertising contracts were negotiated, since top management is interested in getting the department to purchase the required services at a minimum cost

to the firm. Effort would be measured by the expenses incurred by the department, consisting primarily of salaries.

3. Top management may retain for itself all of the important advertising
decisions and delegate to the advertising department only the preparation of
advertising copy, artwork, etc., prepared in accordance with instructions. The
responsibility assumed by the department for the advertising materials would
vary inversely with the detail in which instructions were given. Accomplishment
of the department could probably be measured in terms of the amount of
acceptable advertising copy prepared each period. Effort should be measured
by expenses incurred by the department, consisting mainly of salaries and supplies.

It should be apparent that finding measures that truly reflect departmental
performance is not an easy task. We have already seen that the use of earnings
as a measure of departmental performance is not without its difficulties even
when it is appropriate. When it is not appropriate, as in cases 2 and 3 above,
the use of substitute measures presents more, rather than fewer, difficulties.

There are several principles which can guide management in the selection
of performance measures for subunits of firms. Some of these principles are
interrelated, and some are in conflict; nevertheless, they should all be kept in
mind while the selection is being made.

1. The measure or measures selected should be consistent with the profit
objectives of the firm. Before "units produced" is used as a measure of subunit
accomplishment, management should determine that the firm's profits will be
improved if this subunit produces a larger number of units.

2. The measures selected must be within the control of the subunit being
measured. Again, "units produced" is not an appropriate measure of accomplishment unless the manager of the subunit has the authority to change his
production. This principle also has particular significance to cost accountants.
Subunit expense is the most widely used measure of effort, and part of the cost
accountant's task is to determine which expenses are the responsibility (i.e., within
the control) of the subunit whose performance is being measured.

3. The measure or measures selected should not be subject to artificial
manipulation by the subunit. Measures of effort (or input), such as "hours
worked," are particularly susceptible to this difficulty. As an obvious example,
consider a military air unit whose accomplishment is being measured in terms
of number of air missions flown. The unit may begin flying harmless "missions,"
attempting no contact with the enemy, solely for the purpose of improving
the performance measurement. Of course, almost every measure of accomplishment and effort is susceptible to some manipulation if the management of the
subunit is inclined to do so. Avoiding such practices depends on everyone in
the firm understanding the reasons for, and the importance of, performance
measurement.

4. Measures of accomplishment and effort should be agreed upon in advance
by the top management and the management of the subunit whose performance

is to be measured. A subunit is not likely to perform well if its management does not agree that the measures selected by the top management are relevant and just.

THE ACME AUTO PARTS COMPANY—
A CASE STUDY

The Acme Auto Parts Company has three plants. Two of them are located in the Detroit, Michigan, area and a third is located near Milwaukee, Wisconsin. Company headquarters are located at plant 1 in Detroit. The company manufactures primarily automobile parts that are sold to the "big four" auto makers. In addition it markets a line of specialty metal stampings and moldings, such as rearview mirrors, that are sold through chain automotive stores. The company has also done development work for the military services as well as for the National Aeronautics and Space Administration. It has a reputation for an ability to continually develop new products and more efficient methods of production.

Plant 1 in Detroit houses a stamping and fabrication shop and the central administrative offices of the firm. License plate brackets, wheel covers, generator brackets, mirror backings, battery holders, and similar small subassemblies are manufactured in large quantities, using sheet steel as the primary raw material. Plant 2 in Detroit is a foundry operation that makes molded parts out of aluminum and light metal. Door and window handles, dashboard knobs, and mirror stems are typical products of this plant. Plant 3, in Milwaukee, is similar to plant 1 but is less than half its size.

The organizational structure of the firm is the result of over twenty years of activity in the present line of business. It works well in practice and fits the abilities of the personnel involved. Exhibit 4–1 (page 139) is a schematic diagram of the overall structure of the organization. Each level of management appears on a separate level of the diagram. Relationships of direct authority and responsibility are shown by solid lines. Advisory relationships are shown by dotted lines. Segments of the overall organization chart will be presented elsewhere in an expanded form, but you should refer as often as necessary to Exhibit 4–1 in order to make sure you understand the relationship of each activity to the entire organization.

In general, every relationship in the organizational structure, whether it be direct or advisory, requires some degree of periodic accounting information. The accounting report is a primary means of communication, which is especially vital in this enterprise because of the geographical separation of the three plants. The remainder of Part II will discuss in detail the accounting reports that are employed by managers in the Acme Auto Parts Company. Parts III and IV of the book will show the kinds of reports used by nonmanagers.

EXHIBIT 4-1

ACME AUTO PARTS COMPANY
BASIC ORGANIZATION CHART

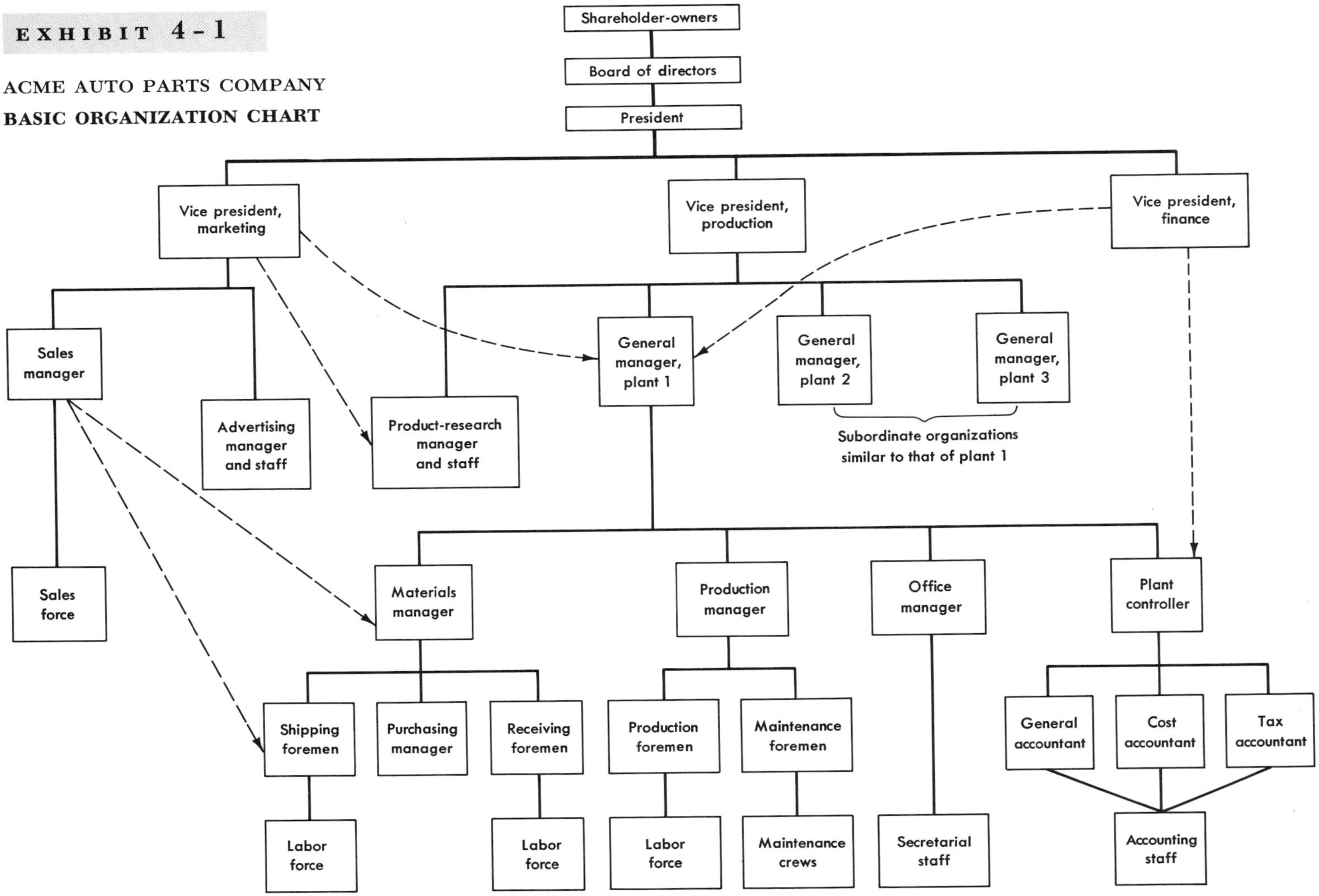

Responsibility Relationships

Several levels of managerial responsibility (and authority) are evident within the structure of the Acme Auto Parts Company. In production operations, for example, there are six responsibility relationships: board of directors ↔ president ↔ vice president, production ↔ plant general manager ↔ production manager ↔ department foremen ↔ labor force. Accounting reports describing the performance of each level to the next superior level must express performance in realistic terms of accomplishment and effort and indicate the degree to which responsibility is accompanied by corresponding authority. In the next two chapters, managerial uses of accounting reports will be discussed in detail. It is important at this time, however, to examine a few broad facets of the problem.

Firm Objectives and Delegations of Responsibility

We have already discussed the accountant's assumption that firms have objectives, even though it is very difficult to distinguish these objectives from the objectives of the individuals in the firm who dominate the firm's activities. From an accounting point of view, the earnings optimization objective seems to be the only important one in the case of Acme Auto Parts. There is no evidence that the firm has strong social or political objectives that would cause it to act in a way contrary to earnings optimization.

The shareholder-owners; their representatives, the board of directors; and the president as chief executive (sometimes the chairman of the board is chief executive) are all primarily concerned with the performance of the firm as a whole, rather than any particular subunit. Thus the information system's principal contributions to these people are the financial statements covering the firm as a whole: statement of earnings and retained earnings, statement of financial position, and statement of working capital flows. (This statement will be introduced later in the chapter and will be studied in detail in Part II of the book.)

The amount of detail in these statements and the frequency of reporting are quite different for stockholders, board of directors, and chief executive. Reports to stockholders and their uses are of little concern to us here. They are discussed in detail in Chapters 17, 18, and 19. Here we shall examine the other two types of reports.

The Board of Directors

Reports to the members of the board, who act as representatives of the stockholders, are of greater importance. Among other things, the board has the responsibility of evaluating performance of the top management, particularly the president, because decisions concerning promotions, compensation, and replacement of the officers rests with the board. The board of Acme Auto Parts meets quarterly, and financial statements covering the quarter just ended are provided each board member a few days before the meeting. These statements provide background information necessary for decisions to be made at the board meeting. The board members' statement of Acme's earnings and retained earnings covering the fourth quarter of 19x1 is shown in Exhibit 4–2.

EXHIBIT 4-2

ACME AUTO PARTS COMPANY

STATEMENT OF EARNINGS AND RETAINED EARNINGS

(in thousands of dollars)

	Fourth Quarter, 19x1		Year Ended Dec. 31, 19x1	
	Budget	Actual	Budget	Actual
Net sales revenues	$5,842	$5,510	$21,719	$20,120
Cost of goods sold	3,302	3,196	12,194	11,547
Earnings margin	$2,540	$2,314	$ 9,525	$ 8,573
Operating expenses:				
Selling expenses	$ 799	$ 771	$3,130	$2,943
Administrative expenses	702	690	2,741	2,709
Total operating expenses	$1,501	$1,461	$5,871	$5,652
Earnings from operations	$1,039	$ 853	$3,654	$2,921
Net nonoperating expense (revenue)	(21)	(27)	81	85
Earnings before income tax	$1,060	$ 880	$3,573	$2,836
Federal income tax expense	424	340	1,500	1,260
Net earnings after tax	$ 636	$ 540	$2,073	$1,576
Retained earnings, beginning	5,103	4,778	4,242	4,242
Gain on sale of equipment			0	56
Total available for dividends	5,739	5,318	$6,315	$5,894
Loss from fire	0	$ 79	0	$ 79
Dividends:				
Preferred	2	2	8	8
Common	190	190	760	760
Total	$ 192	$ 271	$ 768	$ 847
Retained earnings, Dec. 31, 19x1	$5,547	$5,047	$5,547	$5,047

This statement is highly condensed, compared with the one the board members of actual firms receive. An actual statement would include (1) additional columns showing dollar differences between budget and actual, with the larger items footnoted to comments explaining the reasons for the difference; (2) subschedules for several of the items, including sales, cost of goods sold, earnings margin (sales revenue less cost of production) classified by product line, and individual expense items that make up the total of selling and administrative expenses (see Exhibit 4–3); and (3) the same earnings statement for the year 19x0,

EXHIBIT 4 - 3

ACME AUTO PARTS COMPANY

COMBINED STATEMENT OF EARNINGS AND RETAINED EARNINGS

For Year Ended December 31, 19x1

(in thousands of dollars)

Gross sales revenues			$20,650
— Sales returns & allowances		$ 343	
Sales discounts		187	
Total			530
Net sales revenues			$20,120
— Cost of goods sold			11,547
Earnings margin			$ 8,573
— Operating expenses:			
Selling expenses:			
Advertising		$1,467	
Salesmen's salaries		803	
Payroll taxes & fringe benefits		79	
Traveling		246	
Freight charges on outgoing shipments		203	
Depreciation—automobiles		47	
Depreciation—equipment		40	
Miscellaneous		58	
Total selling expenses		$2,943	
Administrative expenses:			
Officers' salaries	$1,326		
Office salaries	817		
Payroll taxes & fringe benefits	52		
Traveling	86		
Credit losses	48		
State & local taxes	174		
Insurance	93		
Office supplies	79		
Depreciation—equipment	34		
Total administrative expenses		2,709	
Total operating expenses			5,652
Earnings from operations			$ 2,921
—Nonoperating items:			
Other expense:			
Interest		$ 165	
.— Other income:			
Rent	$ 60		
Dividends on long-term investments	20		
Total other income		80	
Net nonoperating expense			85

ACME AUTO PARTS COMPANY (CONT.)

Earnings before income taxes		$ 2,836
— Provision for federal income taxes		1,260
Net earnings		$ 1,576
+Retained earnings, 1/1/x1		4,262
+ Gain on sale of equipment		56
Total available for dividends		$ 5,894
— Loss from fire	$ 79	
— Dividend payments:		
Preferred stock ($4/share)	8	
Common stock ($4/share)	760	
Total		847
Retained earnings, 12/31/x1		
(per statement of financial position)		$ 5,047

for comparative purposes. Although the earnings statement is the primary statement used for measuring the performance of management for the period, the board members also receive a comparative statement of financial position (Exhibit 4–4) and a statement of working capital flows (Exhibit 4–5).

EXHIBIT 4–4

ACME AUTO PARTS COMPANY

COMPARATIVE STATEMENT OF FINANCIAL POSITION

As of December 31, 19x0 and 19x1

(in thousands of dollars)

Assets	19x1	19x0
Current assets:		
Cash	$ 504	$ 352
Short-term investments	483	175
Accounts receivable (net)	960	852
Inventories	4,207	3,867
Prepaid expenses	160	170
Total current assets	$ 6,314	$ 5,416
Investments:		
Sinking fund[a]	$ 300	$ 225
Cash surrender value of life insurance policy on company president	30	22
Investment in stock of Cranbrook Auto Parts Manufacturing Company	250	250
Real estate used for investment purposes	625	625
Total investments	$ 1,205	$ 1,122

[a] See glossary.

ACME AUTO PARTS COMPANY (CONT.)

Assets

Long-lived assets:		
Land	$ 125	125
Buildings (net)	1,479	1,553
Machinery & equipment (net)	2,016	1,991
Automotive equipment (net)	185	168
Patents (net)	174	191
Deferred research & development costs (net)	986	726
Total long-lived assets	$ 4,965	$ 4,754
Total assets	$12,484	$11,292

Liabilities and Owners' Equity

	19x1	19x0
Liabilities:		
Current liabilities:		
Accounts payable	$ 1,065	$ 956
Notes payable	150	175
Accrued interest payable	83	74
Prepaid rentals	5	5
Other accrued expenses	346	296
Federal income taxes payable	910	746
Total current liabilities	$ 2,559	$ 2,252
Long-term liabilities:		
5½% note payable (due 7/1/x14)	3,000	3,000
Total liabilities	$ 5,559	$ 5,252
Owners' equity:		
Capital stock:		
Preferred stock (8% cumulative, non-participating, par value $50; authorized and issued 2,000 shares)	$ 100	$ 100
Common stock (no-par value; authorized and issued 200,000 shares)	2,000	1,900
Retained earnings	5,047	4,262
Total owners' equity	$ 7,147	$ 6,262
— Cost of treasury stock[a]	222	222
Net owners' equity	$ 6,925	$ 6,040
Total liabilities and owners' equity	$12,484	$11,292

[a] See glossary.

EXHIBIT 4 - 5

ACME AUTO PARTS COMPANY
STATEMENT OF WORKING CAPITAL FLOWS
For Year Ended December 31, 19x1
(in thousands of dollars)

Working capital provided from:		
Operations:		
Net earnings		$1,576
+ Depreciation & amortization expense		907
Total working capital provided by operations		$2,483
Sale of equipment		100
Sale of common stock		100
Total working capital provided		$2,683
— Working capital used for:		
Acquisition of long-lived assets	$1,162	
Payment of dividends	768	
Contribution to sinking fund	75	
Increase in cash surrender value of life insurance policies	8	
Loss from fire	79	
Total working capital used		2,092
Increase in working capital (per schedule of working capital changes, below)		$ 591

SCHEDULE OF WORKING CAPITAL CHANGES
For Year Ended December 31, 19x1
(in thousands of dollars)

	December 31		Changes in Working Capital	
	19x0	*19x1*	*Increase*	*Decrease*
Current assets:				
Cash	$ 504	$ 352	$152	
Short-term investments	483	175	308	
Accounts receivable (net)	960	852	108	
Inventories	4,207	3,867	340	
Prepaid expenses	160	170		$ 10
Total current assets	$6,314	$5,416		
— Current liabilities:				
Accounts payable	$1,065	$ 956		109
Notes payable (short-term)	150	175	25	
Accrued interest payable	83	74		9

ACME AUTO PARTS COMPANY (CONT.)

Prepaid rentals	5	5		
Other accrued expenses	346	296		50
Federal income taxes payable	910	746		164
Total current liabilities	$2,559	$2,252		
Working capital	$3,755	$3,164		
Increase in working capital during 19x1				591
			$933	$933

At the meeting of the board, the financial statements are discussed by the president, the controller, and other company officers, and in this way the board members form judgments about how well the company has been managed over the period in question. The officers will naturally attempt to place themselves in as favorable a light as possible, but the board members, with the aid of their broad business backgrounds, knowledge of economic conditions, and the financial statements of the company, form their own judgments, not only about the past performance of the management but also about policy matters governing the future of the firm.

The President

The president of Acme Auto Parts has the basic responsibility for earnings optimization for the firm, perhaps to a greater extent than is found in many firms of this size. There are two evidences of this:

1. The chairman of the board apparently takes no operating responsibility, and we find no executive committee or other subcommittee of the board organized to place on the president tighter limits than those described above. The board meets quarterly, rather than monthly as many do. This possibly indicates that the board does not wish to interfere with operations of the firm as long as the president appears to do his job satisfactorily.

2. The president has apparently not delegated responsibility for earnings to his vice presidents. Acme Auto Parts is organized along *functional* lines, meaning that the functions of marketing, production, and finance for the entire firm are separated from each other. It is proper not to subject these functional areas to performance measurement in terms of earnings, because the earnings of each depends on the performance of the others. Similarly, each of the three plants seems to be responsible only for production, not earnings, since the areas of sales and finance have been separated.

It would have been possible to organize the top management of Acme Auto Parts Company so that the president could have delegated earnings responsibility to each of the three plants. The organization would have been as shown in Exhibit 4–6.

EXHIBIT 4 – 6

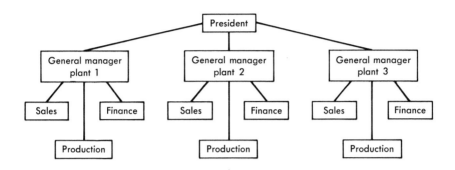

Such a structure is not free from difficulty and is not necessarily better than the existing one. You recall that plant 1 houses the administrative personnel for the entire firm, which means that certain occupancy expenses (in addition to general administrative expenses) of plant 1 should be allocated to plants 2 and 3. Decentralizing the entire finance function among the plants is usually not advisable. Furthermore, greater difficulty is encountered if any of the plants transfers its products to one of the others for further processing or assembly. As we have already seen, earnings measurements of performance of plants are appropriate only to the extent that the plant managers are free to act independently of the general management and of the other plants and have in fact accepted the responsibility for optimizing earnings.

In the Acme Auto Parts Company, earnings optimization can be achieved only when the three functional vice presidents work closely together under the direction of the president. Measuring individual responsibilities in terms of earnings is not possible in this case, with the result that the president must accept full responsibility for earnings. He must also devise other methods of measuring the performance in the marketing, production, and finance areas. As we have seen, the methods he chooses depend entirely on the way in which he wishes to delegate responsibility to his vice presidents.

The president routinely receives performance reports of two kinds:

1. Statements of earnings and retained earnings, financial position, and working capital flows, for the firm as a whole. These are statements of his own performance and are essentially the same reports that go to the members of the board, except that the president receives these statements monthly and the board receives them quarterly.

2. Financial statements of performance in the areas of responsibility of the three vice presidents: production, marketing, and finance. These are not statements of earnings, but contain financial information that relates to the nature of the responsibility delegated in each case. These responsibilities, and the system for measuring and reporting performance, are described in the following sections.

Vice President of Production

Physical output is ordinarily used as one of the measures of accomplishment in the area of production, and the related manufacturing costs (various assets that are transferred into product) as the measure of effort. In the typical case, the performance of the vice president in charge of production (or rather one facet of his performance) is expressed in the ratio

$$\frac{\text{Total manufacturing cost}}{\text{Total output in units}} = \text{Manufacturing cost per unit}$$

This measurement is compared with some standard, or with past experience, to permit management to judge whether performance is good or bad.

The process of identifying manufacturing costs with the related output (called *cost accounting*) is an extremely difficult one in most cases and occupies the full time of thousands of professional accountants. Some of the simpler problems are covered in later chapters, but the difficult ones are beyond the scope of an introductory text. Manufacturing costs are extremely important to management. Past manufacturing costs are vital for performance measurement, and estimates of future manufacturing costs are essential for a great variety of management decisions.

In discussing the Acme Auto Parts Company, we assume that it is possible to measure manufacturing cost per unit in such a way that comparison with some standard is valid and may serve as a means of evaluating one aspect of performance in the production area. Presumably, the lower the cost per unit the better the performance, and an important goal of top management is to reduce this cost to the minimum over the long run.

However, the president of Acme would be a poor manager if he based his judgment of the vice president's performance solely on manufacturing costs per unit. At least three other criteria are highly important in terms of the earnings objective of the firm as a whole, and yet these criteria may be in conflict with the more limited objective of minimizing manufacturing cost per unit. These are:

1. Amount of output. If the vice president of production were permitted to produce as much or as little as he liked, he might produce up to the capacity of the plants if this level of output would result in the lowest cost per unit of output. Maximum output, however, might also result in a large investment in unsalable products, which would be contrary to the earnings objective. On the other hand, the vice president might produce too little in order to avoid costly overtime wages or the use of inefficient equipment. If this should result in *stock-outs*, loss of markets, or loss of customer goodwill, the loss in earnings might more than offset the reduction in manufacturing cost. For these reasons, the vice president of production and the plant managers need to be given production goals. In part, their performance should be measured by the extent to which they achieve these goals. Maximum earnings to the firm as a whole should govern the decision on how high the production goal should be.

2. Rate of output. If the demand for the products is highly seasonal, Acme Auto Parts will probably have to vary its production rate throughout the year. A steady year-round production rate probably will result in the lowest production cost per unit, but the cost of fluctuating inventories may be greater than the saving in production cost.

3. Quality of product. Some criterion for acceptability of product must be specified in order to guard against the possibility of reducing the manufacturing cost per unit by reducing the quality of the output to a point at which its usefulness or sales value would be impaired. This criterion may be implemented in such a way that the cost of spoiled units, or the cost of reworking, can either be identified separately or included as an element in the cost of the good units. Given the criterion of long-run earnings optimization, balancing this cost against the cost of inspection or other safeguards against poor quality is obviously a complex problem.

These illustrations are included in order to demonstrate the nature of the responsibility of the vice president of production of Acme Auto Parts and to explain why he is not free to produce what he likes in the quantity or quality or at the time he likes. If the organization structure assigned to this vice president the responsibility for optimizing earnings, it would also have to grant to him the authority to make all these decisions. Since this has not been done, he and the president must decide on the relative importance of all of the factors that govern his performance.

An Operating Department

There are three levels of managerial responsibility below the vice president in charge of production: the general manager of the plant, the production manager of the plant, and the department foremen. Defining each of these levels involves identifying the nature of the responsibility delegated to the level. The organizational structure specifies that certain responsibilities will be carried out at each level and that certain others will be delegated to a still lower level to be carried out there. In the Acme Auto Parts Company, the department is the lowest organizational level formally recognized in the organizational structure and in the reporting system. Each department is headed by a foreman whose performance is measured in the formal reporting system. There are nine departments under the production manager of plant 1; each submits a weekly performance report to the production manager. One such report appears in the next chapter as Exhibit 5–1.

Of course, the department foreman delegates responsibility to the laborers in his department and measures their performance. But most of the performance measurement is done visually, since the foreman is physically on the scene most of the time and most of the communication is oral rather than written. Time cards and production records are kept for individual laborers and machines, but they are largely for payroll, production, and cost accounting purposes. This system puts a great deal of responsibility on the foreman. At Acme it works well because the foremen are competent and the departments are small enough so that each laborer receives individual attention from the foreman. Let us study the grinding department of plant 1 and note how performance is measured and evaluated.

The Grinding Department.   The foreman of the grinding department has responsibility for the performance of seventeen men and fifteen grinding machines. There are two men who act as machine loaders, relief operators, and general laborers, in addition to fifteen machine operators who operate one machine each. The grinding department is assigned the task of performing a grinding operation on products in a manner set forth by the product-design engineer. The foreman is responsible for completing the task as quickly and as accurately as possible at minimum expense. When the job is completed, the ground parts are sent on to the next production department.

The performance of the grinding department depends on the conditions imposed by the organizational delegation of responsibility and authority. The foreman may be assigned a quota of 10,000 units of part 37-tu, to be ground according to rather loose design specifications within a two-day period. Accomplishment might be expressed in terms of the speed of the output. Performance measurement would compare units per two-day period with expenses during that period. On the other hand, the foreman may be assigned a task of grinding 200 pieces of items 6xl-7 within very close design tolerances, but with no restrictions on time. Here the accomplishment would stress quality, and performance might be measured in terms of expenses per satisfactory unit of product. In the usual situation the foreman may be assigned several tasks simultaneously, and his performance may be measured by using different expressions of accomplishment from time to time.

Whether the task is a quota stressing speed or a problem stressing quality, the accountant will still measure accomplishment in relation to the effort or expenses involved in accomplishing the task. There are many expenses involved in running a grinding department, a few of which are (a) labor wages, (b) grinding wheels used, (c) units of product spoiled, (d) electrical power used, and (e) fire insurance covering the machines.

CONTROLLABLE VERSUS UNCONTROLLABLE EXPENSES.   It is evident even from this sketchy list that there are some expenses the foreman can govern and others over which he has no control. If the basic hourly wage rate is set by a union contract, the foreman's control over labor expense depends on his authority to control the number of hours worked. If he can keep his men working rapidly and transfer them to other production assignments when they finish, he can control labor hours even though he cannot control the wage rate. Furthermore, to the extent that decisions regarding overtime work (at one and a half times the basic wage rate) are within his authority, the overtime premium is within his control. The number of grinding wheels used, the number of spoiled units, and the electrical-power expenses are all dependent on the efficiency of the machine operators. Their efficiency can be controlled by the foreman if he has the authority to train workers properly or replace them if they will not or cannot be trained. Thus these expenses are considered to be within the control of the foreman.

The expense of fire insurance, on the other hand, is obviously not within the control of the foreman. This expense is a result of insurance rates and insurable values about which the foreman can do nothing.

It is seldom an easy matter to determine precisely which expenses are controllable and which are uncontrollable in a given situation. As an example, take the case of the foreman. In addition to the expenses listed above, and many others, his activity will certainly incur the expense of using up the grinding machines. Should this depreciation be considered in measuring his performance? If this expense is merely related to the passing of time, the answer is obviously no. The expense would be incurred no matter what action the foreman took. But suppose that depreciation is related closely to how expertly the machines are operated by the machinists. Since their skill is the foreman's responsibility, should he be held responsible for the machine-usage expense under these conditions?

The real point at issue is that it is vital to measure effort by expenses that are controllable by the organizational unit being measured. If the controllable nature of some expenses is in doubt, they should not be used in performance measurement. A good organizational structure requires that responsibility for accomplishment be matched with the authority to control the expenses by which performance is measured.

Vice President of Marketing

Measuring performance in marketing follows the same pattern as in production. The measures used depend entirely on the nature and scope of the responsibility delegated to the vice president of marketing. In all likelihood there will be several measures used simultaneously that will very possibly conflict with one another.

If, for example, the vice president of marketing accepts responsibility for both sales volume and pricing of products to customers, sales revenue in dollars would be an important measure of accomplishment. In all likelihood there is some relationship between sales dollars and marketing expenses incurred, so that marketing expenses could be a measure of effort, and the ratio

$$\frac{\text{Marketing expense}}{\text{Sales dollar}} = \text{Expense per sales dollar}$$

could be used as a measure of performance.

By itself, however, this approach would be an oversimplification and would lead to difficulties. If the vice president of marketing has the responsibility of building and maintaining customer relations, and if a substantial portion of the effort (expense) in the marketing area is devoted to this activity, then this expense should somehow be related to sales of the future, rather than sales of the present. A cost-conscious marketing executive might be inclined to reduce expenses during periods of reduced sales in order to keep the ratio from rising, when in fact, long-run profit optimization might call for just the opposite policy.

This illustrates the fact that performance measurement in the marketing area is usually more difficult than in production. The relationship between accomplishment and effort in any given period is less apparent, and many qualitative factors, which accountants are not equipped to handle with quantitative measurements, enter in.

This is apparent in the Acme Auto Parts Company. Sales of products to automobile manufacturers do not depend on sales promotion to any great extent. The company is well known in the automotive field, and the "big four" are not influenced by advertising or fast-talking salesmen. Sales to these customers are dependent on (a) the quality of the product, (b) the ability of Acme to meet production deadlines, and (c) price. These three considerations are also primary with respect to the contract work done for the National Aeronautics and Space Administration. As might be expected, advertising and salesmen's activity exert a greater influence on sales made to chain automotive stores, and most of the sales-promotion effort is directed at these customers.

Much of the so-called marketing function is a communication function performed by the vice president of marketing, his assistant, and his sales manager. These people maintain close contact with each of the "big four" customers and make sure that lines of communication are open at all times. They are particularly interested in knowing immediately about projected changes in automobile production schedules, proposed changes in design (whether proposed by Acme or the customer), complaints about and causes of defective products, etc. At least as much automotive-engineering ability as marketing ability is required on the part of the marketing executives at Acme.

The other major function performed by the vice president of marketing is product pricing. He has the final authority on prices of products under each contract with the automotive manufacturers and also with the federal government, subject only to a broad statement of pricing policy drawn up several years ago by the president and approved by the board of directors. There are two other manufacturers of competing products that also have the productive capacity to supply the "big four," and the vice president of marketing must be extremely sensitive to any economic or competitive factor that might call for a change in price. In addition to having as thorough knowledge as possible of the operating characteristics of the competing firms, the vice president of marketing is in constant touch with the Acme vice president of production and the product research manager.

To sum up, Acme's activity in the marketing area differs widely, depending on the type of customer. Most of the salesmen's activity and advertising effort is directed at the chain automotive stores, even though sales to this group of customers are less than one-third of the total annual sales of the firm. Acme has the policy of attempting to build up the business from these customers to make the firm less dependent upon the "big four" and the federal government.

Acme uses the following measures of performance with respect to that portion of the business done with chain automotive stores:

1. Sales in units and dollars, classified by territory and by product.
2. Earnings margin, classified by product.
3. Total sales promotion and advertising expense, as a per cent of sales revenue, classified by territory (no attempt is made to allocate sales promotion expense to various products).
4. Number and average dollar value of customer orders.
   a. Repeat customers
   b. New customers

Measurement of performance of the marketing function with regard to the "big four" is almost entirely subjective, and therefore not amenable to quantitative measurement. The only measurement of performance of the vice president of marketing covering the entire marketing function and issued by the accounting department covers his responsibility as a controller of marketing costs. This is simply a comparison of actual marketing costs with budgeted marketing costs as established at the beginning of the period. The statement is prepared monthly for internal purposes and quarterly for the board of directors. An example appears in Exhibit 4–7.

This statement says very little about performance of the marketing function,

EXHIBIT 4-7

ACME AUTO PARTS COMPANY

SELLING EXPENSES
(in thousands of dollars)

	Fourth Quarter 19x1		The Year 19x1	
	Actual	*Budget*	*Actual*	*Budget*
Advertising	$409	$406	$1,467	$1,597
Salesmen's salaries	199	217	803	841
Payroll taxes and fringe benefits	20	21	79	83
Traveling	59	65	246	261
Freight out	48	50	203	197
Depreciation—automobiles	12	12	47	47
Depreciation—equipment	10	10	40	40
Miscellaneous	14	18	58	64
Total	$771	$799	$2,943	$3,130
Sales revenues	$5,510	$5,842	$20,120	$21,719

since there is no indication of accomplishment during the period. The report may exert an influence, rightly or wrongly, on the vice president of marketing to stay within his budget rather than be forced to explain *over-runs* to the president.

Vice President of Finance

The area of finance in Acme Auto Parts Company, as in most firms, includes both financial management and accounting. Many writers argue that the distinction between financial management and accounting is artificial and unnecessary, and perhaps this is true. However, we are using the former term here to mean determining and maintaining the basic sources of capital for the firm, and the management of cash balances and investments, usually under the authority of a corporate treasurer. We use the term "accounting" to include the entire external and internal financial reporting system, including budgeting, cost controls, asset controls, and financial information reporting for all management decisions, under the authority of the chief accounting officer. This officer is usually called the controller. In the Acme Auto Parts Company, the responsibility for both functions is assigned to the vice president of finance, although the accounting function permeates the entire organization, while the financial management function is carried out entirely by top management.

As is largely true of marketing, performance in the area of finance is virtually impossible to measure, because there is no convincing way to express the accomplishment of the function in quantitative terms. Finance, broadly defined, is entirely a facilitating function, having no separable business objectives of its own. This means that nearly the only performance report on finance is the report

EXHIBIT 4-8

ACME AUTO PARTS COMPANY
FINANCE AND ACCOUNTING EXPENSES
(in thousands of dollars)

	Fourth Quarter 19x1		The Year 19x1	
	Actual	*Budget*	*Actual*	*Budget*
Administrative salaries	$221	$220	$ 647	$ 639
Other office salaries	107	98	419	391
Payroll taxes and fringe benefits	11	10	39	38
Depreciation—office equipment	9	9	34	34
Office supplies	19	20	79	81
Credit losses	11	12	48	45
Interest expense	51	51	165	163
Totals	$429	$420	$1,431	$1,391

on control of financing expenses, i.e., periodic comparison of budgeted and actual expenses. To the extent that the accomplishment of the finance function can be assumed without being measured, then the comparison of budgeted with actual expenses can properly be considered as a report on performance of the vice president of finance. An example is given in Exhibit 4–8.

Qualitative Factors

In appraising the contribution each vice president makes to the earnings of the company, the president of Acme Auto Parts Company must not rely solely on quantitative measures of performance. Two broad classes of qualitative factors must be considered.

1. How well does each vice president cooperate with the other two and with the president in top-management decisions affecting the long-run earnings prospects of the firm? Each officer must avoid favoring the special interest of the particular province he represents and adopt the point of view of the firm as a whole, even when the correct decision is one that might affect adversely the performance measures of one of the areas. Effective participation in this capacity calls for a broad business background as well as an ability to communicate effectively. It is in this capacity that executives at the vice-presidential level develop their abilities to take over positions of even greater responsibility when the opportunity arises.

2. How able is each vice president to act as head of his own organization in such a way as to promote efficiency and high morale among the people in the lower levels? Efficiency in the more routine operations should be reflected in the various quantitative measures of departments in production, marketing, and finance, but the measure of the ability of the vice president as a leader, and particularly as a builder of morale and judge of ability among his own subordinates, is not likely to be reflected in performance reports in any recognizable way. Evaluation of these attributes is essentially subjective, even though they are at least as important as the objective criteria.

SUMMARY

An appropriate organizational structure is a necessary prerequisite of good management. A sound organization matches the delegation of responsibility with the delegation of authority and delineates precisely the superior-subordinate relationships within the enterprise.

Performance measurement within an organization requires that the accomplishment of an area of responsibility be compared with the effort required for that accomplishment. Accomplishment is often difficult to express in quantitative terms, particularly in cases in which the objective of the area of responsibility cannot be entirely separated from the objectives of other areas. Effort is usually expressed in terms of periodic expenses, although the accountant is not always able to establish a convincing relationship between expenses and accomplishment. In his attempt to establish measures of performance for subunits of the firm, which accurately reflect the intent of the organizational structure of that firm, the accountant faces a challenging task.

Questions for Review

4-1. Discuss the relationships among the accounting system, performance measurement, and the balancing of responsibility and authority.

4-2. Identify and give an example of each of the three basic kinds of business activity.

4-3. What is the relationship, if any, between measuring the performance of an individual or department and the existing organizational structure?

4-4. Define and give several examples of "accomplishment."

4-5. Define and give several examples of "effort."

4-6. List the three basic ways to measure performance and give an example of each.

4-7. Define, and give several examples of
  a. circumstances in which costs are controllable.
  b. circumstances in which costs are not controllable.

Problems for Analysis

4-8. The organizational structure, accounting system, and management of a firm are interrelated. A "good" organizational structure can be described as a well-defined superior–subordinate relationship, where the manager has the authority to require certain things from other people. One characteristic of "good" management (from an accounting standpoint) is that it supports an accounting system by encouraging subordinates to provide accounting personnel with accurate cost and revenue input data regarding sales, purchasing, production, and all other business activities. A "good" accounting system is one that provides managers and others relevant and timely information, based upon accurate cost and revenue inputs for decision making.

Using the above definitions of "good," answer the following questions:

a. What effect would poor organizational structure have on the accounting system?

b. What effect would good organizational structure have?

4-9. The foreman of department 1 is responsible for producing stainless steel door moldings for automobiles. These door moldings are mass produced. The foreman of department 2 is responsible for the assembly of power seat devices (including power motors) on seat frames. The power seat device is fairly intricate, and its successful assembly requires a certain degree of skill. The foreman of department 2 has no control over the quality of the power motors. As the plant superintendent, how would you evaluate the performance of each of these two foremen?

4-10. You are attempting to measure the performance of the foreman of the testing department of a manufacturer of gasoline and diesel engines. From the following data, select the items below that you would include in the performance report for this foreman for the month of July, and defend your decision to include or exclude each of these items.

a. wages of department employees for July
b. supplies used during July
c. supplies purchased during July and on hand July 31
d. allocation of machinery cost to July
e. allocation of building cost to July
f. overtime premiums for the employees
g. personal property taxes on the machinery of the testing department

4-11. A foreman who has been surpassing the standards in his department and receiving bonuses for excellence has disapproved the purchase of a new machine for his department that would probably reduce his costs greatly. He has said, "We're doing all right in this department. Why rock the boat?" What leads the foreman to make this error? What would you do to correct the error if you were the plant manager?

4-12. a. List several examples of businesses that conduct a service activity. What services do they render?

b. List several examples of businesses that conduct product-handling activities. Do these types of businesses also render a service? If so, what is the service?

c. List several examples of businesses that perform manufacturing activities. Do these businesses also perform service and product-handling activities? If so, what are they?

4-13. a. How should periodic accomplishment be measured in each of the following departments of the Acme Auto Parts Company?

  1. the grinding department
  2. the shipping department
  3. the sales department
  4. the general accounting department

b. If you were asked to develop a system of accounting reports designed to measure the periodic accomplishment of the above departments, what additional information would you ask for?

c. To what extent is periodic departmental expense a measure of effort in each of the above cases?

4-14. The labor cost per unit of product for a grinding department in one of the Detroit plants was $.14 for July. In Milwaukee, the July labor cost for the same product was $.13 per unit. What additional information would you have to have before you could conclude that labor efficiency in Milwaukee was greater than in Detroit?

4-15. In Detroit plant 1, the maintenance foreman's responsibility is to prevent work stoppages or inefficient operation of machines in the producing department. The maintenance foreman in Detroit plant 2 is responsible for the conduct of regular machine inspections and for their immediate servicing in emergencies.

a. In your opinion, which position has the greater responsibility? Describe the degree of authority each foreman should have to carry out his responsibility.

b. How should accomplishment be measured in each case?

4-16. One salesman for a book company is assigned to a large metropolitan area containing 200 customers within a fifty-block area. These customers normally buy in large quantities. A second salesman's area also contains 200 customers but they are, on the average, ten miles apart and buy in small quantities. Can you develop a measure of performance which would compare the two salesmen fairly for a given period of time?

4-17. a. What advantages and disadvantages do each of the following items have as measures of period performance? (Define "cost" as total departmental expenses for the period.)

  1. cost per unit produced, for the grinding department
  2. sales per dollar of advertising cost, for the advertising department
  3. cost per truckload shipped, for the shipping department
  4. cost per page typed, for the secretarial staff
  5. cost per crew hour, for the maintenance department

b. For each of the examples in part *a*, state one way in which the department head could make his performance look better, at least temporarily, to the detriment of the long-run profit objectives of the company.

4-18. The Moellar Brush Company is a nationwide retailer of household articles. Their products include soaps, cleaners, deodorants, dental supplies, shaving supplies, and many other commodities. The profit margins for the products vary. Their products are marketed by door-to-door salesmen. There are forty salesmen in the central Ohio sales district. Each salesman is responsible for a specific geographical area of central Ohio. The following data pertain to three of these salesmen for one week:

	Salesman		
	1	*2*	*3*
Total sales	$650	$890	$320
Excess of sales price over cost of merchandise sold	$230	$270	$135
Miles traveled	410	280	470
Customers visited:			
New customer stops	20	5	95
Repeat customer stops	64	110	25
Total	84	115	120

Salesman 1 has an established territory in a suburban area of a large city, and has been with the company four years. Salesman 2 has a territory that includes a development of 1,500 apartments. He has been responsible for this territory for three years. Salesman 3 has a suburban territory that includes 400 new homes. He has been with the company for three months.

    a. From the above data, compute and defend the items that you would use in evaluating the salesmen.

    b. Suggest a method of compensating the salesmen. Compute and defend the compensation that you suggest for each salesman. (You may assume that each salesman is reimbursed by the company for automobile expenses.)

    c. What, in your opinion, are the advantages and disadvantages of a written sales policy regarding the responsibilities and compensation plan for the salesmen?

4-19. The Roanoke Mudhens, a professional baseball organization, has hired you to help in player salary negotiations for the forthcoming season. Some of the data regarding the pitching staff for last year appear below.

    a. Rank the three pitchers in order of performance. Describe and defend your criteria for ranking.

    b. What limitations do you see in your criteria? What other information would you need to better evaluate the performance of the Mudhen pitchers?

	Total Pitching Staff (9)	Sam Underhand	Owen Twocount	Bill Gopher
Innings pitched	1,600	283	304	220
Won-lost record	83–79	18–12	16–13	12–12
Completed games	31	9	11	6
Earned run average	3.15	2.96	3.32	2.45
Average attendance[a]	11,815	12,925	11,220	11,940
Salary	$153,000	$22,500	$18,000	$16,000

[a] Average attendance figures are computed by totaling the official attendance for all games started by a pitcher and dividing by the number of starts by that pitcher. For double-headers, each starting pitcher is allotted half the attendance. Includes both home and away games.

4-20. The Tomahawk Electric Company is a privately owned electric utility that operates in a large metropolitan area of the southeastern United States. One of its departments consists of a manager and twelve telephone operators who are responsible for handling telephone calls initiated by approximately 130,000 customers. The calls represent requests for electrical service for a new residence; electrical service for a new occupant (where service was previously provided); discontinuance of electrical service; complaints because of no electricity; complaints because of a large utility bill; and miscellaneous inquiries, such as the status of new service requests and customer accounts.

The company places a great deal of emphasis on customer satisfaction. Since the telephone operators play a key role in shaping the image of the company, the management desires to monitor their activities very carefully. Some problems of performance are: not giving the customer sufficient information, not obtaining adequate and/or reliable information for processing the customer's request, and a backlog of calls which cause some customers to hang up before their call is processed.

The following data pertain to three of these operators for one week:

	Operators		
	1	2	3
Total calls processed (calls and return calls)	350	410	295
Number of large bill inquiries handled by operator	7	2	3
Referred to another department for follow up	3	10	6
Number of return calls to customers required	4	20	15
Calls lost (customer hung up because of excessive delay)	5	3	8
Salary cost (including fringe benefits)	$450	$485	$370

a. From the items above, compute a measure of performance for each telephone operator.

b. Defend each item (used or not used) as a measurement of accomplishment.

c. Rank the telephone operators in terms of their relative performance.

d. Discuss any limitations you see in the performance reports that you have prepared.

e. Should performance for this department be reported for individual operators or for the department? Give reasons for your answer.

f. What types of decision should these performance reports assist a manager in making?

4-21. The Ketchum Collection Agency specializes in collecting delinquent accounts for businesses that wish to use their services. The fee is 30 per cent of all dollars collected. For example, a physician may have $4,000 in delinquent accounts receivable from patients, which he assigns The Ketchum Collection Agency. If the agency collects $1,400, its fee would be $420.

The collectors try to collect the account via telephone, and ask the individual to mail his remittance to the collection agency. When this fails, a field visit with the delinquent payee is required.

The following data pertain to the activities of three of the collectors for one week:

	Collector		
	1	*2*	*3*
Dollar amount collected via telephone	$420	$890	$150
Dollar amount collected via field visit	$780	$810	$500
Dollar amount assigned for collection	$4,100	$3,800	$1,300
Number of accounts collected:			
Telephone	10	15	3
Field visit	20	9	16
Number of accounts assigned	90	95	70
Miles driven	750	400	900
Salary costs	$700	$650	$425
Fringe benefit costs (15% of salary)	$105	$98	$64

Collector 3 has been with the company one year, of which six months was spent as a trainee.

a. From the above data, compute and defend the items that you would use in measuring the performance of the collectors. Rank the performance of each collector.

b. What types of decisions will the measures of performance assist you, the manager of the collection activity, in making? List and discuss briefly.

4-22. The Suwanee Natural Gas Company is a utility operating in a combined urban-rural area of Florida. The company employs meter readers to read each meter monthly. The following data pertain to three of the meter readers for one month:

	Meter Reader		
	1	2	3
Number of meters read	4,650	3,210	4,030
Number of customer complaints of inaccurate readings	22	7	3
Salary and fringe benefit cost of meter readers	$570	$580	$570

Meter reader 2 has a rural route, and readers 1 and 3 have urban routes.

a. From the above data, measure and rank the performance of each meter reader.

b. What types of decisions will these measures of performance assist the manager in making? List and discuss briefly.

4–23. The Accidental Service Company operates a water system that serves the residents of a growing city on the West Coast. The city is experiencing both a rapid increase in the number of residents and frequent annexations of surrounding areas. Both factors create additional demands for water service.

The Company's staff of engineers are responsible for engineering and planning:

1. An increase in the water system to service additional areas.
2. Improvements to the existing system.
3. Provision of service to new customers whose property is adjacent to existing water trunk lines.

The following data pertain to the engineers for one month:

	Engineers		
	1	2	3
Miles of network engineered	3	2	0
Number of requests for new service to be engineered	10	9	35
Estimated man-hours of work-crew time required to implement the engineering plans	2,200	1,950	1,200
Number of projects completed	12	14	32
Number of projects started	15	12	32
Number of projects pending	6	15	0
Salary cost of engineers	$900	$930	$875
Fringe benefits	135	140	130
Cost of draftsmen used (at $4.00/hour)	405	55	20
Automobile expense (at $.10/mile)	34	40	105

a. From the appropriate data, measure and rank the performance of the engineers.

b. Discuss the uses and limitations of these performance measures from the standpoint of the manager of the engineers.

c. Suggest any alternate measures of accomplishment that you think would be useful in performance measurement. Give your reasons.

4-24. Mason's is a fairly large chain of appliance stores, maintaining stores in most of the larger plazas and malls in suburban Chicago. Virtually all sales are on installment. Each store has its own credit manager who is responsible for approving all credit sales, setting limits on credit, and collecting receivables. Data for three stores for last year include the following:

	Store		
	X	Y	Z
Installment sales	$670,000	$875,000	$540,000
Credit losses	$14,000	$62,000	$15,000
Number of credit rejections	172	27	130
Sales value of credit rejections	$61,000	$8,900	$54,000

a. Suppose Mason's management rated the credit managers by one criterion—credit losses as a percentage of installment sales. How would they rate these three managers? What limitations do you see in this measure of performance?

b. Suppose the earnings margin on installment sales is 25 per cent and a study by management reveals that 3 per cent, 5 per cent, and 10 per cent of the installment sales rejected by X, Y, and Z respectively would have resulted in credit losses if the sales had been made. What loss of earnings resulted from the policies of each of the three managers? Of what significance is your answer to the performance measurement of each credit manager?

4-25. John Rialto is the owner of a small chain of movie theaters located in three of the larger cities in the United States. He has neither the time nor the desire to manage these theaters himself, and has hired a manager for each theater, giving each almost complete control over his respective operation. Mr. Rialto limits his own responsibility to the financing and construction or leasing of the theaters, periodic evaluation of the theater managers, and review of cash control.

The managers are given a great deal of responsibility: each determines his own pricing policies, selects the films to be rented, decides whether to handle the concession stand or to lease the space to a vendor, and sets his own hiring and wage rate policies. Mr. Rialto maintains control over operations through the use of a public accounting firm that makes periodic audits of each theater's books. Year-end audits are supplemented by occasional unannounced audits, primarily to verify that adequate cash control is being maintained by each manager. Mr. Rialto receives monthly financial statements so that he can keep an eye on operations.

Mr. Rialto reasons that since he can earn 5 per cent on his money simply by investing in bank certificates of deposit, the managers should be entitled to a share of any profits over a 5 per cent return on total assets. The yearly financial statements are used to determine each manager's bonus, as follows:

1. Total assets on the statement of financial position at year end are used to determine the necessary 5 per cent return.

2. 20 per cent of the difference between this calculated earnings and the actual earnings as shown on the earnings statement (if greater than 5 per cent) is paid as a bonus to the theater manager. (All earnings and rate of return figures are calculated before considering federal taxes.)

The following are the comparative financial statements for the year ended December 31, 19x3.

COMPARATIVE STATEMENT OF FINANCIAL POSITION
As of December 31, 19x3

	Detroit Rialto	Chicago Rialto	Cleveland Rialto
Assets			
Cash	$ 3,400	$ 5,000	$ 4,200
Supplies	400	500	800
Equipment (net)	9,200	8,000	10,000
Buildings (net)	100,000	108,000	0
Land	20,000	23,500	0
Total assets	$133,000	$145,000	$15,000
Liabilities and Owners' Equity			
Accrued payroll	$ 200	$ 250	$ 175
Other accruals	2,200	2,750	1,875
Mortgage payable	94,000	100,000	0
Owners' equity	36,600	42,000	12,950
Total liabilities and equities	$133,000	$145,000	$15,000

COMPARATIVE EARNINGS STATEMENT
For Year Ended December 31, 19x3

	Detroit Rialto	Chicago Rialto	Cleveland Rialto
Revenues:			
Admissions	$160,000	$185,000	$150,000
Concessions	5,000	7,000	4,200
Total revenues	$165,000	$192,000	$154,200

COMPARATIVE EARNINGS STATEMENT (CONT.)

	Detroit Rialto	Chicago Rialto	Cleveland Rialto
Expenses:			
Film rentals	$104,000	$122,000	$ 98,000
Wages	22,000	24,500	20,400
Manager's salary	10,000	10,000	10,000
Building rental	0	0	9,000
Depreciation—equipment	1,150	1,000	1,200
Depreciation—building	5,500	6,000	0
Advertising	6,000	7,000	5,400
Miscellaneous	4,350	5,500	200
Total expenses	$153,000	$176,000	$144,200
Net income	$ 12,000	$ 16,000	$ 10,000

a. Compute the bonuses for the managers of the Detroit, Chicago, and Cleveland theaters.

b. Mr. Rialto apparently considers the bonus paid each manager to be an adequate measure of their relative performances. Why is it important to distinguish between earnings for performance measurement and earnings for a bonus calculation such as the one used by Mr. Rialto?

c. What factors in the rate-of-return calculations, whether used for the bonus calculation or as a measure of performance, jeopardize the comparability between theaters? How would you improve comparability?

d. What subjective factors should Mr. Rialto consider in evaluating his managers?

e. Mr. Rialto seems most interested in the relative performance of each manager. Would it be valuable to compare each manager with some yardstick of performance, such as a 10 per cent return on investment?

4-26. The J. J. Croman Company is a custom manufacturer of truck bodies. The company secures contracts from truck companies throughout the United States. The bodies vary in size from a small half-ton truck body to a tandem truck body with a built-in ladder that will extend as high as fifty feet. Practically all bodies are installed on a new truck chassis supplied by the customer. All bodies are custom-made; a few of the component parts, however, are standardized. The company maintains a small inventory of these standardized parts.

All of the outstanding stock is owned by the Croman family. The company was started twenty-five years ago in the Croman garage and has experienced steady growth since then. At the present time its annual sales volume is approximately $4 million, and the company has slightly over 200 employees on the payroll. A modern building, constructed by the company eight years ago, provides 90,000 square feet of manufacturing space and 10,000 square feet of office space.

An organization chart for the J. J. Croman Company appears on page 167.

The owners, as stockholders, elect the board of directors. The stockholders have delegated to the board of directors the responsibility for the management of the company. To fulfill this responsibility, the board of directors has the authority to hire the officers of the company who will manage the day-to-day operations of the business. The board of directors is accountable to the owners for optimizing long-run profits.

The board of directors has elected a president who is responsible for the implementation of the long-run profit-optimization objective. To fulfill his responsibilities, the president has the authority, delegated to him by the board of directors, to make all the decisions relating to the daily business operations. The president is, of course, accountable to the board of directors for the successful fulfillment of his responsibilities.

The president has appointed three vice presidents, accountable to him, who are responsible for production, sales, and financial controls. The vice presidents have the authority to hire and fire all subordinates under their jurisdictions.

Production

The vice president in charge of production supervises four department heads: the production-research manager, the production-scheduling manager, the purchasing manager, and the factory superintendent. The production-research manager has two responsibilities: first, he is expected to experiment with existing production techniques to discover less costly methods of production; second, he works closely with the sales staff in order to get ideas from the salesmen and customers for product innovations. Product innovations are undertaken only after the officers of the company have given their approval to the proposal. The product-research manager is accountable to the production vice president for the accomplishment of his research and cost-cutting activities in accordance with a predetermined budget.

The production-scheduling manager has the authority to initiate all production orders throughout the plant. He is accountable to the production vice president for scheduling production with a minimum amount of overtime and idle time charges.

The purchasing manager is responsible for having the required materials on hand to meet the scheduled production. The production-scheduling personnel maintain perpetual inventory records for all raw materials, work in process, and finished-goods inventory. When the production-scheduling clerk receives a production request, he checks the bill of materials (a listing of materials necessary to fill the request) against the perpetual inventory records. He immediately reports any shortages to the purchasing manager, who then orders the materials required to meet scheduled production. The purchasing manager is accountable

J. J. CROMAN COMPANY
BASIC ORGANIZATION CHART

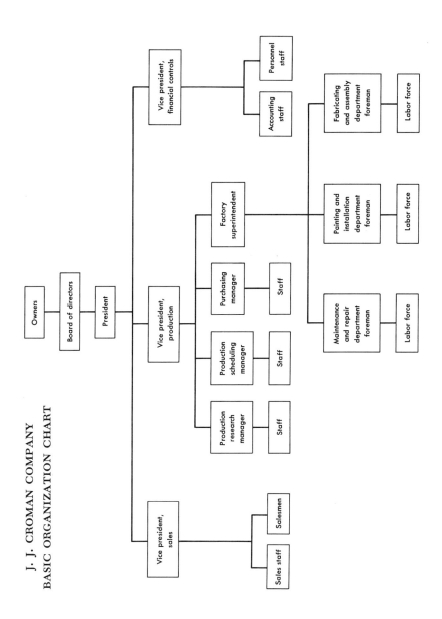

to the production vice president for providing the materials required for production at the desired quality and at the best price.

The factory superintendent has responsibility for the two production departments (fabricating and assembly, and painting and installation) as well as the maintenance and repair department. He has complete authority over the three foremen of these departments. The factory superintendent is accountable to the production vice president for the successful fulfillment of his assigned responsibilities.

The foreman of the fabricating and assembly department is responsible for the construction and assembly of the utility body, and he has complete charge of all activities within his department. The foreman has the authority to hire and fire all department employees. He is accountable to the factory superintendent for the accomplishment of his responsibilities within predetermined operating standards.

The foreman in charge of the painting and installation department has the responsibility for the painting of the truck body and the installation of the truck body on the chassis (which is provided by the customer). He also has the authority to hire and fire his employees in addition to having complete charge of the conduct of the activities within his department. He is accountable to the factory superintendent for accomplishment of his responsibilities in accordance with predetermined operating standards.

The maintenance and repair department foreman has the responsibility for minor additions and revisions to the plant facilities, for implementing changes in the plant layout, and for preventive maintenance on all buildings, machinery, and equipment. He has complete authority over his labor force. The foreman is expected to coordinate his work plans with the production foremen in order to minimize interference with production. He is accountable to the factory superintendent for the projects changing plant layout, etc., in accordance with a prearranged budget. He is accountable to the factory superintendent for minimizing machine breakdowns because of inadequate preventive maintenance.

Sales

The sales vice president is responsible for all aspects of selling, including sales volume, profit margin on sales estimates, and advertising. The sales vice president has complete authority over his employees, including six salesmen who are each responsible for a geographical region in the United States. The salesmen are accountable to the sales vice president for the successful fulfillment of predetermined sales quotas.

The procedure for processing a sales order is as follows: The salesmen accept orders from customers, quoting a contract price that is subject to the approval of the sales vice president. A clerk on the sales staff in the home office checks the order, verifying the completeness and accuracy of the estimated cost of production prepared by the salesmen. The sales vice president reviews the order and approves it by signing the original copy of the order, which is then sent to the customer as confirmation of the sale. A second copy of the order is sent to the production-scheduling manager; a third is sent to the accounting department for customer billing and cost analysis.

Financial Controls

The vice president in charge of financial controls is responsible for securing adequate funds as they are needed to enable the company to fulfill its objectives. The finance vice president uses a cash budget to forecast the company's cash position for the future. He is also the controller—that is, he assists management in controlling the operations of the business by the preparation of performance reports for management use.

The vice president of finance is assisted by the accounting staff. This staff is responsible for sending sales invoices to customers after merchandise has been shipped, and it handles all company bookkeeping—recording, classifying, and summarizing daily business transactions such as sales, purchases, and the receiving and disbursing of cash. The information about these transactions is used by the accounting staff to prepare various reports for management. First, it prepares earnings statements for the officers of the company that measure performance in dollars of the J. J. Croman Company as a whole. Second, it prepares performance reports for use in cost control by management in evaluating production foremen and other line managers. Since these individuals are not responsible for deciding how much to produce or what their operating framework should be, they are judged primarily by whether they keep costs at a minimum. One way to evaluate this is to compare actual costs of completed production orders with their estimated costs. The company president then reviews these reports with the sales vice president to determine what corrective action, if any, should be taken on estimates for new sales contracts. The accounting department also prepares financial statements for nonmanagers—stockholders, investors, and the government. Statements of earnings, statements of retained earnings, and statements of financial position are prepared for financial investors; federal, state, and local tax reports are prepared for the government.

The vice president of finance also has the responsibility for personnel activities, which he delegates to the personnel staff. It hires and fires employees on the recommendations of supervisors throughout the company. The personnel staff also maintains a personnel file for each employee.

a. Point out and discuss any important areas of responsibility in the J. J. Croman Company that are not clearly defined. What are the possible unfavorable consequences of the failure to define these responsibilities clearly?

b. What would be the logic, if any, of placing production scheduling, personnel, and purchasing under the responsibility of a single individual?

c. Write a paragraph describing how you would measure the performance (that is, compare accomplishment and effort) of each of the following:

1. Manager, general accounting department.
2. Manager, cost accounting department.
3. Foreman, maintenance and repair department.
4. Foreman, fabrication and assembly department.
5. Foreman, painting and assembly department.
6. Manager, product and process research department.
7. Salesman in charge of a territory.
8. Sales clerk.
9. Vice president, finance.
10. Vice president, production.
11. Vice president, sales.
12. President of the company.

d. Assume that the vice president in charge of sales receives the following order, already verified by a clerk in the sales department:

J. J. CROMAN COMPANY
SALES ORDER

Sales price		$1,140
— Production costs:		
Fabrication & assembly	$512 (estimated)	
Painting & installation	77 (estimated)	
Total	$589	
Salesman's commission (10%)	114	
Total manufacturing & selling costs		703
Excess of sales price over production & selling costs		$ 437 (estimated)

1. What would the vice president in charge of sales have to consider in his decision to approve or disapprove the sales order?
2. What function has the sales clerk performed?

e. Assume that the sales order was approved on the basis of these estimates at a sales price of $1,140, that the job order is assigned number 445, and that a cost report of the job after it is completed is as shown on page 171.

1. From what you know about the J. J. Croman Company and its activities, is it proper to call the difference between $1,140 and $703 "earnings"? Would you add other costs not shown here? Which ones and why?
2. Does the statement tell you anything about the performance of the production departments? Would you say that the fabrication and assembly department performed poorly? How would you decide?

J. J. CROMAN COMPANY

COST REPORT ON JOB 445

	Estimated	Actual
Production costs:		
Fabrication & assembly:		
Materials (sheet steel)	$278	$301
Labor:		
Cutting & welding	124	127
Assembly	98	92
Supplies	12	16
Total	$512	$536
Painting & installation:		
Labor	$ 60	$ 59
Supplies	17	21
Total	$ 77	$ 80
Salesman's commission (10%)	$114	$114
Total production & selling costs	$703	730

3. What action would you take based on the report on job 445 if you held the following positions?
   a. foreman, fabrication and assembly department
   b. foreman, painting and installation department
   c. manager, production research department
   d. vice president, sales
   e. vice president, production
   f. manager, cost accounting department
   g. president of the company

f. The organizational structure of J. J. Croman Company, the system of accounting reports, and the attitudes of top management about these accounting reports are interdependent factors. The right combination of these factors provides an effective accounting system.

1. List and discuss the factors about the J. J. Croman Company that you believe would contribute to an effective accounting system.
2. List and discuss the factors about the J. J. Croman Company that you believe would hinder an effective accounting system.
3. Accounting has been described by experts as business communication. Do you agree with this description of accounting? Why?

Chapter Five

PERFORMANCE MEASUREMENT: COST CONTROL

INTRODUCTION

Chapters 5, 6, 7, and 8 all deal with measurement of accomplishment and effort. The subject of effort (or costs) is covered more thoroughly, however, because costs are expressed in dollars, and the types of accomplishment discussed in these chapters ordinarily are not. Accountants often have to deal with costs even when accomplishment, and therefore performance, is not measurable at all. Maybe it is the accountant's preoccupation with costs—the negative side of performance—that makes some people think he is a pessimist. The truth is, most accountants are positive thinkers at heart.

COST CONTROL

Cost control is a vital function of business managers, whether the costs relate to current-period expenses or to asset acquisitions that will affect future accounting periods. But when are costs controllable?

They are controllable when managers can determine the steps and take the action necessary to keep costs down. From the point of view of the enterprise as a whole, all costs are controllable by someone at some time. Even major costs such as new factory buildings can be controlled at the time the construction or purchase is being contemplated. Not all costs, however, lend themselves to precise measurements of effort expended on a day-to-day operating basis.

To be useful in measuring performance, costs must be controllable by the person whose performance is being measured within the time period for which the measurement is made. As an example, assume that the grinding department foreman was a member of the committee that authorized the addition of a new factory wing in which the grinding department is currently located. Should the weekly performance report of the grinding department list the weekly depreciation cost on the new building as one of the foreman's controllable costs? No, because the foreman has not been able to minimize the cost during the week under consideration (even though he had a hand in the original decision).

Meaningful performance measurement on a short-term basis requires that assumptions be made about operating conditions within that time period. The usual result of these conditional assumptions is that many costs are considered noncontrollable within the time period covered by most accounting reports.

COMPARISON OF PERFORMANCE

It is not enough merely to know what performance has been during a single time period. There must be some way of finding out whether the performance achieved is good, bad, or indifferent—some balanced judgment of the accomplishment as well as the effort aspects of the performance determination. The relative merits of a given period's performance can be judged only by applying some yardstick of comparison.

Several yardsticks might be used to compare current period performance. One would simply be the past performance of the same organizational unit. For example, the weekly performance report of the grinding department at plant 1 of Acme Auto Parts might show that 150,000 units of item 37-tu were produced at a cost of $17,000, or $.113 per unit. The previous week 100,000 units were handled at a cost of $12,000, or $.120 per unit. What information about departmental performance is provided by this type of comparison?

It appears that the grinding department operated more efficiently in the second week than it did in the first week ($.113 per unit versus $.120). But how can we be sure that this performance is good? It may be that performance in the second week was simply less bad than it was a week earlier. Perhaps good performance should result in unit costs of less than $.10. Furthermore, there is nothing in this report that provides information about the reasons for the different performance in the two periods. A simple time-period comparison may be useful to indicate trends in performance, but it fails to provide adequate indication of the absolute merits of the performance; it fails, also, to explain *why* the performance is better or worse than it should be.

In addition to the above arguments, there may be a practical problem involved in interperiod comparisons of performance: accomplishment may not be comparable in the different periods. In the above example, the grinding department had similar accomplishments (units of item 37-tu) in both weeks. Suppose, however, that in the second week the department worked on a different product or on several different products. How could you make meaningful comparisons between periods in that case? Not very easily!

The performance of two similar departments for the same week might be compared a second way: Suppose that while plant 1's grinding department's performance is $.113 per unit ($17,000 in costs ÷ 150,000 units), that of a similar department in plant 3 is $.19 per unit ($5,700 in costs ÷ 30,000 units). This is an indication of relative efficiency. It appears that the grinding department at plant 1 is performing better than the one at plant 3. But is it true? Are the two departments operating in similar environments? If not, the comparison is not valid and may be wholly unfair to the grinding department foreman in plant 3.

There are many reasons why the comparison of the per-unit production costs of grinding departments in different plants might not be a valid measure of the relative performance of the two departments. Wage rates, material costs, and many other costs not controllable by the department foreman may differ from one location to the other. The experience of the work force, the age of the machines, and working conditions in the two plants may be dissimilar and may have a pronounced effect on operating costs per unit. Finally, you will recall that plant 1 is much larger than plant 3. This may make the former more economical to operate.

Both interperiod and interunit comparisons of performance are therefore limited in their usefulness. How, then, can performance be consistently evaluated to determine whether it is good or bad?

STANDARDS FOR PERFORMANCE

The merits of the performance of an organizational unit during a period of time can be ascertained very well by comparison with a predetermined standard of performance. Standards are scientifically determined estimates of what performance *should be* under stated operating conditions. Standards can be determined for any number of different situations brought about by varying conditions, such as different products, varying order sizes, and nonuniform capabilities of men and machines. Standards can be determined for both the accomplishment and effort aspects of performance. In each case, the purpose of the standard is to provide a basis for comparison of actual performance with standard performance in a given environment.

An *ideal standard*, sometimes called a "perfection standard," is one that is based on the best possible operating conditions, whether these conditions are feasible in a particular situation or not. Such a standard assumes the best possible equipment, workers who never make mistakes, and ideal working conditions.

An *attainable standard* is based on existing operating conditions that cannot be changed quickly. It takes into consideration the facts that the equipment may not be perfect, that even the best worker will make mistakes, that a normal amount of spoilage will occur, etc. It is a standard that can be attained if the operation is performed as well as could be expected under existing circumstances.

The basic concepts employed in accounting standards for performance measurement are the same under all conditions, although the actual techniques may vary slightly. Basically the accounting use of standards involves four steps:

1. determination of the standard of performance
2. measurement of actual performance
3. comparison of actual and standard performances to ascertain plus or minus variances from standard
4. explanation for the variances

In addition to the accounting procedures listed above, management should take corrective action in cases in which the variances indicate poor performance or take advantage of reasons discovered for better-than-standard performance.

Standards and Motivation

In setting standards and standard costs, it must not be forgotten that the basic purpose of the standards is to motivate people to act in the best interests of the firm as a whole, that is, to further its long-run profit objective.

Thus management and the accounting staff are faced with a large and continuous educational problem. Operating personnel must be convinced that standards are useful and necessary guides for the profitable operation of the firm. The use of standards as measures of performance has often created suspicion and resistance among the people they govern. Frequently this adverse attitude has been adopted by labor unions, with the result that standards and standard costs have become a factor in collective bargaining.

One important way of achieving a positive employee attitude toward the use of standards is to require employee participation in standard setting. In cases in which past experience plays an important part in standard setting, the employee or department head whose performance is being measured can contribute greatly to setting realistic standards. In other cases in which more scientific methods are used, the employee must at least be permitted to review the standards and to suggest improvements. In any case, standard costs should have the prior approval of the person whose performance is being measured if the standards are to be effective in controlling costs. An employee will strive to achieve a given standard of performance if he agrees that the standard is fair; if he does not agree or if the standard has been set without his participation and approval, he will resent its use and find ways to "beat the system."

Setting Standards

Standards are well-thought-out estimates made by people who have special knowledge and skills and who are completely familiar with the potential of the organizational unit whose performance is to be measured.

The people who participate in setting standards include the accountants who lend advice about past experience, especially costs. Engineers will be able to predict what the amount of materials should be. Purchasing agents can supply expected price quotations. Operating personnel, including the foreman and labor force, will contribute estimates of the labor time necessary to perform a given task. Time-study engineers will verify these labor-time estimates. In short, standards of performance are set by pooling the estimates of many experts. Past experience will be employed as an indicator whenever possible, but standards are often set without reliance on past performance.

As an example of the type of research that should go into setting standards, take the case of the grinding wheel costs in the grinding department. Management gives this department a grinding operation on a new product, item 37-tu, and sets a standard grinding wheel cost per unit. The product research department will supply metallurgical characteristics of the item to the production engineer. He and his staff will determine the characteristics of the abrasive needed to meet design specifications. An examination of suppliers' catalogs by the purchasing manager might indicate that there are several grinding wheels on the market. Each has slightly different characteristics and prices, and each could do the job satisfactorily. A sample quantity of each might be purchased, and trial runs could be made by the production engineer and the department foreman. The trial runs might indicate that the wheel best suited for the job will cost $5.10 and be able to grind 100 units of item 37-tu before needing replacement.

During the trial runs the time-study engineers would also have observed the operations with stopwatches and motion diagrams in hand and will recommend time standards for the grinding operation as well as for setting up the grinding wheels. These recommendations will be matched with projected wage rates determined by the personnel department to set standard labor costs per unit of item 37-tu.

Standards can be set to emphasize different aspects of performance. In the grinding department there can be standards of quality, standards of quantity, and standards of costs. They can refer to time periods or to individual units of production. For example, you could say that the standard of quality for item 37-tu is plus or minus .003 inches from the designed dimensions. Or you might say that the standard hours of servicing of grinding machines by the maintenance department is twenty hours per month. Or that 150,000 units is the standard amount of item 37-tu that should be produced during a normal week.

Quite often the accountant, in response to management desire, is concerned with the *standard cost* of a unit of product. In setting unit-cost standards, costs such as raw materials, labor effort, and other inputs are estimated for all stages of production and accumulated until the total standard cost of the completed product is determined.

We need not list the many different ways in which standards are employed throughout the business world. It is sufficient to remember that standards of performance can be determined for any type of performance in almost any kind of activity. All that is necessary is a concerted effort on the part of knowledgeable men to estimate what performance should be. Different standards should be set for the differing conditions that may arise.

Keeping Standard Costs up to Date

Not much can be said about this problem here, except to point out that obsolete standard costs constitute the most serious obstacle to the profitable use of standard costs for performance measurement and cost controls. Establishing realistic standards is a very expensive process, and there is a natural tendency to continue to use them long after they become outdated. The conditions on which the standard costs are based are bound to change, and as they change, the standard costs must change if they are to be used effectively. This fact has influenced some managements to decide not to use standards, and if conditions are changing so rapidly that standards cannot be used for a reasonably long period, this decision is probably wise. Obsolete standards can be worse than no standards at all.

While the use of standards for performance evaluation requires that standards be set, the process does not end here. Actual performance must be measured on a comparable basis, and the difference between actual and standard performance must be measured and acted upon.

Comparison of actual performance with standard performance is illustrated in Exhibit 5–1, a standard-performance report for the grinding department at plant 1 of Acme Auto Parts for the week ending November 9. These are the assumptions that underlie the standards indicated:

1. The department will perform one grinding operation on only one piece of product, item 37-tu.

2. The standard quota of 150,000 units is designed to be produced without any overtime work.

3. Standards for controllable costs can be expressed in per-unit terms as well as in total amounts.

How Are Standards Derived?

We shall not discuss the process of accumulating production cost figures in the journals and ledgers of the Acme Auto Parts Company, but it may be helpful if we outline the sources of the information reported in Exhibit 5–1.

EXHIBIT 5 - 1

ACME AUTO PARTS COMPANY, PLANT 1 GRINDING DEPARTMENT

STANDARD PERFORMANCE REPORT

For Week Ended November 9

	Actual		Standard		Total Variance
	Total	*Unit*	*Total*	*Unit*	*(U = unfavorable)* *(F = favorable)*
Accomplishment:					
Output, item 37-tu	150,000		150,000		0
Effort:					
Controllable costs:					
Labor[a]	$ 2,550	$.0170	$ 2,040	$.0136	$ 510 U
Overtime premium[b]	255	.0017	0	0	255 U
Material spoiled	300	.0020	150	.0010	150 U
Grinding wheels[c]	7,500	.0500	7,650	.0510	150 F
Repairs (special)	450	.0030	150	.0010	300 U
Electric power	750	.0050	600	.0040	150 U
Lubricating oil	75	.0005	75	.0005	0
Total	$11,880	$.079	$10,665	$.071	$1,215 U
Noncontrollable costs:					
Depreciation—machine	$ 2,400		$ 2,400		$ 0
Depreciation—plant	1,000		1,000		0
Insurance	50		50		0
Foreman's salary	165		165		0
Maintenance labor	200		300		100 F
Other	1,305		1,400		95 F
Total	$ 5,120	$.034	$ 5,315	$.036	$ 195 F
Total expenses	$17,000	$.113	$15,980	$.107	$1,020 U

[a] Standard labor: seventeen men at $3 per hour for forty hours per week.
[b] Overtime premium: one-half the normal rate per hour (in addition to normal wages).
[c] Standard grinding wheels: $5.10 each at a rate of 100 units of item 37-tu per wheel.

1. Standard production of 150,000 units was obtained from an order from the production manager's office specifying the number of units to be produced each week. The actual production count of 150,000 units was obtained from daily production reports prepared by workmen and verified by physical "count"— finished units are placed in bins of about 500 items each and are "counted" by weighing the bins.

2. The controllable cost standards were obtained from a standard cost sheet for item 37-tu prepared in the controller's office. This sheet lists the following standard costs per unit:

Labor	$.0136
Material spoilage	.0010
Grinding wheels	.0510
Repairs	.0010
Electric power	.0040
Lubricating oil	.0005
Total controllable cost per unit	$.0711

The other cost items were determined in a manner similar to that for the grinding wheels described earlier, except that items such as material spoilage, repairs, and lubricating oil are less susceptible to scientific analysis, and often are determined mainly on the basis of past experience under actual production conditions.

3. The noncontrollable costs are so labeled because they are allocated to the grinding department in a departmental budget. These costs do not change proportionally as production changes, and should not be expressed in per-unit terms. They are not considered within the responsibility of the foreman; they are included in the report simply to keep him and his superiors informed on the total costs of operating the grinding department. Exhibit 5–1 is not typical in this respect, because rarely are noncontrollable costs reported for periods as short as one week. A month is the shortest period commonly used for calculating such items as depreciation and insurance.

4. Actual costs for the grinding department for the week ended November 9 are collected and measured in the controller's department. Several different sources of information must be used:

a. The actual labor hours, overtime hours, and maintenance labor hours are obtained from daily time cards prepared by the workers. Hourly wage rates and the foreman's salary are provided by the payroll department.

b. Spoiled units are discarded into a special bin by an automatic measuring device and counted at the end of each day.

c. Grinding wheels and lubricating oil used are determined as a result of the physical count of grinding wheels and lubricating oil remaining on hand at the end of the week.

d. Special repair and electric power costs are determined by the controller's department in the process of measuring *interdepartmental charges*, i.e., services provided (and costs incurred) by the maintenance department and the power plant, respectively, which are the responsibility of the grinding department.

e. Depreciation, insurance, and other costs are computed in the controller's department and are simply annual calculations of these items reduced to a weekly basis. These items will regularly show no variance in the report except for unexpected changes made in them during the year which were not contemplated when the budget was prepared.

Using the Report

The key figures in Exhibit 5–1 are those found in the far right-hand column, because *variances* represent differences between actual and standard effort. Taking the items as they appear, we see that actual output (accomplishment) was exactly as estimated. The quota was met but apparently at a greater effort than called for by the standard because total actual costs are greater than standard. The overall performance of the department is therefore below standard.

Examination of the individual cost items shows that both normal labor and the overtime premium exceeded the standard set for the 150,000-unit level of output. The department incurred an additional 170 hours of work time, which resulted in an extra labor cost of $510 ($3 per hour times 170 hours) and an overtime premium cost of $255 ($1.50 per hour times 170 hours). Why was it necessary to incur $765 in additional labor cost? Apparently the foreman was not able to control the efficiency of the machinists. Perhaps he allowed too many (or too long) coffee breaks. Or maybe everybody was listening to an astronaut's exploit on the radio instead of concentrating on work. There is a possible tie-in between the need to work overtime and the $300 greater-than-standard special repair costs. It may be that the repair costs were encountered because of machine failure, which, if prolonged, could have called for overtime hours in order to make up for the machine time lost because of the breakdown. In any event, the quota could not be met during normal working hours, and the foreman made the decision to work his crew overtime rather than to produce less than his quota of accomplishment.

The unfavorable spoilage variance of $150 may also be the result of the machine breakdown or inattentive work by the machinists. *Spoilage* is the cost of items 37-tu ruined during processing. The responsibility for this factor rests with the foreman, however, and thus is properly included in those costs over which he has control. He maintains authority to direct his labor force and schedule workloads per machine; he can request better servicing of machines from the maintenance department if he deems it necessary.

The use of more power than standard resulted in the unfavorable power variance of $150. The necessity to work overtime is the most likely cause of this variance, although it might also be owing to inefficient assignment of the workload among the fifteen grinding machines if the machines use differing amounts of power to accomplish the same operation. The foreman would have to continually reschedule the workload in an attempt to minimize his power costs.

Exhibit 5–1 also indicates variances in the noncontrollable costs of routine maintenance and the item listed as "other." These items are included for informational purposes only and should not be considered in judging the performance of the grinding department. Is there any possible tie-in between the favorable variance for noncontrollable routine maintenance costs and the unfavorable variance for "repairs (special)"? If so, of what significance is it in judging the grinding department foreman?

Variance: Quantity and Price

The favorable variance of $150 in grinding wheel expense raises another point. A variance is usually caused by either or both of two factors: the difference between actual and standard quantity, and/or the difference between actual and standard unit price. The variance report merely indicates that total cost was less than standard but does not indicate whether this was because fewer wheels were used, because the cost per wheel was less than expected, or both. Let's examine the possibilities. The total standard and the total actual costs of any item represent the number of units of the item used, expressed in dollars per unit. The total standard grinding wheel cost for the week was $7,650, whereas the total actual cost was only $7,500. Exhibit 5–1 indicates that the total standard cost was based on a predicted use of grinding wheels at a unit cost of $5.10 each and at a rate of 100 units of item 37-tu per wheel. Either the actual cost per wheel was less than the standard cost per wheel, or the actual average production per wheel was more than the 100 units of item 37-tu per wheel specified by the standard, or both.

The general rule used by accountants to separate price and quantity elements in any variance is

Quantity variance = (Actual quantity − Standard quantity) × Standard prices
Price variance = (Actual price − Standard price) × Actual quantity

Adding the two variances, we get:

Total variance = Quantity variance + Price variance
= (Actual quantity × Actual price)
(Standard quantity × Standard price)

This is not the only approach to this problem, but it is conventional and practical. We suggest that you learn to use this method regularly to avoid confusion and promote consistency. Note also that the formulas are arbitrarily stated in such a way that unfavorable variances are positive and favorable variances negative. We hope you will prove to yourself that the formula for the total variance actually is the sum of the other two.

Case 1. Consider the actual grinding wheel cost item in Exhibit 5–1 and assume that 1,500 wheels were used during the week. The average actual output would therefore equal the standard output of 100 units per wheel, and the average actual cost per wheel would be $5. Applying the formulas, we would get:

Quantity variance = (1,500 − 1,500) × $5.10 = 0
Price variance = ($5.00 − $5.10) × 1,500 = −$150 F
Total variance = −$150 F

Case 2. Still using the information in Exhibit 5–1, assume instead that the $7,500 actual expense consisted of 1,471 wheels at $5.10 per wheel.

$$\text{Quantity variance} = (1{,}471 - 1{,}500) \times \$5.10 = -\$150 \text{ F}$$
$$\text{Price variance} = (\$5.10 - \$5.10) \times 1{,}471 = \underline{ 0}$$
$$\text{Total variance} = \underline{-\$150 \text{ F}}^\circ$$

Case 3. Assume that the standard grinding wheel cost is $7,650, as in Exhibit 5–1, but that the actual cost is $7,750, made up of 1,550 wheels used, at an average cost of $5 per wheel.

$$\text{Quantity variance} = (1{,}550 - 1{,}500) \times \$5.10 = \$255 \text{ U}$$
$$\text{Price variance} = (\$5.00 - \$5.10) \times 1{,}550 = -\$155 \text{ F}$$
$$\text{Total variance} = \underline{\$100 \text{ U}}$$

In this case the variances would be in opposite directions. The $.10 savings in price per wheel would not be enough to offset the excess usage of fifty wheels.

Case 4. Using the same standard cost and an actual cost of $8,109 (1,530 wheels at $5.30), we have:

$$\text{Quantity variance} = (1{,}530 - 1{,}500) \times \$5.10 = \$153 \text{ U}$$
$$\text{Price variance} = (\$5.30 - 5.10) \times 1{,}530 = \$306 \text{ U}$$
$$\text{Total variance} = \underline{\$459 \text{ U}}$$

Case 5. If the actual cost were $7,203, consisting of 1,470 wheels at $4.90 per wheel, the variances would be

$$\text{Quantity variance} = (1{,}470 - 1{,}500) \times \$5.10 = -\$153 \text{ F}$$
$$\text{Price variance} = (\$4.90 - \$5.10) \times 1{,}470 = -\$294 \text{ F}$$
$$\text{Total variance} = \underline{-\$447 \text{ F}}$$

It is evident that either or both variances can be favorable, unfavorable, or zero in any given case.

Controllable Versus Noncontrollable Variances

The main purpose in separating a total variance into its price and quantity elements is to make the distinction between controllable and noncontrollable variances. The actual number of grinding wheels used is probably within the control of the foreman and should enter into the appraisal of his performance for the period. It is also likely that the actual price paid for grinding wheels, however, is probably not within the foreman's control and should be reported in the performance report of the purchasing function instead. If the foreman is responsible only for the quantities used, it could be forcefully argued that the performance report of the grinding department foreman should be stated entirely

---

° This solution has been rounded.

in terms of standard-unit prices of all items; the only variances reported would then be quantity variances.

It may be, however, that the foreman is responsible to some degree for unit prices. In the case reported in Exhibit 5–1, the foreman might have intentionally experimented with a grinding wheel of slightly lower quality costing $5.00 per wheel and found it to work as well as the $5.10 wheel called for by the standard. The foreman might have the authority to substitute labor and materials of higher or lower quality (and unit prices) than standard; if so, the effect on quantity variance and output should be reported. Since price and quantity variances in these cases are likely to be in opposite directions, full disclosure and explanation is not possible unless price and quantity variances are shown separately.

Exhibit 5–2 extends the illustration in Exhibit 5–1 to show this separation.

E X H I B I T 5 - 2

ACME AUTO PARTS COMPANY, PLANT 1 GRINDING DEPARTMENT
PRICE AND QUANTITY VARIANCE ON CONTROLLABLE COSTS
For Week Ended November 9

	Total variance	Price variance	Quantity variance
Labor	$ 510 U	$ 0	$ 510 U
Overtime labor	255 U	0	255 U
Material spoiled	150 U	0	150 U
Grinding wheels	150 F	150 F	0
Machine repairs (special)	300 U	85 U	215 U
Electric power	150 U	0	150 U
Lubricating oil	0	0	0
	$1,215U	$ 65 F	$1,280U

Assuming the foreman is responsible only for quantities, his overall performance appears slightly poorer than indicated in Exhibit 5–1.

Another interesting point is the fact that the special repairs cost consists of both price and quantity amounts. The grinding department foreman is responsible for the quantity variance of $215 because his overtime use of the machines required extra effort on the part of the maintenance crew. The price variance of $85 results from having to call in an outside repair specialist at an hourly rate above that paid the Acme Company's maintenance personnel. Do you think this extra hourly rate should be considered a price variance? Who should be held responsible for this variance? The foreman of the grinding department contends that it is the maintenance manager's responsibility to keep his men trained so that outside experts need not be employed. How should controversies of this kind be resolved?

MANAGEMENT BY EXCEPTION

Management's use of standards for evaluating periodic performance makes possible the practice of *management by exception*. Management need not concern itself about actual performance that is at or near standard. If, however, significant variances from standard appear in the periodic performance reports, management devotes time to analyzing these variances and taking proper action. Thus, managerial effort is expended only when exceptional items appear on the standard-performance reports.

Management by exception is a natural and highly important result of setting standards to measure performance. The time of managers at all levels of management is a highly valuable commodity, and the firm cannot afford to have substantial portions of it spent on unnecessary checking of performance and investigation. Standard costs, when properly established, accounted for, and interpreted, provide an automatic means of checking performance and of highlighting trouble spots on which management can concentrate.

How Big Is an "Exception"?

This is a most important question to managers who have the responsibility for performance measurement and cost control. The principle of management by exception makes it mandatory that the manager ignore the small variances, but the definition of "small" is usually left to the manager's judgment and experience. This really means that a manager is likely to act inconsistently from one time to another, depending perhaps on how busy he is with other things. It also means that no two managers are likely to agree on which variances ought to be investigated in the borderline cases.

Statistics have given us some help in solving this problem. It is possible to establish upper and lower *control limits* that permit the manager, with a predetermined level of confidence, to investigate only those variances attributable to other than random causes. If the variance falls outside the control limits, it is presumed to have been caused by something that should be investigated. If it falls within the control limits, it is to be ignored. These techniques have been used in statistical quality control for years, but most of the application to standard-cost variances is still in the experimental stage.

Since a major purpose of standard costs is to keep costs minimal for a given accomplishment, there may be a natural tendency to investigate the unfavorable variances more carefully than the favorable ones. There are not many defensible reasons for this. Favorable variances indicate that performance is exceptionally good and should be rewarded, that the standard is obsolete, or that some other cause that definitely should be ascertained is involved.

Electronic Data Processing and Standard Costs

Electronic computers have made management by exception more efficient by helping to solve two closely related performance-reporting problems that have always given accountants trouble:

1. Reports sometimes come too late to be acted upon. Management action involves investigation into the real causes of the variance to determine whether it should be corrected, and if so, how. If the performance report reaches management too long after the end of the period covered by the report, it is useless. Everyone is far too busy to spend much time checking up on last month, and most people in the firm have forgotten what happened. If action is to be taken to correct a variance, it must be done quickly while the mistake is fresh in everyone's mind.

2. Reports of performance often cover long periods. Even the weekly report in Exhibit 5–1 may cover too long a period. It is useful to know the total units produced and the variances in cost, but how much more useful it would be to know, for example, the variances on individual units, the variances occurring at one time of day as compared with another, or those of one shift compared with another. How can the performance of fifteen machine operators be compared? With one weekly report covering the entire department, none of these things can be done. With manual or even punched-card accounting systems, it may not be economical to provide reports detailed enough to answer these questions. Even weekly reports may contain too many variables averaged together.

With electronic data-processing equipment, great strides have been made toward the solutions to these and other problems. It is now possible and economically feasible to collect and report data much more frequently and in much greater detail than ever before. Accountants, having been partially relieved of the drudgery of the data-collection process, can now devote their efforts to decisions concerning such things as the selection of data to be reported, the persons to be reported to, and time periods to be covered. These are the problems that accountants are trained to solve, and the advent of the large computer makes the work of the accountant far more useful to management than ever before.

CONTROL AND DECISION MAKING

The types of reports we have discussed so far reflect the results of operations. Regardless of the period covered—a day, a week, or a month—they provide the manager only with a report of errors (variances) already made. They do not give him a means of preventing these variances before they occur. For example, how does the foreman of the grinding department prevent his employees from using too much material?

The foreman can maintain some control through a visual inspection of operations. If he notices an unusual number of spoiled units accumulating, he can investigate the cause and immediately take corrective action. However, he can maintain more timely control over material use with a *standard bill of materials* such as the following standard bill for product 79-C:

STANDARD BILL OF MATERIAL
Item 79-C

Description	Part Number	Quantity Required
16 gauge steel	496	3′ × 6′ sheet

The standard bill is used by the stockroom clerk in releasing items from the stockroom to the operator. If the operator is unable to complete the job with the standard materials allowed, he is required to get the foreman's approval before requesting additional materials from the stockroom clerk. This requirement brings the exception to the attention of the foreman immediately.

Even reports as simple as this (other examples are employees' time cards or daily schedules of machine operations) are included in the accounting system and are extremely important in assisting managers at the lower levels in making day-to-day control decisions. In fact, some would argue that accounting makes its greatest contribution in those operational areas where the manager in question must determine for himself the best way of achieving a given objective within known operating conditions. The grinding department foreman operates within the given conditions of fifteen machines and seventeen men. He is unable to control either the wage rates of the men or the acquisition cost of the machines or the factory building. His accomplishment depends on the efficiency with which he operates within his given environment. He has the authority to shift men from machine to machine, to run certain combinations of machines together, to use different grades of grinding wheels, and to schedule the work load per machine. His efficiency in making these choices directly influences the accomplishment of the department, the amount of cost incurred, and thus his performance as shown in accounting reports.

The manager's knowledge that his operations are going to be measured and reported in itself facilitates cost control, but sometimes gives rise to a suspicious and hostile attitude toward the performance-reporting system. This is the result of poor system design. Educational programs often change such attitudes dramatically, by showing the manager how the system operates for his personal benefit, and by pointing out that it is not a way of "pinning the blame" on him for unfavorable variances after they have occurred. It is true that a good performance reporting system pushes the responsibility for cost control down to the lowest level of supervision, but this is where it belongs. It is the manager at the lowest level who makes the ultimate control decisions. Nevertheless, if he is to make these decisions well, he must understand the importance of this function to the company as a whole. In a good reporting system, performance reports are used to broaden the managers' point of view to encompass all departments. This may be done at periodic meetings of managerial staff in which examples from their performance reports are used to illustrate how their operations produced a favorable or unfavorable impact on the firm's overall objectives.

SUMMARY

Cost control is a vital function of business management. All costs are controllable by someone at some time, but not all costs are controllable at all times. Typical uncontrollable costs are those of major facilities and costs that are determined outside the enterprise, such as wages and purchased materials. Accounting reports based on short periods of time must embody certain assumptions about the controllable nature of the costs that enter the performance-measurement process.

Performance must not only be measured but also compared with something if managers are to be able to evaluate the merits of the performance. Evaluation flowing from interperiod or interunit comparisons of performance is subject to serious criticisms. Comparison of actual performance with a scientifically determined standard of performance provides a meaningful and useful method of evaluation. Standards can be determined for both the accomplishment and the expense aspects of performance.

The differences between standard and actual performances are expressed as variations from standard. Total variances can be subdivided into price and quantity variances, which are useful in isolating those aspects of performance over which the organizational unit being measured has authority and control.

The use of standards establishes management by exception, which, when properly employed, allows managers to devote more time to duties other than day-to-day performance measurement. Statistical analysis and electronic data-processing systems increase the timeliness and significance of accounting reports in performance measurement.

Questions for Review

5-1. Under what circumstances are costs controllable by a manager?

5-2. List and compare several yardsticks that can be used to evaluate current period performance.

5-3. Define the standards employed in accounting for performance measurement.

5-4. What is the difference between "ideal" and "attainable" standards?

5-5. What steps are involved in the use of accounting standards?

5-6. Why are variances separated into price and usage?

5-7. What is management by exception?

5-8. List and discuss the management decisions to which a performance reporting system is relevant.

Problems for Analysis

5-9. For each of the following cost items, indicate (a) a set of circumstances that would make the item the responsibility of the foreman of the department to which it is charged, and (b) a set of circumstances that would make the item the responsibility of someone other than the foreman.

1. wage rate of the welding department employees for February
2. cost of materials purchased in January
3. welding supplies used in February
4. portion of real estate taxes allocated to the welding department for February
5. portion of personal property taxes charged to the welding department for February
6. raw materials used by the welding department for February
7. cost of electricity to operate equipment for February
8. salary of the welding department foreman for February
9. labor hours of welding department employees for February

5-10. The Hula-Hoop Company has been operating for the past three years. Its sales volume has increased 400 per cent during this period; earnings, however, have not been satisfactory. Consequently, management has decided to use accounting standards for the performance measurement of the production foremen. The controller and other company officers have determined that the implementation of accounting standards will require the following:

1. determination of the standard of performance
2. measurement of actual performance
3. comparison of actual and standard performances to ascertain variances from standard
4. explanation of the reasons for the variance
5. evaluation of the reasons for below-standard performance
6. implementation of the reasons for better-than-standard performance

Advise the officers of the Hula-Hoop Company about the functions that (a) accountants, (b) engineers, and (c) other management personnel should each perform in implementing the six requirements outlined above.

5-11. Typical variances from standard costs are those of labor prices, labor usage, material prices, and material usage. Assume that the purchasing and personnel departments are responsible for the acquisition of materials and employees. Which, if any, of the variances listed above should be the responsibility of the purchasing agent? Which of the personnel manager? Which of the department foremen? Give reasons to support your answer. Can you think of a situation where the variances listed above might be the responsibility of someone else? Explain.

5-12. The Plastic Container Corporation established a system of standard costs one year ago. The primary purpose of this system was to evaluate the performance of the production foremen. The foremen were fairly well satisfied with the use of the system for the evaluation of their performance for the first few months. However, a few complaints have been received from foremen during the past several months that "the standards are obsolete." Their complaints have often been justified, as operating conditions were changed subsequent to the establishment of the standards. Consequently, management is attempting to revise the standards. Comment on the following considerations:

    a. Should the policy include a provision for the periodic revision of all the standards? Explain.

    b. Should the policy include a provision for the review of individual standards as changes in operating conditions occur? Explain.

    c. Who should initiate requests for a review of standards? Who should establish or revise standards? Explain.

5-13. Explain the advantages of comparing actual costs with standard costs in measuring the performance of a department, as contrasted with comparing actual costs with

    a. actual costs of a prior period for the same department.

    b. actual costs of the same department in another plant.

5-14. Performance reports for the production departments of the Broad Company report actual monthly expenses compared with the actual expenses of the previous month. "We don't believe in standards," the plant manager says. "Each month we simply try to do a little better than we did the month before."

    a. What is your opinion of the plant manager's cost-control policy? Give reasons for your answer.

    b. What probable reaction do the workmen have to this policy?

5-15. Standard labor cost in the assembly department of a firm was determined by studying a skilled assembly worker under normal operating conditions. He averaged sixty completed units per hour in an eight-hour working day. Standard wage rates are $3.00 per hour.

    Assembly operations are performed by twenty assembly workers whose wage rates vary from $2.50 to $3.50 per hour. Actual labor costs are compiled monthly and divided by monthly production totals to arrive at actual labor cost per completed unit. As long as the actual labor cost does not vary more than plus or minus 10 per cent from the standard cost, no investigation is made.

a. What is the standard labor cost per unit? By how much money is the actual labor cost permitted to vary from the standard before the cause of the variance is determined?

b. Comment on and suggest possible improvements in the

    1. method of determining the standard cost.

    2. method of accumulating, reporting, and investigating actual labor costs.

5-16. Under "ideal" conditions, ten pounds of raw material X and fifty gallons of raw material Y are required to make one batch of 1,000 units of finished goods Z. X and Y are mixed, heated, cooled, dried, cut into units, and packaged into boxes of 100 units.

Because of poor working conditions (inadequate space) that will be eliminated only by a new building, approximately 9 per cent of the finished product is spoiled in the packaging operation. (That is, 110 units are required for one box of 100 good units ready for shipment.)

The current purchase price of X is $2.00 per pound. The purchase price of Y is $5.00 per fifty-gallon drum ($.10 per gallon) when purchased in quantities of five drums or less, but if six drums or more are purchased at a time, the price is $4.50 per fifty-gallon drum (or $.09 per gallon). Because of inadequate storage space, the company must buy only one or two drums at a time, and thus pays the higher price.

a. Compute the ideal standard material cost per packaged unit.

b. Compute the attainable standard material cost per packaged unit.

c. Assume that the ideal standard is used with the existing operating conditions, and that during January the company produces at the attainable level. Analyze the variance between standard cost and actual cost.

5-17. In each of the four cases below, compute the portion of the total variance attributable to labor usage and the portion attributable to wage rates.

	Standard			*Actual*			
	Minutes per unit	*Wage rate per minute*	*Unit cost*	*Minutes per unit*	*Wage rate per minute*	*Unit cost*	*Variance per unit*
Case I	20	$.06	$1.20	22	$.07	$1.54	$.34 U
Case II	25	.04	1.00	22	.05	1.10	.10 U
Case III	5	.10	.50	4	.09	.36	.14 F
Case IV	12	.08	.96	13	.07	.91	.05 F

5-18. Each of the following independent situations pertains to a standard cost system for direct material and direct labor:

a. The material price variance is $900 (favorable); the quantity used is 9,000 pounds; and the standard price per pound is $1.00.

Compute the actual price per pound.

b. The labor price (rate) variance is $3,000 (unfavorable); the standard price per hour is $4.00; and the actual price per hour is $4.20.

Compute the quantity of labor used.

c. The standard cost for a transistor is $2.75. The standard quantity of usage per man per day is 180 transistors. The usage variance is $41.25 (unfavorable).

Compute the actual quantity produced.

d. The actual quantity of apple cider produced by an apple press in one day is 1,200 gallons. The standard per day is 1,230 gallons. The variance is $12.90 (unfavorable).

Compute the standard price of the cider.

5-19. The following standard costs per unit of production have been established for direct materials and direct labor:

      Materials: 5 pounds at $2.00 per pound.

      Labor: 10 hours at $4.00 per hour.

Actual data for July are as follows:

      Material purchased and used: 45,200 pounds at $2.02 per pound.

      Labor used: 89,600 hours at $3.95 per hour.

      Actual production: 9,000 units.

Compute the price and usage variances for materials and labor.

5-20. During the month of March, the grinding department foreman decided to experiment with a higher-quality grinding wheel costing $6.50, advertised as longer lasting than the standard wheel costing $5.10. Standards based on the cheaper wheel were not changed. The department produced 125,000 units in March, using 1,050 of the higher-quality wheels compared with 1,250 wheels called for by the standard.

a. Show how this information would appear on the March performance report of the grinding department. Which variances are controllable by the foreman?

b. Was the experiment a success? Why?

5-21. The following information is available for comparable production departments in the five plants of a large manufacturing company:

Department	Material and Labor Costs Standard	Material and Labor Costs Actual	Total Variance	Material Variances Price	Material Variances Usage	Labor Variances Price	Labor Variances Usage
1	$140,000	$142,000	$ 2,000 U	$ 4,500 U	$1,000 F	$2,500 U	$4,000 F
2	75,000	94,000	19,000 U	7,000 U	4,000 U	9,000 U	1,000 F
3	185,000	184,000	1,000 F	6,000 F	4,000 U	1,000 U	0
4	94,000	91,000	3,000 F	1,000 U	2,000 U	5,000 F	1,000 F
5	105,000	111,000	6,000 U	12,000 U	4,000 F	2,000 U	4,000 F

a. Compare the material and labor costs of the five processing departments shown above. Rank the performances of the departmental foremen from best to worst (in dollar amounts). Discuss the reasons for your answer and the assumptions on which it is based.

b. Rank the performance (using percentages) of the departmental foremen from best to worst. Which basis of ranking—dollar amounts or percentages—do you prefer? (Use percentage of total standard cost.)

5-22. The Tasti-Delite Corporation, composed of fifteen restaurants within a twenty-mile radius of a large metropolitan city, enjoys a high volume of sales. The operations of all fifteen restaurants are standardized. The purchasing and accounting activities are centralized in the home office. There are twenty accounting clerks who process invoices, payments to suppliers, and cash receipts. They also maintain inventory records and separate accounts for each restaurant operation, including revenue from food, sundries, and the juke box. The controller and other company officers are considering the installation of some machine accounting system such as a bookkeeping machine, a punched-card system, or electronic data-processing equipment.

a. What are the advantages and disadvantages of machine accounting versus manual accounting?

b. What advantages and disadvantages do you see to a machine accounting system from the standpoint of:

    1. the controller (chief accounting officer)
    2. the treasurer
    3. the vice president in charge of marketing activities
    4. the vice president in charge of purchasing and inventory control
    5. the company president

c. The statement is frequently made that accounting machines are bad for accountants because they eliminate the need for them. The Tasti-Delite Corporation can probably eliminate at least fifteen accounting clerks by the installation of a completely automated data-processing system. Do you feel that machine accounting is advantageous or disadvantageous to the accounting profession? Give reasons to support your conclusion.

5-23. Consider the following direct material and direct labor costs:

	Direct Materials	Direct Labor
Total actual cost	$45,000	$147,000
Total standard cost	40,000	160,000
Total variance	5,000 U	13,000 F
Price variance	10,000 U	21,000 F
Quantity variance	5,000 F	8,000 U

The direct materials standard quantity per unit of output is ten pounds, and the direct labor standard quantity per unit of output is twenty hours. The actual production is 1,000 units.

Compute the following items:
a. Standard direct material cost per pound.
b. Standard direct labor rate per hour.
c. Actual quantity of material used.
d. Actual quantity of labor used.

5-24. The Apollo Company has established the following standards for direct materials and direct labor per unit of product A:

Materials: 4 pounds at $1.00
Labor: 5 hours at $4.00

Actual data for the month of October:

Material purchased and used: 42,000 pounds at $1.10
Labor used: 49,000 hours at $3.80
Actual production: 10,000 units

a. Compute the price and usage variances for direct material and direct labor.

b. Which of the four variances indicate that control action is necessary? Explain.

5-25. The Metal Fabricated Products Company manufactures metal products, including metal chairs used primarily by schools, churches, hospitals, etc.

The standard material and labor cost for a metal chair is as follows:

Material costs:	
Metal legs (4 @ $.06 each)	$ .24
Metal seat	.19
Back frame	.13
Seat frame	.12
Rubber tips (4 @ $.01 each)	.04
Nuts and bolts/set	.14
Total material costs	$ .86
Labor costs:	
5 minutes @ $2.40/hour	.20
Total material & labor costs	$1.06

Operating data for the chair assembly department for the past week:

Day shift			
Materials used:		Seat frames used	2,957
Chairs assembled	2,811	Rubber tips used	11,796
Metal legs used	11,753	Nuts and bolts used (sets)	2,895
Metal seats used	2,886	Labor used:	
Back frames used	2,873	Number of hours	228

Afternoon shift

Materials used:		Seat frames used	2,840
Chairs assembled	2,798	Rubber tips used	11,320
Metal legs used	11,246	Nuts and bolts used (sets)	2,871
Metal seats used	2,810	Labor used:	
Back frames used	2,830	Number of hours	238

Night shift

Materials used:		Seat frames used	1,616
Chairs assembled	1,524	Rubber tips used	6,210
Metal legs used	6,229	Nuts and bolts used (sets)	1,612
Metal seats used	1,596	Labor used:	
Back frames used	1,580	Number of hours	158

a. Prepare a weekly performance report for each of the three shifts. In your opinion, which foreman had the best performance? The worst performance? (Assume that the foremen have no control over labor and material prices.)

b. If you were the production superintendent, what more favorable operating alternatives for the foremen might the performance reports suggest to you?

c. The foreman for the night shift has the responsibility for the assembly and fabricating departments. Consequently, he spends half of his time in the assembly department. Do you think that the production superintendent is wise to have the night-shift foreman responsible for two departments? Discuss.

5-26.   PART I

The cutting department in the Longlife Shirt Company cuts the shirt front, back, collar, sleeves, and cuffs from yard goods. These are essentially machine operations, but feeding the machines to obtain maximum production with minimum spoilage and adjusting for size changes require considerable skill and experience.

The April material usage report for the cutting department is as follows:
Standard cost for April:
    2,181 units × 2 yards per unit   4,362 yards
    4,362 yards × $0.35 per yard $1,526.70
Actual cost for April:
    4,680 yards used (3,505 yards × $0.35; 1,175 yards × $0.50)
    $1,814.25 cost incurred

On the sixteenth working day, a higher-quality raw material costing $.50 a yard was substituted for the standard material at $.35 a yard. The price variance is entirely due to this change. Some of the operators have complained that the new material is harder to work with, and that processing is slower.

The management had made the material substitution both to reduce spoilage (the new material was less likely to tear) and to permit a $.20 increase per unit in selling price without reducing the number of units sold, so it took no action on the report. The usage variance was well within the 10 per cent limitation established by the management for finding the cause of variances. Spoiled units are thrown away, since the material is not considered worth reworking.

a. Compute the material usage and material price variances, assuming that the standard was not changed after the fifteenth working day.

b. Should the standard have been changed after the fifteenth working day?

c. The material-usage standard was established by a study of material usage reports for a considerable number of past periods and discussions with the foreman and skilled operators. The operators agreed that the standard of two yards per unit was about right. What are the disadvantages of this system for setting standards? What other factors might be considered in setting a standard?

PART II

If the plant manager had investigated the cutting department's daily material usage reports, he would have discovered the following information:

1 Working day	2 Good units produced	3 Actual yards used	4 Actual yards/units 3 ÷ 2	5 Actual cost/yard	6 Total cost (3 × 5)
1 (W)	115	242	2.1	$.35	$ 84.70
2 (Th)	119	250	2.1	.35	87.50
3 (F)	94	235	2.5	.35	82.25
4 (M)	88	255	2.9	.35	89.25
5 (T)	109	240	2.2	.35	84.00
6 (W)	110	220	2.0	.35	77.00
7 (Th)	106	201	1.9	.35	70.35
8 (F)	97	223	2.3	.35	78.05
9 (M)	92	285	3.1	.35	99.75
10 (T)	104	218	2.1	.35	76.30
11 (W)	121	230	1.9	.35	80.50
12 (Th)	111	222	2.0	.35	77.70
13 (F)	102	224	2.2	.35	78.40
14 (M)	84	218	2.6	.35	76.30
15 (T)	101	242	2.4	.35	84.70
16 (W)	113	203	1.8	.50	101.50
17 (Th)	114	194	1.7	.50	97.00
18 (F)	94	197	2.1	.50	98.50
19 (M)	92	184	2.0	.50	92.00
20 (T)	109	196	1.8	.50	98.00
21 (W)	106	201	1.9	.50	100.50
	2,181	4,680	Average 2.17	Average $.39	$1,814.25

According to the foreman, there has been considerable absenteeism of machine operators on Monday and Friday. Inexperienced operators ordinarily take their places. The machines run at normal speed on these days, but production is reduced because of a greater number of spoiled units.

a. Considering only the first fifteen working days, prepare a computation to indicate what information the daily production reports provide that was not shown in the monthly averages in Part I.

b. Try to estimate the cost of the absenteeism on Monday and Friday. In your opinion, is the material usage standard of two yards per unit too "loose" or too "tight"? Give reasons for your answer.

c. Assuming that actual material usage will continue as it did during the last six days, does it appear that the decision to use the new material was a good decision? Give your conclusions regarding spoilage, the complaint of the operators, and profitability.

d. Assuming no change in operation other than the use of the new material, prepare a computation to indicate what changes in material standards you recommend for the future.

5-27. Six months ago Henry Franke, fifty-four years old, was promoted to foreman of the finishing department of the Raleigh Furniture Manufacturing Company, and as a result, a long period of inefficient operation and incompetent supervision came to an end. The finishing department had acquired a reputation for internal dissension and high employee turnover. Often it had been a bottleneck at times when high production would have been especially profitable to the company. Under Mr. Franke's supervision, however, substantial changes were made: employee morale improved, production increased, spoilage dropped, and within six months' time the department was "beating the standard" regularly for the first time in years. When asked about his success, Mr. Franke cited his policy of strict adherence to standards. "Good realistic standards are the best tools for controlling an operation of this kind," he said. "I waste no time eliminating possible causes of unfavorable variances."

A few days ago one of the workers proposed an idea to Mr. Franke for a new type of paint-spraying machine that he saw used by a competing factory. The cost of the machine was $10,000; an additional $10,000 would have to be spent for rearrangement of the department layout and installation costs. However, the machine would last for at least ten years (disregarding obsolescence), it would do a better job than existing equipment, and there was about a 75 per cent chance that there would be direct savings of $500 a month in maintenance and labor costs. If the new machine were installed, many of the operating procedures would have to be changed, and a new set of standards developed.

Mr. Franke rejected the proposal to buy the new machine.

a. Do you agree with Mr. Franke's decision? Give reasons. What would you have done in his place?

b. What comment can you make on the organizational structure and policies of this company?

c. Did standard costs have anything to do with Mr. Franke's decision? Why?

5-28. Compare the usefulness of the ideal versus the attainable standard:
   a. in measuring performance of a department or of a worker
   b. in incentive pay plans based on standard performance
   c. as a tool in optimizing profit
   d. in measuring variances between actual cost and standard cost
   e. in their effect on worker morale

Chapter Six COST CONTROL: SPECIAL CONSIDERATIONS

INTRODUCTION

In this chapter we will explore some complications connected with performance measurement and cost control. The first section deals with problems that stem from the failure of actual accomplishment to equal standard accomplishment.

There are two major problems here. The first is measuring the effect of the department's failure to perform its assigned task. Ordinarily this is a difficult problem. If the failure amounts to an inability to meet the production quota, for instance, this failure could have far-reaching consequences. What if the grinding department in plant 1 of Acme Auto Parts Company had produced only 135,000 units instead of 150,000 units in the week ending November 9? Failure to meet the production standard could cause production stoppages in other departments, missed deadlines on contracts, or lost sales because of inventory shortages. On the other hand, the consequences could be immaterial if, for example, there were enough items on hand carried over from previous periods to make up the shortage. In any case, the effect of the failure on the appraisal of the foreman's performance must be judged in terms of the reasons for failure to meet the quota, the authority of the foreman to take unusual steps to make up shortages, the cost of such steps, and the possible consequences in other departments and the firm as a whole. Important as this appraisal is, it is necessarily highly qualitative, and measurement in dollars is rarely possible.

The other problem is that if actual accomplishment differs from standard accomplishment, the total standard costs based on planned accomplishment will

197

no longer be useful for cost control. Since the cost-control aspect of performance is the accountant's primary concern, this problem will occupy a sizable part of this chapter.

ANALYZING THE EFFECT OF VARIATIONS IN ACCOMPLISHMENT

In Exhibit 5–1 of Chapter 5, the actual accomplishment of 150,000 units of item 37-tu was identical with the standard accomplishment, or the quota, for the grinding department. All variances that resulted were due solely to the cost items that made up the effort of the department. Suppose actual accomplishment of the department was only 135,000 units instead of the standard 150,000 units, and that actual costs were $14,755 instead of the standard $15,980. How should the standard performance report reflect these variations?

Direct comparison of actual and standard costs might make all variances appear to be favorable. You might erroneously conclude that the unfavorable accomplishment was not so bad after all because it resulted in what appeared to be highly favorable cost variances. In fact, if actual accomplishment is only 90 per cent of the quota (135,000 is 90 per cent of 150,000) the actual costs *should* be lower than if the quota had been met, and should therefore be lower than the standard cost found on the standard performance report of Exhibit 5–1.

Proper analysis of actual versus standard performance requires that actual costs be compared with standard costs *for the actual level of accomplishment achieved.* There is a standard cost amount for each level of accomplishment. Only when actual costs are compared to standard costs that have been adjusted to the actual level of accomplishment can dependable variances result. Exhibit 6–1 is the standard performance report for the grinding department for the week ending November 16 when accomplishment was only 135,000 units of item 37-tu.

Exhibit 6–1 indicates a favorable total variance of only $56 and an unfavorable subtotal of $24 for the controllable costs. These figures relate an actual cost figure to a standard cost figure based on the *actual* level of operations of 135,000 units. If the standard costs had not been adjusted, there would have been a favorable variance of $1,225 ($14,755 actual costs compared to the standard $15,980 for 150,000 units), and the reader of the report might have misjudged actual performance. The foreman should try to cut costs, but he should not do it by cutting production.

Comparison of standard costs in Exhibit 6–1 and Exhibit 5–1 reveals a somewhat startling fact. Although actual accomplishment (135,000 units) was only 90 per cent of standard performance (150,000 units), the standard costs of $14,811 for 135,000 units are *more* than 90 per cent of the standard costs ($15,980) for 150,000 units. (90 per cent of $15,980 is only $14,372, not $14,811.) If

EXHIBIT 6-1

ACME AUTO PARTS COMPANY, PLANT 1 GRINDING DEPARTMENT
MODIFIED STANDARD PERFORMANCE REPORT
For Week Ended November 16

Accomplishment:	*Actual output*	*Budgeted output*	*Difference*
Total output, item 37-tu	135,000	150,000	15,000

	Actual cost	*Standard cost*	*Variance*
Effort:			
Controllable costs (standard costs adjusted to actual output of 135,000 units)[a]			
Labor	$ 2,040	$ 1,836	$204 U
Overtime labor	0	0	0
Material spoiled	120	135	15 F
Grinding wheels	6,750	6,885	135 F
Repairs (special)	100	135	35 F
Electric power	550	550	0
Lubricating oil	75	70	5 U
Total	$ 9,635	$ 9,611	$ 24 U
Noncontrollable costs:			
Depreciation—machinery	$ 2,400	$ 2,400	$ 0
Depreciation—plant	1,000	1,000	0
Insurance	50	50	0
Foreman's salary	165	165	0
Routine maintenance	285	285	0
Other	1,220	1,300	80 F
Total	$ 5,120	$ 5,200	$ 80 F
Total costs	$14,755	$14,811	$ 56 F

[a] For example, 135,000 units × standard labor costs per unit of $.0136 = $1,836.

accomplishment were 110 per cent of standard (or 165,000 units) for the week ending November 23, what would the standard costs be on the standard performance report? Exhibit 6–2 sets these out and allows a comparison with the figures for the lower accomplishment level presented in previous exhibits.

The fact that the standard cost totals do not vary proportionally with the level of production (92.8 per cent cost at 90 per cent production and only 107.9 per cent cost at 110 per cent production) indicates that *not all costs react in direct proportion to the level of accomplishment.* In order to establish reasonable

EXHIBIT 6 - 2

ACME AUTO PARTS COMPANY, PLANT 1 GRINDING DEPARTMENT
STANDARD COSTS AT DIFFERENT LEVELS OF ACCOMPLISHMENT

Accomplishment (in units)	135,000	150,000	165,000
Percent of 150,000 = unit level	90%	100%	110%
Standard costs:			
Controllable costs:			
Labor	$ 1,836	$ 2,040	$ 2,244
Overtime labor	0	0	102
Material spoiled	135	150	165
Grinding wheels	6,885	7,650	8,415
Repairs (special)	135	150	165
Electric power	550	600	650
Lubricating oil	70	75	80
Total	$ 9,611	$10,665	$11,821
Noncontrollable costs:			
Depreciation—machinery	$ 2,400	$ 2,400	$ 2,400
Depreciation—plant	1,000	1,000	1,000
Insurance	50	50	50
Foreman's salary	165	165	165
Routine maintenance	285	300	315
Other	1,300	1,400	1,400
Total	$ 5,200	$ 5,315	$ 5,330
Total costs	$14,811	$15,980	$17,151
Per cent of 150,000-unit level	92.8%	100%	107.3%

standard costs for the various accomplishment levels, the accountant must be able to predict how different costs will react to changing activity. His ability to predict depends on his understanding of the behavior of costs.

COST BEHAVIOR

Not all costs react in the same manner to changing levels of activity. Almost any product you can think of will serve as an example. The material costs in a bottle of soda pop, for instance, are the beverage itself, the bottle, and the crown (cap). The crown and beverage costs will increase in direct proportion to increased production because each additional unit produced uses a crown and beverage that cannot be used again. The bottle cost may not be so directly related to output because the same bottle can be used several times before it breaks or is lost. And then too, there are some costs, such as the production vice president's salary or fire insurance premiums, that may not vary at all as production activity varies.

The justification for mass production, a main characteristic of the high levels of activity and high living standards in the United States, is based on the fact that total production costs do not go up in direct proportion to production volume. As production volume becomes higher, the average cost per unit becomes lower, and a larger number of units can be profitably sold at a lower price. There is theoretically a point in each industry and factory at which this principle no longer holds, but with most products this point is at a very high production level. Knowledge of cost behavior has been the primary motivating factor behind the desire for higher levels of output in our economy.

Costs tend to fall into four basic behavior patterns. An important point to remember is that the behavior of a particular cost item may combine two or more of the basic patterns. In fact, each cost item in its peculiar environment has its own distinct behavior pattern, which has to be reckoned with when standard costs are estimated for different levels of activity. Nevertheless, the four basic behavior patterns lend themselves well to a general discussion of cost behavior.

Variable Cost Behavior

Variable costs react in direct proportion to changes in activity. The behavior of a variable cost can be better understood by examining Exhibit 6–3, a *cost curve* of variable grinding wheel costs.

Exhibit 6–3 shows that at a zero level of accomplishment there is no cost for grinding wheels. As output increases, the cost increases, and since there is no bend in the curve (mathematically speaking, the slope is constant) the cost increases in direct proportion to each additional unit of output. Thus, when accomplishment drops to 90 per cent of the 150,000-unit level (135,000 units) the cost also drops to 90 per cent of the 150,000-unit level (from $7,650 to $6,885); when accomplishment increases to the 110 per cent level, cost does too.

Variable costs are a result of the level of productive activity regardless of time. Whether it takes one hour or one year to produce 150,000 units, the total cost of grinding wheels, for instance, should be $7,650. Another way of describing a variable cost is to say that the cost per unit is the same regardless of the level of production. Thus, grinding wheel cost is $.0510 per unit, no matter how many units are produced.

Another look at Exhibit 6–2 will reveal that four costs incurred by the grinding department of the Acme Auto Parts Company—labor, grinding wheels, material spoilage, and special repairs—are variable. In each case the cost is 90 per cent of what it would have been at the 100 per cent level of accomplishment

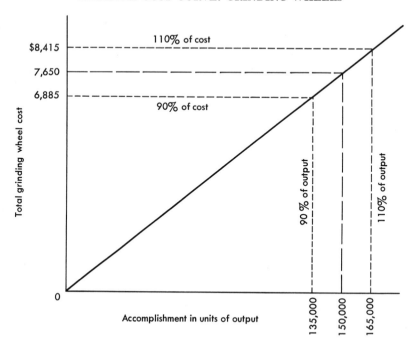

VARIABLE COST CURVE: GRINDING WHEELS

at 90 per cent activity, and 110 per cent at 110 per cent activity. The remaining costs, however, react with a different behavior pattern.

Nonvariable Cost Behavior

In Exhibit 6–2 the behavior of depreciation, insurance, and foreman's salary costs is the same at the three production levels. The total cost remains constant as accomplishment changes. These costs are exhibiting nonvariable cost behavior, and the total cost will remain the same no matter what level of production is achieved. A curve showing this behavior appears in Exhibit 6–4.

The assumption underlying nonvariable cost behavior is that the cost involved is a function of time rather than of level of activity, exactly the opposite of variable costs. Exhibit 6–4 really states that "*for a week* the insurance cost will be $50 no matter what level of output is achieved." Obviously then, for two weeks the cost should be $100 and for a full year $2,600. In fact, the weekly cost of $50 was probably determined by spreading the annual premium over fifty-two weeks. In any event, the assumption is that the total cost is the result of time passing rather than of production activity. The building and equipment must be insured against fire and other hazards whether they are standing idle or working overtime.

While it is entirely possible that a nonvariable cost will remain the same for several accounting periods, it need not. These costs may change because of decisions of management. Management might decide to grant a pay raise to the foreman, for instance. The insurance cost might increase or decrease because of a change in coverage. Even the allocated depreciation cost might be altered to reflect changing assets employed by the business. This is the reason for describing these costs as "nonvariable" (meaning that in the short run they have no clear relationship to production volume), rather than as "constant" or the more traditional "fixed" costs. In the very long run all costs become variable. This is because in the very long run management has time to act on decisions that alter the costs facing the enterprise, and these decisions will be based on predicted levels of output.

For control purposes, it is useful to divide nonvariable costs into *capacity costs* and *programmed costs.* An organization incurs certain costs in order to develop the capacity to provide goods and services to its customers. Examples of these costs include depreciation of buildings, machinery, equipment, and automobiles; real estate taxes; insurance premiums; and key management. These costs are usually nonvariable and are necessary to the continuation of the firm. There is very little that a manager can do to change these capacity costs in the short run.

EXHIBIT 6 - 4

NONVARIABLE COST CURVE: INSURANCE

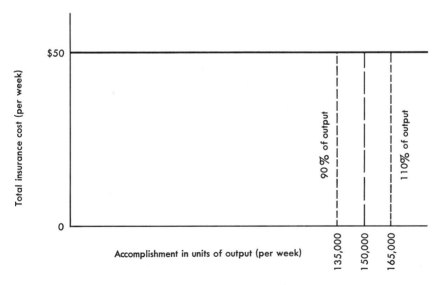

Programmed nonvariable costs result from periodic decisions, usually made by top management, to implement their policies. These costs are more subject to change in the short run (usually once a year, when the budget is formulated) than capacity costs. For example, top management normally establishes and reviews its objectives pertaining to research and development each year. These objectives are then translated into policies and appropriations in the budget. Once the decision is made to embark on a program (for example, research and development and/or advertising) these costs generally reflect a nonvariable behavior pattern.

Programmed costs are generally controlled during the planning phase of operations. The usual performance-measurement procedure in these cases is to compare actual costs with budgeted costs.

You may have begun to suspect correctly that both purely variable costs and purely nonvariable costs are the extremes of possible cost behavior. A few costs actually do follow one of these extreme patterns, but most do not. Most costs have a behavior pattern that is influenced by both time and activity. Two important types of behavior patterns in this category may be called *semivariable* and *semiconstant.*

Semivariable Cost Behavior

Most costs are semivariable in nature, but differ widely from one to another in the way they respond to volume changes. The semivariable cost is one that exhibits nonvariable characteristics at very low volume levels and variable characteristics as activity increases. Electric power, lubricating oil, routine maintenance, and other cost items listed in Exhibit 6–1 reflect semivariable behavior. A chart of the electric power cost, for example, is shown in Exhibit 6–5.

The distinguishing characteristic of the semivariable cost is that its total amount increases as production increases, but the cost per unit is still reduced. The electric power cost, for example, is 91.5 per cent at 90 per cent of production, and 108.5 per cent at 110 per cent of production. But in terms of unit cost, electric power costs $.0041 at the 90 per cent level, $.0040 at 100 per cent, and $.0039 at 110 per cent. The reason for this is that the semivariable cost contains both variable and nonvariable elements.

Even at the zero accomplishment level there still remains some electric power cost. (Exhibit 6–5 shows this at the point where the cost curve intersects the "dollars-of-cost" axis of the chart.) This nonvariable portion of the electric power cost is the grinding department's share of the minimum monthly charge for utilities. For the lubricating oil cost, the nonvariable portion results from the amount of oil needed to preserve the machines even when not used; the variable portion results from oil usage in the production process.

Routine maintenance also has its nonvariable aspect: for example, floors must be swept and machinery oiled even if no production takes place. The mainte-

EXHIBIT 6-5

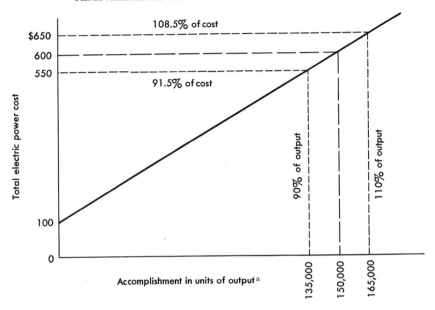

SEMIVARIABLE COST CURVE: ELECTRIC POWER

^a If more meaningful to management, the activity description could be translated into "hours of machine operation."

nance effort increases, however, as accomplishment increases, because with increased usage machines need more care and floors require more cleaning.

From the point of view of the grinding department, the "other" cost category may contain some purely nonvariable costs (such as an allocated portion of officers' salaries) and some variable or semivariable costs (such as heat and water). The overall behavior of this category is, however, that of a semivariable cost.

The same summarization process results in a semivariable total cost for the grinding department as a whole. The total cost figures in Exhibit 6–2 reflect this because at 90 per cent accomplishment the total cost is 92.8 per cent and at 110 per cent activity it is only 107.9 per cent. This pattern is typical of aggregate cost behavior for most business enterprises and is a factor that greatly affects business planning, as we shall see in a later chapter.

Semiconstant Cost Behavior

There are no examples of semiconstant cost behavior in Exhibit 6–2, because the range of activity (from 90 per cent to 110 per cent of production) is not wide enough. If we widen our range of possible activity to include two- and

three-shift operations, we can use the foreman's salary as an illustration. As long
as there is only one shift, the grinding department needs only one foreman at
a nonvariable salary. If, however, the activity level increases so that a second
shift is needed, a second foreman is needed at an additional nonvariable salary.
And, of course, the same would hold true for a third shift. Exhibit 6–6 presents
the cost curve for an assumed semiconstant foremen's salary cost.

EXHIBIT 6 – 6

SEMICONSTANT COST CURVE: FOREMEN'S SALARIES

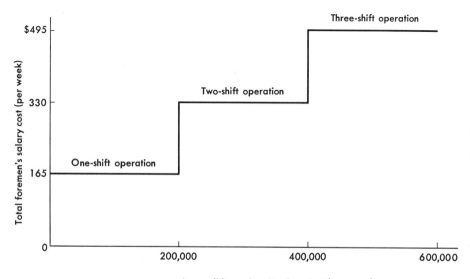

Accomplishment in units of product (per week)

Exhibit 6–6 points out that for one-shift operations, the foreman's salary
is nonvariable. When the second shift is added the cost "stairsteps" to a new
level because an entire second foreman must be added. You cannot add only
a portion of a foreman or add him a little bit at a time.

While there are few costs that exhibit purely semiconstant behavior, many
do have an overall behavior that is partially semiconstant and partially variable
or semivariable, such as the overtime labor cost within the grinding department.

Within the environment of normal one-shift operations there is no need for
any overtime cost until a certain level of accomplishment is reached. Exhibit
6–7 represents the overtime labor cost for the grinding department.

Exhibit 6–7 shows that the overtime labor cost exhibits both nonvariable
and variable characteristics because it is dependent on volume of output but
must be expressed per unit of time (in this example, per week).

EXHIBIT **6-7**

"MIXED" COST CURVE: OVERTIME LABOR

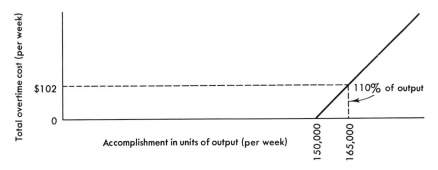

ADDITIONAL COST TERMINOLOGY

Standard Versus Budgeted Costs

Another terminology problem is the use of the words "standard" and "budgeted" as adjectives describing costs. The words can be used interchangeably without really serious confusion, but in this book we will make a distinction common in accounting literature. A *budgeted* cost is any cost that has been predicted for a given future time period. Thus, all of the costs listed under the heading of "standard" in Exhibit 6-2 could just as easily have been called "budgeted" costs, since the list covers a period of one week. (The subject of budgeting is discussed in Chapter 9.)

Standard costs, on the other hand, are often thought of as variable costs only: that is, costs that can be expressed as a constant amount *per unit*, regardless of the level of output or activity. Material, labor, and a few overhead cost items are often the only ones that can be expressed as standard costs. As you have already discovered, semivariable, semiconstant, and nonvariable costs cannot be stated as a constant amount *per unit;* we will call these budgeted costs for the remainder of this book. It is also proper to refer to variable costs as budgeted costs if they are expressed in terms of time periods, rather than units of output.

Flexible Budgets

You should also add the term "flexible budget" to your vocabulary. A *flexible budget* can, and presumably will, be adjusted to the actual level of output in order to compare it with actual costs for cost control purposes, as soon as the actual level of output is known. A *fixed budget*, on the other hand, is based on a predicted output level and not adjusted to actual output. Flexible budgets are preferable to fixed budgets if cost control and performance measurement are the primary objectives. A flexible budget is also properly called a *variable budget.*

Exhibit 6–8 shows the flexible budget that the grinding department foreman for plant 1 would use to control his operations during the operating period. It should be interpreted as follows: The budgeted weekly production cost is $5,440 plus $70.266 per thousand units produced for production levels up to 150,000 units per week, plus $77.066 per thousand units for all units produced over 150,000. For instance, the flexible budget for 160,000 units per week is

	Total	Per thousand
Nonvariable cost	$ 5,440	
Variable cost (for 150,000 units)	10,540	$70.266
Variable cost (for all over 150,000)	770	77.066
	$16,750	

EXHIBIT 6-8

ACME AUTO PARTS COMPANY, PLANT 1 GRINDING DEPARTMENT
FLEXIBLE BUDGET
Item 37-tu

	Per thousand	Per week
Variable costs:		
Labor	$13.60	
Material spoiled	1.00	
Grinding wheels	51.00	
Repairs (special)	1.00	
Electric power	3.333[a]	$ 100
Lubricating oil	0.333[a]	25
Total (up to 150,000 units per week)	$70.266	$ 125
Overtime labor	6.80[b]	0
Total (in excess of 150,000 units per week)	$77.066	$ 125
Nonvariable costs:		
Depreciation—machinery		$2,400
Depreciation—plant		1,000
Insurance		50
Foreman's salary		165
Routine maintenance		300
Other		1,400
Total		$5,315
Total costs	$77.066	$5,440
Rounded	$77.00	

[a] Rounded.
[b] Per thousand units produced in excess of 150,000 units per week.

In other words, the $70.266 and $77.066 per thousand units represent the *marginal* cost per thousand at levels of output of under 150,000 and over 150,000 respectively. The total cost line is shown graphically in Exhibit 6–9.

EXHIBIT 6-9

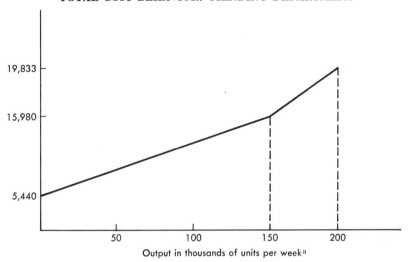

TOTAL COST BEHAVIOR: GRINDING DEPARTMENT

Output in thousands of units per week[a]

[a]Notice that the slope of the line increases at output levels above 150,000 units per week.

Activity Units

Finally, *activity units*, rather than units of output, can be used as measures of departmental accomplishment. As the footnote in Exhibit 6–5 suggests, machine hours could be used instead of units of product if it were more convenient. Machine hours, rather than output, are used as an activity unit in Exhibits 6–10 and 6–11. There are many cost items that cannot be easily related to units of product but can be related to some other activity unit. If the activity unit selected is a fair measure of the accomplishment of the department, it should be used, even though it may not be easily convertible to units of output.

IDENTIFYING COST BEHAVIOR AND ESTIMATING COSTS

At this point it is wise to depart from our somewhat theoretical contemplation of how costs behave and refresh our memories as to why we are concerned with their behavior. Attempting to discern the behavior of costs enables the accountant to estimate more precisely what an item should cost at different levels of accomplishment. As indicated earlier, it is necessary to adjust budgeted costs to actual levels of activity (by using a flexible budget) if the comparison between actual costs and budgeted costs is to be meaningful and useful to the manager.

Estimating costs at various levels of activity depends on the ability of the accountant to identify behavior. There is nothing that can replace experience and sound judgment in this process. There are, however, some simple techniques that help with the task.

The first step in identifying cost behavior is to isolate individual cost elements. It is far easier to identify the behavior of, for example, electric power, gas, and water costs as separate items than it is to identify the behavior of total utility cost as a combined item. Unfortunately, it is also more costly to isolate cost elements than it is to recognize combined groups of costs. A tug of war results between the desire to identify behavior patterns precisely and the desire for economy. The answer lies in compromise. The isolation of costs for behavior identification and estimation purposes should always be as detailed as feasible, but only so long as the costs of obtaining the detailed identification do not outweigh the advantages to be gained. In many situations it is more economical to identify behavior patterns of groups of costs, rather than single items, particularly among the noncontrollable costs. The "other" category of the grinding department is a case in point.

After cost items have been identified and classified, the next step is to examine cost behavior in prior periods. There are several ways in which past behavior can be examined. One of the most common of these is the scatter chart. The technique consists of plotting on a chart actual costs of prior periods against the accomplishment levels of those same periods and then fitting a curve to the various points on the scatter chart.

As an example take the following data concerning the lubricating oil cost of the grinding department:

Week	Actual cost	Hours of machine operation[a]
9/14	$75	560
9/21	70	520
9/28	80	640
10/5	75	600
10/12	80	660
10/19	90	720
10/26	80	640
11/2	75	630

[a] If desired, accomplishment can be translated into units of product by considering the average machine time per unit of product.

Exhibit 6–10 is the scatter chart on which the above information has been plotted. Exhibit 6–11 shows the cost curve that has been fitted to these points. It indicates that lubricating oil cost has a semivariable behavior pattern. The dashed portion of the curve is an assumed extension of the straight line that fits the range of activity covered by the plotted historical data.

There are several methods of fitting a curve to the historical data. The simplest is to place a straightedge on the chart and move it around until the line it makes appears to "fit" the average of all the points. A mathematically correct method employs an arithmetic process called *the method of least squares*. The degree of accuracy desired will dictate the method used.

When only a few data are available, interpolation can be used to obtain an approximation of the line. Suppose we had only two cost figures for lubricating oil—the cost at 520-hour operation and the cost at 720-hour operation. To find the slope and location of the cost curve, we would proceed as follows:

	Cost	Level of activity
Highest point	$90	720
Lowest point	70	520
Difference	$20	200

EXHIBIT 6 - 10

SCATTER CHART OF LUBRICATING OIL COST
(September 14–November 12)

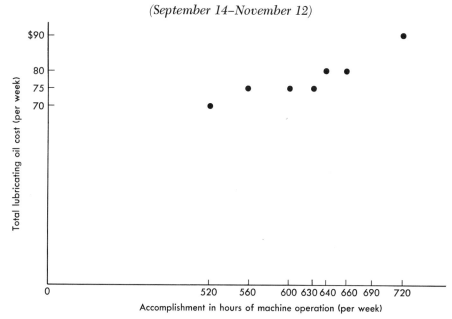

Total lubricating oil cost (per week)

Accomplishment in hours of machine operation (per week)

EXHIBIT 6-11

"FITTED" COST CURVE: LUBRICATING OIL COST

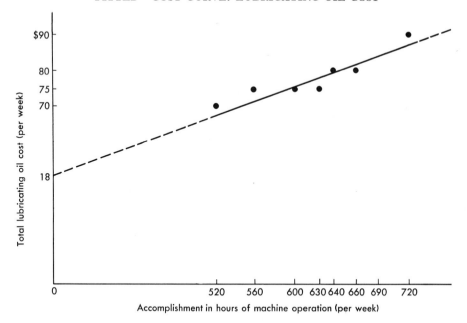

Accomplishment in hours of machine operation (per week)

The variable rate is computed as:

Cost difference $\quad\quad \dfrac{\$20}{200}$ = $.10 variable rate per hour of machine operation
Activity difference

The nonvariable cost component is computed as follows:

Total cost minus variable portion at:
720 hours of activity $90 − $.10 (720) = $18
520 hours of activity $70 − $.10 (520) = $18

Therefore, the cost formula for lubricating oil cost becomes $18.00 per month plus $.10 per machine hour. It is now possible to draw an approximate cost curve for all the intermediate levels of activity. Note that the interpolation method also enables us to separate the cost into its variable and nonvariable components.

The equation for the cost curve can also be solved algebraically if it seems reasonable to assume that the relationship between the expense item and accomplishment level is linear (rarely would there be any reason to assume otherwise).[*]

[*] Using the routine maintenance cost in Exhibit 6–2 as an example, we can substitute into the general equation for a straight line ($y = ax + b$) the values for routine maintenance at 135,000 and 165,000 units of output, which are $285 and $315 respectively:

(1) $315 = 165,000a + b$
(2) $285 = 135,000a + b$

In no case, however, is there 100 per cent assurance that the resulting curve, based on past behavior, will represent cost behavior for the future. The past results may or may not apply to the future. Price and technological change may cause the earlier observations to be out of date. The fitted curve may be biased if these changes follow a pattern. At all times, judgment based on a knowledge and understanding of current conditions must temper any cost behavior predictions flowing from a study of past events. On the other hand, a study of past events is the logical starting place from which to predict the future.

A serious danger in the use of aids such as the scatter chart and interpolation lies in becoming captivated by an apparent scientific correctness about predictions of cost behavior. If the accountant and the manager forget that flexible budgets are based on estimates of what costs should be at different levels of activity, they may trick themselves into unwarranted alarm over minor variances between budgeted and actual results. Performance measurement is necessary to managing an enterprise, but it is not a precise science. It depends upon comparisons of actual results and a standard, or budget, that may have been set by sliding a ruler around on a cluster of dots on a chart. It is necessary to adjust budgets to actual levels of accomplishment in order to obtain more reliable variances, but it is also necessary to temper the significance of the variance by remembering the imperfect accuracy of the process of determining cost behavior.

LACK OF MEASURABLE ACCOMPLISHMENT

Our discussions in Chapters 5 and 6 have dealt thus far with situations in which performance measurement was made easier by recognizable accomplishment and

---

in which a is the slope of the line (increase in routine maintenance per unit produced) and b is the y-intercept (amount of routine maintenance cost at zero production). Subtracting equation 2 from 1:

$$\$30 = 30{,}000a$$
$$a = \$.001$$

This means that for each additional unit produced, one-tenth of one cent is added to the routine maintenance cost. We substitute this value in equation 1:

$$\$315 = 165{,}000 \times .001 + b$$
$$b = \$150$$

Thus at zero output, routine maintenance costs $150. The equation for the routine maintenance line is therefore

(3) $y = .001x + \$150$

Substituting these values for routine maintenance at 100 per cent of standard accomplishment (Exhibit 5–2), we get

$$\$300 = \$.001 \times 150{,}000 + \$150$$
$$\$300 = \$300$$

This means that all three points fall on the line, not common in actual practice. However, it provides added assurance that in this case equation 3 can be used to solve for routine maintenance cost (y) whenever the output level (x) is known.

effort. Not all situations permit such examination. Some activities, such as those carried on in research departments, advertising departments, and certain administrative departments, cannot be objectively measured for short enough periods to permit control of the costs. These are, nevertheless, very important activities making positive contributions toward the profit goal of the enterprise.

For instance, the purpose of a research department is to explore the unknown—to investigate new product possibilities, new production methods, and new uses for existing products or processes controlled by the enterprise. For every usable product or idea that the research department develops, many may finally prove unusable. It is impossible to establish a short-run measure of accomplishment for this kind of activity. "Quotas" would be meaningless. Research-and-development effort requires faith on the part of managers who allocate money for this purpose.

Advertising is another activity for which accomplishment is not always objectively measurable. Management hopes that the advertising program of the firm will result in increased sales. Over a period of time the success of the advertising efforts can be determined because the sales results of the enterprise can be compared with past results, or with those of competitors, but quotas or standards of accomplishment are again meaningless.

Accomplishment in many phases of the administrative activity of an enterprise is also difficult to quantify. Precisely what should be the accomplishment of the corporate president? Or his secretary? What about the accountants' activities within the firm? Their accomplishment is dictated by management's desire for information, which is continually subject to change. Accounting activity, maintenance activity, and many aspects of administrative activity certainly result in positive accomplishment, but they cannot be objectively determined. How then is performance gauged in these situations?

The usual performance measurement procedure in these cases is to compare actual costs with budgeted costs. Costs for a given period are budgeted in a purely subjective manner based on managerial opinion, the amount budgeted in past periods, and the availability of money. Each department is usually required to submit budget requests for funds for the coming accounting period. Since the budget request total usually exceeds the money available, top management may ration the available funds among the requesting departments according to preconceived subjective evaluations of what the accomplishments of each department might be during the period. The manager of the research department, for example, is then authorized to spend the money budgeted for his use. At the end of the accounting period the actual costs of the period are compared to the budgeted costs, and conclusions are drawn about the department head's ability to control costs. There may not have been any recognizable accomplishment during the period. Any that did result can probably not be clearly related to the costs incurred.

There are managerial problems inherent in this situation. The manager in question may be judged solely by his ability to control costs rather than by his ability to conduct successful research (or induce sales, or provide adequate accounting information, or run the company). A good management should try to evaluate actual accomplishment, perhaps by intuition, in addition to observing the department head's control over expenses.

SUMMARY

Accomplishment may vary from standard just as effort does. When accomplishment varies from standard it becomes necessary to restate budgeted costs in terms that reflect the actual accomplishment achieved. This adjustment of budgeted costs to the actual level of accomplishment permits a comparison of actual costs with budgeted costs. A budget that allows for this adjustment is called a flexible budget.

In order to restate budgeted costs in relation to actual accomplishment it is necessary to understand cost behavior. There are four typical kinds of cost behavior: variable, nonvariable, semivariable, and semiconstant. A few costs fit only one of these descriptive types, but most exhibit behavior patterns of mixed characteristics. The majority of costs are semivariable in some degree. This is also true of groups of costs and especially so of total costs incurred by an enterprise.

Cost behavior determination is more an art than a science. There are, however, some semiscientific techniques that help in examining past behavior and thus help predict future behavior. Among these techniques are the scatter chart, which lends itself to visual inspection, arithmetical plotting of a cost curve, or the algebraic method.

Some situations do not lend themselves to objective measurement of performance. These are the functions, such as research, where accomplishment is not objectively measurable. Comparison of actual effort with budgeted effort (costs) is the usual substitute for performance measurement in these situations. This type of comparison is subject to misinterpretation and should not replace management's subjective judgment of performance in terms of both accomplishment and effort.

Questions for Review

6-1. Why should actual costs be compared with standard costs at the actual level of accomplishment achieved?

6-2. Why does the average total production cost per unit usually decrease as production volume increases?

6-3. Define and give an example of each of the following cost behavior patterns:
   a. variable
   b. nonvariable
   c. semivariable
   d. semiconstant

6-4. Give an example of a cost that is related to time and one that is related to activity.

6-5. Define and give an example of capacity costs and programmed costs. What cost behavior pattern do these types of costs generally exhibit?

6-6. At what point is management control generally exercised over programmed costs?

6-7. What is the distinction between standard costs and budgeted costs?

6-8. What is a flexible budget? What are its major uses?

6-9. What is one activity unit, other than units of output, that might be used as a measure of accomplishment? What circumstances would be appropriate for its use?

6-10. Describe the methods of identifying cost behavior and estimating costs that are discussed in Chapter 6.

6-11. How is performance usually measured for activities whose accomplishment cannot be objectively determined? Are there any limitations to this approach?

Problems for Analysis

6-12. The accompanying cost curves represent four types of cost behavior. Identify each curve's cost behavior and give three examples of each behavior pattern.

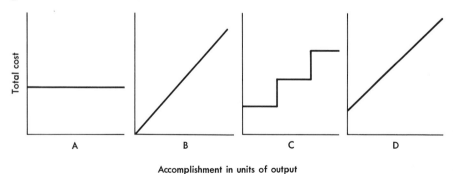

Accomplishment in units of output

6-13. Chapter 5 and this chapter both deal with costs. Explain the differences between the costs discussed in Chapter 5 and the costs discussed in this one. Why is this chapter's discussion important for the accountant? For the manager?

6-14. a. Identify each of the following cost items as variable, semivariable, or nonvariable.

	Units Produced per Month		
	3,000	*4,000*	*5,000*
Materials	$12,000	$16,000	$20,000
Manufacturing supplies	2,250	3,000	3,750
Machine depreciation	2,400	3,200	4,000
Power expense	3,100	4,000	4,900

    b. Prepare charts showing the cost behavior of each item and compute the anticipated cost at 0, 2,000, and 7,000 units of output.

    c. Assuming that the above data are based upon past operating experience, what inherent dangers are there in the exclusive reliance upon past experience in the preparation of a flexible budget?

6-15. The painting department of the Modern Company made studies of its maintenance labor (a semiconstant cost) and power costs (a semivariable cost) of prior periods at three levels of production, with the following results:

Operating level	*Maintenance labor cost*	*Operating level*	*Power cost*
1,500–2,500 units	$120	1,500 units	$140
2,501–3,500 units	240	2,500 units	220
3,501–4,500 units	360	3,000 units	260

The Modern Company has recently negotiated a new contract with the union. The maintenance labor rate is now $3.10 per hour as compared to a previous rate of $3 per hour. Certain improvements have just been made in the machinery that are expected to reduce the power consumption by 20 per cent. These changes in operating conditions are not reflected in the data presented above.

    Indicate what you think the above costs should now be at 3,000, 5,000, and 7,000 units of production.

6-16. The Mullen Company made studies of some of its operating costs to determine how these items changed as the volume of operations changed. Power cost, machine maintenance cost, and manufacturing supplies cost were each studied at operating levels of 25, 40, and 45 units per week, with the following results:

Operating level (units/week)	Power cost	Machine maintenance cost	Manufacturing supplies cost
25	$260	$6,000	$1,250
40	410	6,600	2,000
45	460	6,800	2,250

a. Assuming that the behavior patterns indicated for the above items would exist at *all* other operating levels (including shutdown), how much would you budget for each item at each of the following levels of operation?

Operating level (units/week)	Power cost	Machine maintenance cost	Manufacturing supplies cost
0 (shutdown)	_____	_____	_____
30	_____	_____	_____
50	_____	_____	_____

b. Which cost behavior pattern does each of these three costs represent?

6-17. The North Company's fabricating department has a production quota of 10,000 units for November; on that basis the November budget was prepared as follows:

Raw materials (10,000 lbs.)	$1,000
Machine labor (500 hours)	900
Power	550
Supervision	400
Depreciation	300
	$3,150

Raw material and machine labor are variable costs. Power is variable except for a nonvariable minimum monthly cost of $150. (In other words, total power cost = $150 + $.04 per unit.) Supervision is a semiconstant cost that increases $200 for every 7,500 units produced (that is, $200 for production from 0 to 7,500 units, $400 for production from 7,500 to 15,000 units, etc.). Depreciation is a nonvariable cost. During November, 11,200 units were produced. Actual costs were raw material, $1,140; machine labor, $1,015; power, $630; supervision, $420; depreciation, $300. The amount of raw material and machine labor consumed in production was as follows:

Raw material: 11,900 lbs.
Machine labor: 555 hours

a. Prepare a statement that will reflect the November performance of the department from a cost control standpoint.

b. On what assumptions is your statement in the above requirement based?

c. As the production vice president, what action would you take as a result of this performance statement?

6-18. The Packer Company's cutting department has a production quota of 5,000 units for April; on this basis their April budget was prepared as follows:

Direct materials (15,000 pounds)	$ 3,000
Direct labor (2,500 hours)	10,000
Power—variable	600
Power—nonvariable	150
Maintenance and repairs—variable	250
Maintenance and repairs—nonvariable	400
Taxes and insurance	750
Supervision (increases to $1,200 when production exceeds 5,500 units per month)	600
Depreciation	1,200
Total	$16,950

Actual units produced in April were 6,500, and the following costs were incurred: direct materials, 20,000 pounds at $.18 per pound; direct labor, 3,400 hours at $3.80 per hour; variable power cost, $845; nonvariable power cost, $150; variable maintenance and repair costs, $150; nonvariable maintenance and repair costs, $400; taxes and insurance, $750; supervision, $1,200; and depreciation, $1,200.

a. Prepare a flexible budget, using the format from Exhibit 6–8 expressed in formula form.

b. Prepare a performance report comparing actual performance with the budget.

6-19. After reading an article you recommended on cost behavior, your client is puzzled by the following excerpts from it:

1. "Nonvariable costs are variable per unit of output and variable costs are nonvariable per unit of output."

2. "Depreciation expense may be calculated to be a certain number of dollars each period if the service life of the asset is estimated in terms of time periods, or it may be a certain number of dollars per unit of output if the service life of the assets is estimated in terms of units produced. Therefore, depreciation may be either a nonvariable cost or a variable cost, depending on the method used to compute it."

a. Define the underscored terms. Give examples where appropriate.

b. Explain the meaning of each excerpt to your client. (American Institute of Certified Public Accountants Adapted)

6-20. The Eastern House Company is engaged in the manufacture of box lunches that are sold to various companies in the airline industry. The production quota for August is 100,000 lunches; on this basis the following budget was prepared for the meat department:

Direct materials (50,000 pounds)	$30,000
Direct labor (2,000 hours)	6,000
Power—nonvariable	1,000
Maintenance and repairs—nonvariable	600
Taxes and insurance	900
Supervision	1,100
Depreciation	400
Total	$40,000

Actual production for August was 90,000 lunches, and the following costs were increased: direct materials, 46,000 pounds at $.58 per pound; direct labor, 2,100 hours at $2.90 per hour; power, $1,050; maintenance and repairs, $600; taxes and insurance, $900; supervision, $1,150; and depreciation, $1,200.

a. Prepare a flexible budget, using the format from Exhibit 6–8 expressed in formula form.

b. Prepare a performance report comparing actual performance with the budget.

c. Explain when and how the reports in 1 and 2 above would assist the supervisor of the meat department in controlling costs.

d. Explain when and how the reports in 1 and 2 above would assist the president of the Eastern House Company in controlling assets.

6-21. The following data were accumulated for maintenance and repair costs for the past thirteen weeks of operations:

Week	Units produced	Hours of machine operations	Costs incurred
1	900	500	$340
2	1,200	600	390
3	1,000	550	375
4	1,100	570	380
5	1,400	730	490
6	1,200	680	460
7	850	510	360
8	1,050	580	405
9	1,100	560	375
10	1,200	610	410
11	1,100	580	390
12	1,050	570	395
13	1,300	730	475

a. Use the scatter chart method to determine the nonvariable and variable cost components of maintenance and repair costs.

b. Is "units produced" or "hours of machine operation" a better predictor of maintenance and repair costs? Explain.

c. Use the interpolation method to determine variable and nonvariable cost components.

d. From a managerial standpoint, what is the significance of the difference between your solution to part *a* and your solution to part *c*?

6-22. For each of the following independent cost situations, select the graph that best describes the behavior of the cost. A graph may be selected for more than one answer. All policy decisions and events that caused changes in the behavior patterns of the charted amounts took place in the middle of the time span portrayed in the graphs.

The vertical axes of the graphs represent monthly dollar amounts of cost and the horizontal axes represent the passage of time. The axes intersect at zero.

a. Supervision cost, where the number of supervisors is reduced from five to four.

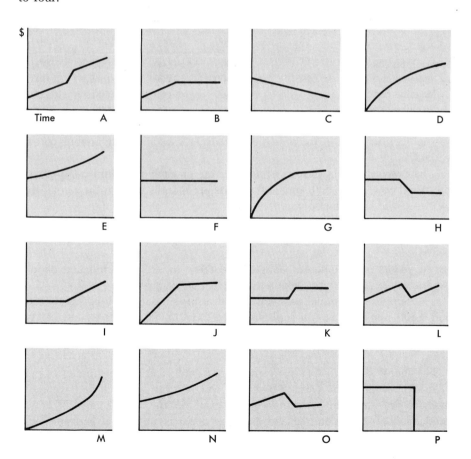

b. Direct materials cost, where prices were rising steadily.

c. Taxes and insurance cost, where the rates were increased thirty per cent.

d. Depreciation cost, where assets become fully depreciated.

e. Depreciation cost, where the charge is changed from $.03 per unit to the straight-line rate.

f. Power costs, where the rate charged the department is increased.

g. Direct labor costs, where the rate of usage is decreased steadily.

h. Rental costs, where the lease terms are changed from a constant amount plus a percentage of gross sales to a constant amount monthly.

i. Direct labor cost, where a 10 per cent rate increase is granted.

j. Direct material cost, where the research and development department developed a production application that reduced the material requirements per unit by 20 per cent. (AICPA Adapted)

6-23. An assembly department of a manufacturing company made studies of labor and overhead costs of prior periods at four levels of production, with the following results:

	Units Produced Each Month			
	7,000	*8,000*	*9,000*	*10,000*
Machine labor	$35,000	$40,000	$45,000	$50,000
Supervision	15,000	17,000	19,000	21,000
Machine repair	8,500	9,000	9,500	10,000
Machine depreciation	3,000	3,000	3,000	3,000

a. Identify each of the above cost items as variable, semivariable, or non-variable.

b. Prepare charts showing the behavior of each item and compute the presumed cost at 0, 6,000, and 11,000 units per month. What is the significance of the cost at 0 production?

c. On what assumptions are your answers in *a* and *b* based? Which of these assumptions would have to be verified before they could be relied upon in an actual case?

d. What other inherent dangers are there in exclusive reliance on past experience in preparing a flexible budget?

e. Suppose additional data reveal that at production levels of 7,500, 8,500, and 9,500 units per month supervision cost is $15,000, $17,000, and $19,000 respectively. What name is given to this type of cost behavior? Prepare a new chart of supervision costs.

6-24. The Williamson Company prepares a budget at the beginning of each year and computes an average budgeted cost per unit for each department to measure departmental performance. For example, the budget calls for annual production of 60,000 units in the stamping department; annual budgeted costs are $90,000 of variable costs and $45,000 of nonvariable costs, or a budgeted average cost of $2.25 per unit. A performance report of the stamping department for the first quarter of the year shows the following:

	Units produced	Variable costs	Nonvariable costs	Average cost per unit
January	5,000	$ 7,000	$ 3,750	$2.15
February	4,000	6,200	3,750	$2.49
January–February	9,000	$13,200	$ 7,500	$2.30
March	4,500	6,800	3,750	$2.34
January–March	13,500	$20,000	$11,250	$2.31

The production manager says, "We recognize that per-unit costs will change as monthly volume of production changes, but if our annual budget is prepared properly, the cost should average out by the end of the year. This way we don't have to adjust the budget up and down from month to month. Besides, we like to keep track of the effect of output changes on our unit costs, and to make sure our department heads are aware of this also."

Criticize the budgeting procedure and method of measuring departmental performance in this company.

6-25. Standard costs for an operating department in a manufacturing concern are as follows:

Raw materials:
  3 lbs. raw material at $.80/pound
Machine labor:
  1½ man-hours at $3/man-hour
Overhead:
  Supervision:
    $600/month for 0–1000 units of output
    $1,200/month for 1,001–2,000 units of output
  Power:
    $400/month for lighting, heating, and air conditioning
    $.50/unit for machine operation
  Machine maintenance:
    $250/month for routine inspections and lubrication
    $.25/unit for repair work
  Machine depreciation:
    $800/month when production/month is 1,000 units or less
    $.80/unit when production/month is more than 1,000 units
  Space costs (building depreciation and utilities):
    $1,000/month

Actual operating data for September follow:

Units produced	1,200
Raw materials used	3,800 lbs. at $1/pound
Machine labor	1,700 hours at $3.20/hour
Overhead:	
Supervision	$1,200
Power	$1,150
Machine maintenance	$ 500
Machine depreciation	$ 960
Space costs	$1,000

Prepare the September performance report for the department, comparing budgeted and actual costs and including any comments that may be helpful in determining the cause of variations.

6-26. The Bristol Plastics Company manufactures plastic toys. Plastic parts are produced in several molding departments and transferred to an assembly department. Production in the molding departments must be scheduled carefully to prevent bottlenecks in production or unnecessary stockpiling of parts inventories. There are pronounced seasonal fluctuations, with the heavy months in the late summer and early fall, at which time the plant operates at full capacity.

One of the molding departments produces plastic bodies for toy trucks and autos. In August, the production schedule called for 20,000 plastic bodies to be transferred to assembly and an inventory of 5,000 bodies to be on hand at August 31. On August 1, there were 2,000 bodies on hand.

The department ran into production troubles early in the month, first because of an interruption caused by the installation of a new machine, and later because of worker resistance to the foreman's attempt to catch up on production. By August 22, 10,000 bodies had been transferred to assembly, and there was no inventory. The foreman decided against (1) adding a second shift, because of the increased cost and the shortage of persons who could be hired temporarily, or (2) scheduling overtime for present workers, because of the increased cost of overtime premiums. By August 31, a total of 15,000 units had been transferred, and there was no inventory.

The August performance report for this department follows below:

a. How many plastic bodies was the department supposed to produce in August? How many were produced?

b. Is the above statement a fair representation of the performance of the department for the month? Explain.

c. Which performance reports would be most likely to reflect the consequences of this department's failure to produce? What factors would you have to consider if you were asked to compute the cost to the company of the department's failure to produce according to schedule?

d. How do you explain the fact that the cost of the new machine does not appear in the performance statement?

MOLDING DEPARTMENT
PERFORMANCE REPORT
For August 19xx

	Budget (at 13,000 units)	Actual
Materials used	$1,200	$1,250
Labor	3,000	2,800
Overhead:		
Supervision	500	500
Machine maintenance	250	250
Power used	125	130
Machine depreciation	1,000	1,000
Total	$6,075	$5,930

6-27. The Brown Company became greatly concerned about the mounting cost of office supplies (stationery, printed forms, stencils, staplers, scotch tape, etc.). For years these supplies had been issued on request to the various offices from a central storeroom, and the only control attempted was to prevent pilferage from the storeroom. Two years ago the controller ordered that a departmental budget system limit each department to a given dollar amount of supplies each year; supplies would be issued only on authority of requisitions signed by the department head. Studies were made of supplies used in each department in prior years, and on this basis the budget was established.

The plan did not work well. By the end of the ninth or tenth month, many departments had already exceeded their budgets, and the controller was forced to authorize the storekeeper to continue to approve requisitions from these departments, since they could not continue to function without supplies. Last year the departmental budgets were adjusted (most of them were increased). Each department head was warned that requisitions in excess of departmental budgets would not be approved.

Before the end of last year, the same problem arose, except that the controller refused to issue additional supplies to departments that had exceeded their budgets. Requisitions were returned to department heads stamped "Disapproved." In one case, a department, unable to answer correspondence, began to telephone long distance on routine matters. In another case, the head of the advertising department, without informing the controller, persuaded a bookkeeper to "transfer" some of his department's unused salary budget to its supplies budget so that additional requisitions would be approved. When the president's secretary told him that she was out of company letterheads and could not replace them, the plan was discontinued.

a. In your opinion, why didn't this plan succeed?
b. What do you recommend?

6-28. In each of the four cases below, briefly discuss the circumstances under which each of the possible accomplishment measurements should or should not be used to evaluate the monthly cost control performance of the department or persons involved. Also, point out the subjective factors that may be important in each case.

    a. A product engineering department. The task of the department is to develop and recommend new products. Costs include salaries, supplies, and space costs.

        1. number of projects started during the month
        2. number of projects worked on during the month
        3. number of projects finished during the month
        4. number of projects accepted by management during the month
        5. man-hours of work by engineers and draftsmen, as indicated by monthly time reports
        6. number of people employed by the department during the month

    b. A sales department, consisting of one sales manager and six traveling salesmen. Costs include salaries, commissions, travel, and sales supplies.

        1. number of orders received during the month
        2. number of calls made during the month
        3. total miles traveled during the month
        4. total dollar amount of orders taken by salesmen during the month

    c. A maintenance department, consisting of one foreman and twelve machinists and helpers. It conducts routine inspections of producing machines and makes repairs in case of breakdowns. Costs include maintenance labor, maintenance supplies, and space costs and depreciation for the machine shop.

        1. total man-hours of maintenance labor during the month
        2. number of machine hours operated in the machine shop
        3. number of breakdowns repaired during the month
        4. number of machine inspections conducted during the month

    d. The accounts payable section of the accounting department, consisting of twenty bookkeepers whose job is to verify information relating to a particular invoice (purchase requisition, purchase order, receiving report, etc.) and to prepare a voucher, which must be approved before payment is made. Costs include salaries, supplies, depreciation of accounting machines, and space costs.

        1. number of bookkeepers on the payroll during the month
        2. number of man-hours in the section during the month
        3. number of invoices processed

6-29. The Zenith Petroleum Company recently established a research department with responsibility for conducting research on new uses for petroleum products and other related projects in which the company might profitably engage. When the budget allocation for this department was discussed, the director of research proposed that he submit to the budget committee each year a list of proposed projects accompanied by cost estimates for each project. The committee could then choose the projects to be worked on, perhaps add others, and approve the cost estimates for budget purposes.

The controller felt that this procedure gave too much authority to the director of research, since there was no way of checking on the validity of the cost estimates. He determined that competing companies, according to their annual reports, seemed to be spending about 2 per cent of sales on research each year, and he proposed that Zenith do the same.

The executive vice president, on the other hand, proposed that the rest of the budget be prepared as it always had been and then research be allocated whatever was left over. He indicated that he had little confidence in the prospects for the department anyway, and thought it would be cheaper to "buy ideas" from competitors rather than to try to discover them.

a. Comment on the proposals for determining the amount to be budgeted for research for the Zenith Company. Make a recommendation of your own.

b. How should the performance of the research department be measured each year? Does it depend on how the budget for it is originally established?

APPENDIX 6A

Accounting Records Using Standards and Flexible Budgets

In Chapters 5 and 6, we discussed standard costs and budgeted costs from the standpoint of the user of cost data. That is, a manager uses standard costs and budgeted costs as measures of what activities ought to cost, compares these costs with actual costs incurred, investigates the causes of variances, and takes whatever corrective action is necessary. This is the process of cost control. In these chapters, it was assumed that only actual costs incurred were entered in the accounts, and that standards and budgets, as well as other operating statistics, were collected and maintained for reporting purposes independent of the accounts.

Now let us consider standards from the standpoint of the accountant. They are highly useful devices for recording cost data in the accounts. Standards permit the accountant to record the (standard) cost of the manufacturing activities as they are carried on, and to report to management the standard cost of manufacturing before the actual cost data are accumulated. Reports based on standard costs are necessarily tentative, because the standards are only estimates, but they are nevertheless very useful to management because of their timeliness. Many elements of actual cost, particularly overhead items, cannot be accurately measured until the end of the accounting period, by which time much of the value of the accounting report has been lost. Of course, the usefulness of reporting in terms of standard costs depends on how accurate the standards are. If the standards are permitted to become obsolete, reports based on them may be misleading.

Here we present material of special interest to students who wish to know more about data collection procedures, or who may desire additional background for advanced accounting courses. We shall give a simple demonstration of how the general ledger accounts can be used to accumulate cost data both at actual and at standard for a manufacturing operation. Plant 1 of the Acme Auto Parts Company is used for illustrative purposes.

Standard costs per unit of item 37-tu are as follows:

Direct material (½ lb. @ $2.00/lb.)	$1.00
Direct labor (¼ hr. @ $2.00/hr.)	.50
Overhead	.90
Total standard cost per unit	$2.40

The methods of computing the direct material and direct labor standards (discussed in Chapter 5) are easily understood, since these are variable costs. The standard overhead cost is different, however, since overhead contains items that are not variable and cannot be identified with physical units of product. Therefore this standard requires explanation.

PREDETERMINED OVERHEAD RATE

Overhead costs associated with the manufacturing process must attach themselves to each unit of product if total product cost is to be known. (Some accountants prefer to say the product "absorbs" overhead, as well as direct costs. The subject of absorption costing and its alternative, variable costing, are discussed in greater depth in Chapter 8.)

Since overhead costs are predominantly time-oriented, one need only spread the overhead per time period over the number of products produced in that time period to make the allocation properly. However, for standard cost accounting purposes we need to predetermine this cost rather than wait for actual production results. The basic requirement then is an estimate of activity levels in the future time period.

The first step in calculating the predetermined overhead rate is to classify overhead items as variable or nonvariable and state them in terms of some *activity level*, such as direct labor hours or units of product. (The flexible budget shown in Exhibit 6–8 is an example.) Total expected overhead costs are then divided by the expected activity level to derive the predetermined overhead rate for the coming year.

Exhibit 6A–1 reflects planned production costs for plant 1 of Acme Auto Parts Company for the next fiscal year.

The overhead rate for plant 1 of Acme Auto Parts Company is predetermined as follows:

$$\frac{\text{Estimated costs}}{\text{Estimated activity}} = \frac{\$2,250,000}{2,500,000 \text{ units}} = \$.90 \text{ per unit of output}$$

When combined with a flexible overhead budget, a predetermined overhead rate permits the calculation of a *budget variance* and a *volume variance* for management's use. The budget variance is the difference between actual overhead costs and the flexible overhead budget at the actual level of activity. The volume variance is derived from the difference between the volume projected in the flexible overhead budget and the actual volume produced times the predetermined overhead rate. The calculation of these variances is illustrated later in this appendix. The budget variance for overhead is similar to the price variance for direct materials and labor discussed earlier. The volume variance is similarly related to the usage variance. Generally, the budget variance is the responsibility of the department manager and the volume variance is the responsibility of top management, perhaps the sales vice president.

EXHIBIT 6A-1

ACME AUTO PARTS COMPANY—PLANT 1
PLANNED PRODUCTION
For Year Ended December 31, 19x0

		Total	Per unit
Accomplishment:			
Total output—item 37-tu[a]		2,500,000 units	
Effort:			
Direct material (1,250,000 pounds at			
$2.00 per pound)		$2,500,000	$1.00
Direct labor (625,000 hours at $2.00			
per hour)		1,250,000	.50
Manufacturing overhead:			
Material spoiled	$ 40,000		
Grinding wheels	127,500		
Repairs (special)	55,000		
Electric power	110,000		
Lubricating oil	28,000		
Depreciation—machinery	460,000		
Depreciation—plant	240,000		
Insurance	8,000		
Foreman's salary	80,000		
Routine maintenance	146,000		
Other	955,500	$2,250,000	.90[b]
Total		$6,000,000	$2.40

[a] Only one product is assumed. This is an intended oversimplification.

[b] The manufacturing overhead cost behavior is:	Total	Per unit
Variable	$ 750,000	$.30
Nonvariable	1,500,000	.60
	$2,250,000	$.90

Let us suppose that during January 200,000 units of item 37-tu were started in production and completed. The beginning and ending inventories are as follows:

	Beginning	Ending
Direct materials	215,000 pounds	180,000 pounds
Work in process	none	none
Finished goods	100,000 units at $2.40	110,000 units at $2.40

The journal entries recording these transactions (at standard) are summarized as follows:

	DR	CR
1. Work in process inventory	480,000	
Direct materials inventory (100,000 pounds at $2.00)		200,000
Direct labor (50,000 hours at $2.00)		100,000
Manufacturing overhead (200,000 units at $.90)		180,000
To charge work in process for 200,000 units		
of item 37-tu started and completed during		
the month of January.		
2. Finished goods inventory	480,000	
Work in process inventory		480,000
To charge finished goods inventory with units		
completed in January (200,000 at $2.40).		

A statement of cost of goods manufactured and sold, at standard, is given in Exhibit 6A-2. This statement could be prepared more frequently (say, once a week) and could include additional information such as comparisons of actual and planned production.

E X H I B I T   6 A - 2

ACME AUTO PARTS COMPANY—PLANT 1

**STATEMENT OF COST OF GOODS MANUFACTURED AND SOLD
AT STANDARD FOR ITEM 37-tu**

For January 19x0

	Per unit	Total
Direct materials	$1.00	$200,000
Direct labor	.50	100,000
Overhead	.90	180,000
Total cost of goods manufactured (200,000 units)	$2.40	$480,000
Beginning inventory of finished goods (100,000 units)		240,000
Total available for sale (300,000 units)		$720,000
Ending inventory of finished goods (110,000)		264,000
Cost of goods sold (190,000 units)		$456,000

For January, the *actual* direct materials and direct labor used in production are as follows:

Direct material = 105,000 pounds @ $1.95 per pound
Direct labor   = 48,000 hours @ $2.30 per hour

The journal entries are as follows:

	DR	CR
1. Direct materials inventory	975,000	
Accounts payable		975,000
To record the purchase of 500,000		
pounds of material at $1.95 per pound		
2. Work in process inventory (at standard cost)	210,000	
Direct materials inventory (at actual cost)		204,750
Material price variance (105,000 pounds at $.05)		5,250
To record the issuance of 105,000 pounds of		
direct material at $1.95 per pound and the		
material price variance.		
3. Direct labor	110,400	
Accrued payroll		110,400
To record direct labor payroll		
costs of 48,000 hours at $2.30		
per hour.		
4. Work in process inventory (at standard cost)	96,000	
Labor price variance (48,000 hours at $.30)	14,400	
Direct labor		110,400
To record the usage of 48,000 hours		
of direct labor in production and the		
labor price variance.		
5. Manufacturing overhead	194,000	
Various accounts (cash, prepaid insurance,		
accounts payable, etc.)		194,000
To record actual manufacturing overhead		
costs for the month of January.		
6. Budgeted manufacturing overhead	185,000	
Manufacturing overhead		185,000
To record the budgeted overhead		
for January (200,000 units × $.30 + $125,000).		
7. Work in process inventory	180,000	
Budgeted manufacturing overhead		180,000
To charge work in process inventory		
for 200,000 units started in production		
and completed during January at the		
predetermined overhead rate of $.90 per unit.		
8. Finished goods inventory	480,000	
Material usage variance (5,000 pounds at		
$2.00)	10,000	
Work in process inventory		486,000
Labor usage variance (2,000 hours at $2.00)		4,000
To charge finished goods inventory with		
the completion of 200,000 units of product		
and record the material and labor usage		
variances.		

	DR	CR
9. Cost of goods sold	456,000	
Finished goods inventory		456,000

To record the cost of 190,000
units sold at standard of $2.40.

The flow of production costs through the general ledger accounts is illustrated in Exhibit 6A–3. The price variances are recorded in the accounts when material and labor are charged to production (work in process inventory account). The usage variances are recorded in the account when completed units are transferred to finished goods inventory.

The inventory cost accounts will appear on the statement of financial position as assets. The direct labor cost account will have a zero balance, since it is simply a clearing account. The material and labor price and usage variance accounts will be reported to the appropriate managers throughout plant 1 for performance measurement purposes and will appear in total on the statement of earnings.

The way the manufacturing overhead figures are derived and posted requires a little explanation. They have to be derived twice in order to obtain budget and volume variances.

Actual production for January was 200,000 units, and actual overhead costs were $194,000.

Predetermined overhead rate: As shown at the foot of Exhibit 6A–1, the predetermined overhead rate is $.90 per unit ($.30 variable and $.60 nonvariable). At the predetermined rate, overhead costs of $.90 × 200,000, or $180,000, should be applied to the work in process inventory.

The flexible overhead budget: Because the nonvariable portion of overhead cannot accurately be assigned to units of product, this is calculated differently:

$.30 per unit produced + $\frac{1}{12}$ of annual budget of nonvariable costs ($1,500,000)

or

$.30 per unit produced + $125,000 = $60,000 + $125,000 = $185,000

But according to the budget this amount of overhead is to be applied to

$\frac{1}{12}$ planned annual output of 2,500,000 units = 208,333 units and January production was only 200,000 units.

Now we can divide the total variance into budget and volume portions, as shown in Exhibit 6A–4.
The budget variance of $9,000 (actual overhead costs compared with budgeted overhead costs) represents excessive costs incurred, and will be reported to the appropriate managers for performance measurement purposes and will appear on the statement of earnings for January. The volume variance of $5,000 is caused by the difference between planned (208,333 units) and actual volume (200,000 units). The volume variance will be unfavorable whenever actual output is less than the planned amount (as in January) and favorable whenever actual output

GENERAL LEDGER AND DIAGRAM OF PRODUCTION COST FLOW
For January 19x0

Direct Materials Inventory

Debited for purchase of actual cost	Credited for materials placed in production at actual cost
(1) 975,000	(2) 204,750

Accounts Payable

	Credited
	(1) 975,000

Direct Labor

Debited for actual labor costs	Credited for labor used in production at actual cost
(3) 110,400	(4) 110,400

Accrued Payroll

	(3) 110,400

Manufacturing Overhead

Debited for actual costs incurred	Credited for budgeted overhead costs
(5) 194,000	(6) 185,000

Various Accounts

	(5) 194,000

Materials Price Variance

Debited for unfavorable variance	Credited for favorable variance
	(2) 5,250

Labor Price Variance

Debited for unfavorable variance	Credited for favorable variance
(4) 14,400	

Budgeted Manufacturing Overhead

Debited for budgeted overhead (actual volume times budget of $.30 per unit + $125,000)	Credited for overhead charged to work in process (actual volume times predetermined overhead rate)
(6) 185,000	(7) 180,000

Materials Usage Variance

Debited for unfavorable variance	Credited for favorable variance
(8) 10,000	

Work in Process Inventory

Debited for actual units placed in production at standard price	Credited for units completed at standard quantities
(2) 210,000	(8) 486,000
(4) 96,000	
(7) 180,000	

Finished Goods Inventory

Debited for units completed at standard	Credited for units sold at standard
(8) 480,000	(9) 456,000

Labor Usage Variance

Debited for unfavorable variance	Credited for favorable variance
	(8) 4,000

Cost of Goods Sold

Debited for units sold at standard	
(9) 456,000	

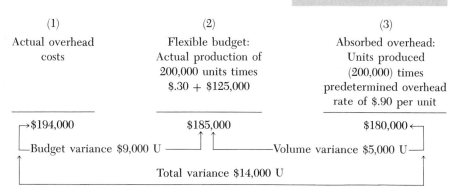

(1)	(2)	(3)
Actual overhead costs	Flexible budget: Actual production of 200,000 units times $.30 + $125,000	Absorbed overhead: Units produced (200,000) times predetermined overhead rate of $.90 per unit

→$194,000 $185,000 $180,000 ←

└─Budget variance $9,000 U ──┘ └────────Volume variance $5,000 U─┘

Total variance $14,000 U

exceeds that planned. Typically, most production operations are cyclical and there will be some months with favorable variances offsetting unfavorable volume variance months like January. At the end of the accounting year, the net volume variance usually appears on the statement of earnings.

The general ledger accounts from Exhibit 6A–3 have been used to prepare the following financial statement for January:

ACME AUTO PARTS COMPANY—PLANT 1

STATEMENT OF COST OF GOODS MANUFACTURED AND SOLD
For January 19x0

	Standard	Actual		Variances	
			Net	Favorable	Unfavorable
Direct materials	$200,000	$204,750	$ 4,750	$5,250 usage	$10,000 price
Direct labor	100,000	110,400	10,400	4,000 usage	14,400 price
Overhead	180,000	194,000	14,000		5,000 budget
					9,000 volume[a]
Cost of goods manufactured	$480,000	$509,150	$29,150	$9,250	$38,400
Add beginning inventory of finished goods	240,000				
Cost of goods available for sale	$720,000				
Less ending inventory of finished goods	264,000				
Cost of goods sold at standard	456,000				
Add net unfavorable variance	29,150				
Cost of goods sold—actual	$485,150				

[a] This variance is normally carried on the statement of financial position as an asset until the end of the fiscal year.

Problems for Analysis

6A-1. Manufacturing costs for the month of April, at standard and actual, for the manufacture of 12,000 units are as follows (planned production is 12,500 units per month):

	Standard costs	Actual costs
Direct materials	6,000 pounds at $2.00	6,300 pounds at $1.90
Direct labor	12,000 hours at $3.00	11,500 hours at $3.20
Overhead	$3.00 per standard direct labor hour: $1.00 for variable overhead $2.00 for nonvariable overhead	$39,000

a. Prepare journal entries to record the manufacturing activity.

b. Prepare a statement of cost of goods manufactured at standard and actual for April.

c. What information from the statement of cost of goods manufactured would be reported to departmental foremen in connection with performance reporting?

6A-2. The following information relates to the production of Innovators, Inc., for the month of September:

Standard Cost Per Unit

	Quantity	Price
Direct materials	3 pounds at $.75 per pound	$ 2.25
Direct labor	2 hours at $3.00 per hour	6.00
Overhead	$4.00 per unit produced	4.00[a]
		$12.25

[a] Planned production for the month is 10,000 units, $1.50 per unit for variable costs and $2.50 per unit for nonvariable costs.

The transactions pertaining to production during September, the first month of the fiscal year, are summarized as follows:

1. Materials purchased on account, $35,000
2. Direct materials used, 31,000 pounds at $.80 per pound
3. Direct labor cost incurred and paid, 21,000 hours at $2.90 per hour
4. Overhead cost for the month:
   Indirect labor cost incurred and paid, $17,000

Depreciation on plant and equipment, 9,000
Real estate and personal property taxes accrued, 4,000
Prepaid insurance expired, 2,500
Miscellaneous factory overhead costs, 7,000

5. Units completed during the period, 10,500. (There was no beginning or ending inventory of work in process.)

a. Prepare journal entries to record the transactions.

b. Prepare a statement of cost of goods manufactured at standard and actual for the month of September.

Chapter Seven

PERFORMANCE
MEASUREMENT:
EARNINGS

INTRODUCTION

This chapter and Chapter 8 are also about performance measurement, but instead of emphasizing cost control, as in Chapters 5 and 6, we are now concerned with profit, or more precisely, *periodic earnings*, as a means of measuring performance. Chapter 2 emphasized that long-run earnings optimization is the basic objective of business firms, and that the decisions of management are presumably directed toward this end. Earnings, properly computed, should therefore serve as a measure of performance of the management of the firm.

Measuring periodic earnings of the firm is probably the most important activity of the accountant, and the subject is not only treated in this chapter but is the central theme of Parts II and III. The reason for this emphasis, and for the divided treatment in this book, is that many people are interested in periodic earnings of the firm for a variety of reasons. Parts II and III cover the interests of stockholders, of creditors, and of the government. While all of these groups are interested in management performance to some degree, they are also interested in earnings for other reasons (dividend prospects, stock-price predictions, liquidity, and taxation).

That various groups are interested in earnings for various purposes leads us to another very important fact, which is that these groups do not define "earnings" in the same way. The question of defining earnings is too controversial and difficult for full development at this point, but it should be understood that "earnings" for purposes of measuring management performance over a period is not the same as "earnings" for computing income taxation, which in turn is not the same as the "earnings" which one might use as an index for determining the amount of a possible wage or dividend increase for that period.

In this chapter we will confine our attention to the use of earnings as an index of management performance. Our interest centers specifically on those report readers who will make decisions based on their appraisal of the management of the firm. Obviously this group includes the stockholder (who may decide to sell his shares if he becomes dissatisfied with the management), but our primary concern is for two other groups of users:

1. The firm's board of directors (representing the stockholders), which has the responsibility for hiring, firing, and rewarding the firm's management, as well as for making suggestions to improve operations.

2. The management itself, which is interested in improving its own performance, as well as in appraising the performance of certain subunits of the firm to which responsibility for earnings has been delegated.

It is obvious that a firm's top management has great interest in how its performance is measured: management naturally wants to look as good as possible to the board of directors and the stockholders. Therefore, it would be extremely difficult for management to be completely objective where there is much room for honest differences of opinion, as is the case in measuring earnings for performance purposes. This means that as far as possible such measurements should be considered an accounting rather than managerial function. For example, it would not be proper for management to specify a definition of its own accomplishment, as it did for the grinding department foreman in Chapters 5 and 6, nor should management specify which costs incurred by the firm are controllable by management and which are not. These questions should be left to the accountant to decide.

Earnings as an index of performance gives rise to some of the most difficult problems faced by accountants. Sometimes the solutions presented in this chapter cannot be easily defended on logical grounds, and in these cases they will merely be described and perhaps criticized. It is most important that you understand the limitations of earnings as a measure of performance, however, and this fact makes this chapter one of the most important in this book.

IDENTIFYING THE EARNINGS CENTER

For performance measurement purposes, an earnings center is a business firm, or unit within a business firm, whose management has the responsibility for bringing in revenues and incurring costs and also has the authority to make decisions that contribute to long-run earnings. The basic distinction between the earnings center and the department discussed in Chapters 5 and 6 is the added responsibility for revenues.

A firm that is responsible for its revenues should have the authority to select and design its products, to select its customers, to set and change selling prices, and to try to force competitors out of business if it chooses to do so. Because of government control over business activity in this country, few firms have a completely free hand in making these decisions. In our regulated industries, such as electric utilities, authority of the management in these areas is extremely limited, and there is serious doubt as to whether periodic earnings are at all useful in measuring management performance in these cases. Regulated industries provide an extreme example, but there are varying degrees of government control and influence over our nonregulated businesses also. Thus management faces limitations on its freedom to optimize long-run earnings. In spite of these difficulties, accountants assume that all independently owned firms have this authority for purposes of measuring management performance, even though the weaknesses in the assumption are well known.

An even more difficult problem arises in identifying subunits of business enterprises as earnings centers. The organization structures of many large corporations indicate that management authority has been delegated to a number of such earnings centers. The management of each earnings center operates (almost) as if it were managing an independent firm.

Many of these corporations attribute much of their success to this *decentralization* of authority. It keeps the top management from having to make operating decisions far from the firms or markets affected by the decisions. Decentralized authority provides incentive for managers of the earnings center to accept responsibility and develop their managerial talents. In those cases in which the authority and responsibility for both costs and revenues have been delegated to earnings centers, the measurement of periodic earnings is probably the best available gauge of performance.

In some cases, decentralization of management has been illusory rather than real, and the use of earnings to measure performance may be unfair to the plant or branch managers in these instances. Earnings computations for these plants may be useful to top management in planning, as for example, in deciding whether to continue a branch or plant, or in determining the best location for it. Earnings computations should not be used for measuring performance of the management personnel in the plant, however, unless these men have all the authority to make their own decisions that the management of an independent firm has.

Identifying an earnings center within an organization, then, is a problem of determining the facts. Generally, in a competitive economy, the assumption that independently owned enterprises are earnings centers is reasonable for performance measurement purposes.

MEASURING EARNINGS
FOR PERFORMANCE MEASUREMENT

The task of measuring earnings is a very difficult one, but it is easy to describe: The *accomplishment* of the firm for a period is measured by the revenues, defined as certain net asset inflows (see Chapter 2) properly associated with the period. The *effort* of the firm for the same period is measured by the expenses, defined as certain asset outflows (or expired costs) properly associated with the revenues of the period. The difference between the revenues and expenses of the period is net earnings or net loss, depending on which is the larger. You may already have discovered that the "weasel word" in this paragraph is "properly."

Defining earnings measurement as a process of associating (matching is a more popular term) expenses with periodic revenues may seem different from the concept of earnings presented in Chapter 2. There, periodic earnings was shown to be the difference in the net assets of the firm between the beginning and the end of the period, excluding dividends and adjustments in contributed capital. But these two definitions are simply different ways of looking at the same thing; as Chapter 3 showed, net asset changes can be broken down into revenue and expense items (plus nonearnings items such as dividends and changes in contributed capital).

On the other hand, the two definitions do have different implications for the measurement of management performance. In particular, the examination of revenue and expense items may reveal that some items are extraordinary or nonrecurring; this fact would not be evident from the financial position statement. It is also possible to identify items which may be considered noncontrollable by management. For these reasons, viewing earnings as a matching of revenue and expense is more useful for performance measurement than the net assets approach discussed in Chapter 2.

Measurement of Periodic Revenues

Basically, measuring periodic revenues is a problem of determining how much the management "accomplished" this period, and theoretically this accomplishment is the total economic values (assets) created while carrying out the firm's activities. For example, a grocery wholesaler must purchase groceries from producers, transport them, store them, insure them, sell them to customers, deliver them, collect cash from customers, pay his bills, and organize, finance, and administer his firm during the entire process. All of these activities are creative in the sense that there is economic usefulness or value attached to them. How can we measure how much the wholesaler "accomplished" last month, or last year, in carrying out these activities? How can we compare his accomplishments in one period with those of another?

The difficulties of finding answers to these questions are apparent. First, the question of whether economic values are created in a given period by any or all of the wholesaler's activities is a matter of opinion. What is of value to one person is unimportant to another. If we are to measure the performance of the wholesaler, we need objective, verifiable evidence that his activities have in fact created values. We cannot rely on the wholesaler's opinion, even though he is the best-informed person, because it is his performance we want to measure, and he is likely to be prejudiced. The accountant is free of prejudice and is fairly well informed, but he does not wish to accept the responsibility of forcing his opinions on the readers of the earnings statement. To establish objective, verifiable values, we need the consensus of a large number of people.

Another related difficulty stems from the fact that, in our example, the wholesaler is engaged in many activities at one time, and the activities are not directly comparable. He buys groceries from producers this month, and this creates value, because he is now in a position to transport, store, sell, etc. He also collects from customers this month, and this also creates value because the cash is more useful in carrying out the other business activities than the customers' accounts receivable. Both of these activities, and all the others as well, are essential to the conduct of the business, but there is no convincing way of determining the values created by each activity.

Because of these difficulties, no attempt is made to measure the values created by these activities of the firm, no matter how theoretically correct it may be to do so! Instead, accountants select a single activity carried on by the firm that seems to be more important than any of the others and that does permit verification of the fact that values have been created. This single activity is not the same for all businesses because certain activities are very important to some businesses and of little importance to others. For example, the act of making a sale to a customer may be more important to the automobile dealer than any other single function he performs. To the grain farmer, making the sale is usually of little importance because he knows he can get the established market price for his grain any time he chooses, with no selling effort at all. In addition to the act of producing grain, the grain farmer is also a speculator, because he is concerned with deciding whether to sell the grain or to hold it in expectation of a higher price at a later time. Selecting the point of sale as the point at which revenue should be measured and recognized is probably appropriate for the automobile dealer. For the grain farmer, the market value at the point of harvesting the grain and the value at the point of sale are both appropriate, because the former market value may best measure his ability as a farmer and the latter his ability as a speculator.

Actually, the selection of the particular activity as the point at which to measure accomplishment is governed by trade practice. The point of sale is obviously appropriate for most product-handling firms. It is also used by most manufacturers, but as we shall see in Chapter 8, this may sometimes be inappropriate. Selection varies considerably among so-called service enterprises, in which no tangible product is sold. The accountant is also influenced by a desire to be conservative, which usually means that he prefers to wait until some event (ordinarily a transaction) occurs that provides evidence that value has been created.

Matching Expenses and Revenues

Once the most appropriate activity is selected, whether the sale or some alternative, and the revenues of the period are measured, the next step is to match the revenues with those expenses that were incurred for the purpose of producing them. There are two appropriate classes of expenses (expired costs) to be matched against (deducted from) the revenues of the period to measure periodic earnings:

1. Expired *product costs*, or *cost of goods sold.* These costs *expire* (i.e., are recorded as expenses) in the period in which the product is sold to customers, regardless of the period in which the costs were incurred. Product costs traceable to units of product *not* sold (e.g., cost of product purchased this period for sale in some future period) are recorded as assets (i.e., inventory) until the period of sale, when they become expenses. Product costs are also sometimes called *inventoriable* costs.

Service enterprises, having no tangible product to sell and having selected some other activity as the point at which revenue should be recognized (e.g., receipt of cash dividends on investments in stocks), often have difficulty identifying costs which are analogous to product costs. Such costs are more likely to be called *direct* costs.

2. Expired *period* costs, or costs expiring this period that were incurred for the purpose of making possible the earning of revenue. It is not possible to trace these costs to the particular units of product sold this period, but it is usually possible to determine that the benefit gained from the costs has been realized and that the amount of expired cost is reasonable and necessary to the operation of the business. Thus period costs are distinguished from *losses*, which are expired costs from which no benefit was gained.

The process of matching periodic revenues with the costs incurred to produce them makes it appear that expense recognition is governed by revenue recognition—that is, that revenues are associated with certain periods of time, and expenses are then associated with the revenues of those periods. In fact, as our discussion of product and period costs indicates, this is only partly true. Product costs, related to products sold or services rendered, are recognized as expenses in the period in which revenue is recognized. Period costs, however—not related to the product or service—are recognized as expenses according to the rules of accrual accounting. Once they are recognized as expenses of a given period, both product and period costs are deducted from the revenues recognized in that period to compute earnings.

A Note on Terminology

There are three sets of adjectives used to classify costs and expenses which overlap each other so much that they are often used interchangeably. It is incorrect to do this, even though the distinctions may seem difficult to understand. They are:

1. The "product"–"period" division distinguishes between costs traceable to units of products purchased or manufactured for resale, and those that are not so traceable. There are varying degrees of traceability, and in borderline cases the distinction depends on the accounting assumptions used in the cost accounting system.

2. The words "direct" and "indirect" also have to do with traceability of costs, but have a broader application. They refer to the traceability of costs to any department, unit, or activity within the firm, whether a product is involved or not. Thus we can speak of the direct and indirect costs of a machine, of a maintenance crew, or of a research and development project.

3. The words "variable" and "nonvariable" refer to the *behavior pattern* of costs, and have nothing to do with traceability. For example, the depreciation cost of a machine is usually nonvariable, but it is a direct cost of (i.e. directly traceable to) the machine. If the machine produces a product, the cost accounting system may provide a method of allocating depreciation cost to the units of product. If so, machine depreciation is also a product cost, even though it is nonvariable. In the next chapter, we shall discuss a system of variable costing (often called direct costing, unfortunately) in which product costs are recorded as period expenses.

Even though there is considerable overlap in these classifications, the distinctions are important. You should learn to use these words carefully in order to avoid ambiguity.

PERFORMANCE MEASUREMENT ILLUSTRATED

It should be clear by now that the measurement of earnings as an index of performance varies widely from one firm to another and depends on the types of activity and transactions carried on by the firm. We cannot provide a survey of all the possible variations, but it may be useful to discuss a few examples to demonstrate the variety of measurement problems that arises. The remainder of this chapter is made up of several illustrations drawn from three types of service activity and a more extensive product-handling illustration. Chapter 8 deals with the more complex problems inherent in measuring the performance of manufacturing firms.

SERVICE ORGANIZATIONS

There are so many kinds of service organizations that the classification is not a particularly meaningful one. They have in common only the fact that they produce or handle no tangible product (that is, something that can be stored and sold to customers in a later period). The absence of a product reduces the usefulness of earnings computations as a measure of performance, because a large share of the costs are period rather than product costs. This means that many of the costs expire (become expenses) in periods in which there is no clear identification with the revenues of that period.

The Attorney

The accomplishment of a practicing attorney can theoretically be measured as the attorney provides legal services for his clients—that is, he earns his revenues in the period in which he performs services. This theory is difficult to implement, because often the dollar value of the services performed for a client cannot be determined until the services have been completed, possibly not until after several accounting periods have passed. In the case of retainers, there is no assurance that any particular amount of services will ever be performed for the client. If the attorney works on only one or two long, important cases at a time, it may be possible and useful to estimate the dollar value of services rendered each accounting period, even though the estimates may have to be corrected in later periods.

In most cases, it is the practice of attorneys (and other professional persons as well, including public accountants) to measure and report their revenue in the period in which the client is billed for services. At this point, the dollar amount becomes almost certain, assuming the client agrees to the amount billed.

An even more conservative method is to wait until the client pays the bill before reporting any revenue. The use of this method eliminates the last bit of uncertainty concerning the amount. It is also useful in cases in which there is substantial doubt as to whether the client will pay his bill. This may be particularly important to physicians, who are more inclined to serve clients without investigating their credit standing beforehand.

In any case, it should be obvious that the attorney is not in business primarily to send bills to clients or to collect cash from them, and either of these methods of recognizing periodic revenue is useful for performance measurement only to the extent that it approximates, period by period, the dollar value of services rendered to clients.

Costs incurred by the attorney in conducting his practice may be grouped in two classes: those costs that can be directly related to the client (that is, those costs that would not have been incurred had it not been for the particular client), and those costs that cannot be related (that is, costs incurred for the joint benefit of two or more clients, or those incurred without regard to a particular client, such as office rent and utilities). Proper accounting for the directly related costs is obvious: These costs should be reported as expenses in the period in which the revenue from that client is recognized.

For example, suppose that for a particular case the attorney buys a highly specialized law book he does not expect to use a second time. The entire cost of the book should first be considered an asset when it is received; this total cost (minus any estimated resale value) should then be considered as an expense, that is, deducted from revenue, in the earnings statement of the period in which the revenue from the particular case is recognized (presumably when the client is billed). To recognize this cost as an expense in the period in which the book was purchased or in the period when the book is paid for, to spread the book's cost (depreciate it) over its physical life, or to wait until the book is disposed

EXHIBIT 7-1

AN ATTORNEY
STATEMENT OF EARNINGS
For June 19x1

Revenues		
Billed value of services rendered to clients (i.e., an estimate of the amounts to be billed to clients as a result of services rendered in June)		$12,500
June retainers (measured on a time basis, since the relationship between the revenue and the specific service rendered or to be rendered is indeterminate)		3,000
Total revenue		$15,500
Expenses		
Direct expenses (expenses incurred on behalf of particular clients in connection with services included in revenues above)		
Travel and entertainment	$2,000	
Detective agency services	2,500	4,500
Contribution to indirect expenses and earnings		$11,000
Indirect expenses		
Library depreciation	$ 200	
Secretarial services	1,000	
Office rent	200	1,400
Net earnings before tax		$ 9,600
Federal income tax		5,600
Net earnings after tax		$ 4,000

of to recognize the expense would be poor accounting practice and would make the earnings statement less useful for performance measurement.

Ordinarily the cost of the attorney's library cannot be related to particular clients. This means that the cost is transferred to expense without regard to any particular revenues. The best procedure in this case is to depreciate the books over the accounting periods beginning with the period of purchase and ending with the period in which the books are no longer useful.

An earnings statement that would be useful for measuring the performance of an attorney is shown in Exhibit 7–1. Detailed explanations are added to illustrate the measurements called for.

As defined in this case, direct expenses are those expired costs directly associated with particular clients. Supplementary records containing the information about this association would have to be maintained. Indirect expenses are measured by the rules of accrual accounting discussed in Chapter 3 for assigning expenses to periods.

The most important expense item is not shown, that is, the cost to the attorney of his personal time devoted to his legal profession. Placing a dollar value on this time may pose a problem, but conceptually it is the amount the attorney could earn in the next best alternative occupation available to him. This value is the so-called *opportunity cost*, that is, the cost of being in the law business measured by the amount he sacrifices by not engaging in the alternative occupation. Comparison of this opportunity cost with his earnings as a lawyer provides a measure of his performance as a lawyer and should be helpful in considering the question of whether he should continue or turn to the alternative occupation. *Implicit costs* such as these are difficult to measure, and usually do not appear in accounting statements.

The Salesman

Consider an individual selling agent or broker who earns commissions on sales of tangible goods, such as appliances, real estate, or the products of a particular manufacturer. Assume he does not own the goods himself, even though he may have physical possession of them (in which case he is a consignee). He may bill the customer under his own name, and/or he may be responsible for cash collections. He may also perform other services, such as delivery or advertising.

In spite of the variety of services performed in individual cases, salesmen invariably consider that accomplishment is recognized (revenue comes into existence) in the period a sale takes place. From the standpoint of the salesman himself, it is the sale that justifies all the other services, since it is the sale for which he is paid a commission and the other services are of relatively minor importance.

Even though the importance of the sale and the relative ease in revenue measurement make the salesman's earnings statement a better measure of accomplishment than the attorney's, effort measurements present much the same problems. Relatively few of the salesman's operating expenses can be assigned to particular sales transactions and most of the expired costs must be assigned to periods rather than directly to revenues. A salesman's earnings statement is given in Exhibit 7–2.

E X H I B I T   7 - 2

A SALESMAN

STATEMENT OF EARNINGS
For June 19x1

Revenue		
Commissions earned		$8,700
Expenses		
Direct		
Packaging and shipping	$ 600	
Advertising	1,000	1,600
Contribution to indirect expenses and earnings		$7,100
Indirect		
Car expense	$ 250	
Bad debt and collection expense	300	
Secretarial services	400	950
Net earnings before tax		$6,150
Federal income tax		3,500
Net earnings after tax		$2,650

Direct and Indirect Expenses

The accountant is constantly faced with the task of distinguishing between direct and indirect expenses (or product and period expenses in the case of mercantile and manufacturing firms). His objective is to classify as many of the expenses as direct, and as few as indirect, as possible, defining direct expenses as those expenses that would not have been incurred if the activities that gave rise to the revenue were not carried on. However, the accountant should not use arbitrary rules of thumb for doing this, because the results would be misleading. In the case of the salesman, for example, the accountant might consider making secretarial services a direct expense by apportioning the secretary's time to the various product lines in some arbitrary manner. If this were done, it might imply to the reader of the earnings statement that secretarial services expense could somehow be reduced if one or more of the product lines were dropped.

Also, whether an expense item is direct or indirect with respect to revenues depends on how revenues are classified. Exhibit 7-2 assumes that commissions-earned revenue can be classified by product lines, and that packaging and shipping expenses and advertising expenses can be identified by particular product lines. On the other hand, car expense can possibly be broken down by geographical area, and bad debt and collection expense by customer or customer class. As is the case with many other accounting concepts, the meaning of direct and indirect expense classifications depends on the facts of the case, the availability of data, and the uses to be made of the results.

The Life Insurance Company

A life insurance company is an example of a single service organization engaged in two related, but dissimilar, lines of business at the same time. In exchange for an insurance premium, the company offers to policy holders the promise of a payment of a certain amount of money to beneficiaries in the event of death of the insured. Since the company must hold substantial sums of money to pay benefits when deaths occur, it also has the problem of investing these funds to earn a return while they are on hand. This investment side of the insurance business is so important that many fear that the financial strength of insurance companies may become greater than is socially desirable. Because of its extremely high social importance, the life insurance industry is subject to greater governmental control than are most other industries.

Certainly it would seem necessary to distinguish between the two businesses carried on by a life insurance company in an earnings statement designed to measure the performance of the company, particularly if comparisons are to be made with other companies that might have different proportions of investment and insurance earnings. Separation of investment revenue from insurance revenue is not at all difficult, but to the extent that much of the administrative and facility costs are incurred jointly (that is, to bring in both investment and insurance revenue, without regard to the separation between the two), complete separation of earnings is not possible. The following are examples of the kinds of revenue and the methods used by accountants to recognize each kind:

1. Interest earnings on bond investments, mortgages, unsecured loans to business firms, etc. A loan contract invariably calls for interest calculated as a function of a given annual rate and is based on a known principal amount outstanding. Earnings are recognized by accountants as a function of the passage of time.

For example, the revenue from a $10,000, 6 per cent bond will be reported in the investor's earnings statements as $50 per month, regardless of when the cash interest is received, assuming that the investor prepares monthly statements and that $10,000 is the cost of the bond.

2. Dividend earnings on investment in stock. Dividends on stock are not contractual and are therefore less predictable than interest. Accountants wait until the dividend is declared before recognizing it as earnings on the stockholders' (insurance company's) earnings statement.

3. Increases in value of securities. Even though many securities, particularly stocks, are purchased for appreciation, rather than dividends, increases in market value of shares owned are not recognized as earned unless the shares are sold. This accounting convention has been adopted for reasons other than performance measurement, and therefore will be discussed more fully in Parts II and III. It may be noted in passing that accountants are much more likely to recognize losses from decreases in market value, even though the shares are not sold.

4. Earnings attributable to shares owned. There is a greater likelihood that earnings attributable to shares of stock owned may be recognized as earnings to the shareowner (even though not evidenced by dividend distributions) rather than increases in market value of the shares. This is particularly likely if the insurance company owns a large proportion of the outstanding shares. Earnings attributable to the shares are at least as important a factor in the decision to purchase as dividends are. It follows that recognition of these earnings may permit a better appraisal of performance than recognition of dividends only. For instance, if the insurance company owns 1,000 shares of X Company stock and the X Company earned $3 per share in a given year, paying only $1 per share in cash dividends, the insurance company could report $3,000 revenue from the investment, rather than just the $1,000 dividend. Accountants, however, are not in full agreement on this point.

5. Earnings from rentals of property owned. Like interest, these earnings are usually contractual and therefore highly predictable, and they are recognized as a function of the passage of time, regardless of the period in which the rent is collected.

Costs incurred by the insurance company to maintain its investment portfolio should be matched against investment revenue. As in the earlier illustrations, most of these costs are necessarily period costs. Examples include the salaries of persons having responsibility for investment decisions and maintenance costs of real estate held for investment. The purchase price of securities owned along with brokers' commissions are examples of product costs. These costs are reported as assets until the securities are sold, at which time they become expenses.

Recognition of insurance premium earnings to a life insurance company represents a rather highly specialized problem that is of no particular interest to beginning students. It may be important to point out, however, that revenue from the sale of a life insurance policy is not recognized at the time of the sale of the policy. Instead, it is reported as earned over the life of the policy in a manner that is also independent of the way in which the premiums are paid. The insurance laws of many states require that insurance companies report all of the salesmen's commissions as expense at the time the policy is sold. Also, companies are usually required to provide reserves against the policy at a rate considerably greater than the rate at which the premium is earned. As a result, earnings statements of life insurance companies often do not give a useful representation of management performance. This is one of the disadvantages resulting from government influence on accounting policy.

PRODUCT-HANDLING ORGANIZATIONS

As has been indicated, product-handling organizations are distinguished from service organizations by the fact that they handle products that can either be sold in the period purchased or stored and sold in a succeeding period. They are distinguished from manufacturers in that the products are sold in essentially the same form in which they were purchased. Any number of borderline examples can be found, however: A television repair shop is essentially a service organization, but it sells the repair parts used, probably at a profit; an automobile dealer is essentially a retailer, but he often offers repair service and financing service as well; many wholesalers perform rather extensive assembly and packaging operations without being considered manufacturers; and most manufacturers carry on extensive product-handling and service functions.

In general, however, product-handling organizations include all retailers and wholesalers, and the designation is useful for accounting purposes. The accounting conventions for revenue and expense recognition are relatively uncomplicated for performance measurement. In the vast majority of wholesaling and retailing operations, the selling function is relatively so important compared with other functions performed (delivery, advertising, credit and financing, etc.) that revenue is recognized at the point of sale, and only then. Most of the other services performed are assumed to play their most important role by contributing to product sales, and their costs are assumed to be recovered in the sale price of the product. (One important exception is the service charge (interest) customers must sometimes pay for credit extensions beyond the normal credit period.)

In performance measurement of product-handling firms, therefore, accounting problems arise in accounting for costs:

1. The first problem is to distinguish between product costs and period costs. As discussed above, this is an extremely important distinction for earnings measurement, because product costs attach to the asset inventory and are deducted from the revenue in the period of the sale of the merchandise. The expiration of period costs is measured in accordance with the rules of accrual accounting.

2. The second problem is to compare actual costs incurred with an estimate of the costs that should have been incurred, preferably standards in the case of variable costs, and budgeted costs for all others. These problems, which were discussed in Chapters 5 and 6, are raised again here for two reasons: First, standard costs are not commonly used in product-handling firms, although there are few convincing reasons why they should not be. Many firms use budgets for period costs but argue that sales volume and revenue are too unpredictable to permit realistic budgeting on a comprehensive basis. Second, where standards are used for product costs, variances from standard should be treated as adjustments to period expenses, that is, added to period expenses if they are unfavorable or deducted from period expenses if they are favorable. This means that, for

performance measurement purposes, merchandise inventories and cost of goods sold should be measured at standard cost. On the other hand, when the earnings figure is to be used for other purposes, particularly by external users, it is sometimes preferable to measure inventories and cost of goods sold at actual cost, even though a standard cost system is employed for internal accounting purposes.

Assume the following situations, oversimplified for illustration purposes. For two months the Pitch Black Coal Company, a wholesale concern, handled the quantities of coal shown in Exhibit 7–3. The selling price per ton is $12 in October and November. The standard purchase price for coal is $7 per ton and the standard freight cost is $3 per ton. Actual costs were as shown in Exhibit 7–4. The earnings statements for October and November are given in Exhibit 7–5.

EXHIBIT 7-3

	Tons of coal October	Tons of coal November
Inventory beginning of month, in tons	3,000	3,400
Coal purchased, per invoice records	4,200	4,600
Available for sale	7,200	8,000
Sold during the month, per sales records	3,500	4,800
Inventory that should be on hand	3,700	3,200
Inventory on hand, by physical estimate	3,400	3,300
Variance	300U	100F

EXHIBIT 7-4

	October Tons	October Total	October Per ton	November Tons	November Total	November Per ton
Coal	4,200	$28,560	$6.80	4,600	$33,350	$7.25
Freight	4,200	13,020	3.10	4,600	13,800	3.00
Selling and administrative expenses		4,800			5,300	

On the financial position statements prepared at October 31 and November 30, the actual quantities of the coal inventories would be priced at standard cost of $10 per ton, or $34,000 and $33,000 respectively. On the statement of earnings these are shown at standard quantities as $37,000 and $32,000. The difference is measured by the quantity variances of $3,000 (unfavorable) and $1,000 (favorable) respectively.

EXHIBIT 7-5

PITCH BLACK COAL COMPANY
STATEMENT OF EARNINGS
For October and November, 19x1

	19x1	
	October	November
Sales ($12 per ton)	$42,000	$57,600
Cost of goods sold, at standard cost		
Inventory, beginning ($10 per ton)	$30,000	$34,000
Purchases ($7 per ton)	29,400	32,200
Freight ($3 per ton)	12,600	13,800
Total	$72,000	$80,000
Inventory, ending (standard quantity—$10 per ton)	37,000	32,000
Cost of goods sold	$35,000	$48,000
Earnings margin	$ 7,000	$ 9,600
Period expenses		
Selling and administration expenses	$ 4,800	$ 5,300
Purchase price variance	420F	1,150U
Inventory quantity variance ($10 per ton)	3,000U	1,000F
Total period expenses	$ 7,380	$ 5,450
Earnings (loss) from operations	$ (380)	$ 4,150

Several points about the statements should be noted:

1. Freight cost is treated as a product cost rather than a period cost, making the total inventoriable standard cost $10, rather than $7.

2. The acceptability of treating the variances as period costs, thus causing the inventories and cost of goods sold to be valued at standard cost of $10 per ton, may depend on the causes of the variances. For example, if unfavorable variances can be shown to result from inefficiency or poor decisions, little objection can be raised. However, variances resulting from obsolete standards mean that the standard cost of $10 per ton should be revised.

3. Notice that the purchase price variance applies to all goods purchased in October and November, regardless of whether the goods are sold or held in inventory, and includes variances resulting from the difference between actual and standard purchase price, as well as the difference between actual and standard freight charges.

4. The statements do not indicate whether an attempt was made to compare actual and budgeted selling and administrative expenses. If it was made, it was made independently of the reporting system.

SUMMARY

Chapter 7 deals with performance measurement of service organizations and product-handling organizations by measuring periodic earnings. Since the assumed objective of the firm is long-run earnings optimization, it follows that the measure appropriate for periodic performance measurement is one that answers the question, How much did the activities of the current period contribute to long-run earnings?

Periodic earnings, defined in Chapter 2 as the increase in the net assets of the firm resulting from certain activities, presents difficult measurement problems. In Chapter 7 we find it more convenient to think of earnings as revenues minus the sum of product and period expenses, in which (a) revenues are measured by selecting one activity (such as the sale of merchandise to customers) and recognizing revenues from all activities as if they were earned by that one activity; (b) expired product costs are matched with those revenues; and (c) expired period costs are associated with the accounting period in which the sale is made, rather than with the product sold. Illustrations of earnings measurements were presented for service and product-handling firms.

Questions for Review

7-1. How is performance measured for the top management of a firm?

7-2. Name several groups of financial statement users that might define earnings differently.

7-3. What groups of financial statement users have primary responsibility for making decisions based upon their appraisal of the management of the firm?

7-4. Why should the accountant, rather than management, define accomplishment for earnings measurement purposes?

7-5. What major responsibilities should management have in order to be considered an earnings center for performance measurement purposes?

7-6. How are earnings measured for performance measurement purposes?

7-7. In actual practice, how is an activity selected for the measurement of accomplishment?

7-8. Distinguish between product and period costs.

7-9. Three concepts of earnings are discussed in this chapter. They are earnings for measuring management performance, measuring taxation liability, and determining possible wage or dividend increases. Why do concepts of earnings differ in these situations?

7-10. Define each of the following terms and describe their use:
  a. variable and nonvariable costs
  b. direct and indirect costs
  c. product and period costs

7-11. Describe the matching process in the measurement of earnings for enterprise performance. Include in your answer the terms "time period," "product costs," and "period costs."

7-12. At what point in the operating cycle is revenue generally recognized? Describe several business situations that would make a departure from the general rule preferable, and justify these exceptions.

7-13. Revenue is normally recorded at the time of sale. Under what conditions (if at all) would you recognize revenue *prior* to the sale? Why?

Problems for Analysis

7-14. The Blue Streak Cab Company owns twelve taxicabs. Each cab has its own driver who is expected to be cruising or on call twelve hours a day, five days a week. Drivers are paid by the hour, and they are permitted to retain all tips. Cab maintenance is done by a mechanic in the company garage.

The manager, concerned about dwindling profits, has suggested a plan for measuring the performance of each driver. "We know the fares recorded on the meter in each cab, and we can easily keep track of gas and oil, maintenance, and repairs for each cab," he said. "Wouldn't total fares minus the driver's wages and cab expenses give us a fair measure of performance for each driver?" It was suggested that the manager discuss each driver's performance with him from time to time, and that a year-end bonus, based on company profits, be awarded to the best two or three drivers. It was felt that such a plan might reduce the driver's temptation to (a) pocket a portion of his fares without reporting them, (b) spend too much working time off the job, and (c) use the cab for personal reasons.

  a. Could each driver be considered an earnings center for performance measurement purposes? What measurement difficulties would you anticipate?

  b. Do you agree with the manager's proposal for measuring driver performance? Why?

  c. Would the bonus plan work? Why?

7-15. The Daisy Dairy Company is engaged in the retail sale of dairy products. There are twelve driver-salesmen who are assigned geographical areas within the service route. Each driver-salesman is paid a salary of $30 per week and a commission of 10 per cent of sales.

Some of the routes are in heavily populated areas and others are in rural areas. The distance driven per driver-salesman per day ranges from forty miles to two hundred miles. Ten of the routes have been in existence for over five years and are well established. Two (11 and 12) have been operated less than one year. Each driver-salesman is permitted to advertise in local news media. The cost of advertising must be paid by him. Sales and mileage data for a recent week are as follows:

Driver-salesman	Sales	Miles driven
1	$2,050	45
2	1,400	80
3	1,725	90
4	1,250	100
5	900	125
6	1,900	130
7	1,800	65
8	1,100	170
9	950	175
10	1,650	110
11	700	195
12	750	180

There have been numerous complaints from driver-salesmen regarding the mileage differential and uniform commission rate. Many driver-salesmen believe that commission rates and salaries should reflect the route density and existing sales level of the route.

a. Could each driver-salesman be considered an earnings center for performance measurement purposes? Discuss fully.

7-16. Wheels, Inc., is engaged in the manufacture of automobiles. It has sales distributors throughout the United States. The company has a wholly owned credit subsidiary, Auto-Credit, Inc., which is engaged in financing automobiles sold through the sales distributors. The general manager of Auto-Credit has been delegated complete authority over the operations except that he is not permitted to expand his automobile financing markets beyond Wheels, Inc., sales distributors. Recently the general manager of Auto-Credit has requested permission to expand his markets beyond company-affiliated sales distributors.

a. Should Auto-Credit, Inc., be considered an earnings center for performance measurement purposes? Discuss.

b. Should the general manager of Auto-Credit, Inc., be permitted to expand his automobile financing market beyond Wheels, Inc., sales distributors? Explain fully the reasoning supporting your decision.

7-17. The following excerpts are taken from the Ling-Temco-Vought, Inc., Annual Report for 1967:

LTV IMPROVES ITS DIVERSIFICATION:
SUBSIDIARIES SEEK SIMILAR STATUS

Companies diversify for many reasons, to: expand technological and operational capabilities; enter new markets; add financial strength; secure protection against economic dislocations; prepare themselves to meet tomorrow's requirements; secure management talent with new skills.

In total, all of these objectives are based on an effort to improve earnings. At LTV we strive for an additional ingredient: the building, to the greatest extent possible, of diversified earnings. Diversification for LTV has been exemplified by our Project Redeployment concept, which has been widely publicized. This concept seeks primarily to reduce LTV's dependence on any one product or technology or business. The concept has worked for us and a record of which we are proud has been established for all to see.

The 1967 example was the redeployment of the former Wilson & Co. into three separate subsidiaries which project LTV into markets for food/meat, sports equipment/toys and pharmaceuticals/cosmetic ingredients/industrial chemicals.

Since diversification exists as an essential key to our growth, we have not hesitated to push duplication of this effort for and within our subsidiaries along the pattern established by the parent company. The 1967 acquisitions by our subsidiaries indicate such efforts are producing results:

LTV Electrosystems broadened its product lines with the acquisition of Memcor, which produces battlefield radio units and other electronic equipment and components.

LTV Ling Altec further penetrated European environmental testing markets by increasing to 100% its 45% interest in the common stock of Pye-Ling, changing the English company's name to LTV Ling Altec, Limited.

Okonite entered the specialty wire and instrument cable markets through the merger of Jefferson Wire and Cable Corporation, Worcester, Mass.

LTV Ling Altec expanded on a major scale into new areas with the acquisition of wholesale and retail electronic sales through Allied Radio Corporation, Chicago, the nation's largest catalog distributor of electronics equipment.

Wilson Pharmaceutical & Chemical Corporation has expanded its distribution of emulsifiers and emollients for cosmetics and related products through Goldschmidt Chemical Corporation, New York City.

Okonite entered the floor covering market through General Felt Industries, Inc.

Wilson Sporting Goods announced an agreement in principle before the end of the year for the merger of Nissen Corporation, Cedar Rapids, Iowa, in a transaction that joins the world's largest manufacturer of trampolines and other gymnastic equipment to the world's largest maker and marketer of recreational products for athletics and sports.

LTV Ling Altec significantly broadened its electronics markets and industrial activities with another acquisition initiated before the close of 1967 and now completed—Escon, Inc., a highly diversified participant in electronic manufacturing and other industrial activities. Shareholders of both companies approved this transaction March 12.

At this writing, LTV is in the process of completing another major acquisition, that of Greatamerica Corporation. The exchange offer for any and all of the Greatamerica shares will remain open until April 1, 1968. At this time sufficient shares have been tendered to give LTV control of Greatamerica and its subsidiaries.

DIVERSIFICATION BY DESIGN TOPPLES DOMINO,
"BIGNESS" THEORIES

LTV has designed built-in objectives of diversification for parent and subsidiary companies. Each subsidiary, in utilizing the "optimum decentralization" concept of Project Redeployment, has positioned itself to effect such diversification. Each is operationally and financially independent of the other, thereby existing as its own profit and credit center. Each is also generally financially independent of the parent corporation. Should a single subsidiary experience trouble, its adversity would not affect the other subsidiaries, and would affect the parent corporation only incrementally.

Motivation to prompt the top executives of our subsidiaries to do their best is also provided by the "optimum decentralization" concept. Each member of a subsidiary management team has an equity position in his company through stock options and ownership, each takes heed of built-in incentive programs. We avoid one-man operations and we strive to build a bank of strong executive talent. We insist that subsidiary managers excel at their work and we believe they do.

With the completion of the Wilson merger, the LTV Dallas corporate staff was strengthened by the addition of some eleven experienced executives and staff people from the Wilson corporate staff, including Mr. Roscoe G. Haynie, and two new LTV Vice Presidents, who were formerly officers of Wilson. Also during 1967, six LTV people were elected vice presidents, another two being added early in 1968. Total employment in LTV reached in excess of 60,000 employees during the year.

As a parent operating company, LTV provides certain services to subsidiary management which they could not provide for themselves without costly duplication to aid them in achieving their goals. Such services include long-range planning, financial planning and controls, legal guidance, industrial relations, public relations, basic research and computer services, and expertise in the area of mergers and acquisitions. We provide these services on a sustained basis and thereby free subsidiary managements to do what they know best: operate their companies in their own competitive markets.

We have found this type of corporate structure mitigates much of the mediocrity and complacency which often comes with "bigness." We have tried, and we believe we have succeeded, to retain the dynamics found in entrepreneur-led companies, by instilling in the subsidiaries much of the spirit that has characterized the growth of LTV since its beginning years. We believe we thus have avoided much of the complacent conservatism and caretaker type of approach to management which so often accompanies "bigness." Project Redeployment, with its attendant principles of responsibility and accountability, plus our own brand of corporate technology, gives us, we believe, an excellent way to properly manage bigness.

Sales and net income for various subsidiaries of Ling-Temco-Vought, Inc., for 1967 are as follows:

LTV AEROSPACE CORPORATION & SUBSIDIARIES
(in thousands)

	1967	1966	Increase
Sales	$343,696	$231,552	48%
Net income	9,578	5,809	65%

THE OKONITE COMPANY & SUBSIDIARIES
(in thousands)

	1967°	1966°°	Increase
Sales	$103,238	$ 90,252	14%
Net income	9,009	7,715	17%

° Includes Jefferson Wire and Cable Corporation on a pooling of interest basis and General Felt Industries for the month of December only.
°° As reported; does not include Jefferson or General Felt.

LTV ELECTROSYSTEMS, INC. & SUBSIDIARIES
(in thousands)

	1967°	1966°°	Increase
Sales	$181,788	$123,564	47%
Net income	5,354	2,644	102%

° Includes Memcor on a pooling of interest basis.
°° As reported; does not include Memcor.

WILSON SPORTING GOODS CO. & SUBSIDIARIES
(in thousands)

	1967°	1966°	Increase
Sales	$ 89,066	$ 83,294	7%
Net income	4,033	4,804	6%

° Pro forma based upon historical results of the present company and/or historical results of divisions of its corporate predecessor.

LTV LING ALTEC, INC. & SUBSIDIARIES
(in thousands)

	1967°	1966°°	Increase
Sales	$102,408	$ 29,242	250%
Net income	2,329	859	171%

° Includes Allied Radio Corporation on a pooling of interest basis.
°° As reported; does not include Allied.

WILSON PHARMACEUTICAL & CHEMICAL CORPORATION & SUBSIDIARIES
(in thousands)

	1967°	1966°	Increase
Sales	$ 39,514	$ 38,609	2%
Net income	1,717	1,463	17%

° Pro forma based upon historical results of the present company and/or historical results of divisions of its corporate predecessor.

a. Evaluate the organizational philosophy of Ling-Temco-Vought from the standpoint of motivating its key executives.

b. How many earnings (profit) centers exist for the company?

c. Do you foresee any limitations, for performance measurement purposes, in any of the earnings centers that you identified in part b?

d. Evaluate LTV's policy of making each subsidiary "generally financially independent of the parent corporation."

e. LTV attempts to motivate top executives "through stock options and ownership" and by providing certain services (such as long-range planning, financial planning and controls, legal guidance, industrial relations, public relations, basic research and computer services, and expertise in the area of mergers and acquisitions) on a centralized basis in order to allow "subsidiary managements to do what they know best: operate their own companies in their own competitive markets." Do you foresee any conflict in these two approaches to motivation?

7-18. Some oil companies are thought of as oil producers, that is, they are engaged primarily in the business of finding, lifting, and selling crude oil. Others are primarily oil refiners and/or marketers, who buy more crude oil than they produce and devote their efforts and investment to refining crude oil into various grades of gasoline, fuel oil, asphalt, etc. and selling these products to wholesalers and users. Still other oil companies are fully integrated, or balanced; they have production, refining, transportation, and marketing facilities of about equal capacity, so that they are equipped to process and sell their own crude oil without purchasing from or selling to other oil companies. There are established market prices for oil properties with known oil reserves, for various grades of crude oil, and for various grades of refined products.

a. How would the managers of an oil company decide whether it is more profitable to be an oil producer, an oil refiner and marketer, or fully integrated?

b. If you were the president of a fully integrated company, how would you compare the performance of the production department with the performance of the refining department? Why is this comparison important?

7-19. Managements of all firms like to keep a close check on their volume of business. Sometimes daily fluctuations are significant, but ordinarily weekly or monthly variations are sufficient. Some of the more important reasons for management's interest follow:

1. Volume is often a valid index of the earnings, and with experience, management can estimate earnings for the period without waiting for all expenses to be computed.

2. Recent fluctuations in volume often indicate what to expect in future periods. Management needs volume estimates in order to plan labor and materials requirements.

3. Volume is a measure of accomplishment for the period. Volume that falls below expectations often calls for significant changes in operating methods.

In each of the cases given below, select the measure or measures of volume that you consider most useful in achieving these purposes. While it may be necessary to have more than one measure of volume in an individual case, the value of having a common denominator for the entire business should not be underestimated. In each case, write a short paragraph defending your answer.

Case I

A retail store handles large gas and electric appliances of several different manufacturers under different arrangements:

1. In most cases, the retailer purchases appliances from the manufacturer and takes the risk of loss in the event of failure to resell to customers. Defective merchandise may be returned to the manufacturer for full credit. The manufacturers suggest retail prices, but the retailer is not bound by them, and often he will sell at lower-than-suggested prices to meet competition. Orders are often taken for models not in stock, which can be filled in about ten days. The retailer may not return the merchandise to the manufacturer if the customer changes his mind.

About half the sales of purchased merchandise are made on terms of "net thirty days," * and the other half on an installment plan providing for about 20 per cent down payment, with the rest to be paid out over twenty-four months. Quoted prices are the same for both types of sales, except that interest and service charges are added to the installment payments.

Bad debts, collection expense, and repossession costs amount to about 1 per cent of sales made on "net thirty days" terms and about 8 per cent of the installment sales. About 15 per cent of the installment sales result in repossessions,

---

* The bill must be paid in full within thirty days of its date.

but the value of repossessed merchandise usually equals the unpaid installment balance.

The company also sells used and repossessed appliances, always on "net thirty days" terms.

2. Some of the new merchandise is handled on a consignment basis, which means that title to it is retained by the manufacturer, who takes the risk of loss if it is unsold. Manufacturers establish retail prices, and the retailer (consignee) earns a commission (from 5 to 15 per cent) of the sales price. Since price reductions are charged entirely against the commission, there is very little price cutting on consignment merchandise. The consignment lines are typically the less well-established lines.

Experience has shown the management that the popularity of various lines will shift as models change, which is usually every year. The busiest months are January, April, May, November, and December; the slowest, July and August.

Case II

A construction company specializes in apartment dwellings and small office buildings. Contracts are usually negotiated for several weeks or months prior to beginning of construction, which often requires more than a year for some of the larger buildings. The construction company will usually handle architectural work, excavation, and electrical, plumbing, and heating installation on a subcontract basis.

Except for purchase of the land, which is accomplished by the ultimate owner, the construction company usually handles its own financing. During the period of construction, construction and subcontracting costs are usually paid for out of the proceeds from bank loans made for the term of construction. The bank loans are paid off when the ultimate owner pays the contract price after construction is completed. Until that time, legal title to the building rests with the contractor.

The purchaser of the building must accept and pay for it on completion, subject only to specifications called for in the original agreement, including reductions in the price because of delays in completion date, etc. In some cases (particularly those in which the purchaser may have a weak credit standing), the contractor may insist on substantial cash payments as construction progresses.

While the volume of building is considerably greater in the warm months than in the cold months, the contractor manages to keep permanent employees busy all year on interior work. Temporary labor is added in the summer months. At a given time, the contractor may have as many as six or eight contracts in various stages of completion.

Case III

A certified public accounting firm consists of three partners and fifteen employees. The firm performs audits, prepares tax returns and gives tax advice, designs and installs accounting systems, and acts as business consultant for business clients and individuals. About 80 per cent of the firm's expenses (almost 90 per cent of which are salaries) is directly allocable to particular clients; the other 20 per cent is considered overhead. Clients are billed in direct proportion to partner and employee time devoted to them at hourly rates commensurate with the level of professional ability required by the assignment.

Although some of the tax and consulting assignments require only a few hours for each client, most of the auditing and accounting assignments extend over several weeks or months. Many of the annual audit assignments are assumed to be continuing engagements year after year; these clients are billed once a year. Others are billed at the end of the engagement or annually, whichever is the shorter period. Terms are thirty days, with special arrangements for payments of larger fees.

Case IV

A steel-castings manufacturer specializes in heavy-duty wheels, axles, springs, and couplings for railroad cars. Since orders for these parts are received from the car manufacturer from one to two months ahead of delivery, and since the steel-castings cycle is less than one month, no inventories of work in process or finished goods are carried. Contracts for these parts are negotiated at infrequent intervals, and only the price is subject to more frequent change. Prices are dependent on manufacturing costs and are adjusted to give constant margins to the steel-castings manufacturer (that is, cost changes are passed on to the car manufacturer). The company has only one customer, and there is no serious competition in the field.

Case V

A textile manufacturer devotes almost all of its efforts to standard cotton goods. The field is highly competitive, and there are many customers. Orders are filled out of substantial finished goods inventories that are carried in order to assure quick delivery to customers. Competition establishes the price. The customers buy in small quantities and the collection problem is serious because it is not always feasible to investigate the credit standing of the customer before filling his order.

7-20. In each of the following, assume that the numbered events occur in the order indicated and that each event occurs in a different accounting period. Indicate the accounting period in which accomplishment (revenue) of the firm should be recognized for purposes of measuring the performance of the firm, period by period. Give reasons to support your selection in each case.

    a. A manufacturing firm (a) acquired and used labor and materials; (b) completed production; (c) sold the product; and (d) collected cash from a customer.

    b. A construction company (a) signed a contract with a customer for a building, specifying the price and other conditions; (b) acquired and used labor and materials; (c) completed construction of the building; (d) legally transferred the building to the customer; and (e) collected cash from the customer.

c. A manufacturing firm (a) received and accepted an order from a customer, specifying the price and other conditions; (b) acquired and used labor and materials; (c) completed production; (d) delivered the product to the customer; and (e) collected cash from the customer.

d. A division of a large firm (a) received a production quota from its home office, specifying the price and other conditions; (b) acquired and used labor and materials; (c) completed production; and (d) delivered the finished product to the home office.

e. A firm of architects (a) signed a contract with a customer to draw some house plans; (b) completed and delivered the plans to the customer; (c) sent the customer a bill; and (d) collected cash from the customer.

f. A retail store (a) purchased goods from a wholesaler; (b) paid the wholesaler's bill; (c) sold goods to a customer; (d) sent a bill to the customer; and (e) collected cash from the customer.

g. A retail store (a) received and accepted an order from a customer for goods not in stock; (b) placed an order for goods with a wholesaler; (c) received the goods from the wholesaler; (d) delivered the goods to the customer; (e) sent the customer a bill; and (f) collected cash from the customer.

h. A retail store (a) received and accepted an order from a customer for goods not in stock; (b) collected cash from the customer; (c) placed an order for goods with a wholesaler; (d) received the goods from the wholesaler; and (e) delivered the goods to the customer.

7-21. Dr. Amos is a general practitioner in the slum district of a large city. His policy is to treat all patients who ask for his services, regardless of their economic circumstances. Consequently, uncollectable fees are a problem. The rate of uncollectable fees varies considerably from month to month. The following information relates to the medical practice of Dr. Amos for the first three years of operations:

	Year		
	1	*2*	*3*
Amount billed to patients	$18,500	$19,000	$22,100
Cash collected from patients	9,000	14,200	11,700
Salary of nurse	3,000	3,000	3,600
Medical supplies purchased	1,350	1,700	2,450
Medical supplies used	900	1,500	2,050
Medical equipment purchased (estimated life of 7 years)	7,000	0	0
Rent	1,800	1,800	2,400
Other expenses	950	1,275	1,594

Prepare a performance report for Dr. Amos for each of the three years of operations. (Defend the amount you indicate as revenue for each of the three periods.)

7-22. The Woodside Billboard Advertising Company sells advertising space on its billboards under three-month contracts, payable by the customer in advance. The cost of erecting billboards along highways is borne by Woodside, and rental to landowners is arranged on an annual basis, also payable in advance.

Woodside's statement of financial position on May 31, 19x5, is as follows:

WOODSIDE BILLBOARD ADVERTISING COMPANY
STATEMENT OF FINANCIAL POSITION
As of May 31, 19x5

Assets			Liabilities and Owners' Equity		
Cash		$ 30,500	Liabilities:		
Prepaid rent[a]		74,000	Customers' deposits[b]		$ 32,500
Billboards	$27,000		Accounts payable		6,500
— Accumulated			Total liabilities		$ 39,000
depreciation	10,500		Owners' equity:		
Net billboards		16,500	Capital stock	$50,000	
			Retained earnings	32,000	
			Total owners' equity		82,000
			Total liabilities and		
Total assets		$121,000	owners' equity		$121,000

	Expiration date	Amount prepaid 5/31/x5		Expiration date	Amount prepaid 5/31/x5
[a] Prepaid rent	6/31/x5	$ 5,000	[b] Customers' deposits	6/30/x5	$11,500
	9/31/x5	10,000		7/31/x5	21,000
	12/31/x5	21,000			$32,500
	3/31/x5	38,000			
		$74,000			

The statement of cash receipts and disbursements for June is as follows:

WOODSIDE BILLBOARD ADVERTISING COMPANY
STATEMENT OF CASH RECEIPTS AND DISBURSEMENTS
For June 19x5

Cash provided from: Deposits on advertising contracts for		
6/1–8/31		$45,000
— Cash used for:[a]		
Payment to landowners on rental contracts for		
7/1/x5–6/30/x6	$38,400	
Other cash expenses	6,900	
Payments on accounts payable	4,000	
Total cash used		49,300
Decrease in cash		$ (4,300)
Cash balance, 5/31		30,500
Cash balance, 6/30		$26,200

[a] Other expenses not paid in cash:
  June operating expenses to be paid in July: $2,000
  June depreciation of billboards: $500

  a. Prepare a schedule showing:
    1. revenue to be reported by month from contracts currently in effect with customers
    2. rent expense by month resulting from contracts currently in effect with landowners
  b. Prepare an earnings statement for June 19x5.
  c. Prepare a financial position statement as of June 30, 19x5.

7-23. Michael Shilling, CPA, is the owner of a public accounting firm that offers three types of service to clients: (1) auditing, which includes examining financial statements and expressing an opinion on them; (2) tax service, which includes preparing returns and giving advice on tax matters; and (3) management services, which includes installing accounting systems and giving advice on financial problems.

Most audit and tax engagements are completed in the month in which they begin, except for engagements that begin late in the month and certain management-service engagements that require several months to complete. In these latter cases, when it is known that the fee will be large, the client will occasionally request an interim billing and will pay some or all of the amount billed.

The billing rates per hour, the hours worked in June (twenty-two working days), and the monthly salary of each accountant are shown below:

Name	Title	Hourly billing rate	Monthly salary	Hours Worked in June Billing time	Hours Worked in June Unassigned
Mr. Shilling	owner	$30		120	56
Mr. Alton	CPA	20	$2,000	176	
Mr. Baldwin	CPA	20	1,500	140	36
Mr. Curtis	staff accountant	10	900	176	
Mr. Dalton	staff accountant	10	700	176	
Miss Elright	stenographer		500		176

Mr. Shilling's unassigned time is spent in administering the firm, talking with prospective clients, etc. Mr. Baldwin spends his unassigned time in tax research, and no attempt is made to assign the stenographer's time to particular clients.

The May 31 statement of financial position and the June statement of cash receipts and disbursements follow:

MICHAEL SHILLING

STATEMENT OF FINANCIAL POSITION
As of May 31, 19x5

Assets		Liabilities and Owners' Equity	
Cash	$ 5,000	Accounts payable	$ 1,500
Accounts receivable [a]	20,000	Michael Shilling proprietorship [b]	23,500
		Total liabilities and	
Total assets	$25,000	owners' equity	$25,000

[a] Of this amount $4,000 is due from clients for completed assignments; $16,000 represents billable charges to clients for engagements unfinished by May 31.
[b] This is the equivalent of "owners' equity" in a corporation's statement of financial position.

MICHAEL SHILLING

STATEMENT OF CASH RECEIPTS AND DISBURSEMENTS
For June 19x5

Cash provided from:		
Collections from clients:		
For work completed in May [a]		$ 4,000
For work completed in June:		
Work begun in previous months	$ 9,000	
Work done in June	10,000	
Total work completed in June		19,000
Total cash provided		$23,000

[a] See statement of financial position for May 31.

MICHAEL SHILLING (CONT.)

— Cash used for:		
Salary payments (ignore payroll deductions)	$ 5,600	
Other cash expenses[b]	3,100	
Payment on accounts payable	1,200	
Total cash used		9,900
Increase in cash		$13,100
+ Cash Balance, 5/31		5,000
Cash balance, 6/30		$18,100

[b] Additional June expenses of $1,000 will be paid in July.

a. How does Mr. Shilling measure his monthly revenue? Describe two other methods he could have used, and discuss the advantages and disadvantages of the three methods.

b. In view of your answer to *a*, is the title "accounts receivable" in the financial position statement an appropriate title? What alternative do you suggest?

c. Prepare a schedule that will help Mr. Shilling measure the performance of his employees (excluding the stenographer). Discuss additional information that would be helpful in refining this measurement.

d. Prepare an earnings statement for the firm for June and a statement of financial position as of June 30.

7-24. Campus-View Apartments, Inc., owns and operates a ninety-two-unit apartment complex. All tenants sign a one-year lease and are required to pay monthly rentals in advance, in addition to a $100 security deposit that is refunded within seven days after vacating the apartment, provided that there has been no unusual damage. Tenants are required to pay their own utility charges.

Campus-View's statement of financial position as of October 31, 19x1, is as follows:

CAMPUS-VIEW APARTMENTS, INC.

STATEMENT OF FINANCIAL POSITION

As of October 31, 19x1

Assets		Liabilities and Owners' Equity	
Cash	$ 8,500	Liabilities:	
Accounts receivable	3,100	Accounts payable for supplies	$ 1,400
Supplies	1,450	Tenant deposits	8,300
Prepaid insurance	975	Accrued interest payable	4,800
Land	105,000	Mortgage payable, 8%	720,000
Buildings and equipment,		Total liabilities	$734,500
$800,000		Owners' equity:	
— Accumulated depreciation		Capital stock	$ 80,000
$86,000	714,000	Retained earnings	18,525
		Total owners' equity	$ 98,525
		Total liabilities and	
Total Assets	$833,025	owners' equity	$833,025

CAMPUS-VIEW APARTMENTS

STATEMENT OF CASH RECEIPTS AND DISBURSEMENTS

For November 19x1

Cash provided from:			
Rentals received from tenants			$14,200
Deposits received from new tenants			600
Receipts from laundry and other vending machines			360
			$15,160
Cash used for:			
Payments on accounts payable		$1,200	
Mortgage payment, November 1:			
Principal	$3,000		
Interest	4,800	7,800	
Management fee		710	
Salaries		800	
Repairs and maintenance		970	
Miscellaneous		160	11,640
Increase in cash			$ 3,520
Cash balance, October 31			8,500
Cash balance, November 30			$12,020

Additional information:
1. Billings to tenants, $13,700
2. Purchase of supplies on account, $370
3. Supplies inventory, November 30, $810
4. Real estate taxes for November (payable on April 30), $1,500
5. Depreciation on building, $1,500
6. Accrued interest for November, $4,780
7. Prepaid insurance, November 30, $890

a. Prepare an earnings statement for November 19x1, with supporting computations.

b. Prepare a statement of financial position as of November 30, 19x1, with supporting computations.

7-25. The data shown below were taken from the books of Sullivans', a men's clothing store:

	October	*November*	*December*
		19x4	
Sales to customers	$20,000	$25,000	$30,000
Purchases at cost	15,000	22,000	19,000
Selling and administrative expenses	3,000	3,500	5,000

Monthly financial statements were prepared, using the following inventory cost amounts:

September 30	$ 9,000
October 31	11,000
November 30	14,000
December 31	12,000

a. Prepare a comparative statement of earnings for October, November, and December 19x4.

b. In January of 19x5, auditors discovered that the inventory counts at October 31 and November 30 contained errors. The October 31 inventory should have been $12,500, and the November 30 inventory should have been $13,500. Prepare a corrected comparative earnings statement for October, November, and December.

c. Explain precisely the effect of each error on reported earnings of the store.

7-26. Franklin Steel Supply buys steel products from a factory at prices that do not include freight. Franklin arranges its own transportation and pays its own freight bills on purchased merchandise. The steel products are sold to local customers on the same basis (i.e., the customer pays the freight to the trucking company).

On February 1, Franklin Steel Supply had 3,000 tons of steel inventory on hand for which they had paid $12 per ton (including freight estimated at $3 per ton), and which had at that time an estimated selling value of $18 per ton.

During February they purchased 2,000 tons of steel for $10 per ton (invoice price), paid $6,000 freight on these purchases, and sold 2,500 tons of steel to customers for $20 per ton, or $50,000. Physical inventory taken on February 28 verified that 2,500 tons of steel were on hand. This inventory has a cost of $13 per ton (includes freight), and probably will be sold for $20 per ton in March.

Assuming that February selling and administrative expenses amounted to $11,000 and that there were no other expenses, prepare an earnings statement for February (ignore income tax).

7-26. The DeLux Hardware Store purchases hardware from several wholesalers and manufacturers for subsequent sale to customers. The merchandise inventory is stored in a warehouse and on the store shelves from the time it is purchased to the time of sale. Store employees take physical inventory at the end of each month (i.e., they count the items on hand and compute the cost of these items), so that the inventory can be controlled (i.e., fast- and slow-moving items are determined, shortages detected, etc.) and so that monthly financial statements can be prepared. The store recognizes revenue (accomplishment) only at time of sale.

Information taken from store records for November and December follows:

	November	December
Sales	$50,000	$65,000
Purchases of merchandise	27,000	36,000
Freight cost on purchases	2,700	3,600
Clerks' salaries	8,000	9,000
Store rent	1,000	1,000
Depreciation of store fixtures	1,500	1,600
Administrative expenses	6,000	5,700

In view of the relationship between freight cost and cost of purchases shown above, it seems reasonable to suggest that an allowance of 10 per cent of purchase cost is a reasonable estimate of the freight cost on any item.

Cost (not including freight cost) of month-end inventories is: October 31, $12,000; November 30, $14,000; December 31, $9,000.

Prepare a comparative statement of earnings for November and December.

Chapter Eight # PERFORMANCE MEASUREMENT: EARNINGS IN MANUFACTURING ORGANIZATIONS

INTRODUCTION

In Appendix 3A we briefly described the essentials of the manufacturing process, for the purpose of demonstrating how double-entry bookkeeping can be adapted to the transactions, internal as well as external, in which "typical" manufacturing organizations engage. That description is extremely important to this chapter, which is devoted to the accounting problem of performance measurement in manufacturing organizations. As in other firms, the principal index of performance is periodic earnings, but there are special difficulties in measuring periodic earnings of manufacturing firms. This measurement, as it relates to the measurement of management performance, is the principal concern of this chapter.

As in firms performing service or product-handling functions, measurement of periodic earnings involves the comparison of accomplishment (output) with effort (input), in which the former is defined as *revenue*, measured in terms of some selected event (not necessarily the sale) that is considered to represent best the primary function of the firm, and the latter is defined as *expense*, measured as the sum of expired product costs and expired period costs. It is the greater variety and complexity of the activities and costs incurred that makes the measurement and interpretation of earnings more difficult for manufacturing firms. Since these firms are characterized by the predominance of manufacturing activity, it appears that accomplishment should be measured in terms of periodic manufacturing output, rather than periodic sales to customers. As we shall see, however, attempting to do this often introduces difficult revenue measurement problems that accountants prefer to avoid, and the result is that the principle of measuring accomplishment on the basis of production is applied only in the minority, rather than majority, of cases. Recognizing revenue at the point of sale simplifies revenue measurement, but it greatly complicates the expense measurement and matching processes because of the difficulty in distinguishing between product and period costs. This difficulty will be explained later in the chapter.

There is an accounting controversy over the question of the right point at which to recognize revenue in manufacturing firms, but this introductory text is not the place to attempt to resolve it. Two points should be kept in mind: First, the practical problem of finding objective measurement methods is a very important one. Management performance, on the other hand, is basically a qualitative, subjective matter, and if the accountant makes too many concessions for the sake of objectivity, his results may not be very useful for performance measurement purposes. Second, circumstances alter cases. There are so many different kinds of manufacturing activity, from farming to shipbuilding to auto-mobile assembly, that performance measurement rules that work well in one case will often be highly inappropriate in another. Without any claim to being exhaustive, we shall examine three important classes of cases in this chapter:

1. Cases in which the manufacturing activity is undertaken in response to a specific order for the product from the customer. In these cases, the sale (defined as the act of transfer of legal title to the goods from the seller to the buyer) at a known price is virtually assured before the manufacture of the product begins. Presumably, the manufacturer is not willing to take the risk of manufac-ture at his own expense without such assurance. Possibly the product is cus-tom-made for the particular customer, or perhaps the quantity involved is very large, as in the case of an order for military equipment from the federal govern-ment. An important subclass of these cases is that of construction contracts requiring many months or years to complete, in which delivery to the customer at completion is a mere formality.

2. Cases in which there is a ready market for the finished product at a known price. In these cases the manufacturer engages in no important selling activity because he has no means of increasing his revenue by doing so. If he can store his product and predicts that the price will increase, he may decide not to sell. Thus he is both a manufacturer and a speculator. Farming is the most important industry in which these conditions apply, although there are also established markets for crude oil, and some precious metals.

3. Cases in which the firm manufactures the product to stock, that is, it also intends to engage in selling the product to customers after it has been produced. In these cases the manufacturer takes the risk of both manufacture and sale, and presumably is able to influence his revenue by his selling effort. Perhaps the majority of manufacturers in the United States conduct their business on this basis.

The remainder of this chapter considers each of these three cases in some detail. In class 1 cases, revenue will be recognized as production takes place. In class 2 cases, revenue will be recognized at the point of completion of production. In class 3 cases, revenue will be recognized only when the product is sold to customers. We shall spend more time on class 3 cases, because it is a difficult problem to account for the cost of a product manufactured in one period and sold in a subsequent period. Since revenue recognition is postponed until the period of the sale, finished goods inventories, valued at product cost, must be reported as an asset until the period of sale so that proper matching of accomplishment and effort will be achieved.

CLASS 1 CASES—PERCENTAGE OF COMPLETION METHOD OF MEASURING REVENUE

In these cases the production is under a firm contract with the customer, in which product characteristics, delivery conditions, and prices are specified and agreed to with the customer in advance. Here the most logical and practical method of revenue measurement is to estimate what portion of the total production called for by the contract is completed each period, and to recognize revenue each period accordingly. If production is being carried out under several contracts simultaneously, individual estimates must be made. As a practical matter, this means that the manufacturer's revenues in any period include the estimated revenue from the production for all contracts worked on during the period, whether the contracts are completed during the period or not. If the contract calls for 120 product units, for instance, and if 30 units are produced in the first month, then 25 per cent of the revenue under the contract should be reported in the first month, whether delivery is made or not. If the contract calls for an apartment building to be constructed in one year, and at the end of the first month one-tenth of the construction is completed, then one-tenth of the total contract price should be reported in that month.

The asset that emerges from this revenue-producing activity is reported as an account receivable from the purchaser, just as if the completed portion of the contract had been sold to the customer. It is not uncommon for the contract to call for periodic cash payments from the purchaser, which may or may not be related to product deliveries under the contract. Such cash payments are deducted from the total accounts receivable as they are received.

Under this method of reporting manufacturing activity, costs become expenses as they are committed to production. In fact, one way of computing the percentage of completion is to compute the percentage of committed costs to the total estimated costs. In any case, there is no accounting inventory of finished or partly finished products, because the costs of this production have already been assigned to revenues of the period. The only inventory shown in the financial position statement is that of raw materials and supplies purchased that have not entered the production process.

To illustrate, assume that on January 1 the Acme Auto Parts Company signed a contract to produce 10,000 units of a special steel casting for a local tool manufacturer, to be completed by February 28. The contract price is $50,000 or $5 per unit, $25,000 to be paid on February 15 and $25,000 on March 15. Acme's financial position at January 1 is as follows:

ACME AUTO PARTS COMPANY

FINANCIAL POSITION

As of January 1, 19x1

Cash	$ 30,000	Liabilities	$ 25,000
Materials	40,000	Capital stock	50,000
Other assets	30,000	Retained earnings	25,000
Total assets	$100,000	Total equities	$100,000

Standard costs per unit are these: materials, $2.00; labor, $1.00; other, $.50. Transactions during January and February were as follows:

	January	February
Units produced	3,000	7,000
Materials used	$6,500	$13,000
Labor (paid in cash)	2,900	7,200
Other product costs		
"Other assets" expired	1,000	1,500
Liabilities incurred	800	2,000
Selling and administrative expenses		
(paid in cash)	1,500	1,500
Cash collected (February 15)		25,000

The earnings statements for January and February are (ignoring income tax):

ACME AUTO PARTS COMPANY

STATEMENT OF EARNINGS

For January and February 19x1

	January	February
Revenue	$15,000	$35,000
Product costs, at standard		
Materials	$ 6,000	$14,000
Labor	3,000	7,000
Other	1,500	3,500
Total product costs	$10,500	$24,500
Earnings margin	$ 4,500	$10,500

ACME AUTO PARTS COMPANY (CONT.)

	January	February
Period expenses:		
Selling and administrative expenses	$1,500	$1,500
Variances	700	800[a]
Total period expenses	$2,200	$ 700
Net earnings	$2,300	$9,800

[a] Favorable variance.

Statements of financial position are as follows:

ACME AUTO PARTS COMPANY
COMPARATIVE STATEMENT OF FINANCIAL POSITION
As of January 31 and February 28, 19x1

	January	February		January	February
Cash	$ 25,600	$ 41,900	Liabilities	$ 25,800	$ 27,800
Accounts receivable	15,000	25,000	Capital stock	50,000	50,000
Materials	33,500	20,500	Retained earnings	27,300	37,100
Other assets	29,000	27,500			
	$103,100	$114,900		$103,100	$114,900

(We recommend that you analyze the transactions for one month and write them in general journal form to demonstrate that these financial statements are correct.) Several aspects of Acme's situation should be noted:

1. The only inventory account used is the materials account. Production costs become expenses as the costs are committed to the production process because revenue from production is recognized at that time. Therefore, there are no accounts for finished goods or work in process.

2. The accounts receivable title is not completely accurate, since it is generally limited to open accounts for completed sales. The asset title "unbilled revenues," often found in practice, suffers from confusing similarity to the revenue title in the earnings statement.

3. The timing and amount of cash collections from the customer have no bearing on the earnings statement.

4. Whether the improvement in per-unit figures between January and February is a good measure of improvement in performance is not clear. A breakdown of the variances item is helpful if it can be assumed that the materials and labor variances are entirely controllable. The "other costs" item is not completely variable, and some portion of that variance must be considered attributable to the increase in February volume.

5. Selling and administrative expenses are period expenses, that is, not traceable or attributable to this contract.

In class 1 cases involving production of a large number of small units, units produced provides a convenient way of determining the percentage of completion at any point in time. This method cannot be used, however, in the case of a long-term construction contract, such as a stretch of highway or a building.

To illustrate, assume a construction company contracts to build ten miles of four-lane highway. Given the facts that several operations need to be performed and that at any time each of these operations may be in process at a different stage of completion, how should an overall percentage of completion be measured? The best answer seems to be on the basis of costs incurred. Assume the total contract price is $10 million and total estimated costs $8 million. If $2 million, $5 million, and $1 million in costs are incurred in three consecutive periods, the percentage of completion during each period would be 25 per cent, $62\frac{1}{2}$ per cent, and 12 per cent respectively, and revenues earned would be $2.50 million, $6.25 million, and $1.25 million. Two major difficulties arise in the use of this method:

1. Some of the costs may be the result of inefficiency and therefore are not adding to the value of the construction. Some method should be found for determining which costs are to be included and which should be charged off as losses in the period incurred. Standard costs are of great assistance in solving this problem.

2. There are many possibilities for error in the cost estimates. The only remedy is to attempt to revise the estimates as the construction progresses, so that errors in estimation are corrected as soon as possible.

Nevertheless, estimating the percentage of completion of a long-term construction project is a difficult problem, whatever method is applied, and in spite of the difficulties mentioned the costs incurred method is frequently used.

CLASS 2 CASES—MARKET VALUE METHOD OF MEASURING REVENUE

The distinguishing feature of this class of cases is that there is an established market price for the finished product, which the producer may realize by sale without any selling effort (expense) on his own part. On the other hand, there is no contract to sell, and the producer is free to hold on to his product if he expects a higher price later on. As a result, his performance is often made up of two elements: (1) gains or losses from production, consisting of the difference between cost of production and the market value of goods produced, measured at the point at which the goods are first ready for sale; and (2) holding gains or losses, measured by the difference between the market value of the goods at the time they are first ready for sale and either the market value at the time they are actually sold (i.e., selling price) or the market value at the end of an accounting period, whichever occurs first. If the sale is automatic at the time the goods are first ready for sale, as in the case where it is impossible to store the product, there would be no holding gain or loss.

Proper accounting in this situation usually requires two additional inventory accounts.

278 MANAGERIAL USES OF ACCOUNTING REPORTS

1. *Work in process inventory,* which is used to measure the *cost* of partly finished product as discussed in Chapter 3. Valuing this inventory at incurred production cost is based on the assumption that there is no market for partly finished product, or that sale of product in a partly finished state is not a feasible alternative. This means that in class 2 cases revenue is recorded at the point at which the goods are completed and ready for sale. It is not necessary to compute a percentage of completion as in the class 1 cases, because revenue is recognized only when completion is 100 per cent.

If the accounting periods are relatively long, as in the case of agricultural accounting on the basis of seasons, or if the production cycle is short, the invested cost in partly completed product is small, and the work in process account may be ignored.

2. *Finished product inventory,* which is used to measure the *market value* of product on hand at any time. Since finished product is recorded at market value, gain or loss from production is recorded at the time of completion as if the goods had been sold. It should be noted that in theory a *holding gain* occurs on finished product on hand whenever there is an increase in market price, and *holding loss* whenever there is a decrease; but except in the most unusual case, in which each increase and decrease in market value is recorded as it occurs, the financial statements will show only the net gain or loss on goods actually sold or on hand at the end of the period, which may be the result of many unrecorded increases and decreases in market value during the period. In other words, the earnings statement will not show whether the producer sold his goods at the most appropriate time.

Assume, for example, that on December 31, 19x0, a farmer has 2,500 bushels of wheat on hand, valued at market price of $1.60 per bushel. His financial position on that date is as follows:

Cash	$5,000	Liabilities	$3,000
Finished product	4,000		
Other assets	6,000	Proprietor's equity	12,000
Total assets	$15,000	Total equities	$15,000

In June 19x1, the farmer harvested 2,100 bushels of wheat when the market price was $1.80, and in October he harvested 2,400 when the market price was $1.75. In July he sold 4,600 bushels at the market price of $1.90, collecting the entire amount in cash. At December 31, 19x1 the market price was $1.50. Additional information regarding his activities is listed below:

Production costs for 19x1:	
Variable (4,500 at $.70)	$3,150
Nonvariable	1,500
Period expenses for 19x1	1,200
	$5,850

Consisting of:		
Other assets written off		$2,500
Liabilities incurred		3,350
		$5,850

The farmer's cash book shows:		
Cash receipts (4,600 at $1.90)		$8,740
Cash disbursements		
Liabilities paid	$4,000	
Other assets purchased	2,000	
Personal withdrawals	2,500	$8,500
		$ 240

The farmer's income statement, with supporting calculations, follows:

A FARMER

STATEMENT OF EARNINGS
For Year Ended December 31, 19x1

Revenue from production		
2,100 bushels at $1.80		$3,780
2,400 bushels at $1.75		4,200
Total		$7,980
Expired product costs		
Variable (4,500 at $.70)	$3,150	
Nonvariable	1,500	4,650
Gains from production		$3,330
Holding gains and losses		
Gains (2,500 at $.30)	$750	
(2,100 at $.10)	210	
	$960	
Loss (2,400 at $.25)	600	360
Gains from production and holding gain		$3,690
Period expenses		1,200
Net earnings (before tax)		$2,400

and his financial position statement is as follows:

A FARMER

FINANCIAL POSITION
As of December 31, 19x1

Cash	$ 5,240	Liabilities	$ 2,350
Finished product	3,600	Proprietor's equity	11,990
Other assets	5,500	Total equities	$14,340
Total assets	$14,340		

(We strongly recommend that you analyze each transaction in terms of its effect on financial position and earnings so that you understand thoroughly how the theory of revenue recognition should be applied.)

A realistic (and hence more complex) illustration would require a work in process account. Apparently the farmer sows winter wheat in the fall and at December 31 has an investment in a wheat crop he harvests in the spring. You may assume that this investment is included in "other assets" as of December 31, 19x0, and that "other assets" at December 31, 19x1 include an investment in the crop to be harvested in the spring of 19x2. Since we have selected the point of harvesting as the point when revenue is realized, this work in process inventory is valued at invested cost and carried as an asset at cost until harvest. At this point it is converted to market value, and gain or loss from production is recorded.

As we indicated earlier, the holding gain and loss results are difficult to interpret. It is not possible to tell whether the decisions to hold or sell are wise, because we have no information on the market price at times when no transaction occurred. A realistic illustration would also include a charge for storage, which would have the effect of reducing the holding gain (or increasing the loss). In any case, this accounting method is an improvement over one which recognizes revenue only at time of sale, because production gain or loss, and holding gain or loss, are separated.

CLASS 3 CASES—RECOGNIZING REVENUE AT THE TIME OF SALE

This method of revenue recognition is probably the most appropriate for the manufacturer who produces goods to stock, that is, adds them to an inventory of finished goods that he hopes will be sold at a later date. If costly selling effort can be anticipated and this effort is expected to be a strong factor in determining the volume of goods to be sold and the price at which the goods are sold, recognition of revenue at any time prior to actual sale to a customer may be regarded as premature. It is difficult to determine the market value of unsold goods where product differentiation is important, as is the case for most consumer products and many others as well. (For example, do red hula hoops sell more than blue or yellow ones? Does an inch difference in diameter affect sales?)

Recognizing revenue at the time of sale is much the simplest solution to the revenue measurement problem. The accountant must estimate (a) the likelihood that customers will return the goods, thus cancelling the sale, or (b) the amount of bad debts, in the case of sales on credit (see Chapter 14); however, these are relatively minor problems. The only real difficulty with the method is in accounting for the cost of finished goods inventories. The cost of these inventories must be reported as assets in the financial position statement until the goods are sold, at which time they are recorded as expense and matched against the revenue from the sale in the statement of earnings. As we saw in

Chapter 3, three types of inventories occur in the financial position statements of manufacturing firms:

1. *Materials and supplies,* the cost of which must be accounted for as an asset whenever these goods are purchased prior to their use in the manufacturing process. In summarized financial statements, *direct materials* awaiting entry as the principal material in the process, and indirect materials classified as overhead, or other manufacturing costs, are included under the same caption.

2. *Work in process,* or partly completed products, the product cost of which must be reported as an asset in cases in which revenue is recognized when goods are finished (as in our earlier illustration of the farmer) or at any later time, such as the sale. Note that in the class 1 cases when revenue was recognized as production was carried on, work in process was matched against the revenue of the period and reported as a receivable.

3. *Finished product inventory,* which must be accounted for as an asset. It is valued on the statement of financial position at product cost.

The schematic diagram in Exhibit 8–1 demonstrates how the three kinds of inventories for manufacturing firms are used in the computation of net earnings. This exhibit should be compared with Exhibit 3A–2 in Appendix 3A.

EXHIBIT 8-1

**INVENTORY CALCULATION FOR STATEMENT OF EARNINGS—
REVENUE RECOGNIZED AT TIME OF SALE**

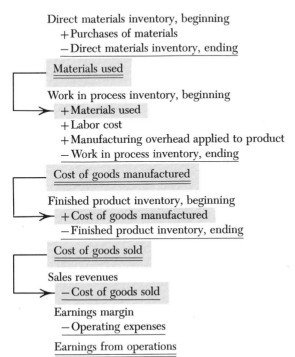

Direct materials inventory, beginning
+ Purchases of materials
− Direct materials inventory, ending

Materials used

Work in process inventory, beginning
+ Materials used
+ Labor cost
+ Manufacturing overhead applied to product
− Work in process inventory, ending

Cost of goods manufactured

Finished product inventory, beginning
+ Cost of goods manufactured
− Finished product inventory, ending

Cost of goods sold

Sales revenues
− Cost of goods sold

Earnings margin
− Operating expenses

Earnings from operations

The shaded areas in the diagram require further explanation:

1. *Materials used,* one of the three principal elements of manufacturing cost, is determined by adding the beginning inventory of direct materials used to direct materials purchased, and deducting the ending direct materials inventory. This is true only if the inventory is limited to *direct* materials. In Appendix 3A, the inventory account materials and supplies included *indirect* materials, which are also an element in overhead. When indirect materials flow through the account, they must be deducted in order for the "materials used" figure to become accurate. (They will be included as part of manufacturing overhead.)

2. *Cost of goods manufactured,* which is the cost of goods *finished* during the period, is determined by adding the beginning inventory of work in process to the sum of the three manufacturing cost elements *entering* the manufacturing process and deducting the ending work in process inventory.

3. *Cost of goods sold,* which is the expense to be matched against the revenue from the sales of the period, is determined by adding the beginning inventory of finished product to the cost of goods manufactured and deducting the ending inventory of finished product.

In the detailed illustration on the following pages, only the last of these three calculations is explained in depth. "Materials used" is given, making this calculation unnecessary, and beginning and ending work in process are assumed to be zero, thus making cost of goods manufactured each period equal to the sum of materials, labor, and other manufacturing overhead costs.

ACCOUNTING FOR FINISHED PRODUCT

Assume that as of June 1 a portion of the foundry in plant 2 of the Acme Auto Parts Company, valued at $12,000, is to be used for the production of lawn sprinklers. The venture is supplied with $1,000 cash, $1,000 materials, and sufficient labor so that the venture can properly be considered a profit center having the following financial position at June 1:

Cash	$1,000
Materials	1,000
Finished product	0
Plant and equipment	12,000
Total assets	$14,000
Liabilities	0
Net assets	14,000

The venture is continued for the months of June, July, and August. The manufacture of a sprinkler requires only a few hours, so that partly finished product (work in process) inventory at any time is negligible. Production and sales figures for the three months are as follows:

	Beginning Inventory	Production	Sales	Ending Inventory
June	$ 0	$1,200	$ 400	$800
July	800	1,000	1,200	600
August	600	800	1,400	0
Total		$3,000	$3,000	

All sales are for cash, and all costs except materials and depreciation are paid in cash in the month incurred. The useful life of the plant and equipment is ten years, and depreciation is therefore $100 per month.

Production costs for the three months are as follows:

	June	July	August
Variable costs per unit			
Materials	$.20	$.25	$.25
Labor	.30	.30	.35
Other	.10	.10	.10
Total variable cost per unit	$.60	$.65	$.70
Variable manufacturing costs (production times variable cost)	$ 720	$ 650	$560
Nonvariable manufacturing costs	360	360	360
Total manufacturing costs	$1,080	$1,010	$920
Units produced	$1,200	$1,000	$800
Total manufacturing costs per unit	$.90	$1.01	$1.15

Selling and administrative expenses (paid in cash) amount to $100 each month. The sales prices per unit were $1.50, $1.25, and $1.25 in the three months. The earnings statements for the venture are as follows:

	June	July	August
Sales revenue			
400 units at $1.50	$ 600		
1,200 units at $1.25		$1,500	
1,400 units at $1.25			$2,530
Cost of goods sold:			
Inventory, beginning of month	0	$ 720	$ 606
Cost of goods manufactured			
Variable costs	720	650	560
Nonvariable costs	360	360	360
Total	$1,080	$1,730	$1,526

	June	July	August
Inventory, end of month			
800 units at $.90	720		
600 units at $1.01		606	
No units on hand August 31			0
Cost of goods sold	$360	$1,124	$1,526
Earnings margin	$240	$ 376	$ 224
Selling and administrative expenses	100	100	100
Earnings	$140	$276	$124

Assets of the venture at the end of each month are as follows:

	June	July	August
Cash	$ 760	$ 1,500	$ 2,530
Materials	760	510	310
Finished product	720	606	0
Plant and equipment (net)	11,900	11,800	11,700
Total assets	$14,140	$14,416	$14,540

(As in other illustrations, you are urged to reconstruct the transactions, record them in journal form, and prepare statements for yourself, at least for the month of June.)

A careful examination of the earnings statement reveals the problems involved in matching expenses (cost of goods sold) with revenues when revenue is recognized at the time of sale. Of the 1,200 units produced in June at the June level of costs, only 400 were sold in June, and the other 800 (cost $720) were sold in July. Six hundred of the units produced in July (cost $606) were not sold until August.

Notice the assumption that the first 800 units sold in July were from the June 30 inventory, and that the first 600 units sold in August were from the July 31 inventory. This is known as the *first-in, first-out* (FIFO) assumption. Other possible assumptions about inventory movements are discussed in Part III.

Production costs per unit increase in this case for two reasons: (1) the variable costs per unit increase, possibly because of price changes or a change in production methods, and (2) the production volume decreases, resulting in higher nonvariable costs per unit. Earnings from sales of products manufactured in a previous month are obviously higher than if the product had been manufactured in the month of the sale. Many theorists argue that the cost assignable to a sale should be the cost of *reproduction* of the article sold, rather than the actual cost of producing the article at the time it was produced. This argument may have special significance in cases in which management performance is the primary criterion, because it would seem that the measurement of effort, as well as accomplishment, should be based on the most current data available.

The basic question, however, is whether revenue from the lawn sprinkler venture should be recognized in the period in which the sprinklers are produced. If costs are a measure of effort, obviously the major effort in this venture is production, not sales, which leads to the conclusion that the revenue should be recognized as the sprinklers are produced. On the other hand, there is no firm contract from a buyer, nor is there assurance that a given sales price will in fact be paid. The price reduction from $1.50 to $1.25 in July may have been unexpected and unpredictable. Possibly only actual sales will provide the evidence that the accountant needs to measure revenue. Under these circumstances, accounting practice heavily favors recognizing revenue only at the point of sale.

Absorption Versus Variable Costing

In the earnings statement for the lawn sprinkler operation, manufacturing costs were separated into variable and nonvariable costs. Both classes were defined as product costs. For example, the $.90 per unit valuation of the 800 units in the June 30 inventory contained only $.60 of variable cost, the other $.30 being nonvariable. Since nonvariable cost is calculated on a per-unit basis by dividing the total nonvariable cost by units of production, the nonvariable cost changes whenever production levels change. Whereas the June nonvariable cost is $.30 per unit, in July it is $.36, and in August it is $.45. The change is entirely attributable to change in the units produced. Thus, expressing nonvariable cost on a per-unit basis can be highly misleading, because the costs cannot really be identified with the units produced.

This kind of costing system is called *absorption or full costing*. The $360 nonvariable cost is treated as a product (i.e., inventoriable) cost because it is clearly a cost of manufacturing, rather than of selling or administration. As long as any units at all are manufactured, these costs will be incurred (theoretically in the amount of $360), and some of them might even continue if the factory were shut down entirely for a month.

Absorption costing is a controversial matter. It is true that costs are traceable to the manufacturing process as a whole, but they can be traced to individual units produced only by arbitrary allocation, as was done in the example employed in Appendix 6A. In the body of Chapter 6 we discussed an alternative costing method, called *variable costing*, in which nonvariable manufacturing costs are treated as period costs. This method has been popular and useful for many accounting purposes. When nonvariable manufacturing costs are treated as period costs, they are not included in period-end inventories of finished products. Instead, they are recorded as expenses according to the rules of accrual accounting, just as selling and administrative expenses are recorded. In the lawn sprinkler illustration, June 30 and July 31 inventories would have been valued at $.60 and $.65 respectively, instead of $.90 and $1.01.

The question of absorption versus variable costing is very important. As the automation of manufacturing processes increases, there is a large-scale substitution of so-called capital goods for direct labor, which in accounting terms is a substitution of nonvariable cost for variable cost. Many manufacturing processes have nonvariable costs that at normal volume amount to many more dollars than the variable cost. Particularly in situations in which the volume of output and inventories fluctuate widely from period to period, absorption and variable costing can have enormously different effects on reported earnings.

Exhibit 8-2 shows how the two methods compare as applied to the lawn sprinkler venture for June, July, and August. You should study all of the figures in this exhibit to make sure you follow the reasoning behind each costing method. Computing the beginning and ending inventory figures is particularly important. Since Acme began on June 1 with no inventory and ended on August 31 with no inventory, the total earnings for the quarter are $550 under either method, but the monthly differences are substantial. It is true that the nonvariable manufacturing expenses are large, and the monthly difference between production and sales is possibly exaggerated. Nevertheless, it may be surprising to learn that such wide differences in earnings can result from an honest difference of opinion over accounting methods.

From the standpoint of measuring performance of the firm, neither method is more correct. Difficulty arises from the fact that accomplishment is measured by monthly sales, while most of the effort is devoted to production. Absorption costing is slightly better for performance measurement because it provides a margin only after deduction of all applicable production costs. It also produces inventory valuations that are likely to be closer to market values than variable costing methods.

IS PERFORMANCE GOOD ENOUGH?

The discussion of the earnings center in Chapter 7 and this chapter has revolved around two problems: identifying the earnings center and measuring earnings. One important problem remains—deciding whether the amount of earnings is sufficient. This problem is similar to the performance measurement of the department foreman in Chapter 4. It was necessary, but not sufficient, to know the foreman's costs; we also had to know what the costs should have been. In the case of the earnings center, we need a valid way of deciding what earnings should have been; or if this is not possible, we need a way of knowing whether the earnings are sufficient to justify continued operation in the same line of business under the same management operating in the same way. Earnings of $1 million a year may be very good or very bad, depending on whether it was earned by a college bookstore or by the General Motors Corporation.

First it is necessary to understand the assumptions underlying the use of earnings as the measurement of performance. Let's examine these underlying

EXHIBIT 8-2

ACME AUTO PARTS COMPANY, PLANT 2 FOUNDRY

COMPARISON OF ABSORPTION COSTING WITH VARIABLE COSTING—LAWN SPRINKLER VENTURE

For Three Months Ended August 31, 19xx

	June		July		August	
	Absorption costing	Variable costing	Absorption costing	Variable costing	Absorption costing	Variable costing
Sales revenues	$ 600	$ 600	$1,500	$1,500	$1,750	$1,750
—Cost of goods sold:						
Inventory, beginning	$ 0	$ 0	$ 720	$ 480	$ 606	$ 390
Variable manufacturing costs	720	720	650	650	560	560
Nonvariable manufacturing costs	360		360		360	
Total	$1,080	$ 720	$1,730	$1,130	$1,526	$ 950
—Inventory, ending	720	480	606	390	0	0
Total cost of goods sold	$ 360	$ 240	$1,124	$ 740	$1,526	$ 950
Earnings margin	$ 240	$ 360	$ 376	$ 760	$ 224	$ 800
—Operating expenses:						
Nonvariable manufacturing expenses		$ 360		$ 360		$ 360
Selling and administrative expenses	$ 100	100	$ 100	100	$ 100	100
Total operating expenses	$ 100	$ 460	$ 100	$ 460	$ 100	$ 460
Earnings from operations	$ 140	$ (100)ᵃ	$ 276	$ 300	$ 124	$ 340

ᵃ This represents a net loss of $100.

assumptions and then turn our attention to the problems involved in measuring investment.

Underlying Assumptions

When measuring and evaluating performance in terms of earnings, it is necessary to keep in mind the basic concept that performance should be judged only in terms of those factors that can be controlled by the person whose performance is under examination. It is often assumed that the management of the enterprise is responsible for, and has authority to control, all factors affecting the firm. The assumed control extends even to "acts of God" or fortuitous acts of government. For example, if poor earnings performance during a period is the result of an extraordinary loss of buildings and equipment caused by a tornado, those judging the performance of the enterprise will hold the managers responsible for the resulting loss of earnings. They will argue that even though the management could not prevent the tornado, they should have forseen the possibility of tornado destruction and guarded against loss of earnings through proper insurance coverage, including a standard business interruption policy.

While the management accepts responsibility for all influences affecting periodic earnings, a more realistic approach to performance measurement is to recognize that there are degrees of control that management can exert over various influences. One of the most important functions of accounting is to emphasize these differences in degrees of control by calling attention to them in financial reports. It would be misleading, for example, to bury the loss from the tornado under the heading of "cost of goods sold" or "depreciation expense." We have already pointed out how conventional accounting fails to distinguish carefully enough between gains and losses from manufacturing and gains and losses caused by price changes of products held in inventory. Management control over factors influencing only the firm in question is assumed to be much greater than control over factors affecting all firms in the industry, such as depressions or changes in the tax laws.

Proper evaluation of earnings performance requires that total earnings be compared to the dollar amount invested in the activity. The relationship of earnings to investment is called the *rate of return on investment*. This can be expressed as follows:

$$\frac{\text{Earnings per period}}{\text{Investment during period}} = \text{Rate of return on investment for period}$$

Proper evaluation of earnings performance, however, requires that special care be taken to ensure that earnings are compared to the proper amount of investment.

Investment

Investment refers to the total assets employed by the earnings center during the period over which the earnings are computed. The firm's assets are as shown in the statements of financial position. These statements have been discussed briefly but will be more thoroughly discussed in Parts III and IV. For the Acme Auto Parts Company, cash, accounts receivable, three types of inventory, and plant would be its principal assets.

The board of directors and top-level officers of Acme Auto Parts are concerned with the total assets employed in the enterprise. They measure their own performance according to the rate of return achieved on this total investment. The overall earnings performance of the company for the year 19x5 would be a 14.5 per cent rate of return if it achieved earnings of $156,000 and had total assets employed of $1,075,000. Here is the formula presentation of this performance result:

$$\frac{\$156,000 - 19x5 \text{ earnings}}{\$1,075,000 - 19x5 \text{ assets}} = \begin{array}{l} 14.5\% \text{ rate of return for 19x5 on} \\ \text{total assets employed in the enterprise} \end{array}$$

The 14.5 per cent return rate for 19x5 can be compared with performances of previous years or of other companies. Such a comparison allows a subjective evaluation by management of the performance of the company. It would be much better, however, if management were to compare the performance actually achieved in 19x5 with a predicted estimate (made at the beginning of the year) of what the performance was expected to be in 19x5. In effect, then, the prediction of earnings for 19x5 is a kind of standard with which to compare actual earnings. Any significant variation between the predicted and actual revenues should be explained, just as are cost variances at the operating levels of the firm. As will be seen in Chapter 9, management should also compare the percentage rate of returns achieved with that percentage rate of return that might have been achieved in some other kind of activity. Again, any significant difference will allow management to draw conclusions and make decisions about changing the nature of the business venture.

Subdivisional Performance

The arguments for a manager's concern about performance of subdivisions of the enterprise have already been stated. Where that performance can be judged in terms of earnings, a difficult problem arises in attempting to allocate to the subdivision its proper share of the total enterprise assets.

In cases like that of the foundry (plant 2) of the Acme Auto Parts Company, when the subdivision is engaged in outside earnings ventures (either under contract or to stock), a breakdown must be made between assets employed in the outside earnings venture and the assets still employed in normal production of regular Acme products. Allocations are made on any basis that seems fair. As an example, assume that there are four metal-melting furnaces in the foundry at the time the plant manager decided to start producing lawn sprinklers. On a production-to-stock basis, only three of the four furnaces are being used to meet normal production. When the manager commits the fourth furnace to melting metal for lawn sprinklers, this asset is considered an investment in the lawn sprinkler venture. The three furnaces still committed to normal production are not a part of this investment. This follows the basic rule that performance should be measured and evaluated only in terms of those factors that the manager can control. He can control the revenue from the sales of lawn sprinklers, and he can control the one furnace that he has committed to this venture. Similar care must be taken in determining the investment in the lawn sprinkler venture represented by other assets such as building space; raw materials; and the cash used to pay employees, insurances, and other general expenses of conducting the activity.

SUMMARY

Chapter 8 is concerned with the problems of evaluating management performance of manufacturing firms by measuring periodic earnings. Emphasis was given to the relationship between the economic circumstances in which the firm operates and the appropriate methods for measuring earnings. Three cases were identified:

1. The case in which goods are manufactured to customers' orders. Revenue should be recognized in accordance with the percentage of completion concept. Since all costs are assumed to relate to the manufacturing activity, and since product costs are matched with revenue as production occurs, the distinction between product and period costs is unnecessary.

2. The case in which finished product can be sold at a known price in an established market. Revenue, measured by the market value of the finished product, should be recognized at the time the production is completed, and matched with product costs associated with completed production. Only in this way is it possible to distinguish manufacturing gain or loss from holding (or speculative) gain or loss.

3. The case in which goods are produced to stock and the firm accepts the risks both from manufacture and from subsequent sale to customers. Revenue recognition is postponed until the point of sale, and product costs are deferred (i.e., treated as assets) from the period of production until the period of sale, when they are matched against revenues. In this case the distinction between product costs and period costs is crucial, and we recognized two alternative methods: (1) absorption costing, in which all manufacturing costs, variable and

nonvariable, were treated as product costs, and (2) variable costing, in which only variable manufacturing costs were treated as product costs.

The chapter also considered briefly the problem of evaluating earnings by means of return on investment calculations for entire firms, for subdivisions of firms, and for special projects.

Questions for Review

8-1. Describe the three classes of manufacturing activities discussed in the chapter, and outline the measurement problems associated with each.

8-2. What is the percentage of completion method of revenue measurement?

8-3. How are holding gains or losses measured under the market value method of measuring revenue?

8-4. For an organization engaged in manufacturing activities, what is the primary justification for recognizing revenue at the time of sale?

8-5. Prepare a schematic diagram showing the three types of inventories for manufacturing firms, how they relate to each other, and how they affect the computation of net earnings.

8-6. What are the important considerations in deciding whether to treat nonvariable manufacturing costs as product or period costs?

8-7. How is rate of return on investment used to evaluate earnings performance?

Problems for Analysis

8-8. Specialties, Inc., has secured an order from Progressive University to produce blazers with special insignia. The delivery schedule in the contract provides for:

2,000 blazers in August
3,000 blazers in September
1,500 blazers in October
1,500 blazers in November

The blazers were delivered according to the contract. The production and cost information for the blazers follows:

Month produced	Number produced	Variable costs
July	2,000	$1.20
August	2,000	1.15
September	2,000	1.05
October	2,000	1.10

Nonvariable costs assigned to the contract were as follows:
Manufacturing costs, $1,200 per month
Selling and administrative costs, $600 per month
The blazers are sold to Progressive for $2.75 each.

a. Prepare monthly earnings statements, in columnar form, for July through November, using the percentage of completion method of measuring revenue.

b. Prepare monthly earnings statements, in columnar form, for July through November, using absorption costing and time of sale (delivery) method of recognizing revenue.

c. Prepare a schedule, in columnar form, reflecting the "differences" in monthly earnings as you measured them in *a* and *b* above.

d. Which earnings measurement method, in your opinion, provides the most realistic measure of performance—percentage of completion, or time of sale (delivery)? Why?

8-9. Mr. Smith owns a 160-acre tract of land. He has signed a contract to have Mr. Jones produce winter wheat on the land. Mr. Jones will have the responsibility for planning, planting, and harvesting of the wheat crop. Mr. Smith is responsible for the storage and sale of the wheat crop. Mr. Smith will receive 40 per cent of the proceeds from the sale of the wheat. The following information relates to the production, storage, and sale of the winter wheat crop:

Wheat harvested in May, 8,500 bushels
Wheat sold in July, 8,500 bushels
Storage cost from May to July, $.05 per bushel per month
Market price of wheat per bushel:
May, $1.90
June, $2.05
July, $2.00

a. Prepare monthly earnings statements, in columnar form, for May, June, and July for Mr. Smith, using the market value method of recognizing revenue.

b. Prepare monthly earnings statements, in columnar form, for May, June, and July for Mr. Smith, recognizing revenue at the time of sale.

c. Which earnings measurement method, in your opinion, reflects the most realistic measure of performance for Mr. Smith?

8-10. Furniture Outlet, Inc., is engaged in the sale of furniture on the installment plan. All furniture is sold with a 10 per cent down payment, and the balance is payable in equal installments over twenty months. Interest of $\frac{1}{2}$ of 1 per cent per month is charged on the amount originally financed. The management of Furniture Outlet, Inc., is considering the recognition of revenue either at the time of sale or at the time of cash collection.

a. Which method of revenue recognition would you recommend? Give reasons to support your answer.

b. What effect do these two methods of revenue recognition have on the timing of the assignment of costs to expense on the statement of earnings? Discuss.

8-11. The Audio Corporation manufactures stereo systems for automobiles and sells them to retail outlets that operate exclusively to sell and install stereo systems. The company has been in operation for six years and has experienced great difficulty from uncollectable accounts of retail outlets. There has been a high turnover of these retailers due in large part to the ill health of the overall economy. Audio's uncollectable accounts ratio to the sales value of shipments over the last six years follows:

Year	Ratio of uncollectables to shipments
1	8 %
2	12 %
3	6 %
4	6 %
5	15 %
6	14 %

In the past, the management of Audio has measured revenue at the time of sale. They are considering the deferral of revenue recognition until the time of cash collection from retailers because of the uncertainty and large variability of collection.

a. Which method of revenue recognition would you recommend—time of sale or time of cash collection? Give reasons to support your answer.

b. What effect do these two methods of revenue recognition have on the timing of the assignment of costs to expenses on the statement of earnings? Discuss.

8-12. The Mott Seed Company produces various types of lawn fertilizer and seeds, which it markets to dealers throughout the United States. The contract with each dealer is that the products may be returned within six months and full credit will be given. The dealer is required to pay for the products in the month following his sale. Dealers are required to submit monthly reports to The Mott Seed Company, indicating items received, items sold, and items on hand together with the cash remittance.

Returns have been substantial in the past; however, management encourages the dealers to maintain a large inventory in order to generate more sales. Credit losses have been very small.

Evaluate the following methods of revenue recognition from a management viewpoint:

a. when items are produced
b. when items are shipped to dealers
c. when items are sold by the dealers
d. when cash is received from the dealers

8-13. The Quincy Equipment Company produces farm implements, which it sells to dealers. The contract with the dealers provides that the equipment (if it is not sold) may be returned at any time, with the dealer being given full credit for the amount billed him. The dealer is not obligated to pay for the equipment until the month after it is sold. He is obligated to make a monthly report of equipment on hand at the end of the month and equipment sold during the month.

Past experience indicates that returns are very large. Despite this experience, the firm is anxious to induce dealers to carry an adequate inventory. The dealers are carefully selected and bad debt losses approximate zero.

Quincy has been recognizing revenue at the time of shipment to the dealers, crediting sales and debiting accounts receivable.

On December 31, 19x1, the account balances were as follows:

Accounts receivable, $2,600,000
Inventory (at cost), $300,000

On that date dealers reported that their inventory, at Quincy's sales price, was $2,400,000.

On December 31, 19x2, the account balances were as follows:

Accounts receivable, $2,100,000
Inventory (at cost), $240,000
Sales (net of returns), $6,000,000

Equipment in the hands of dealers amounted to $2,000,000.

For both years, the production cost was approximately 75 per cent of the sales price. In the sales account is recorded the sales price of goods shipped.

a. Determine the revenue for the year 19x2 if revenue is recognized at the time

1. the equipment is produced. At what amount would the December 31, 19x2 inventory be shown on the balance sheet?
2. the equipment is shipped to the dealers.
3. the equipment is sold by the dealer.
4. cash is received.

b. Evaluate each of the methods from a managerial point of view. Which appears most appropriate?

8-14.   PART I

From the following data, supply the missing information for each of the four months:

	January	February	March	April
Raw materials inventory, beginning	$ 950	$?	$?	$?
Purchases	2,475	3,090	?	2,900
Raw materials inventory, ending	860	?	1,170	1,040
Raw materials used	?	2,865	3,400	?

PART II

From the following data, supply the missing information for each of the four months:

	January	February	March	April
Work in process inventory, beginning	$ 430	$?	$?	$?
Raw materials used (from Part I)	?	?	?	?
Direct labor	1,810	?	2,275	2,165
Variable manufacturing costs	465	510	690	705
Nonvariable manufacturing costs	2,105	2,230	2,200	?
Work in process inventory, ending	?	710	685	670
Cost of goods manufactured	6,800	6,320	?	7,910

PART III

From the following data, supply the missing information for each of the four months:

	January	February	March	April
Finished goods inventory, beginning	$1,270	$?	$?	$?
Cost of goods manufactured (from Part II)	?	?	?	?
Finished goods inventory, ending	1,100	?	2,115	2,270
Cost of goods sold	?	6,310	?	?

PART IV

From the following data, supply the missing information for each of the four months:

	January	February	March	April
Sales revenues	$10,510	$10,705	$?	$?
Cost of goods sold (from Part III)	?	?	?	?
Earnings margin	?	?	4,870	4,375
General & administrative expenses	1,250	?	1,750	1,985
Selling expenses	975	1,120	?	1,400
Earnings from operations	?	1,795	2,175	?

PART V

a. Using the data from Parts I, II, and III, prepare a statement of cost of goods sold for April.

b. Using data from Part IV, prepare a statement of earnings for April.

8–15. Assume that a farmer began the 19x3 season with no corn inventory on hand. During that season and the next two, he produced 5,000, 6,500, and 4,000 bushels of corn, respectively, and he sold 4,500, 5,500, and 5,500 bushels, so that at the end of the 19x5 season he again had no corn on hand. Assume seasonal selling prices per bushel of $1.20, $.90, and $1.10, respectively.

Variable production costs per bushel were the same in all three seasons—$.10 for seed, $.15 for fertilizer, $.25 for labor, and $.20 for machine hire. Nonvariable expenses attributable to corn production amounted to $300 per season. Administrative expenses were $600 per season.

a. Prepare a comparative earnings statement for the three seasons:

1. recognizing revenue on a production basis

2. recognizing revenue on a sale basis (absorption costing method)

Which basis provides the most useful measure of the farmer's performance?

b. How much inventory does the farmer have on hand at the end of the first season? The second season? In the earnings statements above, what recognition should be given the fact that some of the corn was produced in one season and sold in another at a different price?

c. What effect does the method of recognizing revenue have on the reporting of expenses?

8–16. The Ajax Chemical Company manufactures and sells liquid insecticides. The manufacturing process is highly mechanized, requiring little direct labor and comparatively inexpensive direct materials. Two factors make the accounting for manufacturing costs particularly important:

1. An unusually large proportion of the manufacturing cost (depreciation on buildings and equipment, taxes, insurance, etc.) is indirect and does not vary greatly from month to month. For this reason, the management attempts to (a) equalize its production from period to period (since the amount saved by reducing production is very small) and (b) keep its production volume high (since the marginal cost of increasing production is small). Price cutting and low margins are common in insecticides because of the obvious economies of maintaining high volume.

2. Demand is created in part by "epidemics," which are largely unpredictable. This means that fairly substantial inventories of several different insecticides should be on hand at any time. Prolonged storage, however, is expensive.

Through March, April, and May, Ajax produced and sold barrels of insecticides as follows:

	March	April	May
Inventory, beginning	1,500	500	2,500
+ Barrels produced	3,000	3,500	2,500
Total on hand	4,500	4,000	5,000
− Inventory, ending	500	2,500	2,000
Barrels sold	4,000	1,500	3,000

Manufacturing costs for each month were as follows:

Direct materials: $.15 per barrel
Direct labor: $.25 per barrel
Variable manufacturing costs: $.10 per barrel
Nonvariable manufacturing costs: $3,000 per month

Sales amounted to $8,000 in March, $2,800 in April, and $5,400 in May.

a. Ignoring selling and administrative expenses, prepare comparative earnings statements for Ajax:

1. By the variable costing method, using $750 for the beginning inventory (1,500 barrels at a variable cost of $.50 per barrel).
2. By the absorption costing method, using $2,250 for the beginning inventory (1,500 barrels at a variable cost of $.50 per barrel and a nonvariable cost of $1 per barrel). Carry costs per barrel to the nearest cent.

b. Explain *precisely* why the two methods produce different month-to-month earnings.

c. Explain *precisely*, and prove with figures, why the total profit reported over the three-month period is not the same for the two methods.

d. At what price per barrel are the inventories priced at the end of each month? What causes the differences? Are they justified?

e. Which of these methods would make more sense to the manager of this firm? Why?

8-17. The Zephyr Construction Company has just organized and secured a contract to construct a new classroom building for a university.

The contract is for $2,000,000, payable as follows:

$500,000 when construction is 30 per cent complete
$500,000 when construction is 60 per cent complete
$500,000 when construction is 90 per cent complete
$500,000 when construction is 100 per cent complete

A certification from the state engineer regarding percentage of completion is required before cash payments are made to the contractor.

Estimated costs are $1,700,000.

Construction time is estimated at twenty months and will require all of the productive capacity of the company. Its statement of financial position before starting construction follows:

THE ZEPHYR CONSTRUCTION COMPANY
STATEMENT OF FINANCIAL POSITION
As of May 31, 19x2

Assets[a]		Equities	
Cash	$300,000	Capital stock	$300,000

[a] All equipment and facilities required to complete the contract will be leased.

A summary of the transactions during the contract period follows (assume that all costs incurred are paid in cash):

Year 1—June 1, 19x2 to May 31, 19x3:

1. Costs incurred on construction contract, $714,000

2. Certification from the state engineer indicates that the building construction is 40 per cent complete.

3. Received partial payment of $500,000.

Year 2—June 1, 19x3 to May 31, 19x4:

1. Costs incurred to complete construction contract, $1,060,000

2. Certification from the state engineer indicating that the building construction is one hundred per cent complete

3. Received partial payments of $1,000,000. The final payment of $500,000 is expected within thirty days.

a. Prepare journal entries to reflect these transactions and events for each year, assuming that percentage of completion is determined by relating costs incurred to the cost estimate.

b. Prepare a statement of earnings and statement of financial position for each of the two years on the basis of your answer in a.

c. Prepare journal entries to reflect the transactions and events for each year assuming that the percentage of completion is determined from the engineer's appraisal.

d. Prepare a statement of earnings and statement of financial position for each of the two years on the basis of your answer in c.

e. Which method of percentage of completion (engineer's appraisal or costs incurred) gives the most realistic performance measurement? Give reasons to support your answer.

8-18. The Able Construction Company has secured a contract with the state of California for the construction of two miles of concrete highway over a three-year period at a total contract price of $700,000. The company is to receive the contract price in three annual installments of $200,000, $300,000, and $200,000 respectively. The total estimated cost of completing the highway is $500,000.

By the end of the first year the highway was 30 per cent completed, and total costs incurred to date were $150,000. By the end of the second year the highway was 70 per cent completed, and costs incurred totaled $350,000. The highway was completed during the third year, and total costs incurred amounted to $520,000.

a. Determine the revenue and earnings to be reported each of the three years, using the following methods of recognizing revenue:

      1. during the years of production   **2.** in the year of sale

b. Which method of revenue recognition would you recommend in this situation? Explain.

8-19. Hickel's Construction Company has just secured a contract to build a 100-unit apartment project. The contract provides for a contract price of $800,000, payable one-half when the project is 60 per cent complete (as determined by an independent engineer) and the remainder when the project is 100 per cent complete. Estimated construction costs are $720,000.

Hickel's statement of financial position before starting construction follows:

HICKEL CONSTRUCTION COMPANY

STATEMENT OF FINANCIAL POSITION

As of September 30, 19x1

Assets		Equities	
Cash	$140,000	Capital stock	$300,000
Other assets	275,000	Retained earnings	115,000
	$415,000		$415,000

A summary of transactions (for this contract only) during the construction period follows (assume that all costs incurred are paid in cash):

October 1, 19x1 to September 30, 19x2:

    1. Costs incurred on construction contract, $450,000

    2. Certification from independent engineer that the project is 60 per cent complete

    3. Received partial payment of $400,000.

October 1, 19x2 to September 30, 19x3:

    1. Costs incurred to complete construction contract, $280,000

    2. Certification from independent engineer that the project is 100 per cent complete

    3. Received final payment on contract of $400,000.

a. Prepare an earnings statement and statement of financial position under each of the following methods of recognizing revenue:

    1. Percentage of completion

    2. Completed contract

    3. Cash receipts

b. Which method of revenue recognition gives the most realistic measurement of performance for management? Give reasons to support your answer.

8-20. Homestake Mining Company is engaged in the production and sale of gold. By law they are required to sell to the federal government at $35.00 per ounce. Recently, there have been many rumors that the official price of gold may be increased because of the speculative activities of certain foreign governments. The company does not normally hold inventory, but they decided to keep some of the current production in hopes that the federal government would increase the price. Production and sale information for the current year are as follows:

Variable production costs, $17 per ounce
Nonvariable production costs, $30,000 per year
Selling and administrative costs, $20,000 per year
Ounces produced, 10,000
Ounces sold, 8,000
Ending inventory, 2,000 ounces
a. Prepare a comparative earnings statement recognizing revenue:
  1. using the market value method
  2. using the time of sale method (use absorption costing)
b. Which method provides the most useful measure of performance? Why?
c. What effect does the method of recognizing revenue have on the reporting of expenses?

8-21. A trial balance for The Buckeye Manufacturing Company as of October 31, 19x2, is presented below:

THE BUCKEYE MANUFACTURING COMPANY
TRIAL BALANCE
As of October 31, 19x2

Cash	$ 10,000	
Accounts receivable	22,000	
Direct materials inventory, November 1, 19x1	46,000	
Work in process inventory, November 1, 19x1	12,000	
Finished goods inventory, November 1, 19x1	80,000	
Prepaid expenses	4,000	
Land	40,000	
Buildings and equipment	265,000	
Accumulated depreciation—buildings and equipment		$ 27,000
Accounts payable		60,000
Accrued liabilities		8,000
Mortgage payable		100,000
Capital stock		85,000
Retained earnings, November 1, 19x1		36,000
Sales		910,000
Purchase—direct materials	310,000	
Direct labor	190,000	
Factory overhead	165,000	
Selling expenses	35,000	
Administrative expenses	47,000	
Total	$1,226,000	$1,226,000

Inventories on October 31, 19x2, determined by physical count were as follows:

>Direct materials, $52,000
>Work in process, $9,000
>Finished goods, $92,000

a. Prepare the following financial statements:
>1. Cost of goods sold
>2. Earnings
>3. Financial position

b. Journalize the entries required to close revenue and expense accounts to retained earnings.

8-22. A trial balance for The Gator Manufacturing Company as of December 31, 19x3, is presented below:

THE GATOR MANUFACTURING COMPANY

TRIAL BALANCE

As of December 31, 19x3

(in thousands of dollars)

Cash	$ 15	
Accounts receivable	11	
Direct materials inventory, January 1, 19x3	30	
Work in process inventory, January 1, 19x3	14	
Finished goods inventory, January 1, 19x3	65	
Other assets	360	
Liabilities		$ 140
Capital stock		100
Retained earnings, January 1, 19x3		220
Sales		1,450
Purchases—direct material	670	
Direct labor	320	
Manufacturing overhead	260	
Selling expenses	75	
Administrative expenses	90	
	$1,910	$1,910

Inventories on December 31, 19x3, determined by physical count were as follows:

>Direct materials, $28,000
>Work in process, $15,000
>Finished goods, $60,000

a. Prepare the following financial statements:
>1. Cost of goods sold 2. Earnings 3. Financial position

b. Journalize the entries required to close revenue and expense accounts to retained earnings.

8-23. The Beacon Company began business on January 1, 19x4. Unit inventory and production figures for 19x4 and 19x5 were as follows:

	19x4	19x5
Inventory, 1/1	0	3,500
+ Units produced	10,000	9,000
Total units on hand	10,000	12,500
− Units sold	6,500	11,500
Inventory, 12/31	3,500	1,000

Company records reveal the following:

	19x4	19x5
Sales revenues ($2 per unit)	$13,000	$23,000
Variable manufacturing costs ($.75 per unit)	7,500	6,750
Nonvariable manufacturing costs	5,000	5,400
Selling and administrative expenses	4,000	7,000

Prepare three sets of statements comparing the earnings of 19x4 and 19x5, using the following methods:

a. revenues recognized on the basis of production
b. revenues recognized on the basis of sales:
  1. variable costing basis
  2. absorption costing basis

8-24. The Orient Company is engaged in the manufacture and sale of transistor radios. Operating information (for the first month) pertaining to one style of radio at its Cantonian branch plant for July of the current year follows:

Units produced	2,500
Operating costs:	
Direct materials	$ 1.75 per unit
Direct labor	2.20 per unit
Variable manufacturing costs	.70 per unit
Nonvariable manufacturing costs	5,000 per month
Variable selling costs	.40 per unit
Nonvariable selling costs	2,000 per month
Administrative costs	3,500 per month
Units sold	1,800
Sales price per unit	$14.00
Ending inventory—units	700

Compute earnings under the following assumptions (a statement of earnings is not required):

a. Revenue recognized at the point of production
b. Revenue recognized at the point of sale when:
    1. variable costing is used.
    2. absorption costing is used.

8-25. A trial balance for The Keystone Company as of November 30, 19x2 is presented below:

THE KEYSTONE COMPANY

TRIAL BALANCE

As of November 30, 19x2

Cash	$ 14,000	
Accounts receivable	17,000	
Direct materials inventory, December 1, 19x2 (1,000 pounds)	10,000	
Finished goods inventory, December 1, 19x2 (1,500 units)	75,000	
Prepaid expenses	3,000	
Land	80,000	
Buildings and equipment	460,000	
Accumulated depreciation—buildings and equipment		$ 72,000
Accounts payable		115,000
Accrued liabilities		42,000
Capital stock		250,000
Retained earnings, December 1, 19x2		85,000
Sales		1,200,000
Purchases—direct materials (40,000 pounds)	400,000	
Direct labor	195,000	
Factory overhead	390,000	
Selling expenses	50,000	
Administrative expenses	70,000	
	$1,764,000	$1,764,000

Inventories on November 30, 19x2 determined by physical count were as follows:

    Direct materials, 2,000 pounds, $20,000
    Work in process, none at beginning or end of year
    Finished goods inventory, 1,000 units

Current production is 19,500 units. The ending inventory is determined using absorption costing.

Prepare the following financial statements:
    a. Cost of goods sold   b. Earnings   c. Financial position

8-26. The rate of return concept takes into account two factors: the net earnings margin and the turnover of assets. The net earnings margin may be expressed as:

$$\frac{\text{Net earnings}}{\text{Sales}}$$

The turnover of assets may be expressed as:

$$\frac{\text{Sales}}{\text{Total assets}}$$

The rate of return includes the net earnings margin and the turnover of assets as follows:

$$\text{Rate of return} = \frac{\text{Net earnings}}{\text{Sales}} \times \frac{\text{Sales}}{\text{Total assets}}$$

or:

$$\text{Rate of return} = \frac{\text{Net earnings}}{\text{Total assets}}$$

a. What advantages do you see in the consideration of the rate of return computation in two parts (profit margin and turnover of assets), as opposed simply to a consideration of the rate of return expressed as:

$$\frac{\text{Net earnings}}{\text{Total assets}}$$

b. What advantages do you see in the use of rate of return, as opposed to net earnings, for performance measurement?

8-27. The following data pertain to the operations of the Beta Company for a two-year period:

	Year	
	1	*2*
Sales	$10,000	$9,500
Earnings	400	500
Total assets	4,000	5,500

Was performance better or worse in year 2 than in year 1? Show your calculations and give reasons to support your answer.

8-28.   PART I

The J. K. L. Company operates several restaurants in a city with a population of approximately 1 million. The following information pertains to the operations of three J. K. L. restaurants for 19x4:

	Restaurant		
	1	*2*	*3*
Sales	$900,000	$650,000	$300,000
Earnings	22,000	27,000	14,000
Total assets	150,000	220,000	90,000

Compute the rate of return for the three restaurants. Which restaurant performed best? Second best?

The following information pertains to the operations of the same three J. K. L. restaurants for 19x5:

	Restaurant		
	1	*2*	*3*
Sales	$940,000	$690,000	$310,000
Earnings	23,500	30,000	14,500
Total assets	160,000	220,000	90,000

Compute the rate of return for the three restaurants. Rank the restaurants according to performance for 19x5.

8-29. A condensed statement of earnings and retained earnings for the Highland Corporation appears below:

HIGHLAND CORPORATION

**CONDENSED COMBINED STATEMENT OF
EARNINGS AND RETAINED EARNINGS**
For 19x5
(in thousands of dollars)

Sales revenues	$1,500
— Operating expenses	1,390
Earnings from operations	$ 110
— Interest on bonds	12
Earnings before taxes	$ 98
— Federal income taxes	46
Net earnings	$ 52
+ Retained earnings, 1/1	50
Total available for dividends	$ 102
— Dividends	30
Retained earnings, 12/1	$ 72

The asset sections of the Highland Corporation statements of financial position at the beginning and end of the year follow:

ASSETS
(in thousands of dollars)

	December 31		
	19x5		19x4
Current assets		$ 300	$200
Long-lived assets	$1,200		$800
— Accumulated depreciation	500		400
Net long-lived assets		700	400
Total assets		$1,000	$600

a. Compute the rate of return on investment for 19x5. Defend your definition of earnings compared with alternative definitions, giving specific attention to interpretation of interest, federal taxes, and dividends.

b. Discuss the advantages and disadvantages of the following sets of alternatives:

1. Using (a) assets at the beginning of the year, (b) assets at the end of the year, or (c) average assets employed during the year, as alternative definitions of investment. Are there other possible definitions?

2. Measuring investment at the undepreciated cost of long-lived assets, compared with measuring it at original cost without deduction for depreciation.

8-30. The condensed comparative earnings statement and statement of financial position of the Richmond Company for 19x4 and 19x5 are as follows:

RICHMOND COMPANY

COMPARATIVE STATEMENT OF EARNINGS
For Years Ended December 31, 19x4 and 19x5
(in thousands of dollars)

	19x4	19x5
Sales revenues	$2,000	$1,600
— Operating expenses	1,750	1,370
Earnings from operations	$ 250	$ 230
— Non-operating expense[a]	50	50
Earnings before taxes	$ 200	$ 180
— Federal income taxes	94	85
Net earnings	$ 106	$ 95

[a]This expense is the property tax assessed on a piece of property owned by the company, which at present earns no revenue.

RICHMOND COMPANY
CONDENSED COMPARATIVE STATEMENT OF FINANCIAL POSITION
As of December 31, 19x3, 19x4, and 19x5
(in thousands of dollars)

Assets	19x5	19x4	19x3
Current assets	$ 4,500	$ 4,500	$ 4,000
Investments (valued at cost)[a]	1,000	1,000	1,000
Net long-lived assets (cost minus depreciation)	6,500	5,500	5,000
Total assets	$12,000	$11,000	$10,000

Liabilities and Owners' Equity	19x5	19x4	19x3
Liabilities	$ 3,000	$ 2,000	$ 2,000
Owners' equity	9,000	9,000	8,000
Total liabilities and owners' equity	$12,000	$11,000	$10,000

[a] The investment consists of real estate purchased for $1 million in 19x1. Offers to buy as high as $1.5 million have been received, but there is reason to believe that higher offers may be made. The real estate will be sold when a suitable offer is received, but meanwhile it earns no revenue.

After the company had earned an inadequate rate of return on investment for several years, the board of directors made several major changes in management near the end of 19x4, including the appointment of a new president. At the board meeting following publication of 19x5 earnings figures, the new president was criticized because the performance of the company under his leadership did not appear better than that of his predecessor. The new president pointed out that he had lacked time to put many new plans into effect. He also objected to the manner in which rate of return on investment was computed. Specifically, he recommended the following changes:

1. Exclusion of investments from the total assets figure used in the computation, and exclusion of the $50,000 expense from earnings. The real estate had nothing to do with the principal purpose of the company (manufacturing), the president argued. In addition, he felt that since the decision to acquire it had been made long before he appeared on the scene, he was not responsible for its acquisition, although the decision to sell the asset would be made by him.

2. Valuing of the long-lived assets on hand January 1, 19x5, at $3 million. According to the president, these assets were partially obsolete, and they were overvalued on the statement of financial position. The old management had paid too much for them when they were acquired and had depreciated them at rates that were too low. The president estimated the market value of the plant and equipment assets on January 1, 19x5, at approximately $3 million. Therefore, the total assets figure used in the rate of return calculation should be reduced by the loss of $2.5 million, which should have been charged to the old management.

a. Compute the rates of return on investment for 19x4 and 19x5 that you believe should be used to measure the performance of the old and new managements.

b. Write an answer to the president's comments, including the extent to which you agree or disagree with his position, and why.

Chapter Nine PLANNING FUTURE OPERATIONS

INTRODUCTION

Planning the future operations of a business firm is the most important activity of the firm's top management. The planning function combines the short-run and long-run operating goals of the firm with the predictions of economic trends that affect the firm's operations. Translating these goals and predictions into an organized plan of action is generally recognized as an indispensable element in the successful management of a business firm.

The long-run success of a business enterprise rests in the ability of its management to perform this planning function as it relates to the various aspects of the enterprise. Long-range goals and major routes leading to these goals should be planned well in advance by top-level managers, perhaps with the help of the owner-investors. The less broad, but equally important, details of future operations should be thought about and planned for at appropriate managerial levels. It is possible, even in today's highly complex society, to be lucky and occasionally succeed without planning, but consistent success is the reward of the person who has conscientiously tried to anticipate future events.

It has been said with some logic that business planning merely requires the manager to put his feet on his desk, put his hands behind his head, and think. This may actually be what is done during some phases of the planning process and is perfectly acceptable behavior if the manager has made use of the various planning tools available to him. Perhaps the most important benefit from the planning process within a business enterprise is that it does require managers to attempt to anticipate the many factors that will affect their business in the future.

Businessmen engage in two kinds of planning. The first assumes that the environment for his activity will not change. For example, the plant manager of plant 1 of the Acme Auto Parts Company would assume that the buildings and machinery, labor force, products, channels of distribution, and other related activities would remain the same in the future period for which the planning is to be done. The purpose of this type of planning is to enable the manager to make the most of the environment in which he finds himself. Planning within the environment is commonly called *budgeting*.

The second major kind of planning is directed at changing the environment so that the enterprise will find itself in a more favorable position in the future. This kind of planning is concerned with changes of product lines, additions or deletions of plant and equipment, automation, subcontracting versus do-it-yourself possibilities, and similar alternatives.

Planning within the environment and planning to change the environment must be conducted simultaneously. Each is dependent upon the other. The business manager really cannot plan how best to use his existing resources unless he also considers the possibility of changing the scope of those resources. The proper blend of the two types of planning depends on the particular circumstances of each separate business organization. Our purpose here is merely to discuss the nature of each type. The remainder of this chapter discusses the planning that should be undertaken on the assumption that the environment will not change. Chapters 10 and 11 will raise the issues that pertain to changing the environment.

BUDGETING WITHIN THE ENVIRONMENT

Budgeting is undertaken for two reasons. The first, discussed in Chapters 5 through 8, relates to setting the standards for judging certain types of performance. The purpose of budgeting expenses, earnings, and rate of return on investment is to set the guidelines for the day-to-day control of operations. The key factor in control budgeting is to ensure that those factors planned for are expressed in the same terms in which actual performance is measured.

The second reason for budgeting is to help coordinate the efforts of the many different managers and the activities within the enterprise. Proper coordination, for example, can help the treasurer of the Acme Auto Parts Company ensure that there will be sufficient cash available to buy a large order of raw materials three months in the future. Similarly, adequate budgeting will tell the personnel director when he should hire extra workers to meet a temporarily increased production schedule in time to accomplish the necessary advance training.

Responsibility for Budgeting

All budgeting efforts should be sponsored and advocated by the very top levels of management. The managers throughout the enterprise should be made aware that their superiors believe in this planning process and intend to use it as an active tool of management rather than just as a plaything of the accounting department. Without the active support of top management, the budgeting process will not accomplish its objectives.

Managers at all levels of the enterprise should participate in the planning processes. When the planning is primarily concerned with developing control budgets, they should have a positive voice in setting the standards by which their performance will be judged. Their participation in helping to develop budgets will ensure that they are aware of both the factors needing coordination and the methods of achieving it.

Participation in Budgeting

The fundamental purpose of budgeting is to influence the actions of people governed by the budget, so that the long-run profits of the firm are optimized. The people whose actions are to be controlled by the budget must therefore work toward the budgeted objectives. These people must always be conscious of the objectives on which the budget is based, as well as of the reasons for and benefits to be derived from the budgeting process.

The budget should not be used as a punitive device. Ordinarily, people do not respond to punishment or criticism in a desirable way, particularly if there is some possibility that it is unjustified. Instead, management should encourage people to react properly to budgetary control by getting them to assist in establishing the budgetary goals in the first place. If this is not feasible, it is usually possible to obtain prior agreement from the people affected that the budgetary objectives are both desirable and attainable. Only in this way will they willingly accept responsibility for carrying out the budgeted objectives.

The Length of the Budget Period

The length of the budget period is determined by the degree of precision required and the purpose of the budget. The shorter the time period, the more precise the thinking. Most companies engage in budgeting for at least the year ahead and "adjust" their budget every month or perhaps every quarter to reflect corrections of earlier predictions. Some companies also attempt long-range budgeting in which they seek to set broad guidelines that will govern the direction of overall activities. As a general rule, the higher the level of the manager, the longer the period for which he will plan, and vice versa.

Predictions and Goals

Budgeting is more than a forecast about what *will* happen in a future period; it also reflects judgments about what *should* happen. Budgeting helps to set realistic goals, and it controls and coordinates activity. For example, assume that one salesman for Acme Auto Parts forecasts that he can sell $350,000 worth of products next year, based on a given number of calls. After discussing the situation in detail with his sales manager, the salesman estimates that he could sell $425,000 worth of products if he changes his route, increasing the number of calls he makes from 200 to 250. His budgeted sales might be raised to $425,000, rather than $350,000, or to some amount in between. The planning processes undertaken by the salesman and the sales manager will help set a goal and stimulate thinking about how that goal could be accomplished.

The Cost of Budgeting

Since the planning process is costly in terms of manpower, there should be some way of determining whether the system of budgeting will benefit an enterprise more than it costs. Unfortunately, it is very difficult to measure either the costs or the benefits of a budgeting process. Most businessmen believe that it is worth the cost, even though they cannot prove it with financial calculations. However, managers should guard against unnecessary detail in this activity. Occasionally those involved with budgeting become so engrossed in minute refinements that budgets cost more than they should. The degree of refinement should be no greater than that required for the purpose.

Organization for Planning

Budgeting is done most successfully when the enterprise has a definite organizational means of accomplishing the planning. In major firms the overall planning effort is usually in the hands of a planning (or budgeting) committee. At Acme Auto Parts, for example, this committee consists of the vice president of sales, the vice president of production, and the controller. This committee decides what kind of planning will be undertaken, how it will be accomplished, and who will do it. At appropriate times the planning committee requests estimates about future operations from the plant managers, who will in turn request this information from the department heads. In effect, the budgeting process consists of collecting the best predictions about the future from the lower levels of management, through the next higher level of management, all the way up to the planning committee. After collecting these subdivisional budgets, the planning committee coordinates them after many revisions and much consultation with the subordinate managers involved. The result is usually called the operating budget for the given future time period, usually a year. The coordinated plan is then presented to the board of directors, who approve, revise, or disapprove it. If the budget is approved, it is distributed through the enterprise as a road map for operating in the period ahead.

PLANNING AND CONTROL

In Chapters 5 through 8 we were primarily interested in accounting's contribution to the control of business operations. For example, in Chapter 5 we discussed performance measurement for the grinding department foreman at Acme. But this discussion began in the middle of things: Certain planning decisions had to be made before the foreman was assigned his quota of units of output. As Exhibit 9–1 illustrates, planning and control are actually parts of the same cycle. Before the foreman's quota could be set, a sales forecast had to be made and production requirements estimated. The production requirements would then be translated into the units of output needed from the grinding department in each time period.

After the sales forecast and production requirements are approved for the next budget period, the control phase begins. For the grinding department this phase includes ensuring that the quota of units will be produced on a timely basis within the allotted cost allowances. The performance report for the grinding department will be used by the foreman and his superior in evaluating past operations, and this evaluation, in turn, will be used in planning future operations for the grinding department. If the performance report indicates that the quota is not being met on time or costs are too high, planning might include changes in certain operating characteristics (including the qualifications of employees, type of equipment, and/or work methods) of the grinding department.

The planning-control cycle described for the grinding department affects the foreman, his superior, and the accountant. Each responsibility unit in the organization involves a similar cycle. The accountant's job is to educate and motivate the managers throughout the organization to use budgeting and performance measurement reports effectively. The accountant then contributes to the control function only indirectly, by helping motivate line managers to use budgeting and reporting for more effective planning and control decisions.

Exhibit 9–1 includes preoperative, operative, and postoperative decisions. As the exhibit shows, preoperative decisions occur in both the planning and control phases of business operations. Operative decisions occur in the control phase alone; postoperative decisions occur in both planning and control.

EXHIBIT 9 – 1

INTERRELATIONSHIP BETWEEN PLANNING AND CONTROL FOR THE GRINDING DEPARTMENT OF PLANT 1 FOR ACME AUTO PARTS COMPANY

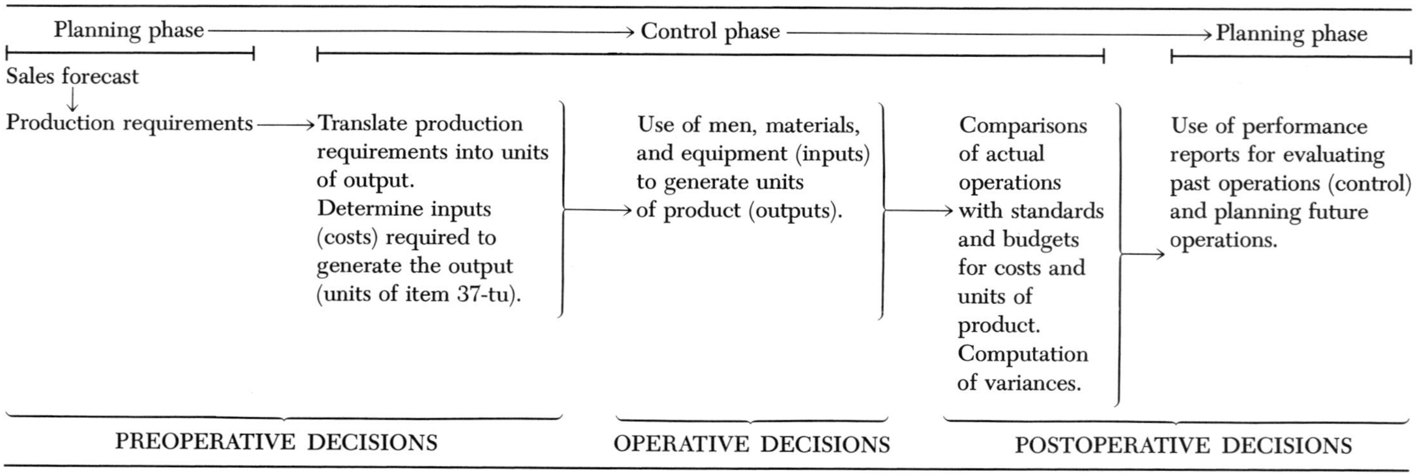

Planning phase ─────────────→ Control phase ─────────────→ Planning phase

Sales forecast
↓

Production requirements ──→ Translate production requirements into units of output. Determine inputs (costs) required to generate the output (units of item 37-tu).

→ Use of men, materials, and equipment (inputs) to generate units → of product (outputs).

→ Comparisons of actual operations with standards and budgets for costs and units of product. Computation of variances.

→ Use of performance reports for evaluating past operations (control) and planning future operations.

PREOPERATIVE DECISIONS

OPERATIVE DECISIONS

POSTOPERATIVE DECISIONS

INTERRELATIONSHIPS
AMONG OPERATING FACTORS

Planning for future operations within a given environment involves many separate objectives. The treasurer wants to know the effect of all operations on his money supply. Top managers generally want to know the possible effect of operations on future earnings. Future earnings have a direct relationship to the future financial strength, and this information is of concern not only to managers, but to creditors and owners as well. The vice president of production, as well as the plant managers and other production personnel, has the responsibility for maintaining the budgeted level of activity and for seeing to it that adequate, but not excessive, inventories of materials, equipment, and workers are available throughout the entire organization.

In most cases, the starting place in developing plans about future operations is the sales budget. This is because most firms have available, or can arrange to acquire, the resources necessary to supply customers with all the goods they will buy, at a price that yields maximum profit. Budgeted sales dollars, made up of the number of units of finished product to be sold to customers multiplied by the estimated sales price per unit, is usually the factor over which management has the least control, and it therefore becomes the prediction on which other budgeted factors will depend.

In a number of situations, however, the sales budget is not the starting place in the budgeting process, particularly if the period is in the near future and relatively short. A retailer or wholesaler may predict that he can sell all of certain products he can buy from others; in other cases, available storage space may be the limiting factor. A manufacturer may find he can sell all he can produce, because of shortages of physical facilities, labor, or sources of capital. Ordinarily these shortages can be corrected over time, and product sales will again become the limiting factor in future periods. In monopoly situations the sales price of the product may be increased during times of such shortage, to the point that the quantity demanded becomes less than supply. The grain farmer, on the other hand, can always sell all his product at the market price (not necessarily a profitable price), and his limiting factor is land, machinery, or labor.

In most cases, the total sales may be at least partially controllable, in that management can vary advertising and other sales promotion expenditures. Theoretically this means that sales promotion expenses provide the starting point for the budget. This is rarely the case, however, because predicting the relationship between sales promotion expenditures and sales ordinarily lacks sufficient reliability.

But no matter what the limiting factor, it must be remembered that earnings, not sales, are the objective of the firm for the budgeted period. Also, you have already learned that maximum earnings for the period immediately ahead are usually secondary in importance to long-run earnings. This means that it may not be wise to increase the sales price per unit simply because the product is temporarily in short supply, or reduce it to try to increase sales so that productive capacity is fully utilized. It may not be wise to curtail sales promotion, research and development, or other nonvariable expenses to increase short-run earnings, if the effect on long-run earnings is adverse.

Knowledge of the relationships among the sales of the firm, the volume of output, and the operating costs for a budget period is obviously very important to the planner and also very difficult to visualize. This is particularly true when it becomes necessary to predict the effect on net earnings of proposed changes in selling price per unit, in predicted volume of production, and/or in variable or nonvariable expenses.

The Breakeven Chart

One popular way of simplifying these relationships so that the management can visualize the operating characteristics of the firm is to plot revenues and expenses on a graph that is usually called a *breakeven chart*. We will use this title, even though it gives undue emphasis to the point of zero profit, or the *breakeven point*, which in fact is usually no more important than any other point on the chart. The breakeven chart depicts the relationship between revenues and expenses, and therefore earnings, at all volumes of output. Exhibit 9–2 shows such a chart.

The total expense (TE) line represents the total expenses faced by the

E X H I B I T 9 - 2   **BREAKEVEN CHART**

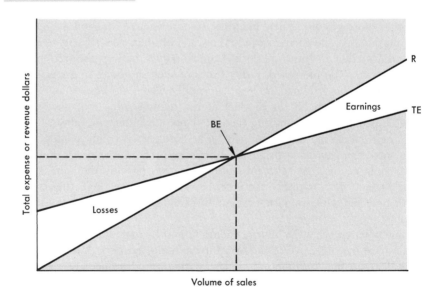

Volume of sales

enterprise at the levels of sales indicated on the horizontal axis of the chart. The TE line is merely the summation of the nonvariable and variable expenses discussed in Chapter 6. (The components of the total expense line are shown in Exhibit 9–3.)

COMPONENTS OF TOTAL EXPENSE CURVE   **E X H I B I T 9 - 3**

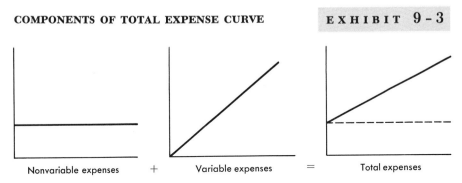

Nonvariable expenses   +   Variable expenses   =   Total expenses

The R line in Exhibit 9–2 represents the total revenues of the enterprise at the various sales volumes represented on the horizontal axis. The breakeven point is at BE, where the revenue and total expense lines cross. As indicated on the chart, sales levels lower than the breakeven point result in loss operations. Sales levels above the breakeven point result in earnings.

Given expense and revenue amounts, the breakeven chart can be illustrated quantitatively. For example, if the selling price of item 37-tu is $1.50 per unit, variable costs $.70 per unit, and nonvariable costs $50,000 per month, it would be necessary to sell 62,500 units per month to break even. The reasoning is as follows: Each additional unit of product sold makes the profit $.80 higher, or the loss $.80 less, because each unit adds $1.50 to revenues and $.70 to expenses. To cover the $50,000 nonvariable expense, sales of 62,500 units, each one providing $.80 toward these expenses, are required ($50,000 ÷ $.80 = 62,500).° The breakeven chart for this situations appears in Exhibit 9–4.

° A more formal approach provides the same result:
The breakeven point is that point at which revenues equal total expenses, or:

Revenues (R) = Variable expenses (VE) + Nonvariable expenses (NE)

If x equals output in units, then

$$R = \$1.50x$$
$$VE = \$.70x$$
$$NE = \$50,000$$

Applying the formula, we get

$$\$1.50x = \$.70x + \$50,000$$
$$(\$1.50 - \$.70)x = \$50,000$$

$$x = \frac{\$50,000}{\$1.50 - \$.70}$$

$$x = \frac{\$50,000}{\$.80} = 62,500 \text{ units per month}$$

EXHIBIT 9 – 4   **BREAKEVEN CHART FOR ITEM 37-TU**

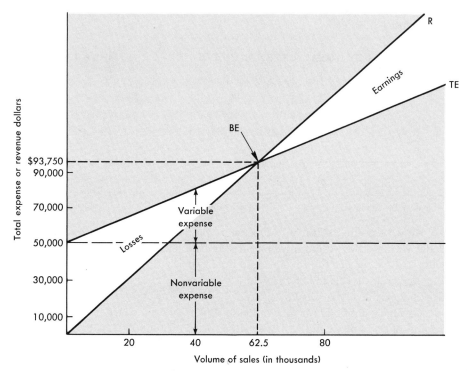

By inspecting Exhibit 9–4 or by arithmetic solution, we can see, for example, that:

1. If the monthly volume were 45,000 units, there would be a $14,000 loss for the month.
2. If the monthly volume were 70,000 units, there would be $6,000 earnings for the month.
3. If the earnings goal for the month were $15,000, 81,250 units would have to be sold.

You should be able to arrive at these results algebraically.

As indicated earlier, the breakeven chart is not of great assistance to the manager who has specific decisions to make. The point of zero profit is not a highly significant point; moreover, the intuitive feeling that the breakeven point is something that should be kept as low as possible is subject to severe limitations. The principal value of the chart is that it demonstrates graphically the difference between variable and nonvariable expenses in terms of their effect on profit at different volumes.

A breakeven chart can be constructed for total enterprise operations, for subdivisional operations, or even for the relationships of expenses and revenues pertaining to a particular product, product line, sales territory, or customer classification. All that is required is knowledge of expense and revenue behavior in relation to volume. Unfortunately it is not always possible to identify these curves with any degree of accuracy. Nevertheless, when they can be ascertained, or even estimated reasonably, it is helpful to managers in visualizing the relationship between expenses and revenues and the resulting effects on earnings.

Refinements in Breakeven Analysis

The breakeven charts in Exhibits 9–2 and 9–4 are based on several assumptions that accountants have to make, either because the illustrations must be simple to be comprehensible or because the information that would permit a more precise measure of estimated profit is not available. Some of these assumptions rather severely limit use of the breakeven chart, while others can be removed if management feels that the cost of the additional research is justified by the benefit to be gained from the additional information.

For example, to draw the revenue curve as a straight line, we must assume that additional units of product can be sold without reducing the selling price per unit. Ordinarily it is not possible to increase the number of units sold, except perhaps within narrow limits, without reducing the price. With most products and markets, therefore, the sales curve will bend as shown in Exhibit 9–5. Notice that the total sales revenues may actually drop at higher volumes if the increase in units sold is not sufficient to offset the drop in the unit price.

MORE REALISTIC SALES REVENUE CURVE   **E X H I B I T 9 - 5**

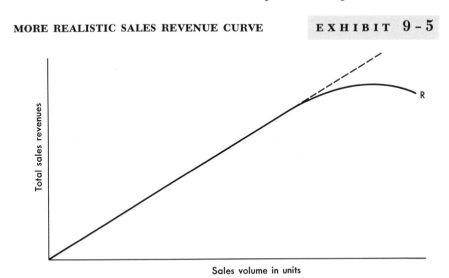

It is probably more logical to assume that the total-expense curve is a straight line, within reasonable output ranges, but there comes a point within a given environment when variable expenses per unit sold will increase. In many cases, this increase results from attempts to produce more than can efficiently be produced within the given environment.

In fact, generalizations about the variable expense per unit at very low or very high levels of output should not be made unless the firm has actually operated at these levels and the expense behavior pattern observed. It is not possible, and (luckily) usually not necessary, to predict revenues and expenses at either extreme on the curve from observations about the more reasonable output levels represented by the middle of the curve.

The breakeven charts are also based on the assumptions that all expenses are either variable or nonvariable, and that the two behavior patterns can be separated and measured. Certainly a realistic expense curve would indicate "jumps" when the plant moved from a one-shift to a two-shift operation, and the curve would also show the effects of the semiconstant behavior patterns discussed in Chapter 6.

Finally, we must remember that the basic data of sales price per unit, variable costs per unit, and nonvariable costs are usually derived from past periods, under market and other environmental conditions that have since changed, and the data may no longer be useful for prediction purposes. Where possible, data from past periods should be adjusted for known changes in conditions before they are used to predict profits for the current period.

INTERRELATIONSHIPS AMONG BUDGETS

Estimates of future sales directly affect the planning for production activity and for material, personnel, and financing requirements. When the planning process can provide an estimate not only of the volume of sales, but also of the pattern in which those sales will occur, further refinements can be developed, such as timetables for materials purchasing, personnel, hiring, and warehouse availability.

The number and nature of individual budgets varies according to the special needs of each firm. A typical situation is that faced by the Acme Auto Parts Company. Assume that top management has already decided that during the coming quarter (three months) there will be no changes in the environment—buildings, equipment, and products will remain the same. Planning for operations within the given environment, then, will require development of budgets for:

1. sales
2. production
3. materials requirements
4. materials acquisitions
5. labor

6. manufacturing expenses
7. selling and administrative expenses
8. cash receipts
9. cash disbursements

Each of these will be discussed in turn. You should be careful to note the relationships among these budgets. The production, materials, and expense budgets depend upon the estimate of sales; the cash budgets in turn depend upon both the sales revenues and the expenses predicted for the future period in question.

The Sales Budget

The sales budget is the result of the combined efforts of many people within and outside of the enterprise. In the case of Acme Auto Parts, sales are highly dependent upon economic conditions within the automobile industry generally, and the automobile industry is dependent upon the economic condition of the country as a whole. Acme's vice president of marketing starts the sales-budgeting process with the "macro" approach—that is, he seeks opinions as to future economic conditions in the nation and their effects on the auto industry. In this regard, he relies upon the statistical information prepared by federal agencies, including the Department of Commerce and the Bureau of Labor Statistics, as well as the business-indicator magazines prepared by the local state university and interpretations of economic conditions in the auto industry trade magazines. In addition he often hires a professor of economics from the state university on a consulting basis to make forecasts of business conditions.

After he has some idea of the economic conditions to be expected in the budget period and their effect on the industry and Acme Auto Parts, the vice president of marketing adopts the "micro" approach—that is, he seeks forecasts of estimated sales from "inside" sources. For example, each salesman is asked to make a forecast of the sales potential in his territory for the sales period. The same request is made of the company officers and those members of the board of directors who have knowledge along these lines.

All the information gathered, whether statistical or personally estimated, is used to formulate a forecast of sales in the future budget period. This sales forecast is then used as the starting place for the development of the sales budget. The sales budget differs from the sales forecast in that the sales budget includes an estimate of what the company *should* accomplish, not just what it could accomplish if everything remained the same. The sales budget will reflect the plans of management to increase the size of the sales force, the amount of advertising expenditures, new product lines, or any other influences the actions of the company may have on its share of the estimated total market for the budget period.

Because of its extreme importance to the rest of the operational budgeting process, the sales budget may take several weeks or even months to develop, and when it is finally formulated it may look deceptively simple. Underlying the simple figures, however, are many hours of research and thought.

The sales budget can take many forms. It can present information by

EXHIBIT 9 - 6

ACME AUTO PARTS COMPANY
SALES BUDGET
For Fourth Quarter 19x5

Month	Item	Units	Average selling price	Revenue	
October	37-tu	500,000	$ 1.50	$ 750,000	
	19-tg	20,000	2.00	40,000	
	77-1x	48,000	1.00	48,000	
	NASA-13	2,000	25.00	50,000	$ 888,000
November	37-tu	700,000	1.50	$1,050,000	
	19-tg	15,000	2.00	30,000	
	NASA-13	1,000	25.00	25,000	
	79-ly	10,000	3.00	30,000	$1,135,000
December	37-tu	800,000	1.50	$1,200,000	
	19-tg	15,000	2.00	30,000	
	79-ly	40,000	3.00	120,000	
	GM-17	80,000	1.00	80,000	$1,430,000
				Total estimated revenue	$3,453,000

production line, sales territory, salesmen, or customer. Actually, it is presented in each of these different ways within the marketing function at Acme Auto Parts. The sales manager uses a budget by sales territory, salesmen, and customer to help control the efforts of his personnel during the budget period. The most important manner of presentation for overall company planning purposes, however, is by product, because it provides the most meaningful information for the preparation of the remainder of the budgets. Exhibit 9–6 is a sales budget by product for the fourth quarter of 19x5.

The Production Budget

When the sales budget for a period has been completed, the production budget can be formulated. Its primary purpose is to facilitate the most advantageous scheduling of production. Ideally, production should occur evenly throughout the year to gain the advantages of a stable work force and a stable level of utilization of facilities. Differences between production and sales will be reflected in inventories of finished goods. Level production volume is often difficult to obtain, however, and there will be periods of production speedup and slack-off during the year. Furthermore, level production may turn out to be more costly in highly seasonal industries if the cost of inventory storage is high or if there is a risk that the value of inventory will decline as a result of price decreases.

The minimum objective in planning production is to ensure that there will be enough of each product available to meet the sales demands for a given time period. Loss of sales and loss of customer goodwill resulting from "stock-outs" are usually more expensive than the costs associated with storage of reasonable amounts of finished goods inventory. Production stoppages resulting from shortages of component parts are usually so costly that great effort is made to avoid these shortages.

The production budget of one product, item 37-tu, is presented in Exhibit 9–7. A similar budget would be developed for each product made by the company, with special care given to proper intermeshing of the separate production schedules.

EXHIBIT 9-7

ACME AUTO PARTS COMPANY
PRODUCTION BUDGET FOR ITEM 37-TU
For Fourth Quarter 19x5

	October	November	December
Estimated sales in units	500,000	700,000	800,000
+ Inventory of finished units desired at end of month to meet sales requirements in early part of next month	200,000	250,000	225,000
Total units required	700,000	950,000	1,025,000
− Inventory of finished units on hand at beginning of month	50,000	200,000	250,000
Production required during month	650,000	750,000	775,000

The Materials Requirement Budget

Assume item 37-tu requires two basic materials in its production. One is type 210 steel, which is melted and cast into the basic shape in the foundry (using one and one-half pounds per unit); the other is a number fourteen, three-and-three-quarter-inch machine bolt, which is purchased and attached at the end of the production process. Exhibit 9–8 is a materials requirement budget for item 37-tu for the fourth quarter of 19x5.

EXHIBIT 9-8

ACME AUTO PARTS COMPANY

MATERIALS REQUIREMENT BUDGET FOR ITEM 37-TU

For Fourth Quarter 19x5

	October	November	December
Production	650,000	750,000	775,000
Materials required:			
Lbs. of type 210 steel	975,000	1,125,500	1,132,500
#14, 3¾" machine bolts	650,000	750,000	775,000

The Materials Acquisition Budget

It can be very costly when production is stopped because adequate materials are not on hand when needed. To help prevent this, the production manager will prepare a materials acquisition budget, which he uses along with the materials requirement budget and the production budget that he has already prepared. The materials acquisition budget ties together the requirements for raw materials with the amounts already on hand, and it indicates the amounts to be acquired during the budget period. A very important factor in developing this budget is the minimum level of inventory desired at all times. Forecasts of future needs, costs of maintaining adequate storage space, costs of having money tied up in inventory, and the risk of price drops are the major factors considered in setting

EXHIBIT 9-9

ACME AUTO PARTS COMPANY

MATERIALS ACQUISITION BUDGET FOR ITEM 37-TU

For Fourth Quarter 19x5

	October	November	December
Units of type 210 steel:			
Required for production	975,000	1,125,500	1,132,500
Required for minimum inventory			
level desired	300,000	350,000	400,000
Total	1,275,000	1,475,500	1,532,500
− Inventory, beginning	250,000	300,000	350,000
Acquisition units required	1,025,000	1,175,500	1,182,500
× Estimated cost/unit	$.15	$.15	$.15
Cost of acquisition units	$153,750	$176,325	$177,375

ACME AUTO PARTS COMPANY (CONT.)

	October	November	December
#14, 3¾″ machine bolts:			
Required for production	650,000	750,000	775,000
Required for minimum inventory			
level desired	150,000	160,000	180,000
Total	800,000	910,000	955,000
− Inventory, beginning	130,000	150,000	160,000
Acquisition units required	670,000	760,000	795,000
× Estimated cost/unit	$.02	$.02	$.02
Cost of acquisition units	$13,400	$15,200	$15,900

minimum inventory requirements. Exhibit 9–9 shows a materials acquisition budget adapted to satisfy the requirements budget presented in Exhibit 9–8.

The Labor Budget

The labor budget, also directly related to the production budget, enables plant and departmental production managers to gauge how many laborers of different types will be needed at different times during the budget period. It enables the personnel manager to plan the hiring or laying off of personnel at the most advantageous times. The board of directors of the Acme Auto Parts Company has set a policy of attempting to maintain a stable labor force. In this case, the labor budget serves as a means of planning the shifting of personnel to different areas of operations within the firm at the best times. The labor budget can become complicated when it is detailed by departments or even parts of departments. It is unnecessary to show an entire labor budget here. Instead, only the labor budget for the grinding department at plant 2 is shown in Exhibit 9–10. A stable labor force of fifteen machinists and two helpers is assumed. The budget shows how that force will be employed during the period examined.

The Expense Budget

Expense budgets can be developed in many different forms. Often they are prepared by department, although in some cases they related to a product line or the kind of expense instead. Whereas the materials and labor budgets serve the dual role of coordinating the production process and helping to control costs, the expense budgets are developed primarily for the control purposes discussed in Chapter 6. The behavior pattern of the expense item is the key factor considered in preparing the expense budgets. An example of the selling expense budget for the Detroit sales territory of the Acme Auto Parts Company for the fourth quarter of 19x5 is presented in Exhibit 9–11. Similar budgets would be prepared for other manufacturing expenses and general and administrative expenses. Note which of the expenses are variable and which are nonvariable.

EXHIBIT 9-10

ACME AUTO PARTS COMPANY, PLANT 2 GRINDING DEPARTMENT

LABOR BUDGET

For Fourth Quarter 19x5

	October					November				December			
Week	1	2	3	4	5	1	2	3	4	1	2	3	4
Machinists 1–7	37-tu ———————————————————————————————————————→ GM-17 ——————→												
Machinists 8–11	19-tg ——→												
Machinists 12–13	77-lx ———————————————————————————————→												
Machinist 14	77-lx ———————————————→				79-ly ——————————→							
Machinist 15	NASA-13 ——————————————————————————→				79-ly ——————————→				79-ly ———→			
Extra machinists (from other departments)										37-tu ———→ (1 man)			

MONTHLY LABOR COST SUMMARY

	October	November	December
Machinists:			
Labor hours	3,000	2,400	2,560
Average wage	$ 3	$ 3	$ 3
Total cost	$9,000	$7,200	$7,680
Helpers:			
Labor hours	400	320	320
Average wage	$ 2	$ 2	$ 2
Total cost	$ 800	$ 640	$ 640
Total departmental labor cost	$9,800	$7,840	$8,340

ACME AUTO PARTS COMPANY, DETROIT SALES TERRITORY
SELLING EXPENSE BUDGET
For Fourth Quarter 19x5

	October	November	December
Budgeted sales	$500,000	$550,000	$650,000
Salaries:			
Sales manager	$ 2,750	$ 2,750	$ 2,750
Office help	1,200	1,200	1,200
Salesmen's commission (at 2.5% of gross sales)	12,500	13,750	16,250
Sales manager's overriding commission			
(at .1% of gross sales)	500	550	650
Advertising (at 2% of gross sales)	10,000	11,000	13,000
Losses on uncollectable accounts receivable			
arising from month's sales (at 1% of gross sales)	5,000	5,500	6,500
Entertainment and miscellaneous (at .5% of			
gross sales)	2,500	2,750	3,250
Space costs (allocated share of utilities,			
insurances, taxes, & depreciation)	850	850	850
Total budgeted sales expense	$ 35,300	$ 38,350	$ 44,450

The Cash Budget

The role of cash in the operations of a business enterprise is like that of the grease in an automobile: Just the right amount is needed to ensure that it runs without friction and that it will continue to run smoothly in the future. Too much grease is wasteful, but too little will cause the automobile to wear out and break down permanently. The basic concept of a cash budget is explained by the schematic outline in Exhibit 9–12.

Quite often it is advisable to subdivide the cash budget into a cash receipts budget and a cash disbursements budget. In any case it is necessary to remember that cash does not ordinarily change hands at the same instant that revenues are earned and expenses incurred. Cash budgets are based on cash receipts and disbursements that may have either a time lead or a time lag compared to the revenues and expenses that generate the cash flow.

The cash receipts and cash disbursements budgets for Acme Auto Parts are shown in Exhibits 9–13 and 9–14, along with their explanatory supplements. Note

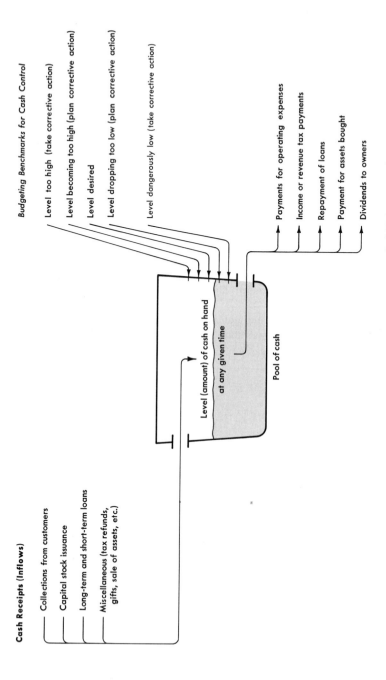

EXHIBIT 9-12   SCHEMATIC DIAGRAM OF CASH RECEIPTS AND DISBURSEMENTS

Cash Receipts (Inflows)

Collections from customers

Capital stock issuance

Long-term and short-term loans

Miscellaneous (tax refunds, gifts, sale of assets, etc.)

Level (amount) of cash on hand at any given time

Pool of cash

Budgeting Benchmarks for Cash Control

Level too high (take corrective action)

Level becoming too high (plan corrective action)

Level desired

Level dropping too low (plan corrective action)

Level dangerously low (take corrective action)

Payments for operating expenses

Income or revenue tax payments

Repayment of loans

Payment for assets bought

Dividends to owners

Cash Disbursements (Outflows)

that the cash receipts and disbursements budgets necessarily include *all* predicted transactions of the budget period, including those pertaining to changes in the environment. These latter factors will be discussed in more detail in Chapters 10 and 11.

EXHIBIT 9-13

ACME AUTO PARTS COMPANY

CASH RECEIPTS BUDGET

For Fourth Quarter 19x5

	October	November	December
Collections from customers:[a]			
From accounts receivable as of 10/1:			
August sales	$ 68,670	$ 0	$ 0
September sales	640,000	72,000	0
From sales in:			
October	88,800	710,400	79,920
November	0	113,500	908,000
December	0	0	143,000
Other sources:			
Sale of temporary investments in securities	30,000	0	0
Collections of last payment for common stock subscribed under officers' stock-option plan	0	0	15,000
Total cash receipts	$827,470	$895,900	$1,145,920

[a] Past experience indicates that collections on accounts receivable from customers can be expected as follows:

In month of sale	10%
In month after sale	80%
In second month after sale	9%
Losses from uncollectable accounts	1%
Total	100%

Total relevant company sales are as follows:

August (known)	$ 763,000
September (budgeted)	800,000
October (budgeted)	888,000
November (budgeted)	1,135,000
December (budgeted)	1,430,000

EXHIBIT 9-14

ACME AUTO PARTS COMPANY
CASH DISBURSEMENTS BUDGET
For Fourth Quarter 19x5

	October	November	December
Payments on materials & subcontract accounts payable[a]	$356,000	$428,000	$ 463,000
Wages & salaries[b]	344,000	356,500	415,000
Payments on utilities, insurance, supplies, advertising, & similar accounts payable[c]	67,000	75,000	133,000
Tax payments:			
Semiannual real estate tax (for 1st half of 19x5)	0	8,000	0
Quarterly payment of state use tax (for 3rd quarter)	3,450	0	0
Quarterly payment of state sales tax (for 3rd quarter)	17,500	0	0
Prepayment of portion of 19x5 federal income tax	0	20,000	40,000
Dividends (to be declared as of 12/10 and paid 12/30)	0	0	37,500
Purchases of machinery & equipment	47,000	8,000	65,000
Total budgeted disbursements	$834,950	$895,500	$1,153,500

[a] See also Schedule A.
[b] See also Schedule B.
[c] A detailed schedule similar to A would normally be attached.

SCHEDULE A

CASH PAYMENTS FOR MATERIALS
AND SUBCONTRACT ACCOUNTS PAYABLE[a]

	Payments		
	October	November	December
Materials purchased in:			
September ($283,838)	$281,000	$ 0	$ 0
October ($341,414)	0	338,000	0

[a]It is company policy to try to pay all accounts payable within thirty days after receipt of the invoice, because it is customary in this industry for vendors to grant a 1 per cent discount for bills paid within thirty days. Subcontracts are paid in full per contract terms, usually one-third when the contract is initiated, one-third at completion, and one-third within thirty days after completion.

SCHEDULE A (CONT.)

	Payments		
	October	November	December
November ($407,070)	0	0	403,000
December ($460,500)	0	0	0
Subcontracts completed by contractor in:			
September ($60,000)	20,000	0	0
October ($90,000)	30,000	30,000	0
November ($75,000)	25,000	25,000	25,000
December ($105,000)	0	35,000	35,000
Total payments for materials and subcontract accounts payable	$356,000	$428,000	$463,000

SCHEDULE B
CASH PAYMENTS FOR WAGES AND SALARIES

	October	November	December
Wage & salary expenses incurred:			
Factory direct labor	$220,000	$226,800	$260,300
Factory indirect labor	34,500	37,600	39,400
General & administrative salaries	40,000	40,000	40,000
Selling salaries & commissions	37,500	43,600	49,300
Total wages & salaries	$332,000	$348,000	$389,000
+ Employer payroll taxes[a]	28,000	32,000	39,000
Total expenses	$360,000	$380,000	$428,000
Disbursements for wages & salaries:			
Paid to employees:			
September	$120,000	$ 0	$ 0
October	120,800	118,550	0
November	0	131,000	140,300
December	0	0	150,200
Employees' share of payroll taxes[b]	75,680	78,430	91,300
Employers' share of payroll taxes[a]	27,520	28,520	33,200
Total disbursements for wages & salaries	$344,000	$356,500	$415,000

[a] Social security, unemployment compensation, workman's compensation.
[b] Social security and withheld income taxes.

Injecting Additional Cash

The management of every enterprise should set a minimum level of cash to be available at any time. Just as the designers of an automobile can determine minimum amounts of lubrication for efficient operation of the vehicle, the cash balances can be determined at the end of any budget period simply by comparing the sales receipts and disbursements in the manner suggested in Exhibit 9–15. If any of these balances fall below the desired minimum level set by management, the treasurer of the company can take proper action to acquire additional cash when needed. He can obtain short-term loans from banks or other money-lending institutions; if long-term additional cash is needed, the treasurer, with the approval of the owners, can sell additional shares of ownership stock or acquire long-term loans. On the other hand, if the budgeted cash balances show a temporary excess over the desired level, the treasurer can invest this excess cash in accordance with corporate policy.

EXHIBIT 9-15

ACME AUTO PARTS COMPANY
CASH BALANCE BUDGET[a]
For Fourth Quarter 19x5

	October	November	December
Cash balance, beginning	$ 46,300	$ 48,620	$ 29,020
+ Budgeted receipts	827,470	895,900	1,145,920
Total	873,770	944,520	1,174,940
− Budgeted disbursements	834,950	895,500	1,153,500
Budgeted balance, ending (from operations)	38,620	49,020	21,440
+ Financing obtained	10,000[b]	0	10,300[e]
− Debts repaid	0	(10,000)[c]	0
− Special items	0	(10,000)[d]	0
Budgeted cash balance, ending (from all sources)	$ 48,620	$ 29,020	$ 31,740

[a] The minimum desired balance is $40,000.
[b] A budgeted loan (a thirty-day note at a bank).
[c] Repayment of the bank loan (with a thirty-day note).
[d] A temporary investment in marketable securities.
[e] Proceeds from the sale of the marketable securities.

The Budgeted Earnings Statement

The information contained in the revenue and expense budgets described is blended into a projected earnings statement for the budgeted period. This statement serves as a guideline against which to compare actual earnings for the period, as was discussed in Chapter 8. Exhibit 9–16 is the budgeted earnings statement for the fourth quarter of 19x5. It incorporates information presented in the earlier examples, plus, of course, assumed figures for those aspects of operations not previously shown in detail.

EXHIBIT 9-16

ACME AUTO PARTS COMPANY
BUDGETED STATEMENT OF EARNINGS
For Fourth Quarter 19x5

Sales revenues			$3,453,000
— Cost of goods sold:			
Finished-goods inventory, 9/30		$ 215,000	
Cost of goods manufactured:			
Materials	$1,283,700		
Subcontracting cost	275,000		
Direct labor	707,100		
Variable manufacturing costs	150,000		
Total cost of goods manufactured		2,415,800	
		$2,630,800	
— Finished-goods inventory, 12/31		190,000	
Total cost of goods sold			2,440,800
Contribution margin			$1,012,200
— Operating expenses:			
Nonvariable labor	$111,500		
Nonvariable manufacturing expenses	85,000		
Total		$196,500	
General & administrative salaries	$120,000		
General & administrative expenses	71,000		
Total		191,000	
Selling salaries & commissions	$130,400		
Selling expenses	45,000		
Total		175,400	
Total operating expenses			562,900
Estimated earnings from operations			$449,300
— Estimated income taxes			110,000
Estimated net earnings, 4th quarter 19x5			$339,300

SUMMARY

In this chapter we have introduced the major function of a business manager—planning. The planning process consists of drawing conclusions and making decisions about the future. Planning for operations within an environment is undertaken to develop budgets suggesting what should happen within the future period. These budgets are used for coordinating the efforts of managers within the enterprise. Budgeted operations for a future period are also used as standards for measuring performance during that period. Budget coordination is achieved because each manager writes down his thoughts about future operations in an organized form understandable to others, and because higher-level managers reconcile the demands of these separate budgets.

Questions for Review

9-1. Contrast briefly the two major kinds of business planning.

9-2. What are two main reasons for budgeting?

9-3. What role should the accountant play in the preparation of the budget? The manager?

9-4. How should the length of the budget period be determined?

9-5. What objective for the firm is assumed in the budgeting process?

9-6. What is the purpose of the breakeven chart?

9-7. A complete (comprehensive) budget is illustrated in the chapter for Acme Auto Parts. Give the sequence in which the budgets are prepared. What is the reason for this sequence?

9-8. What is the purpose of each budget discussed in the chapter?

Problems for Analysis

9-9. Describe as briefly as you can how you think budgeting can assist the manager in planning, coordination, and control.

9-10. The following information pertains to the operations of Gaylord's, Inc., for the fiscal year ending August 31, 19x2:

Estimated sales for the year are 240,000 units (one product), distributed as follows:

September 5%	December 12%	March 6%	June 12%
October 5%	January 4%	April 8%	July 12%
November 8%	February 4%	May 10%	August 14%

Sales for the first quarter of the fiscal year 19x2 are estimated to be $345,600.

Prepare a monthly sales budget in units and dollars for Gaylord's, Inc., for the fiscal year ending August 31, 19x2.

9-11. Gaylord's, Inc., discussed in problem 9–10, prepares monthly budgets to estimate production requirements, materials requirements, and materials acquisition.

a. Finished goods inventory is maintained at 50 per cent of the sales estimate for the following month. The finished goods inventory at August 31, 19x1, is 7,000 units.

Prepare monthly production requirements budgets for the first quarter of the fiscal year, using the budgeted sales from problem 9–10.

b. Two raw materials are required in the production process. Each unit of finished product requires 2 pounds of raw material A, and 3 pounds of raw material B.

Prepare monthly materials requirements budgets for the first quarter of the fiscal year, using the monthly production requirements from *a*.

c. There were 20,000 pounds of item A and 26,000 pounds of item B on hand August 31, 19x1. The company desires as a minimum level of raw materials inventory enough materials to produce 30 per cent of the budget production volume for the following month. Estimated cost of raw materials (beginning inventory and current purchases) is $.30 per pound for item A and $.05 per pound for item B.

Prepare the monthly materials acquisition budget in units and in dollars for the first quarter of the fiscal year, using the monthly production requirements from *b* above.

9-12. Gaylord's, Inc., prepares a quarterly budgeted earnings statement. Prepare a budgeted earnings statement for the first quarter of the fiscal year, using the sales and production data from problems 9–10 and 9–11, in addition to the following:

a. Variable cost per item in the beginning finished goods inventory is $2.50.
b. Direct labor requirements are $1.00 per unit.
c. Variable factory costs per unit are $.30.
d. Nonvariable factory costs are $60,000 per month.
e. Selling expenses:
    1. Salaries, $900 a month

2. Commissions, 3 per cent of gross sales
3. Advertising, 1 per cent of gross sales
4. Uncollectable sales, .4 per cent of gross sales
5. Miscellaneous, 1 per cent of gross sales
6. Space costs (allocated share of utilities, insurance, taxes, and depreciation), $700 per month

f. General and administrative expenses, $4,000 per month.

g. Federal income taxes, 50 per cent of earnings before taxes.

Assume that Gaylord's uses variable costing and that all of the beginning inventory was sold during the current quarter.

9-13. Gaylord's, Inc., prepares a monthly cash budget. Prepare cash budgets for the months of September, October, and November from the following information:

Cash Receipts
1. Obtain the sales data from Problem 9–10. Seventy-five per cent of sales are on account. The sales on account for August, 19x1, totaled $65,000. The pattern of collection from credit customers is expected to be as follows:

In month of of sale	40%
In month following sale	59%
Losses—uncollectable accounts	1%

2. Miscellaneous receipts:

September	$ 900
October	1,300
November	500

Cash Disbursements

1.

	September	October	November
Cash payments to employees	$7,000	$7,200	$6,700
Payments of employee & employer taxes	750	700	650
Payments of utilities, rent, & other operating expenses	8,100	7,800	8,200
Payment for machinery & equipment	19,000	3,100	400
Payment of dividends	4,100	0	0
Payment of federal income taxes	40,000	0	0

2. Obtain the materials acquisition information from problem 9–11. August, 19x1, purchases on account totaled $14,500. All materials are purchased on account. The terms are 2 per cent discount if paid by the tenth of the month following purchase. Assume that Gaylord's always takes advantage of available discounts.

3. The estimated cash balance on August 31, 19x1, was $10,000.

9-14. The Nu-Type Manufacturing Company manufactures a complete line of seat covers for automobiles. The company has been in existence for twelve years, and its sales have increased considerably each year. Nu-Type Manufacturing has exclusive distributorships throughout the country, which provide its only sales outlets.

The sales forecast for the company involves two steps: determining the total market for the product and estimating its share of the market. Demand for seat covers is determined primarily by two factors: estimates of new automobile sales and the number of used automobiles on the market. The company obtains this data from statistics published by the Department of Commerce in its "Survey of Current Business." Annual demand for seat covers has tended to be approximately 11 per cent of the total number of new and used automobiles on the market. The Nu-Type Manufacturing Company estimates that total industry demand for seat covers in 19x6 will be 700,000 sets. Six producers of automobile seat covers account for 90 per cent of the market; numerous small manufacturers account for the other 10 per cent. Nu-Type Manufacturing has increased its share of the market each year. It had 24 per cent of the market in 19x5, and it plans to increase its share to 26 per cent in 19x6. The price to distributors is $6 per set.

The company experiences a seasonal variation in the demand for seat covers. Average monthly sales for the past five years expressed as a percentage of total sales are as follows:

January	4%	April	8%	July	14%	October	7%
February	5%	May	11%	August	14%	November	4%
March	6%	June	13%	September	10%	December	4%

a. Prepare a monthly sales budget for the Nu-Type Manufacturing Company for 19x6.

b. Criticize the company's procedure in sales budgeting.

c. What, if any, additional information should the company include in its sales forecasting?

d. Explain concisely the difference between a sales budget and a sales forecast.

e. As the sales manager for the Pacific coastal region, how would you react to this sales budget?

9-15. The Nu-Type Manufacturing Company, discussed in problem 9–14, prepares monthly budgets to estimate requirements for production, materials, and materials acquisition.

PART I

a. *Production Requirements.* The company schedules production very carefully in order to keep its inventory investment at a minimum. Twenty seat cover sizes, a complete line, are manufactured. Covers are made in five colors: blue, green, gray, red, and tan. Therefore, one hundred sets of seat covers (twenty sizes times five colors) are required in order to have one of every size-color combination in stock. Company policy requires an optimum finished goods inventory of one dozen sets for each size-color combination of seat covers plus 25 per cent of the sales estimate for the following month. The finished goods inventory for December 31, 19x5, was 3,000 sets.

Prepare a monthly production requirements budget for the first quarter of 19x6, using the budgeted sales from problem 9–14.

b. *Materials Requirements.* Two raw materials are required in the production of the seat covers: nylon yard goods and nylon thread. Each set of seat covers requires four yards of nylon goods and thirty yards of nylon thread.

Prepare a monthly materials requirement budget for the first quarter of 19x6, using the monthly production requirements from *a* above.

c. *Materials Acquisition.* The Nu-Type Manufacturing Company had 12,000 yards of nylon goods and 60,000 yards of nylon thread on hand on December 31, 19x5. The company desires the minimum level of raw materials inventory capable of producing 50 per cent of the budgeted production volume for the following month. The estimated cost for raw materials (beginning inventory and current purchases) is $.49 per yard for the nylon yard goods and $.005 per yard for the nylon thread.

Prepare the monthly materials acquisition budget in units and in dollars for the first quarter of 19x6, using the monthly production requirements from *b* above.

PART II

a. The purchasing agent and the shop foreman have had a difference of opinion for quite some time regarding the company's purchasing policies. The purchasing agent prefers to purchase in large quantities. The shop foreman, who has charge of the raw materials storeroom, objects to the large quantities. Do you agree with the purchasing agent or the shop foreman? Justify your position.

b. The company presently manufactures fifteen days in advance of budgeted sales. The financial vice president objects to this policy because, he says, "the large amount of investment in inventory is extremely costly to the company." He feels that manufacturing ten days in advance of budgeted sales would be adequate. What factors should be considered in making this decision?

c. The production manager would like to manufacture at a stable volume throughout the year rather than tailoring production requirements to budgeted sales, the present policy. He states that this would have the following effect: Overall production costs can be lowered by 20 per cent, and employee morale would be increased considerably because layoffs would be minimized. If you were the company's president, what additional information would you need in order to make a decision?

d. Large quantity discounts are available in the purchasing of nylon material. The company presently has five suppliers for nylon goods. The financial vice president has asked the purchasing agent to consider buying from two suppliers in order to take advantage of the quantity discounts. Comment on the advantages and disadvantages of this proposal.

9-16. The Nu-Type Manufacturing Company prepares a quarterly budgeted earnings statement.

a. Prepare a budgeted earnings statement for the first quarter of 19x6, using the sales and production data from problems 9–14 and 9–15, in addition to the information below. (*Hint:* first prepare a budgeted statement of cost of goods manufactured on a variable costing basis and a budgeted schedule of selling expenses.)

1. Variable cost per set of seat covers of the beginning finished goods inventory is $2.85.
2. Direct labor requirements:
   a. Cutting labor: $2 per hour; cutting time per set of seat covers, six minutes.
   b. Sewing labor: $2.10 per hour; sewing time per set of seat covers, ten minutes.
   c. Packing labor: $1.80 per hour; packing time per set of seat covers, three minutes.
3. Variable factory cost per set of seat covers, $.10
4. Nonvariable factory costs, $3,000 per month
5. Selling expenses:
   a. Sales manager, $1,500 per month
   b. Office help, $950 per month
   c. Commissions, 2 per cent of gross sales
   d. Advertising, 2.5 per cent of gross sales
   e. Uncollectable sales, 1 per cent of gross sales
   f. Miscellaneous, .5 per cent of gross sales
   g. Space costs (allocated share of utilities, insurance, taxes, and depreciation), $600 per month
6. General and administrative expenses, $5,200 per month
7. Federal income taxes, 50 per cent of earnings before taxes

b. What is the value to the management of Nu-Type Manufacturing of preparing a budgeted earnings statement?

c. What uses would management make of the budgeted earnings statement at the beginning of the budget period? During and at the end of the budget period?

d. Nu-Type's management has a rate of return objective of $2\frac{1}{2}$ per cent per quarter after federal income taxes. The investment is $1.1 million. Will the present plans for the first quarter of 19x6 enable the management to reach its objective? If not, what action might be taken to improve the planned rate of return?

9-17. The Nu-Type Manufacturing Company prepares a monthly cash budget. Prepare a cash budget for the months of January, February, and March, 19x6, from the following information:

Cash Receipts
1. Obtain the sales data from problem 9–14. All sales of merchandise are

on account. The sales on account for December, 19x5, totaled $40,000. The pattern of collections on accounts receivable from customers is expected to be as follows:

In month of sale	30%
In month following sale	69%
Losses from uncollectable accounts	1%

2. Miscellaneous receipts:

January	$1,400
February	490
March	755

Cash Disbursements

1.

	January	February	March
Cash payments to employees	$8,500	$ 9,000	$ 9,500
Payment of employer & employee taxes	900	1,105	1,465
Payments for utilities, rent, & other operating expenses	6,170	6,945	7,750
Payments for machinery & equipment	2,400	18,500	0
Payment of dividends	5,000	0	0
Payment of federal income taxes	0	0	70,000

2. Obtain the materials acquisition information from problem 9–15. December, 19x5, purchases on account totaled $18,000. All direct materials are purchased on account. The terms are 1 per cent discount if paid by the tenth of the month following the purchase. Assume that Nu-Type always takes advantage of available discounts.
3. The estimated cash balance on December 31, 19x5, was $30,000.

9-18. The Gamma Company has prepared the following unit sales budget for the calendar year 19x6:

January	27,000	July	43,000
February	31,000	August	37,000
March	35,000	September	28,000
April	39,000	October	24,000
May	40,000	November	19,000
June	45,000	December	22,000

Budgeted sales for January are estimated at 24,000 units; for February, 34,000 units. The production cycle is twenty-five days. Company policy is to maintain a finished goods inventory equal to budgeted sales for the next two months.

a. Prepare a monthly production budget for the next calendar year. Assume that there is no work in process inventory at the beginning or end of the budget period. The finished goods inventory at the beginning of the budget period is 58,000 units.

b. Does your production budget provide for a stable or for a varying amount of production each month? What factors should this company consider in deciding whether to maintain a stable or varying production policy?

9–19. Standard Producers, Inc., manufactures generators. There are two producing departments: armature winding and assembly. The company uses a standard cost system.

1. Direct labor standards are as follows:

Standard generator: one and one-half hours for armature winding and one hour for assembly.

Heavy-duty generator: two hours for armature winding and one and a half hours for assembly.

2. The wage rate for armature winding is $1.60 per hour; for assembly, $1.80 per hour.

3. Production requirements in units for the next calendar year are as follows:

	Standard	Heavy-duty
1st quarter:		
January	5,000	2,000
February	4,000	1,500
March	4,000	1,800
2nd quarter	16,000	7,000
3rd quarter	11,000	6,000
4th quarter	19,000	9,000

a. Prepare a direct labor budget in hours and dollars for each period reflected above.

b. What advantages or disadvantages do you see in budgeting monthly for the first quarter and in totals for the remaining quarters?

c. What are the managerial uses of a direct labor budget? Be specific.

9–20. The Sigma Company prepares a monthly cash budget. The following data pertain to the fourth quarter of the current year:

	October	November	December
Sales on account	$95,000	$80,000	$88,000
Cash sales	40,000	41,500	38,000
Dividend income from investments (declared 10/26 & paid 11/10 to stockholders of record 11/3)	0	10,000	0
Purchase of materials on account (2% discount if paid by 10th of month following purchase)	61,000	58,000	59,500
Cash payments to employees	9,500	8,700	8,950

	October	November	December
Payment of employer & employee			
payroll taxes	875	890	850
Payments for other operating expenses	7,400	7,150	7,300
Purchase of equipment	0	0	7,000

1. Collections of accounts receivable have been as follows in the past:

In month of sale	30%
In month following sale	45%
In second month following sale	24%
Losses from uncollectable accounts	1%

2. The cash balance in September was $40,000.

3. The sales on account for August totaled $110,000, and for September, $98,000.

4. The September purchases on account totaled $45,500.

a. Prepare a statement of budgeted cash balances by month for the fourth quarter of the current year.

b. What are the managerial uses of a cash budget?

9-21. The Ultra Company, formed in 19x8, manufactures Chinese foods. The company experienced a steady increase in sales volume, which approximated $1.1 million in 19x3. In 19x4 the sales increased considerably to $1.8 million. Accompanying this desirable increase in sales volume was a very sad circumstance—the company became short of cash. A ninety-day bank loan for $100,000 was negotiated with the local bank within a period of seventy-two hours. This enabled the company to meet its obligations as they came due and thereby avoid financial embarrassment.

The company had never prepared a cash budget in the past. The president of the company became quite concerned over the seriousness of the 19x4 cash shortage. He and the controller agreed that they should prepare a cash budget for 19x5. They accumulated the following estimated data for the first three months of 19x5:

	January	February	March
Sales on account	$80,000	$75,000	$82,500
Cash sales	37,000	34,000	38,200
Collection from sale of scrap	500	550	525
Collection of advance to officers	0	900	0
Purchase of materials on account (2% discount if paid by 10th of month following purchase)	52,000	54,500	55,000
Cash payments to employees	12,500	13,000	13,200
Payment of employer & employee payroll taxes	900	925	940

	January	February	March
Payment of utilities, rent, & other operating expenses	8,500	8,700	8,850
Purchase of equipment	3,000	59,000	5,500
Payment of dividends (to be declared 2/25 & paid 3/15 to stockholders of record 3/5)	0	0	12,500

1. Collections on accounts receivable from customers have been as follows in the past:

In month of sale	12%
In month following sale	76%
In second month following sale	10%
Losses from uncollectable accounts	2%

2. The cash balance on December 31, 19x4, was $10,000.

3. Sales on account totaled $78,000 for November and $81,000 for December.

4. December, 19x4, purchases on account totaled $54,000.

a. Prepare a statement of budgeted cash balances by month for the first quarter of 19x5.

b. What action, if any, should the management of the company take as a result of the budgeted cash balances?

c. Is one month a suitable period of time for cash budgeting in this company? How could the management determine a suitable budget period for cash?

d. How far in advance should the company budget for cash balances? Be specific.

9–22. Cri-Beany, Inc., would like to project their cash receipts and disbursements for the first three months of 19x2. A portion of the trial balance as of December 31, 19x1, follows:

Cash	$ 2,500
Accounts receivable	42,000
Inventory	11,400
Prepaid expenses	1,700
Accounts payable (all for inventory)	14,600
Notes payable	36,500

A 2 per cent discount is given to customers who pay within the first ten days of the month after purchase. The pattern of cash collections is expected to be as follows:

Within the discount period	60%
End of the month following purchase	20%
End of the second month following purchase	17%
Loss from uncollectable accounts	3%

Actual and estimated sales (all on account, at a price of $20.00 per unit) are as follows:

October	$34,000
November	32,000
December	38,000
January	42,000
February	48,000
March	36,000

All of Cri-Beany's materials purchases are payable in the month following purchase. The purchase cost per unit of material is $12.00. Inventory requirements are 200 units plus 50 per cent of the unit sales for the following month.

Estimated selling and administrative expenses are as follows:

Variable, 10 per cent of sales dollars

Nonvariable (includes depreciation of $600 per month), $4,000 per month

The note payable is due February 15.

Prepare a budgeted statement of cash balances by month for the first quarter of 19x2.

9-23. Dura-Products, Inc., manufactures push-type lawn mowers. The company employs twelve salesmen, each responsible for a certain geographical area. The sales manager and president are preparing a sales budget for the next calendar year. They have tentatively agreed on a sales budget of 30,000 regular mowers and 20,000 deluxe mowers for the year. Dura-Products sells the regular mower for $9 and the deluxe mower for $11. Variable costs, excluding sales commissions, are $6 per unit for the regular mower and $7 per unit for the deluxe mower. Sales commissions are 5 per cent of the selling price. Nonvariable costs are estimated to be $98,000 for the coming year. (You may ignore federal income taxes.)

Both the regular and deluxe mowers require the same productive capacity. Total productive capacity for the company is 70,000 mowers per year.

a. Prepare a budgeted earnings statement for the sales manager and president, using the above data.

b. Which alternative would you recommend to management for utilizing the excess productive capacity of 20,000 mowers per year: (a) "pushing" sales of regular mowers through company salesmen by means of additional advertising costing $15,000, or (b) producing regular mowers under "private label" business for $8 each? (Assume that sales commissions will not be required.)

9-24. John and Henry Williams are brothers who started a service station business twenty years ago. The business, called Williams Super Service, has grown steadily, causing several problems. The Williams brothers prepared a budgeted statement of earnings for the year 19x5, and they have just compared the budgeted statement of earnings with the actual statement of earnings. Although total revenues for the year exceed budgeted revenues, net earnings for the year

WILLIAMS SUPER SERVICE

COMPARATIVE STATEMENT OF BUDGETED AND ACTUAL EARNINGS

For Year Ended December 31, 19x5

	Budgeted for 19x5			Actual for 19x5		
	Sales revenues	Cost of goods sold	Earnings margin	Sales revenues	Cost of goods sold	Earnings margin
oline[a]	$202,500	$167,500	$35,000	$211,680	$176,110	$35,570
	7,500	4,550	2,950	8,600	5,250	3,350
essories	26,000	15,900	10,100	19,000	11,500	7,500
	$236,000	$187,950	$48,050	$239,280	$192,860	$46,420
ice revenues			12,000			12,600
l revenues			$60,050			$59,020
Operating expenses:						
Salary of managers[b]		$14,500			$14,500	
Other salaries		18,000			21,000[d]	
Rent[c]		6,500			6,940	
Tools		800			825	
Supplies		2,500			2,275	
Insurance		900			900	
Utilities		4,000			4,090	
Advertising		800			788	
Other expenses		1,200			1,314	
Taxes:						
Payroll		2,050			2,286	
State & local		850			850	
Total			52,100			55,768
rnings before federal taxes			$ 7,950			$ 3,252
— Federal income taxes			2,385			968
et earnings			$ 5,565			$ 2,284

Details of the budgeted and actual sales and cost of sales are as follows:

	Regular		Hi-test		
	Budgeted				
ales revenues	(400,000 gals. at $.30/gal.)	$120,000	(250,000 gals. at $.33/gal.)	$82,500	$202,500
— Cost of goods sold	(400,000 gals. at $.25/gal.)	100,000	(250,000 gals. at $.27/gal.)	67,500	167,500
Earnings margin		$ 20,000		$15,000	$ 35,000
	Actual				
ales revenues	(578,000 gals. at $.30/gal.)	$173,400	(116,000 gals. at $.33/gal.)	$38,280	$211,680
— Cost of goods sold	(578,000 gals. at $.25/gal.)	144,500	(116,000 gals. at $.2725)	31,610	176,110
Earnings margin		$ 28,900		$ 6,670	$ 35,570

John and Henry Williams.
The rental charge is $.01 per gallon of gasoline sold.
The additional volume of gasoline sales (694,000 versus 650,000 gallons) necessitated one additional man for the afternoon shift.

are less than budgeted earnings. They are unable to explain how this happened. The statements and supplementary information are presented on page 345 for your consideration.

a. Explain concisely the purpose of the budgeted earnings statement.

b. What could the company do to improve the profitability of the gasoline sales?

c. Should Williams Super Service attempt to limit the sales volume to 650,000 gallons in order to avoid the additional labor cost?

d. The Williams brothers are concerned over the poor showing of accessory sales. They believe that employees have not been "pushing" these items. Should the Williams brothers continue to sell accessories?

e. Would you make any changes in the budgeting procedure for Williams Super Service in 19x6? Be specific.

9-25. The Mercury Company has just prepared budgets for the next year. According to the budgets, constant costs for the year will be $3 million. The product that the company manufactures sells for $10. The variable cost is $6 per unit.

a. Compute the sales volume required in order to break even.

b. Compute the sales volume required in order to have a 10 per cent rate of return on an investment of $7 million.

9-26. The Gerry Manufacturing Company produces a single product that sells for $8 per unit. Variable costs are $5.10 per unit and constant costs are $700,000 per year.

The Gerry Company is considering the purchase of new manufacturing equipment to replace present equipment. One group of manufacturing equipment would change total constant costs per year to $720,000. Variable costs per unit of output would be $5. The other group of equipment would change total constant costs per year to $1,050,000. Variable costs per unit of output would be $4.50 per unit. This latter equipment would permit the company to automate a large part of its manufacturing operations.

a. Compute the sales volume required to break even under present operating conditions.

b. What sales volume is required to break even if the first group of equipment is installed? If the second one is installed? (Assume that the sales price of $8 per unit does not change.)

9-27. The management of Troll's, Inc., believes that the company should break even at an annual sales volume equal to 60 per cent of capacity. Total capacity per year is 100,000 units. Constant costs are $120,000 per year. Variable cost per unit is $7.

Compute the required sales price per unit in order for the company to break even at an annual sales volume of 60 per cent of capacity.

9-28. Jax's Minit Markets own and operate approximately one hundred neighborhood stores. The following data have been compiled for its operations for the next year:

Sales, $25,000,000
Nonvariable costs, $7,500,000
Variable costs, $15,000,000

Compute expected earnings from each of the following independent situations:

    a. 5 per cent increase in sales volume
    b. 10 per cent decrease in sales volume
    c. 10 per cent increase in variable costs
    d. 10 per cent decrease in variable costs
    e. 15 per cent increase in nonvariable costs
    f. 5 per cent decrease in nonvariable cost

9-29. The Electrical Products Company, founded in the early 1900's, has grown steadily throughout the years. The company's production has expanded into a complete line of electrical products for the automotive industry, including generators, alternators, starters, distributors, and heater motors. The heater motors are produced on a mass-production basis, while the other products are made primarily to customer specifications.

The company is faced with a problem concerning its heater-motor production. About 90 per cent of their heater motors are sold to the "Big Three" in the automotive industry. Until five years ago these companies purchased their entire output from the outside. At that time, they started producing their own heater motors. This production now satisfies about 50 per cent of their requirements. All three companies have stated that they will continue to fill approximately 50 per cent of their heater-motor requirements from outside. The Electrical Products Company has one other competitor for this portion of the market.

Ever since the Big Three started making their own heater motors, they have forced price cuts on the Electrical Products Company. These price cuts are based upon the production costs of the companies in the Big Three. Prices have been cut to such an extent that the company now realizes an earnings margin of about 17 per cent (sales, 100 per cent, minus the cost of goods sold plus operating expenses, 83 per cent). At one time the earnings margin on heater motors was 30 per cent.

Naturally the management is quite concerned over this decline in earnings margin. There is general agreement about the cause of the problem. The Big Three are able to make large investments in capital equipment that reduce their labor cost considerably and permit them to mass produce at a much lower per-unit cost. The Electrical Products Company has just completed an extensive analysis of a proposal to buy new equipment. This new equipment would enable the company to compete on more favorable terms with the Big Three. The management is concerned with the effect that the new equipment would have on its breakeven point. They have accumulated the following data in order to compute their breakeven volume with and without the equipment:

	Total	Costs[a] Nonvariable	Variable
Present production method:			
Materials	$ 600,000	$ 0	$ 600,000
Labor	750,000	0	750,000
Manufacturing costs	1,350,000	500,000	850,000
Selling expenses	80,000	65,000	15,000
Administrative expenses	125,000	115,000	10,000
Total costs	$2,905,000	$ 680,000	$2,225,000
Proposed production method:			
Materials	$ 575,000	$ 0	$ 575,000
Labor	200,000	0	200,000
Manufacturing costs	1,700,000	1,400,000	300,000
Selling expenses	80,000	65,000	15,000
Administrative expenses	125,000	115,000	10,000
Total costs	$2,680,000	$1,580,000	$1,100,000

[a] Cost figures represent production at 100 per cent of capacity. The new equipment would not alter production capacity. Total sales price at 100 per cent of capacity is approximately $3.5 million.

a. Determine the effect of the new equipment on the Electrical Products Company's breakeven sales volume. The breakeven sales volume can be computed as follows:

$$\text{Breakeven point} = \frac{\text{Total nonvariable expenses}}{1 - \dfrac{\text{Total variable expenses}}{\text{Total sales dollars}}}$$

b. Would the new equipment have a favorable effect on reported net earnings? On the breakeven sales volume? Explain.

c. Should the company purchase the new equipment? Justify your conclusions.

d. Are there any limitations to the type of breakeven analysis used in this problem? Be specific.

e. Are there any similarities between budgeted earnings statements and breakeven analysis?

f. Generally, what effect would you expect automation to have on a company's breakeven point?

Chapter Ten **PLANNING**
ALTERNATE COURSES
OF OPERATIONS

INTRODUCTION

A good business manager continuously looks for better ways of conducting his business. Improvement might require the elimination of a current activity or the addition of activities not previously encountered. Planning for changes in the environment occurs simultaneously with the planning directed towards optimizing operations within the environment. The budgets discussed in the previous chapter make sense only when they incorporate the results of all planned changes during the budget period. Planning changes in the environment can be described as a process in which business managers look for, and weigh the consequences of, alternative means of attaining the optimum profits.

THE PROCESS OF PLANNING CHANGES

Successful planning for changes in an environment entails adoption of some aspects of the scientific process of research, such as:

1. Identifying areas where change might be beneficial.
2. Recognizing possible alternatives and then identifying those most logically beneficial.
3. Examining the logical alternatives and quantifying (expressing in dollars of revenues and costs) as many aspects of each alternative as possible.
4. Recognizing and weighing those qualitative factors that cannot be ex-

pressed in terms of dollars and cents but that should be considered in choosing the best alternative.

5. Comparing the relative benefits of each alternative and reaching a decision as to which should be implemented.

The key to successful planning for changing an environment revolves around management's ability to recognize situations where change might be beneficial. Unfortunately there are no universally acceptable rules to follow here. The ability to recognize such situations requires broad familiarity with the operations of the business and events going on outside of the particular enterprise. Recognition of areas in which change may be beneficial might come from anywhere within the firm. At the Acme Auto Parts Company, the production engineering staff is expected to know all the latest developments in, for example, grinding-tool design. When the specialist in grinding equipment estimates that a new development in tool design could be profitably incorporated into the grinding department of his firm, he should originate a study to investigate replacement of the present grinding equipment. The president of the corporation cannot be expected to know of the new developments in grinding equipment, nor can the manager of the foundry. On the other hand, it might be the president who would recognize the feasibility of discontinuing foundry operations within the firm in favor of purchasing castings from another enterprise specializing in that line of work.

Once an area susceptible to change has been recognized, the manager must be careful to ensure that every alternative course of action is considered. For instance, the engineer who recognized the fact that the firm's grinding equipment might be obsolete should not assume that the first new piece of equipment he learns about is the solution to his company's problems. Letters of inquiry, interviews with equipment salesmen, and reading of technical journals should be undertaken in an attempt to learn of other possible alternatives. Similarly, the president who is examining the feasibility of discontinuing foundry operations should ensure that he has considered alternatives such as using forgings or stamped parts rather than castings. It is a major error to jump at the first alternative that is better than the existing method without a concerted effort to investigate the most profitable alternatives.

Each logical alternative should be examined quantitatively and qualitatively. Quantitative measurement expresses in dollars and cents as many aspects of the alternatives as possible. Added revenues, reduced expenses, and the resulting effects on the financial condition of the enterprise should be determined. This procedure will require estimates of future monetary results. Many managers hesitate to quantify the results of alternate courses of action because they feel that the future is impossible to predict accurately. It is more meaningful, however, to estimate that alternative X will increase earnings "by between $17,000 and $25,000" than merely to state that earnings will be increased "substantially." The key to success in choosing among alternatives is the monetary expression of as many factors as possible.

There remain, however, some factors that cannot be expressed in terms of dollars and cents. Among these qualitative considerations might be the effects of a possible course of action on employees or the community. For example, the president of the company might determine from his quantitative calculations that it would add to future earnings if the foundry operations were closed down and castings were purchased from a company in another city. But he would also consider the fact that he might be putting 200 people out of jobs if this were done. The implications of adding to the unemployed in his own community while providing greater employment within another community would be qualitative factors that must be considered before making a final decision. (Similarly the reaction to a request for a contribution to a charitable group depends heavily on qualitative analysis.) Even the engineer, attempting to decide which kind of grinding tool he should buy when replacing the existing equipment, must consider the safety of the operating machinists and the prestige they will feel when operating the equipment. One automobile manufacturer has experienced increased operating efficiency in its engine plant simply because the productive machinery it uses is brightly painted and designed to look streamlined and efficient. It is, of course, impossible to quantify the increased efficiency of operating personnel that results from the pride in working with an attractive piece of equipment.

Chapters 10 and 11 discuss the choices management must make among alternatives, with emphasis on the quantitative measurements that assist management in arriving at decisions. In this chapter we consider short-run decisions that involve no more than an insignificant original investment. In these cases, the relative profitability of the alternatives can be measured in terms of their effect on the reported earnings of the firm for the relatively short period affected by the decision. Chapter 11 is concerned with decisions having long-run consequences, usually requiring substantial capital outlay. In these latter decisions, the time value of money is important, and the profitability of alternatives must be measured by more complicated methods.

The general criterion for short-run decisions is the effect of the decision on net earnings for the period affected by the decision. For example, it must be considered whether adding a new product or accepting a special order will add more to total revenues than to total expenses. If a business manager is deciding upon the desirability of dropping a product, he wants to know whether dropping the product will deduct less from total revenues than it will from total expenses. Proposed changes in operating conditions are approached by determining whether the decision will deduct from some expenses more than it adds to other expenses.

The ideal approach to these decisions is to prepare a complete statement of earnings for the future period affected by the decision. An earnings statement should be prepared for each alternative being considered. There will frequently be just two alternatives: to continue operating without change or to accept the proposed alternative. If each revenue and expense item is independently estimated and reflected on the earnings statement, those expenses and revenues that are affected by the change can be isolated in order to arrive at *differential earnings* (differential revenues less differential expenses).

A shortcut approach is to compute the profitability of the decision in terms of revenue and expense differences only. This is less time-consuming than the preparation of a complete earnings statement; however, the risk of error is substantially higher. These approaches are illustrated below.

THE ROLE OF ACCOUNTING STATEMENTS IN PLANNING

The earnings statement of a business firm for a past period has performance measurement of the firm as its basic objective. It may also shed some light on prospects for future earnings of the firm, *given the operating conditions of the past period.* Since the accounting measurements are limited by operating conditions, the figures in conventional accounting statements must be used with discretion and modified to reflect the conditions presented by the alternatives in question if they are to be used for planning.

A statement of budgeted earnings is more useful to a manager with a decision to make than an earnings statement for a past period. Budgeted statements reflect estimates of the future operating and market conditions that will exist during the period affected by the decision.

Both budgeted statements and statements for past periods, however, include several kinds of costs that are not relevant to any decision. These are costs incurred in the past that, for performance measurement purposes, are applicable to the current period as expenses or future periods as assets.

Sunk Costs

All inventory and plant costs incurred in the past are sunk costs. The costs relevant to management decisions are the market values of these inventory or plant items. Failure to value assets at current market is a deficiency in conventional accounting statements insofar as their use in decision making is concerned. It is not a serious deficiency if the incurred costs are relatively recent and are therefore reasonable approximations of current market values. However, in the case of many plant items, incurred costs are too old and too out of date to approximate current market values, and depreciation methods often do not reflect year-to-year changes in market values of plant assets.

Long familiarity with accounting profits tends to mislead the decision maker. Accounting profits are recorded as the difference between revenues from sale or conversion and the sunk (recorded) cost of the asset sold. In the decision to sell a machine, for example, the decision maker may be influenced by the recorded cost of the item when it was acquired (or cost minus depreciation to the date of sale). If this incurred cost is low, he might be influenced to sell so that a large profit would be recorded; if it is high, he might be influenced not to sell because a recorded loss might be the result. The fact is that, except for the income tax effect of the transaction (discussed below), recorded cost should have nothing to do with the decision to sell or not to sell. The economic cost of selling the machine is the cost of replacing the future services that the machine would have provided had it been retained. The cost of retaining the machine is the price at which it could have been sold. The cost of the machine recorded on the financial statements is not relevant to the decision.

The important exception to this rule is the fact that accounting profit, as defined above, is the basis on which the income tax is computed. Since taxpayers try to keep their income tax payments at a minimum, it is usually desirable to keep accounting profits as low as possible, all other factors being equal. As we shall see in subsequent chapters, the influence of income tax laws on management decisions and on accounting statements is very strong. Income taxes may influence decision makers to carry out transactions in unusual ways. Accountants are often influenced by income taxes in the way they record and report transactions; this is one of the reasons that statement valuations need modification before they can be used as a basis for decisions.

Nonvariable Costs

Another problem in using accounting statements in certain kinds of decisions is that manufacturing cost statements prepared on an absorption costing basis include costs that do not vary proportionally with the volume of production. These nonvariable costs were discussed at length in Chapter 6. If a decision to increase (decrease) output depends in part on how much increase (decrease) in manufacturing costs will result, the total manufacturing cost figure should be ignored. Only the variable portion of the cost is relevant to the decision. This fact provides the principal argument for variable costing, discussed in Chapter 7, in which variable and nonvariable manufacturing costs are reported separately, so that a decision maker can determine more easily the effect on costs of variations in output.

Allocated Costs

A closely related problem in absorption costing systems stems from the allocations of overhead costs to products or to departments. These allocations are made to determine whether the product or department is bearing its share of the costs not directly attributable to it. Because virtually all of these costs are nonvariable, they are subject to the same analytical difficulties as are nonvariable costs that are directly attributable to the department or product involved in the decision. In addition, these allocated costs do not disappear if the product or department is discontinued, and thus they are not relevant to decisions in which these alternatives are involved.

By now perhaps you have concluded that accounting statements are not particularly useful for anything. Certainly it is true that these statements, if they are prepared according to conventional accounting practices, must be used with great caution for any of the business decisions discussed in this chapter and the next. Care must be exercised by the decision maker to determine the particular revenue and cost items relevant to the alternatives involved in the particular decision. In addition, estimates of current rather than past revenues and costs must be obtained.

With all of these limitations, accounting statements still provide the best information available for most business decisions. The accountants who design the accounting systems for collecting and reporting transaction data cannot anticipate all management's needs for data about specific decisions. But accountants can adjust conventionally prepared data to suit the needs of management and conduct special studies to provide data relevant to particular problems when the need arises. Furthermore, we have already discussed the important uses of the conventional statements, the most important being measurement of management performance indicated by accounting profits of past periods.

AN EXAMPLE

To illustrate, assume that the A.B. Company has a vacant building on its property, and that two alternative uses are being considered: (1) use as a storage facility for excess materials, and (2) rental to a tenant for use as a truck garage. Either arrangement can be continued for ten years, the estimated remaining life of the building. The following facts have been ascertained:

1. It is clear that if the building is not used for storage, outside facilities will have to be rented for this purpose. If outside facilities are used for storage, the expense (a variable expense) will be $1 per unit per month. The building has a storage capacity of 1,000 units. It is estimated that in an average month the building would be half full for twenty days and empty for ten days. Additional insurance of $30 per month on the materials will be needed, but no heating, lighting, or protection will be required.

2. The building can be rented as a garage for $400 a month, but heating and lighting amounting to $50 monthly will have to be provided, and $75 will have to be added to the monthly pay of a night watchman, to protect the building and contents.

3. Taxes and depreciation amount to $200 monthly and will continue whichever alternative is selected.

A.B. Company's earnings statements for a typical month reveal the effects of the alternatives on revenues and expenses.

	If vacant	If used for storage	If rented
Revenues	$5,000	$5,000	$5,400
Variable expenses	2,200	1,867	2,200
Contribution margin[a]	$2,800	$3,133	$3,200
Nonvariable expenses	1,900	1,930	2,025
Net earnings before tax	$ 900	$1,203	$1,175

[a]*Contribution margin* refers to the contribution to earnings made by revenues when only variable expenses directly related to the revenues are deducted. (When a product is sold, the contribution margin is traditionally called "earnings margin," that is, sales minus cost of goods sold.)

The alternative approach is to give more emphasis to the *differential* effect of the alternatives:

COMPUTATION OF DIFFERENTIAL EARNINGS

	If used for storage	If rented	Differential if rented
Increase in monthly revenue			$400
Decrease in variable expenses			
($500 × ⅔ of a month)	$333		333
Increase in contribution margin	$333	$400	$ 67
Increase in nonvariable expenses			
Insurance	30		30
Heat and light		50	(50)
Protection		75	(75)
Total	$ 30	$125	$(95)
Difference in net earnings before tax	$303	$275	$(28)

This second approach gives more information, but it becomes confusing when alternatives become more complicated. The first approach, in which the entire earnings of the firm are recomputed under each alternative, provides some assurance that all relevant aspects of the alternatives have been considered.

Notice that the taxes and depreciation on the building, amounting to $200 monthly, are ignored because they will not be affected by the decision. The remaining cost of the building is a sunk cost—it will not be changed no matter which alternative is selected.

The usefulness of variable costing is not emphasized in this illustration, since the particular alternatives do not affect A.B.'s production volume. It is important to note, however, that several nonvariable expense items are affected by the decision and must be considered in the selection of the most profitable alternative.

It is *differential earnings,* not *contribution margin,* that is the crucial criterion in the decision.

PLANNING ALTERNATE COURSES OF OPERATIONS

Decisions that frequently confront a business manager are whether to add a product, whether to accept orders at less than full price, whether to discontinue an existing activity, and whether to make or buy a product. All of these except the make-or-buy decision involve both revenues and expenses, and the controlling criterion in these decisions is the concept of differential earnings. Only if an activity will produce enough revenues to cover the differential expenses of engaging in that activity and will in addition make some contribution towards meeting the existing nonvariable expenses of the enterprise, should it be undertaken or maintained, as the case may be. The make-or-buy decision involves a consideration of the least-cost method of accomplishing a given objective, since revenues are not affected by this type of decision. Each of these four planning decisions will be discussed below.

Add a Product?

The Acme Auto Parts Company manufactures various types of automobile wax and cleaners. It is considering the desirability of adding a combination cleaner and wax to its existing wax and cleaner lines. The new cleaner-wax would be an economy product designed to compete with low-priced cleaner-waxes manufactured by other companies. The existing manufacturing and sales facilities will be adequate for the addition of the cleaner-wax to the product line.

The vice president of marketing estimates an annual sales volume of 200,000 cans of cleaner-wax at a sales price to distributors of $.30 per can. The research and production departments have developed specifications for the new product. They have developed the following per-unit estimates of production costs for the product:

Direct materials	$.15
Direct labor	.04
Variable manufacturing costs	.03
Nonvariable manufacturing costs	
(allocated portion)	.05
Total manufacturing cost/unit	$.27

The estimated selling and administrative expenses per unit are as follows:

Variable selling & administrative expenses	$.04
Nonvariable selling & administrative expenses	
(allocated portion)	.02
Total selling & administrative expenses/unit	$.06

The estimated total costs of producing and selling the cleaner-wax are $.33 per can ($.27 manufacturing costs and $.06 selling and administrative expenses). Since the estimated sales price is $.30 per can, it appears that a loss of $.03 per can would be incurred if the decision were made to add the new product. The full-cost estimate, however, is misleading. You will recall from the earlier discussions of relevant costs that only future costs that will be *different* should be considered in the analysis. Thus only the variable costs are relevant. The allocated nonvariable costs will not be different in the future if the proposal to manufacture the new product is accepted. Therefore, the relevant costs for this decision are as follows:

Direct materials	$.15
Direct labor	.04
Variable manufacturing expense	.03
Variable selling & administrative	
expenses	.04
Total differential costs/unit	$.26

This new estimate indicates that the estimated selling price of $.30 per unit will cover the $.26 per-can differential expenses of producing the cleaner-wax and will make some contribution to the nonvariable expenses of the period. The $.04 per-unit differential is called the differential earnings rather than earnings because by previous definition, net earnings are the difference between revenues and *all* expenses properly assignable to those revenues. To calculate accounting net earnings, all applicable past costs must be considered. Following this principle, the allocated nonvariable expenses of $.07 ($.05 manufacturing expense and $.02 selling and administrative expense) would have to be considered in measuring the earnings from the cleaner-wax venture. The earnings result would be a loss of $.03 per unit sold ($.33 total expense — $.30 selling price). However, each unit sold will generate revenues of $.30 and will incur differential expense of only $.26. Therefore, each unit of cleaner-wax sold contributes $.04 toward meeting the nonvariable expense of the enterprise and in this case *helps to increase earnings* for the firm as a whole.

To emphasize this last point, Exhibits 10–1 and 10–2 give the annual earnings statement for the cleaner and wax product line, as it would appear first without the new product and then with it.

EXHIBIT 10 – 1

STATEMENT OF EARNINGS FOR CLEANERS AND WAXES
WITHOUT NEW PRODUCT
For Next Year

Present sales		$450,000
— Total variable expense	$280,000	
Total nonvariable expense	75,000	
Total expenses		355,000
Earnings from operations		$ 95,000

Examination of Exhibits 10–1 and 10–2 reveals that the addition of the cleaner-wax to the product line will add $8,000 to the earnings of the firm, assuming that the new product would not affect the sale of existing products. It is possible, however, that the new product might in fact either supplant or compete with the sales of existing products. If such were the case, revenues and expenses of present products would have to be adjusted.

Now let us consider a few of the qualitative factors not included in the above analysis. The effect on customer goodwill of adding the cleaner-wax to the product line should be considered. If the new product does not measure up to the quality of existing products, the sales of all the products might be reduced. The effect of this decision on the labor force should be determined. The addition of this new product will probably add several employees to the payroll of the company. In addition, the reaction of competing companies to the introduction of the new product will have to be considered. Can you think of additional

EXHIBIT 10 – 2

STATEMENT OF EARNINGS FOR CLEANERS AND WAXES
INCLUDING NEW PRODUCT
For Next Year

Present sales revenues		$450,000
+ New product sales revenues (200,000 units @ $.30/unit)		60,000
Total revenues		$510,000
— Present variable expense	$280,000	
Differential variable expense (200,000 @ $.26/unit)	52,000	
Total nonvariable expense	75,000	
Total expense		407,000
Earnings from operations		$103,000

qualitative factors that the management of the Acme Auto Parts Company should consider in this product decision?

Accept Orders at Less than Full Price?

The Acme Auto Parts Company has long made a standard water pump pulley that fits almost all makes of automobiles. It has manufactured this product to order for the various automobile manufacturers as well as to stock for the replacement-parts market. The cost of manufacturing and selling the pulley during a normal week of production is listed below. The current selling price is $1 per unit for all customers.

Direct labor	$.17
Direct materials	.28
Variable manufacturing expense	.11
Variable selling & administrative expenses	.04
Total variable expense/unit	$.60
Nonvariable manufacturing expense	
(allocated portion)	.07
Nonvariable selling & administrative expenses	
(allocated portion)	.05
Total expense/unit	$.72

At the present time the productive facilities employed in the production of pulleys are operating at less than full capacity because of a business recession in the industry. A foreign manufacturer of automobiles is not affected by the slowdown, however; it is producing as many cars as it can sell and could sell more if it had greater productive capacity. The foreign automobile manufacturer is attempting to increase its productive capacity by subcontracting the manufacturing of many smaller parts. A representative of the foreign company has approached Acme Auto Parts with an offer to buy 100,000 pulleys during the next three months at a price of $.65 each.

In planning next quarter's production, the top management of Acme must decide whether to accept this offer. At first glance the tendency might be to reject it, because the designated price of $.65 per unit is less than the total indicated expense. However, as shown earlier, as long as the $.65 selling price will cover the differential expenses of producing the additional pulleys and also make some contribution to the nonvariable expenses of the period, the order should be accepted. Care must be taken, however, to ensure that the selling price of $.65 to the foreign automobile manufacturer does not injure the present market at $1 per unit within this country.

If it can be assumed that the normal production can continue to be sold for $1 per unit, then Acme would lose money if it failed to accept the foreign offer at $.65 per unit. The relevant costs in this decision include the variable costs of the normal production cost schedule but exclude any of the allocated nonvariable costs. The allocated nonvariable costs are not differential because they are incurred whether the order is accepted or not. Comparison of the relevant expense of $.60 per unit with the offering price of $.65 per unit reveals that each unit sold to the foreign manufacturer will yield differential earnings of $.05 to the firm and, for this reason, *will help to increase earnings* for the firm as a whole.

A quarterly earnings statement for the water pump pulley product line is shown in Exhibit 10–3 as it would appear if the contract were not accepted, and in Exhibit 10–4 as it would appear if the contract were accepted. Assume that normal quarterly production is 400,000 units and that, owing to the recession, activity has dwindled to 240,000 units (60 per cent of normal capacity). Examination reveals that the foreign contract will add $5,000 (100,000 units at $.05)

EXHIBIT 10–3

STATEMENT OF EARNINGS FOR WATER PUMP PULLEYS
WITHOUT FOREIGN CONTRACT
For Next Quarter

Present sales revenues (240,000 units @ $1/unit)		$240,000
— Total variable expenses (240,000 units @ $.60/unit)	$144,000	
Total nonvariable expenses	36,000[a]	
Total expenses		180,000
Earnings from operations		$ 60,000

EXHIBIT 10–4

STATEMENT OF EARNINGS FOR WATER PUMP PULLEYS
INCLUDING FOREIGN CONTRACT
For Next Quarter

Present sales revenues (240,000 units @ $1/unit)		$240,000
+ Foreign sales revenues (100,000 units @ $.65/unit)		65,000
Total revenues		$305,000
— Total variable expenses (340,000 units @ $.60/unit)	$204,000	
Total nonvariable expenses	36,000[a]	
Total expenses		240,000
Earnings from operations		$ 65,000

[a] The total nonvariable expenses are equal to the normal production level (400,000 units) times the normal allocated expenses per unit ($.09). Or, more realistically, the per unit expense of $.09 was originally obtained by dividing total nonvariable expense by normal production. Because they are nonvariable these expenses do not affect the decision of whether to accept the foreign contract.

to the earnings of the firm if the assumption of an unaffected domestic price and volume of sales holds true.

Discontinue an Existing Activity?

Consider a dilemma faced by Mr. Green, the owner of the local pizza parlor. Some time ago he was induced by a representative of a wholesale beverage distributor to convert about one-tenth (one booth) of the floor space in his establishment into a display area for beverages and to sell soft drinks for the take-home trade. The representative reasoned that many people picking up a pizza for home consumption would also purchase a carton or more of soft drinks at the same time. At first only impulse buying would govern beverage sales. The representative argued, however, that in time customers would identify the pizza parlor as a beverage store as well, and that Mr. Green's overall business would profit.

Mr. Green has engaged in the beverage activity for almost eleven months now and is somewhat dissatisfied with the results shown in his monthly earnings statement. He is afraid that he might be losing money in the beverage business and is trying to decide whether to continue this activity. The earnings results for May are shown in Exhibit 10–5. Mr. Green and his bookkeeper both agree that these figures represent fairly the typical monthly operating results.

The $70 loss shown in Exhibit 10–5 has caused Mr. Green concern. In

EXHIBIT 10 – 5

GREEN PIZZA PARLOR

STATEMENT OF EARNINGS FOR BEVERAGE CARRY-OUT OPERATIONS
For May 19x5

Sales revenues (cartons of beverages)		$500
— Cost of goods sold		410
Earnings margin		$ 90
— Departmental expenses:		
Portion of salary of waiter assigned job of keeping racks full of merchandise in addition to previous duties	$60	
Wages of boy who comes in two hours/day & all day Saturday to sort empty bottles & help fill basement supply shelves	40	
Portion of rent (1/10) of pizza parlor	30	
Taxes (assessed by city on average value of inventory)	10	
Portion of existing liability insurance for customer protection	5	
Additional bookkeeping fees entailed by this activity	15	
Total expenses		160
Net loss		$ 70

deciding whether to discontinue his beverage activity, Mr. Green must determine whether the differential expenses of the beverage activity actually outweigh the earnings margin contributed by it. Three expenses are differential—that is, they result solely from this activity and would be eliminated if the activity were discontinued: the part-time wages of the school boy ($40), the city inventory taxes ($10), and the additional bookkeeping fees ($15). The expenses eliminated would total $65. *If the activity were discontinued, however, the earnings margin of $90 would also be eliminated.* Without the beverage operation, the pizza operations would be charged with an additional $60 of waiter's salary, $30 of rent, and $5 of insurance, or a total of $95 of continuing, nonvariable expenses now allocated to the beverage operations. If the beverage operation is continued, the pizza operation need only overcome the present loss of $70. Thus elimination of the beverage operation would in fact increase Mr. Green's losses by $25. The case of Mr. Green reaffirms the validity of considering only relevant revenues and expenses when deciding among alternatives. When considering the deletion of an existing activity, the relevant revenues and expenses are those that would also be deleted.

Additional Alternatives

It is wise at this time to remind ourselves that the manager should constantly be on the alert to avoid falling into the "decision-making trap." He should not become so engrossed with analyzing two alternatives, such as whether or not to eliminate the beverage line, that he forgets to consider other possibilities. Mr. Green, for example, might very well have considered converting the soft-drink facilities to the display and sale of packaged foods or perhaps using the space for dancing facilities. Acme Auto Parts Company might be able to use the slack in production brought about by the recession to better advantage if they overhauled part of their equipment rather than engaging in the foreign contract.

Whenever additional alternatives enter the realm of consideration, the nature of the quantitative factors may change. The tax cost on the inventory would not be eliminated if the alternative were replacement of beverage sales by packaged foods, rather than elimination of take-home sales altogether. The same might be true of the stockboy's salary and the bookkeeping costs. Revenues might change drastically, however, causing a decision different from that reached previously.

The accountant must be certain that the information he provides concerning differential revenues and expenses is appropriate for the task at hand. His most difficult task lies in the realm of the assumptions he makes when he attempts to present relevant information. The relevance of a particular expense or revenue to a particular decision is dependent upon all other decisions being contemplated at the same time. The accountant must, therefore, attempt to familiarize himself with all possible alternatives, just as the manager must.

Make or Buy?

Assume that the Acme Auto Parts Company is faced with the following alternative. It can either manufacture in its own plants the fastening bracket that attaches item 37-tu to the automobile or it can purchase the bracket ready for assembly from another manufacturer. The decision will be based on the relevant costs involved. Revenue does not enter the picture because the quantity and selling price of the brackets sold will remain the same regardless of whether they are purchased or manufactured within the plant.

Two situations produce the above described alternative choice. On one hand it could be assumed that the fastening bracket is not presently being manufactured by Acme Auto Parts, and therefore the decision would be whether they should continue to buy them or begin to make them. On the other hand Acme Auto Parts Company might already manufacture the brackets. If so, it must decide whether to continue to manufacture them or to start buying the item. The relevant differential costs would not be the same in these two situations.

Assume first that the fastening bracket is a new product and that Acme Auto Parts Company has not started manufacturing at all. In this case the decision to make or buy rests on a comparison between the purchase price from another manufacturer and the differential costs of manufacturing the product within the firm. The vice president of production, with the help of the production research department, has drawn design specifications on the fastening bracket. These specifications were submitted to several machine parts manufacturers, and bids were requested at a production level of 150,000 brackets per month. Three independent manufacturers submitted bids of $.03, $.035, and $.0325 per unit respectively. The vice president of production and his staff analyzed the ability of each of the three manufacturers to meet the required production schedules without interruption and with continued high quality. They acknowledged as the best bid the $.0325 offer because the $.03 per unit offer was made by a manufacturer whose reliability was questionable. The purchase price of $.0325 per unit must be compared with the cost of manufacturing the item internally before a decision can be made as to the best course of action to take. Since production has not started on this item of equipment, the research and production departments must estimate what production costs would be. They estimate costs as follows for a production level of 150,000 units per month:

Direct labor	$1,200
Direct materials	2,500
Equipment rental	1,000
Depreciation—building space	500
Miscellaneous manufacturing costs	800
Total monthly costs	$6,000

The direct labor, direct materials, equipment rental, and nonvariable manufacturing costs can be considered differential in this decision if it is assumed they will be incurred only if the manufacture of brackets is undertaken. Not so with the depreciation of building space. Whether this cost is differential depends upon the status of the building in question in relation to its contemplated use.

Assume that the portion of building space that will be devoted to the manufacture of fastening brackets is already in existence. That is, no additional building facilities need be constructed or acquired. All that is necessary is that some presently unused space in the rear of the shop be cleaned out and devoted to this project. The entire building, including that portion to be employed in manufacturing fastening brackets, is a past cost and thus is irrelevant to the decision at hand. Stated differently, the portion of the building to be devoted to fastener-bracket production does not generate a differential cost because, whether employed in this endeavor or not, the building cost for the enterprise as a whole does not change. (Remember, differential costs are those that would not be incurred except under the proposed alternative.) Based on the assumption that no additional building space is needed, the relevant costs of making 150,000 units of the product in a month rather than buying them become:

Direct labor	$1,200
Direct materials	2,500
Equipment rental	1,000
Miscellaneous manufacturing costs	800
Total monthly costs	$5,500 or $.0366/unit

The $.0366 cost of making the product would be compared with the $.0325 best acceptable price for outside purchasing.

An important factor that should also be considered in this analysis is the uncertainty associated with the cost estimates for making an item. It is entirely possible that the actual cost of making the fastening bracket will exceed the estimated $.0366 per unit. The cost of $.0325 to buy the product, on the other hand, can normally be specified in a contract with the supplier. If no other factors for consideration presented themselves, the manager making the decision should choose to buy rather than make the fastening bracket.

Continue to Make or Start to Buy?

An enterprise that is already manufacturing its own products should continually weigh the possibility of having them manufactured elsewhere. Assume that Acme Auto Parts is already manufacturing its own fastening brackets and that its costs are in fact $.0366 per unit. The vice president of manufacturing discusses the fastening-bracket situation with a friend who runs a parts-manufacturing plant. The friend sends his estimating engineer to Acme Auto Parts, and after careful study the engineer says that his plant can manufacture the same part on a continuous basis of 150,000 units per month for $.0325. The vice president of production for Acme Auto Parts must decide whether to accept this outside offer or not. He must compare the outside price with the costs of manufacturing the bracket within his own firm. If he uses the cost from the list on page 363 he might reach the wrong decision, because that list includes two cost items that are not differential now: depreciation expense for building space and equipment rental (we assume that the equipment rental has already been paid and is not recoverable). These are past costs, not future costs, and therefore should not be considered in reaching this decision. The costs that are relevant in this situation become:

Direct labor	$1,200
Direct materials	2,500
Miscellaneous manufacturing costs	800
Total monthly costs	$4,500/150,000 units, or $.03/unit

A comparison of these relevant manufacturing costs with the purchase price suggested by the outside manufacturer indicates that Acme Auto Parts should continue to manufacture its own fastening brackets for at least another month. When the equipment rental comes due again, another decision will have to be made. The above example emphasizes the point made earlier: The relevance of costs to an alternate-choice situation depends on the nature of the situation, not the nature of the cost. In one case the equipment rental was relevant, in the other, it was not.

Business activity is constantly posing alternatives that require analysis of factual operating statistics. It is the role of the accountant to provide the relevant statistics (in these examples, costs) in an easily understood manner to the decision-making manager. The manager will then employ the information as part of *his* relevant information. He will, of course, have to consider other factors as well as the cost data provided by an accounting report. For example, in the situation discussed above, he should consider the implications of any repeated hiring and laying-off brought about by continuously alternating decisions to make and then buy. It might be wiser to suffer a temporary cost sacrifice by continuing to manufacture and not accepting an extraordinarily low, but probably short-lived, price from an outside contractor. In the long run, his earnings may benefit more from a stable labor force than they would from temporary cost reductions.

SUMMARY

Planning for alternative courses of operations is a decision-making process in which every relevant item of information should be considered. The role of the accountant is to provide relevant quantitative data, usually in the form of estimated revenues and expenses, that the manager can employ as part of his broader scientific process of planning.

Relevant expense and revenue information must pertain to the future and be differential in nature. Revenues and expenses are differential when they are the result of the action being contemplated. Differential expenses may at times include expenses of both variable and nonvariable behavior, depending on the course of action under examination.

The relevant accounting information for some alternate-choice decisions consists solely of costs because revenues are unaffected by the choice. The make-or-buy decision is one example of this kind of situation. There are many alternate-choice decisions in which both revenues and costs are relevant: the decision to add a new product, the decision to accept orders at a price less than full cost, and the decision to discontinue a part of existing enterprise activity.

Questions for Review

10-1. What aspects of the scientific process of research are required for the successful planning of changes in an organizational environment?

10-2. What is the general criterion for the short-run decisions that are discussed in this chapter?

10-3. What are the net earnings and differential earnings approaches to the preparation of an analysis for use in making the decisions discussed in this chapter?

10-4. Why is a budgeted statement of earnings more useful to a manager with a decision to make than an earnings statement for a past period?

10-5. What are sunk costs?

10-6. Under what circumstances are variable costs relevant to the types of decisions discussed in the chapter? Nonvariable costs? Allocated costs?

10-7. What are allocated costs?

10-8. What are differential earnings? Distinguish from contribution margin.

Problems for Analysis

10-9. Discuss the meaning and importance of the following concepts as they pertain to the planning of alternate courses of operations. List two examples of the application of each concept:

    a. sunk costs

    b. differential costs

    c. differential earnings

10-10. The cost records of Kapco, Inc., indicate that it "costs" $1.25 to make a part that could be purchased from a parts manufacturer for $1.10.

    a. Under what circumstances would it be more profitable for Kapco to continue making this part, even though the purchased part may be of the same quality?

    b. What qualitative considerations (that is, those for which the profitability cannot be accurately computed) should also enter into this decision?

    c. Under what circumstances might it be more profitable for Kapco to buy a part from an outsider for $1.25, even if the cost estimates indicated that it would cost only $1.10 to make it?

10-11. The Clark Company is a small manufacturer of parts for aircraft engines. The company has always hired an outside CPA firm to do its tax work, but since it has grown larger, the management has considered adding a tax specialist to its accounting department.

The CPA firm would be expected to prepare federal, state, and local tax returns of all kinds. Many of these are prepared in connection with the annual audit (for which a separate fee is paid), but some of the others are prepared independently. It would also give advice to management regarding the tax effect of proposed transactions on other management decisions. Tax questions related to these decisions can arise any time, often on short notice, and sometimes there have been delays when it has been necessary to contact the CPA firm. Both kinds of tax work involve many hours of study and research by the tax specialist to broaden his knowledge and to keep up with changes, and proposals for them, in the tax laws.

    a. List all the important quantitative considerations in the above decision.

    b. List all the important qualitative considerations in the above decision.

10-12. Bland, Inc., manufactures shaving cream in tubes of two sizes: the regular size, which normally sells for $.65 wholesale, and the economy size (holding twice as much shaving cream), which normally sells for $1. Standard cost information is as follows:

	Regular cost per unit	Economy cost per unit
Direct materials	$.20	$.35
Direct labor	.05	.06
Variable manufacturing costs	.05	.07
Nonvariable manufacturing costs[a]	.10	.15
Total standard cost	$.40	$.63

[a] Nonvariable manufacturing cost is allocated to the two sizes at the normal rate of $60 per machine hour. Machine times are six seconds for the regular size and nine seconds for the economy size.

During July the company anticipated idle capacity of 600 machine hours, and therefore was able to accept either (but not both) of the following special orders: 300,000 regular-size units to be sold for $.35 per unit, or 200,000 units of economy size to be sold for $.55 per unit.

a. Assuming that July profit is management's only consideration, which of the two orders should management accept? Explain.

b. What would your answer be if the choice were between 260,000 units of regular size at $.45 per unit and 240,000 units of economy size at $.65 per unit?

10-13. Bach Resort Motel has operated only during the vacation season, which begins December 1 and ends March 31. An analysis of operating costs reveals the following:

1. Materials and supplies vary directly with motel occupancy; they amount to about $.70 per day per occupied room.

2. Utilities (heat and light) vary directly with motel occupancy; they amount to about $.40 per day per occupied room.

3. Salaries for the motel's staff amount to $4,000 per month when the motel is open. Mr. Bach, the owner, does all the work himself, at no salary, when the motel is closed.

4. Insurance, property taxes, and depreciation amount to $15,000 per year. These costs continue whether the motel is open or not.

The motel has forty rooms and the rent during the vacation season is $10 per day for one or two persons. Not more than two persons are normally allowed in a room. During the vacation season, Mr. Bach can count on 90 per cent occupancy.

Mr. Bach has been considering the possibility of staying open on a year-round basis, which would involve keeping the full staff at the total salary cost of $4,000 per month. Mr. Bach figures that occupancy would average 50 per cent for the remaining eight months of the year if he could keep his price per room at a minimum.

What is the minimum price per room Mr. Bach should charge to justify staying open, assuming that he would be satisfied with $400 per month income to himself for these eight months?

10-14. Jack Raul and John Stevens are owners and operators of the R-S Automatic Car Wash Company. They operate a completely automated car wash. There are eight full-time employees. Each employee receives a salary of $75 per week. The business is open from 10:00 A.M. to 6:00 P.M. each day except Sunday. The volume of business generally fluctuates during the day. Peak hours of activity are usually from 11:00 A.M. to 1:30 P.M. and from 3:30 P.M. to 6:00 P.M. There is very little business during other hours of the day. Consequently, the eight employees have about three hours of idle time each day.

Mr. Raul and Mr. Stevens are attempting to secure additional business that will utilize the idle time of their employees. They are currently negotiating with a used-car dealer about reconditioning his cars for resale. The car dealer sells approximately fifteen cars per month. Mr. Raul believes that his employees could recondition one car per day during the three hours of low activity.

Mr. Raul and Mr. Stevens are attempting to establish a price for reconditioning the cars. They have accumulated the following costs:

Salaries of employees	$600/week
Utilities	200/month
Depreciation on buildings & equipment	350/month
Supplies:	
For car washing	180/month
For reconditioning autos (estimated)	40/month
Taxes & insurance	120/month
Maintenance & repairs	70/month

a. Which of the costs should be considered in establishing a price for the auto reconditioning?

b. What is the minimum price that Mr. Raul and Mr. Stevens should charge for the auto reconditioning?

c. What considerations in the decision to recondition autos are primarily qualitative?

d. What are the advantages and disadvantages to the used-car dealer if he decides to have R-S Automatic Car Wash Company do all of the used-car reconditioning?

10-15. The projected budget of earnings for the Power Mower Company for the next calendar year appears below.

The Power Mower Company manufactures one type of mower, which is sold through its distributors. Present production capacity is for 18,000 mowers per year. The company has received a request from a national chain of discount stores to manufacture 4,000 power mowers (under a private label) at a selling price of $18 per unit. The specifications and costs for these mowers would be the same as for the mowers that are now being produced. The Power Mower Company estimates that acceptance of the private-label business would reduce their regular sales to 9,000 units for the next calendar year.

POWER MOWER COMPANY
BUDGETED STATEMENT OF EARNINGS
For 19xx

Sales revenues (10,000 units)			$240,000
— Cost of goods sold:			
Materials		$80,000	
Labor		35,000	
Variable manufacturing costs		7,500	
Nonvariable manufacturing costs		40,000	
Total cost of goods sold			162,500
Earnings margin			$ 77,500
— Operating expenses:			
Selling expenses:			
Variable		$ 7,000	
Nonvariable		20,000	
Total		$27,000	
Administrative expenses:			
Variable	$ 2,000		
Nonvariable	15,000		
Total		17,000	
Total operating expenses			44,000
Earnings from operations			$ 33,500

a. Prepare a budgeted statement of earnings for the Power Mower Company, assuming that the private-label business is accepted.

b. What qualitative considerations should also enter into this decision?

c. Should the Power Mower Company accept the private-label business or continue to manufacture only for regular sales? Justify your answer.

d. What are the assumptions in your analysis?

10–16. Dreamland, Inc., is an amusement park located in a summer resort area. The season starts on Memorial Day and ends on Labor Day. Average data for each day of the week for the past season are presented below.

The management has given local organizations special prices (on a group

	Number of patrons	*Revenues from rides*	*Revenues from food*
Monday	800	$ 1,900	$ 400
Tuesday	2,100	4,000	1,100
Wednesday	3,909	7,900	1,900
Thursday	2,700	5,100	1,300
Friday	4,500	8,700	2,200
Saturday	10,500	20,200	5,800
Sunday	12,700	26,000	6,900

basis) in order to increase attendance on Mondays, Tuesdays, and Thursdays. Demand for the other four days is generally good without sales-promotion techniques.

The costs of operating the rides (salaries, supplies, maintenance, depreciation, insurance, utilities, and taxes) remain the same regardless of the number of patrons in the park. All rides are $.25 each. The average earnings margin before taxes on food sales is 30 per cent.

The management of Dreamland, Inc., is currently planning for the next season. They are concerned with the poor attendance results on Mondays during the past year and they are contemplating a special price on rides for that day of the week.

a. Prepare a list of the quantitative and qualitative factors that should be considered in developing a policy on the price of Monday rides.

b. Suggest a pricing policy for Monday rides for Dreamland, Inc. Support your policy with an analysis of differential earnings and a list of the assumptions in your analysis.

10-17. The S-L Company is engaged in the manufacture of canvas-top travel trailers. The company has been operating at 50 per cent of capacity by producing 100 travel trailers per period at a total cost per trailer of $700. The selling price per trailer is $1,000. Nonvariable costs account for 40 per cent of the total cost at the current level of production.

a. How many units will be produced at 90 per cent of capacity?

b. What would the differential cost be if volume were changed from 50 per cent to 90 per cent?

c. The sales manager anticipates that sales could be increased to 90 per cent of capacity if the unit sales price of all trailers were reduced from $1,000 to $900.

    1. Should the S-L Company increase sales by reducing the sales price or continue at the current level of operations? Support your answer with computations.

    2. What are the assumptions in your analysis above?

d. Compute the breakeven point:

    1. at 50 per cent of sales capacity.

    2. at 90 per cent of sales capacity.

10-18. Simpson's, now a prosperous eastern chain of over fifty restaurants, began in 1908 as a candy store. The number of candy stores increased and the Simpson name became famous for fine home-made candy. The addition of the restaurant business was gradual, and only in the past five years has it become obvious to the management that, as a profit maker, candy is secondary to food service. Each restaurant continues to feature large candy displays in the lobby, and the company maintains several kitchens devoted exclusively to candy manufacture. Although declining candy sales and higher labor costs have cut into profits, some of the top managers feel that the candy business, and its association with the Simpson name, are effective sales-promotion devices. A few of the top executives have suggested withdrawal from the candy business, so that all management effort can be devoted to the restaurant business.

Recently another alternative has presented itself. Lucky Star, Inc., a reputable and very large manufacturer of low- and medium-grade candy, has offered to operate Simpson's candy business. Lucky Star proposes to lease all of Simpson's candy kitchens, delivery, and sales facilities and to market the candy under the Simpson name, exactly as before, so that the change would not be apparent to Simpson customers. Lucky Star proposes to make a profit by saving in administrative cost, expanding volume by increasing the number of marketing outlets, and slightly reducing the quality, and consequently the cost, of the candy. Lucky Star would have its own labor force and buy its own direct materials. Simpson's only expenses related to the candy business would be property taxes, insurance, and depreciation on leased assets. The proposed rental is $60,000 per month.

Sales and earnings (after allocated expenses and taxes) for the restaurant and candy business for the past five years, expressed in thousands of dollars, are as follows:

	Sales			Earnings		
	Restaurant	*Candy*	*Total*	*Restaurant*	*Candy*	*Total*
19x6	$6,500	$3,500	$10,000	$260	$140	$400
19x7	7,000	3,500	10,500	300	120	420
19x8	7,700	3,300	11,000	335	90	425
19x9	8,800	3,200	12,000	365	65	430
19y0	9,500	3,000	12,500	390	40	430

A condensed earnings statement for 19y0 is shown below:

SIMPSON'S, INC.
STATEMENT OF EARNINGS
For 19y0
(in thousands of dollars)

	Restaurant	*Candy*	*Total*
Sales revenues	$9,500	$3,000	$12,500
— Expenses:			
Materials & supplies	$4,000	$1,200	$ 5,200
Labor	2,850	950	3,800
Depreciation, insurance, & taxes	1,000	500	1,500
General, administrative, & selling expenses[a]	860	275	1,135
Federal income taxes	400	35	435
Total expenses	$9,110	$2,960	$12,070
Net earnings	$ 390	$ 40	$ 430

[a] General, administrative, and selling expenses are allocated to the restaurant and candy business on the basis of sales (figures are rounded).

a. Prepare an estimated earnings statement for 19y1 as it might look if the candy business were abandoned at the end of 19y0. For this purpose you should assume that (1) the depreciable assets associated with the candy business could be sold at no gain or loss to Simpson's, (2) there would be no appreciable saving in one year in general, administrative, and selling expenses, (3) the restaurant business is not likely to be affected by the decision in one year (assume restaurant sales of $10 million), and (4) federal tax rates are 50 per cent of reported net income.

b. Prepare an estimated earnings statement for 19y1 as it would appear if the Lucky Star offer were accepted. Assumptions 2, 3, and 4 stated in *a* above would hold for this purpose also.

c. Discuss the relative long-run and short-run profitability of alternatives and consider both quantitative and qualitative aspects.

10–19. The Witch Company makes and sells brooms. The following facts are taken from the firm's records.

Present sales volume: 500,000 units per year
Present selling price per unit: $.55 per broom
Nonvariable costs per year: $100,000
Variable costs per year: $.30 per broom
Total assets: $100,000

a. What is the present sales breakeven point in dollars?

b. What are the present earnings for a year?

c. How many units must be sold in order for the company to earn a 10 per cent rate of return on total investments?

d. Market research indicates that if the selling price were reduced $.10 per unit, 150,000 additional units could be sold. Would you recommend the price reduction? Show computations to support your decision.

e. If nonvariable costs were increased by 10 per cent, what would the new sales breakeven point be in *dollars?*

10–20. Speedway, Inc., owns an automobile drag strip with a seating capacity of 2,000. Drag races are held on fifty Saturdays per year, and the average attendance is 1,800 per Saturday. Its nonvariable costs per year are $80,000, and variable costs are $0.50 per spectator per race. The price per spectator is $3.50.

The company can increase its seating capacity to 5,000 seats by paying an annual rental fee of $14,000 for the additional seats. Variable costs per spectator will remain the same. Alternative prices and estimated attendance follow:

Price	Estimated attendance
(1) $3.50	1,800
(2) 3.00	2,500
(3) 2.50	3,500
(4) 2.00	4,000
(5) 1.50	5,600

Prepare an analysis indicating which of the five pricing alternatives should be followed, and whether the additional seating capacity should be rented.

10-21. Benny is a tailor specializing in men's suits. Although he keeps his shop open year-round (except for vacation during the last half of July), he finds that the months of September, December, January, and April are considerably busier than the other months.

Benny's father, also a tailor, had coached Benny on how to run the tailor shop: "Always price the suits so you make 20 per cent profit on sales, Benny, and when you figure your costs, make sure you include *all* your costs. Don't leave anything out." Benny has been having trouble applying this rule because of the month-to-month fluctuations in the volume of business, and he asks your help.

"My material and labor costs are easy to figure," Benny says, "but the taxes, insurance, utilities, and depreciation on the shop and sewing machines cost another $2,000 a month whether we make any suits or not. If I follow my father's rule, I would have to charge more for a suit I make in February than I would charge if I made that same suit in December. My prices would be lower in the busy months because higher production makes the cost per suit lower, but this is just the opposite of the result I want. Lately we have been putting together some ready-made suits, just to keep the employees busy in the slack months. Figuring the cost of these suits, and recognizing that the more of this we do the smaller the cost per suit will be, makes it harder to set prices. This is especially true when you don't know what your costs are until the end of the month, and often this comes after we have already sold the suit. My father made a lot of money in this business, but I don't know how he did it with the rules he gave me."

a. Explain, illustrating with figures, why Benny would have to charge more for a suit made in February than one made in December if he followed his father's advice.

b. What general principle should Benny follow in a price policy?

c. Suggest a price policy for Benny.

Chapter Eleven # PLANNING THE ACQUISITION OF FACILITIES

INTRODUCTION

In this chapter we are concerned with acquisitions of major facilities, such as building and equipment. The principles we shall discuss apply, however, to any decision involving the commitment of a large sum of capital for a substantial time period. As in Chapter 10, major emphasis will be given to optimizing earnings and to the relevance of accounting information to the decisions.

The acquisition of facilities usually involves a large cash outlay at the beginning of the project, and estimated cash inflows will continue for some time after the outlay. Thus, the time value of money becomes an important factor in the decision. Because these projects are long-term, they are riskier than the short-term projects discussed in Chapter 10. The decisions discussed there involved very little additional investment, compared with the initial outlays required for the types of decisions that are discussed in this chapter. The large initial investment required and the estimated cash inflows far into the future account for the greater risk associated with these decisions.

FINANCING PROBLEMS

A vital part of the planning for facility acquisition is consideration of the sources of money for this purpose. Money for capital expenditures can come from the funds already in the hands of the enterprise, or it can come from *outside funds,* that is, money specifically borrowed for the purpose or contributed by owners who purchase additional shares of stock. An enterprise that can obtain outside money almost without limit whenever it desires is concerned only with determining how much money it should plan to acquire in sufficient time to do it effectively. An enterprise that for any reason is unable or unwilling to obtain unlimited funds from lenders and owners is faced with the additional problem of rationing the limited funds it has available from internal sources. A given enterprise may fluctuate between internal and external financing from period to period, depending on the supply and demand for funds.

In this chapter we assume that the student has a working knowledge of compound interest, and experience in problem-solving using compound interest tables. A review of compound interest is given in the appendix to this chapter.

EVALUATION OF PROPOSALS

Profitability

From the accounting standpoint, the fundamental yardstick in evaluating capital expenditure proposals, as in judging all other business decisions, is optimization of the firm's long-run earnings. Another way of expressing this is to say that the firm should optimize the present value of expected future net receipts from any long-term investment. For instance, assume that the Emca Investment Corporation has $10,000 in cash. It is hesitating between two alternatives: (1) invest the money in a savings account which will earn 6 per cent annually, or (2) use the money to purchase a parcel of land that, it is estimated, can be sold for $15,000 at the end of five years. Emca may deposit unlimited amounts in the savings account, for any length of time, and may make withdrawals at any time without a waiting period. If the land is purchased and if the selling price turns out to be $15,000 after five years, the rate of return will be slightly more than 8 per cent. In deciding between the two proposals, Emca can apply the following decision rule: *choose the proposal with the higher present value of future net receipts, calculated using the same rate of interest for both proposals.* The present value of the savings account at 6 per cent is $10,000, while that of the land at 6 per cent is $11,409. Thus, Emca should purchase the land.

Simplifying Assumptions

Business decisions are seldom as easy to make as the Emca example implies. In that example we made several very important assumptions that cannot ordinarily be justified in practice. We shall discuss two of these in some detail: the assumption that only two alternatives were available and the assumption that the estimate of future land value was correct.

Alternative Projects

By assuming that depositing the $10,000 in the savings account is Emca's *only* alternative to purchasing the land, we are saying, in effect, that

1. The firm need not worry about having enough cash to meet some emergency need for cash that might arise later, or to take advantage of some third alternative on which the estimated return might be even better than the return on the land. This means that Emca is assuming that it will have the privilege of borrowing unlimited amounts from a bank at no more than 6 per cent, so that no profitable opportunity will be missed due to lack of funds. All emergency needs for cash will be met at a cost of 6 per cent, either by borrowing the money or by withdrawing the saved amount and sacrificing the savings account interest of 6 per cent.

2. Emca need not worry about having to invest in some project on which the return might be less than 6 per cent, since the savings account is assumed always to be available. This means that if the land is purchased and then sold for $15,000 at the end of five years, it will be possible to deposit the proceeds in the savings account at 6 per cent if no better alternative presents itself.

In a more realistic situation, firms may find themselves having to ration limited cash resources among competing projects. It is not reasonable to assume that firms can continue to borrow (or issue shares) indefinitely without increasing the interest cost, and it might be necessary to reject some alternatives even though the return exceeds 6 per cent. In the Emca illustration, there were only two alternatives, and the initial investment and time period were the same for each. In reality, unequal time periods, differences in project costs, and differences in timing of cash inflows make business projects incomparable. Such decisions are beyond the scope of this book. Choosing among competing capital expenditure proposals is a very complicated matter.

The uncertainty of the estimates. All predictions, including those of inflows related to investment proposals, involve uncertainty. Some events are easier to predict than others, but uncertainty can never be completely eliminated. U.S. Government bonds have been described as "riskless" securities, but they do involve a risk, albeit minuscule: If the government is overthrown and the national debt repudiated, the bonds will be worthless. Similarly, the savings account in the Emca Investment Corporation illustration is a "low-risk" investment alternative, but it is always conceivable that the bank could fail, and not be able to honor Emca's withdrawal request.

Nevertheless, the uncertainty in predicting the selling value of the land is much greater. When the predictor says that the selling value of the land will be $15,000 in five years, we are not sure what he means. He could mean that

1. There is a 50-50 chance that the selling value of the land will be less than $15,000 in five years, and a 50-50 chance that it will be greater than $15,000 in five years.

2. There are two chances out of three that the price will be between $13,000 and $17,000.

3. There are nine chances out of ten that the price will be above $15,000.

Countless other interpretations are possible.

Thus predictions of future economic values are not very useful unless accompanied by some statement of the uncertainty involved. These statements are often mathematical and take the form of probability distributions of predicted values. The distributions of any one variable will vary from one predictor to another, depending on his experience and information. One of the major functions of accounting is to provide predictors with information that will permit them to predict economic values with less uncertainty.

In this book we make no attempt to give quantitative expression to the uncertainty of predictions. We shall make predictions only in terms of single values and shall calculate rates of return and present values as if these single values were certain.

It is important to remember, however, that uncertainty cannot be wished away or ignored. It will inevitably influence managers' choices among alternatives, however subjective the influence may be. Managers will insist on higher rates of return on "riskier" investments. For example, in the Emca Investment Corporation, management should not consider purchasing the land if its rate of return were the same as the rate on the bank account, simply because the prediction of the selling price of the land is much more uncertain. How much higher the rate must be will depend on the manager, but only a poor gambler would "go against the odds" and buy the land if the predicted rate of return were 6 per cent or less.

Liquidity.   As the uncertainty in the prediction of future values increases, managers tend to rely less on the profitability measurements on which these predictions are based. In particular, they become increasingly interested in the *liquidity* of the project under consideration, which is the rapidity with which the project will produce cash. If the predictor says that the project will produce enough cash to recover the initial investment within a short time, managers may consider this prediction a sufficient hedge against the uncertainty in the prediction of the rate of return. The time period necessary for investment recovery is called *payback.*

Consider the following example. The two alternatives shown below require an investment of $10,000 each at the beginning of the first year.

In making these payback calculations, we assume that the amounts received in any year are received evenly throughout that year. This calculation is so rough, however, that fractions of a year should probably be ignored.

Payback calculations ignore any cash inflows other than the first investment; thus these measurements give no indication of the relative profitability of the projects. Payback calculations only indicate the relative liquidity of the projects.

	Estimated cash receipts	
Year	Project 1	Project 2
1	$3,000	0
2	3,000	0
3	3,000	0
4	3,000	0
5	3,000	$20,000
Payback	$3\frac{1}{3}$ years	$4\frac{1}{2}$ years

In the example above, we might conclude that there is less uncertainty in project 1 than in project 2, simply because project 1 is more "liquid."

The time-adjusted rate of return on each of the projects in our example is approximately 15 per cent, suggesting that project 1 should be chosen. This is not necessarily the case. Before any choice is made, the decision maker needs to know something about how the $3,000 annual proceeds from project 1 will be invested as they are received. If these amounts can bring more than a 15 per cent annual rate of return until the end of the fifth year, project 1 should be accepted; if not, project 2 should be accepted.

DECIDING TO ACQUIRE A FACILITY

Any proposal for acquiring a facility should be considered in terms of initial investment, dollar advantages, special tax considerations, and yardsticks of economic worth. In this section we shall consider all these factors in the decision from the point of view of the data gatherer and the interpreter.

Initial Investment

Investment in any facility acquisition is made up of several components. By employing the sunk-cost rule discussed in Chapter 10, we eliminate consideration of any investment made in the past and concern ourselves only with the future.

The easiest component of investment to understand is the amount that will have to be paid in order to implement the proposal. This would include the purchase price of a new machine; the acquisition costs of land; the construction costs of buildings; and associated outlays such as legal fees, appraisal fees, and related costs connected with acquiring and putting into working condition any type of facility.

If the proposal concerns the replacement of an existing facility, it is necessary to adjust the amount of investment made in the new facility by the net effect of removing the old one. It is possible that the old facility can be sold for scrap or as used equipment. The proceeds of this sale should be subtracted from the investment made in the new facility. Of course, it is possible that the costs of disposing of the existing facility may exceed the salvage recovery. In such a case the net cost of getting rid of the old facility should be added to the investment made in the new facility. Assume that plant 1 of the Acme Auto Parts Company is contemplating replacing an old grinding machine with a model recently developed by a national machine-tool manufacturer. The purchase price quoted by the manufacturer is $10,000. In addition, there will be freight charges of $450, a sales tax of $300, and an installation charge by the machine-tool manufacturer of $250. Moreover, the new machine requires 440-volt electrical wiring instead of the 220-volt wiring now in plant 1's grinding department. The rewiring cost of $130 must be considered part of the cost of the machine because the rewiring would be done specifically to make the new machine usable. The old grinding machine can be sold to a secondhand dealer for $850, but it is estimated that it will cost $350 to take it out of the plant and ship it to the dealer's warehouse. The net amount of the investment that is contemplated by the proposed replacement of the grinding machine is as follows:

Purchase price	$10,000
Freight charges	450
Sales tax	300
Installation charge	250
Electrical rewiring	130
Total	$11,130
− Net salvage value of old machine	500
Net investment in proposed machine	$10,630

Dollar Advantages

The *dollar advantages* of a given investment proposal are the dollars of earnings that the proposal will generate for the enterprise in the future. When measuring the economic worth, it is always advisable to identify the dollar advantages year by year, or in some cases, even to compute an *average annual dollar advantage.*

Dollar advantages are computed by taking into consideration the net differential inflows and outflows of cash that will be generated by the proposal. Differential inflows and outflows result from:

1. Increases or decreases in revenues that will be generated if the proposal is implemented.
2. Increases or decreases in variable operating costs that will be made possible if the proposal is implemented.
3. Increases or decreases in nonvariable costs, including taxes, resulting from implementation of the proposal.

The proposed grinding machine will generate additional revenue each year of its predicted five-year useful life as follows:

Year	Additional revenue
1	$6,600
2	7,200
3	7,800
4	8,000
5	8,000

The new grinding machine will require variable costs each year as follows:

Direct labor	$1,400
Direct material	0
Variable overhead	600

The new nonvariable costs of insurance and property taxes will be $200 per year. The average annual dollar advantage for this proposed equipment is calculated as follows:

Year	Inflow	Outflow	Annual dollar advantages
1	$6,600	$2,200	$ 4,400
2	7,200	2,200	5,000
3	7,800	2,200	5,600
4	8,000	2,200	5,800
5	8,000	2,200	5,800
Total annual dollar advantages			$26,600

Average annual dollar advantage:

$$\frac{\text{Total annual dollar advantages}}{\text{Life span}} = \frac{\$26,600}{5} = \$5,320$$

Special Tax Considerations

The tax aspects of any capital expenditure proposal need special consideration. This is especially true of certain facets of the federal income tax. Federal, state, and local income taxes may affect an investment proposal in two ways: (1) the net investment required may be affected by a tax gain or loss on the disposal of old facilities released by the new investment, and (2) the earnings for purposes of computing the federal income tax expense may be different from reported earnings throughout the project life and therefore may cause a change in federal income taxes paid. Only the share of earnings that is left to the enterprise after the income tax should be considered when making capital expenditure decisions. In the case of the proposed replacement of Acme's grinding machine, the dollar advantages must be reduced by the amount that the income tax will drain away.

The determination of the tax drain involves a calculation of earnings for federal income tax purposes. Our estimate of earnings will be based upon the simplifying assumptions that (1) cash inflows are taxable revenues, and (2) cash outflows are deductible expenses in the year of the inflow or outflow. Therefore the dollar advantages that were calculated earlier for the new grinding machine represent earnings for federal income tax purposes, except that depreciation (a noncash expense) is deducted before the income tax is calculated.

Assume that the Internal Revenue Service will allow a tax depreciation deduction of 20 per cent of purchase price in each year of the five-year life of the contemplated grinding machine. The purchase price, you will recall, was $11,130, so that the annual deduction is $2,226. The tax rate should be applied to the annual dollar advantages only after subtracting the depreciation deduction. If we assume that the effective tax rate of Acme Auto Parts is 45 per cent, the following calculations show the average after-tax dollar advantage:

Year	Pre-tax advantages	Tax depreciation deduction	Taxable income	Tax drain	After-tax dollar advantages
1	$4,400	$2,226	$2,174	$ 978	$ 3,422
2	5,000	2,226	2,774	1,248	3,752
3	5,600	2,226	3,374	1,518	4,082
4	5,800	2,226	3,574	1,608	4,192
5	5,800	2,226	3,574	1,608	4,192
			Total after-tax dollar advantages		$19,640

$$\text{Average after-tax dollar advantage: } \frac{\$19,640}{5} = \$3,928$$

Tax Effects of Salvage Recovery

In the case of a replacement proposal, the net salvage recovery obtained from selling the old machine may have a tax effect. The federal income tax law states that when an existing asset is sold, the difference between the net selling price and the "tax book value" of the asset must be considered as either a taxable income or, in the case of a sale at a loss, a taxable deduction. The *tax book value* is the difference between the original acquisition cost and the amount of tax depreciation deductions taken prior to disposition. You will recall that the old grinding machine would generate a salvage recovery of $850 minus $350 for removal and shipping expenses, for a net salvage recovery of $500. If the old machine originally cost $8,000 and the total tax depreciation deduction taken for this machine in previous years was $7,300, the tax book value of the old machine would be $700 ($8,000 − $7,300). The difference between the $700 tax book value and the $500 net salvage recovery would result in a $200 special tax deduction in the year in which the old machine was sold. This special tax deduction would decrease the tax drain in the first year and would affect the net investment after taxes in the new machine:

Net investment in proposed machine before federal income taxes		$10,630
− Tax loss deduction on sale of old machine	$200	
× Tax savings (@ 45% rate)	× .45	
		90
Net investment after taxes		$10,540

If the tax book value of the old grinding machine were only $300, the result would be a tax gain on the sale of the old machine that would increase the first year's taxable income by $200 and would affect the net investment in the new machine after taxes in this manner:

Net investment in proposed machine before federal income taxes		$10,630
+ Tax gain on sale of old machine	$200	
× Tax drain (@ 45% rate)	× .45	
		90
Net investment after taxes		$10,720

YARDSTICKS OF ECONOMIC WORTH

As indicated earlier in this chapter, we are defining the economic worth of a proposal as the present value of its after-tax dollar advantages. We are setting aside the more difficult problems of comparing this proposal with alternative proposals that may be in competition for limited funds, and of attempting to measure the uncertainty in the predictions.

To compute the present value of the after-tax dollar advantages, an interest rate (usually called a *discount* rate) is needed. In the Emca Investment Corporation example, this rate was the rate of interest paid by a savings account that was presented as an alternative to the proposal. Acme Auto Parts is not likely to consider such a savings account a reasonable alternative, and in practice, business firms establish *cutoff rates of return* instead. A cutoff rate of return is used just as Emca used the savings account rate of return, that is, to discount the future advantages to a present value. If this present value exceeds the initial investment, the proposal is accepted. If not, it is rejected.

Cutoff Rate of Return

Most financial authorities assert that the proper cutoff rate of return is that rate which represents the average *cost of capital* to the firm. Computing the cost of capital is a difficult and sometimes controversial matter. For the Emca Investment Corporation the cost of capital was 6 per cent, but only because of several very important (and not very realistic) assumptions concerning the conditions under which the savings account could be used. Here we will simply assume that the cost of capital to Acme Auto Parts is 10 per cent after taxes, and that this rate is used as the cutoff rate of return for evaluating capital expenditure proposals.

Profitability Index

Once the present value of expected dollar advantages has been computed, it is divided by the amount of the contemplated net investment in order to obtain the *profitability index:*

$$\frac{\text{Present value of after-tax dollar advantages}}{\text{Net investment}} = \text{Profitability index}$$

An index smaller than 1.00 means that the present value of expected returns is smaller than the contemplated net investment; therefore the proposal would not meet the cutoff rate of return and would be rejected. An index larger than 1.00 indicates that the present value of expected returns is greater than the cost of the investment and that the proposal exceeds the cutoff rate of return.

The after-tax dollar advantages of the Acme Auto Parts Company grinding machine proposal are discounted below. The discount factor is from Table II in the appendix of this chapter, based on a 10 per cent after-tax cutoff rate of return.

Year	After-tax dollar advantages	Discount factor at 10%	Present value at 10%
1	$3,422	.909	$3,110.61
2	3,752	.826	3,099.15
3	4,082	.751	3,065.58
4	4,192	.683	2,863.14
5	4,192	.621	2,603.23
Total present value of future after-tax dollar advantages			$14,741.71

Since the total present value of future dollar advantages ($14,742) is higher than the net investment in the grinding machine ($10,540), the proposal will yield a greater return than the 10 per cent minimum required. The profitability index for this machine is

$$\frac{\$14,742}{\$10,540} = 1.40$$

Estimated Time-adjusted Rate of Return

The profitability index tells us only that the time-adjusted rate of return on Acme's proposal is higher than 10 per cent; it does not tell us what this rate is. To find the rate it is necessary to solve this equation for i:

$$\frac{\$3,422}{(1+i)} \quad \frac{\$3,752}{(1+i)^2} \quad \frac{\$4,082}{(1+i)^3} \quad \frac{\$4,192}{(1+i)^4} \quad \frac{\$4,192}{(1+i)^5} = \$10,540$$

The only practical way of solving equations of this type is by the "trial and error" methods of which the computer is capable. (In Acme's case, the value of i is approximately 25 per cent.)

Payback, the approximate time required for Acme to recover its initial investment of $10,540, is approximately 2.8 years, as can be seen from the fact that the sum of the after-tax dollar advantages for the first three years is $11,256, or about $700 more than the required amount.

ADDITIONAL CONSIDERATIONS

The Judgment Criterion

Thus far, we have been discussing means of identifying which proposals should be implemented, based on considerations of economic worth. We have been concerned only with proposals that lend themselves to some sort of quantitative analysis. But many capital expenditure possibilities facing a given enterprise do not lend themselves to determination of dollar advantage and thus to measurable economic worth. These can be evaluated only qualitatively. Suppose the union representative at Acme Auto Parts submits a proposal for redecorating the employees' cafeteria. He argues that improved lunchroom facilities will increase the morale of the work force and thus increase worker efficiency and overall firm profitability. The union leader, however, would be unable to back his request with a concrete analysis of added revenues, decreased costs, and their relationship to the investment involved. How should management evaluate this proposal? Or suppose the company president is deeply concerned about air pollution, and at his instigation, the board of directors decides to install new antipollution filters in the factory's exhaust system. What criteria did they use in reaching their decision? Certainly the business-relationship value of the act will provide long-run benefits to the enterprise, but will the investment earn sufficient return? There is no way to express such benefits in terms of dollar advantages, and thus qualitative rather than quantitative measures of economic worth must be employed. The manager's *subjective judgment* is the contributing factor in making the decision.

The ability to make correct decisions based on subjective evidence is one attribute that separates superior managers from their lesser counterparts. There is a common belief that good managers are lucky. Probably more correct would be the statement that good managers have an instinctive ability for sound subjective judgment.

Necessary Expenditures

Some capital expenditure decisions require little judgment and no measurement of economic worth because the course of action is necessary to the survival of the business. A meat-packing firm, with a freezing plant that prepares frozen food for the army and for commercial distribution, maintains a standby emergency electric generator in case the public power supply fails. If a routine maintenance examination indicates that the emergency generator has broken down and cannot be repaired, it becomes very obvious that a new generator must be acquired. There is no need to measure economic worth; the only question involved is whether the firm should buy the equipment and stay in business, or not buy the equipment and face possible disaster in event of a public power failure. Similarly, a railroad that is required by the state regulatory commission to install a new kind of grade-crossing signal light need not engage in an examination of economic worth, nor is much judgment necessary. The facts are obvious. Either the new signal lights are installed, or the state commission puts the railroad out of business.

The Ultimate Alternative

The last examples indicate indirectly an alternative course of action that always exists but is often overlooked: going out of business. This is a legitimate course of action, but is not fitted to the psychological makeup of the American businessman. For example, the railroad, when faced with the high cost of refitting all of its grade crossings, should consider the possibility of going out of the railroad business and using its invested capital in another venture that may in the long run prove more profitable. This may be difficult to do, not only because of the psychological "defeat" but also because of legal restrictions and implications. The regulatory commission may not allow the railroad to go out of business. The New Haven Railroad, which provides commuter service from Connecticut into New York City, has tried to go out of business several times. In each case it has been prevented from doing so by the government. The directors of a company who are considering discontinuing an existing line of business and entering another must also consider the wishes of the stockholder-owners, who may not wish to have their money used for a new type of business.

ADMINISTRATIVE PROCEDURES

Because the long-term commitment of funds involves great risk and is important to the long-run profitability of the firm, a great deal of executive time is devoted to planning these expenditures. The administrative procedures used for these projects can be categorized as:

1. originating expenditure proposals
2. screening them
3. considering their financing problems
4. controlling their implementation
5. auditing results after implementation

One possible organization for handling capital expenditure proposals is shown graphically in Exhibit 11–1.

The final authority for making expenditures rests, of course, with the board of directors. They are more concerned, however, with making broad policies for the enterprise, and thus they usually delegate their authority to expend capital to various managers throughout the firm. Again, there are no set rules as to how this authority should be designated. Authority within the Acme Auto Parts Company is designated according to the dollar amount of the expenditure proposal, as follows:

Amount of Capital Expenditure	*Ultimate Decision Maker*
Over $100,000	board of directors or specified top-management committee
$50,000–$100,000	president and/or chairman of board of directors
$25,000–$50,000	vice-president in charge of function
$5,000–$25,000	plant managers
Under $5,000	persons delegated by plant managers

SUMMARY

This chapter has examined the process of planning for changes in an existing environment. Two broad aspects of the capital-expenditure process were discussed: the economic evaluation and the administrative procedures.

EXHIBIT 11-1

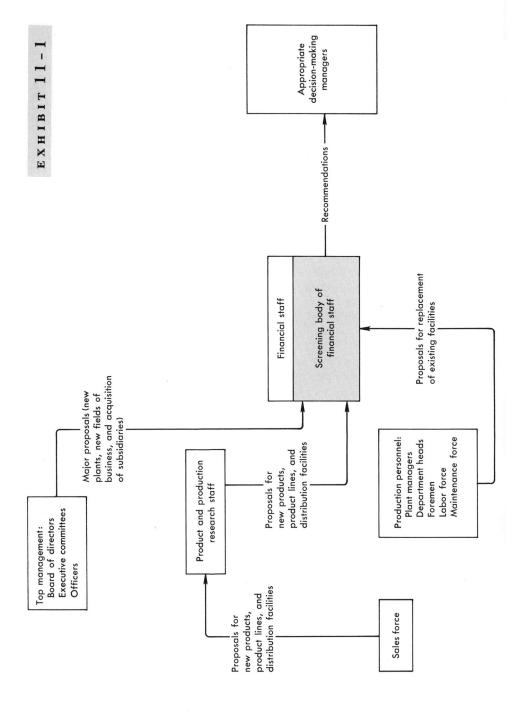

Appropriate decision-making managers

Recommendations

Financial staff

Screening body of financial staff

Proposals for replacement of existing facilities

Top management:
Board of directors
Executive committees
Officers

Major proposals (new plants, new fields of business, and acquisition of subsidiaries)

Product and production research staff

Proposals for new products, product lines, and distribution facilities

Production personnel:
Plant managers
Department heads
Foremen
Labor force
Maintenance force

Proposals for new products, product lines, and distribution facilities

Sales force

The economic evaluation of proposed capital expenditures involves a determination of dollar advantages and investment. Correlation of the two by measuring economic worth indicates the acceptability of the proposal to the firm. Payback and time-adjusted rate of return are two basic yardsticks. The advantages and disadvantages of each were discussed in turn.

In Chapters 10 and 11 we have discussed two broad areas of planning for changes in a business environment. In Chapter 10 we were concerned with operations, adding or dropping subdivisions or product lines, etc., within the enterprise. In Chapter 11 we considered planning for changing the environment by acquisition of productive facilities. In either case, our discussion was directed mainly to the kind of decision that has to be made, and the kind of information needed to make that decision. The real danger of planning for change lies in not being aware of all possibilities for change. Making the decision is a management function; accountants facilitate the process by providing timely and adequate information.

The information required in the planning process is not completely of the kind that comes from the typical accounting system. The typical accounting system is designed to acquire facts about what has happened, not what will happen or should happen. This is not to say that historical information is not useful. On the contrary, the remainder of this book will be devoted to historical information, the reasons why it is acquired, and the uses to which it can be put. The point here is simply that the modern accountant must realize that he should provide information in addition to that traditionally gathered by his system. He should provide long- and short-range estimates of what might transpire for the enterprise in the future. He should present this information to his management in a way that will help the planning process. The various budgets and the forms for originating and evaluating capital expenditure proposals are examples of this type of accounting report. The needs of each enterprise for this kind of information are unique, and therefore it is impossible to generalize about the exact nature of accounting reports to serve this accounting function.

Questions for Review

11-1. What are the major differences between the types of decisions discussed in Chapter 10 and Chapter 11?

11-2. What are the complications in choosing among competing capital expenditure proposals?

11-3. Describe how payback is computed.

11-4. What purpose does payback serve in capital expenditure analysis?

11-5. How are the initial investment and dollar advantages computed in capital expenditure analysis?

11-6. What is the cutoff rate of return? How is it used in evaluating capital expenditure proposals?

11-7. What is the profitability index? How is it used in evaluating capital expenditure proposals?

11-8. What major administrative procedures should be used in the long-term commitment of funds?

Problems for Analysis

11-9. Solve each of the following independent problems:

a. If a firm requires a rate of return of 20 per cent, compounded semiannually, what is the most it should pay for $50,000, to be received in a lump sum in five years?

b. A firm has $30,000 to invest. It requires a return of 12 per cent, compounded quarterly, and it must have the future benefits by the end of three years. What is the expected amount of the benefits if they are received in a single amount at that time?

c. A firm has committed $350 at 12 per cent, compounded monthly, and expects a single benefit of $500. When will it be received?

d. What is the annual interest rate related to an investment that costs $8,800 and will return a single amount of $22,000 in eight years?

11-10. Solve each of the following independent problems:

a. What is the interest rate earned on an investment with an initial cost of $30,000 and expected annual cash returns of $8,500 for five years?

b. Compute the initial investment necessary in order to receive expected annual cash returns of $15,000 per year when the desired rate of return is (a) 10 per cent on ten-year projects, and (b) 16 per cent on fifteen-year projects.

c. Compute the annual cash returns necessary in order to earn a rate of return of 10 per cent on a project that is expected to last five years and have an initial cost of $10,000.

d. A company expects to invest $22,000 in a project, receive annual cash returns of $7,000, and earn 8 per cent on the project. Compute the estimated life of the project.

11-11. How much should a firm invest in a project that will pay $5,000 each year for nine years, plus $10,000 at the end of the tenth year, to earn 16 per cent?

11-12. A firm will receive $1,000 per period for seven periods, plus $5,000 at the end of the eighth period. The initial investment required is $5,000. The firm requires a minimum return of 10 per cent.

a. Should the investment be made?

b. Would it make any difference how long the period is (e.g., a day, a week, a month) if the interest is always 10 per cent per period?

11-13. A farmer whose cutoff rate of return is 12 per cent must decide whether to sell his crop now for $10,000 cash, or wait two years and sell it for $12,000. Ignore such costs as storage and taxes.

a. Which alternative should he select? Why?

b. What assumptions in the farmer's cutoff rate of return should be tested before this decision is made?

11-14. Determine the maximum price to be paid for a building that can be leased out for $10,000 annual rental (the tenant will pay all operating expenses) for fifteen years, and that can then be sold for $20,000. The cutoff rate of return is 10 per cent, compounded annually.

11-15. The XYZ Company has recently installed a new packaging machine that cost $50,000. Now a newly developed standard machine, guaranteed to do exactly the same job, is placed on the market at an installed price of $35,000.

The expected economic life for both machines is eight years. The projected annual out-of-pocket operating costs are $11,000 for the first machine and $8,000 for the new machine.

The company can expect to receive $20,000 from the sale of the first machine. Assume taxes are 40 per cent and that depreciation is straight line (cost ÷ life). After eight years, neither machine will have any salvage value.

Should the company seriously consider acquiring the new machine? Why?

11-16. An investor is undecided between two alternatives: Should he invest $750 in a note that promises to pay $1,000 five years from now, or should he invest the $750 in an opportunity that will yield ten semiannual payments of $100, the first of which will be received in six months?

Which alternative is more attractive? On what assumptions is your answer based?

11-17. For each business enterprise described below, do the following:

a. Outline the administrative procedures that should be followed in processing capital expenditure proposals. Defend each procedure you propose by stating what it will accomplish.

b. Indicate the kind of economic evaluation that should be used by the enterprise, and defend your choice.

1. A local, owner-managed pizza parlor has annual revenue of $35,000 and total assets of $100,000. Annual capital spending averages about $5,000. The owner-manager employs a night-shift manager, two chefs (one each shift), two dishwashers (one each shift), and four waitresses (two each shift).

2. A large international electrical equipment manufacturer has annual revenue of $1.5 billion and total assets of $10 billion. The company has 175 plants or operations, each tied administratively to a corporate vice president. For example, there are thirty-seven plants producing consumers' products (toasters, coffee pots, dishwashers, television sets, etc.), each headed by a plant general manager and all reporting to the vice president of the consumers' products division. There are eleven divisions in the corporation. The most important ones are those for consumer products, heavy machine tools, heavy generators, research and development, and marketing and distribution. Capital expenditures average about $250 million per year.

3. A family owns a chain of eleven supermarkets. Each supermarket is managed by a store manager directly responsible to the corporate president. The managers basically run their own stores; the president is most concerned with opening new stores and setting policies that affect all eleven stores (such as overall advertising policies, mass-purchasing decisions, etc.). Annual revenues average $2 million per store. Total assets are about $5 million for the entire chain. Capital expenditures (other than for new stores) average about $50,000 for the entire chain and are mostly for new store fixtures and storage equipment.

11-18. a. An investment of $7,500 is expected to produce annual dollar advantages after taxes of $800 for twelve years. Can this investment be justified if the cutoff rate of return is 8 per cent?

b. An investment of $1,000 will produce monthly dollar advantages of $50 for five years. Can this investment be justified if the cutoff rate of return is 12 per cent?

c. An investment proposal will produce the following annual after-tax dollar advantages over its six-year life span:

Year	After-tax dollar advantages
1	$2,400
2	3,000
3	3,600
4	3,000
5	2,400
6	1,800

If the company requires a 12 per cent time-adjusted rate of return (after taxes), what is the maximum it should invest in this proposal?

11-19. a. How much would you be willing to pay on January 1 for the right to receive $100 in one year if you required:

    1. a 6 per cent return on your investment

    2. a 10 per cent return on your investment

    3. an 8 per cent return on your investment

b. On January 1, 1972, you deposit $100 in a savings bank that pays 4 per cent interest per annum compounded semiannually. If interest is allowed to accumulate in the account, what will the account balance be on January 1, 1982?

c. On January 1, 19x0, you purchase a used car with no down payment and payments of $40 at the end of each quarter, with the last payment on December 31, 19x4. (Total cash payments: $20 \times \$40 = \$800$.) Assume that the seller is charging you 8 per cent interest per annum, compounded quarterly. What is the equivalent cash price of the car as of the date of purchase?

11-20. The Modern Company is considering the purchase of a new machine to replace one presently being used. The old machine has a tax book value of $8,000. The remaining life is estimated to be eight years. A new machine can be purchased at a cost of $20,000, and will have a resale value of $4,000 at the end of eight years. It is estimated that the old machine can be sold for $4,000. The estimated cost saving if the new machine is purchased is $3,500 per year.

a. Assuming a federal income tax rate of 50 per cent and ignoring salvage value, compute the time-adjusted dollar advantages, using a 10 per cent discount rate on the net investment.

b. Compute the profitability index and the payback period in years for this proposal.

c. Evaluate the time-adjusted rate of return method versus the payback method for making decisions about new equipment.

11-21. Newton Corporation estimates it will have $200,000 available for capital expenditures during 19x0 (plus an additional $30,000 for emergency projects not yet foreseen). A list of the currently foreseen proposals for the year 19x0 follows:

Proposal	Estimated cost	Estimated after-tax annual dollar advantages	Estimated years of useful life
261	$16,000	$ 2,000	18
262	8,000	2,000	6
263	32,000	8,000	4
264	8,000	4,000	2
265	32,000	6,400	7
266	20,000	3,000	20
267	40,000	12,000	5
268	20,000	10,000	3
269	40,000	10,000	5
270	40,000	5,000	18

a. Compute the present value of the dollar advantages and the profitability index for each proposal. Assume a cutoff rate of return of 10 per cent and no salvage value at the end of useful life.

b. What is the payback period in years for each proposal?

c. What additional information would you want before deciding finally which proposals you would approve?

11-22. The Acme Auto Parts Company was recently asked by the National Aeronautics and Space Administration to produce a series of special machined castings for use in destructive ground tests of rocket-booster equipment. The company has decided to accept the offer and now must decide what machinery it will use to accomplish the job. There are two logical machinery alternatives available. An existing multipurpose machine tool can be overhauled and converted to do the job, or a specifically designed machine can be purchased and the existing machine scrapped.

The existing machine cost $30,000 three years ago and has an accounting book value (original cost minus depreciation expense to date) of $18,000. Because of the different depreciation method employed for tax purposes, the tax book value is only $15,000. The production engineer estimates that the machine could be sold in the used-equipment market for $10,000 but that it would cost $1,800 to dismantle it and pack it for shipment. In order to make this machine ready for the NASA job, Acme Auto Parts would have to spend $20,000 on overhauling and conversion. It is estimated that the redone machine would just last throughout the five-year span of the NASA contract.

The new machine, if acquired, would cost $40,000 when purchased from the manufacturer and would require an additional $4,000 for shipping, installation, and break-in expenses. The engineer estimates that it would have a net resale value of $14,000 after its five-year use in the NASA job. He cannot presently foresee any additional use for the machine by Acme beyond the NASA contract.

Here is a tabulation of estimated operating costs for the two alternatives:

	Existing machine after conversion & overhaul	New machine
Costs/unit:		
Labor	$ 8.60	$ 7.15
Material	20.00	20.00
Material wastage	1.00	.50
Power & maintenance	.80	.70
Taxes, insurance, etc.	.60	.65
Selling & administrative	8.00	8.00
Total costs/unit	$39.00	$37.00

Each machine can produce the 5,000 units in the contract (1,000 per year) over the five-year span. (The contract price per unit is $50.)

a. Which yardstick of economic worth should Acme Auto Parts use to evaluate these two investment proposals? Why?

b. Regardless of your answer to *a* above, calculate the payback period and the profitability index for each alternative. Assume a cutoff rate of return of 10 per cent.

c. After making the calculations in *b*, would you change your mind about your answer to *a*? Why?

d. As a manager, which investment would you make?

11-23. Johnson and Jones Company, a small manufacturer of nuts, bolts, and screws primarily for the auto industry, desires to increase its productive capacity and at the same time replace some inefficient facilities. It intends to accomplish this by selling an existing plant (complete with machinery) to a local manufacturer who wants to acquire the facilities. Johnson and Jones Company would then build and equip a new plant more suited to its predicted future needs. It is clearly recognized, however, that the increased capacity of the new plant would be beyond the present market limits enjoyed by the firm. If the production resulting from the increased capacity is to be sold, it will require additional sales effort as well as a slight reduction in prices.

A study made of the proposal indicated the following:

Cost of new plant & equipment (complete)	$1,500,000
Net book value (and tax book value) of existing facility ($200,000 original cost)	60,000
Estimated net proceeds from sale of existing facility	75,000

	Existing facility	Proposed facility
Annual production (in gross[a])	4,000,000	6,000,000
Costs/gross:		
Labor	$.2760	$.2460
Materials	.4550	.4500
Supplies, repairs, & power	.0640	.0595
Taxes, insurance, etc.	.0350	.0200
Selling & administrative expenses	.1500	.1650
Depreciation (5% of cost/year)	.0025	.0125
Total costs/gross	$.9825	$.9530

[a] One gross equals twelve dozen.

The selling price for present production is $1.20 per gross. It is estimated that in order to sell the proposed volume of production, the average price will have to be reduced to $1.15 per gross. (Additional selling costs are included in the increased per-gross charge listed above.)

If you were a member of the screening body of this company, would you recommend the proposed expenditure if the company requires a time-adjusted rate of return of 8 per cent after taxes? (You should limit your analysis to the first six years of the new plant's life, since this is the remaining lifetime for the old facility. Assume that the new plant can be sold for $1.05 million in cash after the six years.)

APPENDIX 11A

The Time Value of Money

The *time value of money* can best be explained by an example. Clearly, $100 cash in hand today is more valuable than the promise of the receipt of $100 at any future time, say one year from today, even if we assume that the promise is 100 per cent certain. This is true because the $100 cash can be invested at interest for one year and the sum will exceed $100 by the amount of interest earned. Understanding the time value of money is essentially a matter of understanding compound interest.

Future Amount of a Single Sum

If we want to know *how much* more valuable $100 cash in hand is compared with the certain promise to receive $100 in one year, we must specify the conditions under which the $100 will be invested, i.e., an interest rate and an interest period. For instance, if $1\frac{1}{2}$ per cent is to be added to the amount on hand each three-month period, the value in one year of $100 deposited January 1 will be given by the formula $P_n = P_0(1 + i) = \$100(1.0614) = \$106.14$, where P_n is the accumulated amount at the end of the year, P_0 is the amount deposited ($100), i is the interest rate per period ($1\frac{1}{2}$ per cent), and n is the number of periods. The formula and arithmetic proof are derived as shown below:

The amount P_1 in the savings account at the end of the first quarter is

(1) $P_1 = P_0(1 + i)^1 = \$100(1.015) = \$101.50$

At the end of the second period it is

(2) $P_2 = P_1(1 + i)^1 = \$101.50(1.015) = \$103.02$

Substituting for P_1 from (1), we obtain

(3) $P_2 = P_1(1 + i)^1(1 + i)^1 = P_0(1 = i)^2$

and at the end of the third period, the amount in the savings account is

(4) $P_3 = P_2(1 + i)^1 = \$103.02(1.015) = \$104.57$

Substituting for P_2 from (3), we have

(5) $P_3 = P_0(1 + i)^2(1 + i)^1 = P_0(1 + i)^3$

At the end of the fourth period, the sum is

(6) $P_4 = P_3(1 + i)^1 = \$104.57(1.015) = \$106.14$

Substituting for P_3 from (5), we get

$$P_4 = P_0(1 + i)^3(1 + i) = P_0(1 + i)^4$$

Interest rates are usually stated on an annual basis (per annum) and annual rates should be assumed if no interest period is specified. Although the phrase is not literally accurate, the above interest rate is usually described as "6 per cent, compounded quarterly." As a result of the quarterly compounding, the effective interest rate is the equivalent of 6.14 per cent on an annual basis.

Since exponential functions are awkward to work with, and since compound interest calculations are quite common, interest tables have been prepared to permit easy calculation of future amounts and present values. Table I° gives the future amount of $1 on deposit at various rates of interest and for various numbers of interest periods. For example, the tabular amount for four interest periods at $1\frac{1}{2}$ per cent† is 1.0615, which produces the answer $1.06 when multiplied by $1.

Here are some examples illustrating the use of Table I:

1. Find the value of $1 at the end of ten years if interest is earned at the rate of 8 per cent.

Answer: $P_n = P_0(1 + i)^n = \$10(1.08)^{10} = \$1(2.1589) = \$2.16$

2. If $10 is left on deposit in a savings bank paying 6 per cent, compounded semiannually, what will be the accumulated amount at the end of four years?

Answer: $P_n = P_0(1 + i)^n = \$10(1 + .03)^8 = \$10(1.2668) = \$12.67$

3. A savings plan promises depositors that it will "double your money" at the end of six years. What is the approximate effective rate of interest (assuming an annual basis, and semiannual compounding)?

Answer: On the row for twelve interest periods in Table I, the tabular amount nearest 2.0000 is in the 6 per cent column, meaning that the effective interest is 6 per cent for each semiannual period. Expressed as an annual rate, this is 12 per cent compounded semiannually.

Present Value of a Future Amount

Present values are of great usefulness to accountants, since many accounting valuations and business decisions are based on present value computations. Basically the problem is to determine the value *now* of an amount of money to be received or paid in the future. As in the illustration above, we must specify

---

° All tables for the computation of the time value of money appear at the end of this appendix.
† Since Table I has only 1 per cent and 2 per cent columns, the amount of $1 at $1\frac{1}{2}$ per cent for four periods is approximated by interpolation, which in this case is the midpoint between 1.0406 in the 1 per cent column, and 1.0824 in the 2 per cent column.

the interest rate and the compounding period. Then we can answer questions such as, How much must be deposited now in a savings account paying 6 per cent, compounded semiannually to accumulate to $100 in two years? The formula $P_n = P_0(1 + i)^n$ applies here, except that the future amount P_n is known to be $100 and P_0, the present value, is the unknown. Solving this equation for P_0, we get

$$P_0 = \frac{P_n}{(1 + i)^n}, \text{ and Table I gives us } \frac{\$100}{1.1255} = \$88.85$$

as an answer to the question. In other words, $88.85 is the *present value* of $100 two years hence, at 6 per cent interest, compounded semiannually.

Table II provides present values of $1 at various rates of interest for various numbers of periods where $P_n = \$1$ so that $P_0 = 1/(1+i)^n$. These amounts are the reciprocals of the amounts in Table I. In manual calculations, it is slightly easier to multiply by a Table II figure than it is to divide by a Table I figure to obtain the present value.

Some examples illustrating the use of Table II follow:

1. How much should you invest for the right to receive $1,000 one year from now if you wish to earn at least 8 per cent, compounded quarterly, on the amount of your investment?

Answer: $P_0 = \dfrac{P_n}{(1+i)^n} = \$1,000(.9238) = \$923.80$ is the maximum investment.

2. On January 1 you sell land to a buyer who agrees to pay $10,000 cash now and $10,000 one year from now. If the interest rate is 8 per cent, what is the sales price of the land?

Answer: $10,000 + $10,000 × .9259 = $19,259.

3. You purchase an automobile with the option of paying $3,000 cash now or $3,600 one year from now. What annual rate of interest is implied if you choose the latter method of payment?

Answer: (Using Table I) $P_n = P_0 (1+i)^n$, or $\dfrac{P_n}{P_0} = (1+i)^n = 1.2(n=1)$

(Using Table II) $\dfrac{P_0}{P_n} = \dfrac{1}{(1+i)^n} = \dfrac{3,000}{3,600} = .8333(n=1)$

The first row of Table I yields 1.2 in the 20 per cent column. The first row of Table II yields .8333 (the reciprocal of 1.2) in the 20 per cent column. The answer is of course 20 per cent, which was obvious by simply examining the facts of the problem.

It should be noted that the interest rate is always expressed using P_0, the present value, as a base rather than P_n, regardless of which variable, P_0 or P_n, is the independent variable and which is the dependent variable.

Future Amounts of Annuities

Tables III and IV contain factors for computing the future amounts and present values, respectively, of *ordinary annuities*. An ordinary annuity is a series of *equal* sums of money to be paid or received at the *ends* of interest periods that occur at regular intervals. In other types of annuities the sum is paid at the *beginning* of each interest period, or is paid only at the end of each two or more interest periods. These latter annuities are not considered here.

Table III is designed to answer such questions as, If $100 is deposited at the end of each quarter in a savings account paying 8 per cent interest, compounded quarterly, how much (including the eighth deposit) will be in the account at the end of two years? This problem can be solved, using Table I, by summing the future amounts of the first seven deposits and adding $100 for the last one. But the same answer can be achieved much more quickly when Table III is used: the amount of the annuity of $1 per period, where i is 2% and $n=8$, is 8.5830. This means that $1 deposited at the end of each period in a fund accumulating interest at 2 per cent per period will amount to $8.583 at the end of the eighth period. Therefore, $100 deposited at the end of each period will amount to $858.30 at the end of the eighth period, including the eighth deposit, which is made at the time of the valuation. Notice that the *amount* of an ordinary annuity of eight payments involves only seven interest periods, since the deposits are made only at the end of each period.

Exhibit 11A–1 will help illustrate the relationship between Table III and Table I. In this exhibit, time runs from left to right, with interest periods and deposits at the end of each interest period as shown.

EXHIBIT 11A-1

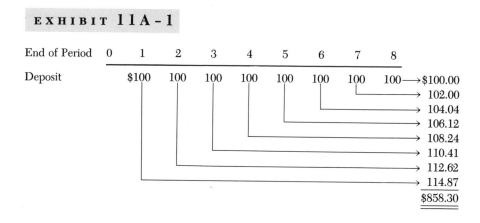

End of Period	0	1	2	3	4	5	6	7	8	
Deposit		$100	100	100	100	100	100	100	100→	$100.00
									→	102.00
									→	104.04
									→	106.12
									→	108.24
									→	110.41
									→	112.62
									→	114.87
										$858.30

The accumulated amount of each of the deposits is obtained by multiplying the appropriate tabular amount from Table I by $100. The sum of these is the same as the figure derived from Table III ($\times$ $100).

Other examples illustrating the use of Table III follow:

1. A man wishes to set aside $1,000 of his earnings each year for retirement. If he deposits $1,000 cash each birthday, beginning with his fifty-sixth, in a fund that pays interest at 8 per cent compounded annually, how much will be in the fund on his sixty-fifth birthday? On his seventieth birthday?

Answers: $14,486.60 and $27,152.10 respectively, assuming that he makes a $1,000 deposit on his sixty-fifth birthday and on his seventieth birthday, immediately before the amounts on deposit in the fund are calculated.

2. You wish to accumulate a $15,000 fund by December 31, 19x5. How much will you have to deposit annually, beginning December 31, 19x1, in a fund to accumulate to this amount if the fund pays 4 per cent interest compounded annually? If it pays 6 per cent?

Answers: Approximately $2,770 per year at 4 per cent interest, or $2,661 at 6 per cent interest, including the deposit made on December 31, 19x5.

3. A man deposits $100 in a fund on the day his grandson is born and $100 annually thereafter, up to and including the grandson's twenty-first birthday. If the fund pays 6 per cent interest compounded annually, how much will be in the fund at that time? (Note that there are actually twenty-two deposits made.)

Answer: $4,339.23

Present Values of Annuities

Table IV gives the present value of ordinary annuities of $1 per period. It shows the sum of the present values of the individual $1 amounts in Table II for the appropriate interest rate and number of periods. The date of valuation of the annuity is the *beginning* of the *first* period rather than the *end* of the *last* period, as in Table III. Table IV is designed to answer such questions as, What single sum must be deposited in a fund on January 1, 19x1, to permit five annual withdrawals of $1,000 each, beginning on December 31, 19x1, assuming the fund pays 6 per cent compounded annually? The answer obtained from Table IV ($n = 5$, $i = 6\%$), multiplied by $1,000, is $4,212.40. The solution is shown diagramatically in Exhibit 11A–2.
Present values of individual payments are computed by multiplying the tabular amounts in Table II by $1,000. Notice that the number of interest periods and the number of payments are the same in the case of present values (as contrasted with future amounts of ordinary annuities, as in Table III), since valuation is made at the beginning of the first period.
    Other illustrations of the use of Table IV follow:

1. A project will return $200 cash at the end of each of the next five years. At the end of the fifth year it will be worthless. How much should I pay for this project if I wish to earn 8 per cent (compounded annually) on my investment?

Answer: From Table IV, for $n = 5$, $i = 8$, the answer is 3.9927($200), or $798.54.

EXHIBIT 11A-2

Date	1/1/x1	12/31/x1	12/31/x2	12/31/x3	12/31/x4	12/31/x5
Withdrawals		$1,000	$1,000	$1,000	$1,000	$1,000

$ 943.40←⎯⎯⎯⎯⎯⎯⎯⎯⎯⎯⎯⎯⎯⎯⎯
   890.00←⎯⎯⎯⎯⎯⎯⎯⎯⎯⎯⎯⎯⎯⎯⎯⎯⎯⎯⎯⎯
   839.60←⎯⎯⎯⎯⎯⎯⎯⎯⎯⎯⎯⎯⎯⎯⎯⎯⎯⎯⎯⎯⎯⎯⎯⎯
   792.10←⎯⎯⎯⎯⎯⎯⎯⎯⎯⎯⎯⎯⎯⎯⎯⎯⎯⎯⎯⎯⎯⎯⎯⎯⎯⎯⎯⎯
   747.30←⎯⎯⎯⎯⎯⎯⎯⎯⎯⎯⎯⎯⎯⎯⎯⎯⎯⎯⎯⎯⎯⎯⎯⎯⎯⎯⎯⎯⎯⎯⎯⎯
$4,212.40

2. How much should I have on deposit on my fiftieth birthday in a fund that pays 6 per cent interest, compounded annually, if I wish to withdraw $1,000 annually on my birthday for ten years, beginning with my sixty-sixth? This problem is diagrammed as follows:

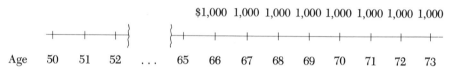

$1,000 1,000 1,000 1,000 1,000 1,000 1,000 1,000

Age   50   51   52   ...   65   66   67   68   69   70   71   72   73

Solving this problem requires two steps. We first use Table IV to calculate the amount that must be on deposit on the sixty-fifth birthday, which is the beginning of the annuity period—one year before the first payment. The tabular amount is 7.3601 ($n = 10$, $i = 6$). So the amount required is $7,360.10 on the sixty-fifth birthday. From Table II, for $n = 15$, $i = 6$, to provide $7,360.10 on the sixty-fifth birthday requires that $7,360.10 × 0.4173, or $3,071.37, be on deposit on the fiftieth birthday.

Problems for Analysis

11A-1. If you deposit a single sum of money in a bank paying 6 per cent interest, compounded semiannually, how long will it take to double the initial deposit? How long will it take at 8 per cent, compounded semiannually? (Ignore fractions of a period). Solve this exercise using Table I and Table II.

11A-2. A series E, U.S. Government Savings Bond costs $18.75 and has a maturity value of $25.00. What is the effective rate of interest if these bonds mature in ten years? In five years? In three years? Solve this exercise, using Table I or Table II, to the nearest $\frac{1}{10}$ of 1 per cent (by interpolation). Demonstrate that the effective interest rate is or is not a linear function of the term of the bond.

11A-3. A loan company advertises 8 per cent interest on personal loans, agreeing to give you $60 now if you sign a note for $100 payable in five years. "Interest" is therefore $8 per year for five years. Calculate the effective interest rate, assuming annual compounding, and comment on the advertising policy of the firm.

11A-4. By January 1, 1980, the X Company must have $1 million in cash on deposit in a fund that pays 6 per cent interest, compounded semiannually. If $350,000 cash is deposited in the fund on January 1, 1971, what additional deposit will have to be made to accumulate the required sum if this deposit is made on January 1, 1976?

11A-5. How much would you be willing to pay for an investment that will return $500 in each of the first two years, $750 in the third year, and can be sold for $1,000 at the end of the fourth year? Assume that you wish to earn 8 per cent, compounded annually, on your investment.

11A-6. By January 1, 19y0, the Y Company must have $1 million in cash on deposit in a fund that pays 8 per cent interest, compounded semiannually. If this $1 million is to be funded by ten equal semiannual deposits in the fund, beginning on January 1, 19x5 (with the last deposit on July 1, 19x9), what will be the amount of each deposit?

11A-7. The E-Z Loan Company advertises "8 per cent simple interest on long-term personal loans up to $1,000". One arrangement provides for the following:

Loan of cash	$1,000
Interest at 8% per year for four years	320
Total	$1,320
Number of semiannual payments	8
Amount of each payment = $1,320 ÷ 8 =	$ 165

Assuming that the money is borrowed on January 1, 19x2, and the first of eight payments is made on July 1, 19x2, what is the effective rate of interest (solve to the nearest whole per cent). Explain the difference between your result and 8 per cent. How much would the semiannual payment be if the interest rate were 8 per cent, compounded semiannually?

11A-8. A person decides to accumulate a retirement fund that will pay him $10,000 annually for fifteen years, with the first withdrawal on his sixty-sixth birthday. If twenty-five equal annual deposits are to be made in a fund paying 6 per cent, compounded annually, and if the first deposit is to be made on his forty-first birthday and the last payment on his sixty-fifth birthday, how much must each deposit be? All funds will remain on deposit until the last withdrawal.

11A-9. An investment will pay you $500 annually for five years at the end of which time it will be worthless. It is a "100 per cent certain" investment and costs $2,000. You have no money, but a bank will lend you the $2,000. What is the maximum rate of interest (compounded annually) you will be willing to pay if your goal is to "break even"? Solve to the nearest whole per cent.

11A-10. A $100,000, 6 per cent, ten-year bond issue matures on December 31, 1980. The $3,000 interest coupon is payable semiannually on June 30 and December 31. What is the equal annual deposit that will pay all principal and interest payments when due if ten deposits are made, beginning on January 1, 1971, in an account paying eight per cent interest, compounded semiannually? (To make this solution simpler, you should assume that four per cent interest compounded semiannually is exactly the same as eight per cent compounded annually. Actually, this is not quite true.)

AMOUNT OF 1 $[P_n = P_0(1 + i)^n$, where $P_0 = 1]^a$

n	1%	2%	3%	4%	5%	6%	8%	10%
1	1.0100	1.0200	1.0300	1.0400	1.0500	1.0600	1.0800	1.1000
2	1.0201	1.0404	1.0609	1.0816	1.1025	1.1236	1.1664	1.2100
3	1.0303	1.0612	1.0927	1.1249	1.1576	1.1910	1.2597	1.3310
4	1.0406	1.0824	1.1255	1.1699	1.2155	1.2625	1.3605	1.4641
5	1.0510	1.1041	1.1593	1.2167	1.2763	1.3382	1.4693	1.6105
6	1.0615	1.1262	1.1941	1.2653	1.3401	1.4185	1.5869	1.7716
7	1.0721	1.1487	1.2299	1.3159	1.4071	1.5036	1.7138	1.9487
8	1.0829	1.1717	1.2668	1.3686	1.4775	1.5938	1.8509	2.1436
9	1.0937	1.1951	1.3048	1.4233	1.5513	1.6895	1.9990	2.3579
10	1.1046	1.2190	1.3439	1.4802	1.6289	1.7908	2.1589	2.5937
11	1.1157	1.2434	1.3842	1.5395	1.7103	1.8983	2.3316	2.8531
12	1.1268	1.2682	1.4258	1.6010	1.7959	2.0122	2.5182	3.1384
13	1.1381	1.2936	1.4685	1.6651	1.8856	2.1329	2.7196	3.4523
14	1.1495	1.3195	1.5126	1.7317	1.9799	2.2609	2.9372	3.7975
15	1.1610	1.3459	1.5580	1.8009	2.0789	2.3966	3.1722	4.1772
16	1.1726	1.3728	1.6047	1.8730	2.1829	2.5404	3.4259	4.5950
17	1.1843	1.4002	1.6528	1.9479	2.2920	2.6928	3.7000	5.0545
18	1.1961	1.4282	1.7024	2.0258	2.4066	2.8543	3.9960	5.5599
19	1.2081	1.4568	1.7535	2.1068	2.5270	3.0256	4.3157	6.1159
20	1.2202	1.4859	1.8061	2.1911	2.6533	3.2071	4.6610	6.7275
21	1.2324	1.5157	1.8603	2.2788	2.7860	3.3996	5.0038	7.4002
22	1.2447	1.5460	1.9161	2.3699	2.9253	3.6035	5.4365	8.1403
23	1.2572	1.5769	1.9736	2.4647	3.0715	3.8197	5.8715	8.9543
24	1.2697	1.6084	2.0328	2.5633	3.2251	4.0489	6.3412	9.8497
25	1.2824	1.6406	2.0938	2.6658	3.3864	4.2919	6.8485	10.8347
30	1.3478	1.8114	2.4273	3.2434	4.3219	5.7435	10.0627	17.4494
35	1.4166	1.9999	2.8139	3.9461	5.5160	7.6861	14.7853	28.1024
40	1.4889	2.2080	3.2620	4.8010	7.0400	10.2857	21.7245	45.2593
45	1.5648	2.4379	3.7816	5.8412	8.9850	13.7646	31.9204	72.8905
50	1.6446	2.6916	4.3839	7.1067	11.4674	18.4202	46.9016	117.3909
55	1.7285	2.9717	5.0821	8.6464	14.6356	24.6503	68.9139	189.0591
60	1.8167	3.2810	5.8916	10.5196	18.6792	32.9877	101.2571	304.4816

aTables I–IV reprinted by permission of Dodd, Mead & Company, Inc., from *Accounting and Economic Decisions* by Donald A. Corbin. Copyright © 1964 by Dodd, Mead & Company, Inc.

TABLE II

PRESENT VALUE OF 1 $\left[P_0 = \dfrac{P_n}{(1+i)^n}, \text{ where } P_n = 1 \right]$

n	½%	1%	2%	3%	4%	5%	6%	8%	10%	12%	16%
1	0.9950	0.9901	0.9804	0.9709	0.9615	0.9524	0.9434	0.9259	0.9091	0.8929	0.862
2	0.9901	0.9803	0.9612	0.9426	0.9246	0.9070	0.8900	0.8573	0.8264	0.7972	0.743
3	0.9851	0.9706	0.9423	0.9151	0.8890	0.8638	0.8396	0.7938	0.7513	0.7118	0.641
4	0.9802	0.9610	0.9238	0.8885	0.8548	0.8227	0.7921	0.7350	0.6830	0.6355	0.552
5	0.9754	0.9515	0.9057	0.8626	0.8219	0.7835	0.7473	0.6806	0.6209	0.5674	0.476
6	0.9705	0.9420	0.8880	0.8375	0.7903	0.7462	0.7050	0.6302	0.5645	0.5066	0.410
7	0.9657	0.9327	0.8706	0.8131	0.7599	0.7107	0.6651	0.5835	0.5132	0.4523	0.354
8	0.9609	0.9235	0.8535	0.7894	0.7307	0.6768	0.6274	0.5403	0.4665	0.4039	0.305
9	0.9561	0.9143	0.8368	0.7664	0.7026	0.6446	0.5919	0.5002	0.4241	0.3606	0.263
10	0.9513	0.9053	0.8203	0.7441	0.6756	0.6139	0.5584	0.4632	0.3855	0.3220	0.227
11	0.9466	0.8963	0.8043	0.7224	0.6496	0.5847	0.5268	0.4289	0.3505	0.2875	0.195
12	0.9419	0.8874	0.7885	0.7014	0.6246	0.5568	0.4970	0.3971	0.3186	0.2567	0.168
13	0.9372	0.8787	0.7730	0.6810	0.6006	0.5303	0.4688	0.3677	0.2897	0.2292	0.145
14	0.9326	0.8700	0.7579	0.6611	0.5775	0.5051	0.4423	0.3405	0.2633	0.2046	0.125
15	0.9279	0.8613	0.7430	0.6419	0.5553	0.4810	0.4173	0.3152	0.2394	0.1827	0.108
16	0.9233	0.8528	0.7284	0.6232	0.5339	0.4581	0.3936	0.2919	0.2176	0.1631	0.093
17	0.9187	0.8444	0.7142	0.6050	0.5134	0.4363	0.3714	0.2703	0.1978	0.1456	0.080
18	0.9141	0.8360	0.7002	0.5874	0.4936	0.4155	0.3503	0.2502	0.1799	0.1300	0.069
19	0.9096	0.8277	0.6864	0.5703	0.4746	0.3957	0.3305	0.2317	0.1635	0.1161	0.060
20	0.9051	0.8195	0.6730	0.5537	0.4564	0.3769	0.3118	0.2145	0.1486	0.1037	0.051
21	0.9006	0.8114	0.6598	0.5375	0.4388	0.3589	0.2942	0.1987	0.1351	0.0926	0.044
22	0.8961	0.8034	0.6468	0.5219	0.4220	0.3418	0.2775	0.1839	0.1228	0.0826	0.038
23	0.8916	0.7954	0.6342	0.5067	0.4057	0.3256	0.2618	0.1703	0.1117	0.0738	0.033
24	0.8872	0.7876	0.6217	0.4919	0.3901	0.3101	0.2470	0.1577	0.1015	0.0659	0.028
25	0.8828	0.7798	0.6095	0.4776	0.3751	0.2953	0.2330	0.1460	0.0923	0.0588	0.024
30	0.8610	0.7419	0.5521	0.4120	0.3083	0.2314	0.1741	0.0994	0.0573	0.0334	0.012
35	0.8398	0.7059	0.5000	0.3554	0.2534	0.1813	0.1301	0.0676	0.0356	0.0189	0.007
40	0.8191	0.6717	0.4529	0.3066	0.2083	0.1420	0.0972	0.0460	0.0221	0.0107	0.003
45	0.7990	0.6391	0.4102	0.2644	0.1712	0.1113	0.0727	0.0313	0.0137	0.0061	0.001
50	0.7793	0.6080	0.3715	0.2281	0.1407	0.0872	0.0543	0.0213	0.0085	0.0035	0.001
55	0.7601	0.5785	0.3365	0.1968	0.1157	0.0683	0.0406	0.0145	0.0053	0.0020	0.0003
60	0.7414	0.5504	0.3048	0.1697	0.0951	0.0535	0.0303	0.0099	0.0033	0.0011	0.0001

TABLE III

AMOUNT OF 1 PER PERIOD $\left[P_n = X \dfrac{(1 + i)^n - 1}{i}, \text{ where } X = 1 \right]$

n	1%	2%	3%	4%	5%	6%	8%	10%
1	1.0000	1.0000	1.0000	1.0000	1.0000	1.0000	1.0000	1.0000
2	2.0100	2.0200	2.0300	2.0400	2.0500	2.0600	2.0800	2.1000
3	3.0301	3.0604	3.0909	3.1216	3.1525	3.1836	3.2464	3.3100
4	4.0604	4.1216	4.1836	4.2465	4.3101	4.3746	4.5061	4.6410
5	5.1010	5.2040	5.3091	5.4163	5.5256	5.6371	5.8666	6.1051
6	6.1520	6.3081	6.4684	6.6330	6.8019	6.9753	7.3359	7.7156
7	7.2135	7.4343	7.6625	7.8983	8.1420	8.3938	8.9228	9.4872
8	8.2857	8.5830	8.8923	9.2142	9.5491	9.8975	10.6366	11.4359
9	9.3685	9.7546	10.1591	10.5828	11.0266	11.4913	12.4876	13.5795
10	10.4622	10.9497	11.4639	12.0061	12.5779	13.1808	14.4866	15.9374
11	11.5668	12.1687	12.8078	13.4864	14.2068	14.9716	16.6455	18.5312
12	12.6825	13.4121	14.1920	15.0258	15.9171	16.8699	18.9771	21.3843
13	13.8093	14.6803	15.6178	16.6268	17.7130	18.8821	21.4953	24.5227
14	14.9474	15.9739	17.0863	18.2919	19.5986	21.0151	24.2149	27.9750
15	16.0969	17.2934	18.5989	20.0236	21.5786	23.2760	27.1521	31.7725
16	17.2579	18.6393	20.1569	21.8245	23.6575	25.6725	30.3243	35.9497
17	18.4304	20.0121	21.7616	23.6975	25.8404	28.2129	33.7502	40.5447
18	19.6147	21.4123	23.4144	25.6454	28.1324	30.9057	37.4502	45.5992
19	20.8109	22.8406	25.1169	27.6712	30.5390	33.7600	41.4463	51.1591
20	22.0190	24.2974	26.8704	29.7781	33.0660	36.7856	45.7620	57.2750
21	23.2392	25.7833	28.6765	31.9692	35.7193	39.9927	50.4229	64.0025
22	24.4716	27.2990	30.5368	34.2480	38.5052	43.3923	55.4568	71.4027
23	25.7163	28.8450	32.4529	36.6179	41.4305	46.9958	60.8933	79.5430
24	26.9735	30.4219	34.4265	39.0826	44.5020	50.8156	66.7648	88.4973
25	28.2432	32.0303	36.4593	41.6459	47.7271	54.8645	73.1059	98.3471
30	34.7849	40.5681	47.5754	56.0849	66.4388	79.0582	113.2832	164.4940
35	41.6603	49.9945	60.4621	73.6522	90.3203	111.4348	172.3168	271.0244
40	48.8864	60.4020	75.4013	95.0255	120.7998	154.7620	259.0565	442.5926
45	56.4811	71.8927	92.7199	121.0294	159.7002	212.7435	386.5056	718.9048
50	64.4632	84.5794	112.7969	152.6671	209.3480	290.3359	573.7702	1163.9085
55	72.8525	98.5865	136.0716	191.1592	272.7126	394.1720	848.9232	1880.5914
60	81.6697	114.0515	163.0534	237.9907	353.5837	533.1282	1253.2133	3034.8164

Note: To convert this table to values of an annuity due (in advance), take one more period and substract 1.000.

TABLE IV

PRESENT VALUE OF 1 PER PERIOD $\left[P_0 = X \dfrac{1 - \dfrac{1}{(1+i)^n}}{i}, \text{ where } X = 1 \right]$

n	½%	1%	2%	4%	5%	6%	8%	10%	16%	24%
1	0.9950	0.9901	0.9804	0.9615	0.9524	0.9434	0.9259	0.9091	0.8621	0.8061
2	1.9851	1.9704	1.9416	1.8861	1.8594	1.8334	1.7833	1.7355	1.6053	1.4568
3	2.9702	2.9410	2.8839	2.7751	2.7232	2.6730	2.5771	2.4869	2.2459	1.9813
4	3.9505	3.9020	3.8077	3.6299	3.5460	3.4651	3.3121	3.1699	2.7981	2.4043
5	4.9259	4.8534	4.7135	4.4518	4.3295	4.2124	3.9927	3.7908	3.2743	2.7454
6	5.8964	5.7955	5.6014	5.2421	5.0757	4.9173	4.6229	4.3553	3.6846	3.0205
7	6.8621	6.7282	6.4720	6.0021	5.7864	5.5824	5.2064	4.8684	4.0386	3.2423
8	7.8230	7.6517	7.3255	6.7327	6.4632	6.2098	5.7466	5.3349	4.3436	3.4212
9	8.7791	8.5660	8.1622	7.4353	7.1078	6.8017	6.2469	5.7590	4.6066	3.5655
10	9.7304	9.4713	8.9826	8.1109	7.7217	7.3601	6.7101	6.1446	4.8333	3.6819
11	10.6770	10.3676	9.7868	8.7605	8.3064	7.8869	7.1390	6.4951	5.0287	3.7757
12	11.6189	11.2551	10.5753	9.3851	8.8633	8.3838	7.5361	6.8137	5.1971	3.8514
13	12.5562	12.1337	11.3484	9.9856	9.3936	8.8527	7.9038	7.1034	5.3424	3.9124
14	13.4887	13.0037	12.1062	10.5631	9.8986	9.2950	8.2442	7.3667	5.4676	3.9616
15	14.4166	13.8651	12.8493	11.1184	10.3797	9.7122	8.5595	7.6061	5.5755	4.0013
16	15.3399	14.7179	13.5777	11.6523	10.8378	10.1059	8.8514	7.8237	5.6685	4.0333
17	16.2586	15.5623	14.2919	12.1657	11.2741	10.4773	9.1216	8.0216	5.7487	4.0591
18	17.1728	16.3983	14.9920	12.6593	11.6896	10.8276	9.3719	8.2014	5.8178	4.0799
19	18.0824	17.2260	15.6785	13.1339	12.0853	11.1581	9.6036	8.3649	5.8774	4.0967
20	18.9874	18.0456	16.3514	13.5903	12.4622	11.4699	9.8181	8.5136	5.9288	4.1103
21	19.8880	18.8570	17.0112	14.0292	12.8212	11.7641	10.0168	8.6487	5.9731	4.1212
22	20.7841	19.6604	17.6580	14.4511	13.1630	12.0416	10.2007	8.7715	6.0113	4.1300
23	21.6757	20.4558	18.2922	14.8568	13.4886	12.3034	10.3711	8.8832	6.0443	4.1371
24	22.5629	21.2434	18.9139	15.2470	13.7986	12.5504	10.5288	8.9847	6.0726	4.1428
25	23.4456	22.0232	19.5235	15.6221	14.0939	12.7834	10.6748	9.0770	6.0971	4.1474
30	27.7941	25.8077	22.3965	17.2920	15.3725	13.7648	11.2578	9.4269	6.1772	4.1601
35	32.0354	29.4086	24.9986	18.6646	16.3742	14.4982	11.6546	9.6442	6.2153	4.1644
40	36.1722	32.8347	27.3555	19.7928	17.1591	15.0463	11.9246	9.7791	6.2335	4.1659
45	40.2072	36.0945	29.4902	20.7200	17.7741	15.4558	12.1084	9.8628	6.2421	4.1664
50	44.1428	39.1961	31.4236	21.4822	18.2559	15.7619	12.2335	9.9148	6.2463	4.1666
55	47.9814	42.1472	33.1748	22.1086	18.6335	15.9905	12.3186	9.9471	6.2483	4.1666
60	51.7256	44.9550	34.7609	22.6235	18.9293	16.1614	12.3766	9.9672	6.2491	4.1667

Note: To convert this table to value for an annuity due (in advance), take one less period and add 1.0000.

Part Three   ALL-PURPOSE
FINANCIAL
STATEMENTS

Persons outside the firm need different kinds of financial information about the firm. Since accounting reports issued to nonmanagers usually become "public" information, and since it is not possible to govern the uses made of them, accountants prepare "generalized" reports consisting of the statement of financial position, the statement of earnings and retained earnings, and the statement of fund flows. These reports are designed to serve the diverse needs of as many nonmanagerial groups as possible. Chapter 12 (and Appendix 12A) and Chapter 13 study the content, arrangement, and terminology of these reports. Chapters 14, 15, and 16 describe the rules, or generally accepted accounting principles, that govern their preparation.

Chapter Twelve GENERAL ACCOUNTING REPORTS

INTRODUCTION

In Chapter 1 we classified nonmanagers as existing and prospective owners and creditors (those with an obvious financial interest) as well as suppliers, customers, employees, and government agencies with some sort of beneficial or overseer relationship to the enterprise. The members of each "outside" group desire information about an enterprise designed to help them draw conclusions and make decisions about the firm. In providing reports to meet these desires, the accountant must choose between two different approaches to supplying information: Should he prepare different kinds of accounting reports designed to meet the particular needs of each group of nonmanagers? Or should a single set of published statements be made available to all users?

Accountants who adopt the first alternative might prepare one set of reports for owners, another set of reports for short-term creditors, another set of reports for long-term creditors (holders of obligations with a maturity in excess of one year from the date of the loan), and separate reports for the various governmental agencies. For example, the owner is primarily interested in the profitability and stability of the enterprise operations. The short-term creditor is interested in the liquidity of the enterprise. The long-term creditor, like the owner, is primarily interested in the profitability and stability of the enterprise operations, because funds for repayment of a long-term loan will ultimately come from profitable operations. Each government agency specifies the type of information that it requires.

The problem is further complicated because the accountant cannot control the use made of the financial statements after they are disseminated for use by the general public. The readers of one kind of report might not fully understand the differences between their report and those used by other nonmanagement groups, and the problem would be magnified greatly when the nonunified accounting reports of one enterprise were compared with those of other companies. Because of the confusion that would result from their widespread usage, "hand-tailored" accounting reports for different nonmanagerial groups are not prevalent in the business world. Instead, managers and accountants rely on a more general method of supplying information to nonmanagers.

The practice of supplying one generalized set of accounting reports for use by all interested groups of nonmanagers is widespread in our country. It is based on the idea that a generally acceptable set of reports will place the same basic information in the hands of all interested parties. Furthermore, if all companies prepare their reports in the same manner, intercompany confusion will be eliminated. Once the basic information is made available to interested parties and is understood by them, they can satisfy their own peculiar needs for information with minor adjustments.

The use of generally accepted accounting principles in the preparation of accounting reports permits one group of nonmanagers to understand the information used by other groups simply because it is presented on the same basis. More important, the use of generally accepted accounting principles for preparing accounting reports for the general public permits a degree of comparability among enterprises of all types, whether they are local pizza parlors or international firms with hundreds of thousands of employees and billions of dollars in revenues.

Most of the generally accepted accounting principles used in preparing the published accounting reports for all nonmanagement groups represent a consensus of opinion among practicing accountants, and their present status is the product of decades of revisions and refinement. The principles relate to both the kinds of information that should be provided and the manner in which it should be presented. It is the purpose of Part III to discuss the importance of these principles and some weaknesses inherent in them because of the generalizing process.

THE ACCOUNTING PROFESSION

Accounting is the process of measuring and communicating economic information so that it may be used to draw conclusions and make decisions. Since information is hand-tailored to fit the needs of each company, accountants who serve only managers need not be familiar with standard accounting procedures and may therefore have many kinds of training and experience. Some corporate controllers (the highest-level accounting officers in an enterprise) have never taken formal college majors in accounting or related subjects. Yet, they make excellent controllers because they have the ability to foresee the kind of information that will be useful to the other managers in their enterprise.

Gathering, analyzing, measuring, and communicating information for nonmanagers in accordance with generally accepted accounting principles, however, requires formal training.

The Certified Public Accountant

Included among the many people who comprise the accounting field today are over 100,000 Certified Public Accountants. It is their primary function to state their opinions regarding the conformity of published accounting reports with generally accepted accounting principles. The nature of this opinion is indicated in Exhibit 12-1, which shows a typical format used by CPA's.

These accountants have not indicated any reservations in saying that the financial statements "present fairly the financial position of the Acme Auto Parts Company as of December 31, 19x1, and the results of operations for the year then ended, and were prepared in conformity with generally accepted accounting principles applied on a basis consistent with that of the preceding year." In some situations it is necessary for the CPA to qualify his opinion. For example, the

ACCOUNTANTS' OPINION E X H I B I T **12-1**

To the Board of Directors and Stockholders
of the Acme Auto Parts Company:

We have examined the Statement of Financial Position of the Acme Auto Parts Company as of December 31, 19x1, and the related Statement of Earnings and Statement of Fund Flows for the year then ended. Our examination was made in accordance with generally accepted auditing standards, and accordingly included such tests of the accounting records and such other auditing procedures as we considered necessary in the circumstances. We made a similar examination in the year 19x0.

In our opinion, the accompanying Statement of Financial Position, Statement of Earnings, and Statement of Fund Flows present fairly the financial position of the Acme Auto Parts Company as of December 31, 19x1, and the results of operations for the year then ended, and were prepared in conformity with generally accepted accounting principles applied on a basis consistent with that of the preceding year.

FERTIG, ISTVAN, and MOTTICE
Certified Public Accountants

Columbus, Ohio
April 2, 19x2

accountant may believe that the financial statements are not fair representations of financial position and operations, or perhaps the enterprise reports do not reflect a "consistent" use of generally accepted accounting principles with the preceding year. The accountant is required by the ethics of his profession (represented by the Code of Professional Ethics of the American Institute of Certified Public Accountants (AICPA)) to indicate clearly those situations in which the accounting reports under examination do not present financial conditions and results of operations fairly.

A favorable opinion by the CPA is not an indication that the accounting statements of the examined firm are "correct." Rather, it indicates that the records have been kept in accordance with generally accepted accounting principles, and the resulting statements are therefore subject to both the favorable and unfavorable aspects of those principles. In essence, the CPA devotes a large part of his efforts to acting as a public conscience in the reporting process between an enterprise management and all other interested nonmanagerial groups. The CPA's opinion is intended to add credibility to managements' financial statements so that third parties (creditors, stockholders, etc.) can rely on them for making decisions regarding the allocation of resources.

In order to familiarize you with the types of accounting reports that are prepared for the nonmanager, this chapter and Chapter 13 will present typical all-purpose accounting reports. The remaining chapters of Part III will discuss the more complex problems associated with measurement of asset and liability items.

GENERAL ACCOUNTING REPORTS

There are four general accounting reports in common use today. Sometimes the four accounting reports are condensed into three by combining the information contained in two of them, but this becomes an organizational matter rather than a change in the concept of presenting information. The four reports are

1. The Statement of Earnings
2. The Statement of Financial Position
3. The Statement of Retained Earnings
4. The Statement of Fund Flows

The remainder of this chapter is devoted to the first three reports; the statement of fund flows is discussed in Chapter 13. (You should refer to Chapters 2 and 3 for a more general discussion of the purposes of the various financial statements and the interrelationship among them.)

Rounding in financial statements. All the financial statements for Acme Auto Parts Company that will be exhibited in this chapter are expressed in thousands of dollars. This means, for example, that rather than reporting gross sales of products as $20,650,420.97, this item is rounded to the nearest thousand dollars, in this case $20,650. In rounding numbers, a digit less than 5 is dropped. If the digit is 5 or greater, the digit to the left is raised by one. In the above example, if gross sales of products were between $20,650,500.00 and $20,651,499.99, the item would be rounded to $20,651.

The process of rounding can be very helpful to the user of financial statements. For example, the user of the statement of earnings for the Acme Auto Parts Company would ordinarily not be influenced by the fact that the net earnings were reported as $1,576,468.32, rather than as $1,576 (thousands). In this example the number of digits reported has been reduced from nine to four. The digits reported on the financial statement have therefore been reduced by over 50 per cent with no sacrifice in the significance or usefulness of the information reported.

THE STATEMENT OF EARNINGS

The statement of earnings of a firm sets forth the revenues earned and the expenses incurred by the enterprise for a given period of time. We are already familiar with the basic concept of the earnings statement because we saw managerial applications of it in Chapters 7 through 10. Exhibit 12-2 shows the earnings statement of the Acme Auto Parts Company for the year 19x5. You will note that the statement of earnings in Exhibit 12-2 maintains the same basic format as that used in Parts I and II of the book. Each heading, subheading, and item in the statement carries significant information to the user of the statement. Some entries require brief explanation.

Heading. The heading for a statement of earnings includes the name of the company, identification of the statement, and the time period involved. Since an earnings statement can be prepared for any desired period, this information is important to the reader.

Gross sales of products. This item represents the total selling price of all goods (or services) sold to customers. Both cash sales and credit sales are included. The term "gross" indicates that this total is the *invoice price* on the bill sent to the customer.

Sales returns and allowances. These are subtractions from gross sales resulting from dissatisfaction of the customer. A sales return represents merchandise returned from customers because of damage or poor quality. Sales allowances are made to customers when it would be impractical to return the goods.

Sales discounts. When a customer buys on credit, he agrees to pay cash at a later date. In order to encourage prompt payment, some businesses allow a discount from the invoice price of credit sales if payment is received within a short time after the sale transaction (usually ten or fifteen days). The discount is usually 1 per cent or 2 per cent of the invoice price. This item represents total discounts taken by customers during the accounting period.

EXHIBIT 12-2

ACME AUTO PARTS COMPANY

STATEMENT OF EARNINGS

For Year Ended December 31, 19x5

(in thousands of dollars)

Gross sales revenues			$20,650
Sales returns & allowances		$ 343	
Sales discounts		187	
Total			530
Net sales revenues			$20,120
Cost of goods sold			11,547
Earnings margin			$ 8,573
Operating expenses:			
Selling expenses:			
Advertising		$1,467	
Salesmen's salaries		803	
Payroll taxes & fringe benefits		79	
Traveling		246	
Freight-out		203	
Depreciation—automobiles		47	
Depreciation—equipment		40	
Miscellaneous		58	
Total selling expenses		$2,943	
Administrative expenses:			
Officers' salaries	$1,326		
Office salaries	817		
Payroll taxes & fringe benefits	52		
Traveling	86		
Credit losses	48		
State & local taxes	174		
Insurance	93		
Office supplies	79		
Depreciation—equipment	34		
Total administrative expenses		2,709	
Total operating expenses			5,652
Earnings from operations			$ 2,921
Nonoperating items:			
Other expense:			
Interest		$ 165	
Other income:			
Rent	$ 60		
Dividends on long-term investments	20		
Total income		80	
Net nonoperating expenses			85
Earnings before income taxes			$ 2,836
Federal income tax			1,260
Earnings before extraordinary items			$ 1,576
Gain on sale of equipment		$ 110	
Fire loss		40	
		$ 70	
Less applicable federal income tax increase		20	50
Net earnings			$ 1,626

Net sales. When returns and allowances and discounts are subtracted from gross sales, the residual is net sales, a key figure in the statement of earnings, which will receive attention in later chapters.

Cost of goods sold. This major item of expense is self-explanatory. Remember, however, that for a manufacturing firm, the cost of goods sold is measured by the *manufacturing* cost of the goods sold this period. It may be good at this time to reread those parts of Chapters 7 and 8 that describe this concept in detail. The cost of goods sold for a wholesale or retail merchandising company is measured by the *purchase* cost of the goods sold and is computed as follows:

Beginning inventory	$
+ Net cost of goods purchased	_____
Total cost of goods available	$
− Cost of ending inventory	_____
Cost of goods sold	$_____

Earnings margin on sales. This key item, the result of subtracting the cost of goods sold from net sales, provides one indication of the effectiveness of the firm's pricing policy. This item is sometimes referred to as the *gross margin.*

Operating expenses. This is a broad term representing all expenses that are incurred in the process of earning the *operating,* as distinguished from *non-operating,* revenue of the firm.

Selling expenses. This group of expenses is associated with the marketing and sales-promotion functions of the firm, including distributing the product (or service) to the customer.

Payroll taxes and fringe benefits. The employer's share of social security taxes, federal and state unemployment taxes, workmen's compensation insurance premiums, group life insurance premiums, hospitalization insurance premiums, and pension fund costs are examples of items frequently included in this category.

Depreciation. Long-lived assets, such as automobiles and equipment, are used over a series of accounting periods; a portion of their cost therefore appears as an expense in each period's statement of earnings. Acme's automobiles are classified as selling expenses because they are used by the sales force. Depreciation of equipment is charged against both selling and administrative expenses, according to the proportion of equipment used by each. The portions of equipment and automobile costs not consumed at the end of the accounting period are reported in the statement of financial position as *long-lived assets.*

Freight-out. This item includes delivery expenses incurred by the firm and associated with the sale of merchandise to customers. (Some accountants prefer to include this item under the cost of goods sold. This is erroneous, because these costs are a cost of selling, not a cost of the item sold.)

Administrative expenses. The items in this category are associated with the general office function of the enterprise.

Officers' salaries. Salaries that are not included as manufacturing or selling expenses are considered administrative expenses and are included in this item. The salary of the president, executive vice president, secretary, treasurer, and other purely administrative personnel are examples. The salaries of other officers might be included elsewhere. For example, the salary of the vice president of manufacturing would be among the nonvariable expenses comprising the cost of goods manufactured.

Credit losses.   Unfortunately, not all credit customers pay their bills. This item represents an estimate of the amount of bad debt losses associated with the sales of Acme Auto Parts during 19x5. In this firm, since the administrative personnel are responsible for approving or disapproving a customer's credit before a sale is made on account, credit losses are considered an administrative expense. In some companies, the sales personnel approve or disapprove a customer's credit, in which case losses resulting from uncollectable sales would be reported as a selling expense.

State and local taxes.   Real estate, personal property, and franchise taxes are examples of the items included in this figure. Keep in mind that some taxes, such as the tax levied on manufacturing equipment and inventories, might be included among nonvariable manufacturing expenses in the cost of goods sold category. Similarly, some of these taxes may be treated as selling expenses.

Insurance expense.   Business-interruption insurance, liability and property-damage insurance, bonding of administrative employees, life insurance on key officers, etc., are generally reported as administrative expenses. Fire insurance premiums on real estate and personal property are generally allocated among manufacturing, selling, and administrative expenses according to the relative protective benefits derived by these functions.

Earnings from operations.   Total operating expenses are deducted from the gross margin to arrive at earnings from operations. This item reflects the entire firm's performance from its principal business activities.

Nonoperating items.   This category includes revenue and expenses not associated with a firm's principal business activities. Interest expense is a financing, as distinguished from an operating, expense; interest, rent, or dividend revenue is "incidental" to a manufacturing firm.

Earnings before income tax.   The net result of nonoperating items is either added to or deducted from net operating earnings to arrive at net earnings before income tax. All costs associated with the period's current revenues, except federal income tax, have been deducted.

Federal income tax.   This represents a tax applicable to the $2,836,000 earnings of the corporation. The $1,260,000 tax is on normal operations. The total tax actually paid is $1,280,000 including $20,000 applicable to the extraordinary items.

Extraordinary items.   Accounting problems associated with these items are discussed later in this chapter.

Net earnings.   This figure represents the net increase to the owners' equity in the enterprise, resulting from operations this year, before possible dividend distributions are taken into account.

Multiple-step Versus Single-step Earnings Statements

Exhibit 12–2 is a *multiple-step* earnings statement. This means that the figures are arranged to draw the reader's attention to certain subtotals having special significance for a person trained in analyzing financial statements—items such as *net sales revenues, earnings margin, earnings from operation, earnings before income taxes,* and *net earnings.* This format, traditionally used in earnings statements for managerial purposes, allows a company to report, among other things, the results of the principal business operations (earnings from operations) separately from the results of sideline activities (nonoperating items) and extraordinary items.

These multiple-step statements, however, are considered by many to be unnecessarily complicated for the average reader, who may be interested only in the items of major significance. A condensed statement that presents these items in simpler form is the *single-step* statement, now used for the annual reports of many large corporations. In this format, all revenues are reported first; all related expenses are added together, and the total is then deducted from total revenues in one step. The single-step form sacrifices detailed information for simplicity, and it serves an important purpose for inexperienced readers. The 19x5 statement of earnings for Acme Auto Parts in single-step form is shown in Exhibit 12–3.

EXHIBIT 12-3

ACME AUTO PARTS COMPANY

STATEMENT OF EARNINGS

For Year Ended December 31, 19x5
(in thousands of dollars)

Revenues		
Net sales		$20,120
Other income		80
Extraordinary gains and losses		
(net of federal income taxes)		50
Total revenues		$20,250
Expenses		
Cost of goods sold	$11,547	
Selling expenses	2,943	
Administrative expenses	2,709	
Interest	165	
Federal income taxes	1,260	
Total expenses		$18,624
Net earnings		$ 1,626

THE STATEMENT OF RETAINED EARNINGS

In a statement of financial position, the retained earnings figure represents all past earnings of the enterprise that have not been distributed to the owners in the form of dividends. The relationship between the retained earnings figure at the beginning of an accounting period and the retained earnings figure at the end of the accounting period is given by:

Retained earnings at beginning of accounting period
+ Net earnings for period
− Dividend distributions during period
= Retained earnings at end of accounting period°

This expression is based on the assumption that net earnings for the period include *all* extraordinary gains and losses. As we shall see below, however, this is not always the case. If Acme Auto Parts had a gain or loss that was recorded in 19x5 but was clearly related to some other year, this item would be reported in the statement of retained earnings, as shown in Exhibit 12-4, rather than in the statement of earnings.

EXHIBIT 12-4

ACME AUTO PARTS COMPANY
STATEMENT OF RETAINED EARNINGS
For Year Ended December 31, 19x5
(in thousands of dollars)

Retained earnings, 1/1/x5		$4,262
Additional income taxes assessed on prior year's earnings		73
Adjusted beginning balance of retained earnings		$4,189
+ Net earnings for 19x5 (per statement of earnings)		1,626
Total available for dividends		$5,815
− Dividend payments:		
Preferred stock ($4/share)	$ 8	
Common stock ($4/share)	760	
Total		768
Retained earnings, 12/31/x5 (per statement of financial position)		$5,047

° It is customary in accounting for proprietorships and partnerships to prepare a statement of owners' equity, which includes both invested capital and earnings retained in the business, and therefore differs from the corporate accounting statement, which includes only earnings retained in the business. See the section of this chapter titled "Form of Organization and Financial Statements."

You will note that Exhibit 12–4 leaves no doubt about which factors have affected the retained earnings figure during the year.

Some accountants prefer to present the statements of earnings and retained earnings in combined form. If this were done for the Acme Auto Parts Company, the combined statement of earnings and retained earnings would appear as shown in Exhibit 12–5 (with the statement of earnings in single-step form).

EXHIBIT 12-5

COMBINED STATEMENT OF EARNINGS AND RETAINED EARNINGS

For Year Ended December 31, 19x5
(in thousands of dollars)

Revenues		$20,120
Other income		80
Extraordinary gain		
(net of federal income tax)		50
Total revenues		$20,250
Expenses		
Cost of goods sold	$11,547	
Selling expenses	2,943	
Administrative expenses	2,709	
Interest	165	
Federal income taxes	1,260	
Total expenses		18,624
Net earnings		$ 1,626
Retained earnings, 1/1/x5	$ 4,262	
Additional income taxes assessed on	73	
prior year's earnings		
Adjusted beginning balance of retained		
earnings		4,189
Total available for dividends		$ 5,815
— Dividend payments		
Preferred stock ($4/share)	$ 8	
Common stock ($4/share)	760	
Total dividend payments		768
Retained earnings, 12/31/x5		
(per statement of financial position)		$ 5,047

Reporting Extraordinary Gains and Losses

The reporting of extraordinary gains and losses is a major accounting problem in the area of general-purpose earnings statements. The problem arises from the need for a single figure that can be labeled the *net earnings* of the firm for the year. The multiple-step earnings statement in Exhibit 12–2 includes several earnings figures that accountants consider important for different purposes. But statement users insist on *one answer* to the question What did Acme Auto Parts earn in the year 19x5? They want to use the answer to determine an earnings trend for Acme over a period of years and to compare Acme's earnings with other firms. Therefore, we need a single definition of net earnings that all accountants will agree to use year after year, so that these comparisons will be valid.

At least three exceptional types of revenue and expense items must be considered in defining net earnings:

1. Nonoperating revenues and expenses, i.e., normal recurring revenues and expenses associated with secondary rather than primary activities of the firm. Typical items include financial revenue and expense of firms primarily engaged in industrial activity.

2. Extraordinary or nonrecurring items of revenue and expense. Typical examples include gains or losses from the sale of long-lived assets or investments, and losses from catastrophe not covered by insurance.

3. Prior-period adjustments. These are revenues and expenses that were recorded this year but would have been recorded in a prior year or years if all of the facts had been known at the time.

Although there is considerable argument among accountants over the treatment of type 1 items in performance statements for internal use (see Chapters 7 and 8), there is general agreement that nonoperating revenue and expense should be included in *net earnings* in published reports. In particular, accountants agree that income tax expense applicable to these earnings should be included.

Type 2 and 3 items present much greater difficulty, and accountants disagree about their treatment. There are two main schools of thought:

1. Advocates of *current operating performance* support the view that type 2 and 3 items should be *excluded* from the net earnings computation, and

2. Advocates of *all inclusive* reporting support the view that type 2 and 3 items should be *included* in calculating net earnings.

In an attempt to resolve the disagreement, the Accounting Principles Board of the AICPA has recently suggested a treatment that, in theory at least, is a compromise between these two extremes: It recommends that type 2 (extraordinary) items be included in net earnings and type 3 (prior-period adjustments) items be excluded.° In practice, this compromise position is much closer to the all-inclusive view than it is to current operating performance, because the board defines prior period adjustments in such a way that few items would qualify to be reported in this manner. Exhibit 12–5 shows "additional income taxes assessed on prior years' earnings" as an illustration, but generally items that would qualify

---

° "Reporting the Results of Operations," Opinion of the Accounting Principles Board No. 9, December, 1966 (New York: AICPA, 1966).

as prior-period adjustments would be rare in modern financial accounting. The board also states that extraordinary items should be included in net earnings, but should "be segregated from the results of ordinary operations and shown separately in the income statement, with disclosure of the nature and amounts thereof."°

There is, of course, no ideal solution to this problem. The best to be hoped for is that the questionable items will be adequately disclosed, so that the statement user can include them or exclude them in computing net earnings, as his individual needs dictate. For purposes of individual, short-run comparisons of net earnings as measures of management performance, the authors of this book recommend the current operating performance viewpoint. On the other hand, for purposes of determining long-run earnings trends involving several years, all unusual items should be included in net earnings. Since accountants cannot dictate the uses of the statements, and since the usefulness of published statements seems to be largely for the long run, the all-inclusive view, as interpreted by the Accounting Principles Board, seems justified.

THE STATEMENT OF FINANCIAL POSITION

The statement of financial position is sometimes called the *balance sheet.* It shows the financial condition of the enterprise (using generally accepted accounting principles) at an instant of time (usually the end of an accounting period). In this sense it is like a snapshot taken with a still camera. A snapshot taken as a tree seed is planted in the ground would show only a plot of freshly dug dirt. A snapshot taken a year later would show a young tree in a stage of early development. A third snapshot taken after another year would show a tree in full bloom. The snapshot of the tree in full bloom does not show the growing process that occurred during the year, but it does reflect all that has occurred during the time between the photographs. The statement of financial position of an enterprise does not in itself show what has happened during an accounting period. Instead, it reflects the results of all that has happened to the business enterprise in the same way as the snapshot reflects the results of the growth of the tree. The statement of financial position sets forth logically the relationship between the assets available for use by an enterprise and the sources of the funds that enabled the assets to be acquired.

You will recall that the basic *accounting equation* was expanded in Chapter 3 so that both the asset side and sources side can be more precisely stated in terms of the categories of assets and sources enjoyed by a typical enterprise. The accounting equation, when expanded to reflect the basic forms and sources of assets, would appear as follows:

° *Ibid.*

Current assets		Current liabilities		Owners' equity
+ Investments	=	+ Long-term liabilities	+	+ Capital stock (amounts contributed by owners at time of investment)
+ Long-lived assets				+ Retained earnings (amounts contributed by profitable operations and left in enterprise as additional investment by owners rather than being distributed as dividends)

The typical statement of financial position is actually more complex than this basic equation. Each of the above captions can be further expanded into several subcategories. The statement of financial position of the Acme Auto Parts Company as of the end of a recent operating year is presented in Exhibit 12–6.

Some of the captions found in Exhibit 12–6 require further explanation. Many of the specific titles correspond to those given in the "Chart of Accounts" in Chapter 3. These are redefined here in greater detail because the definitions are more meaningful in the context of the statement of financial position.

Heading. The heading for the statement of financial position includes the same information as the statement of earnings did: the name of the company, the identification of the statement, and the date of the statement. Note that the statement of financial position is prepared as of a specific day, rather than for a period of time.

Current assets. This category of assets includes cash and other assets that will normally be converted into cash or will be sold or consumed during the next operating cycle or the next year, whichever is longer. The operating cycle represents the average time required to buy or manufacture, sell, and collect for the goods or services sold by the firm. If the operating cycle is less than one year, the time period used for classifying assets as current is typically one year; if the cycle is more than one year, then the time period used is the length of the cycle.

Cash. Only cash that is available for immediate use is included among current assets. Checking accounts and miscellaneous petty cash funds comprise the majority of items included in this figure. Cash that is not available for current use, such as that earmarked for the repayment of borrowed amounts, is reported under the investment classification as restricted cash.

Short-term investments. This category consists of marketable securities that the company intends to convert to cash during the next operating cycle. Management frequently invests surplus cash during the slower phases of operations in an attempt to earn a return on cash that would otherwise be nonproductive. Investments that are not marketable or that management does not intend to sell during the next operating cycle are listed among investments. Short-term investments are usually valued at the original cost or the current market value,

EXHIBIT 12-6

ACME AUTO PARTS COMPANY
STATEMENT OF FINANCIAL POSITION
As of December 31, 19x5
(in thousands of dollars)

Assets

Current assets:		
Cash		$ 504
Short-term investments (market value, $496)		483
Accounts receivable	$1,029	
Allowance for uncollectable accounts	69	
Net accounts receivable		960
Inventories:[a]		
Finished goods	$2,565	
Work in process	898	
Raw materials	744	
Total inventories		4,207
Prepaid expenses		160
Total current assets		$ 6,314
Investments:		
Sinking fund for repayment of long-term notes payable	$ 300	
Cash surrender value of life insurance on company president	30	
Investment in stock of Cranbrook Auto Parts Manufacturing Company	250	
Real estate used for investment purposes	625	
Total investments		1,205

Long-lived assets:
Tangible long-lived assets:

	Cost	Accumulated depreciation	Net book value
Land	$ 125	$ 0	$ 125
Buildings	2,176	697	1,479
Machinery & equipment	3,006	990	2,016
Automotive equipment	450	265	185
Total tangible long-lived assets	$5,757	$1,952	$3,805

Intangible long-lived assets:		
Patents (net)	$ 174	
Deferred research & development costs (net)	986	
Total intangible long-lived assets	1,160	
Total long-lived assets		4,965
Total assets		$12,484

[a] Inventories are valued at cost, which is not in excess of market value. Cost was arrived at on a first-in, first-out basis.

ACME AUTO PARTS COMPANY (CONT.)

Liabilities and Owners' Equity

Liabilities:		
Current liabilities:		
Accounts payable		$ 1,065
Notes payable		150
Accrued interest payable		83
Prepaid rentals		5
Other accrued expenses		346
Federal income taxes payable		910
Total current liabilities		$ 2,559
Long-term liabilities:		
5½% note payable (due 7/1/y5)		3,000
Total liabilities		$ 5,559
Owners' equity:		
Capital stock:		
Preferred stock (8% cumulative non-participating, par value $50; authorized and issued 2,000 shares)	$ 100	
Common stock (no-par value; authorized and issued 200,000 shares, with 10,000 kept in treasury)	2,000	
Total stock	$2,100	
Retained earnings[b]	5,047	
Total owners' equity	$7,147	
− Cost of treasury stock (common)	222	
Net owners' equity		6,925
Total liabilities and owners' equity		$12,484

[b] The contract relating to the 5½ per cent note payable, due July 1, 19y5, provides that dividend payments to stockholders may not exceed 50 per cent of current earnings in any year.

whichever is lower. In Exhibit 12–6 the market value, which was in excess of cost as of December 31, 19x5, was reported parenthetically. Parenthetical reporting of this type makes the financial statements more informative and useful to the user. If the market value (on December 31, 19x5) of the short-term investments were lower than their cost, the market value would have been the basis for valuation.

Accounts receivable. This item represents amounts owed to the company by its customers. These accounts are the result of normal operations and are seldom documented by formal evidence of debt. A debt evidenced by a promissory note or some other formal document is normally reported in notes receivable. An estimate of the amount of accounts receivable that will not be collected— "allowance for uncollectable accounts"—is generally deducted from accounts receivable to show the anticipated amount collectable. Past experiences of the enterprise provide the basis for this estimate.

Inventories. Inventories, like short-term investments, are valued at cost or market value, whichever is lower (in this case, cost). The raw materials inventory is valued at the cost of the items that have been purchased from suppliers but have not entered the manufacturing process by the end of the accounting period. The work in process inventory is valued at the costs of the raw materials, labor, and overhead associated with the items that have entered the manufacturing process but have not been completed by the end of the accounting period. The inventory of finished goods is valued at the total costs associated with the items that are ready for sale.

As earlier discussion has indicated, the value placed on ending inventory affects the figure for cost of goods sold on the statement of earnings. Errors in the ending inventory will also be reflected in cost of goods sold, and therefore net earnings, for the period ended that date.

Prepaid expenses.   These assets result from expenditures that usually will be used up in the next accounting period. Examples are prepaid rent, prepaid advertising, and prepaid insurance. These items possess value to a business because they will benefit future operations.

Investments.   Assets that do not fit the current asset or the long-lived asset category are listed as investment. These are assets that are used in the secondary rather than the primary activities of the firm, and the revenue from them is classified in the earnings statement as nonoperating revenue.

Sinking fund for repayment of long-term notes payable.   This represents a specific fund held in trust by a local bank. The purpose of this fund is to accumulate money to repay the long-term notes payable when they mature in 19x5. The bank trustee may keep the funds in the form of savings deposits within his bank, or if so empowered in his contract, he may invest the money in other types of investments designed to mature by 19x5. The Acme Auto Parts Company adds to this fund every year according to its ability and according to the terms of the long-term notes.

Cash surrender value of life insurance on the company president.   A company will frequently insure the life of its key employees. If such an employee dies, the company may then use the proceeds of the insurance policy to help it through the transition period until the organizational gap left by the death of the valuable employee is satisfactorily filled. The cash surrender value is the amount that could be collected at this time if the policy were cancelled.

Investment in stock of the Cranbrook Auto Parts Manufacturing Company.   This represents an investment in the stock of another corporation. As indicated under short-term investments, if the company does not intend to sell the investment within the next operating cycle or if the investment is not readily marketable, it should not be classified as a current asset. Stocks of this type may be held for investment and/or control purposes. Acme Auto Parts Company is holding this investment with an eye toward a possible merger in the years ahead.

Investment in real estate used for investment purposes.   Long-lived assets that are not used in the operations of the business are also classified as investment assets. The title of this item is self-explanatory.

Long-lived assets.   Assets that are relatively long lived, not intended for resale, and used in the operations of the business are classified in this category.

Long-lived assets are generally valued on the statement of financial position at original cost, adjusted for portions already used up in past accounting periods.

Tangible long-lived assets.   Assets such as real estate, buildings, equipment, and automobiles that possess bodily substance. Land, considered to have an unlimited life, is generally valued at cost. Buildings, machinery and equipment, and automobiles are generally valued at cost minus accumulated depreciation. *Accumulated depreciation* indicates the portion of the asset used up (charged as expenses) in prior accounting periods, and it gives some indication of when the asset might need replacement.

Intangible long-lived assets.   These include legal rights, privileges, and competitive advantages that are useful to the enterprise. Patents, copyrights, franchises, trademarks, goodwill, organization costs, leaseholds, and deferred research and development costs are examples of this type of asset. Intangible assets that have an unlimited life, such as goodwill (in certain cases) and perpetual franchises, are valued at original cost. Intangible assets that have a limited life, such as patents, copyrights, organization costs, leaseholds, and deferred research and development costs are valued at cost minus amortization to date. *Amortization* is the process of allocating the cost of intangible long-lived assets to those accounting periods whose revenues benefit from using the asset. The accumulated amortization figure is usually not shown in the statement of position, as depreciation of tangible assets is. Instead, intangible assets are reported at net cost because the age of the assets and the portion already used up have less significance than in the case of tangible assets.

Patents.   A patent is a temporary monopoly granted by the federal government allowing the recipient to control an invention for seventeen years. Patent costs include legal fees, cost of drawings and models, development expenditures, and patent fees. As indicated above, patents are valued on the statement of financial position at cost less amortization to date.

Deferred research and development costs.   Costs associated with secret processes, development of new products or resources, and the discovery of cost-cutting techniques are included in this figure.

Current liabilities.   Liabilities that come due within the operating cycle or one year, whichever is longer, are classified as *current liabilities.* Amounts owed that do not become due within this period are classified as *long-term liabilities.* As amounts classified as long-term liabilities become due and payable within this period, they are transferred to the category of the current liabilities.

Accounts payable.   Claims of suppliers are reflected in accounts payable. This item represents the company's position as a purchaser of goods and services, whereas accounts receivable represents its position as a seller.

Notes payable.   These are short-term claims of creditors that are evidenced by a formal document, such as a promissory note.

Accrued interest payable.   This represents the interest on the $5\frac{1}{2}$ per cent note from the date of the last interest payment, July 1, 19x5, to the date of the financial position statement, December 31, 19x5.

Rentals collected in advance.   Cash has been received from the tenant for the January, 19x6, rental of the real estate held for investment purposes. The receipt is reflected as a liability rather than as revenue for 19x5, because the rent was not earned in 19x5. The rental receipt is reflected as a current liability because the company has an obligation as of December 31, 19x5, to provide the rental service during January 19x6. The performance of this service will require the use of assets for the payment of 19x6 operating expenses. In January 19x6, when the service is performed, this amount will be transferred from the liability category to the revenue classification "rental income" and will be included in the 19x6 statement of earnings.

Other accrued expenses.   Payroll taxes payable to the federal and various state governments, real estate taxes, personal property taxes, sales taxes, and wages are examples of incurred expenses for which payment has yet to be made.

Federal income taxes payable.   The amount payable to the federal government for federal taxes on 19x5 earnings is shown in this item. The current provision for federal income taxes on the statement of earnings exceeds the federal income taxes payable by approximately $300,000 because a portion of the taxes were paid in advance during 19x5.

Owners' equity.   This represents the ownership in the firm by the stockholders, resulting either from investments made or through earnings retained in the business.

Capital stock.   This category generally represents the amount received by a corporation from the sale of stock. *Preferred stock* and *common stock* are two classes of stock representing different types of ownership interest. The terms "par," "no-par," "cumulative," and "nonparticipating" describe the specific nature of the rights held by that class of owners. Authorized stock refers to the amount of stock specified in the corporate charter that is granted by the state government. The term "issued shares" refers to the amount of the authorized stock that has been issued to the stockholders.

Retained earnings.   This item indicates the total amount of all current and prior periods' earnings that have not been distributed to the owners in the form of dividends. The contract governing long-term notes payable can, as footnote *b* indicates, restrict the amount of dividends that the board of directors can distribute. The board of directors itself can impose limits on distributions if it desires to use its assets for plant expansions or the payment of liabilities.

Treasury stock.   This item represents stock that has been issued and reacquired by the corporation. It is usually retired, or perhaps reissued, as in the case of bonuses or stock-option plans for employees. In this situation there are 190,000 shares of common stock outstanding (200,000 shares issued minus 10,000 shares of treasury stock). Only outstanding shares participate in dividend distributions. The repurchase cost of the 10,000 shares of common stock held as treasury stock is deducted from the total owners' equity because it represents a reduction in that equity.

THE COMPARATIVE STATEMENT

Users of generalized accounting reports often desire to compare the financial information of the current accounting period with that of preceding periods so that trends as well as significant changes can be conveniently noted. A comparative accounting report provides information for one or more preceding periods alongside that of the current period. Exhibit 12–7 is a comparative statement of financial position for the Acme Auto Parts Company. The information as of December 31, 19x5, is the same as that previously presented in Exhibit 12–6,

EXHIBIT 12-7

ACME AUTO PARTS COMPANY
COMPARATIVE STATEMENT OF FINANCIAL POSITION
As of December 31, 19x5 and 19x4
(in thousands of dollars)

Assets	19x5	19x4
Current assets:		
Cash	$ 504	$ 352
Short-term investments	483	175
Accounts receivable (net)	960	852
Inventories	4,207	3,867
Prepaid expenses	160	170
Total current assets	$ 6,314	$ 5,416
Investments:		
Sinking fund	$ 300	$ 225
Cash surrender value of life insurance policy on company president	30	22
Investment in stock of Cranbrook Auto Parts Manufacturing Company	250	250
Real estate used for investment purposes	625	625
Total investments	$ 1,205	$ 1,122
Long-lived assets:		
Land	$ 125	125
Buildings (net)	1,479	1,553
Machinery & equipment (net)	2,016	1,991
Automotive equipment (net)	185	168
Patents (net)	174	191
Deferred research & development costs (net)	986	726
Total long-lived assets	$ 4,965	$ 4,754
Total assets	$12,484	$11,292

Liabilities and Owners' Equity

	19x5	19x4
Liabilities:		
Current liabilities:		
Accounts payable	$ 1,065	$ 956
Notes payable	150	175
Accrued interest payable	83	74
Prepaid rentals	5	5
Other accrued expenses	346	296
Federal income taxes payable	910	746
Total current liabilities	$ 2,559	$ 2,252
Long-term liabilities:		
5½% note payable (due 7/1/y5)	3,000	3,000
Total liabilities	$ 5,559	$ 5,252
Owners' equity:		
Capital stock:		
Preferred stock (8% cumulative, non-participating, par value $50; authorized and issued 2,000 shares)	$ 100	$ 100
Common stock (no-par value; authorized and issued 200,000 shares of which 10,000 shares are in the treasury)	2,000	1,900
Retained earnings	5,047	4,262
Total owners' equity	$ 7,147	$ 6,262
— Cost of treasury stock	222	222
Net owners' equity	$ 6,925	$ 6,040
Total liabilities and owners' equity	$12,484	$11,292

with slight condensing to make the report more readable. Most published accounting reports are in comparative form.

FORM OF ORGANIZATION AND FINANCIAL STATEMENTS

Thus far we have been concerned with the all-purpose financial statements issued for corporations. But corporations are only one of the three basic forms of business organization. There are also proprietorships and partnerships.

The financial statements for proprietorships, partnerships, and corporations are the same except for the owners' equity section of the financial position statement, and the statement of changes in owners' equity. In other words, the principles governing accounting for assets, liabilities, revenue, and expense are independent of the form of organization.

A proprietorship is an unincorporated firm owned by *one* individual. A partnership is an unincorporated firm owned by two or more individuals under expressed or implied conditions as agreed upon by the partners. A corporation is a firm created by a charter granted by the state and is owned by the stockholders under conditions specified in the articles of incorporation. The decision of the owners to operate the firm in unincorporated or corporate form should be based in part on an analysis of the following considerations:

Creation. A proprietorship is formed when the owner commences business activity. There is no formal documentation necessary other than licensing, when appropriate (for example, a taxicab driver-owner). A partnership is created by a contract (preferably in writing) among the partners containing provisions relating to investment, division of earnings and losses, and policy on withdrawal of funds. A contract between partners is referred to as the articles of copartnership.

A corporation is created by filing a formal request with the state indicating corporate name, place of business, original owners, classes of stock, and purpose of business activity.° When this request is approved by the state it becomes the corporate charter. The charter represents authorization by the state government for the corporation to engage in certain specified activities.

Liability of owners. When a corporation receives a charter it becomes a separate entity for legal purposes. The corporation may sue and be sued. Generally, the liability of a corporate stockholder is limited to his investment. This limited liability feature has contributed substantially to the popularity of the corporate form of organization throughout the United States.

Proprietors and partners in a partnership usually do not enjoy limited liability. When a partnership becomes insolvent (cannot meet its obligations as they become due), creditors may look to *any* general partner, regardless of his investment in the partnership. Similarly, a proprietor is liable to the value of all his possessions for debts incurred through his business activity.

Term of existence. The term of a corporation's life is specified in its charter and may be perpetual. On the other hand, a proprietorship or partnership is dissolved in the case of the death, incapacity, or withdrawal of the owner. In large partnerships provision is usually made in the partnership agreement to allow additions or withdrawals of partners without reorganization of the firm.

Transferability of ownership. Ownership of a corporation is divided into transferable units called shares of stock. In most cases shareholders may sell their stock at will without disrupting the activities of the corporation. A partner may sell his interest in a partnership only if the remaining partners agree, and the transaction constitutes the formation of a new partnership. A proprietor may sell his business assets at any time he desires if he can find a buyer.

Distribution of earnings. Earnings of a corporation are distributed to owners in the form of dividends. Dividends are declared by a board of directors elected by the stockholders. Earnings of a partnership are distributed to the

---

° This discussion assumes a profit-seeking corporation, but public corporations (municipalities, etc.) and nonprofit corporations are also created in accordance with the laws of the state.

partners in accordance with the partnership agreement. A proprietorship has no distribution problem.

Federal income taxes. Earnings of a corporation are subject to the federal income tax whether or not they are distributed to stockholders as dividends. In addition, when dividends are declared, the stockholders must pay personal income tax on them. Thus, the earnings of a corporation are taxed twice: first, when the corporation makes them, and second, when the stockholder receives them as dividends.

Generally, proprietorships and partnerships are not subject to the federal income tax. Proprietors pay personal income taxes on business earnings. Partners are required to pay tax on their share of partnership earnings on their personal tax returns whether the earnings are distributed or not. If certain provisions of the Internal Revenue Code are met, a partnership may elect to be taxed as a corporation. If this option is taken, the partnership's federal income tax status becomes similar to that of the corporation.

Financial Statements of Proprietors

In accounting for proprietorships it is impossible to distinguish between contributed capital and retained earnings. All capital items on the financial position statement are shown under the single heading "owner's equity."

Financial Statements of Partnerships

Partners' equity. As with proprietorships, in partnership accounting the distinction between contributed equity and undistributed earnings is usually not made in the statement of financial position. Instead, emphasis is given to the identity and the ownership interests of each partner, as shown in Exhibit 12–8.

EXHIBIT 12-8

FYER AND WATTER
STATEMENT OF PARTNERS' EQUITY
For Year Ended November 30, 19x4

	Fyer	Watter	Total
Balance, December 1, 19x3	$45,200	$36,400	$ 81,600
Investment during the year	0	5,000	5,000
Share of earnings for the year	12,000	6,000	18,000
Total	$57,200	$47,400	$104,600
Less withdrawals for the year	10,000	7,000	17,000
Balance, November 30, 19x4	$47,200	$40,400	$ 87,600

One difference from a retained earnings statement for a corporation, such as Exhibit 12–4, is that details regarding changes in stockholders' investments (other than retained earnings) are not reported for corporations.

The owners' equity section of a statement of financial position for the partnership illustration in Exhibit 12–8 would appear as follows:

EXHIBIT 12-9

FYER AND WATTER
PARTIAL STATEMENT OF FINANCIAL POSITION
As of November 30, 19x4

Owners' equity:		
Fyer	$47,200	
Watter	40,400	
Total owners' equity		$87,600
Total liabilities and owners' equity		$xxxxxx

Unless otherwise indicated, the remainder of this text assumes the corporate form of business organization.

SUMMARY

Published accounting reports prepared primarily for nonmanagers are admittedly highly generalized and summarized. This makes it possible for one set of accounting reports to serve many different groups of nonmanagers. While these reports may not be perfect for any given group, the average degree of acceptability is much higher than it would be if a unique set of reports were created for each interested party.

Accounting reports intended for nonmanagers are prepared according to generally accepted accounting principles. These principles, which we will examine in detail in later chapters, are designed to satisfy most of the people most of the time.

The most commonly employed accounting reports for corporations are these:

1. The Statement of Earnings
2. The Statement of Financial Position
3. The Statement of Retained Earnings
4. The Statement of Fund Flows

The first three reports were discussed in this chapter; the statement of fund flows will be discussed in Chapter 13.

Questions for Review

12-1. What primary interest does each of the following groups of users have in a firm's financial statements?
  a. short-term creditors
  b. long-term creditors
  c. owners

12-2. Why do accountants supply external users of accounting information with a single set of all-purpose accounting reports rather than special-purpose accounting reports?

12-3. What purpose do generally accepted accounting principles serve in the preparation of all-purpose accounting reports?

12-4. What function does the Certified Public Accountant serve in stating his opinion of management's financial statements?

12-5. What purpose does rounding (dropping digits) serve in financial statements?

12-6. Contrast the formats of single-step and multiple-step earnings statements.

12-7. For the financial statement, what are the implications of reporting extraordinary gains and losses from the current operating performance viewpoint? The all-inclusive viewpoint?

12-8. How has the Accounting Principles Board distinguished between prior period adjustments and extraordinary gains and losses?

12-9. Briefly describe the general content of each of the following financial statements:
  a. statement of earnings
  b. statement of retained earnings
  c. statement of financial position

12-10. Define each of the following classifications that typically appear on a statement of financial position:
  a. current assets
  b. investment assets
  c. long-lived assets
  d. current liabilities
  e. long-term liabilities
  f. owner's equity

12-11. What advantages are there in issuing "comparative" financial statements?

12-12. Contrast the partnership and corporate form of organization with respect to

    a. liability of owners

    b. term of existence

    c. transferability of ownership

    d. distribution of earnings

    e. federal income taxes

12-13. Contrast the financial statements of a partnership and a corporation.

Problems for Analysis

12-14. Examine typical annual reports (provided in Appendix 12A) from the following points of view:

    a. Do the words and pictures, along with the accompanying reports, give you enough information to draw conclusions and make decisions about this company? Would your answer be the same if you were an owner? A creditor? The chairman of a regulatory commission?

    b. How much less information would you have had about the company if you had received only the set of accounting reports?

12-15. a. Using the following data, prepare a classified statement of earnings for the U-Like-It Candy Company. The data pertain to the fiscal year ending January 31, 19x5.

Merchandise returned by customers	$ 800
Advertising expense	2,900
Credit losses	900
Freight-out	2,000
Insurance expense	1,100
Depreciation expense—office equipment	700
Depreciation expense—store equipment	1,200
Office supplies	800
State & local taxes	2,100
Office salaries	3,200
Salesmen's salaries	7,800
Traveling expenses	2,000
Rental income	3,000
Interest expense	2,500
Cost of goods sold	68,000

Sales revenues	104,000
Discounts granted to customers	1,200
Provision for federal income taxes	3,000

b. What is the significance of the following items that appear on the statement of earnings?
1. earnings margin from sales of products
2. earnings from operations
3. nonoperating items

12–16. a. Prepare a classified statement of earnings for the Stutz Manufacturing Company from the following data. The statement period is the current calendar year.

Cash & credit sales	$145,000
Capital stock	70,000
Accounts receivable	19,000
Accounts payable	16,500
Advertising expense	3,000
Salesmen's commissions	7,200
Officers' salaries	9,000
Office salaries	4,500
Cost of merchandise for cash & credit sales	82,000
Discounts given to customers	1,200
Fire loss	2,500
Interest income	1,100
Payments received from customers for merchandise not yet shipped	4,000
Dividend payments to stockholders	1,400
Depreciation expense—selling equipment	900
Depreciation expense—office equipment	600
Accumulated depreciation—equipment	9,700
Traveling expense—salesmen	800
Finished goods inventory, 12/31	24,000
Credit losses	1,500
State & local taxes	3,400
Payroll taxes & other fringe benefits	1,800
Office supplies	300
Retained earnings, 1/1	30,500
Provision for federal income taxes	8,800

b. Explain the significance of the time period indicated in the head of your statement of earnings.

12–17. a. From the following information prepare a single-step statement of earnings for the Diversified Corporation for the fiscal year ended March 31, 19x0.

Net sales	$175,000
Cost of goods sold	103,000
Selling expenses[a]	32,000
Administrative expenses	26,000
Gain on sale of equipment	7,000
Rental income	4,000
Dividend income	3,300
Uninsured flood loss	8,700
Provision for federal income taxes	5,800

[a] These expenses have been combined for financial statement purposes.

b. Discuss the advantages and disadvantages of the single-step statement of earnings as compared with the multiple-step statement of earnings.

12-18. The following data pertain to the operations of the Space Age Development Company for the current calendar year:

Sales revenues (net)	$4,150,000
Rental income	120,000
Gain on sale of long-term assets	176,000
Increase due to correction of inventory errors made in previous years	42,000
Cost of goods sold	2,820,000
Selling expenses	467,000
Administrative expenses	378,000
Federal income taxes (current year)	180,000
Loss on sale of short-term investments	79,000
Uninsured fire loss	33,000
Retained earnings, 1/1	946,000
Dividend payments	80,000

a. Prepare a combined statement of earnings and retained earnings.
b. What are the advantages and disadvantages of the combined statement of earnings and retained earnings? Do you prefer a combined statement or separate statements? Give the reasons for your answer.

12-19.

	Beginning of period	End of period
Total assets	$100,000	$143,000
Total liabilities	41,000	49,000
Total owners' equity:		
Common stock[a]	40,000	?
Retained earnings[b]	19,000	?

[a] Proceeds from the sale of stock during the period were $6,000.
[b] Dividends paid during the period amounted to $1,500.

The information above was obtained from the records of the Automatic Vending Company:

a. Compute the net earnings for the period.

b. What is the relationship between earnings, assets, and liabilities?

12-20. Using the following data, prepare a classified statement of financial position for Atlas, Inc., as of December 31, 19x5:

Cash in bank	$1,100
Inventory	3,100
Accounts payable	2,500
Accounts receivable	2,900
Equipment	4,000
Common stock	7,000
Retained earnings	1,600

12-21. a. Using the following data, prepare a classified statement of financial position for Zephyr Enterprises, Inc., for the fiscal year ended November 30, 19x5:

Cash	$10,000
Notes receivable	6,000
Accounts payable	22,000
Common stock	15,000
Preferred stock	5,000
Land	12,000
Accounts receivable	28,000
Inventory	21,000
Equipment	14,000
Notes payable	24,000
Taxes payable	8,000
Retained earnings, 12/1/x4	11,000

b. What were the all-inclusive earnings for the year, assuming that no dividends were declared?

12-22. The following account balances were obtained from the records of Moore, Inc., for the fiscal year ended August 31, 19x5:

	DR	CR
Cash	$ 3,300	
Accounts receivable	8,100	
Inventory	7,500	
Equipment	7,900	
Accounts payable		$ 7,300
Common stock		10,000
Retained earnings, 9/1/x4		9,200
Dividend payments	500	
Sales revenues		4,000

	DR	CR
Cost of goods sold	2,200	
Salaries expense	700	
Rent expense	200	
Miscellaneous expenses	100	
Totals	$30,500	$30,500

Prepare the following financial statements for the fiscal year ended August 31, 19x5:

    a. statement of earnings
    b. statement of retained earnings
    c. statement of financial position

12–23. a. Prepare a classified statement of financial position for the Leisure-Time Corporation from the following data, as of December 31, 19x0.

Land held for investment	$ 5,000
Land used for business	20,000
Unexpired insurance	900
Prepaid rent	1,500
Cash surrender value of life insurance	3,200
Cash in bank	13,400
Accounts receivable	40,600
Accounts receivable (officers)	2,100
Accounts payable	23,500
Note payable (due 6/1/x9)	60,000
Common stock (no-par value; authorized & issued 14,000 shares)	140,000
Inventories (at lower of cost or market):	
Cost	50,000
Market price	54,500
Accrued expenses payable	1,900
Sales revenues received in advance	4,600
Buildings	104,000
Machinery & equipment	96,500
Retained earnings	?
Short-term investments (at lower of cost or market):	
Cost	10,000
Market price	9,700
Allowance for uncollectable accounts	4,600
Patents	8,400
Trademark	700
Accrued wages payable	2,300
Notes payable (due in 90 days)	6,000
Accumulated depreciation—buildings & equipment	40,000

b. What, in your opinion, are the advantages of preparing a classified statement of financial position in lieu of a mere listing of assets, liabilities, and owners' equity?

c. Justify the date indicated in the heading of your statement of financial position.

12-24. Prepare a classified statement of financial position for the Ajax Company as of August 31, 19x0.

Patents	$ 6,600
Sinking fund—cash	1,200
Sinking fund—investments	8,700
Interest expense	3,100
Accrued interest payable	1,300
Preferred stock (par value $10; authorized & issued 1,000 shares)	10,000
Work in process inventory	6,500
Advertising expense	10,500
Rent received in advance	1,000
Automotive equipment	12,000
Cost of treasury stock (common, 1,200 shares)	6,000
Sales discounts	2,400
Federal income taxes payable	9,500
Cash in bank	12,000
Raw materials inventory	14,000
Finished goods inventory	18,500
Prepaid expenses	900
Net earnings for period	9,700
Short-term investments at lower of cost or market:	
Cost	8,000
Market price	7,500
Land	9,000
Buildings (pledged as collateral for mortgage note payable)	70,000
Note payable (due in 6 months)	10,000
Mortgage note payable (due 7/1/x9)	40,000
Accounts receivable	21,000
Accounts payable	24,700
Wages payable	3,200
Common stock (no-par value; authorized & issued 100,000 shares)	45,000
Additional paid-in capital (common)	30,000
Retained earnings, beginning of period	24,100
Dividends paid	4,500
Machinery & equipment	78,000
Accumulated depreciation—building	15,000
Accumulated depreciation—automotive equipment	9,500
Accumulated depreciation—machinery & equipment	42,000
Allowance for uncollectable accounts	1,400
Retained earnings, end of period	?

12–25. The following table computes the cost of goods sold, using both correct and incorrect ending-inventory values:

	Correct information	Incorrect information
Beginning inventory	$1,000	$1,000
+ Net cost of purchases	2,500	2,500
Total cost of goods available for sale	$3,500	$3,500
− Cost of ending inventory	1,200	800[a]
Cost of goods sold	$2,300	$2,700

[a] The mistake in ending-inventory value of $400 is reflected in the cost of goods sold.

a. What effect would the incorrect ending inventory above have on the cost of goods sold for the current accounting period? On net earnings? On retained earnings?

b. What effect would the incorrect ending inventory above have on the cost of goods sold for the following accounting period? On net earnings? On retained earnings?

c. What is the total effect of the ending inventory for the current and following accounting period on net earnings? Retained earnings?

12–26. The following inventory errors were made by Blue Cheese Creamery, Inc., in their ending inventory for the last four months:

	Errors			
	January 31	February 28	March 31	April 30
Ending inventory:				
Eggs	$300	$ 0	$ 0	$0
Butter	0	(400)[a]	(225)	0
Cheese	0	0	(325)	0
Sundries	175	0	0	0
Totals (inventories overstated or understated for month)	$475	$(400)	$(550)	$0

[a] Parentheses indicate understated inventories.

a. What is the effect of these inventory errors in each of the four months above on the cost of goods sold? On net earnings? On retained earnings?

b. What effect do these errors have on the aggregate net earnings for the four-month period?

12–27. Supply the missing data in the following situations:

	A	B	C	D
Accounts receivable, beginning	$	$150	$175	$220
+ Sales on account during period	250		325	300
Total accounts receivable	$	$	$	$
− Payments received on account	280	240		385
Accounts receivable, ending	$150	$175	$220	$

12-28. The Tasti-Delight Ice Cream Company began operations one month ago. Mr. Sligo is the sole stockholder and has asked you, as his accountant, to prepare a statement of earnings for him at the end of the first month of operations. He gives you the following information about his financial position at the beginning and end of the month:

	January 31	January 1
Cash in bank	$ 390	$ 350
Amounts due from customers	875	0
Inventory	2,150	1,600
Prepaid insurance	660	0
Prepaid rent	900	1,200
Accounts payable (for inventory)	$1,200	0
Wages payable	400	0
Common stock	3,150	$3,150
Retained earnings	?	0

An analysis of Mr. Sligo's checkbook reveals the following cash receipts and disbursements for the month:

Cash received from customers on account		$3,500
− Cash payments:		
To creditors on account	$2,350	
For 1-year fire insurance policy (effective 1/1)	720	
To employees	390	
Total cash payments		3,460
Increase in cash during January		$ 40

a. Prepare a statement of earnings for Mr. Sligo for January of the current year.

b. Verify the net earnings reflected on your statement of earnings.

12-29. The following information pertains to Sphinx, Inc., for the fiscal year ended August 31:

	DR	CR
Sales		$125,000
Cost of goods sold	$ 67,000	
Salaries expense	21,000	
Rent expense	12,000	
Other expenses	18,200	
Dividends paid	3,500	
Retained earnings, beginning		10,500
Cash	23,000	
Accounts receivable	26,150	
Inventories	23,940	
Accounts payable		5,100
Common stock		54,190
Totals	$194,790	$194,790

Prepare the following financial statements:

a. statement of earnings

b. statement of retained earnings

c. statement of financial position

12-30. The following information pertains to the Nettles Company for the calendar year ended December 31:

	DR	CR
Cash	$ 1,250	
Service revenues		$ 4,200
Wages expense	1,400	
Accounts receivable	400	
Rent expense	700	
Other expenses	950	
Dividend payments	500	
Supplies inventory	300	
Land	2,000	
Wages payable		50
Accounts payable		250
Buildings (net)	11,500	
Equipment (net)	1,000	
Mortgage payable		11,600
Common stock		3,900
Retained earnings, beginning		0
Totals	$20,000	$20,000

Prepare the following financial statements:

a. statement of earnings

b. statement of retained earnings

c. statement of financial position

12-31. The following data were obtained from the records of the Davis Supply Company for the fiscal year ended June 30, 19x5:

Sales	$4,150,000
Sales returns & allowances	49,050
Sales discounts	50,500
Purchases	2,875,600
Salaries expense	594,875
Rent expense	60,000
Insurance expense	8,500
Utilities expense	19,480
Supplies expense	9,570
Other operating expenses	61,340
Interest expense	30,500
Interest income	2,210
Fire loss (net of federal income taxes)	39,225
Federal income tax expense	190,000
Retained earnings, 7/1/x4	565,000
Preferred dividends paid	10,000
Common dividends paid	58,500
Cash	254,835
Accounts receivable	490,000
Allowance for uncollectable accounts	20,510
Notes receivable	100,000
Inventory, 7/1/x4	475,000
Inventory, 6/30/x5	520,500
Supplies inventory	34,000
Prepaid insurance	21,200
Prepaid rent	5,000
Land	225,000
Buildings	495,000
Accumulated depreciation—buildings	150,000
Equipment	240,500
Accumulated depreciation—equipment	66,520
Accounts payable	50,435
Notes payable	200,000
Other accrued liabilities	75,000
Federal income taxes payable	205,000
Preferred stock ($100 par value, authorized & issued 1,000 shares)	100,000
Common stock (stated value $100, authorized 10,000 shares; issued & outstanding 6,500 shares)	750,000
Paid-in surplus, common stock	63,000

Prepare the following financial statements in good form:

a. statement of earnings (normal-operating concept)

b. statement of retained earnings

c. statement of financial position

12–32. The following data (in thousands of dollars) were obtained from the records of Mergus, Inc., for the calendar year ended December 31, 19x5:

Cash	$ 167
U.S. Government securities at cost	62
Accounts receivable (net)	280
Notes payable (due within 1 year)	22
Accounts payable	110
Accrued liabilities	106
Estimated federal income taxes payable	50
Long-term notes payable	1,871
Preferred stock	80
Common stock	1,448
Retained earnings, 1/1/x5	469
Sales revenues	2,344
Other income	105
Selling expenses	245
Administrative expenses	300
Interest expense	210
Provision for federal income taxes	352
Cash dividends paid	70
Stock dividends paid	125
Land	750
Plant & equipment	3,560
Accumulated depreciation	1,120
Patents (net)	74
Inventory, 1/1/x5	323
Purchases	1,155
Supplies	52
Inventory, 12/31/x5	468

Prepare the following financial statements in good form:

a. combined statement of earnings and retained earnings

b. statement of financial position

APPENDIX 12A

Financial Statements from Industry

In this appendix we present actual financial statements recently published by corporations in their annual reports to stockholders. They are included here to acquaint you with the end product of financial accounting. They will also be used in reference material in later chapters.

The annual reports of most large corporations contain more information of importance to stockholders and other interested parties than is contained in the financial statements. Often, the reports discuss in some detail plans for future activity, including projections going beyond the scope of generally accepted accounting principles. In most large corporations the annual report is the primary (if not the *only*) means of communication between management and non-management.

Federated Department Stores

The Federated Department Stores, Inc., 1970 annual report is a typical example of the highly condensed, general-purpose reporting of our modern U.S. corporate giants. The ten-year summary (pages 452–53) is widely used and gives additional emphasis to long-term trends.

Benrus Corporation and Subsidiaries

The Benrus Corporation and Subsidiaries 1970 financial statements are of particular interest because of the unusual care with which "extraordinary items" are reported, and also because of the prominence given the Statement of Source and Use of Funds.

Nationwide Life Insurance Company

These financial reports of a life insurance company are included here as examples of the strong influence of regulatory agencies on published reports. Note the unusual terminology, particularly in the Condensed Statement of Assets and Liabilities. This report may be useful also in connection with the insurance company illustration discussed in Chapter 7.

R. G. Barry Corporation

The excerpt from the R. G. Barry Corporation 1969 annual report is included here as an illustration of an experiment in financial reporting that may have an important impact on future accounting practice.

Federated Department Stores, Inc.

Consolidated Balance Sheet

Assets

	January 31, 1970	February 1, 1969
Current Assets:		
Cash	$ 50,688,449	$ 53,290,020
Accounts receivable *(page 17)*	386,374,282	345,902,255
Merchandise inventories *(note 1)*	240,046,742	210,419,339
Supplies and prepaid expenses	9,177,556	8,258,923
Total Current Assets	$ 686,287,029	$617,870,537
Other Assets:		
Deferred tax charges	$ 11,390,014	$ 9,228,046
Real estate not used in operations — at cost, less depreciation	26,677,258	12,371,511
Miscellaneous	17,631,293	15,056,036
	$ 55,698,565	$ 36,655,593
Property and Equipment — net *(page 17)*	360,372,502	316,459,225
	$1,102,358,096	$970,985,355

Liabilities

	January 31, 1970	February 1, 1969
Current Liabilities:		
Notes payable and long-term debt due within one year . .	$ 77,399,853	$ 18,012,703
Accounts payable and accrued liabilities	176,592,765	151,950,329
Federal income taxes, current and deferred	75,191,158	72,502,050
Total Current Liabilities	$ 329,183,776	$242,465,082
Provision for deferred compensation	50,323,839	45,701,313
Long-Term Debt, due after one year *(note 2)*	69,531,401	70,792,570
Shareholders' Equity — 43,475,134 common shares outstanding at January 31, 1970 *(page 16)*	653,319,080	612,026,390
	$1,102,358,096	$970,985,355

Federated Department Stores, Inc.

Consolidated Statement of Income

	52 Weeks Ended January 31, 1970	52 Weeks Ended February 1, 1969
Net Sales, including leased department sales	$1,992,668,937	$1,813,771,463
Rental Revenues	6,194,529	4,993,166
	$1,998,863,466	$1,818,764,629
Deduct:		
Cost of goods sold, including expenses exclusive of items listed below	$1,702,115,402	$1,543,306,082
Taxes other than federal income taxes	45,762,656	40,917,253
Depreciation and amortization	26,989,702	24,723,391
Rent expense *(note 5)*	18,547,135	16,856,179
Maintenance and repairs	17,289,229	15,426,844
Retirement expense	13,163,144	12,747,753
Interest expense — net *(note 6)*	5,054,655	2,517,413
Total costs *(note 7)*	$1,828,921,923	$1,656,494,915
Income Before Federal Income Taxes	$ 169,941,543	$ 162,269,714
Federal income taxes:		
Currently payable	$ 80,832,000	$ 77,398,000
Deferred	3,168,000	4,602,000
	$ 84,000,000	$ 82,000,000
Net Income	$ 85,941,543	$ 80,269,714
Earnings per Share of Common Stock	$1.98	$1.85

Accountants' Report

TOUCHE ROSS & CO.
80 Pine Street, New York, N.Y. 10005

Board of Directors and Shareholders,
Federated Department Stores, Inc.

We have examined the accompanying consolidated balance sheet of Federated Department Stores, Inc. and subsidiaries as of January 31, 1970 and the related statements of income, shareholders' equity and source and application of funds for the 52 weeks then ended. Our examination was made in accordance with generally accepted auditing standards, and accordingly included such tests of the accounting records and such other auditing procedures as we considered necessary in the circumstances.

In our opinion, the consolidated financial statements referred to above present fairly the financial position of Federated Department Stores, Inc. and subsidiaries at January 31, 1970, and the results of their operations and the source and application of funds for the 52 weeks then ended, in conformity with generally accepted accounting principles applied on a basis consistent with that of the preceding year.

April 10, 1970   Touche Ross & Co.
                   Certified Public Accountants

Source and Application of Funds

52 Weeks Ended January 31, 1970

Source of Funds:

Net income for year	$ 85,941,543
Depreciation	26,989,702
Disposition of property	17,220,923
Decrease in working capital	18,302,202
Other	9,449,635
	$157,904,005

Application of Funds:

Dividends	$ 42,430,070
Property and equipment	102,574,718
Other	12,899,217
	$157,904,005

Federated Department Stores, Inc.

Ten-Year Summary

Operations *(dollars in thousands)*

Net sales . . . .

Income before federal income taxes . . . .
    Percent of sales . . . .

Federal income taxes . . . .

Net income . . . .
    Percent of sales . . . .

Dividends paid . . . .
Earnings retained . . . .

Capital expenditures . . . . . .
Depreciation . . . .

Taxes other than federal income taxes . .

Per Share of Common Stock[2]

Net income[3] . . . .
Dividends . . . .
Shareholders' equity *(book value)*[4] . . .

Year-End Financial Position *(dollars in thousar*

Accounts receivable[5] . . . . . .
Inventories . . . .
Working capital . . . .

Property and equipment — net . . . .

Long-term debt . . . .
Shareholders' equity . . . .
    Return on shareholders' equity[6] . . .

Statistics

Number of department stores *(at end of year)*
Number of square feet of department store s
    (in thousands) . . . .
Average number of shares outstanding
    (in thousands)[2] . . . . . .

Notes:

(1) The acquisitions of Ralphs in 1967 and Bullock's-Magnin in 1964 were accounted for as poolings of interests. Figures for prior years have not been restated except for the inclusion of Ralphs' accounts in the figures for 1967 through 1964.

(2) Adjusted to reflect 2-for-1 splits on July 5, 1968 and September 9, 1960.

(3) Based on average number of shares outstanding during the year.

(4) Based on number of shares outstanding at end of year.

(5) Before deduction of accounts sold in 1964 and prior years.

(6) Based on the average of the shareholders' equity at the beginning and end of year.

1969	1968	1967[1]	1966[1]	1965[1]	1964[1]	1963	1962	1961	1960
92,669	$1,813,771	$1,680,747	$1,560,663	$1,481,058	$1,401,642	$967,696	$930,009	$886,052	$811,873
69,942	162,270	155,737	143,831	137,143	129,980	88,922	76,633	76,676	67,480
8.5%	8.9%	9.3%	9.2%	9.3%	9.3%	9.2%	8.2%	8.7%	8.3%
84,000	82,000	72,483	67,190	63,691	62,721	45,194	39,447	39,839	34,511
85,942	80,270	83,254	76,641	73,452	67,259	43,728	37,186	36,837	32,969
4.3%	4.4%	5.0%	4.9%	5.0%	4.8%	4.5%	4.0%	4.2%	4.1%
42,430	40,203	35,965	35,423	32,840	31,015	22,068	20,309	18,967	18,043
43,512	40,067	47,289	41,218	40,612	36,244	21,660	16,877	17,870	14,926
02,575	56,918	60,223	55,101	44,133	35,269	19,431	18,795	22,198	16,552
26,990	24,723	22,392	20,452	19,103	18,493	11,809	11,270	10,560	10,033
45,763	40,917	37,433	34,061	30,952	28,634	18,782	18,288	17,136	15,207
1.98	$ 1.85	$ 1.92	$ 1.77	$ 1.69	$ 1.55	$ 1.26	$ 1.08	$ 1.07	$ .96
.97½	.92½	.85	.83¾	.77½	.72½	.63¾	.58¾	.55	.52½
15.03	14.08	13.21	12.13	11.24	10.35	8.98	8.38	7.93	7.43
36,374	$ 345,902	$ 309,848	$ 304,373	$ 283,650	$ 263,679	$207,371	$198,846	$186,286	$174,670
40,047	210,419	194,783	181,216	161,433	150,106	109,297	106,667	99,802	85,311
57,103	375,405	362,642	342,972	336,751	297,159	200,561	188,079	175,806	168,215
37,050	328,831	303,900	274,934	244,979	224,025	130,397	125,548	122,025	112,490
59,531	70,793	72,317	75,657	82,026	62,432	10,662	16,002	18,303	20,678
73,319	612,026	573,512	525,981	487,140	448,666	311,329	289,752	273,649	255,750
13.6%	13.5%	15.1%	15.1%	15.7%	15.5%	14.6%	13.2%	13.9%	13.3%
102	97	98	91	87	84	60	58	54	47
2,595	21,314	20,528	19,369	18,203	17,300	13,870	13,321	12,559	11,624
3,500	43,461	43,392	43,376	43,399	43,446	34,601	34,566	34,475	34,352

Benrus Corporation and Subsidiaries

Consolidated Source and Use of Funds

For the year ended January 31, 1970

Funds provided from:	
Operations:	
Net income	$ 20,634
Add charges to income not requiring funds:	
Depreciation and amortization	364,946
Other charges not requiring funds	370,578
Funds provided from operations	756,158
Proceeds from sale of common stock	1,325,000
Sale of property, plant and equipment (excluding net gain included in net income)	143,276
Working capital of Wells at date of acquisition	108,224
Other—net	2,589
Total funds provided	2,335,247
Funds used for:	
Reduction of long-term debt	428,884
Reduction of other liabilities	330,539
Additions to property, plant and equipment (less mortgage assumed)	353,290
Total funds used	1,112,713
Increase in working capital	1,222,534
Working capital at beginning of year	7,379,675
Working capital at end of year	$ 8,602,209

Benrus Corporation and Subsidiaries

Statement of Consolidated Income and Earned Surplus

	YEAR ENDED JANUARY 31	
	1970	1969
Sales	$27,924,878	$31,975,801
Less sales of discontinued watches and watch components (Note 9)	934,612	
Net sales	26,990,266	31,975,801
Other income	170,721	74,294
Total	27,160,987	32,050,095
Costs and expenses:		
Cost of goods sold (Note 10)	16,705,904	24,857,453
Selling, general and administrative expenses (Note 9)	9,753,941	10,153,464
Interest	1,295,619	1,059,376
Other	10,662	49,378
Total	27,766,126	36,119,671
Loss before federal and foreign income taxes and extraordinary items	605,139	4,069,576
Federal and foreign income taxes—net (credit)	183,635	(419,007)
Loss before extraordinary items	788,774	3,650,569
Extraordinary items (Note 9):		
Income (loss) related to discontinuance of certain watch product lines	400,000	(1,567,576)
Other income (loss)	409,408	(2,807,499)
Total	809,408	(4,375,075)
Net income (loss)	20,634	(8,025,644)
Earned surplus at beginning of year	762,289	8,880,924
Total	782,923	855,280
Dividends ($.15 per share)		92,991
Earned surplus at end of year	$ 782,923	$ 762,289
Earnings per share of common stock (Note 11):		
Loss before extraordinary items	$ .99	$ 5.63
Extraordinary income (loss)	1.02	(6.75)
Net income (loss)	$ .03	$(12.38)

See the accompanying Notes to Financial Statements.

Benrus Corporation and Subsidiaries
Notes to Consolidated Financial Statements

Extraordinary Items

For the year ended January 31, 1970 extraordinary income is as follows:

Related to discontinued watch product lines —Estimated amount recovered, less disposal costs, from sales of inventories of discontinued watch product lines*....	$ 400,000

Other:

Gain on sale of building, net of related tax	$ 216,078
Gain on sale of investment in affiliate	90,879
Credit equivalent to tax benefit from utilization of loss carry-forward	102,451
Total	$ 409,408

* During the year ended January 31, 1969 the Corporation discontinued the production of certain watch product lines and reported as an extraordinary charge the estimated loss to be sustained on liquidation of the inventories of watches and watch components of the discontinued lines. During the year ended January 31, 1970 a portion of such inventories were sold and future sales are anticipated. The estimated amount recovered, less disposal costs estimated to be a pro rata portion of total selling, general and administrative expenses, is $400,000, which has been shown as extraordinary income.

For the year ended January 31, 1969 extraordinary loss is as follows:

Related to discontinued watch product lines — Inventory losses and related net costs resulting from discontinuance of certain watch product lines	$1,567,576

Other:

Inventory losses and related net costs resulting from the discontinuance of the Electronics Division	$ 392,052
Costs relating to the relocation of certain operations	231,139
Cost incurred under prior years' guarantees in excess of provisions made therefor	645,000
Corrections of prior years' pricing errors in inventories	230,000
Write-off of certain leasehold costs previously capitalized	434,176
Net losses from sale and abandonment of fixed assets during current and prior years	358,973
Termination payments to former officers and employees	253,260
Other	262,899
Total	$2,807,499

NATIONWIDE LIFE INSURANCE COMPANY

**CONDENSED STATEMENT
OF ASSETS AND LIABILITIES**

	December 31, 1969	December 31, 1968
Admitted assets:		
Bonds	$192,199,499	$174,058,905
U.S. Government obligations, public utilities and other bonds at amortized cost.		
Stocks	22,951,186	22,864,017
Preferred and common stocks as valued by the law of the State of Ohio or the National Association of Insurance Commissioners.		
Mortgage loans	171,130,244	158,407,451
First mortgage loans on real estate, primarily single family homes.		
Real estate	3,518,511	3,542,959
At cost less depreciation.		
Policyholder loans	20,939,396	16,891,829
Loans to policyholders fully secured by the cash value of policies.		
Cash	2,934,810	2,030,233
Funds held to provide for prompt payment of benefits to policyholders and operating expenses.		
Due and deferred premiums	9,600,282	8,754,705
Outstanding and deferred premiums fully secured by policy reserves.		
All other assets	3,879,191	3,598,188
Accrued interest and miscellaneous assets.		
Separate account assets	24,300,698	24,107,486
Assets of contracts with variable benefits.		
Total admitted assets	$451,453,817	$414,255,773
Liabilities:		
Policy reserves	$306,941,234	$279,919,544
Amounts which together with future premiums and interest will provide full payment of future policy benefits.		
Supplementary contracts	5,323,654	5,899,646
Policy contract claim amounts left to accumulate with interest at request of beneficiaries.		
Policy claims	2,267,219	2,114,582
Claims in the process of settlement and provision for claims not yet reported.		
Policyholder dividend accumulations	46,991,776	41,996,255
Amount of policy dividends left to accumulate at interest.		
Reserve for policyholder dividends	12,840,701	11,507,409
Amount of dividends payable during 1969 to policyholders.		
Tax reserves	1,689,004	1,642,676
Fund set aside for payment of Federal, state, and other taxes.		
Mandatory securities valuation reserve	7,337,946	7,566,154
Reserve for market fluctuation in bonds and stocks.		
Other liabilities	6,537,081	4,990,868
Premium deposit funds, contingency reserves and miscellaneous liabilities.		
Separate account liabilities	23,884,121	23,779,264
Liabilities of contracts with variable benefits.		
Total liabilities	413,812,736	379,416,398
Capital stock		
3,600,000 shares — $1 par	3,600,000	3,600,000
Surplus	34,041,081	31,239,375
Total capital stock and surplus	37,641,081	34,839,375
Total liabilities, capital stock and surplus	$451,453,817	$414,255,773

See accompanying notes to financial statements.

NATIONWIDE LIFE INSURANCE COMPANY

CONDENSED STATEMENT OF INCOME
For the year ended December 31,

	1969	1968
Premium income and other considerations	$77,232,862	$72,241,401
Net investment income	20,351,368	17,752,700
	97,584,230	89,994,101
Benefits to policyholders and beneficiaries	28,251,232	24,414,023
Increase in reserves for future benefits	31,441,218	31,923,652
Operating expenses	18,109,831	16,454,200
	77,802,281	72,791,875
Net income before policyholders' dividend and Federal income taxes...........................	19,781,949	17,202,226
Dividends to policyholders	12,159,250	10,707,683
Net income before Federal income taxes	7,622,699	6,494,543
Federal income taxes	2,557,899	2,132,363
Net income	$ 5,064,800	$ 4,362,180
Net income per share	$1.41	$1.21

STATEMENT OF SURPLUS
For the year ended December 31.

	1969	1968
Balance at beginning of year...........................	$31,239,375	$27,333,265
Additions:		
Net income	5,064,800	4,362,180
Capital gains — (losses):		
Realized, net of taxes	446,355	20,273
Unrealized	(1,104,126)	1,154,532
Other credits, net	321,719	379,711
	4,728,748	5,916,696
Deductions:		
Other charges	535,250	118,250
Cash dividends to stockholders ($.45 per share, $.35 per share in 1968)	1,620,000	1,260,000
	2,155,250	1,378,250
Increase (decrease) in mandatory security valuation reserve	(228,208)	632,336
Increase in surplus	2,801,706	3,906,110
Balance at end of year	$34,041,081	$31,239,375

See accompanying notes to financial statements.

Human Resource Accounting

The information presented on this page is provided only to illustrate the informational value of human resource accounting for more effective internal management of the business. The figures included regarding investments and amortization of human resources are unaudited and you are cautioned for purposes of evaluating the performance of this company to refer to the conventional certified accounting data further on in this report.

During the past year work continued on the development of Barry's Human Resource Accounting System. The basic purpose of the system is to develop a method of measuring in dollar terms the changes that occur in the human resources of a business that conventional accounting does not currently consider.

Basic Concept

Management can be considered as the process of planning, organizing, leading and controlling a complex mix of resources to accomplish the objectives of the organization. Those resources, we believe, are: physical resources of the company as represented by buildings and equipment, financial resources, and human resources which consist of the people who comprise the organization and proprietary resources which consist of trademarks, patents, and company name and reputation.

In order to determine more precisely the effectiveness of management's performance it is necessary to have information about the status of investments in the acquisition, maintenance, and utilization of all resources of the company.

Without such information, it is difficult for a company to know whether profit is being generated by converting a resource into cash or conversely whether sub-optimal performance really has been generated by investments in developing the human resources which we expensed under conventional accounting practice.

Definition

Human Resource Accounting is an attempt to identify, quantify, and report investments made in resources of an organization that are not presently accounted for under conventional accounting practice. Basically, it is an information-system that tells management what changes over time are occurring to the human resources of the business. It must be considered as an element of a total system

"THE TOTAL CONCEPT"
R. G. Barry Corporation and Subsidiaries
Pro-Forma
(Financial and Human Resource Accounting)

Balance Sheet

	1969 Financial and Human Resource	1969 Financial Only
Assets		
Total Current Assets	$10,003,628	$10,003,628
Net Property, Plant and Equipment	1,770,717	1,770,717
Excess of Purchase Price of Subsidiaries over Net Assets Acquired	1,188,704	1,188,704
Net Investments in Human Resources	986,094	
Other Assets	106,783	106,783
	$14,055,926	$13,069,832
Liabilities and Stockholders' Equity		
Total Current Liabilities	$ 5,715,708	$ 5,715,708
Long Term Debt, Excluding Current Installments	1,935,500	1,935,500
Deferred Compensation	62,380	62,380
Deferred Federal Income Taxes as a Result of Appropriation for Human Resources	493,047	—
Stockholders' Equity:		
Capital Stock	879,116	879,116
Additional Capital in Excess of Par Value	1,736,253	1,736,253
Retained Earnings:		
Financial	2,740,875	2,740,875
Appropriation for Human Resources	493,047	—
Total Stockholders' Equity	5,849,291	5,356,244
	$14,055,926	$13,069,832

Statement of Income

	1969 Financial and Human Resource	1969 Financial Only
Net sales	$25,310,588	$25,310,588
Cost of sales	16,275,876	16,275,876
Gross profit	9,034,712	9,034,712
Selling, general and administrative expenses	6,737,313	6,737,313
Operating income	2,297,399	2,297,313
Other deductions, net	953,177	953,177
Income before Federal income taxes	1,344,222	1,344,222
Human Resource expenses applicable to future periods	173,569	—
Adjusted income before Federal income taxes	1,517,791	1,344,222
Federal income taxes	730,785	644,000
Net income	$ 787,006	$ 700,222

of management—not as a separate "device" or "gimmick" to focus attention on human resources.

Objectives

Broadly, the Human Resource Accounting Information System is being designed to provide better answers to these kinds of questions: What is the quality of profit performance? Are sufficient human capabilities being acquired to achieve the objectives of the enterprise? Are they being developed adequately? To what degree are they being properly maintained? Are these capabilities being properly utilized by the organization?

As expressed in our 1968 Annual Report, our specific objectives in development of human resource accounting are: 1) to provide Barry managers with specific feedback information on their performance in managing the organizational resources entrusted to their care so that they can make proper adjustments to their pattern of operations to correct adverse trends or further improve the condition of these resources; 2) to provide Barry managers with additional information pertaining to human resources to assist in their decision-making; and 3) to provide the organization with a more accurate accounting of its return on total resources employed, rather than just the physical resources, and to enable management to analyze how changes

in the status of the resources employed affect the achievement of corporate objectives.

Approach

The approach used has been to account for investments in securing and developing the organization's human resources. Outlay costs for recruiting, acquiring, training, familiarizing, and developing management personnel are accumulated and capitalized. In accordance with the approach conventional accounting employs for classification of an expenditure as an asset, only those outlays which have an expected value beyond the current accounting period deserve consideration as investments. Those outlays which are likely to be consumed within a twelve-month period are properly classified as expense items. The investments in human resources are amortized over the expected useful period of the investment. The basic outlays in connection with acquiring and integrating new management people are amortized over their expected tenure with the company. Investments made for training or development are amortized over a much shorter period of time. The system now covers all management personnel at all locations of the corporation.

Research and development of the system began in late 1966 as a joint

effort between the Institute for Social Research, of the University of Michigan, and R. G. Barry. Representing the Institute in the development of the system were Rensis Likert, Director of the Institute for Social Research; William C. Pyle, Director, Human Resource Accounting Research, who was responsible for much of the theoretical and conceptual work; and Lee Brummet, Professor of Accounting, of the University of Michigan Business School. For Barry, the team members were Edward Stan, Treasurer; Robert L. Woodruff, Vice President, Personnel; and Richard Burrell, Controller.

Applications

There are many potential applications for human resource accounting. Considering outlays for human resource investments which have a useful life over a number of years would have an impact upon the current year's revenue. Recognizing investments in human resources and their useful lives, losses resulting from improper maintenance of those resources can be shown in dollar terms. Estimating the useful lives of investments also provides a basis for planning for the orderly replacement of human capabilities as they expire, supplementing conventional manpower planning. Finally, recognizing investments in human resources will allow management to calculate dol-

lar return on investment on a more comprehensive resource base for a particular profit center.

Summary

From the standpoint of management, knowledge of the human resource investments, maintenance and returns is necessary for proper decision-making and planning long-range corporate growth. As industry becomes increasingly technical, and management becomes progressively more complex, we believe conventional accounting practice will come to recognize human resource accounting in financial reporting.

At this stage, the Human Resource Accounting System at R. G. Barry is best regarded as a potentially important tool of the overall management system. It is not an end in itself, and needs continuing refinement and development.

Typical Investments In Individual Managers

$40,000	
$30,000	
$20,000	
$10,000	

1 First line Supervisor   3 Middle Manager
2 Industrial Engineer   4 Top Level Manager

Chapter Thirteen

THE STATEMENT
OF FUND FLOWS

INTRODUCTION

Although the earnings statement and financial position statement continue to be the most important financial statements issued by corporations to users outside the firm, they are not capable of conveying all of the information required by the users. Much of the needed additional information is contained in supplementary schedules that explain in greater detail the accounts shown in summary form in the basic statements. Footnotes to the statements may describe events or possible future events that have financial significance but that can be expressed only in qualitative terms at the date of the report.

Particularly important to users is information about the events causing changes in the asset and liability items in the financial position statement. The financial position statement shows the *amounts* of these items as of the date of the statement and enables the user to compute the amount of the change from one time to another, but it is not always possible to determine the events that caused the changes. For the user, the amount of the change in an asset or liability is not very helpful unless the reasons for the change are also known.

The combined statement of earnings and retained earnings explains some of the asset and liability changes during the period covered by the statement, because all revenues and expenses can be expressed in these terms, but many other changes are not explained by the combined statement. Consider, for example,

1. Purchases and sales of investments or long-lived assets
2. Long and short-term bank borrowings and repayments
3. Stock issues and redemptions

None of these transactions is reflected in the statement of earnings, and yet they may provide valuable insights into the financial policy and intentions of the management.

The most informative way of reporting these transactions is a *statement of fund flows*, which in the last twenty years has achieved a position of great importance in the annual reports of American corporations. While these statements do not (and should not) have the status of earnings statements, they occupy a prominent place among the standard reports given both to external statement users and to internal management. They are often included within the scope of the opinion given by the CPA auditors.

The major portion of this chapter is devoted to the basic analysis required for the preparation of statements of fund flows and of cash receipts and disbursements, because these statements are prepared differently from the others treated in this book. The differences arise because the conventional accounting system is designed to focus attention on period income and on the interpretation of changes in asset and liability items in terms of revenues and expenses, rather than in terms of funds or cash. For this reason, it is difficult (but not impossible) to obtain the data necessary for these statements directly from the journals and ledgers. Instead, the usual procedure is to convert the figures in the conventional earnings statement and financial position statement to reflect the effect of events on funds or cash. That is, the statement of fund flows and the statement of cash receipts and disbursements are *derived* statements—the information for them is obtained from the basic statements rather than from the books of original entry.

It should be evident that accounting systems could easily be designed so that information for fund and cash statements could be obtained directly from the books of account. This is rarely done in practice, and the procedures for doing so are beyond the scope of this book. As the usefulness and popularity of these statements increase, however, we can expect that reporting companies will provide more direct methods of accumulating the necessary information.

The interpretation and use of fund flow statements are discussed more fully in Chapters 18 and 19.

THE STATEMENT OF FUND FLOWS

The first difficulty with fund flow statements is that there is no universally accepted definition of the term "funds." There are at least four different definitions either used in practice or recommended in the accounting literature. These are (1) cash; (2) cash and marketable securities; (3) cash, marketable securities, and current receivables less current liabilities; and (4) current assets less current liabilities. The significance of the differences among these concepts is best explained in an illustration. Consider first the financial position statement of the Acme Auto Parts Company shown in Exhibit 13–1.

EXHIBIT 13-1

ACME AUTO PARTS COMPANY

COMPARATIVE STATEMENT OF FINANCIAL POSITION
As of December 31, 19x0 and 19x1
(in thousands of dollars)

	19x1	19x0
Assets		
Current assets		
Cash	$ 504	$ 352
Marketable securities	483	175
Accounts receivable (net)	660	852
Inventories	4,507	3,867
Prepaid expenses	160	170
Total current assets	$ 6,314	$ 5,416
Investments	1,205	1,122
Long-lived assets (net)	4,965	4,754
Total assets	$12,484	$11,292
Equities		
Current liabilities	$ 2,359	$ 2,252
Long-term liabilities	3,200	3,000
Total liabilities	$ 5,559	$ 5,252
Owners' equity		
Capital stock	$ 2,100	$ 2,000
Retained earnings	4,825	4,040
Total owners' equity	$ 6,925	$ 6,040
Total equities	$12,484	$11,292

Let us assume that this is all the information we have available, and that we define "funds" as cash (the first of the four possible definitions given above). The statement of funds flows would be as shown in Exhibit 13–2.

Because there is no information about the transactions causing the changes, this statement is not particularly useful. In essence, it is simply a statement of changes in all nonfund (in this case, noncash) items, arranged so that it purports to explain the change in cash. Actually, we have no information other than the financial position statement; the fund flow statement explains nothing.

If we defined funds as the sum of cash and marketable securities, we would prepare a statement of asset and liability changes exactly like the one above, except that the item "increase in marketable securities" would be omitted. Then "increase in funds" would amount to $460, and thus the difference in the sum of cash and marketable securities at the beginning of the year ($352 plus $175) and at the end of the year ($504 plus $483) is explained.

Defining funds as the sum of cash, marketable securities, and current re-

EXHIBIT 13-2

ACME AUTO PARTS COMPANY
STATEMENT OF FUND FLOWS
For the Year 19x1
(in thousands of dollars)

Sources of funds:		
Decrease in receivables		$ 192
Decrease in prepaid expenses		10
Increase in current liabilities		107
Increase in long-term liabilities		200
Increase in capital stock		100
Increase in retained earnings		785
Total sources of funds		$1,394
Uses of funds:		
Increase in marketable securities	$308	
Increase in inventories	640	
Increase in investments	83	
Increase in long-lived assets	211	
Total uses of funds		1,242
Increase in funds		$ 152

ceivables less current liabilities (often referred to as quick assets) introduces complications. The statement of fund flows is as shown in Exhibit 13–3.

EXHIBIT 13-3

ACME AUTO PARTS COMPANY
STATEMENT OF FUND FLOWS
For the Year 19x1
(in thousands of dollars)

Sources of funds:		
Decrease in prepaid expenses		$ 10
Increase in long-term liabilities		200
Increase in capital stock		100
Increase in retained earnings		785
Total sources of funds		$1,095
Uses of funds:		
Increase in inventories	$640	
Increase in investments	83	
Increase in long-lived assets	211	
Total uses of funds		934
Increase in funds		$ 161

The "increase in funds" figure is reconciled with the changes in "fund" items as shown in Exhibit 13–4.

EXHIBIT 13-4

ACME AUTO PARTS COMPANY

SCHEDULE OF FUND ITEM CHANGES

For the Year 19x1

(in thousands of dollars)

	19x1	19x0	Changes in Fund Item Increase	Decrease
Current assets:				
Cash	$ 504	$ 352	$152	
Marketable securities	483	175	308	
Accounts receivable	660	852		$192
Less: Current liabilities	2,359	2,252		107
Increase in funds				161
Total			$460	$460

Finally, if "funds" is defined as current assets less current liabilities (usually called *working capital,* or *net working capital*), the statement of changes would be as shown in Exhibit 13–5.

EXHIBIT 13-5

ACME AUTO PARTS COMPANY

STATEMENT OF FUND FLOWS

For the Year 19x1

(in thousands of dollars)

Sources of funds:		
Increase in long-term liabilities		$ 200
Increase in capital stock		100
Increase in retained earnings		785
Total sources of funds		$1,085
Uses of funds:		
Increase in investments	$ 83	
Increase in long-lived assets	211	
Total uses of funds		294
Increase in funds		$ 791

This result is reconciled with the fund items in Exhibit 13–6.

EXHIBIT 13-6

ACME AUTO PARTS COMPANY
SCHEDULE OF WORKING CAPITAL CHANGES
For the Year 19x1
(in thousands of dollars)

| | December 31 | | Changes in Working Capital | |
	19x1	19x0	Increase	Decrease
Current assets:				
Cash	$ 504	$ 352	$ 152	
Marketable securities	483	175	308	
Accounts receivable	660	852		$ 192
Inventories	4,507	3,867	640	
Prepaid expenses	160	170		10
Total current assets	$6,314	$5,416		
Less: Current liabilities	2,359	2,252		107
Working capital	$3,955	$3,164	$1,100	309
Increase in working capital		791		791
Totals	$3,955	$3,955	$1,100	$1,100

Which Definition Is Best?

There is no obvious answer to this question. The "working capital" definition seems to be used most often in accounting practice, but the other definitions are occasionally found. Firms with large, slow-moving inventories would probably prefer the "quick assets" definition, because changes in inventory balances might have great financial significances and require special emphasis in reporting. Similarly, firms with heavy investments in installment receivables or firms that rely on large short-term borrowings might prefer the "cash and securities" definition. Except for those special cases, it seems reasonable to think of working capital as a single "fund," and we will use this definition in the remainder of this chapter.

Developing the Statement of Fund Flows

In the previous section, we assumed that the only information available was the comparative statement of financial position. As a result, the only usable data were the *amounts* of the changes in various asset and liability items, and the result was a statement of little or no use because we had no information about the events causing the changes. In the following discussion we will introduce additional information about events (usually in summary form rather than individually) that will permit us to explain the relationship of various asset and liability changes to working capital, and thus develop a statement that will provide valuable information not conveniently available to report users any other way.

For example, assume that we also have available the statement of retained earnings for Acme Auto Parts for the year 19x1 (Exhibit 13–7).

EXHIBIT 13-7

ACME AUTO PARTS COMPANY

STATEMENT OF RETAINED EARNINGS

In the Year Ended December 31, 19x1

Retained earnings, January 1, 19x1		$4,040
Net earnings	$1,553	
Less: Dividends declared and paid	768	
Increase in retained earnings		785
Retained earnings, December 31, 19x1		$4,825

This added information can be incorporated into the statement of fund flows and give it added meaning. As shown in Exhibit 13–8, this statement is more informative because it gives emphasis to the dividend as a decision of the firm involving the use of working capital.

EXHIBIT 13-8

ACME AUTO PARTS COMPANY

STATEMENT OF FUND FLOWS

In the Year 19x1

(in thousands of dollars)

Sources of funds:		
Increase in long-term liabilities		$ 200
Increase in capital stock		100
Net earnings		1,553
Total sources of funds		$1,853
Uses of funds:		
Dividends	$768	
Increase in investments	83	
Increase in long-lived assets	211	
Total uses of funds		1,062
Increase in funds		$ 791

Now let us assume the condensed statement of earnings for the year 19x1 is also available (Exhibit 13–9). Several items in this statement have a direct effect on the statement of fund flows. We now see that the statement of fund flows

<table>
<tr><td colspan="3">E X H I B I T   1 3 - 9</td></tr>
</table>

ACME AUTO PARTS COMPANY
CONDENSED STATEMENT OF EARNINGS
For the Year 19x1
(in thousands of dollars)

Revenue:		
Sales revenue		$20,120
Gain on sale of equipment		56
Total revenue		$20,176
Expenses:		
Cost of goods sold[a]	$10,761	
Administrative[a]	2,675	
Selling[a]	2,856	
Depreciation	907	
Interest	85	
Loss from fire	79	
Federal income taxes	1,260	
Total expenses		18,623
Net earnings		$ 1,553

[a] Exclusive of depreciation expense.

was in error to report $1,553 of net earnings as a source of funds; in fact, several adjustments to this figure must be made before the effect of earnings on funds can be properly reported. We find the item of depreciation expense amounts to $907, which we know to be a reduction in long-lived assets and not a reduction of working capital. Therefore, it is incorrect to report only $1,553 as a source of funds when we know that this figure has been reduced by $907 that did not involve a current outlay of funds. Similarly, we find that, had it not been for the reduction due to depreciation, long-lived assets would have increased $1,118 (i.e., $211 plus $907), instead of $211. Giving effect to this new information, we write the statement of fund flows as in Exhibit 13–10.

Let us now further assume two additional pieces of information:

1. The "loss from fire" of $79 resulted from complete destruction of a building having a net book value of $200, on which only $121 of insurance was collected. We know that the $79 loss takes the form of a reduction in long-lived assets, and does not involve an outlay of funds. We also know that the insurance proceeds are a source of working capital that should be disclosed, and that the true increase in long-lived assets, exclusive of the destroyed building (and of course depreciation), is $1,118 plus $200, or $1,318.

EXHIBIT 13-10

ACME AUTO PARTS COMPANY

STATEMENT OF FUND FLOWS

For the Year 19x1

(in thousands of dollars)

Sources of funds:		
Increase in long-term liabilities		$ 200
Increase in capital stock		100
Net earnings	$1,553	
Depreciation	907	
Funds derived from operations		2,460
Total sources of funds		$2,760
Uses of funds:		
Dividends	$ 768	
Increase in investments	83	
Increase in long-lived assets	1,118	
Total uses of funds		1,969
Increase in funds		$ 791

2. The gain of $56 on the sale of equipment resulted from a transaction in which long-lived assets having a net book value of $100 were sold for $156. This means that the proceeds of $156 should be shown as a source of working capital (instead of just the $56 gain reported above as a part of net earnings), and that the true increase in long-lived assets, exclusive of depreciation and net book value of the assets destroyed and sold, is $1,418. The statement of funds now looks like Exhibit 13–11.

The statement has become considerably more complicated, but it also provides information not available from the simpler versions. For example, after the effect of depreciation and the cost of long-lived assets destroyed and sold are eliminated from the original change in long-lived assets of $211, the result of $1,418 can be interpreted as at least a reasonable approximation of the cost of long-lived assets purchased during the year 19x1. Assuming that the purchases involved an outlay of working capital (rather than issue of stock or a long-term debt), they should be reported as a use of funds.

There are three other figures in Exhibit 13–11 that should be broken down into the transactions causing them:

1. The item "increase in long-term liabilities" is the difference between the total long-term borrowings and total repayments during the year. If there were no repayments during the year, the $200 increase could properly be labeled "long-term borrowing," but if there were repayments, they should be shown as a use of funds, and total borrowings as a source of funds. Obviously, this assumes

EXHIBIT 13-11

ACME AUTO PARTS COMPANY
STATEMENT OF FUND FLOWS
For the Year 19x1
(in thousands of dollars)

Sources of funds:		
Increase in long-term liabilities		$ 200
Increase in capital stock		100
Net earnings (exclusive of fire loss and gain on sale of assets:		
$1,553 + $79 − $56)	$1,576	
Depreciation	907	
Funds derived from operations		2,483
Insurance proceeds from destroyed building		121
Proceeds from sale of equipment		156
Total sources		$3,060
Uses of funds:		
Dividends	$ 768	
Increase in investments	83	
Purchase of long-lived assets	1,418	
Total uses		2,269
Increase in funds		$ 791

that the liability was incurred in exchange for working capital rather than for a long-lived asset or investment asset.

2. The increase in capital stock represents the excess of stock issued over stock reacquired. Assuming that stock reacquired (if any) was in exchange for working capital, the transaction should be shown as a use of funds, and total stock issued shown as a source.

3. The increase in investments is the excess of the cost of investments acquired over the cost of any investments that may have been sold. As in the case of the long-lived asset illustrated above, total proceeds from a sale of an investment asset (which would include any gain or loss on the sale) should be shown as a source of funds, and *total* cost of investments purchased reported as a use.

To produce this type of information the accountant must have access to the journals and ledgers of the firm. The technique for preparing the statement of fund flows directly from the books of account (ideally, this is the best way to do it) is beyond the scope of this book. The important task here is to understand that the net difference in any asset or liability item from one time to another may be the result of several highly important offsetting transactions that are not revealed in the financial position statement.

Depreciation and Funds

The statement of fund flows shown in Exhibit 13–11 is not in its most useful form. Of particular importance is the $2,483 figure labeled "funds derived from operations." The addition of depreciation to net earnings may have caused confusion among unsophisticated readers, because these readers are (almost) encouraged to think of depreciation as if it were a source of funds. The real purpose in adding depreciation to net income is to eliminate its effect in order to measure funds derived from revenue and expense transactions. Depreciation is an expense and therefore must be deducted in the process of measuring earnings, but since it does not involve an outlay of funds during the period, it should not be deducted in measuring "funds derived from operations." Unfortunately this point is not clear to many users of financial statements, partly because of accountants' poor presentations.

The best method of guarding against faulty interpretation is to calculate and report the $2,483 figure another way. From the earnings statement in Exhibit 13–7, we find that this amount can be derived as follows:

Funds derived from sales revenue		$20,120
Funds used for operating expenses		
Cost of goods sold	$10,761	
Selling	2,856	
Administrative	2,675	
Interest	85	
Federal income taxes	1,260	17,637
Funds derived from operations		$ 2,483

The items included under "funds used for operating expenses" could be shown in highly condensed form to avoid repeating much of the same information that appears in the earnings statement. The essential point is that only those expense items involving a current outlay of funds (i.e., reduction of a current asset or increase in current liability) are shown. Depreciation expense and the fire loss are not included, since these items were reflected in the reduction of long-lived assets. (The gain on sale of equipment of $56 is also omitted because it is included as part of the $156 proceeds from sale of equipment, shown elsewhere in the statement of fund flows.)

The Statement of Fund Flows in Final Form

We now summarize all of the information and analyses of the working capital transactions of the Acme Auto Parts Company for the year 19x1 to obtain a final version of the statement of fund flows. This version is shown in Exhibit 13–12.

Exhibit 13–12 is an acceptable form for a statement of fund flows when accompanied by a schedule of working capital changes (Exhibit 13–6), but it

EXHIBIT 13-12

THE ACME AUTO PARTS COMPANY
STATEMENT OF FUND FLOWS
For the Year 19x1
(in thousands of dollars)

Sources of funds:			
Operations:			
Funds derived from sales revenues			$20,120
Funds used for operating expenses			17,637
Funds derived from operations			$ 2,483
Investors:			
Increase in long-term debt		$200	
Increase in capital stock		100	
Total funds from investors			300
Liquidation of noncurrent assets:			
Insurance proceeds from destroyed building		$121	
Proceeds from sale of equipment		156	
Total funds from long-lived assets			277
			$ 3,060
Uses of funds:			
To investors:			
Dividends		$768	
Purchase of noncurrent assets:			
Long-lived assets	$1,418		
Increase in investments	83		
Total funds for noncurrent assets		1,501	
Total uses of funds			2,269
Increase in funds			$ 791

is by no means the only acceptable form. A wide variety of fund flow statements are used in practice. Standardization of forms and classifications is probably not necessary or even desirable. Much more important is proper emphasis on those events that have substantial influence on the flow of working capital. These events may vary from year to year, and most certainly will vary from one firm to another, so that flexibility in statement preparation is to be encouraged.

Cash Flow

The figure in the statement of fund flows entitled "funds derived from operations" ($2,483 in the illustration above) has achieved a position of such great importance, particularly among financial analysts, that it has been given a special name—cash flow. Cash flow figures are often reported prominently in corporate annual reports and other media, often in the form of "cash flow per share." This calculation implies a comparison with "earnings per share," and in fact, the "cash flow per share" figures have occasionally been used by analysts as if they were measures of performance or predictors of stock prices, particularly when cash flow is considerably greater than earnings (i.e., when depreciation is large).

One plausible defense of the use of cash flow figures rather than earnings figures is that depreciation measurements are inherently variable and inaccurate. When depreciation expense is large, the earnings figure becomes suspect; the cash flow figure simply bypasses this difficulty.

In general, however, the emphasis on cash flow as a measure of performance is unfortunate, and the possible optimism created by the comparison with earnings is not justified. It is not possible to solve measurement problems simply by ruling out their difficult elements, and the implication that depreciation expense is somehow of questionable status as a cost of doing business is sadly misleading.

There are other objections to the cash flow label that has been attached to "funds derived from operations:"

1. "Funds derived from operations" corresponds to working capital, not to cash. "Funds derived from operations" can be an approximation of cash flow *only on the assumption* that the balances of receivables, inventories, and current liabilities are the same at the beginning and the end of the period.

2. There is some implication that cash flow represents cash (or working capital) that can be disbursed at the discretion of the management. This implication is seriously misleading. At a minimum, some allowance must be made for expenditures required to maintain the productive capacity of the capital equipment before any useful comparison with the net income figure can be made.

This discussion is not intended to discredit the usefulness of the statement of fund flows in any way. On the contrary, we hope we have established our opinion that the statement, properly presented, makes a significant addition to the information provided by the statement of financial position and statement of earnings. Nevertheless, it is important to stress the fact that the fund flow statement should not be used as if it were a substitute for the earnings statement.

THE STATEMENT OF CASH RECEIPTS AND DISBURSEMENTS

In some circumstances, a properly prepared statement of cash receipts and disbursements is more useful than the statement of working capital fund flows as defined above, for the cash receipts and disbursements statement contains additional details about inventories, receivables, and current liability changes. It is for this reason that the statement of cash receipts and disbursements is not preferred in all circumstances; these details are not always important for general analysis.

The statement of cash receipts and disbursements is often called a statement of cash flows; to avoid confusion with the popular use of the term "cash flow," we prefer the former title.

Extending the Statement of Fund Flows

As we have indicated, one way of deriving the statement of cash receipts and disbursements is simply to extend the statement of fund flows ("fund" defined as working capital) so that it includes changes in receivables, inventories, and current liabilities. Extending the statement of fund flows of Acme Auto Parts in Exhibit 13–12 would give the result shown in Exhibit 13–13.

EXHIBIT 13-13

ACME AUTO PARTS COMPANY
STATEMENT OF CASH RECEIPTS AND DISBURSEMENTS
For the Year 19x1
(in thousands of dollars)

Increase in funds (from Exhibit 13–12)			$791
Add:			
Decrease in current receivables		$192	
Decrease in prepaid expenses		10	
Increase in current liabilities		107	
Total		$309	
Deduct:			
Increase in marketable securities	$308		
Increase in inventories	640	948	(639)[a]
Increase in cash			$152

[a] Parentheses denote negative amounts.

Exhibit 13–13 does not show a *good* form for the statement of cash receipts and disbursements; its purpose is to demonstrate the relationship to the statement of fund flows. The reasons for adding and deducting the various items are not difficult to understand. The decrease in current receivables, for instance, simply means that Acme collected from customers a larger amount of cash than the amount of working capital produced by the revenues from sales. The amount of the excess (i.e., the amount of the decrease in current receivables) is a source of cash but not a source of working capital, and it must be added to the working capital sources to compute total cash sources. Conversely, an increase in marketable securities means that more securities were purchased than were sold. Since short-term marketable securities are an element of working capital, the purchase of securities does not involve an outlay of working capital. The transaction does involve an outlay of cash, however, and the increase in cost of marketable securities must therefore be deducted from the change in working capital to compute the change in cash.

Exhibit 13–12 is essentially a statement of changes in working capital, however, and simply adding the adjustments required to account for cash changes does not allow for clear or convenient analysis of the events and conditions affecting flows of cash. In order to prepare a statement that provides for such an analysis, it is necessary to return to the basic financial position and earnings statements as primary sources of information.

Preparing the Statement of Cash Receipts and Disbursements

The Emca Wholesale Corporation has issued the comparative statement of financial position and combined statement of earnings and retained earnings shown in Exhibits 13–14 and 13–15.

In order to derive a statement of cash receipts and disbursements from these data, it will be necessary to rely on several assumptions, as in preparing the statement of working capital flows.

EXHIBIT 13-14

EMCA WHOLESALE CORPORATION

COMPARATIVE STATEMENT OF FINANCIAL POSITION
As of December 31, 19x1 and 19x2
(in thousands of dollars)

	December 31 19x2	December 31 19x1	Increase (Decrease)
Assets			
Current assets:			
Cash	$ 1,940	$ 1,113	$ 827
Marketable securities	2,000	0	2,000
Accounts receivable (net)	5,609	5,167	442
Accrued interest receivable	37	42	(5)
Merchandise inventories	8,911	10,985	(2,074)
Prepaid expenses	173	157	16
Total current assets	$18,670	$17,464	$1,206
Investments	0	105	(105)
Long-lived assets (net)	2,740	2,503	237
Total assets	$21,410	$20,072	$1,338

EMCA WHOLESALE CORPORATION (CONT.)

| | December 31 | | Increase |
	19x2	19x1	(Decrease)
Equities			
Current liabilities:			
Accounts payable	$ 1,547	$ 1,477	$ 70
Accrued expenses	217	169	48
Notes payable	2,300	3,300	(1,000)
Accrued federal taxes	291	314	(23)
Total current liabilities	$ 4,355	$ 5,260	$ (905)
Owners' equity:			
Capital stock	$12,000	$10,000	$2,000
Retained earnings	5,055	4,812	243
Total owners' equity	$17,055	$14,812	$2,243
Total equities	$21,410	$20,072	$1,338

EXHIBIT 13-15

EMCA WHOLESALE CORPORATION

**COMBINED STATEMENT OF EARNINGS AND
RETAINED EARNINGS**

*For Year Ended December 31, 19x2
(in thousands of dollars)*

Revenue:		
Sales		$13,990
Gain on sale of investments		15
Interest earned		72
Total revenues		$14,077
Expenses:		
Cost of goods sold	$ 9,005	
Credit losses	59	
Depreciation	137	
Other operating expenses	2,307	
Loss on sale of long-lived assets	32	
Interest	115	
Federal income tax	1,040	
Total expenses		$12,695
Net earnings after taxes		$ 1,382
Retained earnings, December 31, 19x1		$ 4,812
Total		$ 6,194
Dividends declared and paid		$ 1,139
Retained earnings, December 31, 19x2		$ 5,055

1. Except as otherwise noted, all changes in financial position items between the beginning and the end of the year are assumed to be the result of cash transactions.

2. Accounts receivable (net) represent amounts estimated collectable from trade customers. Of the $13,990,000 total sales, $1,185,000 were cash sales.

3. All merchandise is purchased on account, and all accounts payable are assumed to result from merchandise purchases.

4. Long-lived assets having a net book value of $105,000 were sold for $73,000 cash.

The development of the information for the statement of cash receipts and disbursements follows the same procedure as outlined for the statement of working capital flows earlier in this chapter. In skeleton form, the procedure is shown in Exhibit 13–16.

EXHIBIT 13-16

EMCA WHOLESALE CORPORATION
STATEMENT OF CASH RECEIPTS AND DISBURSEMENTS
For Year Ended December 31, 19x2

Cash receipts:		
Decrease in accrued interest receivable (1)		$ 5
Decrease in merchandise inventory (2)		2,074
Decrease in investments (3)		105
Increase in accounts payable (2)		70
Increase in accrued expenses (4)		48
Increase in capital stock (5)		2,000
Increase in retained earnings (6)		243
Total		$4,545
Cash disbursements:		
Increase in marketable securities (7)	$2,000	
Increase in accounts receivable (net) (8)	442	
Increase in prepaid expenses (4)	16	
Increase in long-lived assets (9)	237	
Decrease in notes payable (10)	1,000	
Decrease in accrued federal taxes (11)	23	
Total		3,718
Increase in cash		$ 827

This statement reveals nothing that is not evident from the financial position statement. It does, however, assure that all cash changes are accounted for and reported. In the following paragraphs we shall calculate each item individually; then we shall arrange them in proper statement form. The paragraphs are keyed with the numbers of the individual items in Exhibit 13–16.

(1) *Interest receipts*

Interest earned, per earnings statement	$72
Add: Increase in accrued interest receivable	5
Cash receipts from interest, 19x2	$77

The explanation is not difficult. The asset "accrued interest receivable" is increased for interest earned and decreased for interest collected. Since the asset decreased $5 during the year, Emca must have collected $5 interest more than it earned.

(2) *Accounts payable paid*

Cost of goods sold, per earnings statement	$9,005
Less: Decrease in merchandise inventory	2,074
Merchandise purchased on account	$6,931
Less: Increase in accounts payable	70
Cash paid on accounts payable	$6,861

This is slightly more complicated, but the reasoning is the same as in (1). A decrease in inventory means that the cost of goods sold during the year is greater than merchandise purchased, by the amount of the decrease (since there were apparently no losses from theft, spoilage, etc.). Furthermore, since all merchandise was purchased on accounts payable (assumption 3 above), and since accounts payable increased $70 during the year, Emca must have purchased $70 more than the amount of cash payments to creditors.

(3) *Proceeds from sale of investments*

Gain on sale of investments, per earnings statement	$ 15
Decrease in investments	105
Total proceeds from sale	$120

(4) *Payments for other operating expenses*

Other operating expenses, per earnings statement	$2,307
Less: Increase in accrued expenses	48
	$2,259
Add: Increase in prepaid expenses	16
Cash paid for operating expenses	$2,275

There is obviously more than one expense item involved in this calculation; otherwise, it would not be possible to have prepaid expenses (i.e., expense items paid for but not consumed) and accrued expenses (expense items consumed but not paid) at the same time. The increase in accrued expenses represents excess of consumed expenses over cash payments (hence it is deducted to compute cash payments), while the increase in prepaid expenses represents an excess of cash payments over consumed expenses (hence it must be added to compute cash payments).

(5) *Capital stock issue*

The capital stock increase, by our first assumption, resulted from an issue of stock for $2,000 cash.

(6) *Interest paid and dividends paid*

An examination of all items affecting retained earnings reveals that the only items not accounted for as a part of other calculations (either above, or in the paragraphs to follow) are interest expense of $115, and dividends declared and paid of $1,139. Since there are no accounts or prepayments related to these items, the amounts also represent cash disbursements, and will be reported as such.

(7) *Marketable securities purchased*

The increase in marketable securities is assumed to have resulted from a disbursement of cash.

(8) *Cash collected from customers*

Cash sales (assumption 2)			$ 1,185
Credit sales		$12,805	
Less: Increase in receivables (net)	$442		
Credit losses	59		
Increase in receivables (gross)		501	
Collections from credit customers			12,304
Total cash collected			$13,489

The increase in receivables represents revenue realized but not collected in cash, and must be deducted from sales revenue to compute cash collections from customers. Since the change in receivables is reported "net" (of credit losses), and since the 19x2 credit losses of $59 represent a noncash reduction of receivables, the effect of the credit losses must be eliminated by adding them back to the receivable increase. The effect of this addition, you will note, is to reduce the computed amount of cash collected.

(9) *Purchase and sale of long-lived assets*

Increase in long-lived assets (net)		$237
Add: Noncash decreases in long-lived assets		
Depreciation expense	$137	
Book value of assets sold (assumption 4)	105	242
Long-lived assets purchased		$479
Proceeds from sale of long-lived assets (assumption 4)		$73

Two statement items are shown here; they will be reported as a disbursement of cash and a receipt of cash, respectively. Note that the loss of $32 reported in the earnings statement is included in the $105 book value of assets sold and, like depreciation, does not involve an outlay of funds.

(10) *Notes payable paid*

The decrease in notes payable is assumed to have resulted from a cash disbursement of $1,000. Without access to the notes payable ledger account, it is impossible to determine total borrowings and repayments.

(11) *Federal taxes paid*

Federal income taxes, per earnings statement	$1,040
Add: decrease in accrued federal taxes	23
Federal taxes paid in cash	$1,063

As in the earlier paragraphs, the analysis here is that the decrease in the liability represents an excess of taxes paid over tax expense incurred.

We now have the individual items of cash receipts and disbursements arranged in logical order for statement purposes; see Exhibit 13–17.

EXHIBIT 13-17

THE EMCA WHOLESALE CORPORATION
STATEMENT OF CASH RECEIPTS AND DISBURSEMENTS
For the Year 19x2
(in thousands of dollars)

Receipts from operations:			
Cash sales			$ 1,185
Collections from credit customers			12,304
Interest collected			77
Total operating receipts			$13,566
Merchandise invoices paid		$6,861	
Other expenses paid		2,275	
Interest paid		115	
Federal taxes paid		1,063	10,314
Cash derived from operations			$ 3,252
Receipts from sale of assets other than merchandise:			
Proceeds from sale of investments		$ 120	
Proceeds from sale of long-lived assets		73	193
Receipts from issues of securities:			
Stock issued			2,000
Total			$ 5,445
Disbursements for dividends		$1,139	
Disbursements for notes paid		1,000	
Disbursements for purchases of nonmerchandise assets:			
Short-term securities purchased	$2,000		
Long-term assets purchased	479	2,479	
Total			4,618
Increase in cash			$ 827

For purposes of comparison, the 19x2 statement of fund flows and schedule of working capital changes for Emca are shown in condensed form in Exhibit 13–18.

EXHIBIT 13 - 18

THE EMCA WHOLESALE CORPORATION
STATEMENT OF FUND FLOWS
For the Year 19x2
(in thousands of dollars)

Sources of funds:		
Operations:		
Funds derived from revenues		$14,062
Funds used for operating expenses		12,526
Funds derived from operations		$ 1,536
Proceeds of sale of noncurrent assets:		
Investments	$ 120	
Long-lived assets	73	193
Investors:		
Stock issued		2,000
Total sources		$ 3,729
Uses of funds:		
To investors:		
Dividends	$1,139	
Purchase of noncurrent assets:		
Long-lived assets	479	
Total uses of funds		1,618
Increase in funds		$ 2,111

THE EMCA WHOLESALE CORPORATION
SCHEDULE OF WORKING CAPITAL CHANGES
(CONDENSED)
For the Year 19x2
(in thousands of dollars)

	December 31		Increase
	19x2	*19x1*	*(Decrease)*
Current assets	$18,670	$17,464	$1,206
Current liabilities	4,355	5,260	905
Net working capital	$14,315	$12,204	$2,111

You should test your understanding of the statement of fund flows by deriving the individual items shown in the statement from the basic financial statements shown in Exhibits 13–14 and 13–15.

COMPARING THE STATEMENT OF FUND FLOWS AND THE STATEMENT OF CASH RECEIPTS AND DISBURSEMENTS

Much can be learned about the content and usefulness of the two statements by comparing the individual items. In particular, there are events that affect cash but do not affect working capital, and other events that affect working capital but do not affect cash. For example:

1. The payment of current notes payable and purchase of short-term securities reduce the cash balance but do not affect working capital.

2. "Operations" provided substantially more cash than working capital because the large reduction in inventory during the year had the effect of reducing working capital but did not require an outlay of cash. The effect of this inventory reduction was offset by the increase in accounts receivable, which increased working capital but did not result in receipt of cash in 19x2.

It is not particularly useful to attempt to make conclusions about which statement is better, because the information conveyed is not the same, and the conclusion as to which statement is better would vary with the circumstances. Published reports do not often contain both statements, and the statement of fund flows is more popular. It should be clearly understood that neither statement should ever be used as a measure of performance of the firm, or as a substitute for the statement of earnings in any other capacity.

SUMMARY

The statement of fund flows provides information to the user beyond that provided by the statements of financial position, earnings, and retained earnings. It explains to the statement user *how* the items comprising funds changed during the accounting period.

Funds can be defined in several different ways:

1. cash
2. cash and marketable securities
3. cash, marketable securities, and current receivables less current liabilities
4. current assets less current liabilities (also known as working capital)

The most commonly used definitions are cash and working capital. In this chapter the derivation of the statement of fund flows for Acme Auto Parts Company was discussed in detail using the working capital definition. Then a statement of cash receipts and disbursements was prepared for Emca Wholesale Corporation and compared with the working capital flows.

One definition of the fund should not be favored over another. Each, with its appropriately prepared statement of flows, is useful. The type of business activity involved, and the needs of statement users, govern which is most useful in each case.

Questions for Review

13-1. What is the basic purpose of a statement of fund flows?

13-2. Why are the statements of fund flows and cash receipts and disbursements referred to as derived statements?

13-3. What are the four definitions of funds discussed in the chapter?

13-4. What type of business organization might use the quick assets definition of funds? The cash and securities definition?

13-5. Why is depreciation expense on the earnings statement not a use of funds?

13-6. Why should the funds statement *not* be used as a measure of performance?

13-7. Contrast the content and usefulness of the statement of cash receipts and disbursements with the statement of working capital flows.

13-8. Compare the statement of fund flows with the statement of earnings, with respect to the objectivity of the measurements.

Problems for Analysis

13-9. Indicate the effect of the following items on the working capital fund.

Depreciation charges for long-lived assets	$100,000
Net loss from operations (excluding charges for depreciation & amortization)	46,000
Net earnings before deducting charges for depreciation & amortization	37,000
Purchase of long-lived assets	74,000
Purchase by a company of its long-term debentures on open market	60,000

Payments received from customers on accounts receivable	21,000
Payment of dividends to stockholders	10,500
Payment to suppliers on accounts payable	17,500
Sale of long-lived assets for scrap	3,200
Sale of merchandise inventory for cash	8,000

13-10. A comparative statement of financial position and a statement of earnings for the Sandy Manor Company are presented below. Following them is a format for a statement of working capital flows and a schedule of working capital changes.

Complete the statement of working capital flows and the schedule of working capital changes. Then compare your solution with the statement of cash receipts and disbursements in problem 13–15.

SANDY MANOR COMPANY

COMPARATIVE STATEMENT OF FINANCIAL POSITION

As of December 31, 19xx

	End of year	Beginning of year	Increase (Decrease)
Assets			
Cash	$150	$200	$ (50)
Short-term investments	50	25	25
Accounts receivable (net)	320	250	70
Inventories	250	200	50
Prepaid insurance	75	100	(25)
Machinery & equipment	180	150	30
— Accumulated depreciation	(75)[a]	(25)	(50)
Total assets	$950	$900	$ 50
Liabilities and Owners' Equity			
Accounts payable	$125	$175	$ (50)
Notes payable (short-term)	75	100	(25)
Accrued payroll	25	25	0
Accrued interest payable	50	25	25
Federal income taxes payable	50	25	25
Capital stock	495	450	45
Retained earnings	130	100	30
Total liabilities and owners' equity	$950	$900	$ 50

[a] Parentheses indicate minus quantities.

SANDY MANOR COMPANY

COMBINED STATEMENT OF EARNINGS AND RETAINED EARNINGS
For Year Ended December 31, 19xx

Sales revenues		$1,000
— Cost of goods sold		625
Earnings margin		$ 375
— Operating expenses:		
Salaries	$73	
Depreciation	50	
Credit losses	27	
Interest	60	
Insurance	18	
Miscellaneous (for cash)	32	
Total operating expenses		260
Earnings from operations		$ 115
— Provision for federal income taxes		40
Net earnings		$ 75
+ Retained earnings, beginning balance		100
Total available for dividends		$ 175
— Dividend payments		45
Retained earnings, ending		$ 130

SANDY MANOR COMPANY

STATEMENT OF WORKING CAPITAL FLOWS
For Year Ended December 31, 19xx

Working capital provided from:		
Operations:		
Net earnings		$
+ Depreciation expense (operating expense not requiring fund outlay)		
Total working capital provided by operations		$
Proceeds from sale of capital stock		
Total working capital provided		$
— Working capital used for:		
Acquisition of machinery & equipment	$	
Payment of dividends		
Total working capital used		
Increase in working capital during year (per schedule of working capital changes, below)		$

SANDY MANOR COMPANY
SCHEDULE OF WORKING CAPITAL CHANGES
For Year Ended December 31, 19xx

	December 31		Changes in Working Capital	
	End of year	Beginning of year	Increase	Decrease
Current assets:				
Cash	$150	$200	$	$
Short-term investments	50	25		
Accounts receivable (net)	320	250		
Inventories	250	200		
Prepaid insurance	75	100		
Total current assets	$845	$775		
— Current liabilities:				
Accounts payable	$125	$175		
Notes payable (short-term)	75	100		
Accrued payroll	25	25		
Accrued interest payable	50	25		
Federal income taxes payable	50	25		
Total current liabilities	$325	$350		
Working capital	$520	$425		
Increase in working capital				
			$	$

13-11. The financial information presented below pertains to the Johnston Manufacturing Company for one fiscal year:

JOHNSTON MANUFACTURING COMPANY
COMPARATIVE STATEMENT OF FINANCIAL POSITION
As of October 31, 19x4 and 19x5
(in thousands of dollars)

	19x5	19x4
Assets		
Current assets:		
Cash	$ 34	$ 28
Accounts receivable (net)	71	65
Notes receivable	9	11
Inventories	152	133
Prepaid expenses	4	6
Total current assets	$270	$243

JOHNSTON MANUFACTURING COMPANY (CONT.)

	19x5	19x4
Long-lived assets:		
Land	$ 40	$ 35
Buildings (net)	121	105
Machinery & equipment (net)	53	54
Patents (net)	16	18
Goodwill	100	100
Total long-lived assets	$330	$312
Total assets	$600	$555

Liabilities and Owners' Equity

	19x5	19x4
Liabilities:		
Current liabilities:		
Accounts payable	$ 69	$ 47
Notes payable	35	15
Accrued expenses payable	6	5
Federal income taxes payable	8	7
Total current liabilities	$118	$ 74
Long-term liabilities:		
Bonds payable (due 6/1/x4)	60	75
Total liabilities	$178	$149
Owners' equity:		
Capital stock	$300	$300
Retained earnings	122	106
Total owners' equity	$422	$406
Total liabilities and owners' equity	$600	$555

JOHNSTON MANUFACTURING COMPANY

STATEMENT OF RETAINED EARNINGS

For Fiscal Year Ended October 31, 19x5
(in thousands of dollars)

Retained earnings, 11/1/x4	$106
+ Net earnings for year[a]	40
Total available for dividends	$146
− Dividend payments	24
Retained earnings, 10/31/x5	$122

[a] Net earnings were calculated after deducting the following expense items:

Provision for credit losses	$4,000
Depreciation—building	2,000
Depreciation—machinery & equipment	5,000
Amortization—patents	2,000

Prepare a statement of working capital flows and a schedule of working capital changes.

13-12. A comparative statement of financial position for Cordials, Inc., is given below.

CORDIALS, INC.

COMPARATIVE STATEMENT OF FINANCIAL POSITION

As of December 31, 19x3 and 19x4

	19x4		19x3	
Assets				
Current assets:				
Cash	$15,000		$18,000	
Accounts receivable (net)	30,000		20,000	
Inventories	45,000		29,000	
Total current assets		$ 90,000		$67,000
Long-lived assets:				
Equipment (cost)	$50,000		$40,000	
Less: Accumulated depreciation	20,000		15,000	
Total long-lived assets		30,000		25,000
Total assets		$120,000		$92,000
Liabilities and Stockholders' Equity				
Current liabilities:				
Accounts payable	$11,000		$10,000	
Notes payable	20,000		15,000	
Federal income taxes	6,000		4,000	
Total current liabilities		$ 37,000		$29,000
Long-term liabilities:				
6% bonds payable in 19x5		0		15,000
Stockholders' equity:				
Capital stock, no-par value	$60,000		$40,000	
Retained earnings	23,000		8,000	
Total stockholders' equity		83,000		48,000
Total liabilities and stockholders' equity		$120,000		$92,000

CORDIALS, INC.

COMBINED STATEMENT OF EARNINGS AND RETAINED EARNINGS

For Year Ended December 31, 19x4

Sales	$200,000
Cost of goods sold	100,000
Earnings margin	$100,000

CORDIALS, INC. (CONT.)

Operating expenses:		
Depreciation	$ 5,000	
Office supplies	1,000	
Other expenses	67,100	73,100
Net earnings from operations		$ 26,900
Less: Interest expense		900
Net earnings before federal taxes		$ 26,000
Provision for federal income taxes		6,000
Net earnings		$ 20,000
Retained earnings, 12/31/x3	$ 8,000	
Less: Dividends	5,000	3,000
Retained earnings, 12/31/x4		$ 23,000

Late in the year, the company retired the bonds at par value, prior to their maturity. Because of this and other significant changes in the company's financial position, management feels that statements analyzing sources and uses of working capital during the year would be useful.

Prepare a statement of working capital flows and a schedule of working capital changes.

13-13. The following financial statements pertain to the earnings and financial position of the Hoosier Company for the current year:

HOOSIER COMPANY
COMPARATIVE STATEMENT OF FINANCIAL POSITION
As of December 31, 19xx

	End of year		Beginning of year	
Assets				
Current assets:				
Cash		$ 2,500		$ 8,300
Accounts receivable	$23,600		$20,000	
— Allowance for uncollectable accounts	100		200	
Net accounts receivable		23,500		19,800
Inventories		17,100		14,600
Prepaid rent		1,200		400
Total current assets		$44,300		$43,100
Long-lived assets:				
Plant & equipment	$40,300		$35,300	
— Accumulated depreciation	13,500		9,000	
Net plant & equipment		26,800		26,300
Total assets		$71,100		$69,400

HOOSIER COMPANY (CONT.)

	End of year	Beginning of year
Liabilities and Owners' Equity		
Liabilities:		
Current liabilities:		
Accounts payable	$ 8,300	$10,900
Accrued payroll	1,600	400
Federal income taxes	2,200	3,100
Total current liabilities	$12,100	$14,400
Long-term liabilities:		
Bank note payable	8,000	10,000
Total liabilities	$20,100	$24,400
Owners' equity:		
Capital stock	$15,000	$10,000
Retained earnings	36,000	35,000
Total owners' equity		45,000
Total liabilities and owners'	51,000	
equity	$71,100	$69,400

HOOSIER COMPANY

COMBINED STATEMENT OF EARNINGS AND RETAINED EARNINGS
For Year Ended December 31, 19xx

Sales revenues		$100,400
— Cost of goods sold		64,700
Earnings margin		$ 35,700
— Operating expenses:		
Salaries & wages	$21,600	
Rent	2,100	
Depreciation	4,500	
Credit losses	200	
Total		28,400
Earnings from operations		$ 7,300
— Nonoperating items:		
Interest expense		100
Earnings before income taxes		$ 7,200
— Federal income taxes		2,200
Net earnings		$ 5,000
+ Retained earnings, 1/1		35,000
Total available for dividends		$ 40,000
— Dividend payments		4,000
Retained earnings, 12/31		$ 36,000

Prepare a statement of working capital flows and a schedule of working capital changes.

13-14. a. Using the following information, compute the cash collected from customers:

Sales	$100,000
Sales returns & allowances	3,600
Sales discounts	1,100
Credit losses	4,000
Accounts receivable (net):	
Beginning	24,000
Ending	25,600

b. From the following information for a retail store, compute:
   1. The amount of inventory purchased from suppliers during the period.
   2. The cash payments on accounts payable during the period.

Cost of goods sold	$83,000
Accounts payable (all for inventory purchases):	
Beginning	9,000
Ending	10,500
Inventory:	
Beginning	20,400
Ending	19,750

c. Determine cash payments for insurance premiums from the following information:

Insurance expense	$450
Prepaid insurance:	
Beginning	220
Ending	195

d. Compute the cash payments for rent from the following data:

Rent expense	$ 325
Prepaid rent:	
Beginning	1,025
Ending	700

e. From the following data compute interest payments during the period:

Interest expense	$1,100
Accrued interest payable:	
Beginning	5,000
Ending	0

f. From the following information determine the cash payments for federal income taxes during the period:

Federal income tax expense	$150,000
Federal income taxes payable:	
Beginning	170,000
Ending	102,000

13–15. A comparative statement of financial position and a statement of earnings for the Sandy Manor Company are presented below. Following them is a format for a statement of cash receipts and disbursements. Complete the statement of cash receipts and disbursements.

SANDY MANOR COMPANY

COMPARATIVE STATEMENT OF FINANCIAL POSITION

As of December 31, 19xx

	End of year	Beginning of year	Increase (Decrease)
Assets			
Cash	$150	$200	$(50)
Short-term investments	50	25	25
Accounts receivable (net)	320	250	70
Inventories	250	200	50
Prepaid insurance	75	100	(25)
Machinery & equipment	180	150	30
— Accumulated depreciation	(75)[a]	(25)	(50)
Total assets	$950	$900	$ 50
Liabilities and Owners' Equity			
Accounts payable	$125	$175	$(50)
Notes payable (short-term)	75	100	(25)
Accrued payroll	25	25	0
Accrued interest payable	50	25	25
Federal income taxes payable	50	25	25
Capital stock	495	450	45
Retained earnings	130	100	30
Total liabilities and owners' equity	$950	$900	$ 50

[a] Parentheses indicate minus quantities.

SANDY MANOR COMPANY
COMBINED STATEMENT OF EARNINGS AND
RETAINED EARNINGS
For Year Ended December 31, 19xx

Sales revenues		$1,000
— Cost of goods sold		625
Earnings margin		$ 375
— Operating expenses:		
Salaries	$73	
Depreciation	50	
Credit losses	27	
Interest	60	
Insurance	32	
Miscellaneous (for cash)	18	
Total		260
Earnings from operations		$ 115
— Provision for federal income taxes		40
Net earnings		$ 75
+ Retained earnings, beginning balance		100
Total available for dividends		$ 175
— Dividend payments		45
Retained earnings, ending		$ 130

SANDY MANOR COMPANY
STATEMENT OF CASH RECEIPTS AND DISBURSEMENTS
For Year Ended December 31, 19xx

Cash provided from:		
Operations:		
Collections from customers		$
— Cash required by operations:		
Payments for inventory	$	
Payments to employees		
Interest payments		
Payments for other expenses		
Payments for insurance		
Payment of federal income taxes		
Total cash required by operations		
Net cash provided from operations		$
Proceeds from sale of capital stock		
Total cash provided		$

SANDY MANOR COMPANY (CONT.)

— Cash used for:		
Payment on notes payable	$	
Purchase of short-term investments		
Purchase of machinery & equipment		
Payment of dividends		
Total cash used	_____	
		_____
Decrease in cash during year (per schedule of cash changes, below)		$ _____

SANDY MANOR COMPANY

SCHEDULE OF CASH CHANGES

For Year Ended December 31, 19xx

Cash balance, beginning	$
— Cash balance, ending	_____
Decrease in cash during year	$ _____

13–16.
PART I

The following data summarize all the transactions of Red's Clothing Store for January. Supply the missing data for these independent transactions:

a.	Accounts receivable, 1/1	$2,190
	Credit sales	3,720
	Cash collections on accounts receivable	3,510
	Accounts receivable, 1/31	?
b.	Prepaid insurance, 1/1	$ 470
	Insurance premiums paid	2,005
	Insurance expense	190
	Prepaid insurance, 1/31	?
c.	Accounts payable, 1/1 (for merchandise)	$1,210
	Merchandise credit purchases	1,870
	Cash payments on accounts payable	1,250
	Accounts payable, 1/31	?
d.	Supplies inventory, 1/1	$ 220
	Supplies purchased for cash	175
	Supplies used	110
	Supplies inventory, 1/31	?
e.	Accrued salaries & wages, 1/1	$ 170
	Salaries & wages expense	865

Salaries & wages paid	890
Accrued salaries & wages, 1/31	?

f. Merchandise inventory, 1/1 $3,040
    Merchandise purchases   1,870
    Cost of goods sold   2,080
    Merchandise inventory, 1/31   ?

g. Accrued rent payable, 1/1 $ 100
    Rent expense   200
    Rent paid in cash   400
    Prepaid rent, 1/31   ?

PART II

Select the appropriate data from the transactions in Part I and prepare the following financial statements:

    a. statement of cash receipts and disbursements
    b. statement of earnings
    c. statement of owners' equity
    d. comparative statement of financial position

You may use the following financial statement formats as guides:

RED'S CLOTHING STORE
STATEMENT OF CASH RECEIPTS AND DISBURSEMENTS
For January 19xx

Cash provided from:		
Collections on accounts receivable		$
— Cash used for:		
Insurance premium payments	$	
Payment of accounts payable		
Cash purchases of supplies		
Payment of salaries & wages		
Rent payment		
Total cash used	————	
Net cash provided from (used for) operations		$
+ Cash balance, 1/1		2,360
Cash balance, 1/31		$

RED'S CLOTHING STORE
STATEMENT OF EARNINGS
For January 19xx

Sales	$
— Cost of goods sold	————
Earnings margin	$

RED'S CLOTHING STORE (CONT.)		
— Operating expenses:		
Insurance	$	
Supplies used		
Salaries & wages		
Rent		
Total operating expenses	————	
Earnings from operations		$ ————

RED'S CLOTHING STORE

STATEMENT OF OWNERS' EQUITY

For January 19xx

Owners' equity, 1/1	$
+ Net earnings for January	————
Owners' equity, 1/31	$ ————

RED'S CLOTHING STORE

COMPARATIVE STATEMENT OF FINANCIAL POSITION

As of January 1 and January 31, 19xx

	January 1	January 31
Assets		
Cash	$	$
Accounts receivable		
Merchandise inventory		
Supplies inventory		
Prepaid insurance		
Prepaid rent		
Total assets	$ ————	$ ————
Liabilities and Owners' Equity		
Liabilities:		
Accounts payable	$	$
Accrued salaries & wages		
Accrued rent		
Total liabilities	$	$
Owners' equity		
Total liabilities and owners' equity	$ ————	$ ————

13–17. From the information given below for A Trading Company, prepare the statement of financial position for December 31, 19x2, following the format indicated.

A TRADING COMPANY

COMPARATIVE STATEMENT OF FINANCIAL POSITION

As of December 31, 19x1 and 19x2

		December 31, 19x1		December 31, 19x2
Assets				
Cash		$ 25,000		$
Accounts receivable		40,000		
Prepaid insurance		5,000		
Merchandise inventory		17,000		
Building & equipment	$120,000		$	
Less: Accumulated depreciation	50,000	70,000		
Land		23,000		
Total assets		$180,000		$
Liabilities and Stockholders' Equity				
Notes payable		$ 35,000		$
Accounts payable		18,000		
Other expenses payable		11,000		
Capital stock		80,000		
Retained earnings		36,000		
Total liabilities and stockholders' equity		$180,000		$

A TRADING COMPANY

STATEMENT OF EARNINGS

For Year Ended December 31, 19x2

Sales		$180,000
Expenses:		
Cost of goods sold	$110,000	
Depreciation	15,000	
Insurance	3,000	
Other expenses	30,000	158,000
Earnings from operations		$ 22,000
Loss on sale of land		4,000
Net earnings		$ 18,000

A TRADING COMPANY

STATEMENT OF CASH RECEIPTS AND DISBURSEMENTS

For Year Ended December 31, 19x2

Receipts:	
Cash sales	$ 35,000
Collections on accounts	140,000

A TRADING COMPANY (CONT.)

Sale of land	7,000
Borrowing on notes	50,000
Total receipts	$232,000
Disbursements:	
Purchases	$100,000
Insurance	2,000
Other expenses	34,000
Notes payable	40,000
Machinery	37,000
Dividends	15,000
Total disbursements	$228,000
Increase in cash	$ 4,000

Additional information:

a. Purchases for the year ended December 31, 19x2, amounted to $118,000. All purchases of merchandise are on account, and "accounts payable" are incurred for merchandise purchases only.

b. All accounts receivable arise from credit sales of merchandise to customers.

c. There are no bad debts.

13–18. The following—a comparative statement of financial position, a statement of earnings, and a statement of cash receipts and disbursements—pertain to Mike's Body Shop, Inc.

Fill in the figures omitted from the statements. (*Hint:* Complete the statements in the following order: (1) statement of earnings, (2) statement of cash receipts and disbursements, and (3) comparative statement of financial position.)

MIKE'S BODY SHOP, INC.

COMPARATIVE STATEMENT OF FINANCIAL POSITION
As of June 30 and July 31, 19x1

	July 31	June 30
Assets		
Current assets:		
Cash	$	$ 6,000
Accounts receivable	4,000	12,900
Inventories	10,000	15,000
Notes receivable	0	7,000
Interest receivable on notes	0	100
Prepaid rent	12,000	6,000
Total current assets	$	$47,000

MIKE'S BODY SHOP, INC. (CONT.)

	July 31	June 30
Long-lived assets:		
Land	$10,000	$ 5,000
Building (net)	16,000	8,000
Total long-lived assets	$26,000	$13,000
Total assets	$	$60,000
Liabilities and Owners' Equity		
Liabilities:		
Current liabilities:		
Accounts payable (for merchandise)	$ 5,000	$ 7,000
Notes payable	0	6,950
Accrued interest payable	0	50
Accrued payroll		500
Total current liabilities	$	$14,500
Long-term liabilities:		
Mortgage note payable	25,500	15,500
Total liabilities	$	30,000
Owners' equity:		
Capital stock	$30,000	$10,000
Retained earnings		20,000
Total owners' equity	$	$30,000
Total liabilities and owners' equity	$	$60,000

MIKE'S BODY SHOP, INC.

STATEMENT OF EARNINGS

For July 19x1

Sales revenues		$105,000
— Cost of goods sold:		
Inventory, beginning	$	
Purchases		
Goods available for sale	$	
— Inventory, ending		
Total cost of goods sold		
Earnings margin		$
— Operating expenses:		
Salaries	$4,000	
Light & power	1,500	

MIKE'S BODY SHOP, INC. (CONT.)

Rent	6,000	
Depreciation		
Total operating expenses	——	
Earnings from operations		$
— Nonoperating items:		
Interest income	$ 150	
— Interest expense		
Net nonoperating income	——	
Earnings before income taxes		$ 11,600
— Federal income taxes		3,600
Net earnings for July		$ 8,000

MIKE'S BODY SHOP, INC.

STATEMENT OF CASH RECEIPTS AND DISBURSEMENTS

For July 19x1

Cash provided from:		
Operations:		
Collections from customers		$
— Cash required by operations:		
Payments to creditors for merchandise	$77,000	
Payments for wages & salaries	4,400	
Payment of federal income taxes	3,600	
Rent payment		
Light & power payments	1,500	
Total cash required by operations		
Net cash provided from operations		$
Proceeds from sale of capital stock		
Proceeds from long-term bank loan		$10,000
Collection of note receivable (with interest)		7,250
Total cash provided		$
— Cash used for:		
Additions to buildings & land	$15,000	
Payment of dividends	4,000	
Payment of notes payable (with interest)	7,050	
Total cash used		
Increase in cash during July		$

13-19. a. Prepare a statement of cash receipts and disbursements from the following information:

BIG JIM'S DISCOUNT STORES, INC.
STATEMENT OF EARNINGS
For Fiscal Year Ended January 31, 19xx
(in thousands of dollars)

Gross sales revenues			$1,017
— Sales returns & allowances		$ 29	
Sales discounts		18	47
Net sales revenues			$ 970
— Cost of goods sold:			
Beginning inventory		$146	
+ Net cost of purchases		592	
Total cost of goods available for sale		$738	
— Ending inventory		174	
Total cost of goods sold			564
Earnings margin			$ 406
— Operating expenses:			
Selling expenses:			
Advertising		$ 50	
Salesmen's salaries		34	
Salesmen's commissions		30	
Payroll taxes & fringe benefits		4	
Freight-out		12	
Depreciation—equipment		35	
Rent		30	
Miscellaneous		9	
Total selling expenses		$204	
Administrative expenses:			
Officers' salaries	$20		
Office salaries	22		
Payroll taxes & fringe benefits	5		
Traveling	7		
Credit losses	14		
State & local taxes	11		
Insurance	5		
Depreciation—equipment	20		
Office supplies	6		
Rent	12		
Total administrative expenses		122	
Total operating expenses			326
Earnings from operations			$ 80
— Provision for federal income taxes			36
Net earnings			$ 44

BIG JIM'S DISCOUNT STORES, INC.

COMPARATIVE STATEMENT OF FINANCIAL POSITION

As of January 31, 19xx
(in thousands of dollars)

Assets	End of year	Beginning of year
Current assets:		
Cash	$ 97	$ 50
Accounts receivable (net)	115	97
Inventories	174	146
Prepaid rent	108	36
Prepaid insurance	51	42
Total current assets	$545	$371
Investments:		
Cash surrender value of life insurance policies	26	20
Long-lived assets:		
Equipment (net)	189	148
Total assets	$760	$539

Liabilities and Owners' Equity	End of year	Beginning of year
Liabilities:		
Current liabilities:		
Accounts payable (for inventory)	$ 48	$130
Other accrued expenses	27	49
Federal income taxes payable	39	33
Total current liabilities	$114	$212
Long-term liabilities:		
6% debentures (due 2/1/x6)	150	0
Total liabilities	$264	$212
Owners' equity:		
Common stock (par value $15; authorized 30,000 shares; issued 20,000 & 15,000 shares respectively)	$300	$225
Paid-in capital exceeding par value of common stock	80	30
Retained earnings	116	72
Total owners' equity	496	327
Total liabilities and owners' equity	$760	$539

b. What is the significance of the item "net cost of purchases" appearing on the statement of earnings?

c. What are the advantages or disadvantages of presenting financial information in thousands of dollars? When do you think rounding on financial statements is justified?

d. The financial statements for Big Jim's Discount Stores, Inc., are prepared for the *fiscal* year ended January 31. Many companies have their fiscal year end just after their busy season. What advantage do you see in this policy? To the accounting department? To the entire company?

e. The form of the statement of financial position for Big Jim's Discount Store differs from those illustrated in Chapter 12. Which form of presentation do you prefer? Discuss.

f. What were the dividend declarations and payments during the year? Verify your answer.

13-20. The following financial statements are for the James Company for the current fiscal year ended October 31:

JAMES COMPANY

STATEMENT OF EARNINGS

For Fiscal Year Ended October 31, 19xx

(in thousands of dollars)

Sales revenues (net)			$229
— Cost of goods sold			152
Earnings margin			$ 77
— Operating expenses:			
Selling expenses:			
Advertising		$ 7	
Salesmen's salaries		9	
Depreciation—store equipment		4	
Miscellaneous		1	
Total selling expenses		$21	
Administrative expenses:			
Officers' salaries	$8		
Office salaries	6		
Depreciation—office equipment	3		
Miscellaneous	2		
Total administrative expenses		19	
Total operating expenses			40
Earnings from operations			$ 37
— Federal income taxes			18
Net earnings			$ 19

JAMES COMPANY

STATEMENT OF RETAINED EARNINGS

For Fiscal Year Ended October 31, 19xx

(in thousands of dollars)

Retained earnings, beginning balance	$28
+ Net earnings for fiscal year	19
Total available for dividends	$47
− Dividend payments during fiscal year	14
Retained earnings, ending	$33

JAMES COMPANY

COMPARATIVE STATEMENT OF FINANCIAL POSITION

As of October 31, 19xx

(in thousands of dollars)

	End of year	Beginning of year
Assets		
Current assets:		
Cash	$ 27	$ 19
Accounts receivable (net)	36	40
Inventories	49	68
Total current assets	$112	$127
Long-lived assets:		
Land	$ 23	$ 15
Store equipment (net)	44	30
Office equipment (net)	41	36
Total long-lived assets	$108	$ 81
Total assets	$220	$208
Liabilities and Owners' Equity		
Current liabilities:		
Accounts payable (all for inventory purchases)	$ 7	$ 8
Notes payable	5	15
Federal income taxes payable	20	15
Other liabilities	3	4
Total current liabilities	$ 35	$ 42
Long-term liabilities:		
Note payable	38	34
Total liabilities	$ 73	$ 76

JAMES COMPANY (CONT.)

	End of year	Beginning of year
Owners' equity:		
Common stock	$114	$104
Retained earnings	33	28
Total owners' equity	$147	$132
Total liabilities and owners' equity	$220	$208

Prepare a statement of cash receipts and disbursements and a schedule of cash changes for the current fiscal year.

13-21. The Marathon Corporation's only record of transactions kept on a continuous basis is its checkbook, in which bank deposits and checks written are recorded. Each month these transactions are summarized and classified, and the following is the statement of cash receipts and disbursements for April:

MARATHON CORPORATION
STATEMENT OF CASH RECEIPTS
AND DISBURSEMENTS
For April 19x5

Cash provided from:	
Cash sales	$ 600
Charge account customers	3,500
Rental income	500
Total cash provided[a]	$4,600
— Cash used for:	
Payments on accounts payable (all for merchandise purchases)	$2,200
Payments of employees' wages	900
Payment for building improvements	1,000
Payment of dividends	200
Total cash used	$4,300
Increase in cash during April	$ 300

[a] All cash receipts are deposited immediately.

Each month Marathon prepares a statement of financial position simply by adding up all of its known assets and liabilities at the time. It began business several years ago with $10,000 paid in for its capital stock. It is a retail store that primarily handles its own merchandise, but it does rent some of its floor space to others on occasion for special sales or displays. These temporary tenants must always pay rent in advance.

The statement of financial position at the beginning and end of April 19x5 is as follows:

MARATHON CORPORATION

COMPARATIVE STATEMENT OF FINANCIAL POSITION

As of March 31 and April 30, 19x5

Assets	March 31	April 30
Cash	$ 500	$ 800
Accounts receivable, customers	1,200	1,300
Merchandise inventory	1,400	900
Store building (net)	15,500	15,800
Total assets	$18,100	$18,800

Liabilities and Owners' Equity	March 31	April 30
Accounts payable—merchandise	$ 700	$ 900
Accrued wages	200	100
Rent received in advance	100	300
Capital stock	10,000	10,000
Retained earnings	7,100	7,500
Total liabilities and owners' equity	18,100	$18,800

Prepare a combined statement of earnings and retained earnings for April for Marathon.

13-22. A statement of financial position for the Jones Wholesaling Company at the beginning of the fiscal year 19x4 is presented below and on the next page.

JONES WHOLESALING COMPANY

STATEMENT OF FINANCIAL POSITION

As of November 30, 19x4 (beginning of fiscal year)

Assets				
Current assets:				
Cash				$ 50,000
Accounts receivable (net)				332,500
Inventories (cost)				380,000
Prepaid insurance				6,100
Total current assets				$ 768,600
Investments:				
In stocks			$ 50,625	
In bonds			35,000	
Total investments				85,625
Long-lived assets:				
Tangible long-lived assets:				

	Cost	Accumulated depreciation	Net cost	
Land	$ 25,000	$ 0	$ 25,000	
Buildings	150,000	15,000	135,000	
Equipment	225,000	55,000	170,000	
Automobiles	15,500	1,500	14,000	
Total	$415,500	$71,500	$344,000	

Intangible long-lived assets:				
Goodwill			28,000	
Total long-lived assets				$ 372,000
Total assets				$1,226,225

Liabilities and Owners' Equity		
Liabilities:		
Current liabilities:		
Accounts payable		$ 150,000
Notes payable		9,000
Accrued expenses payable		40,000
Federal income taxes payable		72,000
Total current liabilities		$ 271,000

JONES WHOLESALING COMPANY (CONT.)

Liabilities and Owners Equity

Long-term liabilities:		
Mortgage payable (due 8/1/x8)		40,000
Total liabilities		$ 311,000
Owners' equity:		
Preferred stock	$275,000	
Common stock	553,000	
Total	$828,000	
Retained earnings	87,225	
Total owners' equity		915,225
Total liabilities and owners' equity		$1,226,225

The following additional information is for the 19x5 fiscal year:

Cash	$ 80,000
Sales revenues	1,703,500
Inventories	410,000
Advertising expense	46,000
Credit losses	14,000
Prepaid insurance	3,200
Buildings	175,000
Accounts payable	160,000
Sales discounts	23,650
Accounts receivable (net)	370,000
Accrued expenses payable	30,000
Office salaries	66,000
Dividend payments	44,675
Purchases	1,086,700
Sales returns & allowances	49,500
Allowance for uncollectable accounts receivable	15,000
Depreciation expense—automobiles	1,100
Accumulated depreciation—buildings	23,000
Equipment	260,000
Accumulated depreciation—equipment	74,000
Land	25,000
Accumulated depreciation—automobiles	2,600
Automobiles	17,900
Investment in stocks	70,000
Investment in bonds	35,000
Salesmen's commissions	93,500
Officers' salaries	27,500
Depreciation expense—buildings	8,000
Miscellaneous office expenses	41,300

Depreciation expense—equipment	19,000
Insurance expense	2,900
Goodwill	26,000
Notes payable	7,500
Preferred stock	275,000
Amortization expense—goodwill	2,000
Miscellaneous selling expenses	32,700
Provision for federal income taxes	104,000
Mortgage payable	40,000
Federal income taxes payable	90,000
Common stock	611,800
Retained earnings, 11/30/x4	?

Prepare the following statements for the fiscal year ended November 30, 19x5:

a. combined statement of earnings and retained earnings
b. statement of financial position
c. statement of working capital flows
d. statement of cash receipts and disbursements

Chapter Fourteen # CURRENT ASSETS AND CURRENT LIABILITIES

INTRODUCTION

The accounting principles discussed in this chapter and the next are primarily rules for the measurement of asset and liability items on the statement of financial position and the measurement of the resulting revenues and expenses in the earnings statement. These rules govern financial statements that will be available publicly to anyone who may be interested, and although it is often convenient and proper to think of stockholders and potential stockholders as the principal users, we know from experience that creditors, employees, government agencies, and others are also interested in published financial information about business firms.

THE USES OF PUBLISHED STATEMENTS

The identification of these nonmanagerial users and their varying uses of the data cause a change from the performance measurement approach of Chapters 7 and 8. It is fairly clear that outside users of financial information are interested in more than just the performance of the management. Investors and potential investors seem to be more interested in earnings figures that will give them some basis for predicting future trends. If current earnings are high, and if a rosy future is indicated, stockholders may not worry too much about whether the management is sound or whether it is simply lucky enough to find itself in a prosperous industry.

Users other than stockholders generally rate management performance among their less important interests. The Internal Revenue Service and other government agencies are primarily interested in whether the firm has fulfilled the requirements of the law. Creditors, particularly short-term creditors, are interested in the firm's liquidity (the amount of cash the firm is likely to produce in normal operations and the amount it could produce in an emergency) and in the firm's stability (that is, its ability to survive periods of economic recession). The special interests of these groups will be discussed in Part III of this book.

The Relationship Between Financial Position and Earnings

Chapter 2 discussed the relationship of financial position and earnings in detail; here we give a simple illustration to reflect a somewhat different viewpoint. Consider the comparative financial position statement of the Bergen Company (Exhibit 14–1).

EXHIBIT 14-1

BERGEN COMPANY

COMPARATIVE FINANCIAL POSITION
As of December 31, 19x0 and 19x1

	December 31	
	19x1	*19x0*
Assets		
Cash	$ 300	$ 500
Accounts receivable (net)	800	600
Inventories	1,000	700
Plant and equipment (net)	1,900	2,000
Total Assets	$4,000	$3,800
Equities		
Current liabilities	$ 200	$ 300
Long-term liabilities	600	800
Total liabilities	$ 800	$1,100
Net assets (owners' equity)	$3,200	$2,700

If this were the only information available, we might conclude that earnings for the year 19x1 were $500, the increase in the owners' equity. This conclusion requires an assumption that all transactions affecting owners' equity also affected earnings. If we knew, for instance, that during 19x1 there were dividends of $200 and issues of stock amounting to $300, we would have to take these items into account, as follows:

Increase in owners' equity, 19x1		$500
Issues of stock	$300	
Dividends	200	
Increase resulting from "nonearnings" transactions		100
Net earnings, 19x1		$400

This calculation also assumes that net earnings are computed on the all-inclusive basis, as described in Chapter 12. If we knew that an extraordinary loss of $150 had been recorded (and therefore included in the $400 figure above) and we wished to adopt the normal-operating approach to earnings, another adjustment would be necessary:

Net earnings, 19x1 (all-inclusive approach)	$400
Extraordinary loss	150
Net earnings 19x1 (normal-operating approach)	$550

It is possible to compute net earnings for a period if the assets and liabilities at the beginning and end of that period are known and if certain other transactions affecting equity (but not affecting earnings) are known. This fact introduces a new dimension to financial accounting, which we explore in this chapter.

Accounting Theory Versus Accounting Practice

Theoretically, the basic objective of the financial position statement is to report how much the firm's assets are worth and how much the firm owes as of the date of the statement. This is the only logical definition of the term financial position, and a user of financial statements who has no knowledge of accounting measurement rules is justified in assuming that accountants are pursuing this objective to the best of their ability.

In practice, however, this assumption is erroneous, particularly in regard to measuring assets. In many instances an asset item is shown at a dollar amount that is significantly different (usually much lower) than the current value of the item, and in many other instances valuable asset items are omitted entirely from the financial position statement.

These differences between accounting theory and accounting practice arise for two reasons:

1. How much an asset is worth at any time involves many assumptions concerning the firm owning the asset, the use to which the asset is put, and the economic environment in which it is used. The definition of value is a matter of opinion. In order to be objective, accountants tend to limit themselves to reporting on historical events rather than current values of assets.

2. It is not practical simply to report earnings as the change in value of the firm between two points in time. Accounting practice calls for a detailed

statement of earnings in which various expense items are matched with the revenues of the period, such revenues and expenses being the result of completed or partially completed transactions and events in which the firm has participated. Management performance cannot be measured, so the argument runs, simply by measuring the amount by which the current value of the firm has changed. Many things affecting the value of the firm may have little or nothing to do with the performance or efficiency of the management.

Because of the emphasis placed on matching revenues and expenses in order to measure management's performance, the statement of financial position suffers as a reflection of current values. Accountants tend to interpret and record transactions and other events in the light of the eventual impact on earnings rather than financial position. The use of one double-entry system for recording purposes thus results in a more realistic statement of earnings but a financial position statement that often bears little resemblance to current value. The system records historical costs, not current values.

Nevertheless, statements of financial position continue to occupy a prominent place in the financial reports of firms. As long as they do, they must be judged by that extent to which they display the current values of the assets and liabilities of the firm.

Conservatism in Published Statements

The fact that the accountant cannot control the uses to which financial statements are put outside the firm has a decided effect on the rules he follows in measuring financial statement items. In most instances, the accountant attests to the fairness of financial statements in his opinion, and thus assumes a degree of responsibility for the representations in the statements. As a result, the measurement rules of accountants tend to be conservative, for many of the asset and liability measurements are matters of opinion, necessarily based on estimates. In short, the accountant tends to favor measurement rules that represent the firm's financial position (and earnings) in a pessimistic light. Here are the most important examples:

1. Rules for estimating asset values that permit estimation "on the low side." There are many rules of this type, as we shall see. One is the tendency to estimate somewhat shorter service lives for long-lived assets than are thought to be most likely. The effect is an overstatement of depreciation expense and an understatement of the financial value of the asset during its life.

2. Rules that permit estimating liabilities "on the high side." The few rules that fall into this category relate to liabilities that stem from estimated expenses or losses that may have to be paid in the future.

3. The rule that requires an "arm's length" exchange of assets between independent knowledgeable parties in order to recognize revenue. The effect

of this rule is to prevent the valuation of any asset at any figure higher than its cost unless the owner actually sells the asset and thus "realizes" the gain. This is an extremely important rule in accounting and is the subject of much controversy.

The effect of these conservative rules is best shown by an example. Here are the assets and liabilities (conservatively measured) of the Apex Corporation at three points in time.

	Beginning of year 1	End of year 1	End of year 2
Assets	$100	$130	$120
– Liabilities	60	85	70
Owners' equity	$ 40	$ 45	$ 50

We assume that no dividends were declared, no capital stock was issued or redeemed, and net earnings were all-inclusive. Then periodic net earnings can be computed as the difference in owner's equity between the beginning of the period and the end, or $5 in each year. Suppose, however, that the application of a conservative rule caused the understatement (for example, with management's best estimates) of assets at the end of year 1 by $10, so that these assets should have been stated at $140 instead of $130. Net earnings for the first year would then be $15, and the net loss for the second year, assuming the measurements at that date were accurate, would be $5. The earnings covering the two-year period are unchanged, and the effect of the undervaluation is simply to shift $10 of income from the second year to the first.

As this illustration shows, the consistent, year-to-year application of conservative measurement rules does keep net asset valuations "on the low side," but it does not necessarily understate net earnings in any given year. In fact, conservatism applied to net asset values at the beginning of a period tends to overstate earnings for that period. The net effect is simply to cause shifts in reported earnings from one period to another. Thus, rules for asset and liability measurement affect periodic earnings of the period just ended as well as earnings of the period to follow.

MONETARY AND NONMONETARY ASSETS AND LIABILITIES

In discussing the rules governing measurement of asset and liability items, it is useful to distinguish between monetary and nonmonetary assets and liabilities:

1. *Monetary* assets are assets that derive their value from the fact that they represent contractual claims to a *fixed number of dollars*. Examples are cash in

bank, accounts and notes receivable, and bonds. This legal claim is of great assistance to the accountant in measuring the values of these assets.

2. *Nonmonetary assets* are assets that derive their value from the fact that they are believed to be useful in producing a marketable product or in rendering a marketable service. Examples are merchandising or manufacturing inventories, plant and equipment investments in real estate, intangible assets, etc. Accountants usually make no attempt at direct measurement of the contribution the various asset items will make. Since there is no claim to dollars, as in the case of monetary assets, and since nonmonetary assets are to be used in earning a profit in whatever activities the firm engages, accountants usually attempt to avoid anticipating this profit by valuing these assets no higher than their cost.

3. *Monetary liabilities* are claims against the firm that will have to be satisfied by payment of a fixed number of dollars. Almost all liabilities recognized on financial position statements are monetary liabilities, although not all of these liabilities are legal claims (i.e., enforceable in a court of law) at the time they appear on the statement. Instead they represent the present value of the best estimate of the amount that will have to be paid when payment is due.

4. *Nonmonetary liabilities* are those measured by some method other than the present value of the estimated dollar payment to be made. The only clearcut example is the case of advance payments made by customers who have no legal or moral claim once the payment is made, as in the sale of a season football ticket on a no-refund basis. The only obligation of the football team is to play the scheduled games. The advance payment is reported as a liability on the financial position statement of the football club until the games have been played, because reporting it as revenue at the time of sale would cause mismatching of revenues and expenses in the statement of earnings.

The distinction between monetary and nonmonetary assets and liabilities is not emphasized in financial position statements, in which liquidity is considered more important. In the study of valuation theory, however, the monetary-nonmonetary distinction is important, as will be evident in the following sections.

The discussions in this chapter and in Chapter 15 are based on the assumption that you have a grasp of the concept of the time value of money as well as a working knowledge of the use of compound interest tables for single amounts and annuities. We recommend that you study the Appendix in Chapter 11 if you are in need of a review.

CURRENT MONETARY ASSETS

Cash on Hand, Cash in Bank

Cash available to the firm for payment of current debts presents no valuation problems. Since the amount will not change before the cash is used, no predictions are required, and cash should be valued at the amount available for use at the date of the financial position statement. The only problem in reporting the available cash arises when cash has been earmarked for purposes other than payment of current debt. Then the sum should be classified as investments rather than current assets. Obviously this treatment is called for in the case of cash held in escrow by a trustee for the purpose of paying off long-term bonds, or as a deposit for future purchase of land. It is less obvious, but nevertheless true, that this treatment is also called for when the firm sets aside cash without formal legal action declaring the intent to use it for some long-term purchase or debt payment.

Short-term Investments

The most popular type of short-term investment made by business firms is the highly liquid, low-return, relatively risk-free security. These securities are properly classified as current assets, provided management intends to liquidate the investment when the expected need for cash arises in the near future. In highly condensed statements of financial position, these securities are often added to cash and shown as a single item, often labeled "cash and marketable securities."

The purpose of short-term investments and the nature of the securities indicate that they should be valued at the present value of expected receipts resulting from future sale or redemption. Sometimes this is done when the securities are short-term government notes or bonds to be held to maturity, but more often the accountant's conservatism leads him to value the securities at acquisition cost or current market (as of the date of the statement), whichever is lower. This would always be the case if the securities were stocks (a questionable investment for this purpose) rather than bonds or notes, because stocks, having no maturity value, are nonmonetary assets. Using the cost or market valuation method means that recognition of expected gains is postponed until liquidation, but that losses are recognized during the accounting periods over which the securities are held.

Assume that the Apex Corporation pays $100,000 for U.S. government securities and $50,000 for X-Ray Company bonds in December; it plans to hold these securities until February, when the need for cash will require that they be sold. On December 31, the quoted market values of these securities are $101,500 and $49,250, respectively. How should these securities be valued on the financial position statement of this date? We find that two rules apply: In the case of the government bonds, the increase in market value is not realized because there has been no sale transaction. The $1,500 is not properly included as revenue, and consequently, the bonds should be reported on the financial position statement at cost ($100,000). In the case of the X-Ray Company bonds, however, valuation at cost ($50,000) would fail to recognize the fact that the bonds are worth only $49,250. Therefore, a loss of $750 is deemed to have occurred and is recorded as a December expense on the earnings statement. The bonds are valued at $49,250 on the statement of financial position. If the two investments were lumped together for statement purposes, they would appear under current assets as

Short-term investment (market value $150,750) $149,250

This is a demonstration of the rule of "lower of cost or market" (LCM), which is an acceptable basis for valuation of both short-term investments and inventories. The rule is difficult to defend on grounds of consistency, but the method is clearly conservative.

Could the loss of the X-ray Company bonds be ignored, since it is more than offset by the unrealized gain on the government bonds? The answer is apparently Yes in the case of short-term investments, because it is permissible to apply the LCM rule to the investments as a group. There is little evidence to show whether many companies actually do offset losses against gains. If this were done in our example, the asset would be stated as

Short-term investments (market value $150,750) $150,000

and no loss would appear in the December earnings statement.

If the $750 loss is recorded as in the first illustration, then $49,250 becomes the remaining "cost" of the X-Ray Company bonds for purposes of future statements. If the bonds are sold in February for $50,000, for example, a gain of $1,250 (not $500) will be added to February revenues.

Some accountants contend that gains from market increases, as well as losses from decreases, should be recorded; that is, all short-term investments should be shown at market values on the statement of financial position, in spite of the fact that such a rule contradicts the realization rule. This practice has not been widely followed. In the case of short-term notes purchased for less than maturity value, where the increase in market value is influenced primarily by the approach of the maturity date of the notes, failure to record the increase in the period in which it occurs is a failure to record interest revenue in the period earned and from the standpoint of the earnings statement is indefensible. For example, assume that notes that mature on February 1, 19x2, at $100,000 were purchased on November 1, 19x1, for $99,100. If these notes have a market value of approximately $99,700 on December 31, 19x1, it would seem reasonable to use that figure for financial position purposes and label the $600 interest revenue in the earnings statement.

Assets arising from interest or dividend revenue earned on short-term investments are often collectable when the security is liquidated and are properly reported as part of the security value until collection is made, as in the case illustrated above. Accrued interest receivable and dividends receivable may be shown as separate items but may be added into the total of short-term investments if collection is to be made prior to maturity. The value of these items is measured by the amount of interest or dividends earned to the date of the financial position statement.

Notes Receivable

These assets are monetary assets, since their value is derived in terms of a fixed number of dollars to be received at a given maturity date. They usually earn interest at a rate specified in a written document called a *promissory note.* Ordinarily notes are received by business firms from customers, with the intention that the principal be paid at maturity and the interest be paid as it comes due. A common type is the installment note, in which the principal is payable at a series of dates (usually monthly), with interest computed on the unpaid balance. These notes often originate in sales of automobiles or appliances. Notes can be bought and sold like bond investments but, strictly speaking, they are not bond "securities," since each note has its own maturity amount and date. Bonds, on the other hand, have standard characteristics as covered in a bond contract involving smaller denominations issued to many investors.

Short-term notes receivable are usually valued on financial position statements at face value, which is the equivalent of the amount to be collected at maturity, assuming that the remaining life of the note is short enough that the discount to present value may be ignored. Accrued interest receivable is valued at the total amount earned (less collections already made), and can either be shown separately or added to the face value of the note. Interest earned is recorded as revenue on a straight-line basis (equal amounts per period), and the discount to present value is also ignored because of the short-term period to the payment date.

The most important exception to these valuation rules occurs when the management has good reason to believe that all or some portion of the note and accrued interest will not be paid by the maker (originator) of the note. When management comes to this conclusion, an entry should be made reducing the assets "notes receivable" and "accrued interest receivable" and reducing the contra account *"allowance for uncollectable accounts,"* which will be explained below in greater detail.

Although notes receivable are supported by written evidence of the debt with specified due dates, etc., they are not necessarily better assets (i.e., have no greater likelihood of collection) than accounts receivable. Some firms require notes only from those customers who are considered poor credit risks or whose credit standing is unknown. The collectability of notes receivable and accrued interest receivable is a matter of constant study by management, or more specifically, the credit manager.

Although customers' notes receivable are not bought and sold by investors, as are short-term bonds, and therefore have no established market value, it is possible for firms to sell notes, usually to banks, subject to certain conditions, and thus collect the cash from the note prior to maturity. Banks usually require the selling firm to remain contingently liable to the bank in case the original maker of the note does not pay on the due date.

The amount of cash the bank is willing to pay for the note is the present value of the future cash receipts from the note. The difference between future cash receipts and the present value of these receipts, or the *discount,* constitutes the bank's revenue resulting from the transaction. For example, assume that the following events take place. On August 1, the Blanton Company, a retailer, receives a $300, ninety-day, 6 per cent note receivable from a customer in exchange for the sale of a refrigerator. On September 1, the Blanton Company "discounts" the note at a local bank whose discount rate is 8 per cent. The Blanton Company agrees to be contingently liable in case the customer does not pay on the due date. On October 29, the due date, the customer pays principal and interest of $304.50 to the Blanton Company. On October 30, the Blanton Company turns over the $304.50 cash to the bank.

These events are recorded on the Blanton Company books as follows (we omit the cost of sales entry since it is not pertinent to this illustration):

Aug. 1	Notes receivable	300.00	
	Sales revenue		300.00
Aug. 31	Assumed interest receivable	1.50	
	Interest revenue		1.50

To record August interest earned. Interest for one month is calculated as 6% × $300 ÷ 12 = $1.50. This entry assumes that Blanton Company financial statements are prepared each month.

Sept. 1	Cash	300.44	
	Interest expense	1.06	
	Notes receivable		300.00
	Accrued interest receivable		1.50

To record discounting the note with the bank at an 8 per cent rate. The computation is as follows:

Value of note at maturity (Oct. 29), principal and interest	$304.50
Less: Discount to present (Sept. 1) value at 8%	4.06
Present value (cash paid to Blanton Company)	$300.44

The $1.06 interest expense is the balance figure in the entry and represents the excess of the bank discount rate of 8 per cent on $304.50, or $4.06, over the interest rate on the note of 6 per cent on $300.00, or $3.00, for the two-month period to maturity.

The Blanton Company is usually required to endorse the note "in blank," which means that if the customer does not pay the note and interest on the due date, the Blanton Company will be liable to the bank. This is a *contingent liability* of the Blanton Company until the note matures and should be disclosed in a footnote to the financial position statement of the Blanton Company. Contingent liabilities are discussed later in this chapter.

| *Oct. 29*   Cash | 304.50 | |
| Due to bank | | 304.50 |

To record collection of the note from the customer. (The Blanton Company is acting as a collection agency for the bank in this case.)

| *Oct. 30*   Due to bank | 304.50 | |
| Cash | | 304.50 |

To record payment to bank. The contingent liability is no longer in effect. If the customer had paid $304.50 directly to the bank, the Blanton Company would have no entry to make. It merely eliminates the footnote from the financial position statement, since the contingent liability no longer exists.

Accounts Receivable

Accounts receivable represent dollar claims against customers for the sale of merchandise or the rendering of a service on credit. Accounts receivable, as distinguished from notes receivable, are seldom documented by written evidence of debt. Since they are expected to be converted to cash within the operating cycle, accounts receivable should be valued on the statement of financial position as current assets and should be measured by the future amount expected to be collected from the accounts. The collection period is usually so short that the difference between future amount and present value is too small to consider. An important exception is the case of installment accounts, which usually cover a period of many months.

Estimating Credit Losses

Generally, credit is extended to customers even though it is known at the time of sale that some proportion of the customers will not pay. An estimation of the amount of accounts receivable that will eventually prove to be uncollectable is necessary to avoid valuing accounts receivable above the estimated cash value. The effect of recording the estimate of uncollectable accounts is to convert an *asset* (accounts receivable) into an *expense* (credit losses). The asset is reduced in order to reflect on the statement of financial position the amount that is actually expected to be collected. The expense is recorded because it is associated with sales revenues in the statement of earnings. Allowing for estimated credit losses in the period of sale *properly matches* this expense with the revenues resulting from all credit sales.

There are two principal methods of estimating credit losses. The first is to estimate the proportion of total sales (or perhaps credit sales only) that will eventually result in uncollectable accounts and apply this proportion to the sales (or credit sales) of each period. The estimate is based primarily on past experience but should be modified by changes in current economic condition, changes in company policy in extending credit, and other factors. This method emphasizes the importance of the earnings statement, because it is obviously designed to achieve as accurate matching of revenue and expense as possible. It is particularly appropriate for firms having a large number of credit customers who purchase in relatively small amounts, because these conditions tend to produce a stable proportion of credit losses to sales from period to period.

The second method of estimating credit losses is to appraise the accounts and notes receivable at the end of the accounting period and estimate their collectability. Often this estimate is based on the age of the accounts (the older the account, the less collectable), and the process is known as "aging" the accounts. Since notes have maturity dates, they are not subject to aging. This method emphasizes the importance of the financial position statement, since it is the individual accounts at the end of the period, rather than the sales during the period, that provide the basis for the credit loss estimated.

To illustrate the first of these two methods, assume that the Young Company estimates that 1 per cent of credit sales will eventually result in uncollectable accounts. Since this is Young Company's first year in business, it has no past experience of its own, and relies on the advice of its trade association for the accuracy of the 1 per cent estimate. Other pertinent facts are summarized at the end of the first and second months of the first year:

	First month		Second month	
	Event no.	*Amount*	*Event no.*	*Amount*
Cash sales	(1)	$100,000	(6)	$110,000
Credit sales	(2)	125,000	(7)	120,000
Cash collected on active accounts	(3)	85,000	(8)	130,000
Estimate of credit losses	(4)	1,250	(9)	1,200
Accounts written off	(5)	800	(10)	1,000
Cash collections on accounts written off			(11)	50

These events are recorded in the ledger accounts as follows:

Cash in Bank			Accounts Receivable			
(1)	$100,000		(2)	$125,000	(3)	$ 85,000
(3)	85,000		(8)	120,000	(5)	800
(7)	110,000		(12)	50	(9)	130,000
(8)	130,000				(11)	1,000
(12)	50				(12)	50

Allowance for Uncollectable Accounts			
(5)	$ 800	(4)	$1,250
(11)	1,000	(10)	1,200
		(12)	50

Sales			Credit Losses	
(1)	$100,000	(4)	$1,250	
(2)	125,000	(10)	1,200	
(7)	110,000			
(8)	120,000			

The first three events require no explanation. Event 4 represents the expense of credit losses for the first month, based on the estimate of 1 per cent of credit sales. It should be interpreted to mean that, on the average, 1 per cent of each period's credit sales will never be collected and this amount should be shown as an expense, or deduction from sales, in each month's earnings statement.

Most students find event 5, the actual discovery of worthless or partially worthless accounts, confusing at first, because they may feel that it is this event that should measure the expense for the period instead of the estimate in event 4. Event 5 cannot be used for this purpose because it is impossible to determine at the end of each period *all* of the accounts that will eventually turn out to be worthless. In fact, our illustration is unrealistic in that the Young Company discovers some worthless accounts in the first month of operation. This is highly unlikely. Furthermore, the problem of identifying the period in which a particular account becomes wholly or partially uncollectable is very difficult, and opinions and practices vary widely from one credit manager to another. As a result, the *only* proper period to record credit losses is the period of the sale, even though the exact amount cannot be determined until a much later period.

Once this line of reasoning is accepted, the rest follows logically. The $1,250 expense in period 1 is credited to a contra account called allowance for uncollectable accounts, which is interpreted as a deduction from accounts receivable on the financial position statement. The contra account is necessary because at the time the expense estimate is recorded, the particular customers who will eventually not pay their accounts cannot be identified. Since accounts receivable is a "control" account (i.e., controlling the individual customers' accounts in a subsidiary ledger), the entry reducing this account will have to be postponed until these particular customers can be identified (see event 5). (Subsidiary ledgers are illustrated in the Appendix to Chapter 3.)

A useful way of looking at event 5 is the following:

(on the statement of financial position)

	Before event 5	After event 5
Accounts receivable	$40,000	$39,200
Less: Allowance for uncollectable accounts	1,250	450
Accounts receivable, net	$38,750	$38,750

The $800 reduction in the accounts receivable control account is offset by the debit to allowance for uncollectable accounts so that the asset "accounts receivable, net" is unchanged. Obviously, we could postpone recording event

5 indefinitely without having any effect on either financial position or earnings. The loss from worthless accounts has already been recorded in event 4, and the identification of some of these accounts in event 5 is of minor consequence. The $450 remaining balance in the contra account at the end of first month means that there are $450 of worthless accounts yet to be identified from the first month's sales (assuming that the estimate in event 4 is correct). The balance in this account is carried forward from period to period as an offset to accounts receivable.

The entries to record events 6 through 10 in period 2 are made exactly as in period 1, but event 11 introduces a new problem. These entries are summarized in journal form:

(6)	Cash	110,000	
	Sales		110,000

To record cash sales in period 2

(7)	Accounts receivable	120,000	
	Sales		120,000

To record credit sales for period 2. Debit entries totaling $120,000 are also made in the accounts receivable subsidiary ledger accounts.

(8)	Cash	130,000	
	Accounts receivable		130,000

To record collections on account for period 2. Credit entries totaling $130,000 are also made in the accounts receivable subsidiary ledger accounts.

(9)	Credit losses	1,200	
	Allowance for uncollectable accounts		1,200

To record expense from credit losses in period 2, at the rate of 1 per cent of credit sales.

(10)	Allowance for uncollectable accounts	1,000	
	Accounts receivable		1,000

To record actual accounts discovered to be worthless (or partially worthless) during period 2. Credit entries totaling $1,000 are also credited to the accounts receivable subsidiary ledger accounts.

(11)	Cash	50	
	Accounts receivable		50
	Accounts receivable	50	
	Allowance for uncollectable accounts		50

To record collection of $50 from a customer whose account had been written off previously.

The first of the two parts of entry 11 records the collection in the normal manner, possibly before the bookkeeper discovered that the account had been written off. The second part of the entry corrects the error made earlier when the account was written off. You will note that it is the opposite of the entry to record event 10. Both the credit in the first part and the debit in the second part of entry 11 are also posted to the particular customer's subsidiary ledger account. The collection may or may not restore the customer to active, current status as a credit customer.

You recall that the Young Company uses a bad debt estimate of 1 per cent of credit sales, which it obtained from a trade association because it is a new firm and has no experience of its own. How can the Young Company determine whether the 1 per cent estimate is correct? This question can be answered by observing the balance in the allowance for uncollectable accounts carried forward from period to period. If the balance increases in proportion to the balance in accounts receivable, it means that credit loss estimates are exceeding write-offs, and that perhaps the 1 per cent should be reduced. If the balance is decreasing in proportion to accounts receivable, the estimate should be increased. This recommendation assumes that worthless accounts are written off promptly as they are discovered and that the changing balance in the allowance account cannot be justified by changes in economic conditions or changes in credit policy.

Accounts receivable should also be reduced by discounts to which customers are entitled (and which they can be expected to use), estimated sales returns, and estimated collection expenses to be incurred in connection with accounts receivable currently on the financial position statement. These items pose difficult measurement problems, which are not illustrated here.

CURRENT NONMONETARY ASSETS

Inventories

There are two generally accepted methods of valuing inventory on financial statements. One of these is the *cost* method, in which cost is defined as the financial outlay needed to acquire the item or, in the case of manufacturing inventories, the amount required to bring it to the stage of completion reached as of the date of the financial position statement. The other method is *lower of cost or market*, which, with some modifications, is the same rule that applied to the valuation of short-term investments.

Of these two methods, the second is by far the most widely used in published financial statements. That is, a loss is recorded when the market value of inventories on the financial position date is substantially below acquisition cost. In recent years, largely because almost continuous general inflation tended to make market values higher than costs either method could have been used with almost the same results. Gains from market increase in inventory are not recorded, because, for reasons we have discussed earlier, most accountants are opposed to including these gains in the net earnings of the period.

In Chapters 7 and 8 we discussed the distinction between product and period costs and the problems associated with computing the cost of inventory. Here we shall review some of these considerations briefly, from a different point of view.

Cost of Purchased Inventories

Wholesalers and retailers buy their inventory items in substantially the same form in which they are sold. This means that the major portion of the acquisition cost of an inventory item is usually the invoice price paid to the seller. However, all costs necessary to bring the item to the location and condition required for sale to customers are properly added to this invoice price. Examples are freight charges associated with acquisition and warehousing costs. All cash or trade discounts available to the purchaser should normally be deducted in arriving at acquisition cost.

In these firms, selling and administration costs are not ordinarily included as inventory costs. The connection between administration and the merchandising activity is usually considered to be too remote to justify such treatment. Selling costs are usually thought of as relating primarily to the goods sold in a given period rather than to the goods on hand at the end of the period. Therefore, selling and administrative costs are treated as expenses of the period in which they are incurred.

Cost of Manufactured Inventories

The cost of raw-material items in the inventory of manufacturers is measured much as in wholesaling and retailing firms. Invoice price (less available discounts) plus freight, handling, and other acquisition and storage costs are properly included.

The cost of work in process inventories includes raw material costs as defined above plus the labor and manufacturing overhead applied to the product up to the date of the financial position statement. As we saw in Chapter 8, there is much controversy over including the nonvariable portion of manufacturing overhead. The generally accepted answer is that nonvariable manufacturing overhead should be included in inventories reported in published statements, for the same reasons advanced in Chapter 8 in support of this practice for performance measurement purposes. (Note that favoring absorption costing over variable costing for published financial statements results in higher inventory values and is contrary to the conservative nature of most of the other rules.)

To illustrate, we assume the following finished product inventory for Acme Auto Parts in the year 19x1:

	Units	Cost	Per unit	Variable	Nonvariable
On hand January 1	50	$ 750	$15	$ 9	$6
Produced during 19x1	450	8,100	18	10	8[a]

[a] $3,600 ($8,100 − $4,500) divided by 19x1 production of 450 units.

During 19x1, 375 units were sold (for $25 per unit), leaving 125 units on hand at December 31. Work in process at any time is very small, and may therefore be ignored.

EXHIBIT 14-2

ACME AUTO PARTS COMPANY

PARTIAL STATEMENT OF EARNINGS

(variable costing compared with absorption costing)

	Absorption costing	Variable costing
Sales	$9,375	$9,375
Cost of goods sold		
Finished goods, January 1		
50 units @ $15	$ 750	
50 units @ $ 9		$ 450
Cost of goods manufactured		
450 units @ $18	8,100	
450 units @ $10		4,500
Total	$8,850	$4,950
Finished goods, December 31		
125 units @ $18	2,250	
125 units @ $10		1,250
Cost of goods sold	$6,600	$3,700
		$5,675
Nonvariable manufacturing expense		3,600
Margin	$2,775	$2,075

Partial earnings statements on absorption costing and variable costing bases appear in Exhibit 14–2. Selling and administrative expenses are not shown, since these expenses are the same in both cases. Notice also that ending inventory per-unit costs are computed solely on the basis of 19x1 production. It would be equally acceptable (assuming year-to-year consistency) to average this production cost with the cost of beginning inventories, in which case ending inventory costs would be $17.70 and $9.90, respectively, instead of $18.00 and $10.00 as shown.

The two methods of costing give rise to a $700 difference in the margin.

In financial-position terms, the difference is explained by pointing out that at the end of the year, the absorption costing inventory includes $1,000 of nonvariable overhead that is to be charged to 19x2 cost of goods sold and that is partially offset by $300 nonvariable overhead in beginning inventory.

Cost measurement of the finished product inventories of manufacturers follows the same rules as measurement of work in process inventories.

As in the case of retailers and wholesalers, the selling and administrative costs of manufacturing firms are treated as expenses of the period in which the costs are incurred.

Although the discussion and illustrations in the remainder of this chapter are confined to retailers and wholesalers, all arguments apply with equal force to manufacturers. Manufacturers, however, encounter complex inventory measurement problems, which are beyond the scope of this book.

The Effect of Inventory Cost Measurement on Earnings and Assets

In Chapter 7 we considered the following calculation:

Inventory, beginning of period
+ Acquisitions during period
Goods available for sale
− Inventory, end of period
Cost of goods sold

From this we concluded that the ending inventory of one period becomes the beginning inventory of the next period. Logic dictates, therefore, that every item of inventory acquired (or manufactured) by an enterprise will influence the accounting reports either as an asset (if included in the ending inventory) or as an expense (if included in the cost of goods sold).

In any one accounting period, the method of dividing the cost of goods available for sale between ending inventory and cost of goods sold will influence both the amount of earnings reported in the statement of earnings and the total assets in the statement of financial position. Accountants have traditionally computed the cost of the ending inventory, subtracted this amount from the dollar total of goods available for sale, and taken the arithmetic residual as the cost of goods sold. Obviously, the smaller the ending inventory total, the larger the cost of goods sold, and vice versa.

Perhaps the most difficult problem in determining inventory costs and cost of goods sold stems from the fact that inventory items are purchased (or manufactured) at varying costs during the year and are often held for a substantial period of time before they are sold or processed further. Prices may change during this time, and the identity of the individual inventory items is often lost. We can illustrate the problem with an oversimplified (and exaggerated) example.

Suppose you are a shoe retailer, and at the beginning of the month you have on hand one pair of shoes of a certain size and style, purchased at a cost of $4 in the previous month. Your transactions during the current month are as follows:

January 5:   You purchased one pair for $5.
January 10: You sold one pair for $8.
January 20: You purchased one pair for $6.
January 25: You sold one pair for $9.
January 31: You have one pair on hand.

What is the earnings margin on sales in January? The answer depends on the way inventory is identified with units sold.

SPECIFIC IDENTIFICATION.   If it is possible to identify physical units of inventory in purchase and sale transactions, there is little doubt as to the historical cost of the inventory or of the goods sold during the period. A used-car dealer, a furniture store, and an appliance outlet are examples of businesses where specific identification of inventory costs may be possible. In each case the inventory consists of relatively few items that are easily identified as distinct units. Situations lending themselves to the specific identification method of determining inventory costs, however, are the exception rather than the rule.

In most situations, however, specific identification is not applicable, for the items of inventory have lost their identity, or are interchangeable. In the illustration above, if the two pairs of shoes on hand at the time of either sale are identical, should our retailer be permitted to sell any pair, as he chooses? The retailer can influence his earnings by picking a $6, $5, or $4 pair, and if the pairs are identical, reported earnings is the only criterion the retailer has in making his choice. Thus he could manipulate his earnings figures by selecting shoes of the higher or lower cost. In this case, a consistent assumption regarding the flow of goods is preferable.

ASSUMED COST FLOW.   The majority of business inventories consist of large numbers of homogeneous items usually accumulated through many separate purchases at different prices. The gasoline in the underground storage tanks of a corner gas station is such an inventory. It is physically impossible to separate and identify each gallon in the tank with its specific cost. Similar difficulties of identification occur with apples in a bin at a supermarket, shelves of hardware at a hardware store, piles of iron ore at a steel mill, etc.

When inventory items intermingle so that specific identification becomes impractical, assumptions must be made as to which acquisitions remain in the ending inventory (and, therefore, which have been sold). Accountants use three basic patterns of assumed flow: *average, first-in, first-out (FIFO),* and *last-in, first-out (LIFO).*

Average cost flow.   In this case the ending inventory cost is assumed to be representative, or an *average,* of the beginning inventory cost and the cost of all items purchased during the period. In the case of the shoe retailer, this average cost is $5 ($4 + $5 + $6 ÷ 3), and the earnings margin is computed as follows:

Sales		$17
Cost of goods sold		
Beginning inventory	$ 4	
Purchases	11	
	$15	
Ending inventory	5	
Cost of goods sold		10
Margin		$ 7

FIFO cost flow. In this case, the cost of the first items acquired (starting with the inventory on hand at the beginning of the period) is the first cost to be assigned to sales revenue and the cost of the most recently acquired items is assigned to the ending inventory. For our shoe retailer the earnings margin is:

Sales revenue		$17
Cost of goods sold		
Beginning inventory	$ 4	
Purchases	11	
Total	$15	
Ending inventory	6	
Cost of goods sold		9
Margin		$ 8

LIFO cost flow. In this case, the cost of the most recently acquired items is assigned to the sales revenue of the period, and the cost of the earliest acquired items, including the cost of items on hand at the beginning of the period, is assigned to ending inventory. The shoe retailer's margin is

Sales revenue		$17
Cost of goods sold		
Beginning inventory	$ 4	
Purchases	11	
Total	$15	
Ending inventory	4	
Cost of goods sold		11
Margin		$ 6

As this example shows, the total of $15 of inventory costs can be assigned to cost of goods sold and ending inventory in accordance with any one of three assumptions regarding the flow of inventory costs throughout the period. Each assumption will produce a different result whenever actual per-unit costs have changed during the period. Managers may select any method they like, and their choice will often be made solely on the basis of the desired effect of their choice on periodic earnings and inventory costs. They are free to ignore the actual physical flow of inventory if they wish to do so. Accounting principles suggest, however, that the same cost method be used period after period. Change of method for federal income tax purposes can be made only with permission of the Internal Revenue Service and requires full disclosure of the effect of the change on earnings and inventory costs.

For the accountant, two basic questions arise in this connection:

1. Should the physical flow of inventory items govern the choice of inventory costing method? We believe the answer is Yes, simply because there is no other objective criterion by which the choice can be made.

Many accountants reject this answer, however. They prefer to select the pricing method that most clearly reflects net earnings for the period. In those firms that experience parallel movements of cost prices and selling prices to the extent that a cause-and-effect relationship can be presumed, it can be argued that the LIFO method provides the best matching and therefore reflects earnings better than the other methods. No one doubts the validity of the earnings measurement objective, but the argument is based on the tenuous assumption that the concept of earnings is sufficiently precise to indicate the correct method. In the absence of such precision, the argument fails.

2. If the physical flow of inventory items need not be followed, and if the concept of net earnings is of no help, how can we decide among the alternatives? The generally accepted rule at present is that any of the three is acceptable, as long as it is consistently used from period to period.

In accounting practice, various outside forces influence the choice of pricing method used. One of the most prominent is the federal income tax.

The federal income tax.   The Internal Revenue Code allows the taxpayer to assume a flow of inventories different from the actual physical flow in determining taxable income for purposes of calculating the federal income tax. As a result, many enterprises employ the LIFO method, although this does not correspond to actual physical flow. This method's popularity stems from the fact that *in a period of rising prices,* LIFO produces the lowest ending-inventory figure (because the inventory bought at the highest price is used up first) and therefore the *greatest expense assigned to the current period.* By raising expenses, LIFO lowers taxable income. Of course, in a period of falling prices, LIFO would lower expenses and raise taxes. But as long as rising prices are expected, the LIFO method provides a tax advantage, and there can be little argument against its use for this purpose. The requirement that this method, if used for tax purposes, be employed in the preparation of general accounting reports remains, however, a highly questionable interference by Congress with the right of accountants to decide on accounting principles.

LIFO: good or bad?   Undoubtedly the second strongest argument favoring the use of LIFO is the fact that it results in a figure for cost of goods sold that is made up of the most up-to-date acquisition or manufacturing cost figures. When LIFO is used, the figure for cost of goods sold in the earnings statement is more closely comparable to the figure for sales than with any other method.

This argument, however, is really an argument for the use of *replacement cost*, not LIFO, in the computation of cost of goods sold. It can be argued with considerable force that the "cost" of making a sale from inventory is really the cost of replenishing the inventory, rather than the cost of the item sold. But this is an argument in favor of LIFO on the grounds that it approximates a departure from historical cost, whereas today LIFO is being used as a method of allocating historical costs.

The strongest argument in opposition to LIFO is that it tends to reduce the usefulness of the statement of financial position. The effect of allocating the more up-to-date costs to cost of goods sold is to allocate the old, out-of-date costs to the inventory shown on the statement of financial position. If the firm maintains a relatively steady physical quantity of inventory from year to year and uses LIFO during a long period of price change, the inventory valuation on the financial position statement can become virtually meaningless.

It is impossible to state a general rule regarding adoption of LIFO flow. The managers of each enterprise must decide for themselves. On the one hand, they can decrease the tax drain on earnings during periods of rising prices while presenting undervalued inventories on the statement of financial position. On the other hand, they can present more reasonable inventory valuations and pay the penalty of higher taxation. If they choose LIFO, they must be prepared to use it for the indefinite future, for the Internal Revenue Service forbids them to switch from the LIFO method to another at will.

Cost determination and perpetual inventory records. In many business situations, the need for continual and current information about materials on hand justifies the added cost of maintaining a continual or *perpetual inventory record*. Such records include every acquistion *and use* of the material, so that a current balance of items on hand is always available.

We are not concerned here with the details of a system of perpetual inventory records; rather, we wish to indicate what happens to the inventory cost figures under the average, LIFO, and FIFO assumptions. As we shall see, FIFO gives the same results as one periodic physical count, but LIFO and the average method give very different figures.

The left-hand column of Exhibit 14–4 presents the acquisitions as well as the dates and quantities in which material x–17 was withdrawn from the inventory at Acme Auto Parts.

The problem is to allocate the total cost between the 650 units of materials used in manufacturing in March and the 200 units on hand at March 31. Using the periodic inventory method, we get the results shown in Exhibit 14–3.

The perpetual inventory record produces different results from the periodic inventory when average and LIFO costing are used, because the perpetual record considers the *timing* of the purchase and use transactions occuring during the month, as Exhibit 14–4 shows.

While the differences in ending inventory figures between the periodic and perpetual systems, and therefore in the costs assigned to the accounting period,

EXHIBIT 14-3

ACME AUTO PARTS COMPANY
INVENTORIES USING PERIODIC METHOD
For March 19xx

	Periodic count	FIFO	Average cost	LIFO
Total cost to be accounted for (200 units @ $1.10, 300 units @ $1.20, 350 units @ $1.40)	$1,070	$1,070	$1,070	$1,070
Inventory at March 31				
250 units @ $1.40	350	350		
250 units @ $1.26 ($1,070 ÷ 850)			315	
250 units at LIFO (200 units @ $1.10 + 50 units @ $1.20)				280
Cost of goods sold	$ 720	$ 720	$ 755	$ 790

are not large in this illustration, they demonstrate that the same set of data can produce several different earnings figures even though generally accepted accounting principles are followed. The situation is further complicated when the *lower of cost or market* (LCM) method of valuation is superimposed over the different cost-determination techniques.

LOWER OF COST OR MARKET.   So far we have been primarily concerned with the problems of arriving at inventory costs. You recall, however, that inventories may be valued on the financial position statement at either historical cost or the lower of cost or market. This is fundamentally the same rule applied to the valuation of short-term investments, and roughly the same arguments in its favor and against it apply to inventories. As was true for investments, for inventories the LCM rule is a one-way street. Inventories may be "written down" when market values decline, but they are not "written back up" if market prices subsequently increase. If a lower market figure is used in one accounting period, it becomes the substitued cost for the next period. Market losses (declines) may be recognized, but, as mentioned earlier, market gains (advances) may not be recognized until the asset is sold.

The major difference in applying the rule to inventories appears in the definition of "market." For the short-term investments, "market" was simply the quoted selling price on the security exchanges at the date of the financial position statement. For inventories, "market" is defined as replacement cost, that is,

1. the cost of replacing a purchased item in the inventory if it were to be purchased in the usual quantities from the ususal vendors under the "typical" purchase agreement, or

EXHIBIT 14-4

ACME AUTO PARTS COMPANY
PERPETUAL INVENTORY SCHEDULE FOR MATERIAL X-17
For March 19xx

	Units	Unit cost [a]	Units on hand	FIFO	Average	LIFO
				Total Cost of Inventory on Hand		
Inventory, March 1	200	$1.10		200 @ $1.10 = $220	200 @ $1.10 = $220	200 @ $1.10 = $220
Used, March 1-5	150		50	50 @ $1.10 = $ 55	50 @ $1.10 = $ 55	50 @ $1.10 = $ 55
Purchased, March 5	300	1.20	350	50 @ $1.10 = $ 55 300 @ $1.20 = $360 $415	350 @ $1.19 = $415	50 @ $1.10 = $ 55 300 @ $1.20 = $360 $415
Used, March 5-18	250		100	100 @ $1.20 = $120	100 @ $1.19 = $119	50 @ $1.10 = $ 55 50 @ $1.20 = $ 60 $115
Purchased, March 18	350	1.40	450	100 @ $1.20 = $120 350 @ $1.40 = $490 $610	450 @ $1.35 = $609	50 @ $1.10 = $ 55 50 @ $1.20 = $ 60 350 @ $1.40 = $490 $605
Used, March 18-31	200		250	250 @ $1.40 = $350	250 @ $1.35 = $337	50 @ $1.10 = $ 55 50 @ $1.20 = $ 60 150 @ $1.40 = $210 $325

[a] In a typical, realistic example, the beginning inventories would not have the same dollar cost for each of the three methods.

2. the cost of reproducing a manufactured item, considering current costs for materials, wages, and overhead.

The LCM rule is employed in inventory valuation when the accountant feels that the acquisition cost of an asset no longer represents a realistic value for reporting purposes because the market value of that asset is less than cost. This is the case for a women's clothing store that is unable to sell inventory of last year's styles. It is also possible even when style or fashion does not govern marketability. Steel, oil, foods, machinery, automobiles—in fact all products—are subject to changing market values. The LCM rule can be applied to all business inventories.

When the LCM rule is used, the value of the inventory is computed twice, once at cost and then again at market, and the lower amount is employed in accounting reports. Exhibit 14–5 shows the calculation for the inventory of Green Hardware Supply. In this exhibit, the LCM figure is diffdierent from either the cost or the market figure because the LCM is calculated for each inventory item individually. The LCM figure will always be smaller when applied on an item-by-item basis than when it is derived on a group-total basis, as long as there are some items having costs lower than market prices. This is because both cost and market-value *totals*, no matter which is lower, would include *individual* items that are not the lower of cost or market. Data on actual practice in inventory valuation are difficult to obtain, but we believe that many firms use group totals rather than item-by-item comparisons to obtain the LCM valuation.

Market or replacement costs are often difficult to obtain, particularly for manufactured products, and occasionally they must be approximated in a rough manner. Under these circumstances the inventory should not be reported as if it had been valued with a high degree of accuracy.

LCM AND ACCOUNTING REPORTS.   The LCM rule is used primarily for

EXHIBIT 14-5

GREEN HARDWARE SUPPLY
CALCULATION OF LCM INVENTORIES

Inventory item	Units	Cost	Market value	Lower of cost or market
X	100	$ 100	$ 120	$ 100
Y	200	360	325	325
Z	50	250	250	250
A	1,000	500	530	500
B	800	420	375	375
C	1,200	1,080	960	960
Total		$2,710	$2,560	$2,510

its effect on the statement of financial position. Valuing assets conservatively, however, also affects the statement of earnings for that period: The LCM rule lowers the value of ending inventory, producing a higher cost of goods sold and therefore a lower earnings margin on sales and lower net earnings. Over several periods, however, the LCM rule does not affect earnings, because a lower ending inventory for one period becomes the lower beginning inventory for the next period, thus raising reported earnings.

Assume that the Green Hardware Supply in the previous illustration had a beginning inventory valued at cost of $3,000, which was lower than market, and purchases for the accounting period of $11,000. The LCM method of inventory valuation, as compared to using historical cost, regardless of market, affects the statement of earnings as shown in Exhibit 14–6. Note that the effect of the lower valuation is reversed in the next period, since $2,560 becomes the new beginning inventory.

EXHIBIT 14-6

GREEN HARDWARE SUPPLY

COMPARISON OF COST OF GOODS SOLD CALCULATION
Using Costs and LCM

	Cost	Lower of cost or market[a]
Inventory, beginning	$ 3,000	$ 3,000
+ Purchases	11,000	11,000
Goods available for sale	$14,000	$14,000
− Inventory, ending	2,710	2,560
Cost of goods sold	$11,290	$11,440

[a] Applied to the entire inventory rather than to individual items.

The cost method of valuing inventories can be strongly defended in accounting theory because it produces more logical matching of expenses and revenues than the LCM method. In spite of this, however, it is doubtful that the cost method is widely used in pratice. Although data on actual accounting practice are difficult to obtain, few managers would permit valuation of inventory at historical cost if they were aware that the inventory had a substantially lower market value at the date of the financial position statement.

Prepaid Expenses

Prepaid expenses (unexpired insurance, prepaid rent, prepaid taxes, office supplies, prepaid advertising, and the like) are valued at that portion of the acquisition cost that applies to future periods. They are carried as assets on the statement of financial position until they have been used up in operations or until it is determined that their value disappeared. They are then recorded in the statement of earnings as expenses or losses of the period in which they were consumed.

The justification for including prepaid expenses as assets is that it provides a more accurate matching of expenses with periodic revenues. The rule of lower of cost or market does not apply as it does in the case of inventories. In other words, accountants are much more inclinded to value prepaid expenses at unexpired cost, even though a lower replacement cost figure might be available. For instance, office supplies on hand having a cost of $500 might be valued at that figure even though they could be replaced at that time for $300. Few accountants would follow this rule in the case of inventories.

CURRENT LIABILITIES

Every business enterprise generates liabilities. Accounts payable, notes payable, and mortgages and bonds payable are liabilities with which you are already familiar. In most cases the liability is identified as a known or estimated amount of money due to a known creditor at some known time in the future. Generally accepted accounting principles suggest that monetary liabilities be shown in accounting reports at the amount of money that is expected to be required to satisfy the debt under the terms of the transaction incurring it.

In this section we discuss current liabilities in order to emphasize the importance of these liabilities in computing working capital. Special features of long-term liabilities are discussed in Chapter 15. However, since problems of estimating liabilities and of disclosing contingent liabilities are the same for both current and long-term liabilities, we shall discuss them here.

Current Monetary Liabilities

Current liabilities are those that will have to be paid within one year or within an operating cycle, whichever is longer. Most firms have operating cycles shorter than one year, and therefore the one-year rule applies. Prominent exceptions include the tobacco and distillery industires, which have long operating cycles because of the time required to age inventories. In these and similar instances, if inventories are included as current assets, current liabilities should include all debts that will come due within the longer operating cycle, including debts incurred in the financing of these inventories.

The purpose of this rather complicated definition is to permit a meaningful comparison between current assets and current liabilities on the statement of financial position. As we shall see in Part IV, short-term debt-paying power, as measured by calculations such as working capital and the current ratio, is important to many statement users.

Commitments

As a general rule, accountants recognize only liabilities that result from past transactions, and do not recognize liabilities that are likely to arise as a result of future transactions. This means that a commitment, legal or moral, to perform an act resulting in future liabilities should not be recognized until the act has occured. Premature recognition of these liabilities would also involve premature recognition of the predicted acquisition of a future asset.

For example, suppose the Able Company signs a contract to purchase 1,000 units of direct material from the Baker Company each month for the next twelve months. Does a liability arise on the date of the contract, and should it be reported in the Able Company financial position statement? Such commitments are common business practice, and unless there is something unusual about the contract, most accountants feel that the delivery of the material would mark the time to recognize the liability.

Disclosure of unexecuted and partially executed contracts is an unsettled issue in accounting pratice. Traditionally, such commitments have not been disclosed, partly because of the large volume of information that would have to be reported in the financial position statement and partly because disclosure might, in certain cases, injure the competitive position of the parties involved. On the other hand, these facts may be of such crucial importance to the firm that an intelligent assessment of financial position cannot be made unless they are known. Recent practice has leaned in the direction of more disclosure, particularly in the case of long-term commitments such as leases (discussed in the next chapter). Failure to disclose such commitments might conceal the firm's most important assets and liabilities, even when the agreements are wholly or partially unexecuted.

Estimated Liabilities

Business liabilities are sometimes created for which specific dollar amounts are unknown, even though the debt may be legally payable and the person to whom it is payable and the date of payment may be known. Typical of this type of liability is the federal income tax. Generally accepted accounting principles suggest that the dollar amount of such liabilities be estimated and included in business accounting reports. For example, the Acme Auto Parts Company ends its accounting year on December 31. During the year the company has computed its earnings, using generally accepted accounting principles, and has calculated its taxable income, using the Internal Revenue Code. The managers and accountants of the company know that by March 15 of the next year they will have to pay the income tax for the year just ended. There is no doubt that the liability exists, when it is due, or to whom it must be paid. The chances are, however, that the exact amount that will eventually have to be paid is not known because some of the items on the tax return are subject to interpretation. The final amount of tax due for any year may well be the result of negotiation between the managers of the company and the agents of the Internal Revenue Service. Generally accepted accounting principles require that an estimated liability for federal income taxes be included in the accounting reports as of December 31, even though the exact amount of that liability is not known. This procedure is employed for all liabilities of this type because any error in the estimate will be less misleading than complete omission of the liability.

Contingent Liabilities

Care must be taken to distinguish between estimated liabilities and contingent liabilities. An estimated liability is known to exist, but its amount is uncertain. The existence of a contingent liability, on the other hand, depends on some future happening. Assume that Acme Auto Parts is being sued for $2,000,000 for patent infringement, and that if the company loses the case, it will have to pay $2,000,000 to the plaintiff. If the company wins the case, it will have to pay nothing. The liability, if incurred, will be $2,000,000, but there is no certainty that it actually will be incurred, since the findings of the court cannot be predicted. Generally accepted accounting principles suggest that contingent liabilities need not be shown as dollar amounts in published accounting reports, but they should be disclosed in footnotes indicating the existence of the contingency, the approximate amount of the money involved, and the fact that the eventual outcome is uncertain. This disclosure of the contingency provides adequate information to the interested reader.

Current Nonmonetary Liabilities

Generally speaking, a nonmonetary liability is one that is valued on the financial position statement at some figure other than the present value of the cash to be paid to satisfy it. The only significant transactions that call for recognition of current nonmonetary liabilities are those in which an asset representing revenue is received by the firm before the revenue is earned. If a tenant pays six months' rent of $1,500 to a landlord on January 1, for the period ending June 30, the entry on the landlord's books on January 1 is:

Cash	1,500	
Rent received in advance		1,500

On January 31 the following adjustment is appropriate, assuming the landlord prepares monthly statements:

Rent received in advance	250	
Rent earned		250

The liability will be valued at $1,250 on the January 31 financial position statement.

The justification for this liability interpretation does not rest on the assumption that the landlord would owe a refund to the tenant if the lease were broken for some reason, although some types of leases might call for such refunds. The justification rests, instead, on the need for timely reporting of the landlord's revenues in his earnings statements. The liability arises because the landlord has the obligation to permit the tenant to occupy the premises for the period involved, and earning the revenue requires that this obligation be satisfied. The value of the liability so reported is obviously not measured by the amount of estimated "outlays" that the landlord will make.

The interpretation of such items as liabilities introduces ambiguity into the definition of liabilities. The phrase "nonmonetary liability" could be construed as a contradiction, and to avoid this problem, some accountants have substituted the title *deferred credits* (i.e., meaning that the credit to revenue has been "deferred" for a time) to indicate that these items are to be reported among the equities but that they are neither liabilities nor owners' equity. Such treatment has done nothing to clarify the ambiguity and should be discouraged.

On the other hand, interpretation of these liabilities as deferred credits to revenue is directly analogous to the interpretation of nonmonetary assets as deferred debits to expense. The justification for including inventories, plant and equipment, etc., among the assets and valuing them on the basis of cost must be that these costs are to be charged to expense in future periods and *not* that these items may have market value. Thus the same ambiguity exists in the definition of assets; this is simply one of the troublesome aspects of accounting.

SUMMARY

This chapter, Chapter 15, and Chapter 16 are concerned with the problems of measuring asset and liability items in financial statements that are available to any and all users outside the firm. In this chapter we discussed the various uses to which these statements may be put, as well as other factors affecting the measurement of the asset and liability items. Generally accepted accounting principles for measuring current monetary and nonmonetary asset and liability items were introduced and appraised. We also considered important alternatives within generally accepted accounting principles for measurement of current assets and current liabilities.

Questions for Review

14-1. Who are the principal nonmanagerial users of published financial statements? What are their more important interests in these statements?

14-2. Theoretically, what is the basic objective of the financial position statement? What are the two main reasons for the differences between accounting theory and accounting practice on the statement?

14-3. Why do accountants limit themselves to reporting on historical events rather than current values of assets?

14-4. What is "conservatism" in published statements? Give several examples of conservatism in financial statements and indicate their effects on net assets. On earnings.

14-5. What is the net effect of conservatism on reported earnings?

14-6. Define and give an example for each of the following terms:
1. monetary assets
2. nonmonetary assets
3. monetary liabilities
4. nonmonetary liabilities

14-7. What is the difference between accounts receivable and notes receivable?

14-8. What is the justification for estimating credit losses on the statement of earnings? On the statement of financial position? What are the two principal methods of making these estimates? When is each generally used?

14-9. Why are selling and administration costs generally not included in inventory costs? How are they treated?

Problems for Analysis

14-10. Define and discuss the significance of the following terms as they are used in accounting:

a. asset	**e.** liability
b. cost	**f.** owners' equity
c. expense	**g.** matching concept
d. revenue	

14-11. Franchise Associates has been operating for the past three years and has recently decided to sell its stock to the public. A CPA firm was engaged to audit its financial statements. Earnings reported for the three years were: year 1, $24,000; year 2, $33,500; and year 3, $39,700. The following errors were discovered during the audit:

	Year 1	Year 2	Year 3
Customer deposits on next year's sales recorded as revenues	$9,500	$12,000	$16,500
Accrued interest receivable omitted	500	450	0
Accrued liabilities omitted	1,250	1,900	2,700
Ending inventory understated	1,500	2,500	
Ending inventory overstated			12,000

    a. Prepare an analysis showing corrected earnings for each of the three years (ignore income taxes).

    b. Prepare the adjusting entries required to correct the books at the end of year 3.

14-12. The financial position statement of Dekline Corporation at the end of its first year of operations follows:

DEKLINE CORPORATION

STATEMENT OF FINANCIAL POSITION
As of End of Year 1

Cash	$ 28,000	Accounts payable	$ 17,000
Receivables (net)	46,000	Accrued liabilities	9,500
Inventory	71,000	Income taxes payable	14,000
Property, plant and		Capital stock	150,000
equipment (net)	114,000	Retained earnings	68,500
	$259,000		$259,000

No dividends were declared in year 1.

You are asked to review the accounting records to determine whether the earnings of $68,500 and statement of financial position are correct. You discover the following errors:

Inventory overstated	$15,000
Prepaid expenses omitted	2,850
Unearned revenue (recorded as revenue earned)	12,300
Accrued expenses omitted (property taxes expense)	1,100

a. Compute the corrected earnings for year 1. Assume a federal income tax rate of 30 per cent.

b. Prepare a revised statement of financial position.

14-13. The following information pertains to the financial position of Dane Corporation, a television repair company.

	April 30	May 31
Cash	$ 3,200	$ 9,600
Accounts receivable (net)	1,100	2,250
Inventory	2,700	2,500
Land	7,000	7,000
Building (net)	24,000	23,500
Equipment (net)	8,000	8,350
Accounts payable		
(all for inventory purchases)	2,900	2,200
Capital stock	20,000	21,000

An analysis of the checkbook stubs reveals the following:

Receipts:	
Services rendered for cash	$ 5,000
On accounts receivable	12,000
Sale of capital stock	1,000
	$18,000
Disbursements:	
On accounts payable (all for inventory purchases)	$ 7,500
For operating expenses	2,600
For purchase of equipment	500
For dividends	1,000
	$11,600

You determine that $200 has been recorded as a reasonable provision for credit losses allocable to May.

Prepare the following financial statements:

a. earnings for May

b. financial position as of May 31

14-14. A comparative trial balance for Rock Company, after closing revenue and expense accounts, follows:

ROCK COMPANY

TRIAL BALANCES

For January 1 and December 31

	January 1	December 31
Cash	$ 10,000	$ 20,000
Accounts receivable (net)	40,000	45,500
Accrued interest receivable	400	350
Notes receivable	6,000	6,000
Inventory	65,000	70,000
Prepaid expenses	5,000	4,000
Land	20,000	20,000
Buildings (net)	60,000	59,000
Equipment (net)	45,000	47,000
	$251,400	$271,850
Accounts payable (all for inventory purchases)	$ 32,000	$ 29,000
Accrued interest payable	700	950
Notes payable	10,000	10,000
Accrued liabilities	4,500	5,700
Capital stock	150,000	160,000
Retained earnings	54,200	75,650
	$251,400	$271,850

An analysis of the cash account reveals the following summary of transactions:

Receipts:	
For cash sales	$ 50,000
Collections on accounts receivable	260,000
For interest on notes receivable	600
For sale of capital stock	10,000
	$320,600
Disbursements:	
For accounts payable	$120,000
For operating expenses	62,000
For interest on notes payable	700
For purchase of equipment	10,000
For dividends	117,900
	$310,600

A reasonable estimate of credit losses resulting from this year's sales is $800.
Prepare a statement of earnings for the year.

14-15. The statement of financial position for Namco Construction Company follows:

NAMCO CONSTRUCTION COMPANY

STATEMENT OF FINANCIAL POSITION

As of November 30, 19x4

Assets		Equities	
Cash	$ 40,000	Capital stock	$130,000
Machinery and			
equipment (net)	120,000	Retained earnings	30,000
	$160,000		$160,000

The company has just been awarded a contract to construct an office building. It has no other contracts at the present time.

Date of contract: December 1

Terms of contract: Estimated thirty months to complete from date of contract

Sales price: $400,000

Cash payment schedule:

$180,000 when the contract is 50 per cent completed

$220,000 upon completion and final acceptance by the customer

Estimated cost of production: $300,000.

The following data relate to the completion of the contract by Namco Construction Company:

November 30, 19x5: Extimated that the contract is thirty per cent completed. Actual costs to date, $95,000. This includes $10,000 for depreciation on machinery. Of the remaining expenses, $35,000 was paid in cash and $50,000 resulted in accounts payable.

November 30, 19x6: Estimated that the contract is 70 per cent completed. Actual costs to date, $220,000. This includes $20,000 for depreciation on machinery. The remaining expenses for the year resulted in accounts payable. Namco collected $180,000 on the contract and paid $165,000 on accounts payable.

November 30, 19x7: The contract was completed during the year, and the remaining $220,000 was collected. Total contract cost amounted to $315,000. This includes $25,000 for depreciation on machinery, and the remaining expenses for the year initially resulted in accounts payable. The entire amount of accounts payable was paid.

a. Prepare a comparative earnings statement for each of the three years and a statement of financial position at the ends of years 5, 6, and 7, for each of the following independent assumptions:

1. Revenue is recognized at the point of production.
2. Revenue is recognized at the point of sale (completed contract).
3. Revenue is recognized at the point of cash collection.

b. What are the circumstances that justify the recognition of revenue at:
1. the point of production?
2. the point of sale?
3. the point of cash collection?

c. When *should* Namco Construction Company recognize revenue from this contract? Discuss.

d. Of what significance are these alternatives of revenue recognition to a user of accounting reports?

14–16. The Automatic Machinery Company has just negotiated a contract for the manufacture of a special-purpose automatic screw machine. The terms of the contract are as follows:

Date of contract: April 1

Terms of contract: Estimated at two years to complete, from date of contract

Sales price: $760,000

Cash payment schedule:

$100,000 at the date the contract is signed

$75,000 when production is 25 per cent completed

$175,000 when production is 50 per cent completed

$175,000 when production is 75 per cent completed

$175,000 when production is 100 per cent completed

$60,000 upon delivery and final acceptance by the customer

The estimated cost of production is $608,000.

The following data relate to the completion of the contract by the Automatic Machinery Company:

April 1: Initiated production.

November 30: Estimated that the contract is 25 per cent completed. Actual costs to date, $150,000.

December 31: Estimated that the contract is 30 per cent completed. Actual costs to date, $180,000.

March 31: Estimated that the contract is 45 per cent completed. Actual cost to date, $300,000.

August 31 (second year): Estimated that the contract is 75 per cent completed. Actual costs to date, $450,000.

December 31 (second year): Estimated that the contract is 85 per cent completed. Actual costs to date, $540,000.

February 28 (second year): The contract is 100 per cent completed and delivered to the customer. Actual costs, $590,000.

March 31 (second year): Notification of final acceptance is received from the customer.

a. Compute the profit on this contract for each of the three years ending December 31 (starting with the year of the receipt of the contract), assuming that revenue is recognized at:

      1. the point of production
      2. the point of sale
   b. What are the circumstances that justify the recognition of revenue at:
      1. the point of production?
      2. the point of sale?
   c. When should the Automatic Machinery Company recognize revenue for this contract? Discuss.

   d. Of what significance are these alternatives of revenue recognition to a user of accounting reports?

14-17. The Dakota Company, which reports on a calendar-year basis, had the following short-term investments in its portfolio for a four-year period:

Year 1

   June 1: The Dakota Company purchased 500 shares of common stock of Spearfish, Inc., at $48 per share.

   November 15: Dakota received a dividend of $1.50 per share.

   December 31: The market value for the Spearfish stock was $52 per share.

   July 1: Dakota purchased $100,000 par-value, $3\frac{1}{2}$ per cent U.S. Government bonds at par.

   December 31: Dakota received a semi-annual interest payment on the bonds.

   December 31: The market value on the bonds was 98 per cent of par value.

Year 2

   February 15: Dakota sold the Spearfish stock for $60 per share.

   June 30: Dakota received semiannual interest payments on the bonds and then sold the bonds for 95 per cent of par.

   December 1: Dakota purchased 1,000 shares of common stock of the Homestake Company at $90 per share.

   December 28: Dakota received a dividend of $2 per share on the Homestake stock.

   December 31: The market value on the Homestake stock was $82 per share.

Year 3

   March 28: Dakota received a dividend of $2 per share on the Homestake stock.

   June 28: Dakota received a dividend of $2 per share on the stock.

   September 28: Dakota received a $2 dividend on the stock.

   December 28: Dakota received a $2 dividend on the stock.

   December 31: The market value on the stock was $85 per share. The company decided to hold the securities until the next calendar year because they anticipated that the market value of the stock would be higher.

Year 4

   January 25: Dakota sold the Homestake stock for $89 per share.

   Show how these securities would be reflected in the statement of earnings and statement of financial position of the Dakota Company for each of the four calendar years. Include the financial statement classification ("current assets," "operating expenses," etc.) in your answer.

14-18.

PART I

The Rushmore Company had the following short-term investments in its portfolio on November 30, the end of its fiscal year:

1. Stock of Dynamics, Inc. Rushmore had purchased 300 shares at a cost of $70 per share. The market value of the stock on November 30 was $75 per share.

2. Stock of Violets Company. Rushmore had purchased 700 shares for $50 per share. The market value of the stock on November 30 was $42 per share.

Show how these securities would be reflected on the statement of financial position and the statement of earnings of the Rushmore Company under each of the following assumptions:

a. Securities are valued on the statement of financial position at cost.

b. Securities are valued on the statement of financial position at LCM value.

c. Securities are valued on the statement of financial position at market value.

PART II

Assume that the securities were sold on December 15 of the next fiscal year at the following prices:

1. Dynamics, Inc., $80 per share
2. Violets Company, $45 per share

a. How would these transactions be reflected on the financial statements in the period of sale according to each of the assumptions above?

b. Evaluate the three methods used above for valuing short-term investments.

c. Relate your evaluation to generally accepted accounting principles for short-term investments.

14-19. Prepare journal entries to record the following transactions of Savings, Inc.

February 1: Received a $1,000, 120-day, 8 per cent note receivable from a customer in payment of an account receivable.

March 1: Discounted the note with the Lewis Bank. The discount rate was 10 per cent and Savings, Inc., endorsed the note in blank.

June 1: The customer paid the Lewis Bank the maturity value of the note.

14-20. Prepare journal entries to record the following transactions of Elso Company.

May 1: Received a $3,000, ninety-day, 7 per cent note receivable from Super, Inc., in payment of an account receivable.

June 15: Endorsed and discounted the note at Capital Bank at an 8 per cent discount rate.

July 29: The note was dishonored by Super, Inc. Elso Company paid Capital Bank for the maturity value of the note.

14-21. Trump Company had the following account balances related to accounts receivable at the end of its fiscal year on June 30, 19x2:

Accounts receivable	$140,000
Allowance for uncollectable accounts	8,000

The following transactions pertain to uncollectable accounts for the fiscal year ending June 30, 19x3.

1. Wrote off uncollectable accounts of $8,200 during the year.
2. Estimated uncollectable accounts for the current year to be 2 per cent of net sales, which were $450,000.

a. Prepare journal entries to record the information in 1 and 2 above.

b. Assuming that accounts receivable at June 30, 19x3 were $160,000, show how accounts receivable, allowance for uncollectable accounts, and credit losses would be reported on the financial statements.

14-22. The Canton Company has just completed its first year of operations. The company has made all sales of merchandise on account. The credit sales for the year amounted to $420,000. The accounts receivable at the end of the year amounted to $71,000. Experience obtained from the trade association for the industry indicates that $1\frac{1}{2}$ per cent of credit sales can be expected eventually to become uncollectable.

a. Compute the estimated credit losses for the year, and make the journal entry to record these losses.

b. Show how the estimated credit losses should be reported in the statement of earnings and in the statement of financial position, assuming that $2,000 is considered uncollectable. Make the entry to record the write-off of these accounts.

c. What is the justification for estimating and providing for uncollectable accounts in the statement of earnings? In the statement of financial position? Explain.

14-23. The Factory Merchandise Mart, Inc., had the following information relative to sales and accounts receivable at the end of its first year of operations on September 30:

Accounts receivable	$ 40,000
Sales	300,000
Sales returns & allowances	6,000
Sales discounts	3,700

Sales and accounts receivable information for the second fiscal year was as follows:

Accounts receivable	$ 56,000
Sales	325,000
Sales returns & allowances	9,400
Sales discounts	4,650

a. Assuming that the company estimates that $1\frac{1}{2}$ per cent of its net sales will eventually become uncollectable, compute the credit losses for the first fiscal year ended September 30.

b. Show how the information pertaining to credit losses would be reflected in the statements of earnings and financial position for the first fiscal year ended September 30.

c. Assume that during the next fiscal year, accounts amounting to $3,950 prove to be uncollectable. How would this information be reflected in the accounts?

d. Show how the information pertaining to credit losses would be reflected in the statements of earnings and financial position for the second fiscal year ended September 30.

e. Are the balances allowed for uncollectable accounts and credit losses the same in part *d* above? If not, what causes the difference?

f. What is the justification for estimating credit losses in the statement of earnings, as opposed to waiting until the uncollectable account is discovered? What is the justification in the statement of financial position?

14-24. The Excelsior Company has a $400 balance for uncollectable accounts at the end of the current year prior to the adjustment for credit losses. Data relating to sales and accounts receivable for the current year are as follows:

Accounts receivable	$ 90,000
Sales	940,000
Sales returns & allowances	14,500
Sales discounts	11,000

a. The company estimates that 1 per cent of gross sales will eventually become uncollectable. How will this information be reflected in the statement of earnings and statement of financial position?

b. What is the justification for estimating credit losses in the statement of earnings? In the statement of financial position?

c. Why are estimated credit losses reflected as "allowance for uncollectable accounts" in the statement of financial position rather than *direct* reductions against accounts receivable?

14-25. The Mudner Electrical Products Company is a wholesaler of a complete line of electrical products. The company buys large quantities of copper wire.

Data relating to the purchase and sale of sixteen-gauge copper wire for the last six months of a calendar year are as follows:

	Pounds	Cost per pound
Inventory, 7/1	5,000	$.59
Purchases:		
7/20	2,100	.61
8/25	3,600	.625
10/1	3,000	.63
11/15	3,700	.64
12/20	3,900	.65

The company sold 17,000 pounds of sixteen-gauge copper wire during the six-month period at $.70 per pound.

a. Using the following methods of determining cost, prepare partial statements of earnings as of December 31, showing the earnings margin on sales:

    1. FIFO

    2. LIFO

    3. Average

b. Explain your choice of inventory method—periodic or perpetual—in your answer to the question above.

c. Why do the three inventory costing methods produce different results?

d. In your opinion, which of the three inventory costing methods is the most appropriate in this situation? Discuss.

14–26. Assume that the Mudner Electrical Products Company in problem 14–25 maintains perpetual inventory records for the sixteen-gauge copper wire. The sale of 17,000 pounds of wire occurred as follows:

Date	Pounds
7/25	2,800
8/15	2,000
8/31	2,100
9/20	1,900
10/10	2,300
11/12	1,700
11/30	2,300
12/22	1,900

a. Using the following methods of determining cost, prepare partial statements of earnings as of December 31, showing the earnings margin on sales:

    1. FIFO

    2. LIFO

    3. Average

b. What differences in the earnings margin on sales are produced by the periodic and perpetual inventory methods, using each of the three costing methods above? Why do these differences occur?

c. Compute the earnings margin on sales, assuming that the purchase of 3,900 units on December 20 had not been made. What effect would making or not making this purchase have on the earnings margin on sales under each of the three costing methods?

14-27. a. Using the three ending inventories computed in problem 14–25, determine the ending inventory and the cost of goods sold, according to the LCM method of inventory valuation. The market price (replacement cost) of copper is $.64 per pound as of December 31.

b. What is the justification for using the LCM method of inventory valuation?

c. Which method of inventory valuation, cost or lower of cost or market, does a better job of matching revenues earned with expenses incurred?

14-28. The following information was taken from the records of Gearly, Inc., for April:

	Units	Unit cost	Total cost
Inventory, 4/1	1,500	$40	$60,000
Purchases:			
4/5	700	40	28,000
4/12	900	41	36,900
4/15	1,200	45	54,000
4/24	1,000	45	45,000
4/30	800	48	38,400

During April the following units were sold:

4/3	900
4/9	800
4/17	1,000
4/26	1,100

a. What was the April cost of goods sold and the April 30 inventory valuation, using the perpetual inventory method:
   1. Assuming cost to be determined on a FIFO basis?
   2. Assuming cost to be determined on a LIFO basis?
   3. Assuming cost to be determined on the average method?
b. What was the April cost of goods sold and the April 30 inventory valuation, using the periodic inventory method under each of the three costing assumptions of part *a* above?

c. Compute the differences between the perpetual and periodic inventory methods, using each of the three inventory costing methods. You might set up a chart as follows:

	Perpetual	Periodic	Difference
Ending inventory, FIFO cost			

14–29.   PART I

Zlatkin Enterprises had 5,000 gallons of fuel oil at $.17 per gallon in its beginning inventory on September 1. Purchases of fuel oil for September were as follows:

Date	Gallons	Cost per gallon	Total cost
9/10	10,000	$.18	$1,800
9/18	15,000	.19	2,850
9/27	15,000	.20	3,000

Sales for the month totaled 38,000 gallons at $.27 per gallon.

a. Compute the earnings margin from the sale of fuel oil for September under each of the following inventory costing assumptions:
  1. FIFO
  2. LIFO
  3. Average

b. Assuming that the market price (replacement cost) of the fuel oil was $.185 per gallon on September 30, compute the earnings margin for September, using the LCM method of valuing inventory under each of the following inventory costing assumptions:
  1. FIFO
  2. LIFO
  3. Average

PART II

Zlatkin Enterprises made the following purchases of fuel oil for October:

Date	Gallons	Cost per gallon	Total cost
10/5	12,000	$.19	$2,280
10/17	14,000	.20	2,800
10/31	10,000	.21	2,100

Sales for the month totaled 30,000 gallons at $.28 per gallon.

a. Using the information from a of Part I above, compute the earnings margin from the sale of fuel oil for October under each of the following inventory costing assumptions:

1. FIFO
2. LIFO
3. Average

b. Using the information from *b* of Part I above and the LCM method of valuing inventory, compute the earnings margin from the sale of fuel oil for October under each of the following inventory costing assumptions:

1. FIFO
2. LIFO
3. Average

c. Evaluate the use of the cost method versus the LCM method of inventory valuation from the standpoint of matching revenues and expenses.

14-30.   PART I

The Grey Company is a wholesaler of plumbing supplies. Their inventory as of August 31, the end of their fiscal year, is as follows:

Inventory item	Units	Cost per unit	Market value per unit
A	100	$ 4.20	$ 4.00
B	240	11.50	10.90
C	600	26.00	26.00
D	750	21.00	19.50
Y	400	7.10	7.45

The inventory at the beginning of the current fiscal year was $32,000, and purchases for the period amounted to $80,000.

a. Compute the ending inventory and the cost of goods sold under the following independent situations:

1. Ending inventory is valued at cost.
2. Ending inventory is valued at lower of cost or market (applied to the entire inventory).
3. Ending inventory is valued at lower of cost or market (applied on an item-by-item basis).

b. Compared with cost, what effect does the LCM rule have on reported earnings for the current year? On the statement of financial position for the current year?

PART II

Assume that the inventory purchases for the following year are $90,000. The total ending inventory at August 31 of the following year is as follows:

Cost	$34,000
Total market value (applied to entire ending inventory)	34,250

a. Compute the cost of goods sold for the second year, assuming that the company values ending inventory at cost.

b. Compute the cost of goods sold for the second year, assuming that the company values ending inventory at lower of cost or market, applied to the entire inventory.

c. Compute the difference in total cost of goods sold for the two years between the cost method of inventory valuation and the LCM method of inventory valuation, applied to the entire inventory.

d. What effect does the LCM method have on reported earnings for the second year? For the two-year period?

e. The statement is made in Chapter 14 that "the determination of periodic earnings requires a *proper matching* of revenues and costs within the given accounting period." In your opinion which method of inventory valuation, cost or LCM, does a better job of implementing the matching concept? Discuss.

14-31. Yanks, Inc., manufactures and sells one model of hair dryers. Information relative to beginning inventory and production for the current year follows:

	Units	Per unit	Variable	Nonvariable
Beginning inventory, January 1	300	$12	$8	$4
Produced during 19x2	1,500	15	9	6[a]

[a] $9,000 divided by 19x2 production of 1,500 units.

1,100 units were sold during the year for $27 each. There was no beginning or ending work in process inventory. Selling and administrative expenses were $5,000.

a. Prepare a statement of earnings on the variable costing basis under each of the following assumed cost flows:
1. FIFO
2. LIFO
3. Average

b. Prepare a statement of earnings on the absorption costing basis under each of the following assumed cost flows:
1. FIFO
2. LIFO
3. Average

c. Do you recommend the use of variable or absorption costing in published financial statements? Discuss.

14-32. Harold's, Inc., manufactures and sells one style of minibike. A summary of operations for 19x7 follows:

	Units	Amount
Raw materials inventory, January 1		$ 30,000
Work in process inventory, January 1		0
Finished goods inventory, January 1	500	500,000
Raw materials inventory, December 31		35,000
Work in process inventory, December 31		0
Finished goods inventory, December 31	600	66,000
Purchases—raw materials		295,000
Direct labor		420,000
Manufacturing overhead		305,000
Selling and administrative expenses		110,000
Sales	1,000	1,600,000

a. Prepare a statement of cost of goods manufactured indicating the cost per unit of finished goods produced during the year.

b. Prepare a statement of earnings for the year under each of the following three assumptions relative to inventory cost flows:

1. FIFO
2. LIFO
3. Average

14-33. Gaylord's, Inc., has computed earnings of $200,000 before income taxes. You have reviewed their accounts and determine the need for the following adjustments:

1. No recognition was made in the accounts for $1,500 of accrued salaries at the end of the year.

2. Accrued interest on notes payable of $2,000 has not been recorded.

3. The account "insurance expense" shows the cost of all insurance premiums paid during the year. Prepaid insurance at year-end amounted to $4,100.

4. A $10,000 deposit on a sales contract was recorded as revenue. Performance under the contract is expected to take place early in the next fiscal year.

5. An inventory of office supplies indicates items of $3,700 on hand at year-end. The office supplies account, which was unchanged during the year, shows a balance of $2,900.

6. The "allowance for uncollectable accounts" account reflects a debit balance of $600. The ending accounts receivable balance is $40,000, of which 4 per cent is estimated to be uncollectable.

7. The federal income tax rate is 30 per cent.

a. Prepare journal entries to record the above information.

b. Prepare a schedule indicating earnings after your adjustments in *a* above.

14-34. A summary of purchases for Unger Company follows:

Purchases $200,000; terms 2/10; n/30 (2 per cent discount if paid within ten days; if not paid then, the full amount must be paid within thirty days).

Paid on account:

    $150,000 within the discount period

    $50,000 after the discount period had passed

Prepare journal entries to record the above information.

14–35. Prepare the current asset section of a statement of financial position for Blundell's Manufacturing Company for the fiscal year ended April 30, 19x5, from the following information:

Cash accounts:	
Petty cash	$ 300
Cash in bank:	
Operating account	40,000
Payroll account	3,500
Dividend account	1,000
Restricted account for preferred stock	
retirement in 19y1	22,000
Accounts receivable:	
Sales to customers	80,000
Travel advance to officers	700
Sales to employees	1,200
IOU in petty cash fund from employee	50
Notes receivable:	
From customers	8,400
From loans to officers	750
From customers (discounted with the local bank)	1,500
Inventories:	
Factory supplies (FIFO cost)	400
Raw materials (FIFO cost)	11,500
Work in process (FIFO cost)	17,000
Finished goods (at lower of cost or market:	
FIFO cost, $60,000; market, $57,000)	?
Prepaid expenses:	
Prepaid licenses	450
Prepaid insurance	700
Prepaid rentals	1,300

14–36. Analyze the effect on current liabilities of the following two independent transactions of Aire, Inc., for the accounting period ended August 31:

    1. Inventory is purchased on account on August 27 for $12,000, with payment due in thirty days.

    2. A remittance of $10,000 is received from a customer on August 27 for merchandise that will be shipped in thirty days.

    Contrast the nature of these two obligations and the methods of discharging them.

14-37. The following list contains current liabilities that frequently appear in published financial statements. Define each of the following items or describe the typical transactions that would create and discharge them.

    a. bank overdraft
    b. accounts payable
    c. notes payable
    d. subscriptions received in advance
    e. accrued interest payable
    f. federal income taxes payable
    g. social security and withholding taxes payable
    h. city income taxes payable
    i. liability for union dues withheld from employees
    j. current installment of 5 per cent serial bonds payable

14-38. The Creighton Company has two long-term obligations:

    1. $5\frac{1}{2}$ per cent twenty-year bonds payable, due on February 1, 19x6.
    2. A $4\frac{3}{4}$ per cent twenty-year note payable, due on May 15, 19x6. The management of the company plans to pay off the bonds payable with cash that has been previously accumulated. The note payable will be paid off by the issuance of another twenty-year note.

    How would you classify these two obligations on the statement of financial position of the Creighton Company for the fiscal year ended June 30, 19x5?

14-39. Somis, Inc., reported the following transactions for its fiscal year ended April 30 regarding an account with one of its customers, the Zoom Company:

    January 15: Somis sold merchandise on account to Zoom Company for $6,500, with payment due in thirty days.

    February 15: The Zoom Company had insufficient cash to pay for the January 15 purchase and persuaded Somis to accept a ninety-day noninterest-bearing note receivable in payment for the account receivable.

    March 31: Somis discounted the note received from the Zoom Company with the local bank, receiving cash of $6,500 less the bank's discount. The local bank required Somis to endorse the note of Zoom so that the bank could require Somis to pay the note in case Zoom failed to do so.

    a. Did Somis incur a liability by discounting its customer's note with the local bank?

    b. How should the discounting of the customer's note be reflected in the statement of financial position of Somis as of April 30?

14-40. The following independent situations represent different kinds of liabilities. Which kind of liability—current, long-term, estimated, or contingent—does each of the following represent?

    a. Accounts payable to suppliers.
    b. Long-term bonds payable, due in 19x5.
    c. [Estimated] federal income taxes payable.

d. A bank overdraft.

e. A promissory note received from a customer, endorsed, and discounted with a local bank.

f. The portion of long-term serial bonds payable that matures in six months.

g. A lawsuit initiated by a customer who claims to have suffered damages because of an inferior product. The outcome of the lawsuit is not determinable at this time.

h. A Company has guaranteed the principal and interest payments on a bond issue of X Company. In case X Company is unable to meet principal and interest payments as they become due, A Company will be liable to the creditors of X Company.

14-41. Prepare the current-liability section of Hasbrouck's Inc., for the fiscal year ended June 30, 19x5, from the following information:

1. Cash (First National Bank), $74,000; overdraft (Dimes State Bank), $6,500.

2. Liability for merchandise purchased on account, $30,000.

3. Estimated liability resulting from one-year product guarantees, $7,000.

4. Revenue received in advance for magazine subscriptions, $80,000. The subscriptions will be earned in the following fiscal periods:

Fiscal year ended June 30, 19x6	$42,000
Fiscal year ended June 30, 19x7	25,000
Fiscal year ended June 30, 19x8	13,000

5. Estimated federal income taxes payable on earnings for fiscal year, $11,000.

6. Customer's note endorsed and discounted with First National Bank.

7. Notes payable, due within one year, arising from the following transactions:

  a. Loan from First National Bank, $8,000.

  b. Loan from officers of Hasbrouck's, $11,500.

8. Social security and withholding taxes payable, $2,500.

9. Interest payable on notes payable, $850.

10. Other accrued expenses payable, $7,000.

Chapter Fifteen LONG-TERM MONETARY ASSETS AND LIABILITIES; INVESTMENTS

INTRODUCTION

In this chapter and the next we discuss presentation (on the statement of financial position) of assets and liabilities whose life spans are longer than the current assets and liabilities discussed in Chapter 14. These longer-lived items fall into the monetary-nonmonetary categories already described. Furthermore, primarily because of the long lives involved, their reported valuation is subject to distortion caused by the changing purchasing power of the dollar in periods of inflation and deflation.

Chapter 15 considers the valuation of long-term monetary assets and liabilities, and then goes on to discuss investments, a special type of nonmonetary asset. Chapter 16 examines other long-lived nonmonetary assets and liabilities and introduces the potential influence of price level changes on financial statements.

LONG-TERM MONETARY ASSETS AND LIABILITIES

Long-term monetary assets and liabilities are investment in bonds or notes receivable or payable, depending on whether the firm being accounted for is the lender or the borrower. In this section we discuss the valuation rules applicable to these items. We also consider briefly some of the important problems related to long-term leases, from the standpoint of the lessee, and to accounting for pension plans of industrial firms, from the standpoint of the employer. A few specialized problems of other long-term liabilities are also touched upon.

Noninterest-bearing Receivables and Payables

The simplest case of the long-term receivable or payable is the noninterest-bearing bond or note. The term "noninterest-bearing" simply means that the interest is implicit in the loan transaction instead of being expressly stated on the face of the note. Assume that on January 1, 19x0, Adams borrows $8,900 from Browne and signs a note of $10,000 face value with a maturity date of December 31, 19x1. Since the amount of money borrowed is only $8,900, the implicit interest rate is almost exactly 6 per cent compounded annually. Entries on the books of both parties over the two-year period are as follows:

	Adams' Books		*Browne's Books*	
January 1, 19x0	Adams borrows $8,900 from Browne and signs a 2-year, $10,000, noninterest-bearing note.			
	Cash 8,900		Note receivable 8,900	
	Note payable	8,900	Cash	8,900
December 31, 19x0	Interest for the first year (6% of $8,900 or $534)			
	Interest expense 534		Note receivable 534	
	Note payable	534	Interest earned	534
December 31, 19x1	Interest for the second year (6% of $9,434 or $566)			
	Interest expense 566		Note receivable 566	
	Note payable	566	Interest earned	566
December 31, 19x1	Adams repays the debt of $10,000			
	Note payable 10,000		Cash 10,000	
	Cash	10,000	Note receivable	10,000

It should be noted that it is incorrect to state the interest rate in this transaction as $5\frac{1}{2}$ per cent (i.e., $550 average interest per year divided by $10,000), for two reasons: (1) The statement would ignore the effect of compounding, and (2) even more important, it would fail to recognize that $8,900 is the true principal, not $10,000, even though the latter figure is the only one stated on the face of the note. The amount of cash changing hands at the time of the transaction is determined by the effective rate of interest agreed upon between the lender and the borrower.

A variation of this transaction occurs with U.S. Government Series E bonds. Here, both the original principal (e.g., $75) and the maturity value ($100) are fixed by the terms of the issue. The entire interest of $25 is paid when the bond matures. However, it is still possible to vary the effective interest rate by varying the maturity date, and therefore the term, of the bond, and this has been done in the past. The bonds were originally issued to mature in ten years, and the effective interest rate was therefore just under 3 per cent.°

But the original ten-year maturity has been reduced on several occasions to increase the effective yield on Series E bonds. To obtain a yield of 4 per cent compounded annually, for example, the Series E bond must mature in approximately seven years and four months, as can be determined from Table II.

Interest-bearing Receivables and Payables

A more direct way of implementing an effective rate of interest is to add to the lending agreement a provision for periodic cash payment of interest over the life of the note, in addition to the payment of the face value at maturity. Consider the agreement between Adams and Browne above ($10,000 face value, two-year note) as an example, adding the requirement that Adams pay Browne $600 in cash at the end of the first year and again at the end of the second year, in addition to the maturity value of $10,000 at the end of the second year. We find that the price of the note is now $10,000, computed as follows:

Present value of $10,000 maturity value (2 years, 6%)(Table II) =	$ 8,900
Present value of an annuity of $600 (2 years, 6%)	
= $600 × 1.8334 (Table IV)	= 1,100
Present value of note (principal)	$10,000

The price of this note is $1,100 higher than the price of the noninterest-bearing note at 6 per cent and the amount borrowed is therefore $10,000 instead of $8,900. Entries on the books of the borrower (Adams) and lender (Browne) are as follows:

Adams' Books		*Browne's Books*	
January 1, 19x0 Adams borrows $10,000 from Browne and signs a 2-year, $10,000, 6% note.			
Cash 10,000		Notes receivable 10,000	
Notes payable	10,000	Cash	10,000
December 31, 19x0 Interest for the first year is accrued			
Interest expense 600		Interest receivable 600	
Interest payable	600	Interest earned	600

° This can be determined by scanning the tenth row (assuming annual compounding) of Table II in the appendix to Chapter 11 for the tabular figure nearest .75, which is the 3 per cent column. The answer is proved by noting that

$$\$100 \times (\text{present value of } \$1, n = 10, i = ?) = \$75$$

and dividing both sides by $100:

$$\text{Present value of } \$1 \ (n = 10, i = ?) = \tfrac{75}{100} = \$.75.$$

	Adams' Books			Browne's Books	
January 2, 19x1	Interest for the first year is paid				
	Interest payable	600		Cash	600	
	Cash		600	Interest receivable		600
December 31, 19x1	Interest for the second year is accrued				
	Interest expense	600		Interest receivable	600	
	Interest payable		600	Interest payable		600
December 31, 19x1	Principal ($10,000) and interest for the second year ($600) is paid				
	Notes payable	10,000		Cash	10,600	
	Interest payable	600		Notes receivable		10,600
	Cash		10,600	Interest receivable		600

Bonds

The price of a bond is established like the price of the interest-bearing note illustrated above, i.e., the sum of (1) the present value of the face or maturity amount and (2) the present value of the interest annuity. There is, however, one added complication: It is not possible for the borrower (issuer) and lender (investor) to agree on the characteristics of the bond at the time the bond is purchased. There is often considerable delay between the time the characteristics of the bonds are established (called an *indenture* in a contract) and the time they are finally purchased by an investor, and conditions in the bond market may change in the meantime. This means that the interest rate on the bond, which is called the *coupon* rate and which establishes the amount of the interest annuity, does not usually agree with the *effective* or *yield* rate of interest, which reflects the price of the bond actually paid to the issuer by the investor. The yield rate also reflects, of course, the amount of money the bond issuer has actually been able to borrow, and the yield rate therefore is also the actual rate of interest the borrower must pay.

Most bonds may be bought and sold many times after issue on highly organized securities markets, and the prices paid in these transactions are established by the market conditions existing at the time. This means, of course, the bonds may sell for more or less than par (the maturity value), depending on whether the coupon rate is higher or lower than the desired yield rate. Only when the coupon rate and desired yield rate happen to be equal will the market price of the bond be the same as its maturity value.

BOND PRICE AT TIME OF ISSUE.   Assume that on January 1, 19x1, the Borrow Company issues bonds having a maturity (face) value of $100,000 on January 1, 19x6. The coupon interest rate is 6 per cent, which means that $6,000 cash interest will be paid to the bondholders on December 31 of each year.°

What price will investors pay for the bonds? The answer depends on how

---

° This illustration is oversimplified to permit easy use of the tables in Appendix 11A. In practice, most bonds are issued for periods of longer than five years, and almost all of them pay interest semiannually. Other complicating factors (such as issue and redemption of bonds on dates other than interest-payment dates) are also ignored here.

much yield they demand on their money. If the investors require a yield of 6 per cent, the price will be:

Present value (1/1/x1) of $100,000 maturity value, 6%	
(Table II), due in 5 years ($100,000 × .7473)	$ 74,730
+ Present value of $6,000 annuity, 6% (Table IV),	
for 5 years ($6,000 × 4.2124)	25,274
Total bond issue price	$100,004[a]

[a] Rounding error of $4.

If the investors are satisfied with a yield of 4 per cent, the bond price they will be willing to pay (ignoring brokerage fees, etc.) is as follows:

Present value (1/1/x1) of $100,000 maturity value, 4%	
(Table II), due in 5 years ($100,000 × .8219)	$ 82,190
+ Present value of $6,000 annuity, 4% (Table IV), for	
5 years ($6,000 × 4.4518)	26,711
Total bond issue price	$108,901

If the investors require a yield of 8 per cent, the price will be:

Present value (1/1/x1) of $100,000 maturity value, 8%	
(Table II), due in 5 years ($100,000 × .6806)	$ 68,060
+ Present value of $6,000 annuity, 8% (Table IV),	
for 5 years ($6,000 × 3.9927)	23,956
Total bond issue price	$ 92,016

Since the bond issue price is a direct function of the yield rate, bond prices are often quoted in terms of yield rates rather than in terms of dollars. If the bond issue price is less than maturity value (that is, if the yield rate is higher than the coupon rate), the bonds are said to have been issued at a *discount*. If the bond issue price is higher than maturity value (that is, if the coupon rate is higher than the yield rate) the bonds are said to have been issued at a *premium*.

BOND VALUATION SUBSEQUENT TO ISSUE. At any time after the date of the issue, Borrow's liability for the bonds can be computed by the same procedure used to determine the original issue price. Suppose that the Borrow Company's original bond price was $108,912 (with a yield rate of 4 per cent). On December 31, 19x1, one year after the date of issue, the bond liability on the Borrow Company's statement of financial position would be as follows:

Present value (12/31/x1) of $100,000 maturity value, 4%	
(Table II), due in 4 years ($100,000 × 0.8548)	$ 85,480
+ Present value of $6,000 annuity, 4% (Table IV),	
for 4 years ($6,000 × 3.6299)	21,779
Total liability, 12/31/x1 (yield rate 4%)	$107,259

If the yield rate is 6 per cent, the bond liability at December 31, 19x1, is $100,000, and at 8 per cent, the liability is $93,376.

The following table emphasizes the effect of the yield rate of interest on the bond issue liability as the bond approaches maturity. Remember that we have assumed that this bond has a maturity value of $100,000 and a coupon rate of 6 per cent (therefore the interest annuity is $6,000 annually) and is due in five years.

	Yield Rate		
	4%	6%	8%
Bond issue price, 1/1/x1	$108,901	$100,000	$ 92,014
Bond liability valuation:			
12/31/x1	107,259	100,000	93,375
12/31/x2	105,550	100,000	94,845
12/31/x3	103,772	100,000	96,434
12/31/x4	101,923	100,000	98,149
12/31/x5	100,000	100,000	100,000

(For practice, you should compute these bond liabilities yourself and verify that the amounts shown in the table are correct.) The table demonstrates that the bond liability approaches the maturity value of $100,000 as the maturity date approaches; the liability is reduced over time in the case of the premium (with the yield rate of 4 per cent) and is increased over time in the case of the discount (with the yield of 8 per cent).

The liabilities we have calculated here would also be the prices investors would be willing to pay on those dates.

ACCOUNTING FOR BONDS.   In this section we shall show how these bonds are accounted for on the books of the Borrow Company (the issuer), and the Lend Company (the investor). Assume for convenience that the Lend Company purchased the entire $100,000 issue on January 1, 19x1, at the price that will yield 8 per cent on Lend's investment. The price is therefore $92,058, so that the bonds were purchased by Lend at a discount of $7,942. Both companies prepare only annual statements, and the fiscal years end on December 31. Interest checks are sent and received shortly after the end of the year. The entries on both the lender's books (left-hand column) and borrower's books (right-hand column) are the following:

Lend Company's Books		Borrow Company's Books	
Investment in			
Borrow bonds	92,014	Cash	92,014
Cash	92,014	Bonds payable	92,014

	Lend Company's Books			Borrow Company's Books	

December 31, 19x1 Interest accrual for 19x1

	Lend Company's Books		Borrow Company's Books	
Accrued interest receivable	6,000		Interest expense	7,361
Investment in Borrow bonds[a]	1,361		Accrued interest payable	6,000
Interest earned		7,361	Bonds payable	1,361

[a] Most accounting textbooks call for recording the liability in two accounts rather than one, i.e., the face amount in one account and the discount (or premium, as the case may be) in another. In this method, all subsequent adjustments to interest expense are made to the discount or premium account, with the account for the face value of the liability remaining unchanged until the bonds are redeemed. There is no important reason for this technicality, and it is not shown here. Significantly, the two-account method does not seem to be widely practiced in accounting for bond investments.

(The $1,361 addition to Lend's investment account (and to Borrow's liability account) is the difference in bond valuation between January 1 and December 31, 19x1, as shown in the 8 per cent column of the table shown previously.)°

January 2, 19x2 Interest for 19x2 paid and received

Cash	6,000		Accrued interest payable	6,000	
Accrued interest receivable		6,000	Cash		6,000

December 31, 19x2 Interest accrued for 19x2

Accrued interest receivable	6,000		Interest expense	7,470	
Investment in Borrow bonds	1,470		Accrued interest payable		6,000
Interest earned		7,470	Bonds payable		1,470

Interest earned (expense) is 8% of the investment (liability) of $93,375 for 19x2.

January 2, 19x3 Interest for 19x2 paid and received

Cash	6,000		Accrued interest payable	6,000	
Accrued interest receivable		6,000	Cash		6,000

(Similar entries for 19x3, 19x4, and 19x5 are not repeated here. In these years the interest earned (expense) by the investor (issuer) is $7,588, $7,715, and $7,852, respectively.)

° Another way to compute the interest earned (or expense) is the yield rate (8 per cent) times the investment (or liability) of $92,014, which achieves the same result, except for rounding errors, as in the annual valuation method shown above. Note that the annual increase in the investment (liability) is interpreted as additional earnings (expense) to the investor (issuer). If the yield rate had been less than 6 per cent when the bonds were issued and the bonds had therefore been issued at a premium, the interest earned (expense) would be less than $6,000, and the difference would be recorded as a reduction in the bond value each year.

The bonds mature at the end of the fifth year, by which time Lend's investment account and Borrow's liability account will be stated at $100,000, the maturity value of the bonds.

January 3, 19x6 The bonds are redeemed by cash payment from Borrow to Lend

Cash	100,000		Bonds payable	100,000
Investment in			Cash	100,000
Borrow bonds		100,000		

UNREALIZED GAINS AND LOSSES. In the above illustration the 8 per cent yield rate, having been established by the issue price of the bonds on January 1, 19x1, remains fixed throughout the life of the bonds and is unaffected by changes in the market (yield) rate of interest that may occur during the life of the bonds. This is consistent with current accounting practice, in which we account for costs and ignore changes in the market value of long-lived assets held or liabilities outstanding.

The cost principle of valuing bonds is based partly on the concept that gains and losses are not "realized" unless the bonds are sold, and partly on the questionable argument that if the market reverses itself before the bonds are sold, the gain or loss is cancelled and should not be reported. The only time accountants depart from this principle is when there is a substantial, seemingly permanent, loss in the market value of the bond, presumably resulting from evidence that the issuer may default on interest or principal payments. In these cases, the bondholder's original cost of acquisition loses its meaning, and his loss is considered to have occurred even though he does not sell the bond. Even when unrealized gains or losses are not recognized, however, parenthetical disclosure of the market price is good accounting practice.

Leases

Long-term lease agreements for the rental of real or personal property are the most important class of contracts giving rise to long-term assets and liabilities. Proper accounting for long-term leases calls for reporting the present value of all future payments required under the lease as a long-term liability. Although this method is seldom used at present, the cost of the contractual right to the use of the property should appear on the asset side of the statement of financial position as the offsetting item. Reporting the financial effect of the lease at its inception therefore increases both sides of the financial position statement by the present value of the remaining lease payments. The liability is a monetary liability, of course, but the asset, consisting of the intangible property right, is a nonmonetary asset.

This method of reporting measures the total resources covered by the lease and employed in the production of income, and the financial obligations to which the company is committed. It also allows users to compare the profitability of companies using leased assets with that of companies that prefer to own their assets outright.

Generally accepted accounting principles do not demand the method we have just described. Instead, unless the lease *is in substance a purchase* of the property, or the lessor and lessee are *related* (e.g., if the lessee is an unconsolidated subsidiary of the lessor), they call for disclosure in footnotes or schedules of rights and obligations under lease agreements "if the omission of this information would tend to make the financial statements misleading."[*] The reason for this recommendation by the Accounting Principles Board seems to be that if the lessor is not acquiring ownership of all or a portion of the property, there is no asset or liability relating to the future rights or obligations under the lease.

We believe that rights and obligations should always be disclosed and that disclosure in footnotes is not sufficient. We also believe that some managers will select leasing rather than purchasing *primarily* because they need not show the asset and liability in the financial position statement. Omitting these items makes several financial ratios (particularly rate of return on total assets, and the debt-equity ratio, discussed in Chapters 18 and 19) appear more favorable than would be the case if the asset were purchased, and in financial terms this difference is not justified. Furthermore, financial statement users tend to gloss over or ignore footnotes, or read them out of the context of the statement of financial position.

On the other hand, footnote information is considerably better than no information at all, and it often used to be the case that lessors reported only (as current expense) the periodic rental accruals required by the lease. With the rapid growth in importance of leasing transactions, however, and with the encouragement of the AICPA, accounting practice in the disclosure of the financial effects of leases seems to be improving.

Long-term Liabilities Arising from Accruals of Current Expenses

The monetary liability items covered thus far have arisen from acquisitions of cash, property, or property rights, and their measurement has been based on the cost of the acquisition. In this section we turn briefly to long-term liabilities arising from accruals of expenses, which are recorded and deducted from the current revenues to measure net earnings of the current period. Deferred compensation of executives' and employees' pension costs are the most common example of this type of liability. Theoretically, these liabilities also arise from the acquisition of assets, but they differ from those previously discussed in that the measurement of the asset is not possible or necessary until the asset is consumed (i.e., becomes an expense). The effect of this difference is that the measurement of the liability at any time is dependent upon the measurement of *operations* (i.e., revenues and expenses) rather than on the measurement of an asset.

The liabilities arising in this manner are monetary liabilities in that they will be settled by cash payment at some future time, but usually the amount

[*] "Reporting of Leases in Financial Statements of Lessee," Opinion of the Accounting Principles Board No. 5, September 1964 (New York: AICPA, 1964).

reported at any time will not reflect the total amount to be paid. Instead, the amount reported will be that portion of the liability attributable to the operations of past periods. As was pointed out in Chapter 14, the liabilities reported at any time are those that arise from *past transactions.* Those arising from expected future asset purchases or from expected expenses attributable to future periods cannot, and should not, be recognized. For example, the liability for employee pensions (discussed in the next section) reported at any time is that portion of the pension liability attributable to the service rendered by employees in the past (as measured by salary and wage expense of past periods). At any particular point in time, this is likely to be substantially less than the total retirement benefit expected to be paid to all employees when they retire.

Pension Liabilities

An employer's agreement to pay retirement benefits to retired employees need not be as legally binding on the employer as his bonds and leases are. If, however, there is a reasonable expectation that a given employee will receive a retirement benefit of a predictable amount at some future date, a liability to that employee should be shown in the financial position statement.

In the most widely accepted interpretation, pension costs "accrue," or accumulate, over the working life of the employee. In other words, the pension expense to the employer is earned by the employee in the normal course of his employment as additional wages, payment of which is delayed until after he retires. This means that the company's liability to him gradually increases until his retirement date, at which time it should equal the present value of the estimated retirement payments to be made. Estimating pension costs involves prediction of many variables, but reasonably objective estimates can be made if the number of employees covered is sufficiently large to permit the use of mortality tables, average employee-turnover rates, and other statistical indexes.

The federal income tax law exerts a strong influence on accounting practice in the area of employee pension plans. The employer is allowed to deduct as expenses the *payments* he makes to a "qualified" pension plan, even though these payments are not taxed as income to the employees until they receive the benefits. This law has provided a strong incentive to employers to adopt pension plans that qualify for the deduction and to make payments (usually to a trustee or insurance company) that are actuarially sound. As a result of the federal income tax law, therefore, pension expense is usually accounted for on a cash rather than accrual basis, and pension liabilities rarely appear in published financial statements.

We should not be misled into reasoning that it is the cash payment that results in the expense; it is the service rendered by the employee. The cash payments are merely the result of the employer's financial arrangement for funding the plan. The expense is incurred whether or not financial arrangements are made to meet it, and the liability accumulates over the working life of the employee regardless of whether the employer has made arrangements to discharge it. Thus, employers who have pension plans but have not arranged for periodic payments should still record pension expense. There is, however, little evidence that they do so.

Other Liabilities

Certain other specialized monetary liabilities are occasionally found in published statements.

LIABILITY FOR PRODUCT GUARANTEES. Firms manufacturing and selling products that are covered by a guarantee should record as current (i.e., period of sale) expenses the estimated future cost of repairs and replacements under the guarantee contract. The reasoning is that the sale revenue of the product includes an element attributable to the guarantee, and proper matching requires that the expenses be recorded in the same period. The entry to record the expenses is

Guarantee expense	X	
Liability for product guarantee		X

When repairs and replacements occur under the guarantee, the entry is

Liability for product guarantee	Y	
Cash (or an appropriate liability)		Y

The balance in the liability account (X-Y) at any time represents the estimated future guarantee costs associated with products already sold to customers.

LIABILITY FOR MAINTENANCE. Firms with heavy investments in plant and equipment must plan to make heavy expenditures for maintenance. Ideally, the actual maintenance work is carried out during periods of low output, when interference with productive activity is at a minimum. But the need to account for maintenance expense on an accrual rather than cash basis is apparent, because the need for maintenance arises and the expense therefore occurs in every period, as a direct result of production. This means that maintenance cost should be recorded and included as a cost of production, as illustrated in this entry:

Maintenance expense (or work in process)	XXX	
Liability for maintenance		XXX

When the actual maintenance work is done, the entry is

Liability for maintenance	YYY	
Cash (or accrued payroll, supplies, etc.)		YYY

INVESTMENTS: NONMONETARY ASSETS

In the remainder of this chapter we discuss those nonmonetary assets classified as investment assets on the financial position statement. These assets derive their value from the expectation of future revenue—either from holding or using the assets, or (in an unusual case) from their sale. Although some of these assets may have well-established current market values, they are nonmonetary because there is no legal claim to future cash. Invariably, the firm's intention is to hold the asset—either for direct production of revenue, such as rent or dividends, or for consumption in a revenue-producing activity. These assets are clearly distinguished from inventories not only by the fact that inventories are current assets, but also because there is no apparent intention to separate the asset from the firm and sell it.

Investments in Stock of Other Companies

Industrial firms rarely invest their resources in the stock of other firms for purposes of long-run dividend income. The usual reason one corporation buys stock of another is to obtain control of the second company. Typical reasons for seeking control of another company are to diversify into new lines or add volume to existing lines; to assure a continuous and controlled source of raw material, or control of a marketing outlet; or to achieve greater efficiency, often in the use of managerial talent.

In theory, complete control is obtained by the ownership of 51 per cent of the stock of a corporation. In practice, the percentage needed varies considerably. Whatever the percentage acquired, however, if it is less than 100 per cent, the new subsidiary must retain its coporate form for the benefit of the "minority" stockholders. Even when the subsidiary is wholly owned, it is sometimes advisable to retain the corporate form rather than to dissolve the subsidiary by merger. In either case, the investment in the subsidiary company appears on the books of the "parent" company as an asset.

In the majority of parent-subsidiary relationships, *consolidated* financial statements are prepared for published report purposes. These financial statements combine the parent company with the subsidiaries as if the combination were a single firm. Exhibit 15–1 shows the consolidated financial position statement of the Hi Company combined with its 80 per cent-owned subsidiary, the Lo Company. Hi Company purchased its shares of Lo Company at a cost of $80,000 when Lo Company was organized.

Several comments about this exhibit are in order. The items in the consolidated financial position statement are the sums of the items in the individual statements, *with all intercompany transactions and balances eliminated.* First, the Hi Company owes $9,000 of accounts payable to the Lo Company; this amount has therefore been deducted from accounts receivable and accounts payable in the third column. Second, the Hi Company investment in the stock of the Lo Company is an intercompany dealing and is therefore not shown in the third column. Of the total $100,000 of Lo Company capital stock, $80,000 has also been eliminated and $20,000 has been transferred to the special "minority interest" category. The $30,000 in this category represents the 20 per cent ownership of the minority stockholders: $20,000 (20 per cent) of the Lo Com-

EXHIBIT 15-1

HI COMPANY AND LO COMPANY

COMPARISON OF SEPARATE AND CONSOLIDATED
FINANCIAL POSITION STATEMENTS
As of December 31, 19xx

	Hi Company	Lo Company	Consolidated
Assets			
Cash	$ 40,000	$ 70,000	$110,000
Accounts receivable	60,000	80,000	131,000
Tangible long-lived facilities	30,000	53,000	83,000
Investment in Lo Company			
(80% of Lo Company's stock)	80,000	0	0
Total assets	$210,000	$203,000	$324,000
Liabilities and Owners' Equity			
Liabilities:			
Accounts payable	$ 35,000	$ 23,000	$ 49,000
Other liabilities	40,000	30,000	70,000
Minority interest in			
Lo Company			30,000
Owners' equity:			
Capital stock	60,000	100,000	60,000
Retained earnings	75,000	50,000	115,000
Total liabilities and owners' equity	$210,000	$203,000	$324,000

pany's capital stock and $10,000 (20 per cent) of its retained earnings. Also eliminated are such intercompany transactions as transfers of product between companies, even though they are recorded as purchases and sales on the individual company records.

The consolidation of financial statements is a virtual necessity where control exists if misleading inferences are to be avoided. The subsidiary is in fact simply a division of a larger firm, and to omit its financial statements because it retains its corporate form is to give a legal technicality a degree of importance it does not deserve.

Nonconsolidated Investments

There are cases of intercorporate investments, of course, in which consolidated statements are not appropriate. The principal case is that in which control does not exist. Another occurs with investment in a foreign company, where there might be danger of expropriation of assets, or where asset values are so difficult to verify that there is no valid basis for preparing the subsidiary financial statement.

Let us illustrate the typical case of a domestic company. Assume that the Allen Company purchased 30 per cent of the outstanding shares of the Blue Company for $50,000 on December 31, 19x0. The Allen Company hopes that sufficient additional shares can be acquired in future years so that control may eventually be achieved. How should the Allen Company account for its investment in the Blue Company in the meantime? There are, it seems, two alternatives:

1. The investment can be reported at the Allen Company's cost of $50,000, with dividend revenue from the investment reported in its earnings statement as nonoperating revenue. Presumably market fluctuations in the Blue Company's stock would not be recognized on the Allen Company's books. This cost method of accounting is consistent with accounting rules as applied to other long-lived assets and is usually recommended for individual investors who purchase small amounts of stock to be held for dividend income over the long term.

2. The investment can be reported at cost, adjusted for all increases and decreases in the owner's equity, as reflected by the Blue Company's financial statements subsequent to the acquisition. This method is called the *equity* method, and we prefer it over the cost method under the circumstances indicated here. Assume, for example, that the Blue Company's owners' equity on December 31, 19x0, 19x1, and 19x2 is the following:

	December 31		
	19x0	*19x1*	*19x2*
Capital stock	$100,000	$100,000	$100,000
Retained earnings	20,000	40,000	30,000
	$120,000	$140,000	$130,000

The Allen Company purchased 30 per cent of the Blue Company's stock when the Blue Company's total owners' equity was $120,000. The Allen Company paid the market price of $50,000 for the shares, $14,000 more than the underlying equity of $36,000 ($120,000 × .30) as reflected in the Blue Company's financial statements.

We now assume that the Blue Company's earnings and dividends for 19x1 and 19x2 are as follows:

	19x1	*19x2*
Earnings (loss)	$25,000	($10,000)
Dividends	5,000	0

Entries on the Allen Company's books over the two-year period, using the equity method, are as follows:

| *December 31, 19x0* | Investment in Blue Company stock (30%) | 50,000 | |
| | Cash | | 50,000 |

To record the original purchase of stock.

| *December 31, 19x1* | Investment in Blue Company stock | 7,500 | |
| | Earnings from Blue Company stock | | 7,500 |

To record 30 per cent of the Blue Company's 19x1 earnings as earnings to the Allen Company.

| *December 31, 19x1* | Cash | 1,500 | |
| | Investment in Blue Company stock | | 1,500 |

To record receipt of the Blue Company's 19x1 dividend. (This is not to be interpreted as additional earnings to the Allen Company. It is instead the conversion of earnings already recorded into cash.)

| *December 31, 19x2* | Loss from Blue Company stock | 3,000 | |
| | Investment in Blue Company stock | | 3,000 |

To record 30 per cent of the Blue Company's 19x2 loss as loss to the Allen Company.

The objective of the equity method is to keep the account "Investment in Blue Company stock" on the Allen Company's books in line with the changes in the underlying equity this stock represents. If we can assume that the Blue Company's accounting procedures are sound, there seems to be little reason for the Allen Company not to recognize its share of the Blue Company's earnings and losses as they occur.

Under the cost method, the investment in Blue Company stock would be reported as a $50,000 asset until additional shares were purchased, or some shares were sold. The $1,500 dividend would be reported as revenue in 19x1. No recognition would be given the profit earned by the Blue Company in 19x1 or the loss incurred by the Blue Company in 19x2.

Purchases Versus Poolings

Let us now change the facts of the Allen Company's investment in Blue Company stock and assume that on December 31, 19x0, the Allen Company acquires a controlling interest in the Blue Company—for example, 90 per cent—paying (in cash or stock) $150,000, the market value of this interest at that time. If we interpret this transaction as a *purchase*, this acquisition is recorded at cost of $150,000, which is then assigned to the Blue Company's assets and liabilities in accordance with their market values and their significance in the acquisition. Presumably the Blue Company's assets and liabilities will be revalued and possibly some value assigned to "goodwill." This is consistent with the accounting rules governing the purchase of any asset and is based on the assumption that, at the time of acquisition, the best available evidence of the value of an asset is its purchase price.

Since a controlling interest in the Blue Company was acquired in this case, and since the Allen Company, the parent company, will report both firms on a consolidated basis, another interpretation is available: that the transaction represents a *pooling of interests*. This interpretation gives a different result: The original acquisition of Blue Company stock will be recorded by the Allen Company not at $150,000, but at $108,000, which is the "book" equity of the shares acquired, according to the Blue Company's financial position statement at the time of purchase (90% of $120,000 = $108,000). This can be recorded in either one of two ways:

1. If the Allen Company acquired the Blue Company's shares by issuing its own shares to the Blue Company's stockholders, the transaction would be recorded as

Investment in Blue Company stock	108,000	
Capital stock		108,000

This entry ignores the current market values of both firms' shares. In the pooling of interest interpretation, the Blue Company's assets and liabilities continue to be valued as they were valued on its books, i.e., as if the acquisition by the Allen Company had not occurred.

2. If the Allen Company paid $150,000 cash for the Blue Company's stock or incurred $150,000 in debt, the original acquisition would be recorded as in the case of a purchase:

Investment in Blue Company stock	150,000	
Cash (or liability account)		150,000

Then the excess of the cost over the equity associated with the Blue Company's shares, or $42,000, called "goodwill," would be written off immediately to the Allen Company's retained earnings, as follows:

Retained earnings	42,000	
Investment in Blue Company stock		42,000

In either case, the Allen Company's share of the Blue Company's assets and liabilities are reported at $108,000, with the individual items valued as they had been valued on the Blue Company's statement of financial position before the acquisition.

The pooling of interests interpretation has little to recommend it, from the standpoint of the users of financial statements. The lower values for assets acquired will inflate return on investment calculations after the merger, because expenses (expired costs) will be lower and the investment base will be lower than if the purchase interpretation had been used. Pooling makes no attempt to allocate the investment cost to the various asset and liability items, and it does not recognize goodwill. These characteristics have an appeal to the managers and accountants, but they sacrifice the interests of the statement users, who need asset and liability information that is as current as possible. We believe that all business combination transactions should be viewed as opportunities to express financial information in current terms, and in the present case, favor not only the recording of the Allen Company's purchase of the Blue Company's stock at the current cost of $150,000, but also, if objective evidence is available, the revaluing of the Allen Company's assets and liabilities so that the financial statements of the combined firms can be expressed on a current basis.

SUMMARY

This chapter presented generally accepted accounting principles applicable to long-term monetary assets and liabilities as well as to investments in ownership shares of other enterprises, a special kind of nonmonetary asset.

When measuring monetary assets or liabilities with long life spans, it is necessary to employ the present value concept. The financial position statement valuation of long-term bonds or notes should be the present value of the future amounts to be received (or paid). This concept was illustrated under a variety of conditions.

Special emphasis was given to the importance of full disclosure of all estimates of future payments to be made under such long-term contractual arrangements as leases and pension agreements, as well as bond indentures.

Historical cost was established as one generally accepted method of valuing long-lived investments. In the case of investments in subsidiary companies, another is the equity method. Downward revision of historical costs, in cases of apparently permanent substantial losses in value, is considered to be generally accepted accounting, although recording value increases is not so considered, regardless of the circumstances.

Questions for Review

15-1. What is a major category of investment assets?

15-2. Distinguish between current assets and long-lived assets.

15-3. Why is the monetary-nonmonetary distinction more useful for asset valuation than the current long-lived distinction?

15-4. If the coupon rate is higher than the yield rate, bonds will sell at a premium. Why? If the coupon rate is lower than the yield rate, bonds will sell at a discount. Why?

15-5. When are gains and losses on bonds (resulting from changes in the yield rate) "realized" in the financial statements?

15-6. In accounting for long-term leases, the long-term asset is nonmonetary and the long-term liability is monetary. Why are they classified this way?

15-7. What is the apparent reason for the Accounting Principles Board's position that property rights resulting from the lease should not be shown on the financial position statement unless the lease "is in substance a purchase"?

15-8. Both the acquisition of assets and the matching of expenses and revenues often call for recognition of liabilities. Give examples of each.

15-9. Contrast the cost and equity methods of accounting for intercorporate investments in stock.

15-10. Contrast the effect of the purchase and pooling of interest alternatives in accounting for business combinations.

Problems for Analysis

15-11. On January 1, 19x1, Adam signs a $10,000 noninterest-bearing note payable to Borman, receiving $7,500 in cash. The note provides that Borman will not call for payment before January 1, 19x5.

    a. If Borman calls for payment on the note at January 1, 19x5, what is the effective interest rate?

    b. If Borman does not demand payment until January 1, 19x7, what is the effective interest rate? (Assume annual compounding in both cases. Solve to the nearest whole per cent.)

15-12. On January 1, 19x1, Caine signs a $1,000 noninterest-bearing, two-year note payable to Dunn and receives $888 in cash. The note provides that Caine may repay the note before the due date at the end of any six-month period (i.e., July 1, 19x1, January 1, 19x2, or July 1, 19x2), but that he must pay a premium that will yield 8 per cent to Dunn. Assume semiannual compounding.

    a. What is the effective interest rate if Caine pays the note at maturity?

b. How much will Caine have to pay if he redeems the note on
1. July 1, 19x1?
2. January 1, 19x2?
3. July 1, 19x2?

15-13. Evans borrows $824 from a loan company, signing a $1,000 noninterest-bearing, two-year note. Assuming semiannual compounding,

a. What is the effective interest rate to the nearest whole per cent?

b. Assuming that Evans prepares quarterly income statements, make the journal entries to record the borrowing transaction, periodic interest accruals, and final payment on the note.

c. Comment on Evans' practice of recording interest on a straight-line basis (in this case, $22 per quarter).

15-14. On January 1, 19x1, Fuerzt borrows $5,000 cash from Gannon. He signs a $5,000 face-value, two-year, 8 per cent note, with $100 interest payable in cash each quarter. Make the journal entries to record the borrowing transactions and interest accruals for four months on Fuerzt's and Gannon's books. Assume that both prepare monthly income statements and that Fuerzt pays the first quarter's interest on April 3, 19x1.

15-15. On January 1, 19x1, Holton borrowed $10,000 from Jacob, giving Jacob a $10,000 face-value, 6 per cent, four-year note. Interest is payable on July 1 and January 1. By January 1, 19x3, the market rate of interest was 8 per cent on loans of this type.

a. Compute the amount of unrealized gain or loss to Holton and Jacob.

b. Explain why the gain or loss occurs, and explain why accountants do not report these gains or losses in financial statements.

15-16. On January 2, 19x7, an investor purchased a $1,000, 6 per cent ten-year bond issued by the Xenin Company on January 1, 19x0, at a price that yields 8 per cent. Interest is payable July 1 and January 1.

a. Compute the price of the bond.

b. Make the journal entries reflecting the purchase of the bond and the interest earned for the year 19x7. Assume that the investor prepares statements semiannually on June 30 and December 31.

15-17. On December 31, 19x7, an investor purchased a $10,000, five-year, 8 per cent bond issued by Yenger Company on January 1, 19x6. The investor paid a price to yield 6 per cent, plus accrued interest. Interest is payable January 1 and July 1.

a. Compute the price of the bond.

b. Give journal entries to record purchase of the bond and receipt of accrued interest on January 2, 19x8, July 1, 19x8, and January 2, 19x9.

15-18. On January 1, 19x5, the A Company issued $10,000 maturity-value, ten-year bonds having a 5 per cent coupon rate of interest payable annually. Compute the issue price at yield rates of 4 per cent and 6 per cent.

15-19. On January 1, 19x5, the B Company issued $10,000 maturity-value, ten-year bonds having a 5 per cent coupon rate of interest, payable $2\frac{1}{2}$ per cent semiannually. Compute the issue price at a yield rate of 4 per cent.

15-20. On January 1, 19x5, five-year bonds having a maturity value of $50,000 were issued at a price to yield 4 per cent annually. Interest is payable annually at a coupon rate of $4\frac{1}{2}$ per cent. Prepare a table showing the issue price, the annual liability valuation for the life of the bonds, and the interest expense to be reported each calendar year.

15-21. On January 1, 19x5, five-year bonds with a maturity value of $100,000 and a coupon interest rate of 5 per cent payable annually were issued for $104,449 cash. Find the annual yield rate.

15-22. On January 1, 19x5, ten-year bonds having a maturity value of $100,000 and a coupon interest rate of 5 per cent payable annually, were issued for $108,155. At this price, the bonds will yield 4 per cent annually to an investor. *Without using the tables in your textbook,* devise a method for computing the annual interest expense and annual liability valuations to be reported in the financial statement of the issuer. Prepare a table showing these annual amounts for the first three years of the life of the bonds.

15-23. On January 1, 19x0, the Zoss Corporation issued $100,000 face-value, 6 per cent, ten-year bonds at a price to yield 8 per cent to investors. Interest is payable annually on December 31. The bonds are redeemable at the option of Zoss Corporation after five years, in accordance with the following schedule:

Redemption date	Redemption price required
12/31/x4	$106,000
12/31/x5	104,000
12/31/x6	102,000
12/31/x7	100,000
12/31/x8	100,000
12/31/x9 (maturity)	100,000

    a. Compute the issue price of the bonds.

    b. Give the entries reflecting the issue of the bonds and the interest expense and payment for 19x0 and 19x1, assuming only annual financial statements.

    c. Assume that by December 31, 19x4, the yield rate on bonds of the type issued by the Zoss Corporation is 5 per cent, and that this rate is expected to remain the same for at least five years. This means that Zoss Corporation could borrow money at this rate for the next several years. Ignoring income tax effects and brokerage fees, when, if ever, would it be advisable for Zoss Corporation to redeem the original issue and issue new bonds yielding 5 per cent?

d. If the answer to *c* occurs prior to 12/31/*x*9, give the entry to redeem the bonds.

15-24. On December 31, the X-Ample Company issued 6 per cent, thirty-year bonds with a face value of $300,000 to yield 4 per cent. The proceeds from the issue were $403,746.

a. What is the stated rate of interest? The market rate?

b. Why are the two rates of interest different?

c. How would the bond issue be reflected on the statement of earnings for the second year of issue? On the statement of financial position on December 31, two years after the issue date? (Include amounts in your answer.)

15-25. Leveraged, Inc., has negotiated a five-year lease with Lease Company for a machine. The machine could be purchased for $100,000. Assume that the machine has a five-year life and no resale value at the end of its estimated life.

The lease agreement specifies a rate of return (on the $100,000 purchase price) to the lessor (Lease Company) of 10 per cent. Annual payments of $28,000 are required at the end of each year of the lease.

a. Prepare the journal entry to reflect this transaction at the time the lease is negotiated, assuming that the present value of the lease payments will be reflected on the statement of financial position for Leveraged, Inc.

b. Show how this transaction would be reflected on the statement of financial position for Leveraged, Inc., at the end of the second year of the lease contract.

c. Does Leveraged, Inc., have any other alternatives in reporting the lease on its financial statements? Discuss.

d. Discuss the financial statement limitations if this transaction is not reflected on the statement of financial position for Leveraged, Inc.

15-26. The Alto Corporation, faced with the need for additional cash, was considering the possibility of increasing its mortgage loan. However, on December 31, 19*x*5, the Alto Corporation sold its long-lived assets, consisting of a warehouse and the land around it, to an insurance company for $100,000 cash. Included in the contract of sale was the agreement that Alto would lease the land and building at an annual rental of $7,500 for a period of twenty years, with an option to renew the lease for a second twenty-year period at the same rental if Alto wished to do so. The sale was consummated on this basis. Alto paid off the old mortgage on the land and building and added the remainder of the cash proceeds from the sale to its cash account. The federal income tax rate on the gain from sale of the real estate is 25 per cent.

Alto's condensed statement of financial position immediately prior to the sale appears as follows:

ALTO CORPORATION

STATEMENT OF FINANCIAL POSITION
As of December 30, 19x5
(in thousands of dollars)

Assets			Liabilities and Owners' Equity		
Current assets		$ 25	Liabilities:		
Long-lived assets:			Current liabilities		$ 5
Land (cost)		40	Mortgage payable		10
Warehouse (cost)	$80		Total liabilities		$ 15
— Accumulated			Owners' equity:		
depreciation	40		Capital stock	$70	
Net warehouse		40	Retained earnings	20	
			Total owners' equity		90
			Total liabilities and		
Total assets		$105	owners' equity		$105

a. Prepare a condensed statement of financial position for Alto immediately after the sale transaction, following the customary practice in disclosing the lease agreements.

b. Write a paragraph comparing the financial effect of this sale-leaseback transaction with the alternative that was available to Alto—retaining title to the property and simply borrowing $100,000 for twenty years, repaying principal and interest on the mortgage loan in annual installments of $7,500.

c. What is the yield rate of interest on the loan transaction described in *b* above?

d. Revise Alto's statement of financial position in *a* to reflect the recommendation in your text for disclosure of lease agreements, using a 4 per cent yield rate of interest on the lease transaction.

15-27. The Palo Company is considering adopting a retirement plan for employees. The following characteristics of the plan have been approved:

1. The amount of the benefit shall be the difference between $300 per month and the employee's social security benefits.

2. An employee may retire at sixty-two if he has had ten years or more of continuous employment with Palo. Retirement at sixty-five is compulsory for all employees.

3. No benefit will be paid if the employee dies or leaves the company prior to retirement. (Palo has a separate group insurance plan.)

4. Employees become covered by the plan automatically either on completion of five years of employment or upon attaining the age of sixty.

5. Palo will pay the entire cost of the plan (the plan is "noncontributory"). Palo officials now have the problem of estimating what this plan will cost

the company, because (1) they wish to record these costs in such a way as to report periodic income properly, and (2) they wish to begin to accumulate assets in a trust fund so that they will have the money to pay pension benefits when they come due. The trustees will invest the fund in securities that will be sold as cash is required.

a. Make a list of all the factors that will have to be predicted in order to estimate the cost of the plan.

b. Write a paragraph recommending a method for recording and reporting pension costs in Palo's financial statements.

15-28. The amount of the benefit under the Jeffries Corporation pension plan is the average salary over the last five years of employment times 2 per cent times the number of years of covered service. Thus if a person's average salary for the last five years prior to retirement is $10,000, and if he has been employed for thirty years, his retirement benefit is $6,000 annually ($10,000 × .02 × 30).

The Jeffries plan is completely financed by the employer. The company makes annual cash payments to a trust fund, and expects the return on the fund to average 6 per cent compounded annually. The payments to the fund will be the equal annual amount required to provide the estimated pension benefit of the "average" employee by the time he retires. The amount required to be on deposit at retirement is $7,722 for each $1,000 of annual retirement benefit to be paid. According to independent actuaries who have worked with Jeffries on the plan, the "average" Jeffries employee has the following characteristics.

1. Average age at retirement—65
2. Average annual salary for last five years, estimated for the current working force—$12,000
3. Average age of entry into the plan—35
4. Percentage of covered employees who will retire under the plan—75 per cent

a. During 19x1, Jeffries had 2,400 covered employees on the payroll. Calculate the amount Jeffries should contribute to the fund in 19x1, based on the above information. (Assume that the funding plan has been in effect for thirty years.)

b. Write a paragraph on each of the following:

    1. Is the amount calculated in *a* an appropriate measure of pension expense for 19x1? Under what circumstances would it *not* be?

    2. What is the proper method of recording and reporting pension expense in Jeffries' financial statements?

c. Dropping the assumption in part *a*, assume instead that, although Jeffries has been in business many years, 19x1 is the first year the pension plan has been in effect. Therefore no funds have been accumulated in prior years for paying retirement benefits. How does this change your answer to *a?* Outline a plan for (1) funding "past service" pension cost and (2) reporting this cost in Jeffries' financial statements.

15-29. During 19x0, the Duro Appliance Manufacturing Company announced a new two-year guarantee plan on all model 19x1 washers and driers. Company engineers estimated that repair costs covered under the guarantee would average $25 per machine sold. Arrangements were made with dealers for stocking repair parts and for reimbursement of labor costs incurred for repair work done under the guarantee.

Quarterly reports from dealers indicate the following sales and service of 19x1 washers and driers:

19x1 models sold 19x1		Work done under guarantee Parts used	Labor
First quarter	5,000	$15,000	$33,000
Second quarter	4,000	20,000	37,000
Third quarter	4,000	28,000	51,000
Fourth quarter	2,000	30,000	57,000

a. Prepare journal entries to record the above on Duro's books, and describe how the information would appear in the financial statements.

b. Late in the 19x1 year, company engineers considered a plan for 19x2 models that would call for a one-year guarantee only and would cover only repairs resulting from defective workmanship. In addition, the company was considering making a two-year service contract available to customers, although one of the unsolved problems was the price that should be charged for such a contract. Give your opinion on the relevance of the 19x1 information to these problems.

15-30. The Parent Company acquired a 70 per cent interest in the Subsidiary Company as of December 31, 19x5. The statements of financial position for the two companies follow:

PARENT COMPANY AND SUBSIDIARY COMPANY

STATEMENTS OF FINANCIAL POSITION

As of December 31, 19x5

(in thousands of dollars)

	Parent Company	Subsidiary Company
Assets		
Current assets:		
Cash	$ 90	$ 75
Accounts receivable (net)	65	40
Inventory	140	107
Prepaid expenses	20	18
Total current assets	$315	$240
Investment in Subsidiary Company	182	0

PARENT COMPANY AND SUBSIDIARY COMPANY (CONT.)

	Parent Company		Subsidiary Company	
Long-lived assets:				
Land	$ 50		$ 30	
Buildings (net)	120		95	
Equipment (net)	70		50	
Total long-lived assets		240		175
Total assets		$737		$415
Liabilities and Owners' Equity				
Current liabilities:				
Accounts payable		$45a		$ 65
Notes payable		30		0
Other current liabilities		90		90
Total current liabilities		$165		$155
Owners' equity:				
Common stock	$300		$160	
Retained earnings	272		100	
Total owners' equity		572		260
Total liabilities and owners' equity		$737		$415

a Of this $45,000 in accounts payable, $15,000 is owed to the Subsidiary Company, as of December 31, 19x5.

a. Prepare a consolidated statement of financial position for the Parent Company as of December 31, 19x5.

b. What is the purpose of preparing consolidated financial statements?

c. What is the significance of an understanding of consolidation accounting to a user of financial statements?

15-31. Five years ago the Black Corporation acquired 70 per cent (7,000 shares) of the outstanding stock of Spires, Inc., for control purposes at a cost of $70,000. Total earnings and dividends for Spires for the past five years were as follows:

Year	Earnings	Dividends
1	$10,000	$6,000
2	11,400	6,000
3	11,000	6,000
4	11,700	6,400
5	12,000	6,400

a. Compute the total income to be reported by the Black Corporation on the investment for the five-year period, assuming:

  1. the cost method of valuation for long-term investments
  2. the equity method of valuation for long-term investments
  b. What would the carrying value of the investment in Spires be (on the statement of financial position) at the end of five years, assuming:
  1. the cost method of valuation for long-term investments
  2. the equity method of valuation for long-term investments
  c. The market value of Spires stock was $16 per share at the end of five years. What effect, if any, would this have on your answer to *b* above?
  d. Is an understanding of the cost and equity methods of valuation of long-term investments essential for a user of accounting reports? Explain.

15–32. The Wall Drug Company had the following transactions in 19x1 pertaining to its investment in the common stock of Research, Inc.:

  January 15: The Wall Drug Company purchased on the open market 10,500 shares of Research common stock for $30 per share. (Research has 20,000 shares of stock outstanding.)

  March 31: Research reported earnings of $2.50 per share for the fiscal year ended February 28.

  April 20: Research declared and paid a dividend of $1 per share.

  August 15: The Wall Drug Company purchased on the open market an additional 2,500 shares for $32 per share.

  The earnings and dividend payments of Research for 19x2, 19x3, 19x4, and 19x5 were as follows:

Year	Earnings per share	Dividends per share
19x2	$2.70	$1.25
19x3	2.85	1.25
19x4	3.00	1.40
19x5	2.80	1.40

  a. Compute the income to be reported on the investment each calendar year from 19x1 through 19x5 by the Wall Drug Company, assuming:
  1. the cost method of valuation for long-term investments
  2. the equity method of valuation for long-term investments
  b. What was the carrying value of the investment in Research on December 31, 19x5 (on the statement of financial position), assuming:
  1. the cost method of valuation for long-term investments
  2. the equity method of valuation for long-term investments
  c. The market value of Research stock was $28 on December 31, 19x5. What effect, if any, would this have on your answer to *b*?
  d. What is the significance of an understanding of the cost and equity methods of valuing long-term investments to a user of financial statements? Explain.

15-33. On January 1, 19x1, the P Company acquired all of the outstanding shares of the S Company by issuing 5,000 shares of its common stock to S Company shareholders. S Company's only important asset was a piece of land that P Company intended to use as a plant site in a few years but would be used as a parking lot in the meantime. The land was carried on S Company books at $50,000, but three appraisers' estimates were $100,000, $110,000, and $112,000. There had been no market for S Company stock, but P Company stock had a market price of $20 per share at January 1, 19x0.

Statements of financial position of the two companies immediately before the above transactions were as follows:

STATEMENTS OF FINANCIAL POSITION
As of December 31, 19x0

Assets	P Company	S Company
Current assets	$350,000	0
Land	100,000	50,000
Buildings and equipment (net)	200,000	0
Total assets	$650,000	$50,000
Equities		
Capital stock, $10 par, 50,000 shares	$500,000	
$25 par, 1,000 shares		$25,000
Retained earnings	150,000	25,000
Total equities	$650,000	$50,000

a. Prepare journal entries for P Company to record the acquisition of S Company and subsequent merger of P and S Companies giving effect to

1. The pooling of interests interpretation
2. The purchase interpretation with
   a. goodwill recognized
   b. goodwill not recognized

b. Assuming that P and S Companies are not merged and that S Company is retained as a wholly owned subsidiary company, prepare consolidated financial position statements as of January 1, 19x0, giving effect to each of the interpretations listed in *a.*

c. Write a paragraph defending the pooling interpretation and indicate why you believe this interpretation is or is not consistent with the other generally accepted accounting principles.

15-34. PORTFOLIO EVALUATION, AMERICAN ECONOMIC ASSOCIATION STYLE[°]

The American Economic Association holds, for investment, a portfolio of common stocks and bonds. Each year end, it reports, to its members, the value

[°] Reprinted from *Financial Analysts Journal,* Vol. 23, No. 5 (September–October, 1967), p. 158. Reprinted by permission of Financial Analysts Journal.

of the portfolio, the income received, and the changes in the portfolio that have taken place during the past year. For the year of 1966, this information is presented in the May, 1967, *American Economic Review.*

Following this year's report, there is printed a Committee proposal to change radically both the method of evaluating the portfolio, and accounting for income received. Milton Friedman, the noted economist, was the Chairman of the Committee on Financial and Investment Policies. Its findings are as follows:

"Currently, income from equities is reported as the sum of dividends received and capital gains realized. . . . This method has three main defects. First, it takes no regular account of earnings of enterprises plowed back rather than paid out as dividends. Second, it does not recognize the market's evaluation of changes in the future prospects of the enterprises whose stocks we own. Third, it makes income depend on the accident of when securities are sold. The first leads to an understatement of income; the second, in principle, might lead to either understatement or overstatement, but in practice has led to understatement. The third produces wide fluctuations in recorded income that do not necessarily correspond to changes in the amount available for expenditures without impinging on capital."

To adjust for these "defects," the Committee proposes three remedies. To recognize the import of retained earnings, they propose: "Instead of recording as income simply dividends received, we propose including also retained earnings."

Changes in market prices would be treated as follows: ". . . We propose computing for each year the changes in the market value of the stocks in our portfolio adjusted for (a) retained earnings and (b) changes in the general price level. Adjustment (a) will be made by subtracting retained earnings as calculated above. Adjustment (b) will be made by subtracting the product of the start of the year market values of the portfolio times the percentage change in a price index. We propose to use as the price index the implicit GNP deflator. . . ."

The adjustment to be made for the timing of sales is as follows: "By recognizing, as in the previous paragraph, all changes in market value, we would remove the fortuitous element in our present method arising from the timing of sales. But, including all such gains would give undue significance to short-term market fluctuations. Since the objective is to take account of longer-term movements in stock prices, we propose spreading the gain as calculated in the previous paragraph over three years, including one-third in the year to which the calculation refers and one-third in each of the next two years. The number "three" was selected as roughly corresponding to the duration of cycles in stock market prices in the post-World War II period."

Here is the final formula that was worked out: "This treatment would make the Association's income from equities in each year equal to dividends received in that year plus our share of earnings plowed back that year plus one-third of market appreciation in that year (adjusted for retained earnings and price-level change) plus one-third of adjusted appreciation in the preceding year, plus one-third of adjusted appreciation in the second preceding year."

In its conclusion, the Committee expresses appreciation to the A.E.A.'s accountants, Arthur Andersen & Co., who have "expressed the informal opinion that the method of reporting income proposed is in conformity with generally accepted accounting principles."

The proposed A.E.A. approach to portfolio accounting is one which seeks to measure the actual economic changes in composite values, including the change in the value of currency, that occur in a portfolio over time. Although there may be justifications in economic theory for this method of valuation, is it a method our profession would approve?

Evaluate the recommendations of the American Economic Association for accounting for its investment portfolio. Include in your evaluation a contrast with generally accepted accounting principles. Also consider usefulness to the financial statement users.

15-35. An issue of bonds bearing interest at 5 per cent and maturing in twenty years involves obligations or commitments entered into by a corporation. A twenty-year lease contract also involves obligations or commitments by the corporation leasing the property.

    a. Compare these two commitments in terms of what is deemed appropriate by the accounting profession today, describing in some detail accepted accounting treatment with supporting reasons therefor.

    b. How do *you* evaluate the theoretical aspects of these two commitments? Discuss.

Chapter Sixteen **LONG-LIVED NONMONETARY ASSETS AND LIABILITIES; PRICE LEVEL**

INTRODUCTION

In this chapter we consider assets that are relatively long-lived, not intended for resale, and used in the operations of the business. These assets are generally valued on the statement of financial position at their original costs, adjusted for the portion already allocated to expense in past accounting periods (that is, the original costs less accumulated depreciation for tangible assets, or amortization for intangible assets). Examples of tangible long-lived assets include land, buildings, and machinery. Except for land, tangible assets have physical service lives and usually a residual resale value. Among those assets classified as intangible are patents, franchises, deferred research and development costs, and purchased goodwill. We describe the methods of depreciation and amortization that are in general use. Long-lived nonmonetary liabilities are also discussed, as is the accounting for price level adjustments made advisable by long-lived periods of inflation (or deflation).

TANGIBLE LONG-LIVED ASSETS

Tangible long-lived assets present many problems of measurement. The most important are determining acquisition cost, finding substitutes for acquisition cost, treating subsequent outlays, and calculating depreciation.

Determining Acquisition Cost

The acquisition of a long-lived nonmonetary asset often occurs over a period of time during which many events related to the acquisition occur. Most of the events requiring interpretation are those in which costs are incurred. The accountant must analyze the events in order to decide whether the cost should be *capitalized* (debited to the asset account, thus increasing the cost of the asset) or whether it should be treated as an expense or a loss. The rule he follows is that *the total cost of the facility should include all costs required to make the asset ready for its intended purpose.*

To illustrate, assume that the Acme Auto Parts Company acquires a new grinding machine for plant 3. The following transactions occur:

1. The purchase price of the machine is $14,000 plus sales taxes of $500. The invoice is paid in time to receive credit for a cash discount of 2 per cent, or $280.

2. Freight charges paid to transport the machine to the factory are $1,300.

3. Expenditures related to installation are as follows:

    a. $700 paid to salvage company (includes $1,000 cost of removal of old machine less $300 credit for sale of scrap)

    b. Concrete foundation for new machine, $370

    c. Uncrating and installation of new machine, $250

    d. Repair of damage from faulty installation, $120

4. Expenditures related to breaking-in and adjusting the new machine are as follows:

    a. Labor, $150

    b. Cost of spoiled material, $125

One solution to the question of the total cost of the machine, with the basic arguments and assumptions, follows:

Purchase price, less cash discount, including taxes	$14,220
The cash discount, offered as an inducement to pay the invoice on time, is not revenue to the purchaser. In fact, if Acme had missed the discount, good accounting would record it as a $280 loss in the period of purchase.	
Freight charges	1,300
The decision to capitalize the freight cost is not a difficult one. Assuming that the amount is reasonable, it clearly applies to the acquisition. The alternatives of treating the expenditure as either an expense of the period of purchase, or a loss, are unacceptable.	
Installation, including foundation	620
The $700 paid to the salvage company should have been considered a part of the cost of the old machine. Since this expenditure was not anticipated, the least harmful	

expedient is to consider it a loss this period. The cost of the faulty installation is clearly a current loss, since it can produce no future revenue.

Breaking-in and adjustment costs	275
The reasoning applied to the freight cost applies here also.	
Total capitalized cost	$16,415

The $370 cost of the new foundation is included in the acquisition cost of the machine on the assumption that the foundation is of a specific design suited only for use by the grinding machine in question. When this particular machine is abandoned, the foundation will also have to be torn out and replaced. It is quite possible, of course, that the foundation is more generally useful and could support many different machines, including future replacements for the grinding machine. If this latter situation were the case, the costs of the foundation would be more correctly included in total assets as a part of the building rather than the machine. This type of cost could be classified under an asset heading called "building improvements."

The total capitalized cost derived here would probably not be accepted by all accountants. Our solution to the question is only one of many possible answers.

Substitutes for Acquisition Cost

There are times when a business enterprise acquires assets by means other than purchase or construction, and it is necessary to determine a substitute for the acquisition cost. Among the situations requiring development of such substitutes are acquisitions of assets by donation, barter or exchange, and issuance of capital stock.

Acquisition of assets by gift is rare. Nevertheless corporations have received land, buildings, franchises, and similar assets from municipalities in exchange for a commitment by the corporation to locate in that city. These so-called gifts really amount to investments by the community in its future well-being, but the gifts must nevertheless be reflected in the accounting reports of the recipient. Generally accepted accounting principles suggest that the currently prevailing market price of the property be used as a substitute for an acquisition cost. If such market price is not readily available, it can be estimated by a competent independent appraiser. The substitute value for acquisition cost will, of course, have to be balanced on the equity side of the financial position statement. It is usually shown as a type of paid-in capital, with full disclosure of the exact source of the asset.

Firms may trade assets, with or without cash included in the transaction. Investors have been known to exchange one farm for another, a factory building in one city for a factory building in another, an apartment hotel in New York City for an oil well in Texas. An exchange of one asset for another should be thought of as the sale of the old asset and the purchase of the new one, which usually results in the recognition of a gain or loss on the asset given up. The problem for the accountant is to measure the cost of the asset received; this may be established either by the fair market value of the asset given up, or the fair market value of the asset received, whichever is the more objectively determinable.

To illustrate, assume the Olney Corporation trades an old delivery truck and $3,000 cash for a new truck. Let us assume that the cash value of the old truck, as determined by several offers from used-truck dealers, is $1,000. Let us also assume that the "sticker price" on the new truck is $4,500 and that the new-truck dealer is therefore offering a trade-in allowance of $1,500 for the old truck. What is the cost of the new truck to the Olney Corporation?

There is conflicting evidence here. The $1,000 offers from used-truck dealers contradict the $1,500 trade-in allowance. If these offers are considered reliable, the "sticker price" on the new truck must be considered inflated by $500. If the "sticker price" can be judged a true cost equivalent (would the new-truck dealer have demanded $4,500 cash for the truck?), then the $1,000 offers are unreasonably low. On the basis of the evidence submitted, it would appear that the used truck has a cash value of $1,000 and the cost of the new truck should be $4,000. This reasoning is based on the fact that the $1,000 offers were subject to competitive pressures, since there were several of them, and the "sticker price" on the new truck was not.

Given this solution, and assuming that the old truck was carried on the Olney Corporation books at $2,000 ($3,500 original cost less $1,500 accumulated depreciation), the entries to record the trade are as follows:

Accounts receivable—truck dealer	1,000	
Accumulated depreciation—trucks	1,500	
Loss on trade-in	1,000	
Trucks		3,500

To record trade-in of old truck

Trucks	4,000	
Cash		3,000
Accounts receivable—truck dealer		1,000

To record purchase of new truck

To take another example, a real estate development firm desires to gain control of a competing firm. It therefore exchanges with a stockholder of the competing firm a large parcel of land for a controlling interest in stock held by that individual. The land originally cost the firm $70,000 but now has a fair market value of $80,000. The value of the stock received in the exchange is not determinable because it has never before been sold or traded, and the assets of the competing firm are mainly options on land, the value of which is also indeterminable. Since the value of the asset received cannot be determined, the $80,000 value of the asset given up is used to indicate the exchange price. A gain of $10,000 (the $80,000 exchange price less the $70,000 cost) is recognized on the land. If the current market value of the land were not determinable for any reason, its $70,000 cost would determine the exchange price. No gain or loss would be recognized under these circumstances.

Treatment of Subsequent Outlays

Physical facilities such as buildings, equipment, and machinery often require outlays of funds after they have been installed and have been operating for some time. A part may break or a general overhaul may be necessary. Technological developments may even require a complete rebuilding of certain parts of the machine. The accountant must decide how to treat each of these different outlays in relation to generally accepted accounting principles. Generally, he has to choose between two broad alternatives.

On the one hand, he can treat all subsequent outlays connected with a particular facility as maintenance expense. Each outlay would be charged to the accounting period in which it was incurred, regardless of whether changes in the original facility had long-run significance. On the other hand, the outlays can be treated as the acquisition of additional facilities and added to the original cost of the asset. In practice the accountant must decide which treatment should be accorded to each subsequent outlay, based on its particular merits. To help in making this decision, generally accepted accounting principles suggest the following guides:

1. A cost incurred for the purpose of maintaining the estimated service potential of the facility when it was originally acquired should be treated as a repair or maintenance expense and charged to the accounting period in which it is incurred.

2. A cost incurred to alter the service potential of the facility by lengthening its useful life, increasing its output capacity, improving the quality of its output, or restoring service potential expired in past periods should be treated as an addition to asset values.

Take the case of a large diesel engine used in a pumping station of an oil pipeline company. The engine was originally acquired two years ago at a cost of several thousand dollars. Assume that during the past period three outlays were made for this engine. In one case a new fuel pump, costing $150, was installed to replace one that had failed. Assuming that the average life of the fuel pump is two years and the replacement is to be expected, this outlay would be treated as an expense of the period (a repair or maintenance) because the service potential of the asset was merely maintained at that originally contemplated before the outlay became necessary.

On the other hand, a new lubricating-oil filtering system was installed at a cost of $167. The reason for this installation was improved service-life potential (with cleaner oil the engine would not wear out so quickly). This outlay would therefore be capitalized.

The third expenditure, of $435, was for a complete overhaul of the engine, including new valves, piston rings, and bearings. After the overhaul the engine had nothing it did not have when it was new. Nevertheless, the outlay would probably be capitalized because the original service potential of the facility was increased by lengthening the engine's life. An outlay of this nature is often called a *betterment,* to indicate that no actual additions were made to the original facility. Betterments generally require a new estimate of useful life for depreciation purposes.

Proper treatment of subsequent outlays is another area in accounting where principles are broadly defined and where careful analysis by the accountant has great influence on the eventual impact of the information presented in the accounting reports of the firm. How would you treat the cost of repainting the interior of an apartment building? Or reroofing a factory? Or putting new tires on a large cross-country moving van?

Depreciation of Long-lived Tangible Assets

The acquisition cost of assets such as buildings, equipment, and machinery encompasses two economic components. One portion of acquisition cost is the amount that will be used up as the asset is employed in the revenue-seeking endeavors of the enterprise. This portion is called the *depreciable cost* of the asset. The second portion is any residual acquisition cost left over after the asset has served its period of usefulness to the enterprise. The name usually given to this portion is *resale value.* This apportionment is described by the formula:

Depreciable cost = Acquisition cost − Resale value

Resale value is an estimate of either the dollar proceeds from the sale of the asset as scrap (metal, wood, bricks, etc.) or the dollar proceeds from the sale of the asset on the used-facility market.

As an example of how resale value is considered in setting the depreciable cost of an asset, assume that Acme Auto Parts purchased a new grinding machine at a total acquisition cost of $12,000. This machine was designed specifically to grind one kind of product on a special order from the National Aeronautics and Space Administration. It was estimated that the order for 17,500 of these special castings would take approximately eighteen months to complete. At the time the special grinding machine was acquired, there was no foreseeable use for it within the company beyond the terms of the NASA contract. The property accountant and the production engineer estimated that the resale value of the grinding machine would be $7,000 after use by Acme. The depreciable cost to Acme, therefore, was $5,000 (the $12,000 acquisition cost minus the estimated resale value at the end of its usefulness to Acme).

Resale value can be a negative figure as well. This occurs when an asset can only be sold at a price that is less than the costs of removal from the premises. In many cases where assets have a life of several years or more, accountants will merely assume a zero resale value rather than attempt to determine a net resale value after disposal costs.

The process of depreciation is defined in accounting as the allocation of depreciable cost to those accounting periods whose revenues will benefit from the using up of the asset. With the exception of land, tangible assets have a limited useful life, usually measured in periods of time. Two factors must be considered in estimating useful life: physical wear and tear, and obsolescence. An estimate of the useful *physical* life, limited by wear and tear, is compared with an estimate of the useful *economic* life, limited by obsolescence, and the shorter of the two lives is used for depreciation purposes.

The *physical* life of an asset is dependent on two principal, and closely related, factors. The first of these is the use to which the asset is put. Many types of assets can be put to alternative uses and used under varying conditions. The lives of delivery equipment, for example, will vary with the weight carried and with the conditions of delivery (e.g., whether urban or cross-country).

The second factor in physical life is the maintenance policy. Certain assets, if carefully maintained, can be made to last almost indefinitely. On the other hand, neglect can result in a very short life indeed. Somewhere between these extremes is an optimum policy in which the average annual cost of the asset (depreciation and maintenance combined) is at a minimum. Ideally, the life of the asset when this optimum policy is in effect should be selected as the physical life of the asset. However, as we shall see, in the usual case the physical life does not establish the life of the asset for depreciation.

Obsolescence is the phenomenon that establishes the useful service life of most depreciable assets. Two general types of obsolescence must be considered: obsolescence of the asset itself, which occurs when technological improvements or style changes make it economically advisable to replace the old asset, and obsolescence resulting from the conditions of use of the asset. For example, factory buildings of expanding firms become too small, and machinery that can be used only in production of an obsolete product is also obsolete.

Obsolescence, as defined here, is a broad concept, and it is not difficult to understand why it should be the controlling factor in determining the service lives of most depreciable assets, particularly in an economy such as ours, in which technological changes are occurring at a rapid rate. In fact, the major reason that physical service lives continue to influence accounting estimates is that obsolescence is very difficult, if not impossible, to predict in many cases, and sometimes it is (wrongly) ignored.

The Pattern of Use

Once the useful life has been estimated, a pattern for spreading the depreciable cost over the useful life must be determined. The pattern used for accounting purposes should correspond as closely as possible with the actual physical pattern of depreciation after both wear and tear and obsolescence are considered. Three typical patterns are employed by accountants to reflect the depreciation affecting business facilities: production basis, straight line, and declining. The production basis of depreciation is related to the *use* of the asset. The straight-line and declining patterns relate to the *time* the asset is available for use.

PRODUCTION-BASIS PATTERN. In some cases it is possible to express the length of useful life in terms of units produced rather than in terms of time. As an example, the soft-drink bottling industry uses rather complicated high-speed automatic machinery to fill bottles with soda pop and put the crowns (caps) on the bottles. Most bottling concerns purchase this equipment with the thought that it will satisfactorily handle a certain estimated number of soft drink bottles during its lifetime. The accountant might therefore state its lifetime in terms of millions of bottles handled. Under this method, depreciation is computed by dividing the depreciable cost by the number of bottles to determine the "unit cost of depreciation." The total amount of depreciation in any given time period during the lifetime of the asset is found by multiplying the unit cost by the number of units produced in that time period. For example, if a bottling machine has a depreciable cost of $50,000 and will last for 20 million units, the depreciation factor per bottle will be as follows:

$$\frac{\$50,000}{20,000,000 \text{ bottles}} = \$.0025 \text{ per bottle}$$

If the bottling machine processes 600,000 bottles in 19x1, its annual depreciation for that year will be $1,500 (600,000 bottles × $.0025 per bottle). Obviously, the amount of depreciation per time period can vary greatly, depending on the activity level achieved by the enterprise in that period. If the demand for soft drinks increased until a distributor had to run three shifts per day rather than one, the increase in depreciation expense resulting from the increased use of his bottling machine would reflect this immediately.

STRAIGHT-LINE PATTERN. The straight-line pattern of depreciation assumes that throughout its estimated useful life to the enterprise the asset in question will contribute equally in each time period to the generation of revenues. For example, a blacktop parking lot constructed for a supermarket might be considered to have a straight-line pattern of depreciation because the lot will be able to handle the same number of customers' cars in each year of its estimated useful life. The calculation of the amount of depreciation per accounting period when assuming a straight-line pattern is relatively easy:

$$\frac{\text{Depreciable cost}}{\text{Number of periods of useful life}} = \frac{\text{Depreciation expense per}}{\text{accounting period}}$$

The name "straight line" comes from the chart that can be made showing the change in asset balance per year over useful life. Exhibit 16–1 is such a chart. Since the same amount of depreciation occurs each year, the year-end asset balance shown on the chart is reduced by equal amounts each year, thus producing a straight diagonal line.

EXHIBIT 16–1

THE EFFECT OF STRAIGHT-LINE DEPRECIATION ON ASSET VALUES

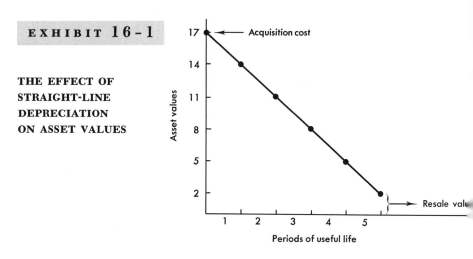

The straight-line pattern of depreciation is very popular for two reasons. First, it is rather easy to calculate the amount of depreciation per period. Second, for many assets, it is impossible to prejudge what the actual pattern of use will be; the straight-line pattern is the one least likely to be subject to bias, since each period receives the same depreciation charge.

DECLINING PATTERN.   The declining pattern of depreciation assumes that the asset in question will contribute more toward the earning of revenues in the earlier stages of useful life than it will in the later stages. An apartment building is typical of this kind of asset. A brand new apartment building with an estimated useful life of forty years will be able to command higher revenues in rentals per apartment when it is new and fashionable. During the course of its useful life, the apartment building will begin to show the signs of wear and tear, increasing maintenance costs, style obsolescence, and neighborhood obsolescence. With each progressive year it will command less and less rental value per apartment, assuming no inflation, and revenue per period will show a declining pattern. The need to match revenues with the associated costs requires that the depreciation expense per period be treated correspondingly.

A valid use of a declining pattern of depreciation occurs when it is felt that obsolescence will exert a strong influence on the life of the asset, but there is no way of predicting when it will occur. The declining pattern reflects this anticipation on the part of management.

A chart reflecting the declining pattern of depreciation is presented in

Exhibit 16-2. With each additional year of useful life the depreciation expense per year becomes smaller. As a result, the line connecting the year-end asset balances will curve downward to the right.

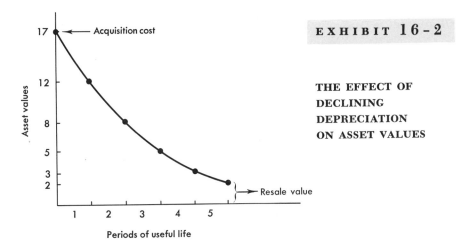

EXHIBIT 16-2

THE EFFECT OF DECLINING DEPRECIATION ON ASSET VALUES

Two ways of calculating a declining pattern are in general use today. Both are suggested in the Internal Revenue Code as methods of reflecting declining patterns of depreciation for federal income tax purposes. While it is not required by the code that the pattern of depreciation used for tax purposes be employed for general accounting purposes, there is nothing that prohibits this. Therefore in order to reduce bookkeeping costs, many firms use the same pattern for both purposes. This is in accord with generally accepted accounting principles as long as the pattern employed conforms logically to economic depreciation. Unfortunately, many taxpayers have continued to use the tax method for general accounting purposes when it seems unwarranted according to basic accounting principles. It may be an excusable "stretching" of the principles, however, considering how nebulous the whole process of estimating depreciable lives and depreciation pattern is.

The two widely used tax methods for calculating a declining depreciation pattern are the *double-declining-balance method* and the *sum-of-the-years'-digits method*.

THE DOUBLE-DECLINING-BALANCE METHOD. This method of calculation achieves a declining pattern similar to that illustrated in Exhibit 16–3. The curve resulting from the double-declining-balance calculation is based on the assumption that the amount of depreciation to be charged off each year is a function of the remaining asset value at the beginning of that year.

The calculation is made by applying a percentage to the *remaining original cost* (original cost minus depreciation to date) of the asset. (Note that for this calculation resale value is not employed.) The allowable percentage can be no

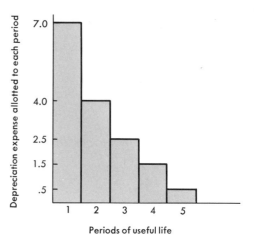

EXHIBIT 16-3

**DOUBLE-DECLINING-
BALANCE PATTERN
OF DEPRECIATION**

greater than twice the straight-line percentage. An asset lasting five years would have a 20 per cent straight-line percentage and thus an allowable 40 per cent for purposes of making the double-declining-balance calculation. Exhibit 16–5 compares the calculation of the straight-line pattern with the double-declining-balance pattern and with the sum-of-the-years'-digits pattern as well.

THE SUM-OF-THE-YEARS'-DIGITS METHOD. The pattern achieved with this method of calculation is shown in Exhibit 16–4. The declining straight line represents a constant rate of change in the depreciation of the asset.

The calculation is made by adding the digits for the years of useful life. An asset lasting five years would have a sum of the years' digits of 15 (1 + 2 + 3 + 4 + 5). The depreciable cost (resale value is considered) would then be allocated to the five years of its life as follows: the first year, $\frac{5}{15}$; the second year, $\frac{4}{15}$; the third year, $\frac{3}{15}$; the fourth year, $\frac{2}{15}$; and the fifth year, $\frac{1}{15}$. Exhibit 16–5 compares the three accepted methods of calculating depreciation

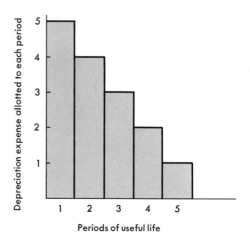

EXHIBIT 16-4

**SUM-OF-THE-YEARS'-
DIGITS PATTERN
OF DEPRECIATION**

EXHIBIT 16-5

COMPARISON OF DEPRECIATION PATTERNS

Year	Straight Line			Sum of the Years' Digits			Double Declining Balance		
	Depreciation expense	Remaining depreciable cost	Book value	Depreciation expense	Remaining depreciable cost	Book value	Depreciation expense	Remaining depreciable cost	Book value
1	$ 3,000	$15,000	$17,000	$ 5,000	$15,000	$17,000	$ 6,800	$15,000	$17,000
2	3,000	12,000	14,000	4,000	10,000	12,000	4,080	8,200	10,200
3	3,000	9,000	11,000	3,000	6,000	8,000	2,448	4,120	6,120
4	3,000	6,000	8,000	2,000	3,000	5,000	1,469	1,672	3,672
5	3,000	3,000	5,000	1,000	1,000	3,000	203	203	2,203
		0	2,000		0	2,000		0	2,000
	$15,000			$15,000			$15,000		

on an asset with an estimated life of five years, an acquisition cost of $17,000, and a resale value of $2,000.

It is wise to keep in mind that the examples of calculation indicated above are greatly simplified. There are many refinements and restrictions in actual use that are not of concern at this time.

Recording Depreciation

In its simplest form, the entry to record depreciation is

Depreciation expense	XXX	
Allowance for depreciation		XXX

As you already know, the debit to the expense account has the effect of reducing the earnings for the period, and consequently, reducing retained earnings on the statement of financial position. The offsetting credit reduces the long-lived asset total, since the account "allowance for depreciation" is treated as a contra account or reduction of the cost of the asset to which it applies.

The reasons for using the contra account, rather than making the credit entry directly to the asset account, are not strong, because the essential effect on the statement of financial position is the same with either method. The contra account is used partly because the added information provided is considered useful. For example, compare these two presentations:

(Using the contra account)		*(Not using the contra account)*	
Long-lived assets		Long-lived assets	
Buildings—cost	$1,000,000	Buildings—net of depre-	
Allowance for depre-		ciation	$200,000
ciation	800,000		
Undepreciated cost	$ 200,000		

The presentation at the left gives an indication of the age of the building as well as its original cost, while the presentation at the right does not. In addition, depreciation is a rough estimate that, under unusual circumstances, may be subject to correction during the life of the asset. For example, suppose the building in the above illustration was being depreciated on a straight-line basis over a twenty-year life (no salvage value), or $50,000 per year for sixteen years. Assume further that it is now clear that the original service life should have been twenty-five years, or $40,000 per year. If it is decided to correct this error in the records, the proper entry would be

Allowance for depreciation—buildings	160,000	
Correction of prior periods' income		160,000

Depreciation would then be recorded at $40,000 per year for the remaining nine years of the life of the asset. (It is wrong to simply allocate the remaining $200,000 over the remaining life of nine years, because this introduces a compensating error. This erroneous solution is the only one acceptable for federal income tax purposes, however.)

An analysis of the entry that records depreciation, which merely reduces both sides of the financial position statement, should make it abundantly clear that depreciation, per se, provides no "funds" (however defined) for the firm. The one qualification one may wish to consider is that depreciation is a tax deduction, and the firm's tax outlay is therefore lower than it would have been had depreciation not been deducted. The relationship between depreciation and funds is covered elsewhere in this book, and need not be elaborated here.

INTANGIBLE LONG-LIVED ASSETS

Intangible long-lived assets are legal rights, privileges, and competitive advantages that are relatively long-lived, not intended for resale, and used in the operations of the business. Several examples follow:

Patents. A patent represents a temporary monopoly that is granted by the federal government to an inventor and gives him the exclusive right to sell or use his invention for seventeen years.

Copyrights. A copyright represents the exclusive right given by the federal government to reproduce or sell literary or artistic work. A copyright extends for twenty-eight years and is renewable for a second twenty-eight-year period.

Trademarks. A symbol or name that is used by a company to identify its product is a trademark. Trademarks have an unlimited legal life if they have been registered with the federal government.

Franchises. A government body or a business firm may grant certain rights and privileges to the recipient of a franchise. A typical government franchise is the exclusive right to operate a public transportation system. Manufacturers' franchises are often grants of exclusive rights to a distributor to sell the manufacturer's product within a specified territory.

Organization costs. The costs associated with the organization of a company should be carried as intangible assets. Legal fees and printing costs are examples of costs that are generally incurred in the organization of a company.

Leasehold improvements. A tenant who has secured a lease on real estate and has made improvements that have become part of this real estate has acquired a leasehold improvement. The tenant has incurred a cost for the purpose of improving the real estate, and this cost gives him the *right* to benefit from the improvement during the period of the lease. When the lease itself is shown as an asset, the leasehold improvement may be added to this asset account for amortization purposes if the life of the improvement is at least as long as the life of the lease.

Goodwill. Goodwill exists when a business has earnings that exceed a *normal* rate of return on its assets. A favorable business location, good employees and managers, and good customer relations are some of the factors that contribute to excess earnings. However, only *purchased goodwill*—that is, excess earning power paid for in acquiring an existing business—should be carried as an asset on the statement of financial position. Businesses that have developed their excess earning power over a period of years would not show goodwill on their statements of financial position.

Deferred advertising costs.   Advertising costs that are expected to produce revenues in one or more future accounting periods should be carried as intangible long-lived assets.

Deferred research and development costs.   Costs incurred for the development of new products and/or improved methods of operations are properly classified as intangible long-lived assets. Research and development costs have become the lifeblood of many of our leading industries. A high percentage of sales revenue in many companies results from products that were not in existence five or ten years ago.

Valuation of Intangible Long-lived Assets

The same principles apply to the valuation of intangible as well as tangible long-lived assets, and the previous discussion on determining acquisition costs and substituting for acquisition costs applies equally.

Intangible assets, like some tangible assets, are frequently developed as a result of activities within a business enterprise. Therefore, it is possible for an intangible asset to be included on the statement of financial position of the developer if he has made *identifiable* outlays in its development. This is especially true of patents and deferred research and development costs that are frequently the result of research or engineering effort by company employees. The cost of experiments, salaries of researchers, building equipment, etc., can frequently be determined quite accurately. According to good accounting practices, these costs should be capitalized as intangible long-lived assets.

Measurement Difficulties

Intangible long-lived assets—particularly patents, goodwill, deferred advertising costs, deferred research and development costs, and trademarks—are frequently the most important assets of a business in terms of expected economic benefits. However, in many cases, these assets do not appear on the statement of financial position. This omission is partly due to the difficulty of measuring costs associated with future benefits. For example, if the General Motors Corporation sponsors a weekly television show on a national network, the company hopes to receive benefits from this advertising in the current accounting period as well as in future accounting periods. The difficult question is, *How much* of the current cost associated with advertising expenditures can be expected to benefit future accounting periods and can thus be properly capitalized as an asset? The same problem described in connection with deferred advertising costs also applies to research and development costs. Because of measurement difficulties, costs for these items are usually accounted for as current expenses. It is common practice *not* to capitalize the cost unless the future benefit is fairly certain and the amount of the cost associated with the future benefit can be objectively determined. It is most important, however, for a user of financial statements to consider whether assets such as these exist even though they do not appear on the statement of financial position. It is difficult for him to determine this, however, unless he has inside information.

Another factor influencing accounting practice in the area of intangibles is the fact that "expensing" outlays for intangibles is considered "conservative," which, unfortunately, is sometimes thought to be a synonym for "good." There is some evidence that this general attitude is slowly giving way to increased recognition of the need for unbiased measurements, but in accounting for intangible assets, little progress has been made. Displays of large amounts of intangible assets on a firm's financial position statement are very likely to be interpreted as a sign of the firm's financial weakness. In fact, some financial analysts follow the practice of omitting intangibles when calculating financial ratios, presumably because they feel that such assets are of questionable validity. It is small wonder that a financially strong firm is tempted to "expense" intangibles, as long as it can continue to report satisfactory earnings to shareholders. When this is done, the matching (of revenues and expenses) criterion is ignored, and the likelihood increases that users will be misled regarding the earnings potential of the firm.

The following item sometimes appears on the statement of financial position:

> Intangible long-lived assets:
> Trademarks and goodwill $1

The appearance of an asset valued at $1 on a statement showing total assets of several million dollars may appear a bit unusual or perhaps ridiculous. The purpose of this nominal valuation of $1 is to disclose to the reader of the statement that such assets exist. In the usual case, a sizeable intangible asset has been amortized down to $1, which was then retained on the books, in order to convey the impressions that (1) the benefits from the unreported asset continue and that (2) the firm is financially strong enough to absorb these costs prematurely. In this case, poor accounting may create a good "image."

Human Resource Accounting

One of the most interesting experiments currently being conducted in the area of intangible assets is called *"human resource accounting."* Defined as "an information system that tells management what changes over time are occurring to the human resources of the business," human resource accounting was developed jointly between the Institute for Social Research of the University of

Michigan, and the R. G. Barry Corporation.° In this system, outlay costs for recruiting, acquiring, training, familiarizing, and developing management personnel are accumulated and capitalized. These investments in human resources are amortized over the expected useful life of the investment. The basic objective is to provide "managers with specific feedback information on their performance in managing the organizational resources entrusted to their care. . . ."†

Expensing Intangibles

A change in accounting for intangible assets will doubtless be a long time in coming, but every effort should be made to bring about this change. It must be remembered that competent managers, in making decisions to spend large sums for research, must have high expectations of a profitable return on these investments. If these expectations are certain enough to justify the expenditure, they are certain enough to report as assets on the financial position statement. Virtually all the nonmonetary asset values on the financial position statement find their justification in the expectations of management, and there is no reason why intangibles should require a higher level of certainty than buildings or machinery. Conversely, if management's expectations of reward for the expenditures are highly uncertain, then one must question their competence to make wise investment decisions.

Another factor that encourages accountants to treat advertising and research cost as expenses in the period incurred is the fact that these items are immediately deductible for tax purposes. The firm need not follow its tax-reporting methods in its published reports, but because of the highly subjective nature of the problem, most accountants do, for lack of a better alternative.

For example, assume that the Meno Electronics Corporation spends $100,000 in 19x5 on a research project that the company expects will produce revenues for ten years, beginning in 19x6. The accountant is trying to decide whether to record the research costs as an asset that will be amortized over a ten-year period, or as a 19x5 expense. Assuming that he wants the Meno tax return to agree with the published statements, the alternatives are as shown in Exhibit 16–6.

Deducting the research costs in 19x5 does not "save" $50,000 in taxes; it merely delays tax payment until future years. Deducting the item currently provides a hedge against the possibility that the future years might be loss years; since no taxes would have to be paid in loss years anyway, future deductions might not bring any tax benefits. Equally important is the fact that the company has the use of $50,000 in cash it would otherwise not have, and $50,000 on which it can earn a return.

° R. G. Barry Corporation Annual Report, 1969. (See Appendix 12A.)
† *Ibid.*, pp. 12–14.

EXHIBIT 16-6

	Research costs are expensed and deducted for tax purposes	Research costs are capitalized and not deducted for tax purposes
Assets		
Working capital	$ 500,000	$ 450,000
Long-lived assets	1,000,000	1,100,000
Total assets	$1,500,000	$1,550,000
Liabilities and Owners' Equity		
Long-term liabilities and owners' equity	$1,500,000	$1,550,000
Earnings before taxes and research costs	$400,000	$400,000
— Research costs	100,000	
Earnings before taxes	$300,000	
— Federal income taxes (50%)	150,000	200,000
Net earnings	$150,000	$200,000

Amortization of Intangible Long-lived Assets

Once the cost of intangible assets has been established for purposes of the statement of financial position, the accountant is faced with a further problem of determining the length of the life and the pattern over which this cost should be amortized. (To accountants, the word "depreciate" seems inappropriate when applied to intangibles because of the absence of a physical service life, but the two words mean much the same thing. Sometimes accountants also use "amortize" when referring to the write-off of tangible assets.) As in the case of tangible assets, the length of the life is determined by the expectations of benefits from the expenditure.

Patents and copyrights have legal lives that establish maximum service lives for these assets, but the economic lives are usually much shorter than the legal lives. Franchises and leases have maximum lives established by law or by contract.

The amortization of deferred research costs presents difficult problems. As indicated earlier, however, the management must have had some minimum period in mind over which the benefits from the expenditure would be realized when the expenditure for the research was authorized. The accountant can do no better than to select that same period as the useful service life of the asset, subject, of course, to possible changes in these expectations at a later time when better evidence becomes available.

Purchased goodwill and organization costs can have useful service lives that are indefinitely long; that is, they are as long as the life of the firm. Much management effort is devoted to enhancing the goodwill and perpetuating the life of the firm. This means that the intangible assets should be reported as assets as long as these efforts seem to be successful, and they should not be amortized until the evidence indicates that the goodwill is disappearing. In the case of organization costs, amortization would theoretically begin only when the end of the life of the firm can be predicted. As a practical matter, most accountants prefer to amortize these assets, perhaps over a long life such as forty or fifty years, so that the annual amounts are small. Admittedly, there seems little to be gained by carrying these assets on the statement of financial position indefinitely.

As for patterns of amortization, it appears that the straight-line method is almost universally used, at least for the intangible assets discussed in this section. There seems little reason to select the production basis or one of the declining-balance methods. The straight-line method has the advantages of simplicity and the fact that it does not favor one accounting period over another.

NONMONETARY LIABILITIES: AN EXAMPLE

Deferred Income Tax Liability

Some of the most difficult and controversial accounting problems arise in the accountant's attempt to assign federal income tax expense to the accounting periods in which it is incurred. The problems arise because the federal income tax law levies a tax on a "business income" that often differs from the accountant's "net earnings before income taxes." One fairly easy solution to the problem of accounting for tax expense is to assign to each period the expense that is *legally* assessed by the taxing authorities. Many accountants support this practice both from a theoretical as well as a practical point of view. The liability for federal income tax would always be the amount legally payable, and thus a monetary liability.

When this accounting interpretation is implemented, however, some confusing results may appear in the financial statements. Consider this example: The Able Company reports $40,000 as the proper amount of depreciation expense to arrive at its net earnings for the year 19x0. Assume, however, that the tax law permits the Able Company to deduct $100,000 depreciation to arrive at taxable net income for that year because the law permits "accelerated" depreciation, which Able Company feels is not appropriate for reports to stockholders. If we account for Able's income tax expense as suggested above, the result will look like this:

	Able Company's tax return 19x0	Able Company's report to stockholders 19x0
Net earnings before depreciation and income taxes (assume)	$500,000	$500,000
Depreciation		
For tax purposes	100,000	
For accounting purposes		40,000
Taxable income	$400,000	
Net earnings before tax		$460,000
Federal income tax (assume a 40% rate)	$160,000	160,000
Net earnings after tax		$300,000

The problem arises because the deduction of $60,000 excess depreciation allowable for tax purposes (on which the tax reduction is $24,000) in 19x0 means that depreciation for tax purposes in future years will have to be reduced by $60,000 on these particular assets. In other words, the taxpayer is simply permitted to speed up his depreciation on a given group of assets.

If we wish to report that the $24,000 tax saved in 19x0 will have to be paid later, then a $24,000 nonmonetary tax liability should be shown at the end of 19x0; the 19x0 tax expense should be $184,000 (40% of $460,000), not $160,000; and the entry to record federal tax expense on Able's books should be as follows:

Federal tax expense	184,000	
Federal income tax payable (current)		160,000
Federal income tax payable (deferred)		24,000

The justification for the $184,000 expense instead of $160,000 is based on the matching principle. As a result of 19x0 operations, so the argument runs, $184,000 of income tax expense has been incurred, some of which will be paid currently ($160,000), and the remainder in some later year or years. Controversy arises, however, over the question of whether the $24,000 will *ever* be paid. If this question can be answered affirmatively, then the above solution is correct. But if it can be shown that Able Company will continue to expand its depreciable assets and will continue to use accelerated depreciation for tax purposes indefinitely, then the liability is most certainly nonmonetary; it can even be argued that the $24,000 liability will not be paid and therefore is not a liability at all, and that 19x0 profits are understated.

This is only one example of the many complex problems in accounting for federal income tax expense in financial reports. For those who wish to study the subject in greater detail, additional discussion and illustrative examples are contained in the Appendix to Chapter 17.

FINANCIAL STATEMENTS AND INFLATION

Once we begin talking about monetary values, we run into a problem that many people feel constitutes a fundamental flaw in accounting practice. The problem arises from the fact that the value of the accountant's measuring unit, the dollar, is not stable in terms of purchasing power. General inflation, or reduction in the purchasing power of the dollar, has been occurring at varying rates of speed over a period of many years.

Anyone who holds cash or bonds, or who depends for spending money on the collection of a fixed number of dollars, will find that his purchasing power decreases during a period of inflation. Certainly the importance of a fixed number of dollars as an economic resource can be expressed only in terms of what that number of dollars will buy, and changes in this purchasing power result in gains and losses even though the number of dollars remains the same.

Gains and losses in purchasing power of monetary assets and liabilities are important factors in business decisions, although the effect on all firms is by no means the same. Firms having large investments in monetary assets, such as banks and insurance companies, have a much different problem than, say, a public utility with a heavy investment in plant and equipment financed primarily by long-term bond issues. In all firms, however, the ability to predict long-run and short-run movements in purchasing power is an indispensable talent of managers. Several phenomena in recent years can reasonably be traced to the expectations of investors and businessmen that the recent inflation (i.e., the decline in purchasing power) is likely to continue in the future:

1. Investors have tended to purchase stocks (nonmonetary assets) rather than bonds (monetary assets) to avoid the loss in purchasing power of the bond when inflation occurs.

2. Business firms have tended to buy inventories and capital assets (nonmonetary assets) before they are needed, in anticipation of higher prices later on.

3. Individuals and business firms have tended to use borrowed funds, thus incurring monetary liabilities, in anticipation of repayment with "cheaper" dollars at some later time.

Many accountants and others feel that conventional accounting practice is deficient in assuming that the changes in the purchasing power of the dollar have occurred slowly enough to be ignored in financial statements. Most accounting writers, and also the AICPA, are concerned about the problem and have made various recommendations for change, experimentation, and publication of supplementary information about the effect of inflation on the financial affairs of business firms.

The most comprehensive price level index in the United States is the Gross National Product Implicit Price Deflator (GNP Deflator), issued by the Department of Commerce. This index, beginning with its base year of 1958, has moved as follows:

Year	Index	Purchasing power
1958	100.0	$1.00
59	101.6	.98
60	103.3	.97
61	104.6	.96
62	105.7	.95
63	107.1	.93
64	108.9	.92
65	110.9	.90
66	113.9	.88
67	117.6	.85
68	122.3	.82
69	128.1	.78

This index may be used to convert dollars of any year into the dollars of any other year so that comparisons will not be distorted by the fact that the dollar measurements in different years are not the same. If you accept the assumption that the GNP Deflator is a valid measure of price-level change, then you must recognize that dollar measurements arising in different periods must be adjusted by this index to reflect a dollar of *common* size before the sum or difference between the various dollar amounts has any meaning. Assume, for example, that Acme Auto Parts Company purchased one machine for $10,000 in 1964 and another machine for $12,000 in 1967. It is not really accurate to say that the total cost of the two machines is $22,000. We should convert the second machine into 1964 dollars as follows:

$$\$12{,}000 \times \frac{108.9}{117.3} = \$11{,}140$$

add the $10,000 cost of the first machine, and report that the cost of the two machines is $21,140 1964 dollars. Or we can express these figures in 1969 dollars by converting both as follows:

$$\$10{,}000 \times \frac{128.1}{108.9} = \$11{,}760$$

$$\$12{,}000 \times \frac{128.1}{117.6} = \underline{13{,}100}$$

Total cost of the machines $24,860   1969 dollars

Inflation is a common phenomenon and is much more severe in many other countries of the world than in the United States. Businessmen and individuals are heavily influenced by past inflation in their expectations of future inflation, and intelligent decision makers have learned to govern themselves accordingly.

Generally accepted accounting principles do not include adjustment of dollar figures of various years into common dollars for purposes of financial reports. The reasoning is simply that the change in the value of the U.S. dollar has been slow enough that such adjustments are unnecessary. You will note that the GNP Deflator movement has been significantly faster since 1965, and more and more accountants are beginning to doubt whether this rate of inflation can continue to be ignored in financial statements. In June of 1969, the AICPA issued "Financial Statements Restated for General Price-Level Changes,"[*] in which adjusted financial statements were recommended as supplementary information to be included in annual reports to stockholders. The technique for making these adjustments is beyond the scope of this book, not because it is difficult, but because it is of interest primarily to professional accountants. The following (highly unrealistic) example will illustrate the concept.

An Illustration

Assume that Price Corporation is organized on January 1, 19x0, by issuing common stock for $25,000 cash and issuing 8 per cent, five-year notes for $75,000 cash. Land costing $80,000 is purchased that same day, and no other transactions occur during the entire year. The financial position statements, at the beginning and end of the year, prepared in accordance with conventional accounting practices, are as follows:

PRICE CORPORATION
COMPARATIVE STATEMENT OF FINANCIAL POSITION

| | *Assets* | | | *Equities* | | |
| | *19x0* | | | | *19x0* | |
	January 1	*December 31*			*January 1*	*December 31*
Cash	$ 20,000	$ 20,000	Notes payable		$ 75,000	$ 75,000
Land	80,000	80,000	Accrued interest			6,000
			Capital stock		25,000	25,000
			Retained earnings		0	(6,000)[a]
	$100,000	$100,000			$100,000	$100,000

[a] Parentheses denote deficit.

The negative retained earnings (deficit) is the loss resulting from interest on the notes, with no offsetting revenue.

[*] Statement of the Accounting Principles Board, No. 3, June 1969 (New York: AICPA, 1969).

Now let us assume that the general price level index, which we accept as the measure of inflation, is 100 at the beginning of the year, 106 at the end of the year, and averages 103 for the year. The following financial position statement should be presented as supplementary information in the report:

PRICE CORPORATION

COMPARATIVE STATEMENT OF FINANCIAL POSITION

(expressed in December 31, 19x0 dollars)

	Assets			Equities		
	19x0				*19x0*	
	January 1	*December 31*			*January 1*	*December 31*
Cash	$ 21,200	$ 20,000	Notes payable		$ 79,500	$ 75,000
Land	84,800	84,800	Accrued interest			6,000
			Capital stock		26,500	26,500
			Retained earnings			(2,700)[a]
	$106,000	$104,800			$106,000	$104,800

[a] Parentheses denote deficit.

The following points should be noted:

1. The January 1 financial position statement, expressed in December 31 dollars, is obtained by multiplying each figure in the conventional statement by 106/100. The "dollar" has shrunk by six percentage points during the year, and the adjustment is necessary to retain the economic significance of the January 1 financial position statement. For example, the $84,000 figure for land says in effect that on January 1, 19x0, land was purchased at a cost of the equivalent of $84,000 *December 31 dollars,* and the $79,500 notes payable figure says that on January 1 the company borrowed the equivalent of $79,500 *December 31 dollars.* It is important to note that the $84,000 is *not* intended to be an estimate of the December 31 value of the land, nor is the $79,500 intended to reflect the current value of the liability.

2. The purchasing power of the dollar dropped six percentage points during the year, but legal agreements did not change. Accordingly, the bank carrying Price Corporation's checking account is obligated only to the extent of $20,000 December 31 dollars. Similarly, Price Corporation is obligated to pay only $75,000 principal on the note and $6,000 annual interest, both liabilities being expressed in December 31 dollars. In the eyes of the law, a dollar is a dollar, regardless of what it will buy. Therefore, monetary assets (cash in this case) and monetary liabilities (notes and accrued interest payable) retain their legal status, and we find that the Price Corporation has to absorb a loss as a result of holding cash and enjoying a gain resulting from the liabilities.

3. The considerations in 2 affect the retained earnings as shown below:

PRICE CORPORATION
STATEMENT OF EARNINGS
For the Year 19x0
(expressed in December 31, 19x0 dollars)

Interest expense	$6,175	
Net operating loss		$6,175
Purchasing power gains and losses		
Gain on notes payable	$4,500	
Gain on interest payable	175	
	$4,675	
Loss on holding cash	1,200	
Net gain in purchasing power		$3,475
Deficit, 12/31		$2,700

The interest expense accrues over the entire year, during which the average value of the index is 103. In December 31 dollars, the interest expense is 106/103 × $6,000, or $6,175, but since the liability is a monetary liability, the company gains $175 December 31 dollars in purchasing power as an offsetting factor.

This illustration brings into sharp focus the distinction between monetary and nonmonetary assets and liabilities. Even though it is oversimplified, the illustration also explains why predictions of inflation are likely to influence management's actions. The gain on monetary liabilities is a major factor in offsetting the interest expense on the loan. Managers are influenced to borrow and invest the cash in nonmonetary assets (such as land) that will not shrink in value as the purchasing power of the dollar declines. If the Price Corporation had invested $100,000 in land instead of $80,000, the loss in purchasing power of the cash balance would have been avoided. The illustration provides some evidence of the relationship between interest rates and inflation, and it suggests the reason why small increases in interest rates may not be effective in slowing down an "overheated" economy, as long as managers expect the inflationary trend to continue.

The authors are inclined to agree with the AICPA that financial statements adjusted for change in purchasing power of the dollar should be included as supplements in annual reports to stockholders because of the additional information they provide regarding the influence of inflation on management. It should be kept in mind, however, that such adjustments do not have the effect of reflecting the "value" of the firm, which is the basic purpose of financial statements. Financial statements adjusted for inflation adhere strictly to the conventional accounting principles of historical cost, with one faulty assumption removed (the assumption that the change in the purchasing power of the dollar may be ignored). Adjusted financial statements are therefore also based on historical cost expressed in dollars of uniform purchasing power. Accounting for assets and liabilities in terms of their current value is another matter and it will be dealt with briefly in the next section.

FINANCIAL STATEMENTS AND PRICE CHANGES OF INDIVIDUAL ASSETS AND LIABILITIES

It is entirely realistic to assume circumstances in which the prices of individual nonmonetary asset and liability items change without change in the general price level. Such price changes are considered unrealized gains and losses and are not usually recorded and reported by accountants (except when the current prices of inventory items fall below cost). More generally we can define gain or loss from price changes as the amount of the price change that cannot be accounted for by the change in the value of the dollar. For example, if the current value of an inventory item increases from $100 to $110 during a period in which the general price level index increases from 100 to 106, we define the unrealized gain as $4. If the general price level moved from 100 to 97 during this period, the unrealized gain on the inventory item would be $13.

In fact, price-level adjusted statements follow the same concept of gain or loss. Even when the current number of dollars assigned to a monetary asset or liability does not change, an unrealized gain or loss occurs when the general price-level index does change. The reason for emphasis on monetary assets is that the law makes it certain that the number of dollars assigned to the monetary items will remain the same.

In the illustration in the previous section, we made no attempt to ascertain the current value of the nonmonetary asset "land" or the nonmonetary owners' equity item "capital stock." These items were stated at historical cost expressed in December 31 dollars so that measuring and reporting unrealized gain or loss would not be necessary.

Since we assume that the basic objective of the financial position statement is to approximate the current value of the firm, it is difficult to justify failure to reflect current values as closely as possible. The justification is even more difficult if the statements are to be included in the report as supplementary information. Certainly gains and losses on monetary assets are not basically any different from nor are more important than gains and losses on nonmonetary assets, similarly defined.

Nevertheless, there are differences between monetary and nonmonetary assets and liabilities that may justify the Accounting Principles Board's recommendation to report gain or loss on monetary items but not on nonmonetary items:

1. Since they are not established by law or contract in dollars, current values of nonmonetary assets must be defined. In the case of long-lived nonmonetary assets, the amount of future cash that will be received through use of the asset has very little meaning, because invariably the asset is used jointly with many other assets, and future cash receipts attributable to a particular asset cannot be determined.

2. This means that some substitute for current value must be selected. The accountant must choose between *current replacement cost* ("entry value"), which is the amount in current dollars it would cost to replace or reproduce the productive capacity of the asset, and *net realizable value* ("exit value"), which is the amount in current dollars the firm would receive from immediate sale of the asset.

3. Either one of the substitute values in 2 above, or both, may be very difficult to measure in a given case. Since management's intent is to use the asset, rather than to replace it or sell it, current values must be determined hypothetically, often on the basis of evidence not susceptible to objective verification.

4. Even if current market values are easily determinable, many accountants feel (in the case of inventories, for example) that an actual sale must take place to justify reporting gain or loss. It must be remembered that in addition to a legally fixed dollar amount, monetary assets have a legally fixed (or highly predictable) maturity or collection date. On the other hand, an item of inventory not sold at a time when the market value is known is presumably being held because the market is expected to go higher. In the absence of an actual sale or contract to sell, the future cash to be received is not known.

Whether this case for omitting current value data on nonmonetary assets is convincing, particularly from reports that are presented as supplementary information (and presumably not covered by the auditors' opinion), is a matter of opinion. Certainly accountants do not want to take responsibility for reporting values that are simply unsupported guesses or whims of the management. On the other hand, when current values are highly objective, the failure to report them is difficult to defend. In our opinion, a major fallacy in the reasoning of many accountants is the notion that since the current values of *some* assets cannot be determined, it is wrong to report current values of *other* assets that can be established. It is always possible to cite examples of asset items on which the accountant has no choice but to report on the basis of historical cost, but this should not be used as a justification for omitting the current values of other assets that are measureable.

SUMMARY

This chapter dealt with the cost measurement problems associated with long-lived nonmonetary assets—tangible asset costs, such as plant and equipment costs; and intangible asset costs, such as patents, and research and development costs. These measurement problems appear first at the time of acquisition, and additional problems arise throughout the estimated life of the asset. These problems are accentuated by the influences of conservatism, the federal tax law, and, particularly in the case of intangibles, the desire of management to keep the financial position statement free of questionable assets. The chapter also dealt briefly with the complex question of the liability for deferred federal income taxes.

The chapter concluded with a discussion of the significance of conventional financial statements during and following a period of change in the general price level. Recommended adjustments to counteract this effect were discussed, and the relationship of these adjustments to specific price changes was evaluated.

Questions for Review

16-1. What three requirements must be met in order to classify an asset as long-lived on the statement of financial position?

16-2. By which method are long-lived assets generally valued on the statement of financial position?

16-3. How does the accountant decide which costs should be capitalized in arriving at the total acquisition cost for a long-lived asset?

16-4. What guidelines should be followed in measuring substitutes for acquisition costs?

16-5. What guidelines should be followed in accounting for costs incurred subsequent to acquisition of a long-lived asset?

16-6. What factors should be considered in developing a depreciation policy for long-lived assets?

16-7. What major factors should be considered in selecting a method of depreciation for a long-lived asset?

16-8. Describe the major measurement problems associated with long-lived intangible assets.

16-9. What situation may create a deferred income tax liability?

16-10. What impact has inflation had on financial statements in the United States in recent years?

16-11. Distinguish between general price level changes and price changes of individual assets and liabilities, and indicate the significance of this difference in financial reporting.

16-12. Under what circumstances would the double-declining-balance method of depreciation be more desirable for federal income tax purposes than straight-line depreciation? Explain.

Problems for Analysis

16-13. The following two quotations are from corporate annual reports. Evaluate each of these excerpts.

From the May Department Stores Company: "We obtain an exceptionally high cash flow from depreciation per dollar of sales for a department store company because we own the bulk of our real estate. This flow of funds into the business provides an important source of capital for future growth."

From the Pennsalt Chemicals Corporation: "Due to improved earnings, funds generated internally from depreciation, amortization and retained earnings amounted to $8,441,000, the highest in the Company's history. The magnitude of this figure is important, in that it is the principal means by which future growth of the Company is sustained. These are the funds that are available for investment in new plants and facilities, which in turn will provide additional earnings in subsequent years."

16-14. Wiggins, Inc., incurred the following costs pertaining to a recently acquired milling machine for use in its manufacturing activity. Determine which of these costs should be capitalized:

1. Invoice for milling machine, $11,000°
2. Freight, $90
3. Building-structure reinforcement to accommodate new machine, $1,200
4. Accessories to improve machine's safety for employees, $425
5. Training for machine operators, $350
6. Damage suit from employee injured during installation of machine, $1,650
7. Routine maintenance inspection thirty days after machine was put into operation, $20

° A 2 per cent cash discount of $220 was received for payment of the invoice within the discount period.

16-15. The Embers Company acquired a delivery truck on January 1 of the current year and incurred the following costs:
1. Invoice for truck, $2,600
2. Air conditioner, $300
3. Radio, $60
4. Lettering truck with company name, etc., $80
5. Installation of special racks for ease of handling deliveries, $160
6. Minor engine tune-up 60 days after truck's acquisition, $30

The truck is thought to have an estimated life of four years, with a resale value of $200. The company has capitalized the invoice cost of $2,600 and established a depreciation charge of $960 for the first calendar year of use.

a. Determine the amount of costs that should be capitalized in connection with the acquisition of the delivery truck.

b. What method of depreciation is the company using for the delivery truck?

c. Illustrate the effect on net earnings over the life of the delivery truck of the errors that the company made in determining the acquisition cost of the delivery truck.

16-16.   PART I

The Sparta Creamery Company is a wholesaler of butter, eggs, cheese, shortening, and other food products to restaurants, hotels, and motels. There are six salesmen-drivers who are responsible for certain areas of the city (the approximate population of which is 600,000). The company reports on a fiscal year ending January 31.

On February 1 of the current year the company purchased a new truck to be used on one of the delivery routes. The estimated life of this delivery truck is five years. The costs associated with the purchase of the truck are as follows:

1. Invoice from dealer (chassis only), $1,800
2. Transportation from dealer to company (fifty miles), $32
3. Installation of special-purpose enclosed body, $1,350
4. Installation of cooling equipment for truck body, $175
5. Liability and collision insurance premium for one year, $180
6. Lettering truck with company name, etc., $65
7. Radio, $58
8. Rearview mirrors, $21
9. Four heavy-duty tires for rear wheels (Original tires were traded in for $205. Net cost of new tires: $310 − $205 = $105.), $310

Determine the amount of these costs that should be capitalized.

PART II

Assume that the Sparta Creamery Company incurs the following costs on the truck during the first three years of operation:

1. First six months of operation:
   a. Complete engine tune-up, $40
   b. Radio repair, $8
   c. Tire repair, $12
2. Second six months of operation:
   a. Installation of heater, $78
   b. Complete engine tune-up, $46
   c. Purchase of new tire, $61
   d. Repair of damaged fender, $70
3. Second year of operation:
   a. Purchase of 3 new tires, $190
   b. Installation of seat cover, $12
   c. Paint touch-up, $32
   d. Replacement of broken windshield, $48
4. Third year of operation:
   a. Major engine overhaul (estimated to extend life of truck one additional year), $425
   b. Replacement of muffler and shock absorbers, $110
   c. Relining and repair of brakes, $62
   d. Purchase of two new tires, $81

a. Which of the above costs should be capitalized and which expensed?

b. What assumptions are implicit in your decision to capitalize or expense?

c. What factors should a company consider in the establishment of a policy regarding capitalization versus expensing of acquisition costs?

d. Do accounting principles place any restrictions on the flexibility of such a policy?

16-17. Growth, Inc., incurred the following costs for a building site to be used for the construction of a new office building:

1. Paid $25,000 cash for land and building. Six months earlier an appraised valuation, reported for a different purpose, placed values on the land and building at $15,000 and $10,000 respectively. The liability for unpaid taxes of $1,400 was assumed.
2. Paid cash of $2,400 for the removal of the old building.
3. Additional payments included:
   a. Title insurance and other closing costs, $1,250
   b. Surveyor's fee, $200
   c. Building permit, $425
   d. Grading of site, $800

Prepare journal entries to record the above transactions.

16-18. A building was constructed by the employees of Sem's, Inc., a manufacturing firm. From the following amounts that were expended, determine the amount to be capitalized in the building account:

1. Building permit, $300
2. Architect's fee, $15,000
3. Surveyor's fee, $175
4. Materials purchased, $108,200 (includes $110,000 less discounts of $1,800)
5. Labor cost, $60,500
6. Payroll taxes on labor cost, $4,200
7. Executives' salaries paid during period of construction, $45,000. 20 per cent allocated to building construction; 80 per cent allocated to other operations.
8. Factory overhead during construction, $100,000. 15 per cent allocated to building construction; 85 per cent allocated to regular production.
9. Estimate of profit that could have been earned if employees working on building construction had worked on regular products for sale, $15,000. (You determine that this is a reasonable estimate and that products, if manufactured, could have been sold.)
10. Landscaping costs, $3,700
11. Paving costs, $8,100
12. Fence for the parking lot, $3,900

16-19. The Farber Corporation was recently organized for the purpose of manufacturing safety equipment for automobiles. The charter authorized the issuance of 10,000 shares of no-par value stock. The first few transactions of Farber were as follows:

June 1: It issued 1,000 shares of stock for $1,200 cash.
June 3: It issued 1,500 shares of stock for $1,950 cash.
June 5: It issued 2,000 shares of stock in exchange for equipment.
The fair market value of the equipment was $2,650.

a. Determine the basis (in accordance with generally accepted accounting principles) for recording the acquisition of the equipment.
b. If the fair market value of the equipment could not be determined, what would your answer be?

16-20. The Holding Company has extensive investments in stocks, bonds, and real estate. The company has recently negotiated for the acquisition of a twenty-unit apartment building in exchange for 10,000 shares of Electronics, Inc., stock, which was acquired in 1957 at a total cost of $114,000. The fair market value of the 10,000 shares is now $280,000.
a. What should be the basis for recording the acquisition cost of the apartment building?
b. What effect would this transaction have on
   1. the statement of financial position for the Holding Company?
   2. the statement of earnings for Holding?

16-21. The Buckeye Milling Company purchased 8,000 shares of Hoosier, Inc., stock for $52 per share in 19x3. In 19x5 the Buckeye Company acquired a building that was appraised at $430,000, in exchange for 7,000 shares of its Hoosier stock. The market value of the stock at the time the building was acquired was $66 per share.

    a. What basis should Buckeye use for recording the acquisition of the building?

    b. What effect would this transaction have on

        1. the statement of financial position of the Buckeye Company?

        2. the statement of earnings for the Buckeye Company?

16-22. Martin Company is considering the acquisition of land in exchange for some of its capital stock. From each of the following independent assumptions, prepare the journal entry to record the transaction:

    a. The owner of the land agrees to accept 10,000 shares of stock as payment in full. The corporation's shares were originally issued two years earlier at $10 per share.

    b. Assume the same facts as in *a* above, and also that the owner was asking $125,000 for the land prior to the agreement to sell to Martin Company. If your journal entry differs from *a*, explain why.

    c. If the board of directors of Martin Company valued the land at $110,000, how would you record the transaction?

    d. Assume that Martin Company's stock was currently selling for $11 per share on the New York Stock Exchange. Would this have any bearing on your answer to *a*? To *b*? To *c*? Explain.

16-23. The Builtmore Construction Company recently traded in an old road grader for a new one. The old grader was carried on the books as follows:

Original cost	$14,000
Accumulated depreciation	$ 8,500

The invoice price of the new grader was $18,700. Builtmore paid a cash difference of $15,700.

    a. Give two possible alternatives to the question of (1) the cost of the new grader and (2) the gain or loss on the old grader.

    b. Select the best alternative and give your reasons for your answer.

16-24. On September 15, Talis Company purchased a new machine. An old machine was traded in and $25,000 cash was paid. The original cost of the old machine was $28,000, and accumulated depreciation on September 15 amounted to $24,000. The list price of the new machine is $30,000, and the fair market value of the old machine is determined to be $2,000.

    a. Prepare three independent journal entries to record this transaction, each one reflecting a different interpretation of the transaction.

    b. How do you decide which of these solutions is preferable?

16-25. Three medical doctors recently formed a corporation for the purpose of purchasing a twenty-unit brick apartment building. The building was purchased on July 1 at a cost of $130,000. The building was twenty-two years old at the date of purchase. The new owners estimated that the remaining life of the building was twenty-five years from the date of purchase.

Which of the following expenditures (made during the first two years of ownership) should be capitalized, and which expensed?

September 15: The corporation paid $1,750 to have the exterior trim painted. The work was completed during July and August.

November 1: It paid $900 for extensive repair and alterations to a five-room apartment for a new tenant. The tenant signed a three-year lease on the apartment.

December 10: It paid $175 to Ace Plumbers, Inc., for service calls made during November.

April 1: It received a $2,300 invoice for the cost of installing air conditioners in ten apartments.

July 20: It paid an invoice of $300 from Nurseries, Inc., for trees and shrubs.

September 30: It paid a local painting contractor $700 for painting all the hallways in the building.

16-26. The Norwood Electric Company recently acquired a used truck for use in its business. The following transactions relate to the purchase and use of the truck:

January 20: Norwood Electric purchased the used truck for $1,300.

February 2: The company purchased two new tires for $90.

February 6: It overhauled the engine at a cost of $150.

February 25: It purchased a two-way radio for $190.

February 26: It had the truck painted and lettered with the company name, etc., at a cost of $130.

February 28: It installed new seat covers for $12.

March 1: It started using the truck in the business operations on this date.

April 15: It purchased a new tire for $47 to replace a recently damaged tire.

May 31: A minor engine tune-up costing $35 was required.

July 25: The company repaired body damage resulting from a recent accident at a cost of $90.

Determine which of the expenditures listed above should be capitalized, and which expensed.

16-27. The Ace Company purchased a special-purpose milling machine for $43,000. The useful life of the machine is five years, with a salvage value of $3,000. Total service is estimated at 20,000 machine hours, as follows:

Year	Hours of use per year
1	4,500
2	4,000
3	4,000
4	4,000
5	3,500

a. Prepare a depreciation schedule comparing the following depreciation patterns for this asset:
   1. straight line
   2. double declining balance
   3. sum of the years' digits
   4. production basis

b. Give a justification for using each of the four methods included in your depreciation schedule above.

c. What factors should Ace consider in developing a depreciation policy for this machine? Discuss.

d. What are the possible objectives of providing for depreciation?

16-28. Bright Company acquired a machine on January 1 of the current year at a cost of $20,000. The estimated life of the machine is six years, with a salvage value of $2,000. The company reports on a calendar-year basis.

a. Determine the amount of depreciation on this machine for the calendar year of purchase and each year thereafter, assuming the following depreciation methods:
   1. straight line
   2. double declining balance
   3. sum of the years' digits

b. What is the book value of this machine at the end of the second calendar year under each of the three depreciation methods?

16-29. The Nike Company acquired tabulating equipment costing $65,000, with an estimated resale value of $5,000 at the end of its estimated economic life of four years.

Determine the depreciation expense for each year of the estimated economic life of the equipment, and calculate the book value at the end of the fourth year, using the straight-line, sum-of-the-years'-digits, and declining-balance (150 per cent of the straight-line rate) methods of depreciation.

16-30. Motor Transport, Inc., leases trucks and automobiles. On January 2 of the current year, the company acquired a new tractor-trailer truck at a cost of $12,000. The resale value of the truck is estimated to be $1,000 at the end of its four-year useful life.

Motor Transport has secured a four-year lease on the truck from the Continental Coal Company at $500 per month, starting at the date of purchase.

Net earnings from all operations of the company before depreciation on the new truck and federal income taxes, is estimated to be $70,000 for the next four years.

a. The company is considering the use of either double-declining-balance or straight-line depreciation on the new truck. Prepare schedules comparing the effect of the two methods on net earnings and on the cash balance for each of the next four calendar years. Assume that all revenues, expenses, and federal income taxes are paid in cash in the period they apply to, that the federal income tax rate is 50 per cent, and that the beginning cash balance is zero.

b. What should the objectives of the management of Motor Transport be in selecting a depreciation method

    1. for financial reporting purposes?

    2. for federal income tax purposes?

c. Are the objectives in the above question the same? If not, would it ever be desirable to select one method of depreciation for financial reporting purposes and another method for federal income tax purposes? Discuss.

16-31. The Urban Trucking Company accounts for truck tires separately from the trucks, since the service life of a tire is normally shorter than the trucks. Information concerning tire costs is as follows:

A truck tire costs $100 new. The average service life of a tire is 60,000 miles without recapping, but if the casing is not damaged, the tire can be recapped at a cost of $40 and used for another 60,000 miles. It is the policy of the Urban Trucking Company never to recap a tire more than three times, and considering damaged casings, blowouts, etc., tires average about two recappings each. Used tires have no scrap value.

At March 31, 19x2, the following balances appeared on the statement of financial position:

Tires	$75,000
Less: Accumulated depreciation	50,000
Undepreciated cost	$25,000

Prepare journal entries to record the following transactions for the year ended March 31, 19x3:

April 10, 19x2: Had seventy-five tires recapped at a cost of $40 each.

June 30, 19x2: Purchased 100 new tires at $100 each.

September 1, 19x2: Discarded 250 tires.

January 2, 19x3: Had 150 tires recapped at $40 each.

March 31, 19x3: During the year the company had in service fifty trucks that averaged 40,000 miles per truck for the year. Each truck uses ten tires. Record depreciation on the tires for the year.

16–32.

PART I

It is possible for a company to defer federal income taxes by selecting an accelerated depreciation method (double declining balance or the sum of the years' digits) in lieu of the straight-line method of depreciation for tax purposes.

The following illustration assumes the purchase of an asset for $11,000, with an estimated salvage value of $1,000 and an estimated life of five years. The asset is purchased on January 2, 19x5. The following illustration assumes a tax rate of 50 per cent. The federal income tax deferral resulting from the adoption of double-declining-balance depreciation in lieu of straight-line depreciation for tax purposes is as follows:

Year	Double declining balance	Straight line	Difference in depreciation[a]	Difference in federal income tax[a]
19x5	$ 4,400.00	$ 2,000.00	$ 2,400.00	$(1,200.00)
19x6	2,640.00	2,000.00	640.00	(320.00)
19x7	1,584.00	2,000.00	(416.00)	208.00
19x8	950.40	2,000.00	(1,049.60)	524.80
19x9	425.60	2,000.00	(1,574.40)	787.20
Total	$10,000.00	$10,000.00	$ 0	$ 0

[a] Parentheses indicate the increases that would have been caused by using the straight-line instead of the double-declining-balance method.

What are the effects of using an accelerated depreciation method, such as double declining balance, for federal income tax purposes? Discuss.

PART II

The following illustration assumes the purchase of a new machine (the same type of machine discussed in Part I) for $11,000, *each year* for ten years. Each machine has an estimated life of five years and an estimated salvage value of $1,000. The tax effects of using double-declining-balance depreciation compared with straight-line depreciation are shown on the next page.

a. What are the differences in the effect on federal income taxes between the illustration in Part I and that in Part II?

b. What is the significance of the $4,819.20 in the illustration in Part II?

c. What factors should the management of a corporation consider in adopting a depreciation method for federal income tax purposes?

16–33. Large corporations frequently have the following item appearing under intangible assets:

Trademarks & goodwill $1

Discuss the objectives that management might have in using this method of reporting.

MACHINE

Year of purchase	1	2	3	4	5	6	7	8	9	10	Total tax deferral
19x0	$1,200.00										$1,200.00
19x1	320.00	$1,200.00									1,520.00
19x2	(208.00)[a]	320.00	$1,200.00								1,312.00
19x3	(524.80)	(208.00)	320.00	$1,200.00							787.20
19x4	(787.20)	(524.80)	(208.00)	320.00	$1,200.00						0
19x5		(787.20)	(524.80)	(208.00)	320.00	$1,200.00					0
19x6			(787.20)	(524.80)	(208.00)	320.00	$1,200.00				0
19x7				(787.20)	(524.80)	(208.00)	320.00	$1,200.00			0
19x8					(787.20)	(524.80)	(208.00)	320.00	$1,200.00		0
19x9						(787.20)	(524.80)	(208.00)	320.00	$1,200.00	0
	$ 0	$ 0	$ 0	$ 0	$ 0	$ 0 [b]	[b]	[b]	[b]	[b]	$4,819.20

[a] Amount of additional tax outflow generated by using double-declining-balance depreciation rather than straight-line depreciation.
[b] The totals for these columns will be zero after the machines are fully depreciated.

16–34. a. List six intangible long-lived assets discussed in this chapter, indicating the proper accounting treatment (capitalizing versus expensing and/or the pattern of amortization) for each item.

   b. Discuss the problems in implementing accounting theory with respect to accounting for intangible long-lived assets.

   c. What is the significance of these problems to a user of financial statements?

16–35. *Case A:* The Armco Company has spent the past fifteen years developing a brand name for its nationally distributed ice cream. Advertising and other public-relations endeavors are primarily responsible for the development of the brand name. The management of the Armco Company is unable to isolate all of the costs associated with the development of the brand name because of the variety of purposes in public-relations efforts.

Case B: The Modern Company recently acquired a company that was a national distributor of ice cream. The purchase price included a payment of $120,000 for the brand name associated with the distribution of the ice cream.

   a. What is the nature and type of asset discussed in these examples?

   b. How would this asset be reflected on the statement of financial position for the Armco Company? For the Modern Company?

   c. Assume that the asset discussed above possesses approximately equal value for both companies. Does the statement of financial position for each company convey the same information to the statement user? If not, how might this information be better presented?

16–36. On January 1 of this year, the Sailor Sporting Goods Company negotiated a ten-year lease on a new building located in a shopping center of a large metropolitan area. The building has an estimated life of thirty years. The terms of the lease provide for monthly payments of $400. In addition, the lessee has the right to make certain alterations to the building subject to the approval of the lessor. The company made the following expenditures before opening the new building for business on January 10:

   January 1: $2,100 for installing a new store front
   January 5: $700 for a sign that was designed for installation on the new building and had an estimated life of eight years
   January 7: $240 to install the sign
   January 9: $1,800 for materials for and installation of built-in showcases, with an estimated life of fourteen years.
   January 10: The company opened the new store for business.

   a. What is the nature of these expenditures?

   b. How would you account for these expenditures?

   c. Show the effect of these transactions on the statements of earnings and financial position at the end of the second year of the lease.

16–37. The Swift Delivery Corporation was organized on December 31, 19x0. Mr. Neely, the major stockholder, invested $4,000 cash to purchase a new truck to be used in the business. It was estimated that the truck would have a five-year life and no salvage value at the end of five years.

Mr. Neely is the only employee. Collections are received from customers in the period in which services are performed, and all bills and expenses, including federal tax, are paid in cash in the years to which they apply. Mr. Neely pays himself a dividend at the end of each year equal to the net income after taxes. The financial statements for the five-year period are reflected below and on the following page.

SWIFT DELIVERY COMPANY

COMPARATIVE STATEMENT OF FINANCIAL POSITION
As of December 31, 19x0, 19x1, 19x2, 19x3, 19x4, and 19x5

	19x0	19x1	19x2	19x3	19x4	19x5
Assets						
Cash	$ 0	$ 800	$1,600	$2,400	$3,200	$4,000
Equipment (net)	4,000	3,200	2,400	1,600	800	0
Total assets	$4,000	$4,000	$4,000	$4,000	$4,000	$4,000
Liabilities and Owners' Equity						
Common stock	$4,000	$4,000	$4,000	$4,000	$4,000	$4,000
Retained earnings	0	0	0	0	0	0
Total liabilities and owners' equity	$4,000	$4,000	$4,000	$4,000	$4,000	$4,000

SWIFT DELIVERY COMPANY

**COMPARATIVE COMBINED STATEMENT OF EARNINGS
AND RETAINED EARNINGS**
For Years Ended December 31, 19x1, 19x2, 19x3, 19x4, and 19x5

	19x1	19x2	19x3	19x4	19x5
Revenues	$7,000	$6,500	$6,800	$6,200	$6,000
— Operating expenses:					
Salaries	$3,000	$3,000	$3,000	$3,000	$3,000
Supplies	500	400	450	400	400
Repairs	300	350	400	450	500
Depreciation	800	800	800	800	800
Total operating expenses	$4,600	$4,550	$4,650	$4,650	$4,700
Earnings from operations	$2,400	$1,950	$2,150	$1,550	$1,300
— Federal income taxes (50%)	1,200	975	1,075	775	650
Net earnings	$1,200	$ 975	$1,075	$ 775	$ 650

SWIFT DELIVERY COMPANY (CONT.)

	19x1	19x2	19x3	19x4	19x5
+ Retained earnings, beginning	0	0	0	0	0
Total available for dividends	$1,200	$ 975	$1,075	$ 775	$ 650
− Dividend payments	1,200	975	1,075	775	650
Retained earnings, ending	$ 0	$ 0	$ 0	$ 0	$ 0

SWIFT DELIVERY COMPANY

COMPARATIVE STATEMENT OF CASH FLOWS

For Years Ended December 31, 19x1, 19x2, 19x3, 19x4, and 19x5

	19x1	19x2	19x3	19x4	19x5
Cash provided from:					
Revenues	$7,000	$6,500	$6,800	$6,200	$6,000
− Cash used for:					
Salaries	$3,000	$3,000	$3,000	$3,000	$3,000
Supplies	500	400	450	400	400
Repairs	300	350	400	450	500
Income taxes	1,200	975	1,075	775	650
Dividends	1,200	975	1,075	775	650
Total cash used	$6,200	$5,700	$6,000	$5,400	$5,200
Net cash provided from operations (equals depreciation)	$ 800	$ 800	$ 800	$ 800	$ 800

On December 31, 19x5, Mr. Neely found it necessary to replace the old truck in order to continue his delivery business. However, a new truck (comparable to the 19x0 model) now costs $4,800. Mr. Neely is concerned because the cash balance (on the December 31, 19x5, statement of financial position) showed only $4,000. (The typical situation would include a portion of the assets in forms other than cash, such as accounts receivable and inventory.)

Mr. Neely approaches you with the following questions:

a. Since depreciation was provided in accordance with generally accepted accounting principles, and since Mr. Neely limited himself to reported earnings in determining his dividend, is there reason to believe that Mr. Neely should have had enough money in the business to buy a new truck at the end of the five years?

b. Was Mr. Neely's "capital investment" being taxed?

c. How could Mr. Neely have avoided this problem?

d. Would a double-declining-balance method of depreciation have been helpful?

e. If a problem exists, what could accountants do to correct it?

16–38. The Vernor Manufacturing Company manufactures and sells power lawn mowers. Included in their factory equipment are four machines purchased as follows:

Date acquired	Cost
19x0	$15,000
19x3	15,000
19x6	15,000
19x9	15,000

Each machine has an estimated life of fifteen years. You may ignore salvage value. Depreciation should be computed for the entire year in the year of acquisition.

a. Determine the value to be reported as machinery (you may ignore accumulated depreciation) on the statement of financial position as of December 31, 19x9, and as depreciation expense on the statement of earnings for 19x9, ignoring price level changes.

b. Recompute the values determined above in 19x9 dollars, using the Gross National Product Implicit Price Deflator (GNP Deflator, page 609) to adjust for price level changes.

c. In this situation, what effect does common-dollar reporting have on the statement of financial position? On the statement of earnings?

d. What advantages and disadvantages do you see in adjusting for price level changes? Discuss.

e. Do you have a recommendation that might help solve the price level problem in financial reporting? Discuss.

16–39. The Flying Eagle Company has three machines purchased at the following dates and amounts:

Date acquired	Cost
19x2	$10,000
19x5	11,200
19x9	11,700

Each machine has an estimated life of ten years and no resale value.

a. Determine the asset value (ignoring accumulated depreciation) to be reported as machinery on the statement of financial position as of December 31, 19x9, and as depreciation expense (straight-line method) on the statement of earnings for 19x9, ignoring price level changes.

b. Recompute the values determined above in 19x9 dollars, using the GNP Deflator Index from the text to adjust for price level changes.

c. What effect does common-dollar reporting in this situation have on the statement of financial position? On the statement of earnings?

16–40. The XYZ Corporation was organized on January 1 of the current year to buy and sell portable television antennas. The following transactions occurred during the first calendar year of operations:

January 1: The corporation issued capital stock for $100,000 cash.

January 1: It purchased equipment for $50,000 with an estimated life of six years and a salvage value of $2,000.

January 15: It purchased 2,000 units of inventory for $6,000 cash.

February 28: It purchased 3,000 units of additional inventory for $10,500 on account.

April 30: It paid a $3,000 invoice to an independent research company to cover the cost of a project recently undertaken for the corporation. The ultimate success of this project is not definite, although XYZ is confident that the project will increase revenues over the next three years, starting around July 1 of the current year.

June 15: It sold 1,600 units of inventory on account for $16,000.

June 30: It purchased a one year insurance policy for $2,400.

June 30: It purchased a one-year insurance policy for $2,400.

June 30: It paid $6,000 in salaries and wages for the first six months. (You may ignore payroll taxes.)

September 15: It purchased 1,500 units of inventory for $5,250 on account.

October 31: It sold 2,200 units of inventory on account for $24,200.

December 15: It received $16,000 cash from customers.

December 31: It paid $6,000 in salaries and wages for the last six months.

December 31: It recorded depreciation and insurance expense.

December 31: It sold equipment that had cost $5,000 (with an estimated salvage value of $200) for $3,800 cash.

December 31: The federal income tax payable, if any, is estimated at 30 per cent of taxable income.

a. Prepare two sets of financial statements reflecting the above data for the calendar year; use the perpetual inventory method for both.

    1. For the first set of financial statements, assume:

      the FIFO method of costing inventory

      the straight-line method of depreciation

      the all-inclusive earnings concept

      that research costs are capitalized if a future benefit is anticipated

    2. For the second set of financial statements, assume:

      the LIFO method of costing inventory

      the double-declining-balance method of depreciation

      the normal-operating concept

      that research costs are expensed as incurred

b. Describe the differences in the two sets of financial statements that will occur in subsequent years, and explain why they will occur.

c. Do generally accepted accounting principles place any constraints on the selection of alternative accounting procedures? Discuss.

d. What is the significance of this problem to a user of financial statements?

Part Four NONMANAGERIAL USES OF ACCOUNTING REPORTS

In Part IV of this book, we will discuss how reports are used outside the firm. The principles governing the preparation of these reports have been covered in Chapters 12 through 16. Chapter 17 will deal with the accounting needs of government agencies concerned with control or taxation of business enterprises. For the reader wishing to delve more deeply into the subject, Appendix 17A presents a more detailed discussion of accounting for income taxes. Chapter 18 will cover the special interests of creditors or potential creditors of the firm. Chapter 19 will deal with uses of accounting reports by owners or potential owners, or by people such as investment counselors, who act in behalf of owners.

Chapter Seventeen # ACCOUNTING REPORTS FOR GOVERNMENT USERS

INTRODUCTION

In our current age it is impossible to conduct any business activity without giving due concern to the rules and regulations imposed upon that activity by society. Enforcement of these rules and regulations is the function of many government agencies. Our purpose here is not to argue for or against the desirability of government influence in business affairs, but merely to accept its existence and to point out the many ways in which accounting reports are used in the government-business relationship.

The influence of governmental activities on the preparation of accounting reports stems from two distinct governmental requirements. On one hand, the government needs to generate its own revenues through many different taxes. Each tax requires its own special tax return, which is one kind of accounting report. On the other hand, the government's regulatory function requires the filing of periodic reports to enable a regulatory agency to draw conclusions and reach decisions regarding the lawfulness of the activity engaged in by the enterprise filing the reports. Each of these two areas will be discussed in turn.

TAXES AND ACCOUNTING REPORTS

The amount of effort expended in a typical business enterprise in order to properly report its activities under the various revenue statutes (tax laws) is immense. Here is a partial list of the tax reports filed by a typical manufacturing firm such as the Acme Auto Parts Company:

Federal tax returns:
1. Estimate of federal income tax for next calendar year.
2. Annual federal income tax return, including several subsidiary schedules.
3. Monthly, quarterly, and annual returns connected with employees' withholdings for income tax and social security.
4. Special returns required when payments are made to certain types of suppliers or contractors.
5. Quarterly and annual manufacturer's excise tax returns.
6. Monthly, quarterly, and annual returns connected with federal unemployment compensation.

State and local tax returns:
7. State annual income tax return.
8. Annual income tax returns for each municipality in which the enterprise engages in business activity, and which levels a city income tax.
9. Monthly, quarterly, and annual state sales or use tax returns.
10. Monthly, quarterly, and annual city and county sales and use tax returns.
11. County or state business personal property tax return.
12. Monthly, quarterly, and annual returns connected with state workers' unemployment compensation and workmen's compensation (for absence due to injury).
13. State and local excise taxes on products manufactured or sold within localities.
14. State corporate franchise taxes.

When the multiplicity of filing times is considered—the same return may be filed monthly, quarterly, and annually—it may be found that a typical business files as many as thirty-five to fifty different tax returns in a single year, each requiring many supporting schedules. This total is considerably increased for those enterprises that conduct business activities in more than one location. A large national and international organization may file several hundred returns because of its activities in each of the fifty states and in many foreign countries. Each return constitutes an accounting report that must be prepared under specified regulations.

Differing Rules of the Game

Notice that several tax returns in the above list are called "income" tax returns. You are aware of the tremendous economic importance of the tax levied by the federal government on the income of both individuals and business firms. Taxes on income levied by state and local taxing authorities are also very important.

One source of confusion among businessmen and among some accountants is the fact that "income" as defined by a particular taxing authority usually does not correspond in all respects with "earnings" as defined according to accounting principles. This is not surprising when we consider that a taxing authority is much less concerned with the accountants' idea of net earnings than with (1) raising required revenues, (2) using the income tax as a device to stimulate one or more segments of the economy, (3) minimizing possible hardship that may stem from tax payments, and (4) maintaining equity among taxpayers. Conversely, there is no reason to believe that net earnings as defined by accountants would or should achieve the above purposes. Furthermore, when one considers the influence of lobbying and other political maneuvering on income tax bills considered by Congress, it is perhaps surprising that accountants' net earnings and taxable income correspond as much as they do.

On the other hand, one of the basic theories of the income tax is that the tax is levied on the basis of some measurement of the taxpayers' "ability to pay," and historically, accountants' net earnings have been considered such a measurement. As you learn more about accrual accounting, however, you begin to understand that accountants' net earnings should be used as a base for taxation only after careful consideration and probable modification to achieve the objectives of the taxing authority.

The Federal Income Tax on Corporations

To illustrate in greater detail the nature of the information called for by the Internal Revenue Code, the federal income tax return is shown in Exhibit 17–1. This exhibit, you will note, includes an earnings statement and a statement of financial position. The taxable-income computation, starting on line 1 of page 1 and continuing through line 30 on page 1, constitutes the earnings statement. Schedule L on page 4 constitutes the financial position statement. The title of Schedule M on page 4 indicates that there are differences between taxable income calculated under the terms of the tax law and net earnings (as reflected in the net change in retained earnings) calculated on the taxpayer's "books," which (it is assumed) are prepared using generally accepted accounting principles.

Taxable Income Defined

The basic differences between the accounting reports included in Exhibit 17–1 and those prepared for more general use lie in the embodied definitions. Under generally accepted accounting principles, earnings for a period consist of the revenues of that period minus the costs incurred in generating those revenues. One of these costs is the income tax itself, which must be considered in calculating net earnings for "book" purposes, but which, of course, is the *result* of the definitions embodied in determining taxable income. The definition of

EXHIBIT 17-1

Form 1120

Department of the Treasury
Internal Revenue Service

U.S. Corporation Income Tax Return

For calendar year 1969 or other taxable year beginning
............................, 1969, ending ...., 19 ....
(PLEASE TYPE OR PRINT)

196

Check if a—

A Consolidated return ☐

B Personal Holding Co. ☐

C Business Code No. (see page 7 of instructions.)

Name

Number and street

City or town, State, and ZIP code

D Employer Identification

E County in which loca

F Enter total assets from 14, column (D), Sche L (See instruction R)

$

IMPORTANT—Fill in all applicable lines and schedules. If the lines on the schedules are not sufficient, see instruction N.

GROSS INCOME

1 Gross receipts or gross sales .... Less: Returns and allowances ....
2 **Less:** Cost of goods sold (Schedule A) and/or operations (attach schedule) . . . .
3 Gross profit . . . .
4 Dividends (Schedule C) . . . .
5 Interest on obligations of the United States and U.S. instrumentalities . . . .
6 Other interest . . . .
7 Gross rents . . . .
8 Gross royalties . . . .
9 Net gains (losses)—(separate Schedule D) . . . .
10 Other income (attach schedule) . . . .
11   TOTAL income—Add lines 3 through 10 . . . .

DEDUCTIONS

12 Compensation of officers (Schedule E) . . . .
13 Salaries and wages (not deducted elsewhere) . . . .
14 Repairs (do not include capital expenditures) . . . .
15 Bad debts (Schedule F if reserve method is used) . . . .
16 Rents . . . .
17 Taxes (attach schedule) . . . .
18 Interest . . . .
19 Contributions **(not over 5% of line 28 adjusted per instructions—attach schedule)** . . .
20 Casualty or theft losses (attach schedule) . . . .
21 Amortization (attach schedule) . . . .
22 Depreciation (Schedule G) . . . .
23 Depletion . . . .
24 Advertising . . . .
25 (a) Pension, profit-sharing, stock bonus, annuity plans (attach Form 2950) . . . . . .
    (b) Other employee benefit plans (see instructions) . . . .
26 Other deductions (attach schedule) . . . .
27   TOTAL deductions on lines 12 through 26 . . . .
28 Taxable income before net operating loss deduction and special deductions (line 11 less line 27) .
29 **Less:** (a) Net operating loss deduction (see instructions—attach schedule)
    (b) Special deductions (Schedule I) . . . .
30 Taxable income (line 28 less line 29) . . . .

TAX

31   TOTAL TAX (Schedule J) . . . .
32 Credits: (a) Tax deposited—Form 7004 application for extension (attach copy). . .
    (b) 1969 estimated tax payments (include 1968 overpayment allowed as a credit—do not include any "quick refund" of overpayment of 1969 estimated tax applied for on Form 4466) . . . .
    (c) Credit from regulated investment companies (attach Form 2439) . . .
    (d) Credit for U.S. tax on nonhighway gas and lube oil (attach Form 4136)
33 TAX DUE (line 31 less line 32). See instruction G for tax deposit system . . . . . ▶
34 OVERPAYMENT (line 32 less line 31) . . . . ▶
35 Enter amount of line 34 you want: Credited to 1970 estimated tax ▶   Refunded ▶

Under penalties of perjury, I declare that I have examined this return, including accompanying schedules and statements, and to the best of my knowledge and belief it is correct, and complete. If prepared by a person other than the taxpayer, his declaration is based on all information of which he has any knowledge.

CORPORATE SEAL

Date   Signature of officer   Title

Date   Individual or firm signature of preparer   Address

c59—16—80

hedule A—COST OF GOODS SOLD (See instruction 2)

- nventory at beginning of year . . . . .
- Merchandise bought for manufacture or sale .
- Salaries and wages . . . .
- Other costs (attach schedule) . . . . .
- Total . . . .
- Less inventory at end of year . . . . .
- Cost of goods sold—Enter on line 2, page 1 .

Method of inventory valuation ....

s there any substantial change in the manner of determining quan-
es, costs, or valuations between opening and closing inventory?
☐ No ☐. If "Yes," attach explanation.

Schedule C—DIVIDENDS (See instruction 4)

1 Domestic corporations subject to 85% deduction .
2 Certain preferred stock of public utilities . . .
3 Foreign corporations subject to 85% deduction .
4 Dividends from wholly-owned foreign subsidiaries subject to 100% deduction (section 245(b)) . .
5 Other dividends from foreign corporations . . .
6 Includable income from controlled foreign corporations (Subpart F; attach Form 3646) . . .
7 Foreign dividend gross-up (section 78) . . . .
8 Qualifying dividends from affiliated groups (section 243(b)) . . . .
9 Other . . . .
10 Total—Enter here and on line 4, page 1 . . .

hedule E—COMPENSATION OF OFFICERS (See instruction 12)

1. Name of officer	2. Social security number	3. Title	4. Time devoted to business	Percent of corporation stock owned		7. Amount of compensation	8. Expense account allowances
				5. Common	6. Preferred		

Total compensation of officers—Enter here and on line 12, page 1 . . . .

edule F—BAD DEBTS—RESERVE METHOD (See instruction 15)

ear	2. Trade notes and accounts receivable outstanding at end of year	3. Sales on account	Amount added to reserve		6. Amount charged against reserve	7. Reserve for bad debts at end of year
			4. Current year's provision	5. Recoveries		
4 .						
5 .						
6 .						
7 .						
8 .						
9 .						

edule G—DEPRECIATION (See instructions for Schedule G)

ayers using Revenue Procedures 62–21 and 65–13: Make no entry in column 2, enter the cost or other basis of assets held at end of year in column 3, and enter the accumulated depreciation at end of year in column 4.

1. Group and guideline class or description of property	2. Date acquired	3. Cost or other basis	4. Depreciation allowed or allowable in prior years	5. Method of computing depreciation	6. Life or rate	7. Depreciation for this year
otal additional first-year depreciation (do not include in items below) ⟶						
uildings						
urniture and fixtures						
ansportation equipment . . .						
achinery and other equipment .						
her (specify)						
tals						

ss amount of depreciation claimed in Schedule A and elsewhere on return . . . .
lance—Enter here and on line 22, page 1 . . . .

edule H—SUMMARY OF DEPRECIATION

	Straight line	Declining balance	Sum of the years-digits	Units of production	Additional first-year (section 179)	Other (specify)	Total
der Rev. Procs. -21 and 65–13							
her . . .							

c59—16—80699-1

Form 1120 (1969)   Pag

Schedule I—SPECIAL DEDUCTIONS

1 (a) 85% of line 1, Schedule C . . . .

   (b) 62.462% of line 2, Schedule C (Fiscal year corporations, see page 6 of instructions.) . . . .

   (c) 85% of line 3, Schedule C . . . .

   (d) 100% of line 4, Schedule C . . . .

2 Total—May not exceed 85% of (line 28, page 1, less the sum of lines 3 and 5 of this schedule). The 85% limitation does not apply to a year in which a net operating loss occurs . . . .

3 100% of line 8, Schedule C . . . .

4 Dividends paid on certain preferred stock of public utilities (see instructions) . . . .

5 Western Hemisphere trade corporations (see instructions). . . . .

6 Total special deductions—Add lines 2 through 5. Enter here and on line 29(b), page 1 . . . .

Schedule J—TAX COMPUTATION (Fiscal year corporations, see page 6 of instructions)

1 Taxable income (line 30, page 1) . . . .

2 Surtax exemption (line 1, $25,000, or amount apportioned under section 1561, whichever is lesser) . . . . .

3 Line 1 less line 2 . . . .

4 (a) 22% of line 1 . . . .

   (b) 26% of line 3 . . . .

   (c) If multiple surtax exemption is elected under section 1562, enter 6% of line 2 . . .

5 (a) Income tax (line 4, or line 24 of separate Schedule D, whichever is lesser) . . .

   (b) Tax Surcharge—10% of line 5(a) . . . .

6 Foreign tax credit (attach Form 1118) . . . .

7 Line 5 less line 6 . . . .

8 Investment credit (attach Form 3468) . . . .

9 Line 7 less line 8 . . . .

10 (a) Personal holding company tax (attach Schedule 1120 PH) . . . .

    (b) Tax Surcharge—10% of line 10(a) . . . .

11 Tax from recomputing a prior year investment credit (attach Form 4255) . . . .

12 Total tax—Add lines 9, 10, and 11. Enter here and on line 31, page 1 . . . .

Schedule K—RECORD OF FORM 503 FEDERAL TAX DEPOSITS (List deposits in order of date made—See instruction G)

Serial number of Form 503	Date of deposit	Amount	Serial number of Form 503	Date of deposit	Amount	Serial number of Form 503	Date of deposit	Amoun

G Date incorporated ....

H (1) Did you at the end of the taxable year own directly or indirectly 50% or more of the voting stock of a domestic corporation?
                                   Yes ☐ No ☐

   (2) Did any corporation, individual, partnership, trust, or association at the end of the taxable year own directly or indirectly 50% or more of your voting stock? . . . . Yes ☐ No ☐

      (For rules of attribution, see section 267(c).)

      If the answer to (1) or (2) is "Yes," attach a schedule showing:
       (a) name, address, and identifying number; and
       (b) percentage owned.

      If the answer to (1) above is "Yes," also show the taxable income (or loss) from line 30, page 1, Form 1120 of such corporation for the taxable year ending with or within your taxable year.

I Did you have any contracts or subcontracts subject to the Renegotiation Act of 1951? Yes ☐ No ☐. If "Yes," enter the aggregate gross dollar amount billed during the year. ....

J Did you claim a deduction for expenses connected with: Yes   No

   (1) Entertainment facility (boat, resort, ranch, etc.)? . . ☐   ☐

   (2) Living accommodations (except employees on business)? . . . . ☐   ☐

   (3) Employees' families at conventions or meetings? . ☐   ☐

   (4) Employee or family vacations not reported on Form W–2? . . . . ☐   ☐

K Taxable income (or loss) from line 30, page 1, Form 1120 for:
1966 ...., 1967 ...., 1968 ....

L Refer to page 7 of instructions and state the principal:
Business activity ....
Product or service...

M Were you a member of a controlled group subject to the provisio
   (1) Section 1561? . . . . Yes ☐ N
   (2) Section 1562? . . . . Yes ☐ N

If answer to (1) or (2) is "Yes," check type of relationship:
   (a) parent-subsidiary   ☐
   (b) brother-sister   ☐
   (c) combination of (a) and (b)   ☐   (See section 1563.)

If answer to (2) is "Yes," does section 1562(b)(1)(A) apply (n plication of 6% additional tax under section 1562)? . Yes ☐

N Were you liable for filing Forms 1096 and 1099 or 1087 for th endar year 1969? . . . . Yes ☐ N

If "Yes," where were they filed? ....

O Were you a U.S. shareholder of any controlled foreign corpor Yes ☐ No ☐. (See sections 951 and 957.) If "Yes," attach 3646 for each such corporation.

P Did you ever declare a stock dividend? . . . . Yes ☐ ₧

Q During this taxable year, did you pay dividends (other than dividends and distributions in exchange for stock) in excess o earnings and profits? Yes ☐ No ☐. (See sections 301 and If "Yes," file Schedule A, Form 1096. If this is a consolidated ᵣ answer here for parent corporation and on Form 851, Affili Schedule, for each subsidiary.

e59—16—

Schedule L—BALANCE SHEETS

ASSETS	Beginning of taxable year		End of taxable year	
	(A) Amount	(B) Total	(C) Amount	(D) Total
Cash				
Trade notes and accounts receivable . . .				
(a) Less allowance for bad debts				
Inventories				
Gov't obligations: (a) U.S. and instrumentalities .				
(b) State, subdivisions thereof, etc. . . .				
Other current assets (attach schedule) . .				
Loans to stockholders				
Mortgage and real estate loans				
Other investments (attach schedule) . . .				
Buildings and other fixed depreciable assets .				
(a) Less accumulated depreciation . . .				
Depletable assets				
(a) Less accumulated depletion				
Land (net of any amortization)				
Intangible assets (amortizable only) . . .				
(a) Less accumulated amortization . . .				
Other assets (attach schedule)				
Total assets				
LIABILITIES AND STOCKHOLDERS' EQUITY				
Accounts payable				
Mtges., notes, bonds payable in less than 1 yr.				
Other current liabilities (attach schedule) .				
Loans from stockholders				
Mtges., notes, bonds payable in 1 yr. or more.				
Other liabilities (attach schedule)				
Capital stock: (a) Preferred stock				
(b) Common stock . . .				
Paid-in or capital surplus (attach reconciliation) .				
Retained earnings—Appropriated (attach sch.) .				
Retained earnings—Unappropriated . . .				
Less cost of treasury stock	(	)	(	)
Total liabilities and stockholders' equity . .				

Schedule M–1—RECONCILIATION OF INCOME PER BOOKS WITH INCOME PER RETURN

Net income per books . . . .
Federal income tax . . . .
Excess of capital losses over capital gains .
Taxable income not recorded on books this year (itemize)
Expenses recorded on books this year not deducted in this return (itemize)
(a) Depreciation . . $
(b) Depletion . . . $
Total of lines 1 through 5 . . . .

7 Income recorded on books this year not included in this return (itemize)
(a) Tax-exempt interest $
8 Deductions in this tax return not charged against book income this year (itemize)
(a) Depreciation . $
(b) Depletion . . $
9 Total of lines 7 and 8 . . . .
10 Income (line 28, page 1)—line 6 less 9 .

Schedule M–2—ANALYSIS OF UNAPPROPRIATED RETAINED EARNINGS PER BOOKS (line 24 above)

Balance at beginning of year . . . . .
Net income per books . . . .
Other increases (itemize)
Total of lines 1, 2, and 3 . . . .

5 Distributions: (a) Cash . . . . .
(b) Stock . . . . .
(c) Property . . . . .
6 Other decreases (itemize)
7 Total of lines 5 and 6 . . . .
8 Balance at end of year (line 4 less 7) . .

taxable income for federal income tax purposes is presented below:

Economic inflows to the enterprise
  — Nonincome items (i.e., return of invested capital)
  — Items explicitly excluded from taxation under federal constitution
  — Items specifically excluded by congressional statutes
= Gross income
  — Deductions allowed by statute (similar to accounting expenses but not identical)
  — Special deductions for certain kinds of businesses
= Taxable income

Gross income for purposes of the federal income tax differs in details from the concept of revenues used for general accounting purposes. These differences are mostly in the nature of items that are excluded from the tax definition while admitted to the accounting definition. For example, interest earned on investments in bonds of state and local governments (or their legal subdivisions) is excluded from gross income for federal income tax purposes. This is also true of the interest earned on certain federal bonds issued prior to subsequent changes in the tax law. Perhaps the most striking difference in the concept of revenues lies in the tax distinction between ordinary income and capital gain. Under the current tax law, certain types of gains resulting from transactions in *capital assets*—sales of investments and long-lived assets, for example—are taxed at rates only half (or less) as great as ordinary income. Ordinary income generally includes such revenues as gross profit from the sale of goods and services, interest, and rents. Generally accepted accounting principles do not make such a distinction between the types of revenue (except perhaps where extraordinary items are not shown on the earnings statement but are instead carried directly to retained earnings under the normal-operating concept).

Revenues for accounting purposes are further delineated from gross income for tax purposes because of the special deductions on page 3, Schedule I, lines 1 to 5, of Exhibit 17–1. These items amount to exclusions from revenues for tax purposes but not for more general accounting purposes.

Even more striking differences become evident when one examines the cost side of the earnings computation. Basically, generally accepted accounting principles require that all expenses (current period costs), whatever their nature, be subtracted from revenues in the computation of earnings on page 1 of the exhibit. This is not true, however, for tax purposes. The deductions listed on lines 12 through 27 on page 1 of Exhibit 17–1 do not include all costs encountered by the enterprise. The deductions from gross income allowable for federal tax purposes are limited to those specified in the Internal Revenue Code.

Among the cost items that are not allowed as tax deductions are donations to political organizations, entertainment expenses beyond certain maximum limits, certain types of federal tax payments (excise taxes in particular), and, in the case of small corporations, excessive salaries paid to officer-stockholders. In each case there is a social, moral, economic, or political reason for not allowing the particular deduction in question. Yet all of these would be legitimate costs on an earnings statement prepared according to generally accepted accounting principles. The result is a difference between an earnings statement and a tax return for the same company in the same accounting period.

Income Tax Influences on Financial Accounting

In earlier chapters we sometimes spoke of the accounting treatment of items "for tax purposes," with the implication that the tax treatment was in some way relevant to the question of the accounting treatment for financial reporting. Except in the case of LIFO inventories, there is no compelling reason why the tax laws need even be considered in decisions about financial accounting. As a practical matter, however, we find that the influence exists in more than this exceptional case. As mentioned earlier, "taxable income" varies from "net earnings" as defined according to generally accepted accounting principles because the Internal Revenue Code is designed to serve political and social needs as well. To the extent that the Internal Revenue Code, with all its inadequacies, tends to be adopted as a model for financial accounting, it has acted as a deterrent to the improvement of financial accounting.

One of the obvious reasons for the influence of the Internal Revenue Code stems from the cost of record keeping. Differences between tax accounting and financial accounting often call for supplementary records in support of these differences as reported in Schedules M-1 and M-2, page 4 of Exhibit 17–1. Differences between tax and accounting depreciation, for example, often require elaborate records that can be eliminated if accounting depreciation is adjusted to conform to the depreciation provisions in the tax law.

There are more important reasons than bookkeeping economy, however. The lack of a measurable concept of accounting income is perhaps the most important. If the accountant and his employer or client lack conviction as to which measurement methods are the most useful, or if they fail to understand the importance of the published figures, they may select the tax method as the best accounting method simply for lack of a better alternative. The provision in the Internal Revenue Code that the LIFO inventory method must be used for financial statement purposes if used for tax purposes is a case in point. The provision was presumably written into the law to prevent taxpayers from adopting LIFO unless they felt it was also appropriate for accounting purposes. Unfortunately, the effect of the provision has been to cause many LIFO taxpayers to report to stockholders on a LIFO basis when they probably would not otherwise have done so.

The conviction regarding the need for strong accounting principles, and the feeling among many accountants as to what these principles should be, is growing stronger. Differences between tax accounting and financial accounting now appear in published statements with much greater frequency than was once the case, indicating that accountants are much more concerned about financial accounting principles.

The influence of income tax on accounting principles may be undesirable, but the tax has at least one desirable influence on accounting. The Internal Revenue Code requires that business firms keep records that are adequate to provide support for the representations in the tax return. Many small business firms would not keep adequate records were it not for the tax requirement. These firms are finding that the contributions to better management decisions and the benefits from improved control over the enterprise far exceed the cost of the records.

State and Local Taxes

The number of states, municipalities, and other taxing subdivisions enacting income tax legislation is increasing at a geometric rate. Many of these statutes are fashioned as closely to the Internal Revenue Code as possible so that taxpayers can use substantially the same figure for local income tax as they use for federal income tax purposes. Not only is this economical from a bookkeeping standpoint, but also it saves the even more important cost of the research time of the tax experts who must learn to use all the federal, state, and local tax provisions. Unfortunately, not all taxing authorities recognize the importance of uniform tax provisions, with the result that the cost of administering state and local income taxes in addition to the federal income tax is very high.

Rather than attempt to describe the large number of different kinds of taxes on business firms levied by taxing authorities, we will mention briefly only a few of the more important ones:

1. *Taxes on assets.* Taxes levied on personal and real property are a most important source of revenue for local governmental units, particularly counties and school districts. Asset valuations used for taxing purposes ordinarily are based on arbitrary procedures that usually have little to do with proper asset valuations for financial accounting purposes. For instance, assessed values of real estate are often established at figures representing only a certain percentage of market values.

Personal property taxes are usually levied on inventories, accounts and notes receivable, and investments. The tax is often based on the asset valuations used on the financial statements of the taxpayer. This taxing method is satisfactory from an administrative standpoint, but it may influence accountants to minimize asset values in order to minimize taxes. This influence is of course undesirable from the financial accounting point of view.

2. *Taxes on revenues.* Many sales taxes are paid by customers, since the tax is added to the amount of the purchase, but many other sales taxes are paid by the business firm. These taxes ordinarily do not present any unusual administrative problem, nor is there a pronounced effect on accounting procedures.

3. *Excise taxes.* These taxes are not unlike sales taxes from the standpoint of administrative cost, except that these taxes apply to specified goods and services. As in the case of sales taxes, no important accounting problems are caused by excise taxes.

REGULATORY AGENCIES AND ACCOUNTING REPORTS

The uses made of accounting reports by government regulatory agencies are all related to the fact that the agencies are required by statute to oversee the conformance of private business enterprises with some aspect of the law. When nonconformance is discovered, an agency may take action ranging from simple corrective recommendations to legal steps. In many cases the actions of an agency can have a vital effect on the profit-making capacities of the enterprise involved. For instance, within the past few years, the federal Civil Aeronautics Board disapproved a merger between Pan American Airways and Trans World Airlines that would have made the combined firm the world's largest international air carrier. This merger was refused in spite of the fact that the board had approved in the preceding year a merger between United Airlines and the now defunct Capital Airlines. Similarly, the Justice Department, the Federal Power Commission, the Interstate Commerce Commission, and many other agencies have made decisions and issued edicts directly affecting many private business concerns. In most cases, government agencies employ accounting reports of some nature in drawing conclusions and reaching decisions.

It is not feasible to discuss or even list at this time all of the more than 200 government agencies (both federal and state) requiring accounting reports from business firms. You will be exposed to most government-business relationships in your other business and economics courses. We suggest, however, that as you learn of these relationships you attempt to ascertain the significance of the accounting information used to communicate between the parties involved.

To see what kinds of accounting problems business enterprises can have with regard to regulatory agencies, we will take a brief look at the functions of two agencies. The first, the Securities and Exchange Commission, affects directly the accounting reports of large, widely owned corporations. The second, a typical state public utilities commission, can dictate, within limits, the economic welfare of business firms falling under its control.

The Securities and Exchange Commission

The Securities and Exchange Commission (the SEC) affects, in one way or another, most of the larger domestic and many foreign corporations. Its primary duty is to administer the following statutes:

1. the Securities Act of 1933
2. the Securities Exchange Act of 1934
3. the Public Utility Holding Company Act of 1935
4. the Trust Indenture Act of 1939
5. the Investment Company Act of 1940
6. the Investment Advisers Act of 1940

These statutes deal with government control over securities exchanges, securities dealers, and corporations issuing securities (stocks and bonds). Our interests here are with those regulations governing certain accounting actions by corporations.

All corporations having securities listed for trading on national securities exchanges (just one of which is the New York Stock Exchange) are required to file an application for registration with the SEC. The application contains a great amount of significant information about the company, its method of operation, its kinds of securities, and the personnel comprising its management. In addition the companies must file detailed annual financial reports as well as other occasional reports, so that the information on file will be current. The information on file with the SEC is available to the public.

Managements of listed companies must also conform to SEC rules when they solicit *proxies* (authorization to vote the shares of stockholders who cannot attend stockholders' meetings). In many cases the request for a proxy must be accompanied by a *proxy statement* containing financial accounting information specified by the SEC.

A corporation considering the sale of stocks or bonds to the general public must also comply with SEC regulations. If the proposed sale does not fall into the class of exempt offerings (very few do), the company must file a full-blown *registration statement* with the SEC, and the securities may not be sold until the SEC notifies the firm that the statement is effective. Permission is not granted until the SEC has reviewed the information in detail and is satisfied that there is no misleading information or significant omission. When permission is granted by the SEC, the firm may then publish a *prospectus* (containing the information included in the approved registration statement), which is made available to all parties interested in purchasing the securities. Accounting reports comprise the major part of the information contained in the registration statement and thus also in the prospectus.

Accounting for the SEC

Under the Securities Act of 1933, the SEC is authorized to define accounting terms used in the statute and to prescribe the forms in which required information is to be set forth as well as the items or details to be shown in accounting reports. The powers include prescription of methods to be followed in keeping records, valuing assets and liabilities, depreciating assets, recognizing revenues and expenses, and preparing reports.

The principal accounting regulation of the SEC is regulation S-X. This regulation sets forth the rules to be followed as to form and content of the accounting reports filed with the commission. The accounting rules required by the SEC are amended by the issuance of a continuing series of "releases" as well as occasional written opinions of the SEC chief accountant. Those persons concerned with accounting for affected firms, as well as the involved CPA's, must familiarize themselves with the accounting requirements set forth in regulation S-X and the Accounting Series Releases.

The SEC does not attempt to dictate accounting principles for use in general reports published by affected companies. The rules and regulations it promulgates pertain only to the reports and statements that must be filed with the commission itself. However, in its decisions and in the Accounting Series Releases, it has stated its opinions concerning a limited number of accounting principles and practices. For the most part, however, the SEC is willing to rely on generally accepted accounting principles as they exist or develop over the years. In cases where SEC regulations and generally accepted accounting principles do differ, it is usually because the commission specifies certain forms or requires additional information. In many cases, for example, when extraordinary gains or losses are properly included in the statement of retained earnings under generally accepted accounting principles, the item must be given special treatment in an SEC filing.

The commission must take responsibility for the reports filed with it, and occasionally it will overrule some of the generally accepted accounting principles or practices when it deems them faulty for its purposes. In one Accounting Series Release, the view was expressed that in the final analysis, the commission must weigh the value of all expert testimony (as to what is generally acceptable accounting) and rely on its own judgment of what is sound accounting practice.°

Furthermore, the SEC firmly believes that income tax accounting under the Internal Revenue Code does not represent sound accounting principles or practices. One of the major difficulties encountered by the SEC is that reports in registration statements are often prepared on a tax basis but are certified by CPA's as being in conformance with generally accepted accounting principles. Generally speaking, however, the fact that the SEC does require a CPA's opinion with all reports filed with the commission precludes any major disagreements between SEC accounting rules and generally accepted accounting principles.

THE 10-K FORM. The 10-K form is most commonly used for filing annual reports under the Securities Exchange Act of 1934. The report must be filed with the SEC within 120 days after the close of each fiscal year, and its information is available to the public. The annual 10-K report consists of ten items, which

---

° Accounting Series Release No. 73 (1952), p. 11.

require discussion or the presentation of specified information; only item 10, however, requires certification by a CPA. The contents of the ten items are outlined below:

Item 1: The securities registered on exchanges, including the title of the issue and the exchanges on which registered.

Item 2: The number of stockholders of each issue at the latest practicable date.

Item 3: The parents and subsidiaries of the registrant, showing the percentage of voting securities owned.

Item 4: Any changes in business—that is, changes in the nature of operation, reorganization, fiscal year, etc.

Item 5: The principal holders of securities, including the names and number of shares and percentage of voting securities owned of record or beneficially if over 10 per cent.

Item 6: The directors of the registrant, including each name, office held in registrant, present occupation, and shares of stock and securities owned.

Item 7: The remuneration of directors and officers, including the name of each receiving over $30,000 per annum and the total remuneration paid to the group.

Item 8: The option to purchase securities, including for each person named in item 7 above and for all as a group the number of shares under option, the purchase price, the exercise date, the consideration received for granting, and the market price.

Item 9: The interest of management and others in certain transactions if officers, directors, or principal security holders had a material financial interest in any transaction between the registrant and such person or others.

Item 10: Financial statements and exhibits:

    a. The financial statements for the fiscal year must be prepared in accordance with regulation S-X.

    b. Financial statements must be certified by an independent public accountant. Regulation S-X states:

> The accountants' certificate shall be dated; shall be signed manually; shall identify without detailed enumeration the financial statements certified; shall contain a reasonably comprehensive statement as to the scope of the audit made; shall state whether there have been any changes in accounting principles or practices and the accountants' opinion as to such changes; and shall state clearly the opinion of the accountants in respect of the financial statements of, and the accounting principles and procedures followed by, the registrant and its subsidiaries.

    c. Generally, financial statements will include:

    1. statement of financial position
    2. statement of earnings

3. statement of retained earnings
4. notes to financial statements
5. applicable schedules

The State Public Utility Commissions

Electric companies, gas companies, telephone companies, and to some extent public transportation companies usually enjoy a legal monopoly within their area of operations. Because of the inherent inefficiency of duplicate facilities, most states are careful to grant operating franchises to only one enterprise of each type within given municipalities or other geographical subdivisions. The states retain, however, the right to prevent abuse of the monopoly position by the firms that enjoy it.

As you will learn in your basic economics courses, a firm in a monopoly position is able to obtain long-run optimum profits continuously at a level far above that which would be available if the firm faced some degree of competition. The state legislatures have all set up public utilities commissions (PUC's) whose basic function is to act, via law and regulations, as a substitute for the competitive forces that affect nonmonopoly business firms.

The primary method of regulation used by the PUC's is to fix the rate of earnings that each utility company can enjoy. This is usually accomplished by adjusting the prices that the utility can charge its customers for the services it provides. The desired price is derived from the following chain of logic:

(1) Total owners' net investment $\times$ PUC-dictated % rate of return on investment = Maximum dictated earnings utility company can enjoy
(2) Maximum earnings + Operating expenses = Maximum revenues allowed to firm
(3) Maximum revenues allowed $\div$ Units of service (e.g., kilowatt-hours of electricity) sold to customers = Customer rate per unit of service

Obviously the calculations involved are greatly complicated by factors such as the recognition of different classes of customers and different qualities of service. For the accountant the major areas of concern are the determination of both the operating expenses and the dollars of owners' net investment in the enterprise. Most PUC's have dictated earning rates of between 5 per cent and 7 per cent for regulated utilities, depending on the economic condition and risk inherent in their locality. Examination of the above formulas will reveal that the only way the owners can increase their return on investment with a given rate of return would be to increase the reported dollar total of their net investment (assets minus liabilities) or their reported operating expenses, for calculation purposes, but not in fact. This of course means that in order to prevent manipulation of earnings via incorrect accounting practices, the PUC's feel they must dictate, very specifically, the principles by which public utilities account for their costs (both assets and expenses). The PUC's make extensive use of accounting reports filed with them and prepared under their rules in making decisions about how to substitute for competition.

Accounting for Public Utilities Commissions

Any discussion of public utility accounting must necessarily be general because of the differences in requirements among the fifty states. The PUC's, like the SEC, tend to require many supplementary accounting reports. And it is almost universally true that accounting regulations of the PUC's differ somewhat from generally accepted accounting principles. Some notable differences are worthy of discussion here.

Under the rules of some states, long-lived tangible assets (the major portion of total assets for most utilities) are not listed on the statement of financial position at acquisition cost. Instead, they are shown at the acquisition cost to the person first devoting them to public service, which may be far below the cost to the current owner. For example, suppose that the Edison Electric Company were to buy an existing generating plant from the Columbus Light and Power Company for $7 million. That figure would be the actual acquisition cost for Edison. If, however, the Columbus Light and Power Company had originally constructed the plant at a cost of $4 million fifteen years earlier, the $4 million figure would have to be used by Edison. The excess $3 million would have to go into an "adjustment" account that would be amortized as dictated by the Ohio PUC. In some other states, rates of return are based on the replacement cost of plant and equipment assets.

Many state PUC's also require that any accumulated-depreciation figures on long-lived tangible assets be shown as a liability on the statement of financial position rather than as a subtraction from cost on the asset side of the report. Also, most PUC accounting rules require special accounting for transactions with affiliated companies in a manner unnecessary under generally accepted accounting principles. About thirty states, notably Wisconsin and New York, specifically require some form of perpetual-inventory records for long-lived tangible assets as well as normal inventories.

A unique (and presumably effective) type of accounting regulation has been practiced in New Jersey, Oregon, and Washington. In these states, utilities have been required to submit their operating budgets to the state PUC for advance approval so that operating expense conditions can come under closer accounting scrutiny by the commissions.

One major difference between generally accepted accounting principles and regulated utility accounting lies in the area of tax deferrals, discussed as a long-term liability in Chapter 16. Generally accepted accounting principles suggest that where a delay in payment of income taxes is achieved by using a declining depreciation pattern for tax purposes and a straight-line pattern for accounting purposes, the tax reduction should not all be used to increase earnings (after taxes) in the current year. Instead, part of the tax reduction (and increased earnings) should be deferred to offset the increased taxes (and reduced net earnings) of future years. Most state PUC's disagree. They require the utilities to recognize the reduced taxes of the current year in the current year rather than deferring them as offsets of increased taxes in later years. This "flow through" requirement, of course, increases the utilities' reported current-year earnings, which then brings pressure from the PUC for reduced rates to customers. Since the PUC's are generally more willing to reduce rates to customers than to increase them when reported earnings become lower at the later date, the managements of the utility companies are justifiably concerned about this divergence from generally accepted accounting principles.

Once again we should emphasize that our purpose in this section of this chapter has been to illustrate the uses of accounting reports by governmental regulatory agencies with brief discussions of just two of them. The SEC represents an agency that requires many reports from business firms and requires the firms to adhere, somewhat closely, to generally accepted accounting principles within these reports. The state PUC's also use accounting reports supplied by business firms but quite often require these reports to be prepared under distinctly different accounting rules. A firm falling under the jurisdiction of one or more regulatory agencies has to maintain the records necessary to comply with the requirements of all agencies concerned. In addition, of course, the managers must be prepared to prepare many different tax returns as well as general reports for the nonmanagerial public.

NONREGULATORY USERS
OF ACCOUNTING INFORMATION

Some government uses of business accounting information are not directly connected with regulation. Most notable of these are the statistic-gathering efforts of the Department of Commerce and the Bureau of Labor Statistics. These agencies publish economic statistics of all sorts, among which are the National Income Accounts (Gross National Product figures), the Consumers Price Index, and the Wholesale Price Indexes. In some cases the various states also publish statewide or regional statistics of a similar nature.

A major share of the raw data for these statistics comes from accounting reports provided by private business enterprise. These reports may be among those already submitted to other government agencies (such as the SEC annual reports that are available for public use) or may be specifically designed to satisfy the particular needs of the statistic-gathering bureau. In the latter case the report often is part of a questionnaire supplied by the bureau.

In almost all cases, compliance with the reporting needs of the statistic-gathering agency is voluntary (or incidental to other required action) from the point of view of the business firm. If statistical validity is to be achieved, therefore, the agency involved must be certain that the information it receives is comparable among the sample employed. For this reason, most information-gathering efforts attempt to apply generally accepted accounting principles.

It is logical to assume that usage of accounting information will continue to expand in the years immediately ahead. Certainly the reporting burden of business managements will increase correspondingly.

SUMMARY

The vast majority of governmental agencies use accounting information to help them draw conclusions and make decisions regarding the firms providing the information. Their basic duty is to determine conformance with the law of the land.

Revenue-collection agencies attempt to ascertain the reasonableness of the tax returns filed by taxpayers under many different taxing statutes. In most cases the accounting principles employed in the taxing statutes differ considerably from generally accepted accounting principles. The federal income tax on corporations was used as an example to show some of these differences, and the reports necessary under the law were illustrated.

Two examples, the SEC and the state PUC's, were used to show the influence of governmental regulatory agencies on accounting principles and practices. Several hundred regulatory agencies influence private business efforts in this country.

Some governmental agencies use accounting information simply to provide statistics regarding economic conditions within the nation or its economic subdivisions. In most cases they rely on information already provided to taxing authorities or regulatory agencies.

Questions for Review

17-1. What are the two major governmental requirements for accounting reports?

17-2. List several examples of tax reports required by local, state, and federal government agencies.

17-3. In what ways are the objectives for the measurement of accounting earnings and the definition of taxable income different?

17-4. List the major kinds of state and local taxes.

17-5. Why do regulatory agencies require accounting reports?

17-6. List the statutes administered by the SEC.

17-7. How much control does the SEC exert over financial statements that are filed with the commission?

17-8. What is an area of difference that a state public utility commission may have with a utility company's management over deferred income taxes?

17-9. Describe several nonregulatory government uses of accounting information.

Problems for Analysis

17-10. In the present era, one could almost make the general statement that an enterprise management that did not in effect "keep more than one set of books" was negligent in its quest for optimum long-run earnings.

    a. Does this statement mean that more than one accounting system is required to generate the data required for the reports? Discuss.

    b. What is the nature of the additional "sets of books" discussed above?

17-11. The following data appeared in Schedules M-1 and M-2 of the Calico Company's federal income tax return for the calendar year 19x3:

Schedule M-1		Schedule M-2	
Line 1	$106,000	Line 1	$ 27,000
Line 2	35,946	Line 2	106,000
Line 5	1,000	Line 4	133,000
Line 6	142,946	Line 5 (a)	20,000
Line 7	2,000	(b)	15,000
Line 9	2,000	Line 7	35,000
Line 10	140,946	Line 8	98,000

    a. Compute the net earnings, after federal income taxes, as reported in the statement of earnings by the Calico Company for 19x3. (Assume the all-inclusive concept.)

    b. Prepare a statement of retained earnings for the Calico Company for 19x3.

    c. What purpose or purposes do Schedules M-1 and M-2 serve for the taxpayer? For the Internal Revenue Service?

17-12. The following items appear on the U.S. Corporation Income Tax Return, form 1120:

a. Page 1, line 29b provides for special deductions that are computed on page 3, Schedule I. Line 2 of Schedule I provides for an 85 per cent deduction of dividends reported in Schedule C on page 2. Why do you think the Internal Revenue Code provides for this deduction?

b. Page 2, Schedule E provides for information relating to the compensation of officers. What purpose would Schedule E serve for the Internal Revenue Service?

c. Schedules F and G on page 2 provide for bad-debts expense and depreciation expense respectively. Why would the Internal Revenue Service provide separate schedules for the details of these two expense items?

d. On page 4, Schedule L provides for balance sheets (or statements of financial position) at the beginning and end of the tax year. Why do you think the Internal Revenue Service is interested in this information?

e. The Internal Revenue Service performs an "office audit" of most tax returns filed by taxpayers. If you were responsible for performing an office audit of a corporate tax return, what information would you be interested in? (Hint: Use the various sections of the form 1120 in deciding upon the information you would use.)

17-13. The following is an example of the annual report form 10-K, as filled out by Beta Enterprises, Inc. Note that the financial statements for Beta are referred to as "consolidated statements." Beta Enterprises has a controlling interest in two companies: the Gamma Equipment Company and Jones, Inc. The financial statements of Beta Enterprises are therefore consolidated to reflect the combined operations of the parent company (Beta Enterprises, Inc.) and its subsidiaries (Gamma Equipment Company and Jones, Inc.). (See Chapter 15 for a discussion of consolidated reporting.)

Item 1: Securities registered on exchanges:

ANNUAL REPORT FORM 10-K

BETA ENTERPRISES, INC.,
AND SUBSIDIARIES

Title of class	Name of each exchange on which registered
Preferred (no-par)	"over the counter"
Common (no-par)	"over the counter"

Item 2: Number of stockholders:

Title of class	Number of holders
Preferred (no-par)	15
Common (no-par)	400 (approximate)

The annual and proxy material was submitted to shareholders of record April 1, 19xx. Four copies of this material were mailed to you on the same date they were posted to shareholders.

Item 3: Parents and subsidiaries of registrant:

Registrant: Beta Enterprises, Inc.

The registrant, Beta Enterprises, Inc., owns:

1. 90 per cent (9,000 of 10,000 shares outstanding) of the common stock of the Gamma Equipment Company
2. 80 per cent (40,000 of 50,000 shares outstanding) of the common stock of Jones, Inc.

Item 4: Changes in business:

None

Item 5: Principal holders of voting securities:

No person of record owns or is known by the registrant to own beneficially more than 10 per cent of the outstanding voting securities of the registrant.

Item 6: Directors of registrant:

Name	Principal occupation	Securities beneficially owned
J. P. Smith, Sr.	chairman of board of registrant	2,500 shares (preferred) 100 shares (common)
J. P. Smith, Jr.	president of registrant	2,000 shares (preferred) 800 shares (common)
C. R. Root	vice president of registrant	500 shares (preferred) 200 shares (common)
R. S. Moss	secretary-treasurer of registrant	900 shares (preferred) 350 shares (common)
P. D. Graf	attorney	100 shares (common)
H. H. Wilson	vice president of Wilson Company (investment bankers)	50 shares (common)

Item 7: Remuneration of directors and officers:

Name of individual or group	Capacities in which remuneration was received	Aggregate direct remuneration
J. P. Smith, Sr.	chairman of board of registrant	$40,000
J. P. Smith, Jr.	president of registrant	75,000
C. R. Root	vice president of registrant	42,000
R. S. Moss	secretary-treasurer of registrant	37,500
	Total remuneration paid to officers and directors of registrant	$194,500

Item 8: Option to purchase securities:

Neither the registrant nor its subsidiaries has any stock-option plan.

Item 9: Interest of management and others in certain transactions:

None

Item 10: Financial statements and exhibits:°

BETA ENTERPRISES, INC., AND SUBSIDIARIES

CONSOLIDATED STATEMENT OF FINANCIAL POSITION

As of December 31, 19x0

(in thousands of dollars)

Assets			
Current assets:			
Cash			$ 720
Marketable securities, at cost (market value, $372)			350
Accounts receivable		$ 740	
Notes receivable		11	
Total		$ 751	
— Allowance for uncollectable accounts		35	
Net accounts & notes receivable			716
Inventories:ᵃ			
Finished goods		$ 90	
Raw materials & work in process		240	
Total inventories			330
Prepaid expenses			22
Total current assets			$2,138
Investments:			
Real estate used for investment purposes		$ 14	
Cash surrender value of life insurance		80	
Total investments			94
Long-lived assets:			
Tangible long-lived assets, at cost:ᵇ			
Land	$ 290		
Buildings	140		
Machinery & equipment	1,512		
Leasehold improvements	18		
Total	$1,960		
— Accumulated depreciation & amortization	687		

ᵃ See note 2 of the accompanying notes to financial statements.

ᵇ See notes 3, 4, and 7 of the notes to financial statements.

° Seventeen schedules related to financial statements are referred to in regulation S-X. The schedules may be omitted if they do not apply to the registrant. Only two of the seventeen schedules are included in this example: Schedule VII for intangible assets and Schedule XVI for supplementary earnings-statement information.

BETA ENTERPRISES, INC., AND SUBSIDIARIES (CONT.)

Assets		
Net tangible long-lived assets	$1,273	
Intangible long-lived assets:		
Goodwill & trademarks[c]	370	
Total long-lived assets		1,643
Total assets		$3,875

Liabilities and Owners' Equity		
Liabilities:		
Current liabilities:		
Current maturity of long-term liabilities		$ 47
Accounts payable		180
Estimated U.S. & foreign income taxes[d]		160
Accrued salaries		90
Accrued taxes other than income taxes		29
Accrued profit-sharing contribution[e]		32
Other accrued liabilities (e.g., interest)		11
Total current liabilities		$ 549
Long-term liabilities:[f]		
Mortgage payable	$ 220	
Notes payable	31	
Total long-term liabilities	$ 251	
— Allocation to current liabilities	47	
Net long-term liabilities		204
Total liabilities		$ 753
Minority interest in subsidiaries		120
Owners' equity:		
Capital stock:		
Preferred stock, (no-par value; authorized, issued, and outstanding 24,000 shares at stated value)	$240	
Common stock (no-par value; authorized 20,000 shares; issued and outstanding 12,000 shares at stated value)	600	
Total capital stock	$ 840	
Paid-in surplus	830	
Retained earnings	1,332	
Total owners' equity		3,002
Total liabilities and owners' equity		$3,875

[c] See note 1 of the notes and see Schedule VII.
[d] See note 5 of the notes.
[e] See note 6 of the notes.
[f] See note 7 of the notes.

BETA ENTERPRISES, INC., AND SUBSIDIARIES
CONSOLIDATED STATEMENT OF EARNINGS
For Year Ended December 31, 19x0
(in thousands of dollars)

Net sales revenues			$4,560
— Cost of goods sold			3,154
Earnings margin			$1,406
— Operating expenses			920
Earnings from operations			$ 486
— Nonoperating items:			
Other expenses:			
Interest on long-term debt	$ 20		
Provision for credit losses	15		
Loss on disposal of plant & equipment	11		
Amortization of goodwill[a]	28		
Total other expenses		$74	
— Income from investments		10	
Net nonoperating expenses			64
Earnings before income taxes			$ 422
— Provision for income taxes:			
Federal income taxes	$184		
Foreign income taxes	33		
Total income taxes			217
Net earnings			$ 205

[a] See note 1 of the accompanying notes to financial statements.

BETA ENTERPRISES, INC., AND SUBSIDIARIES
CONSOLIDATED STATEMENT OF PAID-IN SURPLUS
For Year Ended December 31, 19x0
(in thousands of dollars)

Proceeds in excess of stated value of beginning balance:	
Common stock sold (net of $156,000 commission and expenses incurred related to underwriting)	$830
Paid-in surplus, ending balance	$830

BETA ENTERPRISES, INC., AND SUBSIDIARIES
CONSOLIDATED STATEMENT OF RETAINED EARNINGS
For Year Ended December 31, 19x0
(in thousands of dollars)

Retained earnings, beginning balance	$1,157
+ Net earnings for year	205
Total available for dividends	$1,362

BETA ENTERPRISES, INC., AND SUBSIDIARIES (CONT.)

— Dividend payments:		
Preferred stock ($.50/share)	$12	
Common stock ($1.50/share)	18	
Total dividend payments		30
Retained earnings, ending balance		$1,332

BETA ENTERPRISES, INC., AND SUBSIDIARIES
NOTES TO FINANCIAL STATEMENTS
December 31, 19x0
(in thousands of dollars)

1. Factors in consolidation:

The consolidated financial statements include the accounts of the company and its subsidiaries as follows:

Gamma Equipment Company

Jones, Inc.

Goodwill and trademarks amounting to $370, which arose from the acquisition of the subsidiary companies, are being amortized by charges to operations over a twenty-five-year period commencing in 19x0.

All material, intercompany balances, and transactions have been eliminated in preparing the consolidated financial statements.

2. Inventories:

Inventories as of December 31, 19x0, were valued at the lower of cost (FIFO) or market. Opening and closing inventories used in computing the cost of goods sold for the year ended December 31, 19x0, were $310 and $330 respectively.

3. Depreciation, amortization, etc.:

Depreciation and amortization have been calculated on a straight-line basis, based on estimated lives of major classes of property, except that subsequent to December 31, 19x8, depreciation has been calculated on a sum-of-the-years'-digits or declining-balance basis on certain machinery and equipment. The range of estimated lives used in computing depreciation and amortization was approximately as follows:

Item	Years
Buildings	30
Machinery & equipment	5–8
Furniture & fixtures	10
Transportation equipment	3–7
Leasehold improvements	Period of lease

Depreciation expense charged to operations for the year ended December 31, 19x0, aggregated $205.

4. Investment credit:

The investment credit of $24 allowed under the Revenue Act of 1962 has been included as a reduction of the provision for U.S. income taxes and U.S. income taxes payable.

5. Taxes on income:

Income tax returns of the company have been examined through 19x9, and all assessments have been paid.

6. Profit-sharing retirement plan:

Effective December 31, 19x6, a noncontributory profit-sharing pension plan was adopted for all employees of the company who have completed two years of continuous employment. Benefits for disability, retirement, or death are provided for under the plan. The rate of contributions each year is determined by the board of directors. The amount of $32 was charged to operations for the current period in connection with the profit-sharing retirement plan.

7. Long-term liabilities are summarized as follows:

5¾% mortgage, due January 19x7, payable in monthly installments, secured by real estate	$ 60
6½% mortgage, due January 19x6, payable in monthly installments, secured by real estate	165
Noninterest-bearing note, due June 19x8, payable in monthly installments, secured by machinery & equipment	26
Total long-term liabilities	$251
— Portion allocated to current liabilities	47
Net long-term liabilities	$204

SCHEDULE VII

BETA ENTERPRISES, INC., AND SUBSIDIARIES

INTANGIBLE ASSETS

For Year Ended December 31, 19x0
(in thousands of dollars)

COLUMN A	COLUMN B	COLUMN C	COLUMN D Deductions		COLUMN E
Item	Beginning balance	Additions at cost	Charged to profit & loss or income	Charged to other accounts	Ending balance
1. Goodwill & trade name acquired upon purchase of Gamma Equipment Company assets	$250	$0	$11	$0	$239

BETA ENTERPRISES, INC., AND SUBSIDIARIES (CONT.)

Item	Beginning balance	Additions at cost	Charged to profit & loss or income	Charged to other accounts	Ending balance
	COLUMN A	COLUMN B	COLUMN C	COLUMN D *Deductions*	COLUMN E
2. Goodwill acquired upon purchase of Jones, Inc., stock	137	0	6	0	131
Total intangible assets	$387	$0	$17	$0	$370

SCHEDULE XVI

BETA ENTERPRISES, INC., AND SUBSIDIARIES

SUPPLEMENTARY STATEMENT OF EARNINGS INFORMATION[a]

For Year Ended December 31, 19x0

(in thousands of dollars)

Item	To cost of goods sold	To operating expenses	Total
	COLUMN A	COLUMN B *Charged directly to Statement of Earnings*	COLUMN C
1. Maintenance & repairs	$ 42	$12	$ 54
2. Depreciation & amortization of long-lived assets	$201	$14	$215
3. Taxes other than income taxes:			
Payroll	$ 32	$ 9	$ 41
Real estate & personal property	4	3	7
City and state income	0	5	5
Miscellaneous	1	4	5
Total other taxes	$ 37	$21	$ 58
4. Rents	$ 10	$14	$ 24
Royalties	0	54	54
Total rents & royalties	$ 10	$68	$ 78

[a] There were no management or service contract fees during the period.

a. What purpose does the certification by accountants of financial statements and exhibits serve?

b. Most companies voluntarily publish an annual report and furnish all stockholders with a copy of it. The annual 10-K report is an additional report requirement. What purpose, if any, does the 10-K report serve that a typical annual report does not serve?

c. The annual 10-K report consists of ten items. What is the purpose and importance of each item?

d. The following questions pertain to the financial statements and exhibits included in Beta's 10-K report. Discuss each question from the standpoint of conformity to generally accepted accounting principles:

1. What basis of valuation was used for marketable securities? What justification is there for treating marketable securities as a current asset and the cash surrender value of life insurance as an investment?

2. What method is used in arriving at inventory cost? What method of inventory valuation was followed?

3. What is the basis for valuing long-lived assets? What method or methods of depreciation were used?

4. What is the nature of the asset "cash surrender value of life insurance"?

5. What is the source of the asset "goodwill and trademarks" for Beta Enterprises? What is the basis of valuation? Is this asset being amortized?

6. How was the annual liability "profit-sharing contribution" determined?

7. What is the difference between the long-term liabilities "*mortgage* payable" and "*notes* payable"?

8. What is the meaning and significance of the following terms found under owners' equity: "par-value stock," "stated value stock," "authorized stock," "issued stock," and "outstanding stock"?

9. What is the apparent reason for differentiating between "paid-in surplus" and "retained earnings"?

10. What justification, if any, is there for listing "provision for uncollectable accounts" under "other charges" on the consolidated statement of earnings?

APPENDIX 17A*

Accounting for Income Taxes

In preparing financial statements for external users, the accountant attempts to measure earnings and net assets as accurately as possible in accordance with generally accepted accounting principles. "Taxable income," however, is defined by law, not by accountants. Congress enacts tax laws (contained in the Internal Revenue Code) for the purpose of raising revenue for government operations and, in some cases, to accomplish public policy objectives.

The different objectives in measuring accounting earnings and taxable income create some significant differences between the two. Differences between accounting earnings and taxable income arise in the following general areas: (1) permanent differences between accounting earnings and taxable income, (2) allocation of income taxes within a reporting period to extraordinary gains and losses and prior-period adjustments, (3) operating loss carryback and carry-forward, and (4) differences in timing of revenue and expense recognition.

Permanent Differences Between Accounting Earnings and Taxable Income

In adopting certain public policy objectives, Congress has created permanent differences between accounting earnings and taxable income. For example, interest received by an investor in state or municipal bonds is not taxable for federal income tax purposes. Political campaign contributions are not deductible by the donor. In certain cases, extractors of natural resources such as oil and gas are allowed deductions (percentage depletion) in excess of the cost of the natural resources. Good financial statement reporting requires footnote disclosure when these permanent differences have a material effect on a corporation's income tax liability.

Allocation of Income Taxes Within a Reporting Period to Extraordinary Gains and Losses and Prior-period Adjustments

It is generally accepted that extraordinary items and prior-period adjustments (discussed in Chapter 12) should be reported net of income taxes. This treatment permits the earnings-statement user to evaluate the effect of income taxes on

* A tax rate of 50 per cent on ordinary income and 25 per cent on capital gains is assumed throughout this appendix, unless otherwise specified.

earnings from operations. Provision for federal income tax expense on these items can be reported on the financial statements in three different places: (1) as a deduction from earnings from operations, (2) as an addition to or subtraction from extraordinary gains and losses on the statement of earnings, and (3) as an addition to or deduction from prior-period adjustments to the beginning balance in the statement of retained earnings.

Operating Loss Carryback and Carryforward

Congress permits a corporation to offset an operating loss against earnings of the preceding three years and against earnings of the next five years. The offset against prior earnings is referred to as a *loss carryback* and future earnings as a *loss carryforward*. This permits a corporation to have a claim for refund of income taxes previously paid or a potential future tax saving against future earnings.

Loss Carryback

Assume that a corporation suffered a $40,000 net operating loss for the current year (year 5) and its earnings for tax purposes for the preceding four years were as follows:

Year 1	Year 2	Year 3	Year 4
$10,000	$12,000	$18,000	$20,000

The carryback would affect the entire current loss by applying $12,000 against year 2, $18,000 against year 3, and $10,000 against year 4. Assuming a 50 per cent tax rate, the corporation would have a claim for a tax refund amounting to $20,000 that would be recorded by the following journal entry:

Claim for refund of income taxes   20,000
   Refund of income taxes   20,000

The refund of income taxes would be reported on the earnings statement as follows:

A CORPORATION

PARTIAL STATEMENT OF EARNINGS
For Year 5

Loss before taxes	$40,000
Less refund of prior year's income taxes due to operating loss carryback	$20,000
Net losses after tax	$20,000

Loss Carryforward

If a corporation has not reported earnings in the three preceding years for tax purposes, it is permitted to carry the operating loss forward as an offset against earnings for the next five years. There are several alternative accounting treatments of a potential tax savings resulting from an operating loss carryforward:

1. The entire $40,000 operating loss can be reported in the loss year without showing any recognition of the potential loss carryforward in the statement of financial position. If a tax reduction results in any of the carryforward years as a result of using the carried forward loss (or any portion of it), either of the following treatments may be used:

a. The tax reduction can be recognized as a correction of the previous operating loss by the following journal entry (assuming $40,000 earnings and a 50 per cent tax rate):

Provision for income taxes	20,000	
Correction of prior year's earnings		20,000

The provision for income taxes would be deducted on the earnings statement in the normal manner to give net earnings. The correction of prior year's earnings would be a prior-period adjustment against the beginning balance in the retained earnings.

b. The tax reduction may instead be reflected in the year that the tax savings result. Assuming $40,000 of earnings before taxes in the carryforward year, net earnings of $40,000 after taxes would be reported with no deduction for "provision for income taxes" on the statement of earnings. (The $40,000 loss carryforward would reduce taxable income to $0. Thus no taxes would be payable against income for that year.)

2. Another alternative is to record the potential tax savings in the loss year as follows:

Potential claim for refund of income taxes	20,000	
Tax savings due to potential refund		20,000

The "potential claim for refund of income taxes" account would be reported as an asset and amortized to provide for income taxes when earnings are reported. The "tax savings due to potential refund" account would be reported in the statement of earnings as a reduction of the operating loss in the loss year.

Alternative 1a—correction of prior year's earnings when the tax benefit is realized—has the advantage of properly stating earnings after tax and is preferable to alternative 1b—not reporting the tax benefit from the preceding loss year. Alternative 2—recognizing the potential tax saving in the loss year, is desirable if the corporation has a well-established earnings history and the probability is high that it can absorb the operating loss carryforward through earnings in the next five years.

The Accounting Principles Board of the AICPA has taken the position that "tax benefits of loss carryforwards should not be recorded in the accounts until they are actually realized, except in unusual circumstances when realization is assured beyond any reasonable doubt at the time the loss carryforwards arise. . . . When the tax benefits of loss carryforwards are not recognized until realized in full or in part in subsequent periods, the tax benefits should be reported in the results of operations of those periods as extraordinary items." °

Differences in Timing of Revenue and Expense Recognition

Timing differences occur when transactions affect taxable income in one reporting period and earnings for financial reporting in another reporting period. There are four types of transaction that cause timing differences:†

1. Revenues or gains are included in taxable income later than they are included in earnings for financial reporting. For example, revenues on long-term contracts are reported as earnings on a percentage of completion basis (see Chapter 7) and reported for tax purposes when the contract is completed.

2. In computing taxable income, expenses or losses are deducted in a later reporting period than they are deducted in computing earnings for financial reporting. For example, estimated costs of guarantees and product warranty contracts are deducted from earnings in the period of sale and are deducted in computing taxable income in the period when cash is disbursed.

3. Revenues or gains are included in the tax return in a reporting period before they are reported as earnings on the financial statements. For example, rents collected in advance are reported in the tax return in the period when cash is received and are reported as revenue on the financial statements in the period earned.

4. Expenses or losses are deducted in determining taxable income in a period before they are deducted on the statement of earnings. For example, accelerated depreciation methods, such as sum of the years' digits, create a deduction for tax purposes in an earlier reporting period if the straight-line method is used on the statement of earnings.‡

When differences occur between taxable income and financial statement earnings, the accountant must "allocate" income taxes according to Opinion Number 11 of the Accounting Principles Board.§ Interperiod income tax allocation causes the recognition of tax effects of transactions in the same period they are recognized in computing earnings for financial statement purposes.

° "Accounting for Income Taxes," Opinion of the Accounting Principles Board, No. 11, December 1967 (New York: AICPA, 1967), p. 173.

† "Interperiod Allocation of Corporate Income Taxes," Accounting Research Study, No. 9 (New York: AICPA, 1966).

‡ "Accounting for Income Taxes," Opinion of the Accounting Principles Board, No. 11, December 1967 (New York: AICPA, 1967), pp. 161–62, 184–85.

§ *Ibid.*, p. 169.

The interperiod allocation of income taxes will create either a "deferred income tax expense" (asset) account or a "deferred income tax liability" account. A deferred income tax expense would result from the types of timing differences discussed under 2 and 3. A deferred income tax liability would result from the timing differences in *1* and *4.*

Illustration of Deferred Income Taxes

Assume that Greenbrier Apartments, Inc., negotiates a two-year lease with a tenant on January 1 of the current year for $190 per month and requires the first and last months' rent at the time the lease is signed. The last month's rent would be reported on the tax return in year 1 and on the earnings statement in year 2. The timing differences are illustrated below:

Year	Statement of earnings	Taxable income	Differences
1	12 months @ 190 = $2,280	13 months @ 190 = $2,470	$190
2	12 months @ 190 = $2,280	11 months @ 190 = 2,090	(190)
	$4,560	$4,560	$ 0

Interperiod tax allocation would result in the recognition of income tax expense each year based on the amount shown in the statement of earnings, and the difference between taxes accrued and taxes paid would appear as deferred tax expense on the statement of financial position. Journal entries for interperiod tax allocation for the two years would be (assuming no other transactions):

Year 1	Provision for income taxes	1,440	
	Deferred federal income tax expense	95	
	Federal income taxes payable		1,535
Year 2	Provision for income taxes	1,440	
	Deferred federal income tax expense		95
	Federal income taxes payable		1,345

The statement of earnings for year 1 would appear as follows:

GREENBIER APARTMENTS, INC.
PARTIAL STATEMENT OF EARNINGS
For Year 1

Earnings from operations		$2,280
Less: Income taxes:		
Current taxes payable	$1,535	
Less: Estimated taxes relating to earnings of future years	95	1,440
Net earnings		$1,440

Illustration of Deferred Income Tax Liability

Assume that Pilot Corporation purchases an item of equipment for $3,000 with an estimated life of three years and no resale value. They use double-declining-balance depreciation on their tax return and straight-line depreciation in computing earnings for financial statement purposes. Assume earnings, other than depreciation of the equipment, of $75,000 in each of the next three years. The timing differences are illustrated below:

| | Statement of Earnings | | | Tax Returns | | |
| | (1) Earnings before depreciation | (2) Straight-line depreciation | (1−2) Earnings from operations | (3) Double-declining-balance depreciation | (1−3) Taxable income | (4) Difference |
Year						
1	$ 75,000	$1,000	$ 74,000	$2,000	$ 73,000	$(1,000)
2	75,000	1,000	74,000	667	74,333	333
3	75,000	1,000	74,000	333	74,667	667
	$225,000	$3,000	$222,000	$3,000	$222,000	$ 0

ᵃParentheses denote deficit.

Note that the statement of earnings and the tax return report the same earnings of $222,000 over the three-year period.

Journal entries for interperiod tax allocation for the three years would be:

Year 1	Provision for income taxes	37,000	
	Deferred income tax liability		500
	Federal income taxes payable		36,500
Year 2	Provision for income taxes	37,000	
	Deferred income tax liability	166	
	Federal income taxes payable		37,166
Year 3	Provision for income taxes	37,000	
	Deferred income tax liability	334	
	Federal income taxes payable		37,334

The statement of earnings for year 1 would appear as follows:

PILOT CORPORATION
PARTIAL STATEMENT OF EARNINGS
For Year 1

Earnings from operations		$74,000
Less: Income taxes:		
Income tax liability for the year	$36,500	
Estimated income taxes related to earnings of future years	500	37,000
Net earnings		$37,000

Evaluation of Interperiod Tax Allocation

Proponents of interperiod tax allocation argue that the provision for income taxes on the statement of earnings includes the tax effects of transactions entering into the computation of earnings for the period. Interperiod tax allocation permits a proper matching of revenues and expenses in measuring earnings for the period. As stated earlier, it is required by the Accounting Principles Board of the AICPA.

Those who argue against the interperiod allocation of income taxes assert that most timing differences are "permanent" and not "temporary." Consider the following illustration.

A company purchases an asset for $11,000, with an estimated salvage value of $1,000 and an estimated life of five years. The asset is purchased on January 2, 19x5. The tax rate is 50 per cent. The federal income tax deferral resulting from the adoption of double-declining-balance depreciation in lieu of straight-line depreciation for tax purposes is as follows:

Year	Double declining balance	Straight line	Difference in depreciation[a]	Difference in federal income tax[a]
19x5	$ 4,400.00	$ 2,000.00	$ 2,400.00	$(1,200.00)
19x6	2,640.00	2,000.00	640.00	(320.00)
19x7	1,584.00	2,000.00	(416.00)	208.00
19x8	950.40	2,000.00	(1,049.60)	524.80
19x9	425.60	2,000.00	(1,574.40)	787.20
Total	$10,000.00	$10,000.00	$ 0	$ 0

[a] Parentheses indicate the increases that would have been caused by using the straight-line instead of the double-declining-balance method.

At the end of the five-year life, the total depreciation for tax purposes and earnings measurement purposes is equal. Therefore, the tax deferral in years 1 and 2 of the asset life has been offset in years 3, 4, and 5.

If the company maintains its investment in equipment, a "permanent" tax deferral results, as shown in Exhibit 17A–1.

This exhibit indicates that a company that maintains or increases its investment has a "permanent" deferral of income taxes. Price Waterhouse and Co. studied the tax allocation experiences of one hundred companies from 1954 to 1965, and found that tax deferrals for these companies resulted primarily from accelerated depreciation for tax purposes and reporting of installment sales on the tax return when cash was collected and on the statement of earnings in the period of sale.[*] Of the companies studied, approximately $1 billion was charged

[*] "Is Generally Accepted Accounting for Income Taxes Possibly Misleading Investors?" Price Waterhouse and Co. (New York: 1967).

EXHIBIT 17A – 1

						Machine					Permanent tax
Year of purchase	1	2	3	4	5	6	7	8	9	10	deferral[c]
19x0	$1,200.00										$1,200.00
19x1	320.00	$1,200.00									1,520.00
19x2	(208.00)[a]	320.00	$1,200.00								1,312.00
19x3	(524.80)	(208.00)	320.00	$1,200.00							787.20
19x4	(787.20)	(524.80)	(208.00)	320.00	$1,200.00						0
19x5		(787.20)	(524.80)	(208.00)	320.00	$1,200.00					0
19x6			(787.20)	(524.80)	(208.00)	320.00	$1,200.00				0
19x7				(787.20)	(524.80)	(208.00)	320.00	$1,200.00			0
19x8					(787.20)	(524.80)	(208.00)	320.00	$1,200.00		0
19x9						(787.20)	(524.80)	(208.00)	320.00	$1,200.00	0
	$ 0	$ 0	$ 0	$ 0	$ 0	$ 0	[b]	[b]	[b]	[b]	$4,819.20 [b]

[a] Amount of additional tax outflow generated by using double-declining-balance depreciation rather than straight-line depreciation.

[b] The totals for these columns will be zero after the machines are fully depreciated.

[c] Assuming asset replacement each year.

against earnings for deferred taxes, and credits to earnings for payment of deferred taxes approximated $20 million. It appears that the "present value of expected future payments of tax deferrals" is nil when the postponement is indefinite. It also seems that interperiod tax allocation should be used only when tax differences are expected to be "temporary" and should not be used when the postponement of taxes is expected to be indefinite.

Illustration of Reconciliation of Taxable Income with Statement of Earnings

Assume that Cipher Corporation reports earnings after tax of $110,000, shows a provision for taxes of $110,000, and has the following differences between taxable income and earnings for financial statement purposes for the current year:

	Included on statement of earnings	Included on tax return	Differences (earnings in excess of taxable income)
Expenses:			
Depreciation charges	$40,000	$70,000	$30,000
Campaign contributions	5,000	0	(5,000)
	$45,000	$70,000	$25,000
Revenues:			
Municipal bond interest	$10,000	$ 0	$10,000
Rental income received in advance	0	4,000	(4,000)
	$10,000	$ 4,000	$ 6,000
Net difference	$35,000	$66,000	$31,000

These differences are reported on the tax return, Schedule M-1, as shown in Exhibit 17A-2.

Schedule M-1 provides a reconciliation of differences between the statement of earnings and taxable income (in this example $220,000 − $189,000 = $31,000). Remember from the preceding discussion that municipal bond interest and campaign contributions are included in the "permanent differences" category and depreciation and rental income items are in the "differences in timing of revenue and expense recognition" category.

EXHIBIT 17A-2

Schedule M–1—RECONCILIATION OF INCOME PER BOOKS WITH INCOME PER RETURN				
1 Net income per books	110,000	7 Income recorded on books this year not		
2 Federal income tax	110,000	included in this return (itemize)		
3 Excess of capital losses over capital gains .		(a) Tax-exempt interest $...............		
4 Taxable income not recorded on books this		Municipal bond interest		
year (itemize) Rental income				10,000
received in advance	4,000	....		
		8 Deductions in this tax return not charged		
5 Expenses recorded on books this year not		against book income this year (itemize)		
deducted in this return (itemize)		(a) Depreciation . $...............		
(a) Depreciation . . $...............		(b) Depletion . . $...............		
(b) Depletion . . . $...............		....		
campaign contributions				30,000
	5,000	9 Total of lines 7 and 8		40,000
6 Total of lines 1 through 5	229,000	10 Income (line 28, page 1)—line 6 less 9 .		189,000

Questions for Review

17A-1. What are the four general areas of difference between accounting earnings and taxable income?

17A-2. List three examples of "permanent differences" between accounting earnings and taxable income.

17A-3. When is the allocation of income taxes within a reporting period required by generally accepted accounting principles?

17A-4. Describe what is meant and give the preferred treatment in accounting for

    a. an operating loss carryback
    b. an operating loss carryforward

17A-5. List and give examples of the four types of timing differences that may indicate the need for interperiod allocation of income taxes.

17A-6. Describe the accounting treatment required by the Accounting Principles Board of the AICPA for timing differences between taxable income and accounting earnings.

17A-7. Discuss the advantages and disadvantages of interperiod tax allocation.

Problems for Analysis

17A-8. The Contrast Corporation uses interperiod tax allocation procedures when accounting earnings differ from taxable income. In analyzing each of the independent situations below, assume accounting earnings before tax of $1 million and a tax rate of 40 per cent. Assume further that the item of revenue or expense was included in calculating accounting earnings before tax.

1. On its earnings statement, the corporation reported gross profit of $75,000 from installment sales and reported profit of $20,000 on the amount collected in its tax return.

2. Reported pension expense of $400,000 on its earnings statement and $220,000 on its tax return for actual transfers of cash to the pension fund.

3. Reported service contract revenue of $70,000 on its earnings statement for amounts earned during the period; and reported $110,000 on its tax return, the total amount collected from its customers.

4. Reported depreciation expense of $140,000 in its earnings statement and $200,000 in computing taxable income.

a. Prepare the journal entry to record income tax expense for the current year for each of the four "independent" situations.

b. What amount of net earnings will be reported in the earnings statement in each situation?

17A-9. For the preceding five-year period, Volume Company reported the following:

	Taxable income and earnings before tax (loss)	Federal income taxes paid (refund)
Year 1	$ 25,000	$12,500
Year 2	22,000	11,000
Year 3	30,000	15,000
Year 4	46,000	23,000
Year 5	79,000	39,500
Year 6	(190,000)	(?)

Assume that the Company had earnings before tax of $20,000 in year 7, $35,000 in year 8, and $40,000 in year 9. Assume a 50 per cent tax rate in each of the nine years.

Prepare journal entries to record income taxes for years 6, 7, 8, and 9, following procedures recommended by the Accounting Principles Board of the AICPA.

Chapter Eighteen

ACCOUNTING REPORTS FOR CREDITORS

INTRODUCTION

People lend money to a business enterprise because they are interested in obtaining a return on the investment they make in the lending process. The return can be in the form of money or goodwill and continued happy relations with the enterprise. The underlying reason in each case, however, can be assumed to be the profit motive. A bank will lend money because it expects to earn an interest return each year. A supplier will sell on credit because he hopes to retain the "borrower" as a permanent and satisfied customer.

Creditors are usually divided into three groups on the basis of how rapidly the debt matures. *Short-term creditors* are those who expect to be repaid within one year or within one average operating cycle of the debtor, whichever is longer. Debts owing to these creditors are shown as current liabilities (defined in Chapter 12) in the statement of financial position of the debtor. *Intermediate-term creditors* expect to be repaid within five years. *Long-term creditors* expect to be repaid at a future time longer than five years away. For purposes of financial statement analysis, the intermediate- and long-term creditors can usually be put in the same category, just as the obligations to these creditors are all classified as long-term liabilities, because their interests in the financial statements of the debtor (or potential debtor) are substantially the same.

Two other user groups also receive some attention in this chapter. One of these groups consists of *employees* and *potential employees*. These persons have the same interests as creditors, to the extent that they desire information relevant to the continuing ability of the employer to maintain a given level of employment and to meet wage and salary payrolls. Employees also have interests that coincide with the interests of the stockholders. The other group is *customers* of the firm, whose interests are not well defined, but who wish to form some general conclusions about the ability of the firm to continue to supply products of suitable quality, in sufficient quantity, and at competitive prices.

In this chapter we will assume that a standard set of accounting reports (that is, an earnings statement, a statement of financial position, a statement of retained earnings, and various fund flow statements) prepared using generally accepted accounting principles is available to the creditor under discussion. We will discuss how he can make use of the information provided and, where necessary, we will indicate certain shortcomings he may encounter. Uses by short-term creditors will be discussed first, then those of intermediate- and long-term creditors, and finally we will discuss briefly the interests of employees and customers. Keep in mind, however, that there is considerable overlapping of usage among the different groups of creditors. Moreover, the interests of creditors and owners overlap, for all are basically concerned with (1) evaluating the quality of management in terms of optimizing its available opportunities and minimizing the effects of adversity on the firm; and (2) determining the financial soundness of the enterprise under consideration. Our primary emphasis in this chapter is to focus on the financial soundness of the enterprise.

WHO ARE THE SHORT-TERM CREDITORS?

Trade Creditors

In terms of the number of individuals and the business transactions involved, trade creditors comprise the most prevalent group of creditors. Trade credit usually results in an account payable (for the debtor) and an account receivable (for the creditor); occasionally the relationship is evidenced in a more formal manner by promissory notes that specify a rate of interest and maturity date.

Purchase and sale of goods and services on credit are such common transactions that we occasionally forget how important the credit aspect of the transaction is to both the debtor and creditor. In most cases, interest or discount on credit purchases is not explicitly recognized, and consequently there is a natural tendency for the purchaser-debtor to delay payment as long as possible, since it apparently costs him nothing to do so. By delaying payment, the debtor is able to finance his purchase of other assets, operating expenses, and other debt payments with a minimum of funds from the owners. He is therefore able to increase the rate of return on his owners' investment. In a real sense, he is temporarily able to finance the operations of his firm with creditors' funds at no apparent cost to himself.

Similarly, the seller-creditor gains by receiving payment as early as possible, for opposite and equally obvious reasons. He is able to operate his business on a minimum of funds if he makes early collection from his customers. He also minimizes the risk of bad debts from customers of questionable credit standing.

On the other hand, the purchaser wants to maintain a reputation for making prompt payments, because this is the mark of a well-managed, well-financed firm, and this can be a great advantage in obtaining additional credit when it is needed. As we shall see later, the purchaser should always take advantage of cash discounts if they are offered. The seller finds that he can expand his volume of business by extending credit or that he must do so to remain competitive, and he does not wish to antagonize his customers by demands for "cash on the barrelhead." To reconcile these conflicting objectives, credit purchase and sale agreements include explicit or implicit terms for payment, often within thirty days of the sale or by the tenth day of the month following the month of sale.

Credit transactions are also a great convenience to both purchaser and seller. The receipt and disbursement of cash can be handled at different times and by different persons than those who have responsibility for purchase or sale, receipt or shipment, of goods. The functions of cash receiving and cash disbursing can be centralized and mechanized. The accounting system can be made more efficient, and better accounting control over the firm's assets is achieved.

Commercial Lenders

Commercial lenders include banks, finance companies, factors (creditors who buy accounts receivable from debtors), commercial paper houses, and personal loan companies. The business intent of the commercial lender is not unlike that of the trade creditors. The trade creditor's primary concern is selling the goods or services he has available. The credit he extends is a convenience that allows him to sell his goods or services. The commercial lender also renders a service by extending credit, which is his stock in trade. Money is the asset, and the commercial creditor is an individual or institution who seeks earnings from the interest payments received for the use of that money by the borrower.

The most common commercial creditors are the commercial banks, which lend money on both a short-term and long-term basis. A primary function of a bank is to obtain money from depositors and lend that money to borrowers at an interest rate. A commercial bank will lend on almost any terms and for any length of time consistent with the policy it follows and the qualifications of the borrower. Most short-term loans are for periods of thirty, sixty, ninety, or 120 days, and typical interest rates range from 6 per cent up to 10 per cent in most states.

Finance companies, factors, and commercial paper houses all provide valuable service as commercial lenders, usually under more restricted circumstances than the banks. All of these institutions need substantially the same financial information from debtors.

Customers

Customers sometimes provide short-term credit by making advances on their purchases; that is, they make a payment before they receive delivery of the goods or services. This practice is most common when long-term contracts are involved. The builder of a road or a large dam may have to spend millions of dollars over a several-year period before that project is completed. He may not have enough funds of his own to enable him to complete the project without outside financing. The customer often makes an advance payment on the total purchase price to facilitate, and perhaps ensure, the completion of the contract. This type of credit is also used by businesses that provide a very scarce product or are in a near-monopoly (nonregulated) market position; they can demand advanced payment because they hold a strong position when bargaining with their customers.

Government Agencies

The federal government has instituted several agencies, the best known of which is the Small Business Administration, that are empowered to lend money to business firms under special circumstances. More often than not, the money is lent on a long-term basis, but occasionally, short-term loans are negotiated. Most business enterprises prefer not to deal with these agencies for short-term funds because the red tape involved in acquiring the loan is so great that they cannot receive the money in time to do them any good. Where long-term loans are concerned, this is not so vital a factor, and for this reason the governmental agencies are most practically considered as long-term creditors rather than short-term creditors.

THE DECISION TO EXTEND CREDIT

The decisions of short-term creditors to extend credit in a given case, like the general criteria that must be met in order to justify granting credit, are governed, of course, by the long-run profit optimizing objective. Since credit is the commercial lender's stock in trade, he must lend money to make a profit, but he still must decide to whom he should lend, the amount of the loan, the period, and the interest rate. All of these factors will vary, depending on the credit standing of the applicant. The decisions of the trade creditor are not fundamentally different, although there is at least the theoretical possibility that he can avoid the problem by limiting himself to cash customers.

It should be noted, however, that refusal to grant credit in a given case may cause the merchant to lose the profit on the sale that would otherwise be made. This may be a considerably greater "opportunity" loss than the interest loss to the banker on a refused loan application. This helps to explain why a given customer might be allowed to purchase an appliance for $500 on sixty-day terms, even though he is refused a $500, sixty-day, 8 per cent loan at the bank. By the same token, a banker with unlimited funds to lend will be more liberal in his credit policy (all else being equal) when the interest rate is 10 per cent than when it is 8 per cent.

Thus it is not possible to classify potential debtors into hard and fast categories of "good," "fair," and "poor" credit risks, because a given debtor at a given time may be a good risk in one case and not in another. It also means that there are no clear-cut rules to follow in evaluating a potential debtor's financial statements for credit purposes. This fact makes the decision problem more difficult, but in no way does it reduce the importance of the expectation that the debtor will repay, which is the principal question on which the debtor's financial statements are used.

THE INFORMATION NEEDS OF
SHORT-TERM CREDITORS

The fundamental question the potential short-term creditor asks about his prospective borrower is, What assurance have I that I will receive principal and interest payments from this borrower when they come due? The answer to this question could conceivably be stated in terms of statistical probability, or "odds," that the repayments would be made, but ordinarily all the potential short-term creditor hopes to receive is information that will permit him to conclude that the assurance is "good," "fair," or "poor." Included in the answer to this question is the consideration that the repayments should be made in the ordinary course of business affairs—that is, in a way that will not cause undue hardship on the borrower, such as mortgage foreclosure, bankruptcy, or other financial catastrophe.

The financial statement that provides maximum information relevant to the answer to the above question would be the borrower's cash budget covering the proposed period of the loan. This statement would show the uses to be made of the borrowed money, the available sources of cash for repayment, and the cash position of the debtor after repayment. The only concern of the prospective creditor would center around the reliability of the projections.

The Small Business Administration and some commercial banks ask the potential borrower to submit cash budgets as a part of the loan application. Assurance is given that the information will be kept confidential. In most cases, however, prospective borrowers are reluctant to submit cash budgets, and competition among lenders is such that most of them do not feel they can afford to ask for such information. The prospective borrower can always go to another lender who does not ask for a cash budget. Trade creditors are usually in an even poorer position to request cash budgets from credit purchasers.

This means that, in the ordinary case, the prospective lender will at best have available only the statement of financial position, the earnings statement, and funds statement of the borrowing firm covering the past period or periods.

In general, the assurance of prompt payment from the debtor depends on:

1. The relationship of current assets to current liabilities and the liquidity of the current assets, as reflected in the statement of financial position.

2. The past record of the firm with regard to its ability to generate cash from operations, and its past record of borrowing and repayments of debt, as indicated by the funds statement.

3. The earnings performance of the management, as indicated by the earnings statement.

To the short-term creditor, the past earnings record of the firm is relatively less important than it is to intermediate- or long-term creditors. This is because the earnings of the borrowing firm are usually not reflected in increased cash or increased liquidity of current assets within the period of the short-term loan. Long-term creditors are more seriously concerned with earnings, as we shall see later, because as the relevant period of time lengthens, the relationship between earnings and funds becomes more direct. The short-term creditor is interested in earnings only because earnings are an indication of the caliber of management of the borrowing firm.

The interests of the short-term creditor have usually centered around the relationships that appear in the statement of financial position, and with the composition of current assets and current liabilities in particular. The wider use of funds statements in recent years should meet the approval of the short-term creditor, because he stands to learn a great deal by studying them.

The following paragraphs describe some of the more commonly used relationships that are important to the short-term creditor.

The Current Ratio

The prospective short-term creditor can get a fairly good idea of the prospective borrower's ability to repay the short-term debt by examining the borrower's current ratio. This is the ratio obtained by dividing the current-assets figure by the current-liabilities figure shown on the statement of financial position. You will recall from Chapter 12 that current assets include cash and other assets that can be expected to flow through an operating cycle during the next accounting period. Current liabilities are those falling due during the next operating cycle and/or those that will require the use of current assets in order to meet the obligations.

It is impossible to state what a "good" current ratio ought to be. Many people have the uninformed opinion that a ratio of 2 to 1 is the minimum acceptable ratio indicative of a sound financial position. This is not a sound conclusion, primarily because of wide differences among industries. For example, a public utility might be an excellent short-term credit risk even though its current liabilities exceeded its current assets. This is because public utilities carry little or no inventories, and also because their revenues are highly predictable. A manufacturer of heavy machinery, on the other hand, might be a poor risk with a current ratio of 3 or 4 to 1 because of heavy inventories, a long operating cycle, and perhaps strong cyclical fluctuations in sales and cash receipts.

One of the principal difficulties in using the current ratio is that the calculation includes inventories. Not only does the importance and liquidity of inventories vary widely from one industry to another, but variations in valuation methods make comparisons extremely difficult. As you learned in Chapter 14, inventories shown on the statement of financial position on a LIFO basis are of no assistance in appraisal of credit position. Bankers seem to favor the LCM method because of its conservatism.

The importance of the current ratio is not in the absolute figures involved, but rather in their movements from year to year. It is particularly useful for the short-term creditor to know that a borrower's current ratio is presently 1.8 to 1, a year ago it was .9 to 1, and two years ago it was .5 to 1. By examining the trend of the current ratio he is able to ascertain that the borrower is developing a stronger current position that might indicate that his operations are becoming more acceptable from the short-term credit point of view. It is also helpful to determine the relationship between the current ratio of the borrower under examination and that of other firms in the same line of business. Trade and industry publications, government business statistics, and experience can all indicate the typical ratio to be expected in a particular line of endeavor. Comparison of the typical ratio with the particular ratio of the borrower under examination again will provide a clue to help the short-term creditor reach a decision about making a loan and the terms of any loan he will make.

The Quick Ratio

This ratio compares only the most liquid assets—that is, cash, temporary investments, and receivables—to the total current liabilities. Obviously the ratio will be smaller than the current ratio, but again it is difficult to state arbitrarily what a satisfactory quick ratio is. The relationship to typical industry figures provides the most important clue as to the significance of the quick ratio at a given time for a given firm. Where inventories predominate in the current-asset section of a firm's balance sheet, and when these inventories are relatively slow to turn into cash, the quick ratio is probably a better indicator of ability to repay than is the current ratio. Two points deserve special attention:

1. Temporary investments are properly treated as the equivalent of cash, assuming that these investments pass the test of marketability discussed in Chapter 14 and that management intends to convert these investments into cash as the need for cash arises.

2. The liquidity and collectability of open accounts receivable can be estimated by

a. computing the "turnover" of accounts receivable by dividing the net sales by the average accounts receivable outstanding. For example for Acme Auto Parts (see Chapter 12), the average turnover of accounts receivable for 19x5 is computed as follows:

$$\frac{\text{Net sales}}{\text{Average accounts receivable}} = \frac{\$20,120,000}{\dfrac{\$960,000 + \$852,000}{2}} = 22 \text{ times per year}$$

This comes to roughly once every seventeen calendar days.

b. comparing "allowance for uncollectable accounts" with "accounts receivable," as reported in the statement of financial position, and by comparing "credit losses" with "net sales revenues" in the statement of earnings. (You should review Chapter 12 for the definitions of these items.)

c. preparing an "aging schedule" of accounts receivable. In an *aging schedule*, the outstanding accounts are classified according to the age of unpaid balances, usually in thirty- to ninety-day intervals. Obviously, the older the balance, the more questionable the collectability. This schedule must be prepared by the borrower, since it requires information from the detailed accounts receivable ledger.

These three additional analyses are usually limited to open accounts receivable from trade customers. Notes receivable, and particularly installment notes receivable, must be evaluated separately, since they have specified due dates.

The Inventory Turnover

From the point of view of the short-term creditor, much of the usefulness of inventories as a current asset involves the speed with which the inventory is converted into cash. This conversion time can be estimated by computing the inventory turnover, expressed in the Acme Auto Parts example as:

$$\frac{\text{Cost of goods sold}}{\text{Average inventory}} = \frac{\$11,547,000}{\dfrac{4,207,000 + 3,867,000}{2}} = 2.8 \text{ times per year}$$

This comes to roughly once every four and one-third months.

Qualifications About Ratios

Ratios are tricky, and unless they are used with considerable caution and sophistication, they can be misleading. Any ratio is simply the expression of the relationship between one quantity and another. It can have no significance greater than the significance of either of the quantities used, and sometimes its significance is less than either. For instance:

a. A would-be borrower could (1) "hound" his customers for early cash payment just before the year's end, and (2) use all available cash to pay his creditors faster than usual, with the result that the borrower could improve his current ratio and quick ratio as well as his accounts receivable turnover, and thereby impress a would-be creditor with a credit position that is in fact abnormal. Such tactics are called "window dressing" in the statement of financial position. Note that the dollar amount of net working capital and the dollar amount of net quick assets remain unchanged.

In many cases, the use of actual dollar amounts is less confusing than ratios in many phases of financial statement analysis. An exaggerated example would be if you were considering lending $500,000 to a business firm for six months, you would be much more impressed with the fact that the firm has $100,000 of current assets and $20,000 of current liabilities than with the fact that its current ratio is 5 to 1.

b. Calculations involving year-end inventories are open to question for a number of reasons, one of which, of course, is the use of the LIFO cost valuation method. The end of a fiscal year is often the time when inventory balances are lowest, often because firms select a date as the end of the fiscal year with this object in mind. For example, many department stores select January 31 as the end of the fiscal year because the January sales reduce inventories to the lowest point. This inventory figure produces a misleading inventory turnover result compared with the turnover calculated at other times of the year. Where possible, monthly moving averages should be used.

The short-term creditor's interest in the current position of the borrower is logically in reference to his own creditor situation. The prospective short-term creditor must be careful not to forget that the analysis he makes of existing accounting reports does not take into account the situation that will prevail if he enters the creditor relationship. The prospective short-term creditor should therefore examine the current ratio, the quick ratio, a cash-budgeting situation, and any other factors as if he had already extended his credit. For example, suppose a firm's accounting reports showed that its present current ratio was 1 to 1, consisting of $30,000 in current assets ($5,000 cash, $10,000 receivables, and $15,000 inventories) and $30,000 of current liabilities. You are considering lending this firm $20,000 for ninety days so that it can purchase more inventory with which to operate. After the loan the current ratio would still be 1 to 1 ($50,000 current assets and $50,000 current liabilities). The quick ratio would have decreased, however, from .5 to 1 ($15,000 to $30,000) before the loan to .3 to 1 ($15,000 to $50,000) after the loan. Most probably the expected inventory turnover position, as well as the nonmonetary considerations mentioned previously, would govern the granting of the loan.

TYPICAL PRACTICES OF
SHORT-TERM CREDITORS

Special Inducements to Pay

As mentioned earlier, the supplier of goods and services is in need of cash just as is the purchaser; trade creditors may thus take special pains to induce their customers to pay their debts rapidly. It is a diminishing, but still common, practice in this country to grant special discounts to purchasers of goods and services who pay their bills early. For instance, Acme Auto Parts regularly purchases lubricating oil from a local distributor in the Detroit area. As a business practice, this distributor has sold to Acme on the following terms: If the bill is paid within ten days of receipt of the invoice, a 2 per cent discount is granted; if the bill is not paid within this period, the full amount should be paid at the end of thirty days from the date of invoice. The oil distributor is recognizing his need for cash and is willing to sacrifice 2 per cent of his price in order to receive the money twenty days sooner. From Acme's point of view, *it is most advantageous to take advantage of the cash discount,* if at all possible.

Suppose Acme purchased $10,000 worth of supplies under terms of 2/10, n/30 (the customary way of describing the terms described in the above paragraph). On the ninth day after the date of the invoice, the treasurer of Acme realizes that he will not have enough cash on hand to pay the oil distributor until the end of the thirty-day period. The alternatives at that point are to borrow money from a bank in order to take advantage of the cash discount or to disregard the cash discount and pay the bill at the end of the thirty-day period from cash generated from sales during that period. The correct decision would be to borrow the money from the bank, if at all possible. The total savings from taking advantage of the cash discount would be 2 per cent of $10,000, or $200. In effect, the company can "earn" $200 by paying twenty days early. The total cost of borrowing $10,000 from a commercial bank for twenty days, even if the interest rate were 8 per cent, would be only $44.44.° Therefore Acme Auto Parts can

---

°Interest is calculated as follows:

$$\text{Principal} \times \text{time (in years)} \times \text{interest rate} = \text{Interest amount}$$

Thus:

$$\$10,000 \times \frac{20}{360} \times \frac{8}{100} = \$44.44$$

In reverse, the rate of interest per year granted by the supplier is not 2 per cent but rather 36 per cent, calculated as follows:

$$\$10,000 \times \frac{20}{360} \times \frac{x}{100} = \$200$$

$$x = 36\% \text{ annual interest rate}$$

actually "earn" $155.56 (as compared with not borrowing the bank money) by borrowing in order to take advantage of the cash discount terms of the supplier.

From this brief description of cash discounts, we can draw the conclusion that short-term creditors who attempt to speed up payment of trade credit by granting cash discounts do so at a high price. *They too could have borrowed the money from a bank at a much lower interest cost than is involved in the discount.* Therefore, the only economically valid reason for granting cash discounts is to disguise a price cut as a cash discount. It is a unique way of granting a price cut, because it penalizes the customer who does not pay rapidly. Cash discounts should not be confused with "trade" discounts (usually for purchase of large quantities), which are granted regardless of the payment method.

Lending on Discount

Many short-term creditors, especially commercial banks, deduct the interest from the face amount of the loan at the time of the loan rather than adding it to the face amount at the completion of the loan period. This process, lending on discount, requires examination because of the hidden implications involved in the rate of interest charged.

A normal loan of $1,000 for a period of one year at a 6 per cent rate of interest would enable the borrower to have possession of $1,000 for a full year and to return $1,060 to the lender at the end of that year. A discounted loan of $1,000 at 6 per cent would give the borrower only $940 for a period of a year, and he would have to pay back $1,000 at the end of that year. The borrower, however, has not borrowed money at a 6 per cent rate of interest. He has paid $60 for the privilege of having possession of $940 for one year. This amounts to a 6.38 per cent rate of interest, not 6 per cent. This same principle can be seen by realizing that if the borrower actually needed to have possession of $1,000 during the year, he would have to pay back $1,063.80 at the end of the year. The same 6.38 per cent true rate of interest is in evidence.

The implication of the above example is simply that at the same "stated" rate of interest, a discounted loan costs more than a loan with "interest to follow" (payable at the end of the loan period). The borrower then should always attempt to borrow with interest to follow, but the very fact that he must borrow money implies that he may be willing to take it on any terms. The creditor, on the other hand, can achieve a higher rate of return on his investment if he can lend the money at a discount rather than with simple interest.

The Need for Collateral

Many people in the business of lending money attempt to assure repayment by requiring the borrowers to put up "collateral" for the loan. Collateral is an asset pledged by the borrower to encourage him to repay the loan. In the event of *default* (nonpayment) of the loan, the pledged asset comes under the control of the lender, who can sell it and use the proceeds of the sale to pay back the loan.

The collateral demanded by short-term creditors can vary greatly, depending on the specific kind of borrowing involved. A large business concern in need of $100,000 for five days in order to meet its month-end payroll could probably borrow the money from a commercial bank without putting up specific collateral. The bankers would lend the money, basing their decision on the general credit standing of the enterprise, as evidenced by a history of satisfactory borrowing and repayment. On the other hand, if the same business concern buys several new delivery trucks with borrowed money, it may be required to use those same delivery trucks as collateral on the loan. This is also true, of course, for individuals who buy automobiles, washing machines, television sets, and houses on the installment plan.

In most cases the specific collateral used to protect short-term creditors consists of assets purchased with the money borrowed. There really is very little need in such situations for the creditor to analyze the value of the asset used as collateral if he is also the seller of that asset. The manufacturer who agrees to sell a turret lathe to Acme and accept payment in the form of a 120-day note at 6 per cent interest need not make a specific analysis of the value of the turret lathe used as collateral for the loan; he already knows more about the value of this asset than anyone else.

When third parties lend money, using newly purchased assets as collateral, they must expend greater efforts to determine the value of those assets as collateral. The local banker who is willing to lend you money on a used car you have just purchased will not only seek the details about the make, year, and model number of the car but will also examine its physical condition. It is the usual practice of "third party" creditors to accept as collateral for their short-term loans only items whose value can be determined readily. The local banker can buy a "Blue Book" that tells him the approximate low, middle, and high values for specific makes and models of automobiles. It would be very easy to borrow $1,000 using a two-year-old Ford in good condition as collateral, even though the market value of that car might be only $1,300. It might be very difficult to borrow $1,000 against a custom-made "special" even though it might cost several thousand dollars. The banker is relatively sure of the value of the Ford, but there is no way of being positive of the market value of the hand-made special. There are many sources of information available to creditors about "generally acceptable" kinds of collateral. Diamond rings, household furniture, delivery trucks, machine tools, inventory, and even real estate serve quite well as collateral, the lending value of which is readily ascertainable.

Most short-term creditors rely very little on the indications of asset value found in the typical statement of financial position when estimating the worth of assets pledged as collateral. In most cases the assets involved are not yet included among the assets of the borrower. In those cases where an existing asset is being offered as collateral, the lender prefers to use some measure of current market value, rather than the original acquisition cost, to gauge his position in the event the borrower defaults. Accounts (or notes) receivable, since they are valued at the amount to be collected, can be accepted at the position statement value.

WHO ARE THE LONG-TERM CREDITORS?

Banks and Government Agencies

These lenders were discussed previously as short-term lenders. Both are also prime sources of long-term loans, but generally in smaller amounts, usually less than $300,000.

Small Business Investment Companies

SBIC's are privately owned firms that derive part of their original capital in the form of loans from the federal government. They are chartered to make long-term investments in new (or relatively new) businesses that have difficulty obtaining funds from other sources. They typically advance funds on a loan basis, but with provisions that the loan can become an ownership (rather than creditor) relationship if the borrowing firm falters in its operations or financial position. Usually SBIC's lend no more than $100,000 to any single enterprise, and often the amount is less than that figure. Because of the risks involved in these investments, the SBIC's charge higher interest rates than do banks, and for this reason are thought of as sources of last resort by the borrowing firms.

Insurance Companies

Insurance companies collect premiums from insurance buyers with the full realization that eventually these funds will be returned (to some of the buyers) in the form of insurance proceeds. In the case of life insurance companies in particular, the time span during which funds are held by the company can be quite long—several decades or more. This means that these companies have large sums of money available for long-term investment. An extremely large part of the long-term lending for real estate and building purposes is done by insurance companies. Their loans may range from $5,000 on a home mortgage to $500,000,000 on a large-scale urban-renewal program.

Pension Trusts and Unions

Similar to insurance companies are the numerous trustees of funds accumulated under pension plans set up by employers, employee groups, fraternal societies, and labor unions. Contributions are made, usually to a legal trust, with thought to eventual (but usually distant) repayment to the retired persons. In the meantime the trustees are expected to invest the funds in income-producing ventures. Long-term loans backed by high-grade collateral are important types of investment allowed under the trust relationship.

The Bond-purchasing Public

In Chapter 12 we discussed the bond as a kind of promissory note evidencing indebtedness. Written evidence of some kind accompanies almost all long-term credit relationships. While banks favor long-term notes, most long-term creditors prefer to use bonds as the written evidence of the debt because of their negotiability. If necessary, the original lender can "sell" his bond to another lender in order to obtain cash immediately. This practice has become so common that most security exchanges deal in bonds as well as stocks, and bonds are repurchased and resold every day.

The existence of active bond exchanges, plus an ample supply of different kinds of bonds, has enabled the general public to enter the business of lending money to business firms of all kinds and sizes. Many infants own corporate bonds purchased for them by relatives. Usually bonds are issued in amounts of $1,000, but several well-known large corporations have issued them in amounts as low as $100 in order to attract funds from the general public.

When a bond issue is publicly held, it often carries no specific collateral (the bond is called a *debenture bond*). Only the general credit standing of the borrowing firm stands behind the debt. Usually a bank or other financial institution is legally appointed to act in behalf of the bondholding public in the event of default of either the interest payments or the principal.

THE INFORMATION NEEDS OF LONG-TERM CREDITORS

Long-term creditors use accounting reports to give them information about existing borrowers as well as potential borrowers. The nature of long-term debt is such that the creditor must be constantly aware of influences that could be detrimental to his investment over a long period of years. The accounting report is one means by which he can keep track of his investments.

The long-term creditor is concerned with the answer to the same fundamental question that the short-term creditor asks himself: What assurance have I that I will receive principal and interest payments from the borrower when they come due? Although the long-term creditor's concern extends over a much longer period of time, he is interested in all the short-run measurements that are the primary concern of the short-term creditor—that is, the current and quick ratios, receivables and inventory liquidity, and the working capital position. Even if the long-run prospects looked good, the prospective long-term creditor might wisely refuse to lend money if the short-run measurements indicated that the prospective borrower might not survive long enough to take advantage of the long run. The long-term creditor also considers two additional factors:

1. *Earnings.* You have already learned that periodic earnings, as computed by generally accepted principles of accrual accounting, are not direct indicators of debt-paying power in the short run. This is especially true of firms that are in the process of expansion. In the long run, however, periodic-earnings projections provide the best evidence that the prospective borrower will not only be in existence but will be in a financial condition that will permit debt payments when the debts come due. Furthermore, in the long run an able management of the borrowing firm is the best protection a creditor has. Periodic earnings are the best available evidence of this ability.

2. *Long-run stability.* This can be defined rather vaguely as the apparent ability of the firm to survive fluctuations in its business fortunes over a period of years. Some industries are much more sensitive to cyclical movements than others, but every firm should have some "safety factor" that will permit it to live through a reasonable period of losses. For the long-term creditor, this safety factor is represented by the size of the owners' equity, which does not have to be "paid back" at any specified future time, compared with the size of existing long-term debt, which does.

Report Analysis for Long-term Creditors

The Safety of Periodic Interest Payments

The long-term creditor reasons in the following manner when attempting to ascertain whether or not his interest payments will be met: "Interest is an expense to the borrower and, as such, payment must be met from revenues." The long-term creditor who is examining the prospective borrower will want to know if the added expense of his interest payments can be met by the existing excess of revenues over expenses (earnings) before income taxes are considered (interest is also a tax deduction). For example, assume that a firm presently has revenues of $300,000 and expenses of $280,000 (not including income taxes) and wants to borrow $200,000 at 6 per cent interest. The interest expense on the proposed loan will be $12,000 per year. The long-term creditor can safely assume that if the $20,000 of earnings before taxes and interest expense are typical and if they can be continued in the future, his interest payments can be met as they fall due. He can also ascertain that this situation does not hold much safety. If earnings were to drop even slightly, the interest payment might be in danger.

The long-term creditor, after examining the earnings situation of the prospective borrower, will set limits for his lending to a particular enterprise based on the degree of safety he requires concerning interest payments. Most commercial banks require a safety factor of 3 or 4 to 1; that is, average earnings should be three or four times as great as the amount of the interest payment that will be required in the future. The *times-interest-earned ratio* is a measurement of the risk involved regarding year-by-year payment of interest.

A wise investor will not rely solely on the past earnings of the firm as an indication of interest safety. His concern should be for the earnings the borrower will generate after he has put the borrowed money to use. Long-term lenders often put into the bond (or note) agreement clauses that penalize the borrower if certain conditions are not maintained. For example, a currently outstanding bond issue of a large steelmaker requires the firm to earn no less than three times the bond interest during the period of the loan (forty-seven years). In the event earnings fall below the 3-to-1 level, the bondholders have the right to either (1) immediate repayment of principal or (2) election of three members of the board of directors of the firm which would give the bondholders a direct influence in management.

Tests of Collateral

The long-term creditors require collateral only if they feel the borrowing firm might fail or might not generate enough earnings in the future to build up a fund with which to repay the debt. In addition they realize that over the long term, some kinds of pledged assets will decline in value through use or obsolescence. Basically, however, their concern for collateral assets centers around the value of such assets in liquidation, if needed, and not on their original acquisition cost. Accounting reports prepared using generally accepted accounting principles provide very little information about current values of specific assets, which is the important measurement in evaluating collateral.

The best test of any collateral position is an indication that the collateral will never be required as such. Most long-term lenders therefore minimize tests of collateral in deference to other evidence concerning the safety of the loan's principal.

The Safety of the Principal

Long-term creditors must be repaid at the end of the term of their loan. Since repayment depends upon the financial condition of the firm at the time the loan falls due, the long-term financial condition of a business, unlike its short-term condition, is inevitably related to operating performance. Analysis of long-term ability to repay must therefore involve a study of the firm's earnings potential as well as its solvency. Long-term creditors thus are concerned with long-run profitability, just as are owners, and discussion of the major portion of their analysis procedure can be delayed until the next chapter. A few special tests will be mentioned now, however, because they are used principally by creditors.

1. The lender may gain insight into how efficiently management uses assets by employing the *asset turnover ratio.* Asset turnover is determined by dividing the average investment in assets over the year into the net sales, or net revenue, for the year. The higher the ratio, presumably, the higher the efficiency in use of assets. It is not possible to set arbitrary limits of goodness or badness for the ratio, but trend analysis over the years plus comparison with industry figures will enable a potential or existing creditor to get some idea of asset utilization.

2. Creditors are also concerned with their position in relation to all other creditors, as revealed in the statement of financial position. The terms (interest rate, due date, collateral if any, and restrictive clauses) of all liabilities should be clearly set forth in the statement.

3. The ratio of the total long-term debt to owners' equity provides a gauge to evaluate the financial policy of the firm. The safety of the principal is generally greater when this ratio is low, indicating a conservative policy and relatively high stability.

Again, the best assurance of repayment lies in continuously profitable operations coupled with an increase in liquid funds. These are easy to ascertain for the past but difficult to predict for the future. Generally speaking, however, long-run future profitability stems from the efficient use of assets and sound financial management. Financial statements for past periods provide information about past managerial ability and profitability that can be used to predict the firm's future ability to repay debt.

ACCOUNTING REPORTS FOR EMPLOYEES AND CUSTOMERS

Employees and customers enjoy a beneficial relationship to the business enterprise with which they deal. Continuation of the relationship is perhaps more vital to employees than to customers, because the latter group can more easily establish new economic ties. In either case, however, the success of the business relationship revolves around the continuing ability of the firm to employ and pay its personnel and to supply its customers (with appropriate terms of trade credit).

Employees and customers share to a great extent the interest of the long-term creditor. Their primary concern is with periodic payments in the form of wages or a continued supplier relationship, but they are also aware that the future depends upon the continued profitability of the enterprise. Labor union leaders in particular have admitted publicly that they rely heavily on the published accounting reports of business firms when formulating union strategy in wage negotiations. They attempt to determine to what extent they can push for a higher wage package and at the same time enjoy a reasonable assurance of enterprise continuity. The majority of their analyses will be discussed in Chapter 19.

TYPICAL REPORTS ILLUSTRATED

The financial statements that are commonly available for creditors, owners, employees, customers, and others are the statement of financial position, the combined statement of earnings and retained earnings, and the statement of working capital flows. These statements for the Acme Auto Parts Company for the two years ended December 31, 19x5, are shown in Exhibits 18–1 to 18–6; some statements are expressed in dollars, others in percentages. Brief comments about the significance of the statements and ratios are included as aids in analyzing the debt-paying ability of Acme Auto Parts, from the point of view of both short-term and long-term creditors.

Percentage statements in greater detail, such as those showing each current asset as a percentage of total current assets or of total assets, are also occasionally prepared. Exhibit 18–1 demonstrates the *shifts* in asset composition and equity composition from year to year. It would seem that Acme Auto Parts is gradually becoming more liquid, considering the increase in percentage of current assets and the decrease in percentage of current liabilities. Also the percentage of assets contributed by owners is slowly increasing. Both of these trends are healthy from the creditors' viewpoint (although not necessarily from the owners', as we shall see), but the period of two years is too short to get a definite trend, and the movements are slight.

The earnings statement expressed in percentages is ordinarily of greater interest to owners and to managers than to creditors, since its usefulness is primarily as an indicator of efficiency of management. The *operating ratios,* as the percentage of various expense items to net sales are called, are discussed more fully in the next chapter. The analysis of working capital changes in percentages is rarely seen in practice but is presented here as a suggested variation that may prove useful.

The statement of working capital flows in dollars, as shown in Exhibit 18–3, should be particularly useful to long-term creditors because of their interest in the sources of the assets with which the debt will eventually be paid. Of particular importance is the size and regularity of fund inflows from operations. This is the one source that can be hopefully counted on to recur year after year. Many analysts rank this statement on the same order of importance as the statement

EXHIBIT 18 – 1

ACME AUTO PARTS COMPANY

COMPARATIVE STATEMENT OF FINANCIAL POSITION
As of December 31, 19x3, 19x4, and 19x5
(in thousands of dollars)

	19x5	19x4	19x3
Assets			
Current assets:			
Cash	$ 504	$ 352	$ 407
Short-term investments	483	175	15
Accounts receivable (net)	960	852	799
Inventories (lower of cost or market)	4,207	3,867	3,909
Prepaid expenses	160	170	147
Total current assets	$ 6,314	$ 5,416	$ 5,277
Investments:			
Sinking fund	$ 300	$ 225	$ 150
Cash surrender value of life insurance	30	22	15
Investment in affiliated company	250	250	250
Investment in real estate	625	625	625
Total investments	$ 1,205	$ 1,122	$ 1,040
Long-lived assets:			
Tangible long-lived assets:			
Land	$ 125	$ 125	$ 122
Buildings & equipment (net)	3,680	3,712	3,614
Intangible long-lived assets (net)	1,160	917	1,001
Total long-lived assets	$ 4,965	$ 4,754	$ 4,737
Total assets	$12,484	$11,292	$11,054
Liabilities and Owners' Equity			
Liabilities:			
Current liabilities:			
Accounts payable	$ 1,065	$ 956	$ 1,528
Notes payable	150	175	725
Accrued interest payable	83	74	69
Rentals collected in advance	5	5	5
Other accrued expenses	346	296	169
Federal income taxes payable	910	746	698
Total current liabilities	$ 2,559	$ 2,252	$ 3,194
Long-term liabilities:			
Note payable (5½%, due 7/1/y4)	3,000	3,000	2,000
Total liabilities	$ 5,559	$ 5,252	$ 5,194

ACME AUTO PARTS COMPANY (CONT.)

	19x5	19x4	19x3
Owners' equity:			
Capital stock:			
Preferred stock (8% cumulative, non-participating, par value, $50; authorized and issued 2,000 shares)	$ 100	$ 100	$ 100
Common stock (no-par value; authorized 200,000 shares)	2,000	1,900	1,900
Retained earnings	5,047	4,262	3,910
Total owners' equity	$ 7,147	$ 6,262	$ 5,910
— Treasury stock (cost)	222	222	50
Net owners' equity	$ 6,925	$ 6,040	$ 5,860
Total liabilities and owners' equity	$12,484	$11,292	$11,054

of earnings, and they point out the advantage that stems from eliminating the highly subjective, sometimes artificial depreciation figure from this statement. There is merit in this view from the creditors' standpoint, because creditors are primarily interested in flows of liquid assets. The assertion has less validity for owners, although the statement of working capital changes has increased in general popularity in recent years.

The Current Ratio

12/31/x3	1.6 to 1
12/31/x4	2.4 to 1
12/31/x5	2.5 to 1

The improvement during 19x4 seems to have been caused by the borrowing of $1 million on the long-term note, coupled with substantial reductions in accounts and notes payable. The net effect is the substitution of a long-term liability for a short-term liability, thus improving short-run debt-paying power.

The heavy inventory position of Acme makes the current ratio difficult to evaluate. The creditor is probably thankful that the inventories are conservatively valued (that is, on the "low" side), as discussed in Chapter 14.

The Quick Ratio

12/31/x3	.38 to 1
12/31/x4	.61 to 1
12/31/x5	.76 to 1

This ratio puts a different light on the short-run debt-paying power of Acme. The situation is improving, and well it might, for the benefit of short-term creditors. The presence of substantial temporary investments at the end of 19x5 would indicate that Acme is not being "hounded" by creditors, and if the improvement continues steadily, short-term creditors apparently don't have too much to worry about.

EXHIBIT 18-2

ACME AUTO PARTS COMPANY
COMPARATIVE COMBINED STATEMENT OF
EARNINGS AND RETAINED EARNINGS
For Years Ended December 31, 19x4 and 19x5
(in thousands of dollars)

	19x5		19x4	
Sales revenues (net)		$20,120		$17,477
— Cost of goods sold		11,547		10,701
Earnings margin		$ 8,573		$ 6,776
— Operating expenses:				
Selling expenses	$2,943		$2,009	
Administrative expenses	2,709		2,392	
Total operating expenses		5,652		4,401
Earnings from operations		$ 2,921		$ 2,375
— Nonoperating items:				
Interest expense		$ 165		$ 170
— Rental income	$ 60		$ 50	
Dividend income	20		20	
Total income		80		70
Net nonoperating expense		$ (85)		$ (100)
Earnings before taxes		$ 2,836		$ 2,275
— Federal income taxes		1,260		1,064
Net earnings		$ 1,576		$ 1,211
+ Retained earnings, 1/1		4,262		3,910
Gain (loss) on sale of equipment		56		(91)
Total available for dividends		$ 5,894		$ 5,030
— Loss from fire	$ 79			
Dividend payments:				
Preferred stock	8		$ 8	
Common stock	760		760	
Total deductions		847		768
Retained earnings, 12/31		$ 5,047		$ 4,262

EXHIBIT 18-3

ACME AUTO PARTS COMPANY

COMPARATIVE STATEMENT OF WORKING CAPITAL FLOWS

For Years Ended December 31, 19x4 and 19x5

(in thousands of dollars)

	19x5		19x4	
Working capital provided from:				
Operations:				
Sales & other revenues		$20,200		$17,547
— Fund expenses		17,717		15,495
Net working capital from operations		$ 2,483		$ 2,052
Sale of equipment		100		176
Issue of common stock		100		0
Issue of long-term note		0		1,000
Total working capital provided		$ 2,683		$ 3,228
— Working capital used for:				
Acquisition of long-lived assets	$1,162		$1,125	
Dividend payments	768		768	
Contribution to sinking fund	75		75	
Increase in cash surrender value of life insurance	8		7	
Purchase of treasury stock			172	
Loss from fire	79			
Total working capital used		2,092		2,147
Increase in working capital		$ 591		$ 1,081

EXHIBIT 18-4

ACME AUTO PARTS COMPANY

CONDENSED COMPARATIVE STATEMENT OF FINANCIAL POSITION

As of December 31, 19x3, 19x4, and 19x5

(in percentages of total assets)

	19x5	19x4	19x3
Assets			
Current assets	$ 50	$ 48	$ 48
Investments	10	10	9
Long-lived assets	40	42	43
Total assets	$100	$100	$100

ACME AUTO PARTS COMPANY (CONT.)

	19x5	19x4	19x3
Liabilities and Owners' Equity			
Current liabilities	$ 21	$ 20	$ 29
Long-term liabilities	24	26	18
Owners' equity	55	54	53
Total liabilities and owners' equity	$100	$100	$100

EXHIBIT 18-5

ACME AUTO PARTS COMPANY
CONDENSED COMPARATIVE STATEMENT OF EARNINGS
For Years Ended December 31, 19x4 and 19x5
(in percentages of net sales)

	19x5	19x4
Sales revenues (net)	$100	$100
— Cost of goods sold	57	61
Earnings margin	$ 43	$ 39
— Operating expenses:		
Selling expenses	$ 15	$ 11
Administrative expenses	14	14
Total operating expenses	$ 29	$ 25
Earnings from operations	$ 14	$ 14
— Nonoperating items (net)	0	1
Earnings before taxes	$ 14	$ 13
— Federal income taxes	6	6
Net earnings	$ 8	$ 7

The Accounts Receivable Turnover

19x4   21 times per year
19x5   22 times per year

Virtually no change in the accounts receivable turnover during a period of substantial increase in sales is a good sign, because collections will often lag behind sales during expansion periods.

EXHIBIT 18-6

ACME AUTO PARTS COMPANY

**CONDENSED COMPARATIVE STATEMENT OF
WORKING CAPITAL FLOWS**

For Years Ended December 31, 19x4 and 19x5
(in percentages of total funds provided)

	19x5	19x4
Working capital provided from:		
Operations	$ 92	$ 64
Sale of equipment	4	6
Issue of common stock	4	0
Issue of long-term note	0	30
Total working capital provided	$100	$100
— Working capital used for:		
Acquisition of long-lived assets	$ 43	$ 35
Payment of dividend	29	24
Contribution to sinking fund	3	2
Other uses	3	6
Total working capital used	$ 78	$ 67
Increase in working capital	$ 22	$ 33

The Inventory Turnover

19x4   2.7 times per year
19x5   2.8 times per year

Acme's ability to increase sales without some drop in inventory turnover is both surprising and encouraging. The heavy investment in inventories makes inventory turnover an extremely important ratio to watch. Acme should make every effort to keep its investment in inventories at a minimum level consistent with its expansion plans and the necessity for balanced inventories. Improvement in inventory turnover would release funds that would improve Acme's quick-asset position substantially. If Acme's inventories are unusually low at December 31, the average monthly investment may be an even higher percentage of the total, and the turnover slower, than these figures indicate.

The Times-interest-earned Ratio

Interest coverage of the long-term notes, using before-tax earnings, is

19x4   14 times
19x5   18 times

This seems comfortable, and the improvement is substantial. If Acme is expanding and needs financing, it might well consider the possibility of additional borrowing. The interest is deductible for tax purposes, and earnings, if they continue, seem high enough to support additional debt.

The Asset Turnover

$$19x4 \quad 1.5 \text{ times per year}$$
$$19x5 \quad 1.7 \text{ times per year}$$

This ratio is difficult to evaluate. The improvement is consistent with the movement of all Acme's 19x5 ratios and indicates improving asset utilization. If inventories could be reduced without reducing sales, this ratio could be improved even further.

The Ratio of Long-term Debts to Owners' Equity

$$12/31/x3 \quad .35$$
$$12/31/x4 \quad .50$$
$$12/31/x5 \quad .43$$

This relationship is perhaps seen in better perspective on the percentage statement of financial position, in which each item is expressed as a percentage of total liabilities and owners' equity. In any case, it is useful as a measure of stability, and reduction in this ratio constitutes improvement in the financial stability of the firm.

General Conclusion

It is reasonable to conclude that Acme's credit standing is good, assuming that there are no opposing factors that we do not know about. The long-term prospects for financial solidarity and payment of long-term debt seem good. Earnings and interest coverage are more than adequate, from the creditors' viewpoint. Short-term liquidity has not been good, but it was substantially improved by the reduction of short-term debt in 19x4, and it has improved since that time. The reduction of the heavy investment in inventories would provide an opportunity for further improvement if such a reduction is possible without hindering sales volume or efficiency.

SUMMARY

Creditors are concerned with the eventual repayment of principal, the periodic payment of interest by the borrower, and the soundness of any assets employed as collateral for the loan. They use accounting reports whenever possible as sources of information about these facets of the borrower's financial condition.

Short-term creditors include banks, suppliers, finance companies, factors, governmental agencies, and occasionally customers. Because of the relatively short-lived length of their loans, they are primarily interested in the current financial condition of the borrower. The current ratio, quick ratio, inventory turnover, and receivables analyses are among those used by these creditors.

Long-term creditors include banks, governmental agencies, investment companies, trusts, pensions, unions, insurance companies, and the bond-purchasing public. Long-term creditors are as concerned about payment of periodic interest as they are about eventual repayment of debt. The information they seek thus relates primarily to the earnings potential of the borrower. The times-interest-earned test is significant to many long-term lenders, as is the asset turnover and the relationship with other creditors.

Employees and customers are also concerned with the overall, long-run financial stability of the business firm with which they enjoy a beneficial relationship. Their interests are therefore similar to those of the long-term creditor.

Questions for Review

18-1. What three categories of creditors were discussed in the chapter? What was the basis for assigning creditors to these three categories?

18-2. To what extent do the interests of creditors and owners in an enterprise overlap?

18-3. Why does the rate of return on owners' investment usually increase with the increased use of short-term credit?

18-4. What types of institutions are categorized as commercial lenders?

18-5. Contrast the credit analysis policies of trade creditors and commercial lenders, and explain the reason for the difference.

18-6. What fundamental question should the prospective creditor ask about the short-term borrower? Which financial statement provides maximum information relevant to this question?

18-7. State how the following ratios are derived, and explain their meaning to the short-term creditor in the analysis of financial statements.
  a. current ratio
  b. quick ratio
  c. inventory turnover

18-8. Why should a customer usually take advantage of a cash discount even if he has to borrow and pay interest? Compare the annual interest cost of 2/10, n/30 terms with an 8 per cent loan.

18-9. Would you rather borrow money using a discounted loan or an interest to follow loan? Why?

18-10. What are the major categories of informational needs of the long-term creditor?

18-11. State how the following ratios are derived, and give their meaning to the long-term creditor in the analysis of financial statements:
  a. times-interest-earned ratio
  b. asset-turnover ratio

18-12. What information can the statement of working capital flows provide to the long-term creditor?

18-13. What major interests do stockholders and creditors have in the firm?

Problems for Analysis

18-14. Mr. Brown and Mr. Smith are presidents of two local manufacturing companies of approximately the same size. Their views on the desirability of short-term credit are as follows:

Mr. Brown would prefer not to have any short-term creditors. His company purchases most of its merchandise from suppliers on a COD basis. There are no short-term bank loans. Accrued liabilities for taxes and wages are paid in the normal manner as they become due. However, employees are paid each Monday for the wages earned during the previous week.

Mr. Smith's philosophy is to use short-term credit freely. His company purchases all merchandise on account and pays for these purchases on the last day of the discount period. Short-term loans are made with the local bank to provide for peak seasonal activities. Accrued liabilities for taxes and wages are paid in the normal manner as they become due. Employees are paid on the Wednesday following each biweekly pay period.

    a. Criticize Mr. Brown's and Mr. Smith's philosophies on short-term credit.

    b. What factors should management consider in formulating a policy pertaining to short-term credit?

18–15. The Renaldo Company purchased merchandise on account from Sproats, Inc., on July 1 amounting to $12,000. The terms of the purchase were 1/10, n/30. The Renaldo Company is unable to pay the invoice within the discount period unless it borrows funds from the local bank at 6 per cent interest.

    Should the Renaldo Company borrow funds from the local bank or forfeit the discount on the invoice from Sproats? Support your answer with calculations showing the cost and the approximate rate of interest under each method.

18–16. The Perkins Company was recently organized for the purpose of manufacturing wooden toys. The company recently applied for a $5,000 loan from the local bank and was turned down. Ludwig's Lumber Company has agreed to sell merchandise on account to the Perkins Company. The terms will be n/30, and the credit is limited to $5,000 per month. Ludwig's expects to have an earnings margin averaging 30 per cent on sales to the Perkins Company.

    Can you justify the conflicting positions taken by the bank and the lumber company regarding the extension of credit to Perkins? Support your analysis by any calculations that you deem necessary.

18–17. Describe the significance and uses of the following ratios and computations:

    a. current ratio
    b. quick ratio
    c. accounts receivable turnover
    d. inventory turnover
    e. asset turnover
    f. long-term debt to owners' equity
    g. times interest earned

18–18. Describe the informational needs of the short-term and long-term creditors. Give reasons for any significant differences in their needs.

18–19. Describe the difference between a discounted loan and a normal loan. Use a 120-day, 8 per cent loan for $2,500 to illustrate the difference, if any, in effective interest rates between the two types of loans.

18–20. Financial statements for the Cape Company for 19x5 and 19x4 are presented as follows:

CAPE COMPANY

COMPARATIVE STATEMENT OF FINANCIAL POSITION
As of December 31, 19x4 and 19x5
(in thousands of dollars)

	19x5	19x4
Assets		
Current assets:		
Cash	$ 40	$110
Accounts receivable (net)	290	170
Inventories (FIFO cost)	320	150
Unexpired insurance	50	30
Total current assets	$ 700	$460
Long-lived assets:		
Land	$ 90	$ 90
Buildings (net)	260	210
Equipment & fixtures (net)	190	120
Total long-lived assets	$ 540	$420
Total assets	$1,240	$880
Liabilities and Owners' Equity		
Liabilities:		
Current liabilities:		
Accounts payable	$ 170	$ 40
Notes payable	100	0
Wages payable	20	10
Federal income taxes payable	210	160
Total current liabilities	$ 500	$210
Mortgage payable (due 1/1/y0)	150	150
Total liabilities	$ 650	$360
Owners' equity:		
Common stock	$ 300	$300
Retained earnings	290	220
Total owners' equity	$ 590	$520
Total liabilities and owners' equity	$1,240	$880

a. Prepare comparative statements of earnings and financial position in percentages for the Cape Company. Comment on any significant shifts in assets, liabilities, etc., for the two years. Describe the significance of these changes from the standpoints of short-term and long-term creditors.

b. Compute the ratios discussed in this chapter for the Cape Company for the two-year period. Include comments about the significance of the statements and ratios from the standpoint of the debt-paying ability of the company.

CAPE COMPANY

COMPARATIVE COMBINED STATEMENT OF EARNINGS AND RETAINED EARNINGS

For Years Ended December 31, 19x4 and 19x5
(in thousands of dollars)

	19x5	19x4
Sales revenues (net)	$1,800	$1,250
— Cost of goods sold	1,160	740
Earnings margin	$ 640	$ 510
— Operating expenses	280	220
Earnings from operations	$ 360	$ 290
— Federal income taxes	160	140
Net earnings	$ 200	$ 150
+ Retained earnings, 1/1	220	160
Total available for dividends	$ 420	$ 310
— Dividend payments	130	90
Retained earnings, 12/31	$ 290	$ 220

18-21. The financial statements presented herein pertain to the earnings and financial position of Trolls, Inc., and Sheiks, Inc., for the fiscal year ended January 31, 19x5. Both companies manufacture house trailers.

TROLLS, INC., AND SHEIKS, INC.

STATEMENTS OF FINANCIAL POSITION

As of January 31, 19x5
(in thousands of dollars)

	Trolls	Sheiks
Assets		
Current assets:		
Cash	$ 250	$ 120
Short-term investments	400	
Accounts receivable (net)	180	230
Inventories (LIFO cost)	320	410
Unexpired insurance	40	30
Total current assets	$1,190	$ 790
Long-lived assets:		
Land	$ 150	$ 180
Buildings (net)	340	370
Equipment (net)	190	230
Total long-lived assets	$ 680	$ 780
Total assets	$1,870	$1,570

TROLLS, INC., AND SHEIKS, INC. (CONT.)

	Trolls	Sheiks
Liabilities and Owners' Equity		
Liabilities:		
Current liabilities:		
Accounts payable	$ 70	$ 110
Notes payable		100
Wages payable	30	40
Federal income taxes payable	190	210
Total current liabilities	$ 290	$ 460
Bonds payable (due 8/1/y6)		300
Total liabilities	$ 290	$ 760
Owners' equity:		
Common stock	$ 800	$ 500
Retained earnings	780	310
Total owners' equity	$1,580	$ 810
Total liabilities and owners' equity	$1,870	$1,570

TROLLS, INC., AND SHEIKS, INC.
STATEMENTS OF EARNINGS AND RETAINED EARNINGS
For Year Ended January 31, 19x5
(in thousands of dollars)

	Trolls	Sheiks
Sales revenues (net)	$2,100	$2,350
— Cost of goods sold	1,270	1,510
Earnings margin	$ 830	$ 840
— Operating expenses	470	460
Earnings from operations	$ 360	$ 380
— Federal income taxes	170	180
Net earnings	$ 190	$ 200
+ Retained earnings, beginning balance	680	260
Total available for dividends	$ 870	$ 460
— Dividend payments	90	150
Retained earnings, ending	$ 780	$ 310

a. Prepare comparative statements of earnings and financial position in percentages for Trolls and Sheiks. Comment on the significance of differences in assets, liabilities, etc., for the two companies from the standpoints of short-term and long-term creditors.

b. Compute the ratios discussed in this chapter for the two companies. Include comments about the significance of the statements and ratios from the standpoint of the debt-paying ability of the two companies.

18-22. Growth Enterprises, Inc., is a wholesaler of electrical supplies. Comparative financial statements are presented for every two years from 19x0 through 19y0. Mr. Grimes, the company president, is considering additional creditor financing of approximately $150,000.

Analyze the financial statements of Growth Enterprises to determine whether you would consider making the loan to the company:

    a. as a short-term creditor with a six-month note.

    b. as a long-term creditor with a ten-year note.

Your analysis should include use of the following ratios for the ten-year period, where appropriate: the current ratio, the quick ratio, the accounts receivable turnover, the inventory turnover, the times interest earned, the asset turnover, and the long-term debt to owners' equity.

GROWTH ENTERPRISES, INC.

COMPARATIVE STATEMENT OF EARNINGS

For Alternate Years Ended December 31, 19x0–y0

(in thousands of dollars)

	19y0	19x8	19x6	19x4	19x2	19x0
Sales revenues (net)	$2,250	$2,210	$1,920	$1,750	$1,400	$1,120
— Cost of goods sold	1,628	1,590	1,350	1,190	905	705
Earnings margin	$ 622	$ 620	$ 570	$ 560	$ 495	$ 415
— Operating expenses:						
Selling expenses	$ 238	$ 230	$ 210	$ 170	$ 146	$ 120
General & administrative						
expenses	220	216	221	205	195	185
Total operating expenses	$ 458	$ 446	$ 431	$ 375	$ 341	$ 305
Earnings from operations	$ 164	$ 174	$ 139	$ 185	$ 154	$ 110
— Interest expense	20	20	17	9	2	0
Earnings before taxes	$ 144	$ 154	$ 122	$ 176	$ 152	$ 110
— Federal income taxes (50%)	72	77	61	88	76	55
Net earnings	$ 72	$ 77	$ 61	$ 88	$ 76	$ 55

GROWTH ENTERPRISES, INC.

COMPARATIVE STATEMENT OF RETAINED EARNINGS

For Alternate Years Ended December 31, 19x0–y0

(in thousands of dollars)

	19y0	19x8	19x6	19x4	19x2	19x0
Retained earnings, 1/1	$179	$177	$191	$178	$162	$137
+ Net earnings	72	77	61	88	76	55
Total available for dividends	$251	$254	$252	$266	$238	$192
— Dividend payments	75	75	75	75	60	30
Retained earnings, 12/31	$176	$179	$177	$191	$178	$162

GROWTH ENTERPRISES, INC.

COMPARATIVE STATEMENT OF FINANCIAL POSITION
For Alternate Years Ended December 31, 19x0–y0
(in thousands of dollars)

	19y0	19x8	19x6	19x4	19x2	19x0
Assets						
Current assets:						
Cash	$ 60	$ 171	$ 125	$ 147	$116	$ 90
Accounts receivable (net)	390	340	280	215	146	120
Inventory	635	590	510	470	340	260
Prepaid expenses	42	34	30	28	19	12
Total current assets	$1,127	$1,135	$ 945	$ 860	$621	$482
Long-lived assets:						
Land	$ 115	$ 115	$ 115	$ 115	$ 80	$ 80
Buildings (net)	188	192	208	220	130	140
Equipment (net)	200	168	180	195	120	65
Total long-lived assets	$ 503	$ 475	$ 503	$ 530	$330	$285
Total assets	$1,630	$1,610	$1,448	$1,390	$951	$767
Liabilities and Owners' Equity						
Liabilities:						
Current liabilities:						
Accounts payable	$ 442	$ 409	$ 340	$ 301	$122	$ 75
Note payable (5%)	150	160	100	60	40	0
Wages & local taxes payable	90	85	70	50	35	25
Federal income taxes payable	72	77	61	88	76	55
Total current liabilities	$ 754	$ 731	$ 571	$499	$273	$155
Long-term liabilities:						
Debentures (6%, due 6/1/94)	200	200	200	200	0	0
Total liabilities	$ 954	$ 931	$ 771	$ 699	$273	$155
Owners' equity:						
Common stock (no-par value)	$ 500	$ 500	$ 500	$ 500	$500	$450
Retained earnings	176	179	177	191	178	162
Total owners' equity	$ 676	$ 679	$ 677	$ 691	$678	$612
Total liabilities and owners' equity	$1,630	$1,610	$1,448	$1,390	$951	$767

18-23. Use the statements of earning and financial position for Beta Enterprises, Inc., presented on pages 654–59 of Chapter 17, for the following analysis:

Compute the ratios presented in this chapter for Beta Enterprises. Include comments about the significance of the statements and ratios in terms of the debt-paying ability of the company.

18-24. The financial statements for Canyon Lake Enterprises, Inc., for the fiscal year ended July 31, 19x5 are presented on pages 705 and 706.

CANYON LAKE ENTERPRISES, INC.

COMPARATIVE STATEMENT OF FINANCIAL POSITION

As of July 31, 19x3, 19x4, and 19x5

(in thousands of dollars)

	19x5	19x4	19x3
Assets			
Current assets:			
Cash	$ 20	$ 50	$ 45
Accounts receivable (net)	50	38	40
Inventory (LIFO cost)	170	115	110
Prepaid insurance	16	18	15
Total current assets	$256	$221	$210
Long-lived assets:			
Land	$ 75	$ 75	$ 75
Buildings (net)	120	125	130
Equipment (net)	80	68	60
Total long-lived assets	$275	$268	$265
Total assets	$531	$489	$475
Liabilities and Owners' Equity			
Liabilities:			
Current liabilities:			
Accounts payable	$ 54	$ 38	$ 26
Notes payable	50	30	30
Accrued salaries payable	4	2	3
Federal income taxes payable	13	11	9
Total current liabilities	$121	$ 81	$ 68
Long-term liabilities:			
Bonds payable (5¼%, due 6/1/z5), par value	$100	$100	$100
Note payable (due 8/1/79)	50	50	50
Total long-term liabilities	$150	$150	$150
Total liabilities	$271	$231	$218
Owners' equity:			
Capital stock:			
Preferred stock (6%, par value $100; authorized 500 shares, issued and outstanding 500 shares)	$ 50	$ 50	$ 50
Common stock (authorized 3,000 shares, issued and outstanding 2,000 shares)	100	100	100
Total capital stock	$150	$150	$150
Retained earnings	110	108	107
Total owners' equity	$260	$258	$257
Total liabilities and owners' equity	$531	$489	$475

CANYON LAKE ENTERPRISES, INC.

COMPARATIVE STATEMENT OF EARNINGS
For Years Ended July 31, 19x4 and 19x5
(in thousands of dollars)

	19x5	19x4
Sales revenues (net)	$355	$305
— Cost of goods sold	240	210
Earnings margin	$115	$ 95
— Operating expenses:		
Salaries	$ 37	$ 28
Insurance	3	3
Depreciation	11	10
Utilities	6	4
Miscellaneous	9	6
Total operating expenses	$ 66	$ 51
Earnings from operations	$ 49	$ 44
— Nonoperating expense:		
Interest	12	10
Earnings before taxes	$ 37	$ 34
— Federal income taxes	12	10
Net earnings	$ 25	$ 24

CANYON LAKE ENTERPRISES, INC.

COMPARATIVE STATEMENT OF RETAINED EARNINGS
For Years Ended July 31, 19x4 and 19x5
(in thousands of dollars)

	19x5	19x4
Retained earnings, beginning balance	$108	$107
+ Net earnings for fiscal year	25	24
Total available for dividends	$133	$131
— Dividend payments:		
Preferred stock	$ 3	$ 3
Common stock	20	20
Total dividend payments	$ 23	$ 23
Retained earnings, ending	$110	$108

a. Prepare comparative financial statements in percentages.

b. Compute the ratios presented in this chapter for Canyon Lake Enterprises, Inc.

c. Use the information from *a* and *b* above, in addition to the comparative financial statements, to make a written evaluation from the standpoint of

    1. a prospective short-term creditor.

    2. a prospective long-term creditor.

Chapter Nineteen **ACCOUNTING REPORTS FOR STOCKHOLDERS**

INTRODUCTION

In this chapter we will discuss the special interests that corporate stockholders and prospective stockholders have in the financial statements of a corporation. For this purpose we will classify stockholders, or owners, as:

a. *Preferred stockholders:* those stockholders whose ownership interest includes some sort of special privilege compared with the interests of common stockholders. Ordinarily this privilege takes the form of a prior claim on dividend distributions over the claims of common stockholders. This privilege is usually granted in exchange for a limitation on the amount of dividend to be distributed to the preferred shareowners.

b. *Common stockholders:* Two types of relationships between the common stockholders and the corporation must be distinguished. First, in the *closely held company,* a small number of stockholders, often the members of a family, own substantially all of the shares. An important aspect of this arrangement is the fact that the stock is rarely bought or sold, and hence its market value is not easily determined. Second, in the *publicly held corporation,* there are many stockholders, each owning a relatively small proportion of the total stock outstanding. There is ordinarily a well-established market price for the stock in this case, either because of its "listing" on one or more of the stock exchanges or because of frequent "over the counter" transactions.

The use of financial statements by owners of stock in the publicly held company will receive by far the greatest attention in this chapter. Most of the information in the published annual reports of corporations is directed at the common stockholders, and most generally accepted accounting principles are based on the assumption that the common stockholder is the principal user of financial statements. Whether common stockholders do in fact deserve such attention has never been established, but it is convenient to assume that this group is of first importance. This is because the interests of the common stockholders, as the company's residual owners, tend to be broader than those of other groups. For example, common stockholders are interested in short-run and long-run debt-paying power (the primary interest of creditors), because if the firm is poorly financed or fails to keep its debts paid as they come due, the position of the common stockholder is adversely affected. Common stockholders are interested in management performance because they are ultimately responsible for the selection of the management, through their representatives, the board of directors. In addition, common stockholders are interested in the earnings and dividend potential, and it is toward this end that most of the information in financial statements is directed.

Before turning to the common stockholder in publicly held companies, brief attention will be given to preferred stockholders and to the stockholders in closely held companies.

PREFERRED STOCKHOLDERS

There are several ways in which a preferred stock could be preferred relative to common stock, but only the dividend preference will be considered here, because it is the most common type. The dividend preference entitles preferred stockholders to a dividend distribution at a predetermined rate before any distributions are made to common stockholders in any year. If the dividend preference also covers any undeclared preferred dividends from prior years, the preferred stock is called *cumulative preferred stock*. In exchange for the dividend preference, the preferred stockholder gives up a claim to any dividend distributions above the stated rate. Any standard book on corporation finance will contain descriptions of the economic and legal positions of various groups of preferred stockholders.

In terms of their needs for information contained in financial statements, preferred stockholders are much the same as the long-term creditors discussed in Chapter 18. This is particularly true if there is a redemption feature in the preferred stock that calls for return to the stockholder of an amount representing principal after a period of time. In any case, preferred stockholders consider their dividend prospects in much the same way that bondholders consider the safety of interest obligations. The difference between preferred stock dividends and bond interest is that the interest becomes a legal obligation independent of earnings, while preferred dividends are paid only when declared by the board of directors.

This is true even if the preferred stock is cumulative. Preferred dividends are therefore contingent not only on earnings (either of the current period or retained from previous periods) but also on the company's need for cash, as indicated by the board's decision to declare or not to declare the dividend.

In spite of the hybrid nature of preferred stock, preferred stockholders are legally classed as owners of the firm and are included in the owners'-equity category in the statement of financial position. The amount of preferred equity in the statement of financial position is properly the dollar amount originally paid to the company for the shares currently outstanding. In the statement of financial position of Acme Auto Parts, this amount is $100,000, which in this case happens also to be the par amount of the shares issued. If the company had issued the shares for more or less than par, a premium or discount would be added to or deducted from the $100,000 in the statement of financial position. Such premium or discount is not properly shown as gain or loss in the statement of earnings, nor should it be added to or deducted from retained earnings on the statement of financial position.

COMMON STOCKHOLDERS
IN CLOSELY HELD COMPANIES

In general, the interests in financial information of common stockholders in closely held (as contrasted with publicly held) companies are much like the interests of managers. Many of these owners are also officers in the firm; but even if not, they or their attorneys will usually be members of the board of directors. As such, these stockholders may have a great deal to say about the financial policies of the firm. At the very least, decisions regarding dividends on common stock will be made only after the financial condition and income tax status of the stockholders are taken into account. Therefore, these stockholders take direct or indirect part in the decision-making process of the firm.

It follows from this that, in the ordinary case, common stockholders in closely held companies are kept well informed about the financial affairs of the company, often on a month-to-month or even more frequent basis. Their requests for additional information beyond that usually contained in a published annual report will undoubtedly be honored, and their questions, often on highly confidential matters, will be answered. This means that the owner of stock in the closely held company need not rely heavily on the published financial information, as must the owner of stock in a publicly held company.

Finally, the stockholder in the closely held company is not often confronted with the decision to sell his shares or to buy more. His own financial affairs are often so intertwined with the affairs of the company that the decision to sell may never be thought of as a feasible possibility.

Valuing Shares in a Closely Held Company

There are circumstances, however, that make it highly desirable, and sometimes absolutely necessary, to place a "reasonable" market value on the shares of a closely held company. The ownership of these companies does change hands from time to time, and when this happens or when it is contemplated, the information contained in financial statements becomes extremely important. This is because the absence of a market price for the shares may influence the parties to rely on the reported financial position and earnings of the firm to establish a reasonable sales price for the shares. Also, in the case of shares of stock in the estate of a deceased person, it is necessary to place a value on the shares for purposes of the federal estate and state inheritance taxes. If the stock has no readily determinable market value, the financial statements of the company are an important influence in establishing a value for the shares.

As you have already learned, financial statements based on generally accepted accounting principles seem at times to be almost as misleading as they are useful when it comes to valuing assets and equities.

For example, suppose that one stockholder owns all the outstanding shares of the Peerless Company, whose condensed statement of financial position is given in Exhibit 19-1.

EXHIBIT 19-1

PEERLESS COMPANY
CONDENSED STATEMENT OF FINANCIAL POSITION
As of December 31, 19x5
(in thousands of dollars)

Assets		*Liabilities and Owners' Equity*	
Cash & accounts receivable	$ 50	Current liabilities	$ 20
Inventories	150	Long-term liabilities	100
Plant & equipment (net)	390	Capital stock (100 shares)	300
		Retained earnings	170
		Total liabilities and owners'	
Total assets	$590	equity	$590

If our stockholder decides on December 31, 19x5, that he would like to investigate the possibilities of selling the shares, he has the problem of deciding what the shares are worth to him as an investment. He needs some sort of benchmark value to serve as a minimum price below which he will not wish to sell.

Book Value

One value that could conceivably be used for this purpose is the financial position value, usually called the *book value*. The book value of the Peerless shares is $470,000 (capital stock plus retained earnings), or $4,700 per share. Obviously the computation and significance of this figure is subject to the rules and difficulties of measuring assets and liabilities that were discussed in Chapters 14, 15, and 16. If the owner of Peerless had no knowledge of accounting, he might conclude from the company's statement of financial position that the book value of the Peerless stock is the amount of cash he would receive if Peerless were to liquidate—that is, sell all its assets for cash, pay off its debts, and return the difference of $470,000 to the owner. If this were true, the figure would be very useful to the owner, because he could then make an informed choice between liquidation of the company and sale of his shares to the highest bidder. Clearly, if the noncash assets could be sold for the amounts shown, and if the liabilities reported are the only ones that would have to be paid, then the company is in fact "worth" $470,000 (the book value or owners' equity) to the owner in liquidation. However, you know that there are likely to be great differences between the values of assets reported on the financial position statement and their cash values in the event of sale. If the inventories are valued at LIFO, for example, this difference may be very large. The valuation of plant and equipment assets, reported net of depreciation accumulated since acquisition, is not likely to correspond to the value in liquidation, for many reasons you have studied.

This could be interpreted as a criticism of conventional financial position statements. Conventional statements are based, as you know, on the *going-concern* assumption—that a profitable business entity will have an indefinitely long life—and not on the assumption that the business will be sold or liquidated on the date of the financial position statement. However, we have no way of determining the cases in which this assumption is valid and the cases in which it is not. Even more important is the fact that we have no evidence that the assumption is particularly relevant to the user of financial statements even when it is true. Certainly the owner of Peerless finds the financial statements deficient, and he may not be impressed with the validity of the assumptions on which they are based. Finally, the very fact that we must calculate earnings and financial position for short time periods calls into question the validity of the going-concern assumption, even in the general case, i.e., in general-purpose financial statements.

Capitalizing Earnings

Our stockholder will thus get a more accurate indication of the value of his stock if he looks at the earnings statements of Peerless rather than its financial position statements. Suppose a condensed comparative earnings statement of Peerless for the past three years were as shown in Exhibit 19–2.

EXHIBIT 19-2

PEERLESS COMPANY

COMPARATIVE STATEMENT OF EARNINGS

For Years Ended December 31, 19x3, 19x4, and 19x5

(in thousands of dollars)

	19x5	19x4	19x3
Sales & other revenues	$625	$610	$540
— Cost of goods sold	370	355	300
Earnings margin	$255	$255	$240
— Operating expenses	200	190	180
Earnings from operations	$ 55	$ 65	$ 60
— Federal income taxes	27	32	30
Net earnings	$ 28	$ 33	$ 30

Here is a logical, but oversimplified approach to our owner's valuation of his Peerless stock by using these earnings statements: Since the best available alternative investment will yield the owner 5 per cent (after taxes) on his investment, the average earnings of $30,000 after taxes is "worth" $600,000 ($30,000 ÷ .05 = $600,000) to the owner. If he sells the stock at this price and invests the proceeds in the "best alternative" investment, he will break even. Theoretically, he would be indifferent to an offer of $600,000, he would refuse a smaller offer, and he would accept a larger one.

This approach to valuation, called *capitalizing earnings,* is subject to many pitfalls and qualifying assumptions. You have learned about many of these in earlier chapters, but it may be useful to list some of the more important ones again as questions that might be asked of the owner of Peerless:

1. The $600,000 price obtained by capitalizing earnings is substantially greater than the $470,000 book value. Does this mean that the book value is understated, that earnings are overstated, that both are true, or that neither is?

2. Is the "best alternative" investment comparable with Peerless stock? Is the risk greater or less—that is, does it call for a higher or lower capitalization rate than 5 per cent?

3. The capitalization process as shown assumes that the average earnings of $30,000 will continue forever (although twenty-five to forty years is a reasonable approximation of forever in this case). Is there evidence supporting this assumption of continued earnings for the long run?

4. Are earnings for the past three years a reasonable basis for predicting future earnings, or were these exceptional years? Would some other basis serve better for this prediction?

5. How can we be sure that reported earnings are computed in such a way that the use of past earnings as a basis for prediction is justified? What conclusion should we draw concerning the effect of price level changes on earnings, the adequacy of depreciation rates, the accounting interpretations given possible leases or pension plans, or past and future expenditures for research and development?

These difficult questions are not presented here to convince you that capitalizing past earnings is an incorrect way to value securities of closely held companies (the method is often used by experts), that financial statements are useless for this purpose (they provide the best information available), or that it is impossible to predict the future on the basis of the past (we have no choice but to try when there is a decision to make). These questions are presented in an attempt to introduce some healthy skepticism into the use of objective financial statements for the purpose of establishing subjective values, to point out the necessity for allowing a wide margin of error, and to emphasize the need for additional information that usually is not found in financial reports of past periods.

COMMON STOCKHOLDERS IN PUBLICLY HELD COMPANIES

Common stockholders in publicly held companies differ from stockholders in closely held companies in these important respects:

1. They do not have the interests and informational needs of the management. They are ordinarily not interested in, nor are they usually competent to judge, managerial performance. Two possible exceptions occur in the cases of (a) the stockholders who actually attend the annual meetings and raise questions about the management or (b) voting stockholders who occasionally are asked to participate in an attempt to change the management. Ordinarily, the small stockholders' interest in management is limited to whether the management is acting legally.

2. There is a reliable market price for the stock at any time, so that the stockholder can buy or sell any time he wishes with relative ease.

3. There is little or no direct stockholder influence on management decisions such as dividends.

4. Although stockholders are legally entitled to see the corporate records, available stockholder information, as far as the company itself is concerned, is usually limited to the information in the interim and annual published reports. In addition, stockholders may obtain information published in several investment services, or they may seek the advice of security analysts who often have available additional information about particular companies.

Stockholders in Consolidated Companies

Stockholders may have majority or minority interests in either the parent or the subsidiary firm of a consolidated corporation. Exhibit 15–1, on consolidated financial position statements (page 571), suggests some of the informational problems faced by consolidated stockholders. Typically, only the figures for the consolidated Hi-Lo Companies (the right-hand column) would appear in published accounting reports. The separate statements of the parent and the subsidiary corporation normally would not be shown. The result is a clouding of information, especially for the minority stockholders of the subsidiary firm.

The minority stockholder has no way of successfully analyzing the strengths or weaknesses of his investment position unless he receives the separate reports of the subsidiary company. The consolidated report gives no clues as to which assets or liabilities belong to his company or what its income was. Thus, there is no way for him to evaluate the past earnings performance of the firm or to estimate future performance. Since he owns no stock in the parent company, he is not protected by the separate performance of that firm.

In many cases, especially with publicly held firms, the minority stockholders adjust their stockholding positions according to past dividend returns, the current market price, and blind faith. Certainly business managers could improve the quality and quantity of information provided for these owners.

Stockholder Objectives

Stockholders in publicly held companies should be classified into two groups for purposes of determining their needs for financial information. These are as follows:

1. *Speculators,* who ordinarily pay little or no attention to financial information on individual companies. Speculators are much more interested in short-run fluctuations in stock prices caused by those external influences that affect the entire securities market or particular industries.

2. *Long-term investors,* who make up the principal audience for the corporate annual report and whose investment decisions will be affected by the earnings and dividend prospects of the individual corporation. This is the group we are concerned with.

This analysis is primarily concerned with the long-term investor's decision to buy the shares of a corporation for investment purposes or to sell shares already held for the purpose of purchasing an alternative investment. The decision is not unlike the decision of the stockholder of the closely held company described above, except that the investor is constantly confronted with many alternatives among which he may choose if he so desires, a situation made possible by the fact that quoted market prices of many possible investment stocks are readily available. We are concerned more with the influence of financial reports on the prices of individual stocks and on investors' decisions than with short-run market "swings" caused by economic or political influences.

Earnings Prospects

Aside from the external influences that affect the entire securities market or large segments of it, it is generally conceded that prospects for future earnings have a more pronounced effect on the price of the stock of individual firms than any other factor. In other words, when an investor is faced with a decision to buy or sell a particular common stock, his most important prediction concerns the future earnings of the company in question. Having predicted future earnings, he derives a stock value, consciously or subconsciously, by a capitalization method such as the one discussed in the case of the Peerless Company. He then compares this value with the market value of the shares. If the market value is higher, he theoretically refrains from buying and/or sells the shares he owns. If the market value is lower than the value based on his prediction of future earnings, he theoretically buys the stock. This process has become so basic in securities transactions that rules of thumb that relate reported earnings to stock prices, called *price-earnings ratios*, have been used by securities dealers and experts to serve as guidelines in securities transactions. For example, average stock prices of various firms in the steel industry might be described as "thirteen times earnings" at some particular time. This means that the stock price averages thirteen times the most recent annual reported earnings per share for steel companies. If one of the steel stocks happens to be selling at ten times earnings at this time, and if there were no known reasons for the variation from the average, this particular stock might be considered an exceptionally good bargain.

It is not our purpose here to discuss the decision-making process of investors in common stocks in great detail; our specific purpose is to stress the crucial importance of the reported earnings figures in determining the stock prices of individual companies, and, in general, to stress the importance of financial reporting to investors. It is also important to note that while only *future earnings* are really relevant to investors' decisions, *past earnings* are used in price-earnings ratios as guides in determining the fairness of stock prices. Past earnings are thus assumed to be useful as predictors of future earnings. Differences in future earnings prospects for different firms and industries are reflected by different ratios. For example, companies in relatively mature industries (in which future earnings are not expected to increase rapidly, such as oil and steel) might sell for twelve to fifteen times past earnings; other companies that are expected to grow and increase future earnings (such as electronics and chemicals) might sell for twenty times past earnings or more.

DIVIDENDS AND GROWTH. An interesting point to be emphasized here is the fact that reported earnings seem to be more important to prospective investors than cash dividends paid to stockholders by the various companies. At

first it might appear that future dividend prospects might be of greater importance, but this is not the case. The primary reason for this is that the "return
on investment" to the stockholders can take two forms: (a) cash dividends or
(b) proceeds from the sale of stock. If the stockholder predicts a rising market
price for the stock being considered for purchase, and if he plans to sell the
stock after the price has gone up, he may buy it now, even though the dividend
prospects are poor. In fact, there is evidence to indicate that stock values derived
from dividend prospects and values derived from predicted market price increases
are to some extent contradictory. Companies that declare annual cash dividends
in amounts that bear a high ratio to annual earnings are normally not expanding,
as evidenced by the fact that they have no compelling need for cash. On the
other hand, expanding companies (known as growth companies) often have poor
dividend records, low cash balances, and poor dividend prospects for the immediate future because they prefer to use cash funds already in the business to
expand rather than to issue more shares or to borrow. If the decision to expand
is made, the cash funds are invested in additional productive facilities, and the
past earnings are added to the owners' (or stockholders') equity. The decision
to expand is an indication of financial optimism and of even more prosperous
times ahead. This optimism is reflected in the stock price, often to a greater
extent than if the dividends had been paid and the opportunity for expansion
passed up.

PREDICTING FUTURE EARNINGS.   In the following discussion, it is important
to keep in mind that past earnings are important only to the extent that they
assist in predicting future earnings. The step from past earnings to future earnings
is a big step that must be taken very carefully, and only after many quantitative
and qualitative aspects of the company's operation have been taken into account.
For example, rosy earnings prospects are of little value if the company's credit
standing becomes poor before the prospects become realities. This means that
the stockholder must also satisfy himself as to the future debt-paying power of
the company, described in Chapter 18 as the primary interest of the creditor.
Changing economic conditions and changing competitive conditions within the
industry must be evaluated. All the risks of prediction mentioned in connection
with the Peerless Company, including recognition of those generally accepted
accounting principles that hinder, rather than assist, good prediction must be
taken into account.

EARNINGS PROSPECTS ILLUSTRATED

The remainder of this chapter contains an illustration in which the earnings
prospects of Acme Auto Parts are compared with Zero Industries, Inc. Zero
Industries is also a manufacturer of subassemblies for the auto industry. Very

few of the products are in competition with those of Acme products, and it is safe to conclude that the fortunes of both companies are partially dependent on the fortunes of the auto industry. Comparative statements of financial position in condensed form for both companies are given in Exhibit 19–3.

EXHIBIT 19-3

ACME AUTO PARTS COMPANY and ZERO INDUSTRIES, INC.

CONDENSED COMPARATIVE STATEMENTS OF FINANCIAL POSITION

As of December 31, 19x3, 19x4, and 19x5

(in thousands of dollars)

	Acme Auto Parts			Zero Industries		
	19x5	*19x4*	*19x3*	*19x5*	*19x4*	*19x3*
Assets						
Current assets	$ 6,314	$ 5,416	$ 5,277	$4,309	$4,601	$4,327
Investments	1,205	1,122	1,040	620	564	581
Long-lived assets	4,965	4,754	4,737	3,942	3,909	3,888
Total assets	$12,484	$11,292	$11,054	$8,871	$9,074	$8,796
Liabilities and Owners' Equity						
Liabilities:						
Current liabilities	$ 2,559	$ 2,252	$ 3,194	$ 862	$1,072	$1,058
Long-term liabilities	3,000	3,000	2,000	0	250	250
Total liabilities	$ 5,559	$ 5,252	$ 5,194	$ 862	$1,322	$1,308
Owners' equity:						
Capital stock:						
Preferred	$ 100	$ 100	$ 100			
Common	1,778	1,678	1,850	$5,600	$5,600	$5,600
Retained earnings	5,047	4,262	3,910	2,409	2,152	1,888
Total owners' equity	$ 6,925	$ 6,040	$ 5,860	$8,009	$7,752	$7,488
Total liabilities and owners' equity	$12,484	$11,292	$11,054	$8,871	$9,074	$8,796

These statements of financial position reveal little about the earnings of the two companies, but there is at least one item of general interest that will be useful: Zero derives a much greater proportion of its assets from owners and a smaller proportion from creditors than does Acme. We can also see that the assets of both firms are about equally distributed between current and noncurrent assets and that the firms are of comparable size.

Condensed comparative statements of earnings and retained earnings of the two firms are presented in Exhibit 19–4.

EXHIBIT 19-4

ACME AUTO PARTS COMPANY and ZERO INDUSTRIES, INC.
COMPARATIVE COMBINED STATEMENTS OF
EARNINGS AND RETAINED EARNINGS
For Years Ended December 31, 19x4 and 19x5
(in thousands of dollars)

	Acme Auto Parts		Zero Industries	
	19x5	19x4	19x5	19x4
Sales & other revenues	$20,256	$17,456	$17,453	$17,021
— Cost of goods sold	$11,547	$10,701	$ 9,898	$ 9,651
— Operating expenses:				
Selling expenses	2,943	2,009	2,455	2,216
Administrative expenses	2,709	2,392	2,419	2,480
— Nonoperating expenses:				
Interest	165	170	13	13
Fire loss	79	0		
— Federal income taxes	1,260	1,064	1,291	1,277
Total expenses	$18,703	$16,336	$16,076	$15,637
Net earnings	$ 1,553	$ 1,120	$ 1,377	$ 1,384
+ Retained earnings, 1/1	4,262	3,910	2,152	1,888
Total available for dividends	$ 5,815	$ 5,030	$ 3,529	$ 3,272
— Dividend payments:				
Preferred stock	$ 8	$ 8		
Common stock[a]	760	760	1,120	1,120
Total dividend payments	$ 768	$ 768		
Retained earnings, 12/1	$ 5,047	$ 4,262	$ 2,409	$ 2,152

[a] Assume the following additional information about the common shares of the two companies:

	Acme Auto Parts		Zero Industries	
	19x5	19x4	19x5	19x4
Average common shares outstanding	173,000	175,000	280,000	280,000
Book value per share, 12/31	$38	$35	$29	$28
Earnings per share	$9	$6	$5	$5
Market value per share, 12/31	$150	$75	$70	$50
Dividends per share	$4+	$4+	$4	$4

Earnings Analysis

There are several methods for comparing the "profitability" of one firm with
another, and because of the extreme importance of profitability, a security
analyst, an investor, or a prospective investor probably should consider all of

them. The fundamental objective, of course, is to provide a basis for prediction of future earnings; in a venture as hazardous as this, even an expert cannot afford to ignore any approach that might prevent errors. The following methods will be discussed in this chapter:

1. the dollar amount of earnings per share
2. earnings in relation to revenues
3. the rate of return on investment
4. cash flows and working capital flows
5. the price-earnings ratio

The Dollar Amount of Earnings per Share

Certainly no careful investor would limit his investigation to the dollar amount of earnings per share or merely project the trend indicated. On the other hand, a great deal can be learned from examining the dollar figures. For example, the fact that 19x5 was a far better year than 19x4 for Acme, while Zero's earnings were steady, may be significant, considering the fact that the fortunes of both firms are partially dependent on the fortunes of the auto industry. If the auto industry improved over the period, then the reasons for Zero's failure to improve should be carefully examined.

Another important aspect is the possibility that earnings may be affected by extraordinary gains or losses during the period under examination. Acme's fire loss, and the gains and losses on sales of equipment included as other revenue (see Chapter 12 for detailed statements), were not sufficiently large to be important. If these items had been large compared with net earnings, they would have been eliminated from the earnings figure used for prediction purposes, because such items would not be expected to occur again.

Earnings in Relation to Revenues

For comparative purposes, periodic earnings are often related to the revenues of the period. Percentage figures for Acme in relation to Zero follow:

Earnings as Per Cent of Revenues

	19x5	19x4
Acme	7.7	6.4
Zero	7.9	8.1

Zero seems to have an edge here, in spite of the fact that the ratios are much closer in 19x5 than in 19x4.

Earnings as a percentage of revenues is generally considered to be a useful measure of management efficiency, particularly if the entire earnings statement is expressed in percentages, as illustrated in Chapter 18. The principal difficulty in such analysis by an outsider is the fact that he has no sure way of determining the behavior pattern of various expense items. Obviously, earnings as a percentage of sales will vary widely as the volume of business varies if any significant portion of the expenses are nonvariable expenses. For example, how much of Acme's improvement is attributable to the fact that the volume increased in 19x5, and how much is attributable to better cost-reduction practices (that is, efficiency)?

Earnings as a percentage of sales is also often used as a basis for judging price policy in those cases in which there is a presumed relationship between expenses and selling prices. For example, in recent years strong political pressure has been brought to bear on some of the steel companies whenever they increase steel prices. Earnings as a percentage of sales for these companies is cited as evidence that profits were high, perhaps too high, and that the price increases are not justified. In contrast, low percentages of earnings to total revenues are often given considerable publicity in some industries (for example, grocery chain stores) as evidence of "low, low prices," or possibly as evidence of hardship. The use of this relationship for these purposes is likely to lead to highly misleading conclusions, as we shall see.

The Rate of Return on Investment

Probably the most widely accepted definition and measure of profitability is the rate of return on investment. This ratio has many variations, but basically it relates earnings to the total resources (investment) committed to the production of those earnings. For example, Acme Auto Parts employed on the average $11,888,000 in assets during 19x5 (half the sum of $12,484,000 and $11,292,000), if we ignore for the moment all the problems of measuring assets from the Acme statement of financial position. Ignoring still other complications, we could assert that these assets earned $1,553,000, a return of approximately 13 per cent on the assets employed. The corresponding percentage for 19x4 is 10 per cent. This same computation for Zero Industries produces a rate of return slightly in excess of 15 per cent for both 19x5 and 19x4.

The ratio of earnings to investment can be expanded to:

$$\frac{\text{Earnings}}{\text{Sales}} \times \frac{\text{Sales}}{\text{Assets}}$$

It is thus easily seen that rate of return on investment can be analyzed as the product of profit margins (earnings/sales) and asset turnover (sales/assets). This analysis is useful in explaining the differences in operating conditions among firms in various industries. For example, a steel manufacturer and grocery chain might both show a rate of return on investment of 5 per cent, even though the profit margins may be widely dissimilar:

	Profit as per cent of sales	Asset turnover (times/year)	Rate of return on assets (%)
Steel company	6.0	.8	5
Grocery chain	1.5	3.3	5

This demonstrates that the relatively high margins of the steel company are necessary to keep even with the grocery chain because of the comparatively high investment in assets required in the steel industry, resulting in slow asset turnover.

This breakdown is also useful to management in determining why its rate of return on investment may vary from year to year. The effect on the rate of return on assets of changes in profit margins due to changes in price policy or changes in operating costs, or the effect of additional investments in assets, can be more easily evaluated.

COMPARABILITY BETWEEN COMPANIES. The rate of return on investment calculation is the most popular index of profitability because it involves fewer qualifications than the other measurements. In addition, managers are inclined to measure their own performance by this index, and they tend to make decisions that will produce a maximum rate of return on investment. Nevertheless comparisons between companies, and even between years for the same company, must be made with great care. For example, these questions point out possible differences in accounting methods that may affect comparison between Acme and Zero:

1. Do both companies value inventories by the same method?
2. Are the depreciation rates comparable?
3. Are there differences between the companies in accounting methods for research and development expenses? For repairs and maintenance?

You can think of other differences in accounting method that might affect the comparison.

EARNINGS TO WHOM? One of the differences between Acme and Zero noted earlier is the fact that Acme obtains almost half of its total assets from creditors (half of this amount from long-term creditors to whom interest is paid), while Zero obtained only slightly more than 10 per cent of its capital from creditors as of December 31, 19x5, after it paid off the last of its long-term debt. This difference affects the comparability between firms, as expressed by the rate of return on investment calculation.

From the standpoint of management's measuring its own performance, comparability between firms is affected only by the amount of interest on the debt. In theory, management is not concerned with the source of the assets committed to the firm; it is concerned instead with the efficient use of *all* assets, regardless of source. Interest on the debt is a much greater expense to Acme than to Zero, and since this interest may, from management's viewpoint, be viewed as a distribution of earnings rather than as a cost of producing revenue (that is, an expense), the interest expense does spoil the comparability between the firms. It is for this reason that interest expense is often treated as a non-operating expense in a detailed earnings statement. (See Chapter 18.) From the standpoint of the management, operating earnings are a better measure of earnings than net earnings.

From the standpoint of the stockholders, on the other hand, Acme's larger debt spoils the comparability between the firms, but for a different reason; Acme's stockholders have a smaller investment in Acme than Zero's stockholders have in Zero. In addition, interest on Acme's debt, an irrelevant distribution of earnings from the standpoint of management performance, is a bona fide cost of doing business from the standpoint of Acme's stockholders. Earnings (return) for both groups of stockholders are *net,* and the proper measure of investment is share-owners' equity rather than total assets.

From the point of view of Acme's common stockholders, the presence of the preferred stock introduces another complication of exactly the same kind. The preferred dividend is merely an earnings distribution from the point of view of the management and the creditors, but it is an expense from the standpoint of the common stockholders, because it must be paid before the common stock-holders are entitled to claim the remainder of the earnings for themselves.

To summarize, the rate of return on investment, when used as an index of management performance, should use an earnings figure computed before any earnings distributions (interest or dividends) are taken out and an investment figure that measures total assets employed.

	Acme		Zero	
	19x5	*19x4*	*19x5*	*19x4*
Rate of return on total assets	14 + %	11 + %	15 + %	15 + %

(The effect of interest on federal tax expense is ignored in this computation.)

When viewed from the point of view of the common stockholder, earnings are defined as the net remaining figure after all prior claims for interest and dividends have been met, and investment is defined as the portion of the share-owners' equity that attaches to the common shares.

	Acme		Zero	
	19x5	*19x4*	*19x5*	*19x4*
Rate of return on common-stock equity	24%	19%	17 + %	18%

These measurements indicate that Zero has used its total assets slightly more efficiently than Acme; however, because Acme relies more heavily on borrowed funds, the cost of which is smaller than the earnings, Acme's common stockholders are earning a better return on their investment than Zero's common stockholders.

Leverage. Acme's use of long-term borrowed capital, on which it hopes to earn more than the cost of borrowing, is sometimes referred to as the use of *leverage*. The phrase "trading on the equity" is also used to describe this practice. A full-fledged discussion of the advantages and disadvantages of the use of borrowed capital (and preferred stock) is properly left to a book on corporation finance. Nevertheless, the advantage to Acme's common stockholders is obvious as long as it can predict an earnings rate in excess of $5\frac{1}{2}$ per cent, the interest expense of carrying the long-term debt. There is risk in leverage, of course, which Zero apparently prefers to avoid, as evidenced by its retirement of its small long-term debt in 19x5.

The effect of leverage is particularly important in today's economy, which is characterized by high income tax rates and a rising price level. Interest expense is deductible as a cost of doing business; therefore the real cost of borrowed funds is the net cost after considering the effect of the interest deduction. Inflation also encourages borrowing (compared with issuing more stock) because of the prospect of repaying the debt with cheaper dollars than the dollars borrowed.

INFLATION AND THE RATE OF RETURN ON INVESTMENT. Problems in interpretation of financial statements that result from the accountant's erroneous assumption of the stable dollar were discussed in Chapter 16. There is no widely used measurement that is likely to be affected more seriously by inflation than the rate of return on investment, for two very important reasons:

1. Reported earnings will be overstated, principally because depreciation expense is stated in terms of dollars of an earlier year.

2. Owners' equity as reported in the conventional statement of financial position will be understated, compared with what the owners' equity would have been had all the assets been stated in terms of current dollars.

This means that measuring the rate of return on investment compounds this error. Thus

$$\frac{\text{Overstated earnings}}{\text{Understated investment}} = \text{Doubly overstated rate of return}$$

It can be argued that these errors "wash out" when rate of return is used as a basis for comparison of profitability between firms, but this argument may not be valid. If the relative size of investment in long-lived assets of the two firms is about the same, and if the companies are about the same age, then rate of return on investment may be used in spite of the bias introduced by inflation. The first condition seemed to exist in the illustration of Acme and Zero, but we have no information about the age of the two companies. If one of these companies were relatively old and the other company relatively new, the rate of return reported by the older company would tend to look better in comparison, but the comparison would be a false one.

Cash Flows and Working Capital Flows

Difficulties with lack of uniformity in accounting methods among firms and difficulty with the distortions introduced by inflation have influenced some accountants and statement analysts to stress the importance of the statement of cash receipts and disbursements. Occasionally it has even been suggested that the cash statement be used in place of the earnings statement as a measure of profitability. You should review Chapter 13 if you are somewhat hazy on this subject.

This suggestion is highly controversial. It is wrong to try to deny or minimize the limitations in the measurements taken from conventional earnings statements and statements of financial position. As statements of cash inflows and cash outflows, cash receipts and disbursements statements are free of the accounting decisions that necessarily underlie asset and earnings measurements. These statements, if properly prepared, are statements of historical fact and as such are completely objective. This attribute is appealing, but it necessarily carries with it the disadvantage of having highly questionable predictive value.

Furthermore, the rules of thumb used by some statement analysts are not properly labeled "cash flow." At worst, "cash flow" has been defined as the conventional accounting earnings figure except that the depreciation and amortization expense is omitted. This cash flow has occasionally even been reported on a "per share" basis, creating the implication that it is to serve as a substitute for earnings. This practice seems to be most popular in those situations in which earnings per share might not create the optimism for the future that management would like to create.

The usefulness of a cash receipts and disbursements statement (consisting of cash provided minus cash used, appropriately classified) in an annual report is not at issue here. As a statement that is relevant to the appraisal of the *liquidity* of the firms (*not* profitability), its value has been proven by extended use. For this purpose, however, the authors are inclined to recommend the analysis of working capital flows (also discussed in Chapter 13) as having certain advantages over a statement dealing only with cash. The analysis of working capital flows is a simpler statement because it is not concerned with changes in individual current asset and current liability items. The statement of working capital flows gives emphasis to those transactions having a more permanent effect on the liquidity of the firm. Perhaps most important, this statement is less likely to be confused with, or presented as if it were a substitute for, net earnings.

The comparative statements of working capital flows for Acme and Zero are presented in Exhibit 19–5. These statements provide important comparisons of the firms regarding dividend policy, tendency (or lack of it) to make use of borrowed capital, and long-lived asset acquisitions as well as the adequacy of working capital inflows from operations in providing the funds for these activities. It is often accompanied by a statement of changes in items of working capital.

EXHIBIT 19-5

ACME AUTO PARTS COMPANY and ZERO INDUSTRIES, INC.

COMPARATIVE STATEMENTS OF WORKING CAPITAL FLOWS
For Years Ended December 31, 19x4 and 19x5
(in thousands of dollars)

	Acme Auto Parts		Zero Industries	
	19x5	*19x4*	*19x5*	*19x4*
Working capital provided from:				
Operations:				
Sales & other revenues	$20,200	$17,547	$17,453	$17,021
— Fund expenses	17,717	15,495	15,195	14,794
Net working capital from operations	$ 2,483	$ 2,052	$ 2,258	$ 2,227
Issue of long-term note	0	1,000		
Other sources	200	176	188	312
Total working capital provided	$ 2,683	$ 3,228	$ 2,446	$ 2,539
— Working capital used for:				
Acquisition of long-lived assets	$ 1,162	$ 1,125	$ 1,009	$ 982
Payment of long-term debt			250	0
Dividend payments	768	768	1,120	1,120
Other uses	162	254	249	177
Total working capital used	$ 2,092	$ 2,147	$ 2,628	$ 2,279
Increase (decrease) in working capital	$ 591	$ 1,081	$ (182)	$ 260

The Price-earnings Ratio

The importance to the investor of the stock's market price need not be elaborated. This market price should theoretically correspond with the owners' equity per share (book value) as reflected in the statement of financial position, and if this were the case, the price-earnings ratio and the rate of return on investment would be the same. However, the practice of valuing assets at historical cost, coupled with the economic and political influences on the securities markets, which may not have anything to do with Acme or Zero, make this impossible. From the standpoint of the investor, the *book value* per share (or the price paid when each was purchased) is not particularly helpful, and instead he uses the market value of the shares as a measure of his investment. If he is contemplating a stock purchase, this price is the required investment; if he is considering sale of shares already held, the market price is his cost (that is, the sacrifice connected with not selling).

Subject to the important qualification that political and economic events, market actions and reactions, and waves of optimism and pessimism affect all or major portions of the securities markets, *net earnings* are the most important single factor affecting the market price of shares. This means that the price-earnings ratio, when compared with that of other companies or the industry, is a means of judging the "reasonableness" or "adequacy" of the market price of the stock at any given time. The price-earnings ratios for Acme Auto Parts and Zero Industries are as follows:

	Acme	Zero
12/31/x4	12	10
12/31/x5	17	14

Since the price-earnings ratios of both companies moved in the same direction and proportionally over the period of a year, the movement might be attributed to "external" factors that affected the industry or the entire market. For our purposes, the significant fact seems to be that Acme is rated higher than Zero. The relevance of this fact to a possible investment decision is beyond the scope of this book, so the principal possibilities for this preference are merely listed:

1. Acme's expanding sales volume may be projected to higher levels of sales and profits in the future.

2. Acme's tendency to use more borrowed funds may be in its favor in a market that is generally optimistic, because that is the time when trading on the equity is looked on with approval. The higher risk that Acme is taking is apparently ignored or is offset by other factors.

3. It is entirely possible that the market is wrong and will correct itself when this becomes generally known. Assuming this to be the case, now would be the time to sell Acme and buy Zero.

4. The relative riskiness of the type of activity of the two companies may call for a higher price-earnings ratio for Acme. Investors are reluctant to pay as high a price for an interest in a high-risk enterprise as they would in a more stable and secure company.

CASH DIVIDENDS.   It can be argued that it is the cash dividends, not earnings, that are really important to the investor; that in fact earnings are important only because they are the forerunner of dividends to be declared sooner or later. As we have seen earlier in this chapter, however, high cash dividends may be interpreted by investors as an indication that expansion and growth are not being contemplated. In any case, the relatively generous cash dividend policy of Zero has done little to advance the price of its shares. On the other hand, if Zero were to reduce its dividend below $4, it would probably affect the stock price adversely.

STOCK DIVIDENDS AND STOCK SPLITS.   A so-called *stock dividend* is a transaction in which additional shares are issued by the corporation to existing stockholders. The word "dividend" is used to describe this transaction because management sometimes tries to create the impression that the shares issued are really the equivalent of cash, since they can be sold in an established market. This impression is misleading, however, and the word dividend is an unfortunate label. The issue of additional shares to existing stockholders on a pro rata basis merely makes each share a proportionally smaller part of the ownership of the firm and in fact is often a hint that cash dividends will not be forthcoming because past earnings have been permanently reinvested in the business. The stock dividend is a common device for growth companies that need all available cash for expansion purposes but still want to demonstrate the company's profitability in a tangible way. The stock dividend, *not* a distribution of assets in any sense of the word, is nevertheless an indication that the company is expanding and healthy.

A "stock split" transaction should be interpreted the same as the stock dividend. The difference lies in the fact that a stock split usually involves a larger number of new shares issued. A stock split usually requires trading in old stock certificates and receiving more than one new stock share for each old one. The primary reason for the stock split is to reduce the *market price* per share, so that a larger number of smaller investors will be interested in buying the stock.

Ordinarily, stock dividends and stock splits are transactions initiated by financially healthy companies. In spite of the fact that no distribution of assets is forthcoming in either case, the transactions are popular among stockholders and usually are accompanied by an increase in the total market price of the stock of the company.

Prospects for Future Earnings

Regardless of all the financial statement and market ratios based on past data, the fact is that the best prediction of *future earnings* is the only important information an investor should look for in financial statements. All the discussion above is useful only to the extent that it permits the investor or the security analyst to make a more intelligent prediction of future earnings than he would be able to without the data relating to past periods. The accountant is not much better equipped to make this projection than is the investor; all the accountant can do is make sure that the ratios he uses are relevant to the prediction and that his figures are as free of misleading biases as possible.

The President's Letter

Sometimes the investor is assisted in this most difficult step by the expository material in the corporate annual report, in addition to the figures in the financial statements. Many annual reports devote considerable space to development of new products, new research projects, and other activities affecting the future, to the extent that such information is publishable without injuring the competitive position of the company. One of the most authoritative sources of this kind of information is the president's letter, found in the annual reports of most leading companies. The illustration shown in Exhibit 19–6 is taken from the 1969 annual report of the Federated Department Stores, Inc.

EXHIBIT 19–6

LETTER TO SHAREHOLDERS

Dear Fellow Shareholder:

We are happy to report that your company achieved record sales and earnings in fiscal 1969.

Sales for the year ended January 31, 1970 totaled $1,992,668,937 compared with $1,813,771,463 for the 1968 fiscal year. This is an increase of 9.9%.

Income before taxes in 1969 was $169,941,543 compared with $162,269,714 in 1968. Income after taxes in 1969 was $85,941,543 compared with $80,269,714, an increase of 7.1%. Earnings per share were $1.98 compared with $1.85 in 1968.

Perhaps the most significant development in 1969, other than the results themselves, was the announcement of a new top management organization. For some time we had been sensitive to the fact that your company's top management was stretched too thin. Federated has grown rapidly. Both the present and predictably greater size of the corporation demanded more help at the top.

In addition, it was clear that the continued, vigorous growth of our department store divisions—which represent our prime profit opportunity—required additional manpower at the level of corporate management.

With this in mind, we took two steps. We formed a four-man policy committee consisting of the chairman, the president, the chairman of the executive committee and the vice-chairman. This group will be primarily concerned with corporate matters. It will set the objectives and appraise the results of the operating divisions and it will oversee the development of the company's venture businesses.

In addition, we named four of Federated's top merchants to the new post of group president. All have had long experience as principals of our department store divisions. They are Ross F. Anderson, Alfred H. Daniels, William P. Keeshan and Harold Krensky. Their primary assignment will be to supervise the development and implementation of the long-range growth plans of the department store divisions.

Subsequently, the four group presidents and Eugene B. Walsh, a vice president of Federated and former general manager of Ralphs Industries, were elected to the Board of Directors, while four veteran members, with a combined Board service of 85 years, retired. The retiring directors were Paul M. Mazur, a Lehman Brothers partner who participated in the formation of Federated and served its Board for 33 years; James S. Schoff and J. Edward Davidson, who, as president and chairman of the Bloomingdale division initiated Bloomingdale's great postwar transformation; and Walter W. Candy, Jr., a former president of Bullock's, who, following its acquisition by Federated in 1964, became a director and vice president of Federated.

As we have previously reported, 1969 also was noteworthy because of the record expansion of our physical facilities. A net of 2,223,000 square feet of new store space was added. New department stores were opened by Abraham & Straus at Smith Haven, Long Island; by Lazarus at Richland near Mansfield, Ohio; by Shillito's at Beechmont Mall in Greater Cincinnati; by Rike's at Dayton Mall in South Dayton; by the Boston Store at Southridge in Greater Milwaukee; by Levy's in Tucson; and by Burdine's at Pompano, Florida. Our Gold Circle discount division added four new stores—three in Dayton and one in Columbus. Ralphs added nine supermarkets in Los Angeles (three older stores were closed). In addition, a number of existing department stores were enlarged and modernized to accommodate increasing customer traffic.

The geographic distribution of Federated's department stores sales in 1969 was essentially unchanged from its historic pattern, accentuating the national character of our business and our concentration in the nation's strongest economic areas. The East and Northeast provided 37% of our sales; the Midwest 25%; the South and Southwest 22%; and the Pacific Coast 16%.

There were no new developments in our international situation in 1969. We continue our investment in Galerias Preciados in Spain. In addition, we have $20 million overseas and it remains our intention to use this money for foreign investment when an attractive opportunity is found. Meantime, it is invested in short-term securities and is earning more interest than it is costing us.

The dividend was increased again in 1969. The indicated annual rate was boosted from ninety-five cents to one dollar effective with the October distribution. It was the eighth increase in ten years. The dividend rate doubled in the 1960's.

Looking to 1970 we are neither optimistic nor pessimistic about our prospects. We know that a good deal of steam has gone out of the economy. We know inflation has not yet been checked, and, therefore, that we face persistent upward pressure on all the costs of doing business. At the same time, we also know that the 15% increase in Social Security payments and the scheduled elimination of the income tax surcharge are stimulants to our kind of business. On balance, we expect continued growth in 1970, although at a somewhat slower rate of gain than that of the past few years.

For the more distant future we are unblushingly optimistic. Perhaps never in our history has this nation faced quite as many problems as it faces today. But it is also true, we believe, that our country has the will, the resources and the stamina to face them successfully.

Beginning on page four of this report we have spelled out our growth philosophy in some detail. As you will see, those plans are based on the belief that our country will continue to grow and that your company must be prepared to grow along with it—rapidly and profitably. We plan to open approximately 1,450,000 square feet of new store space in 1970. About 950,000 square feet will be for our department store divisions. Another 350,000 will be discount space for our Gold Circle and Gold Triangle divisions, with the remaining 150,000 devoted to new supermarkets for our Ralphs Grocery division in the Los Angeles area.

In closing the books on 1969 we want to thank our employees and our suppliers for another year of devoted effort. We particularly want to salute our four retiring directors—men whose counsel and friendship have meant a lot to us and to the continuing growth of your company.

Respectfully submitted,

Ralph Lazarus, *Chairman of the Board*
J. Paul Sticht, *President*

By Order of the Board of Directors, April, 1970

SUMMARY

In this chapter we have emphasized the uses of accounting information by the stockholders of a corporation. Brief attention was given to the stockholder in the closely held firm, whose point of view is much the same as the point of view of the manager. The interests of investors and prospective investors in publicly held firms were given much greater stress, because these investors are the ones for whom accountants can provide the greatest service and the ones to whom the information in the corporate annual report is primarily directed.

Common stockholders can be classified in terms of their objectives and needs for financial information:

1. Speculators, whose primary concern is the prediction of future stock prices, particularly in the short run. Accounting reports are of little use to these persons.

2. Investors, whose primary concern is the prediction of future earnings, particularly in the long run. The remainder of the chapter was devoted to the informational interests and needs of these investors. The relevance of accounting information to the prediction of future earnings was demonstrated by the use of an illustration comparing Acme Auto Parts with Zero Industries. The effect of dividend policy and its relationship to growth, the importance of the firm policy relating to the use of borrowed capital, and the impact of various accounting methods were discussed. The standard information included in the published annual report of a corporation was discussed as information relevant to changes in market prices of securities.

The rate of return on investment was suggested as the most widely used index of profitability of the firm and, with important qualifications, was recommended as a useful basis for prediction of future earnings. Rate of return was considered both from the management viewpoint and the common stockholders' viewpoint, and its breakdown into components of profit margin and asset turnover was demonstrated. The use of statements of cash receipts and disbursements and statements of working capital flows as statements providing information relevant to short-run and long-run liquidity of the firm, and the misuse of these statements as substitute measures of profitability, were stressed.

Questions for Review

19-1. Describe the two types of relationship between common stockholders and the corporation that were discussed in the chapter.

19-2. Why is information in annual reports geared primarily to the needs of the common stockholders?

19-3. In what ways are the informational needs of the preferred stockholder and bond investor similar?

19-4. What approaches are available in arriving at a market value for stock in a closely held company?

19-5. How is the price-earnings ratio computed and used in security analysis?

19-6. Evaluate the uses and limitations of each of the following methods of comparing the profitability of one firm with another:
  a. the dollar amount of earnings
  b. earnings in relation to revenues
  c. the rate of return on investment
  d. cash flows and working capital flows
  e. the price-earnings ratio

19-7. What is leverage?

19-8. What impact does inflation have on the measurement of return on investment?

19-9. In analyzing the financial statements of two corporations, would you expect greater uniformity between funds statements or earnings statements? Why?

Problems for Analysis

19-10. Explain the meaning and uses of the following items:
  a. book value per share of common stock
  b. market value per share of common stock

c. trading on the equity
d. stock dividends
e. stock splits

19-11. Contrast the use of return on investment (including the investment amount) as it may be applied
    a. by the management of a company
    b. by the stockholders of a company

19-12. The Random Corporation has outstanding 10,000 shares of 8 per cent preferred stock with a $100 par value and 20,000 shares of $75 par-value common stock. Net earnings and total dividend declarations for the first three calendar years of operations are as follows:

	Net earnings	Total dividends declared
19x6	$250,000	$ 0
19x7	325,000	200,000
19x8	420,000	280,000

    a. Compute the total amount of dividends that each class of stockholders would be entitled to receive in 19x7 and 19x8 under each of the following independent assumptions:
        1. The preferred stock is noncumulative and nonparticipating.
        2. The preferred stock is cumulative and nonparticipating.
        3. The preferred stock is cumulative and participating after an 8 per cent return has been paid to common stockholders.
    b. What are the possible objectives of a preferred-stock investor? Of a common-stock investor? Discuss.

19-13. Indicate how the following terms differ in meaning and how they are treated in the financial statements:
    a. market value   f. issued stock
    b. book value   g. outstanding stock
    c. par value   h. stock dividend
    d. no-par value   i. stock split
    e. authorized stock   j. consolidated accounting

19-14. The following ten-year summary pertains to the operations of a large corporation with decentralized operations. There are three other companies of approximately the same size, in addition to numerous small companies, in the same industry.

	19y1	19y0	19x9	19x8	19x7	19x6	19x5	19x4	19x3	19x2
Net sales	$4,100[a]	$4,250	$4,050	$4,300	$3,900	$3,600	$3,400	$3,600	$2,910	$2,550
Net earnings	$210	$305	$260	$240	$210	$212	$201	$168	$157	$130
Cash dividends declared (common stock)	$170	$170	$170	$170	$170	$170	$130	$130	$120	$90
Number of shares of common stock issued	40	40	40	40	40	40	40	40	40	40
Market-price range of stock (high & low for year)	$110–$75	$108–$78	$82–$55	$60–$48	$68–$50	$58–$43	$49–$32	$31–$20	$26–$17	$22–$17
Total assets	$2,600	$2,600	$2,300	$2,300	$2,200	$1,900	$1,800	$1,800	$1,500	$1,400
Plant expenditures	$140	$100	$100	$160	$200	$160	$175	$160	$130	$100
Depreciation & amortization	$115	$120	$130	$120	$110	$90	$80	$70	$60	$60
Average number of employees	270	265	260	258	252	249	242	240	240	230

[a] All figures except price range of stock are expressed in thousands.

a. Analyze the data for the ten-year period from the standpoint of
   1. dividend and growth potential for an investor.
   2. return on investment. Include trends in earnings margin and asset turnover in your analysis.
b. Sales volume increased approximately 65 per cent over this period.
   1. How does this increase in sales volume compare with the number of employees? Discuss.
   2. How does this increase in sales volume compare with the total assets employed? Discuss.
c. What additional information would you require before making a decision to buy stock in this company? Discuss.

19-15. The predicted earnings after taxes of the Thompson Corporation are $300,000 annually. Compute an estimated price at which the company could be sold to yield rates of return to the purchaser of 6 per cent, 8 per cent, and 10 per cent, assuming

a. that the estimated earnings will continue indefinitely.
b. that the estimated earnings will continue for twenty years, at the end of which time the earnings will probably drop to zero.

19-16. In each case below, fill in the blanks:

Case	Sales	Net earnings	Total assets	Earnings as per cent of sales	Asset turnover	Rate of return on total assets (%)
1	$10,000	$ 700	$14,000	—	—	—
2	50,000	___	___	5	1.2	—
3	___	1,200	___	6	—	10
4	___	___	20,000	—	.9	8
5	40,000	___	30,000	6	—	—

19-17. In each case below compute rate of return before taxes on an investment:
a. from the point of view of the management.
b. from the point of view of the common stockholders.

Case	Assets	Liabilities	Earnings from operationsa	6% interest on liabilities	Net earnings	Return on investment (a) (b)
1	$150,000	$ 0	$30,000	$ 0	$30,000	
2	150,000	50,000	30,000	3,000	27,000	
3	150,000	100,000	8,000	6,000	2,000	

a Before interest and federal taxes.

19-18. Condensed financial statements of the PQR Company follow:

PQR COMPANY

CONDENSED COMPARATIVE STATEMENT OF FINANCIAL POSITION
As of December 31, 19x3, 19x4, and 19x5
(in millions of dollars)

Assets	19x5	19x4	19x3	Liabilities and Owners' Equity	19x5	19x4	19x3
				Liabilities:			
Current assets	$ 48	$ 45	$ 35	Current liabilities	$ 40	$ 30	$ 25
Investments	10	10	10	Long-term liabilities	50	55	45
Long-lived assets	107	105	95	Total liabilities	$ 90	$ 85	$ 70
				Owners' equity:			
				Capital stock:			
				Preferred	$ 20	$ 20	$ 20
				Common	50	50	40
				Retained earnings	5	5	10
				Total owners' equity	$ 75	$ 75	$ 70
				Total liabilities and			
Total assets	$165	$160	$140	owners' equity	$165	$160	$140

PQR COMPANY

CONDENSED COMPARATIVE STATEMENT OF EARNINGS
For Years Ended December 31, 19x3, 19x4, and 19x5
(in millions of dollars)

	19x5	19x4	19x3
Sales & other revenues	$200	$190	$185
— Operating expenses:			
Manufacturing, selling, & general expenses	$179	$169	$164
Depreciation & amortization	8	7	5
— Interest expense	3	3	3
— Federal, state, & local taxes	6	6	7
Total expenses	$196	$185	$179
Net earnings	$ 4	$ 5	$ 6

PQR COMPANY

COMPARATIVE STATEMENT OF RETAINED EARNINGS
For Years Ended December 31, 19x3, 19x4, and 19x5
(in millions of dollars)

	19x5	19x4	19x3
Retained earnings, 1/1	$5	$10	$ 8
+ Net earnings	4	5	6
Total available for dividends	$9	$15	$14

PQR COMPANY (CONT.)

	19x5	19x4	19x3
— Dividend payments:			
Preferred stock	$1	$ 1	$ 1
Common stock	3	3	3
— Correction of prior year's depreciation	0	6	0
Total deductions	$4	$10	$ 4
Retained earnings, 12/31	$5	$ 5	$10

PQR COMPANY

COMPARATIVE STATEMENT OF WORKING CAPITAL FLOWS
For Years Ended December 31, 19x3, 19x4, and 19x5
(in millions of dollars)

	19x5	19x4	19x3
Working capital provided from:			
Operations:			
Net earnings	$ 4	$ 5	$ 6
Depreciation & amortization	8	7	5
Total working capital from operations	$12	$12	$11
Loans from long-term creditors	0	10	5
Issue of common stock[a]	0	10	0
Total working capital provided	$12	$32	$16
— Working capital used for:			
Dividend payments	$ 4	$ 4	$ 4
Purchase of long-lived assets	10	23	10
Payment of long-term debt	5	0	0
Total working capital used	$19	$27	$14
Increase (decrease) in working capital	$ (7)	$ 5	$ 2

[a] Common shares outstanding as of December 31: 19x5, 500,000; 19x4, 500,000; 19x3, 400,000.

A few days after publication of the PQR report, the financial page of a local paper came out with the following article:

PQR Company has announced 19x5 earnings per share of $_____, compared with $_____ in 19x4 and $_____ in 19x3. 19x5 sales were $200 million, up _____ per cent from last year. Although earnings dropped slightly, cash flow per share amounted to $_____, compared with $_____ in 19x4 and $_____ in 19x3, not including a depreciation correction of $6 million in 19x4. This means that funds are more than adequate to cover the 6 per cent bond interest, a 5 per cent preferred dividend, and a $6 per share common dividend. Company officials predict that the additional depreciation recovery resulting from correcting depreciation rates in 19x4 will add at least $2 million per year to cash flow for several years to come. Funds made available from earnings and depreciation will be more than sufficient to provide financing for the increasing investment in plant required to maintain productive capacity, the high dividend, and the orderly program of debt retirement.

    a. Fill in the blanks in the article.

    b. Write a letter to the editor of the financial page regarding the PQR release, and clarify any misleading interpretations you believe it contains. What does the writer probably mean by "cash flow"?

    c. Rewrite the statement of working capital flows to correct the handling of depreciation.

19-19. Comparative statements of financial position and earnings statements of the AB Company and the XY Company are shown below. Both companies own

AB COMPANY AND XY COMPANY
CONDENSED STATEMENTS OF FINANCIAL POSITION
As of December 31, 19x5
(in thousands of dollars)

Assets			Liabilities and Owners' Equity		
	AB	*XY*		*AB*	*XY*
Current assets	$ 700	$ 450	Current liabilities	$ 50	$ 70
Long-lived assets:			Mortgage payable	500	2,000
Land	40	100	Capital stock (par		
Apartment build-			value, $100)	400	1,500
ing & equipment	2,400	3,900	Retained earnings	110	100
— Accumulated					
depreciation	(2,080)	(780)	Total liabilities &		
Total assets	$1,060	$3,670	owners' equity	$1,060	$3,670

AB COMPANY AND XY COMPANY
CONDENSED COMPARATIVE STATEMENTS OF EARNINGS
For Years Ended December 31, 19x4 and 19x5
(in thousands of dollars)

	19x5		*19x4*	
	AB	*XY*	*AB*	*XY*
Rental revenues	$250	$325	$250	$325
— Operating expenses:				
Salaries	$ 55	$ 55	$ 53	$ 51
Repairs & maintenance	24	16	22	15
Depreciation	80	130	80	130
— Interest expense	25	95	30	105
— Federal income taxes	30	7	29	5
Total expenses	$214	$303	$214	$306
Net earnings	$ 36	$ 22	$ 36	$ 19

and operate apartment houses of comparable size in the same neighborhood, although the building owned by AB was built in 1940 and the building owned by XY was built in 1960. (Hint: For purposes of this problem, it would be helpful for you to find out how inflation is usually measured and how much inflation we have had in the United States since 1940. See Chapter 16.)

    a. Compute (for both companies)

        1. the rate of return on investment from management's point of view.

        2. the rate of return on investment from the stockholders' point of view.

    b. Assume that the stocks of both of these companies have been recently traded on the market at fifteen times each company's earnings. Compute the approximate market prices of the stocks. From the evidence submitted, which would you prefer at these prices?

    c. How do you explain the fact that the mortgage on the AB building is higher than the book value of the building?

    d. Discuss the possible misleading conclusions in the interpretations of the rates of return figures computed in *a* above. What would be necessary to make the financial statements of the two companies comparable?

19-20. The Picadilly Corporation is a chain of men's clothing stores organized in 1953. About thirty stores were in operation during the 1950's, and this number was expanded to forty stores in 1967 and to forty-five stores in 1971. Most sales are on regular thirty-day charge accounts, but charge customers are carefully screened because the merchandise is low priced and appeals to low-income purchasers. A comparative statement of financial position and a comparative statement of earnings and retained earnings for the Picadilly Corporation for 1968–71 are as follows:

PICADILLY CORPORATION

COMPARATIVE STATEMENT OF FINANCIAL POSITION
As of December 31, 1968–71
(in thousands of dollars)

	1971	1970	1969	1968
Assets				
Current assets:				
Cash	$ 8,500	$ 7,000	$ 6,000	$ 3,500
Accounts receivable	20,000	15,000	14,000	12,000
Inventories (FIFO cost)	50,000	35,000	28,000	22,000
Total current assets	$ 78,500	$57,000	$48,000	$37,500
Buildings & equipment	$ 60,000	$50,000	$30,000	$30,000
− Accumulated depreciation	12,000	10,000	9,000	8,000
Buildings & equipment (net)	$ 48,000	$40,000	$21,000	$22,000
Total assets	$126,500	$97,000	$69,000	$59,500

PICADILLY CORPORATION (CONT.)

	1971	1970	1969	1968
Liabilities and Owners' Equity				
Liabilities:				
Current liabilities:				
Accounts payable (for merchandise)	$ 10,000	$ 8,000	$ 7,000	$ 4,500
Notes payable (bank)	3,000	2,000	1,000	0
Federal income taxes payable	7,000	6,500	6,000	5,000
Total current liabilities	$ 20,000	$16,500	$14,000	$ 9,500
Bonds payable (due 10 years after issue)	40,000	20,000	0	0
Total liabilities	$ 60,000	$36,500	$14,000	$ 9,500
Owners' equity:				
Capital stock (1 million shares)	$ 25,000	$25,000	$25,000	$25,000
Retained earnings	41,500	35,500	30,000	25,000
Total owners' equity	$ 66,500	$60,500	$55,000	$50,000
Total liabilities and owners' equity	$126,500	$97,000	$69,000	$59,500

PICADILLY CORPORATION

COMPARATIVE COMBINED STATEMENT OF EARNINGS AND RETAINED EARNINGS

For Years Ended December 31, 1969, 1970, and 1971
(in thousands of dollars)

	1971	1970	1969
Sales revenues	$100,000	$90,000	$70,000
— Cost of goods sold	60,000	52,000	38,000
Earnings margin	$ 40,000	$38,000	$32,000
— Operating expenses:			
Selling expenses	$ 11,000	$11,000	$10,000
Administrative expenses[a]	13,000	13,000	10,000
Total operating expenses	$ 24,000	$24,000	$20,000
Earnings from operations	$ 16,000	$14,000	$12,000

[a] The figures for administrative expenses include small amounts of interest on the bank notes and $1,000 depreciation in 1969, $1,000 depreciation in 1970, and $2,000 depreciation in 1971.

PICADILLY CORPORATION (CONT.)

	1971	1970	1969
— Bond interest expense	2,000	1,000	0
Earnings before taxes	$ 14,000	$13,000	$12,000
— Federal income taxes	7,000	6,500	6,000
Net earnings	$ 7,000	$ 6,500	$ 6,000
+ Retained earnings, 1/1	35,500	30,000	25,000
Total available for dividends	$ 42,500	$36,500	$31,000
— Dividend payments	1,000	1,000	1,000
Retained earnings, 12/31	$ 41,500	$35,500	$30,000

a. Prepare a comparative statement of cash receipts and disbursements.

b. Assume that you are the investment manager of a large insurance company, and that the Picadilly president comes to you with plans to expand to a total of sixty stores by 1973. It is estimated that this will require $30 million, and the Picadilly president asks you if your company would be interested in providing the money in exchange for either of the following: (1) $30 million in 7 per cent Picadilly bonds, to mature in ten years from the date of issue. $40 million of similar bonds are already held by other investors (see financial position statement). (2) 500,000 shares of common stock at $60 per share. The one million shares currently outstanding were issued for $25 per share when the company was organized. Dividends of $1 per share per year have been maintained since that time, but profits well in excess of the dividend have been earned and reinvested in the business, so that retained earnings per share are over $40 (see financial position statement), making the book value per share more than $65 ($66.50, to be exact).

> 1. Do you believe investment in Picadilly's expansion is desirable from the standpoint of the insurance company? Support your conclusions by a careful analysis of the financial statements. (Don't forget to use the cash receipts and disbursements statement.)
> 2. If the decision to invest in this expansion has already been made, which would be the better buy for the insurance company—the bond issue or the stock issue?

c. Is the decision to expand a wise decision from the standpoint of the management?

d. If the decision to expand has been made, which is the better way to raise money from Picadilly's standpoint—stocks or bonds?

19-21. Financial statements for the Zippo Company for 19x5, 19x4, and 19x3 are presented below.

ZIPPO COMPANY

COMPARATIVE STATEMENT OF FINANCIAL POSITION
As of December 31, 19x3, 19x4, and 19x5
(in thousands of dollars)

	19x5	19x4	19x3
Assets			
Current assets:			
Cash	$ 90	$ 150	$ 125
Short-term investments (lower of cost or market)	0	0	90
Accounts receivable (net)	240	210	160
Inventories (LIFO cost)	470	385	235
Prepaid expenses	50	40	30
Total current assets	$ 850	$ 785	$ 640
Investments:			
Cash surrender value of life insurance policy on company president	$ 60	$ 50	$ 40
Investment of 80% of outstanding stock of subsidiary (cost)	80	80	80
Total investments	$ 140	$ 130	$ 120
Long-lived assets (cost):			
Land	$ 60	$ 60	$ 60
Buildings (net)	300	265	270
Machinery & equipment (net)	225	235	180
Patents (net)	30	35	40
Deferred research & development costs (net)	165	170	130
Total long-lived assets	$ 780	$ 765	$ 680
Total assets	$1,770	$1,680	$1,440
Liabilities and Owners' Equity			
Liabilities:			
Current liabilities:			
Accounts payable	$ 185	$ 150	$ 115
Notes payable (6%)	120	120	80
Accrued interest payable	15	15	14
Sales revenues received in advance	0	0	40
Federal income taxes payable	90	80	65
Total current liabilities	$ 410	$ 365	$ 314
Long-term liabilities:			
Bonds payable (6%, due 1/1/91; par value, $400)	$ 493	$ 497	$ 501
Deferred federal income taxes payable	70	88	60
Total long-term liabilities	$ 563	$ 585	$ 561
Total liabilities	$ 973	$ 950	$ 875

ZIPPO COMPANY (CONT.)

	19x5	19x4	19x3
Owners' equity:			
Common stock (par value $20; authorized 20,000 shares)	$ 240	$ 240	$ 200
Proceeds in excess of par value from sale of common stock	200	200	140
Retained earnings	357	290	225
Total owners' equity	$ 797	$ 730	$ 565
Total liabilities and owners' equity	$1,770	$1,680	$1,440

ZIPPO COMPANY

COMPARATIVE STATEMENT OF EARNINGS

For Years Ended December 31, 19x4 and 19x5

(in thousands of dollars)

	19x5	19x4
Net sales revenues	$2,050	$1,800
— Cost of goods sold	1,420	1,239
Earnings margin	$ 630	$ 561
— Operating expenses	410	370
Earnings from operations	$ 220	$ 191
— Interest expense	29	26
Earnings before taxes	$ 191	$ 165
— Provision for federal income taxes	75	60
Net earnings	$ 116	$ 105

ZIPPO COMPANY

COMPARATIVE STATEMENT OF RETAINED EARNINGS

For Years Ended December 31, 19x4 and 19x5

(in thousands of dollars)

	19x5	19x4
Retained earnings, 1/1	$290	$225
+ Net earnings for year (per statement of earnings)	116	105
Gain on sale of equipment	25	0
Total available for dividend payments	$431	$330
— Loss on sale of securities	$ 0	$ 10
Fire loss	20	0
Dividend payments	54	30
Total	$ 74	$ 40
Retained earnings, 12/31	$357	$290

Choose the most appropriate alternative for the following statements:*

a. The proceeds from the sale of short-term investments in 19x4 were as follows: (1) $90; (2) $80; (3) $100; (4) $200; (5) some other amount.

b. The valuation of short-term investments at lower of cost or market is a generally accepted accounting principle. The rationale underlying this accounting principle is (1) that it is more objective than other methods of asset valuation; (2) that it provides for losses but does not anticipate gains; (3) that the equity method cannot be computed for these types of investments; (4) none of these.

c. Accounts receivable (net) as of December 31, 19x4, means (1) that credit losses pertaining to 19x4 sales have been deducted from accounts receivable in the statement of financial position; (2) that estimated credit losses pertaining to all items in accounts receivable on the statement of financial position have been deducted; (3) that not all accounts receivable have been recorded in the accounts; (4) that depreciation has been provided for; (5) none of these.

d. Inventories at LIFO cost means (1) that declines in the market value of the inventory have been provided for; (2) that the specific-identification method of cost determination has been used; (3) that the inventory probably consists of coal or iron ore; (4) that the inventory cost was arrived at by assuming that the last items purchased were the first items sold; (5) none of these.

e. If you were comparing the financial statements of the Zippo Company with one of its competitors (both companies operating in the U.S.) that valued its inventory at FIFO cost you would expect (1) that the cost of goods sold would be about the same percentage of net sales for both companies; (2) that the competitor had better merchandising policies than the Zippo Company; (3) that the cost of goods sold percentage would probably be higher for the competitor than the Zippo Company; (4) none of these.

f. The LCM method of inventory valuation is generally accepted. In the past twenty-five years a company operating in the United States would probably have greater differences between cost and lower of cost or market if it arrived at inventory cost by one of the following methods: (1) specific identification; (2) FIFO; (3) average; (4) LIFO; (5) none of these.

g. The Zippo Company paid premiums amounting to $45 on the life insurance policy of the company president for the calendar year 19x4. Therefore, the insurance expense in the statement of earnings resulting from this premium payment would be as follows: (1) $45, (2) $55, (3) $35, (4) $40, (5) none of these.

h. The investment in stock of the subsidiary was purchased on January 1, 19w6. Between that time and December 31, 19x5, the company had total earnings of $70 and paid dividends totaling $40. If the Zippo Company had valued this investment using the equity method since 19w6, the asset value on December 31, 19x5, would be as follows: (1) $110; (2) $116; (3) $104; (4) $136; (5) $80; (6) none of these.

---

* All figures are in thousands of dollars.

i. The acquisition cost of long-lived assets includes all costs necessary to bring an asset to a condition in which it is usable for the purpose intended. The cost (or cost minus depreciation or amortization) method of valuation for these assets is justified primarily (1) because it is conservative; (2) because it is usually less than the market value of these assets; (3) because it generally reflects the resale value of these assets; (4) because these assets are generally purchased for use in the business and are not intended for resale; (5) by none of these.

j. Zippo Company uses the straight-line method of depreciation in computing earnings. If a competing company uses an accelerated method of depreciation (declining balance or sum of the years' digits), you would expect the reported earnings of Zippo Company to be (1) lower than the competitor; (2) about the same as the competitor; (3) none of these.

k. The book value of equipment sold in 19x5 was $80. Therefore, the proceeds from the sale of this equipment were (1) $80; (2) $105; (3) $55; (4) $10; (5) none of these.

l. The category "deferred research and development costs" indicates (1) that certain research and development projects will be undertaken in the future; (2) that the company anticipates that future benefits will be derived from these expenditures; (3) none of these.

m. The 6 per cent note payable at December 31, 19x5 (1) will probably mature before December 31, 19x6; (2) will probably mature sometime after December 31, 19x6; (3) is neither of these.

n. The category "sales revenues received in advance" indicates (1) that the company has a liability to some of its customers for product guarantees; (2) that the sales for the period are greater than expected; (3) that customers whose accounts were originally considered to be worthless have paid their accounts; (4) that the company has an obligation to some of its customers to render a service or deliver a product in the future; (5) none of these.

o. The bonds payable were issued to yield 4 per cent. The bond-interest expense reported in the statement of earnings for 19x5 would be (1) approximately $24; (2) approximately $30; (3) approximately $15; (4) approximately $20; (5) none of these.

p. The deferred federal income taxes probably resulted from (1) reporting a larger tax provision on the financial statements than on the tax return; (2) reporting a smaller tax provision on the financial statements than on the tax return; (3) provision on the financial statements for contingent federal income taxes resulting from Internal Revenue Service examinations; (4) a special arrangement with the Internal Revenue Service to pay a portion of the current taxes at a later time; (5) none of these.

q. The stockholders received the following dividends per share in 19x5: (1) $2.70; (2) $20; (3) $4.50; (4) $5.40; (5) $1.50; (6) $3; (7) none of these.

r. The indicated proceeds from the issuance of common stock as of December 31, 19x5, were (1) $240; (2) $40; (3) $440; (4) $797; (5) none of these.

s. Zippo Company reports earnings on (1) the normal-operating concept; (2) the all-inclusive earnings statement concept; (3) the going-concern concept; (4) the entity concept; (5) none of these.

19-22. Use the comparative financial statements of Canyon Lake Enterprises, Inc., in problem 18–24, for the following analysis:

    a. Compute the rate of return before taxes on investment

        1. from the point of view of the management.

        2. from the point of view of the common stockholder.

    b. Assume that the predicted earnings after taxes of Canyon Lake Enterprises are $30,000 annually. Compute an estimated purchase price for the company at a rate of return of 6 per cent, assuming that the estimated earnings will continue indefinitely. Is goodwill indicated in the computed purchase price? Explain.

THE BOOK IN RETROSPECT

This book has covered the fundamentals of two accounting subjects—the uses of accounting data by managers (Part II) and the uses of accounting data by nonmanagers (Parts III and IV)—as well as the background common to both subjects (Part I). This organization of the book is based on the premise that the differences between the two subjects are more important than the similarities and, therefore, that the two should be dealt with separately. Part I, while it introduces basic concepts and terminology and describes a system that provides information required for both managerial and nonmanagerial uses, does not attempt to define or circumscribe the accounting system in either the managerial or nonmanagerial areas.

The approach to management accounting in Part II is based on the assumptions that the objectives of managers in using accounting data are known and consistent with the objectives of the firm. Managers may wish to evaluate the performance of a person or of a division of a firm over a given period in relation to certain objectives (Chapters 4 through 8); or they may wish to plan activities (Chapter 9) or foresee the consequences of alternative decisions (Chapters 10 and 11). The accountant has to ascertain the information needed by these managers, supply it in usable form, and make sure that its uses and limitations are understood.

The assumptions underlying the use of accounting information by nonmanagers make this subject (usually referred to as financial accounting) much more difficult for students and researchers. There are many classes of nonmanagerial users, and sometimes their objectives are not clearly known. Even when they *are*, they may be inconsistent with, or contrary to, the objectives of the firm. In these cases, by supplying the nonmanagerial user with the accounting information he requires, the accountant can be acting against the best interests of the reporting firm. Hence, in supplying accounting information for nonmanagerial uses, it is not possible for the accountant to be guided solely by the needs of the user.

It is for this reason that the financial accounting section of the book has two Parts—III and IV. Part III defines financial accounting information as that dealing with financial position, earnings, and fund flows (Chapters 12 and 13). It also describes the measurement methods accountants use when reporting assets, liabilities, and equities in financial position statements, and periodic changes in these items in earnings and fund flows statements (Chapters 14 through 16). Since the relevance of the information to the objectives of nonmanagerial users will not always be clear, about all the accountant can do is report as much information (of assumed importance) as possible, consistent with the objectives of the reporting firm, and make sure that the uses and limitations of the information are understood.

Part IV (the second part of the financial accounting section) returns the reader to the points of view of various nonmanagerial users of financial information and describes the uses they normally make of the information contained in financial position statements, earnings statements, and fund flows statements. Governmental regulatory users (actually a special case, since these users specify the information to be reported) are covered in Chapter 17. Chapters 18 and 19 deal with creditors' and owners' uses, respectively, describing the techniques of these users in financial statement analysis—their methods for establishing relationships between the financial information provided and the decisions and judgments they must make based on this information.

GLOSSARY

This glossary is intended as a teaching device rather than as a definitive reference. Simplicity rather than precision has been the guiding criterion in defining terms, and definitions conform to the contexts in which the terms are used in this book.

Absorption costing. A method of product costing in which all production costs, variable or not, are classified as product costs, are identified with units of inventory, and are therefore subject to division between the asset inventory and the expense cost of goods sold at the end of a period.

Accomplishment. The measured output or activity—such as units of product of an individual or machine, labor hours of a service department, or sales dollars of a firm—of the earnings center or cost center being accounted for.

Accounting equation. The equation:

$$\text{Assets} = \text{Liabilities} + \text{Owners' equity.}$$

When used for analyzing business transaction, all the terms of the equation, but particularly owners' equity, may be broken down into many subdivisions. *Synonyms:* balance-sheet equation, bookkeeping equation.

Accounts receivable turnover. A measure of accounts receivable liquidity, expressed as net sales divided by average accounts receivable for the period.

Accumulated depreciation. That portion of asset cost used up (charged as an expense) in prior accounting periods and shown as a reduction in tangible long-lived asset cost on the statement of financial position. *Synonyms:* accrued depreciation, allowance for depreciation, depreciation to date, reserve for depreciation.

Activity unit. A unit used to express accomplishment and predicted changes in costs in cases in which revenues or units of production may not be used.

Administrative expense. An operating expense associated with the administrative function. *Synonym:* general expense.

Aging schedule. A schedule classifying accounts receivable according to the age of the unpaid balances.

All-inclusive earnings statement concept. The concept that earnings include all non-recurring and extraordinary items of gain or loss. A statement of earnings with this as a basis will reflect all current changes in retained earnings except dividends. *Synonym:* clean-surplus concept.

Allocated cost. An indirect cost assigned to a unit of product or activity or to a department.

Allowance for uncollectable accounts. An estimate (as of the statement date) indicated on the statement of financial position of the amount of accounts receivable that will be uncollectable. *Synonyms:* allowance for bad debts, estimated uncollectables, reserve for bad debts.

Amortization. The process of allocating the cost of assets, particularly intangible assets, to expense or to product. For tangible long-lived assets the term "depreciation" is preferred.

Asset. Any item of value to the firm that is available for current or future use and is measurable in monetary terms. *Synonym:* resources.

Asset turnover ratio. A measure of asset utilization, expressed as net sales divided by average investment in assets over the period.

Attainable standard. A standard that can be attained under existing operating conditions.

Auditor's opinion. A report issued by a Certified Public Accountant to accompany financial statements that he has examined. The report attests to the fairness of the financial statements in depicting the actual financial condition and operations of the company in accordance with generally accepted accounting principles consistently applied with preceding years. *Synonym:* short-form audit report.

Authorized shares. The shares of stock that a corporate charter specifies may legally be issued.

Average costing of inventory. A method of arriving at inventory cost in which the weighted average of the cost of the beginning inventory and all acquisitions is used to compute the cost of the ending inventory and the cost of goods sold.

Bonds. Written promises by a borrower to repay lenders.

Bonds payable. The liability that arises when bonds are issued (sold).

Book value. (1) The value of shares derived from the statement of financial position; owners' equity divided by outstanding shares. (2) The value of an asset as shown on the statement of financial position.

Bookkeeping system. The methods employed to record and process transactions and other accounting events that are reflected in accounting reports.

Breakeven chart. A graph showing the breakeven relationship between revenues, variable expenses, and nonvariable expenses at varying volumes of output.

Budget. A formal financial plan for all or part of the operations of a firm for a specific future period that expresses corporate objectives in financial terms and controls operations.

Budgeted cost. Any cost included in a budget.

Capitalized earnings. An assessment of a firm's worth determined by dividing estimated earnings of a business by a specified rate of return.

Cash discount. A discount granted to a purchaser for early payment. For example, a 2 per cent discount from invoice cost might be granted if payment were made within ten days of an invoice date, with the full invoice price due within thirty days otherwise. This would be expressed as "2/10, n/30."

Closely held company. A company in which a small number of stockholders own most of the shares.

Collateral. Assets pledged as security for amounts borrowed. *Synonym:* mortgaged assets.

Common dollar. A dollar of a specified purchasing power; a "historical" dollar that has been adjusted by means of an index relating prices prevailing at different periods of time.

Common stockholder. A stockholder who owns the residual interest (that subordinate to all other debt and stock interests) in a corporation. *Synonym:* common shareowner.

Comparative financial statement. A statement that includes information from both previous accounting periods and the current accounting period. *Synonym:* comparative report.

Conservatism. A tendency in financial reporting to understate assets and overstate liabilities in relation to their most likely values. An accountant with this approach attempts to anticipate no gains and to provide for all losses.

Consolidated accounting report. A financial statement that combines results of operations and the financial position of a parent company and one or more subsidiaries.

Consumers' Price Index. An index published by the Bureau of Labor Statistics sometimes used to measure the change in the purchasing power of the United States dollar.

Contingent liability. A liability the existence of which is uncertain because it depends upon some future event, such as the outcome of pending lawsuits or future performance under a contract.

Contribution margin. The excess of sales revenues over variable expenses; the amount available to cover nonvariable expenses and earnings.

Controllable expense. An expense controllable by the organizational unit during the time period under examination.

Copyright. The exclusive right given by the federal government to reproduce or sell a literary or other artistic work.

Cost. An outlay measured in assets given up (and/or liabilities assumed) in order to acquire another asset. All costs are assets until consumed in the production of revenues, at which time they become expenses.

Cost-behavior pattern. A pattern of variation in cost resulting from changes in activity.

Cost of goods sold. The cost to the seller of inventory sold, measured by the total purchase cost (to a retailing or wholesaling firm) or the total manufacturing cost (to a manufacturing firm).

Credit losses. The amount of sales in the current period estimated to be uncollectable and shown as an operating expense deducted from the earnings margin on the statement of earnings. *Synonyms:* bad-debts expense, defaulted customers' accounts, losses from uncollectables.

Cumulative preferred stock. Preferred stock that gives the owner a dividend preference for undeclared dividends of the current and prior years before common stockholders can be paid a dividend in the current year.

Current asset. Cash or any other asset that will normally be converted into cash or sold or consumed during the next year or the next operating cycle, whichever is longer.

Current liability. A debt that will become due within the next year or the next operating cycle and/or that is expected to be paid with current assets. *Synonym:* Short-term liability.

Current ratio. A measure of liquidity obtained by dividing current assets by current liabilities.

Cutoff rate of return. The minimum time-adjusted rate of return that is acceptable to management.

Declining depreciation pattern. A pattern of depreciating assets that allocates a greater amount of cost to earlier accounting periods of use. Two common methods of calculating a declining pattern of depreciation are the double-declining-balance method and the sum-of-the-years'-digits method.

Deferred advertising costs. An asset that represents advertising costs incurred in the past that are expected to benefit future accounting periods.

Deferred research and development costs. An asset that represents costs incurred for research and development that are expected to benefit future accounting periods.

Depreciable cost. The portion of long-lived asset cost that is subject to depreciation, computed as acquisition cost minus estimated resale value.

Depreciation. The reductions in usability of a tangible long-lived asset over time, caused either by wear and tear or obsolescence.

Depreciation expense. The cost of tangible long-lived assets periodically allocated to operating expenses or to product cost.

Differential cost. The difference in cost that results from selecting an alternative course of operation. *Synonyms:* incremental cost, marginal cost, relevant cost.

Direct cost. A cost that can be identified with a product, service, or department; a cost that would not be incurred if the product, service, or department were not in existence.

Earnings. The excess of revenues over expenses (that is, the increase in net assets from operations) during a specified period. *Synonyms:* income, net earnings, net income.

Earnings center. A business firm, or unit within a business firm, whose management has the responsibility for optimizing the earnings of the firm or unit—that is, for bringing in revenues and incurring expenses.

Earnings from operations. Net sales minus cost of goods sold and operating expenses, reflecting the firm's performance from its principal business activities. *Synonyms:* net earnings from operations, net operating income.

Earnings margin. Net sales less cost of goods sold. *Synonym:* gross margin.

Earnings per share. Earnings divided by number of shares of stock outstanding.

Effort. The cost incurred in achieving output or accomplishment.

Equities. The various items of liabilities and owners' interests comprising the half of the accounting equation equal to assets. Often stated as those items comprising the sources of assets or representing claims against the assets.

Estimated liability. A liability that is assigned an estimated amount because its true amount is unknown.

Expense. The sacrifice or consumption of net assets in the process of earning revenues.

Federal income tax expense. The tax attributable to the periodic net earnings of a corporation. *Synonym:* provision for federal income taxes.

First-in, first-out (FIFO) costing of inventory. A method of computing the cost of the ending inventory and the cost of goods sold in which the beginning inventory and the first items acquired are assumed to be the first items sold.

Fixed budget. A budget based on a predicted output level and not adjusted for the differences between predicted and actual output.

Flexible budget. A budget that is adjusted to the actual level of output as soon as it is known, in order to compare budgeted costs with actual costs for cost control purposes. *Synonym:* variable budget.

Freight-out. A selling expense measured by the costs associated with the delivery of goods to customers. *Synonyms:* delivery expense, transportation out.

GNP Implicit Price Deflator. A price level index used to state GNP (Gross National Product) in common dollar terms. Often used as a measure of changes in purchasing power of the United States dollar.

Going-concern assumption. The assumption that a business firm will continue to exist indefinitely.

Goodwill. A long-lived intangible asset, evidenced by anticipated earnings in excess of a normal rate of return on assets other than goodwill.

Gross margin. The excess of net sales over the cost of goods sold. *Synonyms:* gross profit, margin, earnings margin.

Gross sales. The total selling price of all goods (or services) sold, without deduction for returns, allowances, or discounts.

Historical dollar. A dollar in which a transaction was expressed at the time it took place, without adjustment for subsequent changes either in the value of the item involved or in the purchasing power of the dollar.

Ideal standard. A standard based on the best possible operating conditions, whether or not these conditions exist or are feasible in a particular situation. *Synonym:* perfection standard.

Indirect cost. A cost that cannot be identified with a product, service, or department except by arbitrary allocation; a cost that would continue even if the product, service, or department were discontinued.

Inflation. A reduction in the purchasing power of the dollar, usually measured by changes in the Consumers' Price Index or the GNP (Gross National Product) Implicit Price Deflator.

Intangible long-lived asset. A legal right, privilege, or competitive advantage that is expected to benefit future operations beyond one year. *Synonyms:* deferred charge, intangible fixed asset.

Intermediate-term creditor. A creditor who expects to be repaid within one to five years. Debts to these creditors are shown on the statement of financial position under long-term liabilities.

Inventory turnover. A measure of inventory liquidity (that is, the rate at which inventory is sold) expressed as cost of goods sold divided by average inventory for the period.

Investment. An asset not directly associated with the principal business purpose of the firm and therefore not properly classified as a current or long-lived asset. *Synonyms:* nonoperating asset, other asset, permanent investment, sundry asset.

Issued shares. The number of authorized shares of stock that have been issued to stockholders.

Last-in, first-out (LIFO) costing of inventory. A method of computing the cost of the ending inventory and the cost of goods sold in which the last items purchased are assumed to be the first items sold or used.

Leasehold improvement. A long-lived intangible asset of a lessor, measured by the cost incurred for improvements in leased property.

Leverage. The practice of investing borrowed funds instead of owners' funds, so that if earnings on the investment exceed the cost of borrowing, earnings to the owners are increased by the amount of the excess. *Synonym:* trading on the equity.

Liability. A commitment to make a future payment arising out of a past transaction.

Long-lived asset. An asset having a useful life longer than one year or one operating cycle, not intended for resale, and used in the operations of the business. *Synonyms:* long-term asset, tangible and intangible fixed asset.

Long-term creditor. A creditor who expects to be repaid at a time more than five years in the future. Debts to these creditors appear on the statement of financial position under long-term liabilities.

Long-term-debt/owners'-equity ratio. A measure of enterprise stability computed by dividing long-term liabilities by owners' equity.

Long-term liability. A debt that will not become due within one year or one operating cycle. *Synonyms:* fixed liability, long-term debt, noncurrent liability.

Loss. (1) The negative of periodic earnings. (2) The negative profit (or gain) on a single transaction. (3) The disappearance or consumption of an asset without corresponding revenue or accomplishment. *Synonym:* net loss.

Lower of cost or market (LCM). A method of valuing inventory and short-term investments for financial reporting purposes at either cost or market value (usually replacement cost), depending on which is lower. The LCM valuation method may be applied to each item, to subgroups of items, or to the total of all items in the category.

Management by exception. The management practice of investigating only significant variations in actual performance (or exceptions) from a predetermined standard.

Marginal cost. The cost related to one course of action instead of its alternative. *Synonym:* differential cost, incremental cost, relevant cost.

Material amount. An amount that, if not properly disclosed in the financial statements, would alter the decisions of users of the financial statements or cause them to be misled in some important respect.

Monetary asset. Any asset that is usually not income producing, such as cash, short-term bonds, or other receivables that are measured by the amount of cash realizable from them.

Mortgage note payable. Written evidence of a debt for which certain of the borrower's assets, usually real estate, have been pledged.

Net assets. The excess of a firm's assets over its liabilities. *Synonym:* owners' equity.

Net sales revenues. The excess of gross sales revenues over the sum of sales returns, sales allowances, and sales discounts.

No-par value stock. Shares of stock that do not have a par value. Such shares may or may not have a "stated" value.

Nonmonetary asset. An asset such as merchandise, a prepaid expense, a long-lived asset, or an investment asset that is measured by the amount of incurred cost remaining in the asset after allowing for consumption and loss.

Nonoperating item. An expense or revenue item (including a nonrecurring gain or loss) not directly associated with a firm's principal business activities or with the particular year in which it is reported.

Nonvariable cost. A cost item that does not increase with an increase in volume of output or activity. *Synonyms:* constant cost, fixed cost.

Normal-operating earnings concept. The concept that excludes from earnings material, extraordinary, and nonrecurring items of gain or loss. These items are reported in the statement of retained earnings so that the statement of earnings reflects only the results of current operation. *Synonyms:* current-operating concept, current-operating performance concept.

Note payable. A liability evidenced by a written promise to pay called a promissory note.

Obsolescence. The decline in the value of an asset caused by decreased usefulness due to technological factors or to a decline in demand for the product of the asset.

Operating cycle. The average length of time required to invest cash in inventory (or materials and labor), convert the inventory to accounts receivable, and convert the accounts receivable to cash.

Operating expenses. Selling and administrative expenses.

Organizational cost. A cost, such as legal fees, usually interpreted as an intangible long-lived asset, associated with the formal organization of a company.

Outstanding shares. The number of shares of stock currently held by shareholders, computed by deducting treasury shares from issued shares.

Owners' equity. The amount invested by owners in a firm's total assets either as an initial investment or through earnings retained in the business, computed as the excess of total assets over total liabilities. *Synonyms:* net assets, net worth, partners' equity, proprietorship, stockholders' equity.

Par value of bonds. The maturity value of bonds that is used as a basis for quoting bond prices (for example, "98 per cent of $1,000 par value") and calculating periodic interest payments. *Synonyms:* face value, redemption value at maturity.

Par-value stock. A legally authorized per-share value for stock.

Participating preferred stock. Preferred stock that shares in any dividends paid on common stock above a stated rate.

Patent. A seventeen-year monopoly granted by the federal government to an inventor, giving him the exclusive right to sell, use, or make his invention.

Payback period. The time required to recover cash in the amount of the net investment of a capital budgeting proposal.

Period cost. A cost that is not related solely to current production and is treated as an expense of the period to which it is allocated.

Preferred stockholder. A stockholder whose ownership interest includes a special privilege, such as preference over common stockholders for dividends or for assets in liquidation.

Prepaid expense. An incurred cost other than an inventory or long-lived asset cost that will become an operating expense in the near future.

Present value. The current value of amounts of money to be received in the future, calculated by discounting the future amounts (at an acceptable discount rate) to the present.

Price-earnings ratio. A ratio—the market price of the stock divided by expected earnings per share—used as a basis for comparing stock prices.

Price level change. A fluctuation in the purchasing power of the dollar in the form of inflation or deflation, usually measured by changes in either the Consumers' Price Index or the GNP Implicit Price Deflator.

Price variance. The portion of the total variance from standard cost that is attributable to the difference between actual and standard unit prices, calculated according to the formula: (Actual price − Standard price) × Actual quantity.

Principal. The amount borrowed or loaned in connection with notes or bonds receivable or payable.

Product cost. A cost related to a product and reported as an asset (inventory) until the revenue is recognized by sale of the inventory.

Production-basis depreciation pattern. A method of depreciating assets according to the units produced by an asset during the accounting period, so that the amount of depreciation expense is proportional to periodic production.

Profit. The increase in assets or decrease in liabilities, measured by the excess of revenues over expenses that results from a transaction of the firm with outsiders (other than owners). *Synonym:* gain.

Profitability index. A ratio computed as present value of after-tax dollar advantages divided by net investment, used to evaluate and rank budgeted proposals for capital expenditures in relation to a cutoff rate of return.

Prospectus. A document made available to parties interested in purchasing securities and containing financial and other information pertinent to the securities.

Proxy. An authorization to vote the shares of stockholders who do not attend a stockholders' meeting.

Publicly held company. A company owned by many stockholders; its shares may be traded on one or more stock exchanges.

Purchase discount. A reduction in purchase price granted by the seller at the time of payment to encourage prompt payment of invoices.

Quantity variance. The portion of the total variance from standard cost attributable to the difference between actual and standard quantities used, calculated according to the formula: (Actual quantity − Standard quantity) × Standard price. *Synonym:* usage variance.

Quick ratio. A measure of short-run liquidity obtained by dividing the sum of cash, temporary investments, and accounts receivable by current liabilities.

Rate of return on investment. A measure of performance computed as earnings per period divided by average investment in assets over the period.

Registration statement. A statement filed with the Securities and Exchange Commission for the purpose of obtaining approval to offer securities for sale to the public.

Relevant cost. A cost relevant to the specific alternatives or issues under consideration. *Synonyms:* differential cost, incremental cost, marginal cost.

Resale value. The estimated salvage value of a long-lived asset at the end of its service life. *Synonyms:* salvage value, scrap value.

Revenue. An increase in a firm's net assets; a measure of accomplishment computed as assets received and/or liabilities discharged in the process of selling goods to customers, providing services to customers or clients, or earning dividends, interest, rent, etc.

Revenue received in advance. The liability that arises when a customer advances cash or other assets in anticipation of a sale to be made or a service to be rendered. The liability becomes revenue when the sale is made or the service rendered.

Sales allowance. A reduction in the sales price of sales previously made because of damage, market changes, etc.

Sales discount. A reduction in the sales price granted at the time of payment to customers who purchase on account. Its purpose is to encourage prompt payment.

Sales return. The cancellation of a sale because of the return of merchandise to the seller by a customer.

Selling expense. An expense associated with the selling function of the firm, such as an outlay for sales salaries or supplies, advertising, deliveries, or market research.

Semiconstant cost. A cost that varies proportionally to volume of activity (output), but in discrete steps rather than in a continuous pattern.

Semivariable cost. A cost including both a nonvariable element (bearing no relationship to volume of activity or output) and a variable element (varying proportionally to volume of activity or output).

Short-term creditor. A creditor who expects to be repaid within one year or within one average operating cycle of the debtor, whichever is longer. Debts that are owed to these creditors are shown on the statement of financial position under current liabilities.

Short-term investment. An investment utilizing temporarily excessive cash balances; securities that management intends to convert to cash within the next operating cycle. *Synonyms:* marketable securities, temporary investment.

Standard. A predetermined measure, usually expressed in units of material or labor, of activity or effort under specified operating conditions.

Standard cost. A predetermination of what a cost should be under specified operating conditions.

Statement of cash receipts and disbursements. A financial statement showing the sources and uses of cash for a specific period. *Synonym:* statement of cash flows.

Statement of earnings. A financial statement showing the revenues earned and the expenses incurred by the enterprise for a specified period. *Synonyms:* income statement, profit-and-loss statement, statement of operations.

Statement of financial position. A financial statement showing enterprise assets and its sources at a specified time. Sources of assets, sometimes preferably thought of as *claims* against the assets, are liabilities and owners' equity. *Synonyms:* balance sheet, statement of financial condition, statement of resources.

Statement of fund flows. A financial statement reflecting sources and uses of funds for a specific period. Funds are usually defined as working capital (current assets minus current liabilities), but occasionally also as cash, cash and short-term investments, total current assets, and even total assets.

Statement of retained earnings. A financial statement that reflects changes in retained earnings for a period and forms the connecting link between the statement of earnings and the statement of financial position. *Synonyms:* statement of earned surplus, statement of reinvested earnings, statement of retained income.

Statement of working capital flows. A financial statement reflecting sources and uses of working capital (current assets minus current liabilities) for a period. *Synonyms:* statement of fund flows, statement of net working capital flows.

Stock dividend. The issuance of additional shares of stock to existing stockholders by a corporation that receives nothing in return. As a result, the same owners' equity is represented by a larger number of shares after the dividend. Retained earnings are transferred to capital stock on the statement of financial position.

Stock split. An issuance of stock similar to a stock dividend except that the old shares are usually called in and a larger number of new shares are issued to existing stockholders. The intended effect is to reduce the market value per share, increase the marketability of the shares, and thus increase the market value of the total shares outstanding.

Straight-line depreciation pattern. A method of depreciating assets that allocates the same amount of cost to each complete accounting period of use.

Sunk cost. A cost associated with present assets that was incurred in the past and is therefore irrelevant to a contemplated decision regarding the sale or other disposition of the assets.

Tangible long-lived asset. An asset that (1) has a service life longer than one operating cycle, (2) is identifiable by its physical properties, rather than as a legal or economic right, and (3) is intended for use rather than resale. *Synonyms:* plant and equipment, property, tangible fixed asset.

Time-adjusted rate of return. A rate of return based on present values of future amounts, used as a measure of profitability in evaluating capital expenditure.

Trade discount. A reduction in the sales price granted to customers at the time of sale, usually for the purchase of large quantities. The reduced price is properly interpreted as the selling price.

Trademark. The exclusive right, granted by the government, to use a symbol or name to identify a product, a service, or a company.

Treasury shares. Stock that has been issued to stockholders and later reacquired and held by a corporation, usually for a purpose other than retirement.

Variable cost. A cost that changes in direct proportion to a change in the volume of activity.

Variable costing. A method of product costing in which only variable production costs are accounted for as product costs and identified with units of inventory. These costs are thus subject to division between the assets inventory and the cost-of-goods-sold expense at the end of the period. Nonvariable costs are treated as period costs, whether or not they are production costs. *Synonym:* direct costing.

Variance. A difference between actual performance and standard (or budgeted) performance.

Working capital. Current assets minus current liabilities. *Synonym:* net working capital.

Yield. The actual interest rate earned by a bond purchaser, determined by equating the actual purchase price of the bond (the amount loaned) with the present value of future interest receipts. *Synonyms:* yield rate of interest, effective rate of interest, market rate of interest.

INDEX